EASTERN WAYS OF BEING RELIGIOUS

Gary E. Kessler

California State University, Bakersfield

Mayfield Publishing Company
Mountain View, California
London • Ontario

Library of Congress Cataloging-in-Publication Data

Eastern ways of being religious [compiled by] Gary E. Kessler.
    p.   cm.
  Includes bibliographical references.
  ISBN 0-7674-1225-7
  1. Asia—Religion.   2. Africa, Sub-Saharan—Religion.
  I. Kessler, Gary E.
  BL1032.E377   1999
  200'.95—dc21   99-33847
                                                    CIP

Manufactured in the United States of America

10   9   8   7   6   5   4

Mayfield Publishing Company
1280 Villa Street
Mountain View, California 94041

Sponsoring editor, Kenneth King; *production editor*, Carla White Kirschenbaum; *manuscript editor*, Margaret Moore; *text and cover designer*, Linda Robertson; *design manager*, Glenda King; *manufacturing manager*, Randy Hurst. The text was set in 9.5/11.5 Janson by G&S Typesetters, Inc. and printed on 45 # Chromatone Matte by Banta Book Group.

Cover image: Andrew Hall/Tony Stone Images

To Lucia and Caleb, may you live in a peaceful world.

Contents

Preface

Eastern Ways of Being Religious provides both primary source material and secondary interpretative studies for students who wish to learn about different religions. Instructors can use this book alone or in conjunction with a standard textbook on world religions. My intention is to provide material useful for lower-division world religion courses or introductory religious studies courses. The material gathered here can also serve as background reading for courses in philosophy of religion, sociology of religion, and psychology of religion.

Most collections of sources now available for use in world religion courses concentrate on scriptural texts and exclude secondary interpretations. *Eastern Ways of Being Religious* provides source material from various historical periods to give students some sense of how a religious tradition has developed along with introductory overviews and scholarly studies of specific issues. The first three chapters pay more attention than most textbooks to how one goes about studying religion in an academic setting and to the problems associated with defining religion. In addition, this text pays more attention to issues relating to women and religion than is usual in survey textbooks.

I wrote this book to provide students and instructors with sources for interpreting religion and with examples of scholarly approaches to the study of religion. The scholarly studies model for students how one goes about utilizing sources for enhancing one's understanding of a religious tradition. The interplay between primary sources and secondary interpretations show students how to approach the interpretation of religious sources in a scholarly and responsible way.

Organization

Each chapter, after the first three, has an introductory essay providing an overview of a specific religious tradition. These general essays give students a macro-view of the tradition before they plunge into more specific information.

A section titled Sources follows the introductory overview. Here students will find a selection of some of the most influential formative scriptural texts or oral traditions and important later commentaries along with texts representing other developments in belief and practice. I have chosen these sources not only because of their importance to the tradition in question but also to represent such various dimensions of each tradition as the experiential, mythic, ritual, doctrinal, ethical, and social dimensions. The material is not organized explicitly according to these dimensions because many of the selections embody more than one in a unified narrative. Thus, I have judged it best not to cut up unified narratives in brief selections in order to fit these preconceived categories. Selections dealing with women have also been included because this is frequently a neglected topic in the study of world religions (although the situation is, I am happy to say, improving rapidly).

The final section of each chapter dealing with a religious tradition is titled Contemporary Scholarship. Here I include recent interpretative essays that model different approaches to the study of religion—from the philosophical and historical to the theological and sociological.

Pedagogical Features

As I wrote this book, I kept in mind student needs as well as the pedagogical problems instructors in religious studies encounter while teaching about different ways of being religious, and I have tried to meet these needs and solve these problems in a variety of ways. The following list highlights some of the pedagogical features found in *Eastern Ways of Being Religious*:

- reading questions that help students interpret the selections

- introductions that supply students with background information and an interpretative context
- emphasis on developing comparative and interpretative skills
- suggestions for further readings at the end of each chapter
- pronunciation guides
- information on internet resources for studying religion
- maps to aid students' grasp of religious geography

Special Features

I have also incorporated a number of special features that not only make *Eastern Ways of Being Religious* different from most other textbooks on the market but also enhance student learning. These include:

- a unique organization (overview, sources, scholarly essays)
- combining primary sources with secondary interpretative articles
- providing both "outsider" and "insider" perspectives
- modeling different scholarly approaches (historical, anthropological, philosophical, phenomenological, sociological, and theological)
- providing discussions of problems involved in defining religion, a description of the field of religious studies, and methods for studying religion

Acknowledgments

California State University, Bakersfield provided a sabbatical and the Centre for Studies in Religion and Society at the University of Victoria provided a fellowship that enabled me to get this project started. I particularly wish to thank the Centre's director, Harold Coward and his staff for their kind help and support. Ken King, the religion editor at Mayfield, gave encouragement and creative ideas and the helpful staff at Mayfield saw to the production details. Margaret Moore cleaned up my prose and made the book more readable. Katy Kessler did research, listened patiently to my ideas, and offered constructive advice. Barbara McNaughton and Mona Aguliar helped with the permissions and duplicating tasks. I also wish to thank Wendell Charles Beane, University of Wisconsin at Oshkosh; Katherine Carlitz, University of Pittsburgh; Dell deChant, University of South Florida; Kai-Wing Chow, University of Illinois; Frederick M. Denny, University of Colorado at Boulder; John Grimes, Michigan State University; Rita M. Gross, University of Wisconsin at Eau Claire; Stephen L. Harris, California State University at Sacramento; Howard L. Harrod, Vanderbilt University; Russell T. McCutcheon, Southwest Missouri State University; Michael Molloy, Kapiolani Community College; Professor Robert Platzner, California State University at Sacramento; Gerald Michael Schnabel, Bemidji State University; James S. Thayer, Oklahoma State University; Dr. Dan Vaillancourt, Loyola University Chicago, John Whittaker, Louisiana State University, and Mark R. Woodward, Arizona State University. I find it regrettable that I could not incorporate all of their thoughtful suggestions. Whatever errors and limitations remain are of my own doing.

I invite students and instructors alike who use this book to provide me with their thoughts and ideas. My goal is to provide useful material for understanding some of the ways humans express their religiosity. No one person can ever hope to master the vast amount of literature available on religion. We need to pool our knowledge and experience. Your advice can help make this book better should a need for a new edition arise.

Gary E. Kessler, California State University, Bakersfield, e-mail: gkessler@csubak.edu

PART 1

INTRODUCTION

1

A Challenge

It is 10 A.M. on a Sunday morning in British Columbia, Canada. A girl is beginning her Sunday school lesson. On Saturday, some Jewish boys in Italy were studying commentaries on Genesis at a synagogue. In Philadelphia, Islamic students gathered at a mosque on Friday to pray and to study the Qur'an. In Bangkok, Thailand, a thirteen-year-old boy is studying the Buddhist Sutras in preparation for taking monastic vows.

INSIDER'S AND OUTSIDER'S PERSPECTIVES

Like the people I have just described, those of you who have studied religion in Sunday school, Synagogue school (*beth midrash*, or house of study), or Bible study classes or have studied the Qur'an in a mosque have studied from an insider's point of view. The **insider's** view is that of someone who participates in a particular religious tradition. This sort of study presupposes religious commitment and promotes an understanding that will lead to greater commitment. It promotes the interests and furthers the causes of a specific religious organization.

The academic study of religion is different from the insider's study. In the academic study, the student stands outside all religious traditions and studies religions from the viewpoint of the methods and standards associated with the secular academy. The **outsider's** viewpoint does not presuppose any kind of religious commitment, although it does presuppose a commitment to the standards of the academy. Its goal is neither to increase nor to decrease an individual's religious faith, although it may have profound effects on that faith.

For the insider, the study of religion is itself a religious activity. For the outsider, it is not, at least not in a sectarian sense. The difference between the two

ways of studying religion is like the difference between speaking a language and studying how a language is spoken. The latter is a **meta,** or second-order, activity because it stands outside the actual **first-order** practice it seeks to understand. The academic study of religion is a second-order activity that involves observing those who worship.

The controversial ruling of the U.S. Supreme Court on prayer in public schools noted the difference between the insider's and outsider's perspectives by distinguishing between the teaching *of* religion and the teaching *about* religion. The teaching *of* involves sectarian instruction while teaching *about* does not. According to the Court, nothing in the ruling prohibiting prayer in public schools should be understood to forbid teaching *about* religion in public schools.

If I were to ask you to list the advantages and disadvantages of each of these viewpoints, it would not take you long to create a list. On the one hand, the outsider's viewpoint presents a greater hope for achieving objectivity, which is particularly valuable when studying many different religions. On the other hand, the insider's viewpoint presents a greater hope for sympathetic understanding of one particular religious tradition. It can appreciate nuances and feelings that the observer can easily miss.

The situation is like the relationship between you and a psychological counselor. You know yourself from the inside and hence have a unique advantage when it comes to self-knowledge. However, your very intimacy can lead to self-deception, distortions, and blind spots that an outside, trained observer like a counselor can detect almost immediately.

There can be considerable conflict between the insider's view and the outsider's view. The values that each hold appear opposed. The outsider appeals to such values as critical reason, disinterested and unemotional judgment, impersonal observation, and detached analysis. The insider's approach certainly involves the use of reason, but it is tempered by a personal, passionate, and involved pursuit of faith as well as knowledge. At its worst the outsider's approach can lead to a radical depersonalization of the subject matter, taking the vitality out of religions by reducing them to causal factors far removed from the living reality. For example, some scholars claim that religion originates in fear of higher powers—that religious faith is just another form of fear. This hardly seems plausible given the richness and diversity of religions, even if some fear does play a role in religions.

At its worst the insider's approach can become so defensive and prejudicial that it ceases to be honest, distorting facts and ignoring or suppressing evidence. For example, some insiders regard all religions other than their own as the "work of Satan"—that all other religions have the devil as their father! This kind of attitude reduces the comparative study of religion to a combination of **apologetics** and polemics. It reveals nothing about the ways in which "others" understand themselves.

I have identified the academic study of religions with the outsider's viewpoint in contrast to the insider's viewpoint. However, the picture I have painted is distorted. None of us are completely inside or outside in our viewpoints. Even if we practice no religion, religious traditions and values have so permeated our cultures and societies that, like fish, we live in a sea already containing religious currents. There is no view totally outside everything and no view totally inside. These extremes are "ideal types" that characterize the very ends of a continuum. The real situation is more complex. The outsider can be as prejudiced as the insider, although in a different direction, and one might make a plausible case that the outsider is as much committed to promoting the interests of the academic "church of reason" as the insider is committed to promoting the interests of her or his church.

You probably are beginning to see how challenging the academic study of religion can be. It requires a scrupulous self-consciousness about how fairly you are treating others who may have very different values and beliefs from your own. The "other" is always threatening to some extent, and the "religious other" can be very threatening because often it is a good person who believes in her or his way of life as sincerely as you believe in your own. It is difficult in such a situation to sustain the belief that other people are totally wrong religiously.

The academic study of religion challenges you to develop the qualities of openness, honesty, critical intelligence, careful reading and listening, and critical tolerance. We will examine each of these qualities in turn.

OPENNESS

To be open in the academic study of religions is to be always ready to be surprised. It is a constant willingness to regard tentatively the categories, classification systems, labels, and names with which we pigeonhole religious phenomena. We must realize that they are revisable and incomplete. It is not a refusal to draw conclusions nor is it a noncommittal willingness to entertain anything and everything. To be open is to recognize that however helpful classification systems, explanations, and theories can be, they may be wrong and in need of revision as additional evidence comes to light. As a student of religion, you should welcome, as does the student of physical science, evidence that you might be wrong, because if you are wrong and it can be shown, you have learned something new and thereby come that much closer to understanding.

HONESTY

Honesty involves responsibility to yourself, others, and your subject matter. By responsibility I mean the ability to respond in a nonprejudicial way to what you learn. To be prejudiced is different than being biased (although the words are often used interchangeably). Prejudice means prejudgment. Bias means a particular slant, outlook, or perspective. Even the honest person is biased because human beings see, of necessity, what they take to be real from a certain viewpoint. There cannot be a view from nowhere just as there cannot be a view from everywhere. However, the honest person understands his or her biases and constantly is mindful of them, thereby attempting to overcome whatever limitations the biases might impose. Using again our analogy with studying a language, we might characterize honesty in terms of the ability to responsibly study the "language" of religion and at the same time to be aware of the perspective embedded in the meta-language we use to describe religion.

CRITICAL INTELLIGENCE

Critical intelligence is a formidable phrase smacking of abstractions, destructive intentions, and obscure theories. True, critical inquiry may be destructive of some cherished beliefs and deep-seated prejudices. However, its goal is not destruction for the sake of destruction. Its goal is construction. If critical inquiry tears down, it does so in the hope of building up.

To be critical involves a number of intellectual skills including both analysis and synthesis. In analysis we seek to take things apart, to break wholes into basic elements. Just as you may have taken a clock apart in order to see what makes it tick, engaging in the academic study of religion challenges you to take apart religious rituals and beliefs to see what makes them work. However, synthesis—putting things back together—is also required. We must be ever alert for the discovery of previously unseen relationships and for the sudden insight that what we took to be contradictions are reconciled in a greater harmony. Our task as academic students of religion is not only to analyze religion but also to synthesize its various parts so that the underlying and often unexpected convergences come to light.

At the heart of critical intelligence is the pursuit of truth. Although we live in an age of relativism when phrases like "the pursuit of truth" sound outdated, such a pursuit cannot be given up even when we are uncertain there is any truth to be found. To look for truth in our studies of religions necessitates criteria regarding what is going to count as truth. The task of articulating such criteria is by no means easy and is also an ongoing task. However, there are generally acceptable standards available for what is to count as truth, and the student of religion ought to employ them and seek to improve them.

Arguments supporting a particular conclusion must be carefully examined to see if the premises are true and whether the conclusion follows from the premises. Consistency in theory and its application is a hallmark of the pursuit of truth. Evidence must be carefully examined for reliability and checked out. If I claim that the essence of religion is fear and present evidence to support that claim, then I must also check for counterevidence and counterexamples. If there are none, so much the better for my claim. However, if there are some, I must be prepared to modify my claim. I also need to check to see if my terms are defined precisely enough to be useful. For example, I do not know if the admonition of some religions to "fear God" counts as evidence for my claim or not unless I know that the fear I am talking about and the fear they are talking about mean the same thing.

Crucial to the search for truth is the ability to question. Most of us are too easily satisfied with superficial answers and stop questioning too soon. The willingness to continue to raise questions even when you think you understand and to pursue alternative answers is an indispensable tool in the quest for truth. Moreover, there is an art to questioning that involves carefully examining your questions, seeking to find out whether they are correctly formulated and lead in useful directions. The student of religions is challenged to remind herself or himself that questioning is not an end in itself; rather, its purpose is to lead the way to answers.

CAREFUL READING
AND LISTENING

Careful reading and listening is a deceptively simple phrase. Doesn't every student read and listen? My experience has been that while I think I am reading or listening, I am not always doing so. As a teacher, I am used to students asking questions. The more I teach the more I become accustomed to certain questions. This has sometimes lulled me into not listening fully. The student may be in the midst of a question or comment, and I find myself already formulating a reply in my mind. I become so preoccupied with formulating my reply that I cease to listen. Also, comments, questions, and textual materials are often deceptive in that the words say one thing, but the person behind the words may be saying something else. We need to listen and to read for hidden meanings. This is especially important when dealing with religious texts such as sacred writings, which contain many different levels of meaning. The student of religions needs to become sensitive to as many different levels of meaning as possible. There is great joy in studying religions when you are surprised by a new level of meaning in some familiar saying or ritual action. Religious rituals and experiences contain a symbolic richness that will unfold for the student who reads and listens carefully.

Careful reading and listening requires sympathetic imagination. Imagination is one of the student's greatest assets. Through it we can project ourselves, at least partially, into the worldview of a shaman doing magical healing, a yogi in meditation, a prophet proclaiming a judgment she or he hopes will never come true, and a Christian or a Muslim at prayer.

The ability to imagine is the ability to play, to make-believe. Such an ability is invaluable to the student of religions as he or she struggles to comprehend cultures, beliefs, practices, and experiences that seem very different and strange. Sympathetic imagination requires projecting oneself into the viewpoint of another.

Such projection, of course, can easily lead to distortion and deception. We project ourselves into the shoes of another, and insofar as we all share in a common humanity and a common world, such a projection is possible and valuable. However, insofar as the other is truly alien to us and utterly strange, imagination must acknowledge its limits and beware of manufacturing false similarities at the expense of real differences.

CRITICAL TOLERANCE

Sympathetic imagination is indispensable in studying religion, but it must be balanced by critical intelligence, honesty, and openness. The student of religion must learn to cultivate all of these qualities in such a way that they complement one another. Sympathetic imagination and openness promotes tolerance for those who are different, and critical intelligence promotes a tolerance tempered by critical evaluation. We can and should come to understand religious tragedies such as Jonestown or Heaven's Gate, but we cannot condone mass suicide and violence.

Sometimes it is easy to know where to draw the line between understanding and tolerance. At other times it is more difficult. We can understand why some religions sacrificed humans and thought it was right to do so, and we have no difficulty condemning such a practice should it occur today. However, what should we say about the sacrifice of animals, which still takes place in religious settings? Should it be tolerated? What should be done about the repressive treatment of women in Afghanistan? Should we tolerate fundamentalist sects that advocate beating children?

As these questions indicate, there is no simple way

to balance sympathetic understanding and critical intelligence in all situations, but it is a challenge worth meeting. The study of religions can be as difficult and as exciting as learning to understand and appreciate another human being, another culture, another way of life. At its best, the study of religions can show you how to see what the world is like through the eyes of another. It can disclose the depths of human suffering and the heights of human joy, and can challenge you to examine the limits of toleration. The simple act of praying, making a sacrifice, lighting incense, or eating a humble meal can reveal symbolic richness, a sense of proportion and grace, a feeling of awe and mystery that enlarges your soul.

1.1 SPIRITUAL REGRET

The qualities of openness, honesty, critical intelligence, and reading/listening with sympathetic imagination that need to be cultivated by the student of religions might be termed virtues in the sense of excellences. People who have these qualities we generally admire more than people who are closed-minded, dishonest, uncritical, and careless in their reading and listening.

In the study of religions, we frequently find religions other than our own that attract us. For example, I was raised a Christian in the Lutheran Church, but I have been very attracted to Zen Buddhism (among other religions) and even spent some time practicing meditation in a Zen monastery. As you study the religions represented in this book, you may find yourself in a similar situation. How should you best respond? One option is to convert. However, perhaps you have good reasons for not converting such as still being deeply committed to your own tradition or to a nonreligious perspective. Such situations, argues Lee H. Yearley (the author of the following lecture), call for the development of *new* religious virtues, in particular, the virtue he calls **spiritual regret.**

You are probably aware of traditional religious virtues such as faith and hope but may be less aware that various virtues and vices have been added to that list in response to particular historical circumstances. For example, the Walloon Synod of Leydon (seventeenth century), which was mostly made up of French Protestants (Huguenots) who had been persecuted by Roman Catholics, condemned religious toleration (especially toward Roman Catholics) as a vice and a heresy. To them, tolerance meant a lax complacency toward evil. Religious intolerance became, for the Huguenots, a religious virtue. Since then, religious tolerance, at least in some circles, has once again become a virtue and intolerance a vice. Yearley thinks today's circumstances require the development of other religious virtues besides toleration. The times require us, he argues, to recognize new religious virtues such as spiritual regret. He acknowledges objections to his position but still maintains that spiritual regret is a better response to religious pluralism (the existence of many different religions) than either complacency or parochialism (the denial of the need to learn about other religions sympathetically).

Lee H. Yearley is the Walter Y. Evans-Wentz Professor of Religion at Stanford University. He delivered this lecture as part of the University Lecture Series in Religion at Arizona State University in 1994.

As you read his lecture, write brief answers to the following reading questions. They will help you catch key ideas and clarify your own thoughts about Yearley's arguments.

LEE H. YEARLEY

New Religious Virtues and the Study of Religion

READING QUESTIONS

1. As you read, make a list of all the words and ideas you do not understand or are uncertain about. Discuss them with a classmate, look them up in a dictionary, or bring them up in class for discussion and clarification.
2. What is Yearley's subject, and what will he argue?
3. Describe in your own words the four ways of "solving" the problem of religious plurality. Does any of these four ways characterize your own view? If so, which one? If none, what is your own view, and how does it differ from these four?

From Lee H. Yearley, *New Religious Virtues and the Study of Religion* (Arizona State University, Department of Religious Studies, 1994, pp. 1–10, 12–17, 19–22. Reprinted by permission of the author. Endnotes deleted.

4. What does Yearley mean by "articulation of the implicit," and what role does this play in recognizing a new virtue?
5. According to Yearley, what are the characteristics of someone who is modern? Do you consider yourself modern in Yearley's sense? Why or why not?
6. Why do the new virtues like spiritual regret produce both joy and sadness? Do you think the word *regret* is the best word to use in order to describe this virtue?
7. How would you, in your own words, characterize the virtue of spiritual regret? If you have ever felt spiritual regret, describe the situation.
8. Why, according to Yearley, is imagination important for studying comparative religions?
9. What are "sophisticated complacency" and "sophisticated parochialism"? Why does Yearley reject these two types of "principled opposition to imaginative religious voyaging"?

I. INTRODUCTION

Teaching about religion produces numerous situations that set us back on our heels no matter how seasoned we may think we are. Three examples, all with undergraduates: A knowledgeable, reflective Irish-Catholic appears at my door and with evident perplexity and some pain tells me how the Taoist work we just finished makes more sense to her than do those Catholic works that have underpinned her understanding of life. Weeks later, a highly intelligent East Asian Buddhist talks with me at length about how best to understand Aquinas's ideas about sin, ideas she finds compelling but that seem to have no evident place in the religious world she inhabits.

Third, several weeks of lecturing on the Confucian tradition to a large required course leads several Asian American students to tell me, an aging white male, that I had articulated for them ideas that they live from but had barely understood much less evaluated. Indeed, they speak about how they had always felt odd, so different were many of their basic inclinations about say proper attitudes to parents, but now they see those attitudes as manifesting, however confusedly, a long and deep tradition.

Much can, of course, be said about each example and the general situation they illustrate. I want here, however, to discuss how they highlight what I believe is a new and crucial demand on us both as teachers of religion and as people interested in religious positions or committed to them. It involves meeting the teaching challenges and constructive challenges presented by a new understanding of not just religious diversity but of religious goods that are integral but alien. My subject, then, is how best to respond not just to what is often called today the religious "Other" but to the religious "Other" that attracts us.

My focus is not on how we ought as a matter of public policy deal with religious diversity. I do think what I will say is relevant to those issues; I sometimes even think we will not be able to work out the public problems until we work out the private ones. My topic today, however, is what we should do when facing or teaching about alien but tempting religions.

I believe the best way to talk about these situations is to use a language that relies on ideas about virtues. Ideas about virtue, and what they imply, generate understandable suspicions in many people. There are, however, rich traditions—in the West and elsewhere—that have argued a language that employs ideas about virtue provides us with the best way to talk about crucial features of our lives, and I hope to persuade you this approach has much merit. In these traditions virtues are human excellences, aspects of what we call character. Put more abstractly, they are those characteristic patterns of feeling and motivation that reflect a life plan the fulfillment of which is thought to be all important.

If we think in terms of other people's perceptions, virtues are those admirable characteristics that a significant number of people in a society think reflect instances of human excellences. This formulation, however, points up a perplexing feature of my enterprise. I will argue that we need to manifest new virtues, especially new religious or spiritual virtues. These virtues are not generally recognized; they are, at best, only implicit in people's ideas about human excellence.

These new virtues appear when we face what is implied by the diversity of integral religious goods. My example of such a new religious virtue will be the virtue of spiritual regret. That virtue deals with the recognition that various, legitimate ideals of religious flourishing exist and that although some of them move you deeply you cannot manifest them, indeed may not even want to manifest them.

Cultivating such new virtues involves, I believe, acquiring skills that are intimately involved with the disciplined study of diverse religions. That study can occur, of course, in many places, but it surely does have a place in higher education, and I want to talk about how best to cultivate it. Finally, I will end by examining, if briefly, my understanding of what will in the future be, I believe, a most serious debate. The debate is between those who accept some version of the position I describe here and those who would accept much of what is said here but are in principle opposed to the new virtues described—indeed might even call them vices.

Much to do then; let us begin by discussing how apparent religious differences have been treated.

II. How Apparently Alien Religions Have Been Treated

Basic to the idea I will be examining is the notion that genuine goods, especially religious goods, can differ substantially enough to present a person with sharply divergent life plans, plans which are both legitimate and appealing. This is, I believe, a novel idea. Divergences and conflicts among apparent goods surely have been recognized. Nevertheless, the notion that the conflicting goods are truly legitimate ones is not found, I think, in the Western tradition or in those non-Western traditions with which I am familiar. In all those earlier traditions a central claim, one that underlies all other claims, is that there is a single goal. That is, there is either a single, limited form of ideal human excellence or a harmony among somewhat different forms.

People who adhered to a tradition have, needless to say, recognized that other traditions seemed to pursue different goals. But they "solved" the seemingly irreducible plurality among religious ideals in one of four ways. Allow me to use labels for the proponents of each position in order to give a brief typological account: the first sees the adherents of another religious position as simply "in error"; the second sees them as "less developed"; the third sees them as "more developed"; and the fourth sees them as "only apparently different."

Each of these positions vis-à-vis apparent plurality required that its adherents manifest specific virtues—for example the virtue of righteous indignation or the virtue of tolerance. That is, the ideas contained in the positions were supposed to inform one's character. They were to be incarnated in a personal excellence that appeared when one faced divergent religious goods.

The first approach is to see the religiously alien as in error, as "heretics," as mistaken versions of one's own truth. One brings them into the structure of one's own tradition and places them as unorthodox or aberrant members. (A variant of this is to make the religiously different part of a larger cosmological scheme in which it represents some version of the forces of evil.) Those who differ may then be candidates for conversion, extinction, or possibly benign neglect.

A second approach is to employ a developmental scheme in which the religiously alien is seen as a lower stage of development. That stage may have integrity, may even have represented an appropriate response in some contexts. But the hierarchy of developmental stages is clear and the adherent's religion is of a higher sort than is the alien religion.

A third approach uses similar presuppositions about the final state but claims that another tradition represents that to which the home tradition aspires. One's own tradition represents imperfectly what is more fully seen elsewhere. A final approach has been to argue that the differences between oneself and the other are probably only apparent. A lack of information and physical or psychological distance from the religious other means little thought need be given to the issue of differences in religious fulfillment.

These four approaches continue, I believe, to underlie most contemporary Western and non-Western theological attempts to relate religions to one another. They also, therefore, underlie the picture of what virtues are needed when dealing with other religions. That situation says much about the grip of basic paradigms; it underlines for instance how fundamental has been the idea that there is finally a single goal. It also, I think, says much about people's failure to take sophisticated comparative work seriously enough to grapple with the challenges and possibilities it presents.

Some things have, of course, changed. Thankfully, in much of the modern West the inclination to convert the religiously alien or to destroy them if conversion fails has died or at least abated. (Tragically this is far less true in other areas of the world where sophisticated religious accounts are still used to justify terrible acts.) Variants of the last three responses are, however, alive and well today. That is, contemporary approaches reflect features of the traditional strategies for dealing with the religious alien. One approach is to deny that any real differences are present or that all apparent differences can be explained developmentally. This can take the form, for instance, of finding abstract similarities among religions or incorporating into one's own religion features of other religious views. Another strategy is simply to view other religions as one would view exhibits in a museum or specimens in a zoo. They then can be admired as unchallenging but different, be looked on as odd but interesting instances or even mutants of a single species. These approaches all can appear in woefully unsophisticated or even downright foolish forms. But they also appear in elaborate academic garb—which we will presume for the moment is not foolish.

The perseverance of these traditional ways of dealing with religious diversity is, however, far from the whole tale. In various ways and with various people, both inside and outside the academy, awareness grows that something is amiss in these ways of formulating matters. Yet just what is amiss usually remains unclear and new approaches, much less solutions, seem even more murky. Most important to us, no clear idea exists of what new human virtues are called for by this unease about traditional solutions and virtues. In fact, it is even unclear if we can make sense of the idea of truly new virtues.

III. ARTICULATING THE IMPLICIT: THE THEORETICAL BASIS OF NEW RELIGIOUS VIRTUES

The whole idea of new virtues seems to be questionable, to require not only explanation but defense. This problem has various facets and we will examine some of them only when treating my example of a new religious virtue: spiritual regret. That example can also give texture, concrete density, to our initial more abstract discussion. For now, however, let us turn to the most fundamental of the theoretical questions.

Virtues are qualities that, as I put it earlier, most people in a society think reflect admirable qualities. With a new virtue, however, most people will not *explicitly* affirm that a quality is admirable. Nevertheless, I believe they have a general perspective that allows for or even produces an *implicit* affirmation of the quality's admirableness. Therefore they can be persuaded that a quality is a new virtue because it gathers up or focuses attention on discrete and valuable but heretofore inchoate features of their overall perspective. To move from an implicit affirmation of something to an explicit affirmation is for people to become more articulate about the important ideas and attitudes they possess but have no adequate vocabulary for expressing. This "articulation of the implicit," this making explicit what was inchoate, underlies the idea of new virtues.

The idea that nuanced language about virtues enables people to understand themselves in fuller and more subtle ways than they otherwise could, and therefore also to live better lives, has been a standard defense of the significance of virtue theory. It is a defense which rests on controversial but to my mind compelling ideas: that, for example, we often are strangers to ourselves and we find it exceedingly difficult to think well, using ordinary language, about those things that matter most to us. Conventional virtue theory moves from this view to urge closer analysis and better understandings of traditional virtues. I am here arguing that it provides the grounding for new virtues as well.

I believe, then, that people's general perspective implicitly contains or allows for the idea that virtues, like spiritual regret, which manifest different ways of responding to alternative religious views are new virtues. I realize that many people might not initially think they refer to admirable qualities. I aim, however, to show that these qualities deserve to be defined as virtuous and hope thereby to make explicit for people what is implicit in their perspectives. Nevertheless, I also realize that such an inquiry is always a "two-way street." It involves the risk that the persuader can be persuaded. People can have principled objections, as we will see, to labeling a quality like spiritual regret a virtue. They can even see it as a vice, a human deformation. And they may convince me I am wrong.

In fact, unlike some believers in articulation, I think the process may produce not just significant agreements but also deep disagreements. If the disagreements turn out to be shallow so much the better but I think it a mistake to predict they will. Even if deep disagreements result, however, the process of articulation is still very important. The ability to formulate clearly and thereby to discuss well what may be deep disagreements is extremely important to a society like the one we inhabit. Such formulations and discussions are also critical to us personally as the disagreements may well reflect unresolved conflicts between different parts of our views about life. The key point in both cases is that we need to be able to talk about these issues. We need to have, if you will, a "what is X" discussion of the kind that was the staple of many classical Western analyses of various matters, notably the character of virtues like courage or moderation.

The new "what is X" discussion that is needed aims to make explicit the new religious virtues that appear when we think out the implications of three specifically modern emphases or themes and the reactions they generate. Academics who dare to utter the word "modern" can subject themselves, I know, to a barrage of questions or at least quizzical glances, but allow me to proceed.

First is an emphasis on the significance of autonomy, on the importance either of having chosen to be a person of a certain sort or of having consciously affirmed that you choose to be as you have been determined to be by various external forces. Put simply, moderns want to be able to say "It is my life." . . . Second is a valuing of that understanding of self which arises from introspection and retrospection, from reflecting upon one's present self and history. People should feel obligated to grasp as well as they can who they are and what they have been.

These two notions underlie the modern presumption that the "integrity" or "authenticity" of an individual is of crucial value. They also, in turn, generate the modern concern with hypocrisy or insincerity. Whatever may be the problems associated with these ideas (and those problems can be substantial), features of this perspective remain compelling to most people and for good reason. Possessing integrity can, for example, rightly be called a virtue or excellence that ranks with being just or benevolent.

The third modern theme is an understanding of the diversity of possible forms of human actualization, religious or non-religious, that are present in the world. It arises from ideas that are probably less widely shared than the valuing of individual integrity. One is the idea that all our lives are inevitably embedded in specific cultures and are shaped by commitments that are underdetermined by the reasons that support them. We live in ways that we cannot fully justify by the reasons that we have for living that way. This notion rests, in turn, on the belief that our way of life is only one among many.

These ideas form or reinforce the notion that people cannot legitimately appeal to authoritative supports that they might well have invoked before. People, then, must be conscious of the real conflicts that are present about what is the best way to live. That is, I believe, a very difficult thing to do, or at least to do consistently. It involves, at its core, the dual recognitions that many legitimate goods exist and that whatever goods you pursue, they are but one among many possible sets of goods.

Understanding this will always present some problems. But it poses a specific problem for people who wish to be autonomous and reflective about themselves, a problem that underlies the need for new virtues. That a person who desires to possess integrity affirms only one among the different kinds of human excellence he or she could affirm is the notion that lies at the center of the notion that new virtues, like spiritual regret, are needed.

The peculiar character and weight of these virtues arises from the state that follows from this situation, a state where joy and sadness interact. That is, at the heart of the character of these new virtues is the idea that to encounter any real good is to be drawn by it, to find it attractive, and thus to enjoy it. Enjoyment or joy, then, becomes the mark of having recognized a good. This joy remains even if that good must also remain unavailable, unavailable just because of the integrity of the self that meets the alien good. That situation, in turn, must produce sadness because the good cannot be fully realized. People must, then, both encounter goods that draw them and encounter their own integrity, an integrity that makes impossible a full acceptance of the alternative good. That circumstance, a circumstance which defines these virtues, produces both joy and sadness. To feel only sadness would signal that one had not fully encountered the good. But to feel only joy would signal a failure to encounter fully the good of one's own integrity. . . .

IV. INTERLUDE: THE IDEA OF VIRTUE

Although I think the best way to talk about the full encounter with other religious goods involves ideas about virtues, I realize that for many today the word "virtue" has an archaic ring. It often seems to be associated with problematic ideas like priggish scrupulosity; or to be restricted to narrow areas like sexual activity, or to reflect fixed unjust social hierarchies like that found in virtually all traditional societies.

Given that, let me say something about what I mean by the idea of a virtue, drawing my examples from the realm of ethical virtues. For me a virtue is a human excellence or example of human flourishing. It is a permanent addition to the self, part of what makes people who they are, a feature of what we call character. One of my friends, for example, possesses or even exemplifies the virtue of generosity. If she sees a troubled person, she is immediately inclined to give her time or money to that person. I, on the other hand, see a troubled person and often think of other things, for example how much work I have to do or what helping the person will cost me psychologically and financially. I then probably also get tangled up in the question of whether being generous will, in the long term, be good for the troubled person. I might finally do generous things but I am not a generous person in the sense my friend is; she possesses the virtue and I have at best a semblance of it.

Virtues, then, display some characteristic pattern of desire and motivation. They are not simple thoughts that occur and pass: I do not manifest a virtue if I think how compassionate it would be to invite that lonely person to dinner as I walk on past them. Nor are they emotional states that pass quickly: I am not virtuous if I feel very strongly that I should at least talk to my lonely acquaintance but realize the movie is about to start and move on. . . .

V. AN EXAMPLE: SPIRITUAL REGRET AS A NEW, CORRECTIVE VIRTUE

Spiritual regret is one of those virtues that concerns the appropriate response to the recognition that extremely varied, legitimate religious ideals exist and that no person can possibly manifest all of them. Like all virtues it is corrective of a corresponding human weakness, in this case the tendency to overlook the challenge produced by the presence of other integral and even tempting religious goods. It is also new in that it both responds to challenges that were not fully understood before and develops capacities that were previously undeveloped.

Before examining just how it is both "new" and "corrective," a word more about its general character. Spiritual regret, it needs to be underlined, is a virtue and not simply an emotional reaction or even a passing thought or attitude. All those characteristics of virtue mentioned earlier are present: for instance, it is a part of one's character and manifests a general picture of what you think a good life is. Some legitimate uses of the word "regret" do refer to passing emotional perturbations and therefore one can easily think of spiritual regret as a simple emotion. But I want to talk about it as a virtue, one aspect of which often is the presence of a specific emotion — or more accurately the propensity to feel that emotion in appropriate ways in specific situations. The important and complicated virtue of regret has a similar structure.

Spiritual regret arises when we recognize three things. First, that various, legitimate ideas of religious flourishing exist. Second, that conflict among them means that no single person can come close to exhibiting all of them. Third, that those ideals or states which one can pursue or possess will usually be largely determined by forces either beyond one's immediate control or beyond anyone's control. This regret can arise in different forms at different times in one's life. It seems, however, normally to be linked to maturity, to a well understood fund of experience.

Examples of spiritual regret are, I think, myriad. They range from reading texts, most notably for me classical Confucian and Taoist texts, to personal encounters with extraordinary people from other traditions, most notably for me five days of meetings, with five other people, with the Dalai Lama. The most striking example I know occurred when I spent two hours very early one morning in Korea on a cliff high above the East Sea looking at the Sokkurum Buddha. A large granite statue of the Buddha in meditation carved in the 8th century C.E. and flanked by wall carvings of disciples and guardians, it sits in a recessed grotto. One of East Asia's greatest statues, the figure draws one's attention, or at least drew mine, with a magnetic power and generates a mysterious kind of peace or at least stillness. The spiritual vision presented there was as powerful and as tempting as I have ever seen. Yet I wanted it neither for myself nor for those about whom I care most. I wanted the religious goods expressed in the Sokkurum Buddha to exist, and even to be incarnated by many people, and yet did not want the people I cared about most to possess them.

Of the various reasons for that judgment, the one which most haunts me concerns my response to the transcendence of normal human pain and turmoil that I saw. This was true even though the statue was not completely "self-enclosed"; it manifested a calmness and luminosity that involved contact with the world. Statues which expressed that "self-enclosed" kind of perfection, one which would be disturbed by any contact with the world, could be seen within miles of the Sokkurum Buddha in the now largely deserted surrounding hills. They generated in me, at best, a muted admiration. In contrast, the poise, self-possession, and equanimity I saw in the Sokkurum Buddha contained a compassion aimed toward a world the pain and frustration of which was well understood. Nevertheless, that world was distant in a way I found both compelling and disturbing.

The experience was one about which much can be said, ranging from comments about my own possible lack of understanding, or even self-deception, to theoretical issues about the relationship of the mystical and ethical aspects of religion. Most important here, the experience exemplifies many features that contribute to a virtue like spiritual regret, and it can help us understand the virtue's character and newness.

The notion that this or any virtue can be new requires, as noted, both explanation and defense. At least it does for those people who believe ideas about virtue only make sense when coupled with ideas about a constant human nature, all of whose capacities are evident at any time. "Newness" implies that specific historical and cultural complexes, particular chronological features, can be relevant to the identification of a virtue or can even determine it. It means that virtues can be called "era specific." They can be seen as excellences at one age or period but at another they will be unidentified or seen as indifferent qualities or even vices.

In defending the idea that virtues can be new, let me start with the relatively benign notion that specific virtues can be said to have histories that determine their form and value both in people and in civilizations. That is, the character of a virtue changes over time, even though its structural form stays steady enough that we can identify its various manifestations as belonging to the same general category. This kind of change in a specific virtue is perhaps especially evident when dealing with personal histories. Innocence differs significantly for a five-year-old, a thirty-year-old, and a fifty-year-old. An attitude toward odd people or events that is appropriate and even charming in a five-year-old is suspect in a thirty-year-old and positively problematic in a fifty-year-old.

We see a similar phenomenon in civilizations. Courage in Homer, in Aristotle, and in Aquinas is still courage; an identifiable structure is there. But courage's paradigmatic actions have changed from a warrior's defeat of a dangerous enemy to a saint's acceptance of death in martyrdom. The primary instances of courageous dispositions and actions thus appear to be fundamentally different. A new, important, and perhaps even crucial attribute of human goodness has surfaced. (The significance of such changes and difficulties in identifying them are other reasons, incidentally, why attention to comparative method is crucial, even when dealing with the history of one's own tradition.)

The situation with spiritual regret resembles that which we find with the example of courage. As we discussed, people have often recognized the divergences and conflicts among religious goods, and identifiable structures for thinking about the issue and acting well were present. Spiritual regret, however, responds to that situation in a new way. It arises from the sense, however implicit, that the traditional ways of dealing with distinctions among religions are deficient, that they fail to meet adequately the specific demands the modern situation produces. Therefore the virtues that manifest those traditional ways, virtues like toleration or righteous indignation, are also in error or incomplete.

Like all virtues, spiritual regret can productively be thought of as being *corrective*. That is, ideas about this and other virtues rest on a picture of human weakness and need. Virtues correct some difficulty thought to be natural to human beings, some temptation that needs to be resisted or some motivation that needs to be made good. Courage, for example, corrects the inclination to be dissuaded by fear from doing what should be done. Similarly, normal regret can be said to correct the tendency to self-deception and the inclination to forgo painful or nuanced accounts of one's past.

What the virtue of spiritual regret corrects most generally is the human propensity to overlook differences among legitimate goods. It corrects the inclination to subsume different goods under one's own or to deny that different goods are really goods. More specifically, spiritual regret corrects the common human unwillingness to face fully what is involved in a plurality of religious goods. It therefore also corrects the propensity to kinds of idolatry or envy; to see diverse spiritual goods only in one's own image or to feel antipathy toward spiritual goods that one does not possess. The virtue deals, then, with the new need to face fully fundamentally different religious ideals. Moreover, it also deals with the weaknesses present in those basically flawed or overly simple ways of conceiving and responding to those differences that we examined earlier.

This correction can occur, however, only if people understand both what needs correction and why it must be corrected. That is they must, first, be able to grasp the character of genuine religious differences and, second, they must also believe that a virtue is needed to deal with that new recognition. The grasping of differences involves, I believe, the acquisition of a skill—the skill that appears in the activity of accurate and imaginative comparisons between religious phenomena. The accepting that a new virtue is necessary involves a normative judgment about how best to deal with the situation— and that judgment is one that has principled opponents. Let us end by examining these two subjects.

VI. TRAINING OF THE ACADEMIC RELIGIOUS IMAGINATION

The correction which spiritual regret produces can appear only if the skill of comparison is well developed. That can occur only if one not only has the imagination to enter into other religious visions but also educates that imagination, and believes one should exercise that imagination. The crucial points, then, about what is involved in dealing with powerful but alien religions all revolve around the idea of imagination. The first concerns the role of imagination in understanding; the second concerns the need to educate it; and the third concerns the belief it should be used.

To focus on the imagination may seem odd. But I would argue that the capacity to imagine is as important as the capacity to deliberate when the subject is how best to live and therefore what are the virtues we should pursue. Moreover, the capacity to imagine underlies, I think, all significant comparative work whether it involves our subject, the understanding of different religions, or even related subjects such as understanding more fully people we may think we know well.

I believe all people have the capacity to enter imaginatively into other religious visions. Like virtually all capacities or potentialities that can generate skills, however, it can be actualized only if it is trained. That training can be hard to come by. Travel, reading, temperament, and sustained attention to the people around one can surely help. Moreover, portions of the media, especially television, often do present foreign religious perspectives and more than occasionally do so in very striking ways. Nevertheless, the training to understand and appreciate those perspectives is for many people available only in educational institutions. They are one of the few places, and I am often tempted to say only places, it can occur. Indeed, I would even argue that media presentations and many kinds of travel usually foster the kind of tourist mentality that leads people away from rather than toward complex understandings.

Obviously a position like mine can carry the rancid odor of self-justification or even self-aggrandizement. Such suspicions are surely understandable, whether they arise from observers within or outside of the profession, but several comments may alleviate them. First, the general purposes of education often differ dramatically from what higher education can accomplish. I do believe the purpose of education, when defined most generally, is to develop all those human excellences a culture thinks are important. But few American institutions of higher education either have the time or possess the ethos to develop most ethical or religious virtues. Indeed, it would be self-deceiving and probably silly to believe that such institutions can fundamentally change the ethical and religious dispositions that have been formed by the powerful forces of family and culture.

That does not mean, however, that education cannot develop skills. These skills, in turn, will inform virtues in ways we discussed earlier. Given higher education's character many of the virtues it informs will be intellectual ones, and the contribution of the acquired skills will be direct and basic. Other virtues, however, will be ethical or religious ones, and the contribution of both the acquired skills and the resultant intellectual virtues will be less direct and basic. I think the disciplined and imaginative understanding of other religious perspectives is one skill that can be developed in higher education. Moreover, the development of this skill is not only valuable in itself but it also contributes much to the growth of other virtues—intellectual, ethical, and religious. We can help train people's imagination in this area, then, and therefore aid in the development of virtues such as spiritual regret. . . .

VII. ENCOUNTERING THE PRINCIPLED OPPOSITION

Presuming needed development of the imagination has occurred we are still left with our third question, the question of whether full human flourishing demands that the power should be exercised. This question involves dealing with many daunting issues, and here I will just sketch out the competing positions and what are, I think, the major issues separating them.

People have and surely can argue that the imaginative

voyaging I recommend is unnecessary or even destructive. They may see it, for example, as a kind of voyeurism or self-torture. Opposing positions have many variants, but they all fit into two groups, groups that represent, to my mind, the different major alternatives. Both are integral views and have powerful spokespeople; both can even provide opportunities for virtues like spiritual regret.

The first response is avowedly secularist; it is areligious or antireligious if we employ any conventional notion of being religious. Most in this category share what has been called the modern ideal of the affirmation of ordinary life and therefore will distrust the heroic. They will also embrace at least some kind of pluralism and remain suspicious of grand claims. At the core of this position is, I believe, a kind of *sophisticated complacency*, especially a complacency about the need to respond to the kinds of questions religions deal with. The aim, then, is to help people overcome their fears about the importance of the answers they give to religious questions.

This position can easily produce a debilitatingly banal vision of human fulfillment. But it can also produce a powerful view where pride of place is always given to moral not religious questions and to realistic, practical solutions. Moreover, it can share the spiritual ideal of disciplined detachment from many normal human concerns which underlies the notion of human excellence. . . . It can, then, represent a powerful spiritual alternative to what I have been arguing for; it may, for example, hold to the dramatic notion that regret of any sort ought not be part of a well-lived life.

The second response includes people who would claim to be religious however conventionally or unconventionally they take that term. For them imaginative voyaging and the virtues like spiritual regret that it aims to produce represent at best a problematic ideal, at worst a significant vice or religious deformation. They could, for example, classify spiritual regret as a virulent case of primordial pride, a violation of humility, an attempt to encompass all possible goods and to become "god-like."

Most important for these people are the implications to be drawn from human finitude. Especially important are the limits that must be observed if a full religious life is to be lived. Proponents of this position argue that imaginative voyaging undercuts the only possible basis for active, and perhaps saving, participation in a religious community. Such participation, it is said, requires one to limit the sorts of religious questions one entertains. It may even require, on religious grounds, that one treat the claims of fundamentally different religious perspectives with ironic distance or cultivated neglect rather than with intense attention. They argue, then, for a kind of *sophisticated parochialism*, an intentional and reasoned closing off of perspectives.

Any full response to these two principled opponents involves, as noted, dealing with questions I cannot examine fully here. However, let me sketch out the most crucial features of the rationale for my position. I think imaginative voyaging, and what it produces, is necessary for three related reasons. We need it, first, if we are to meet fully both the demands and the possibilities our current religious situation places before us. That is, we face a situation which requires new responses from us if any religious ideas are to meet the criteria of appropriateness and plausibility. That in turn presents striking new opportunities to rethink what we are committed to and why. We also need it if we are to see the new kinds of spiritual discipline the current situation makes possible. That is, the particular asceticism which characterizes scholarly inquiry into different religions—for instance, the cultivation of thinking without assenting—can be seen as part of a discipline the spiritual implications of which extend beyond scholarship, at least as it is narrowly defined. Finally, we need it if we are to operate well and perhaps even survive in the present world. That is, our contact with diverse religious ideas and practices grows at a pace that places striking new demands on us about how best to understand and to judge them.

I want, then, to defend the significance of virtues like spiritual regret. Nevertheless, I also agree with some features of the positions presented by the principled opposition. Most important, I agree there are areas where such virtues are inappropriate and can, at times, even be called vices. Indeed, seeing where virtues like spiritual regret ought not function is an extremely important part of this kind of analysis, just as courage is best understood in the context of foolhardiness and timidity. Separating out areas where they are appropriate from areas where they are not is critical for seeing both what the virtues are and what their deformations are. Let me end with a few brief comments on this subject.

Some confrontations that might seem to be occasions for, say, spiritual regret are not. They are not appropriate occasions because one cannot accept the option presented and still remain oneself in any meaningful sense. In one such area, really entertaining the option is impossible because of either the *theoretical* or the *ethical* webs of belief a person has. Those two webs of belief differ in important ways but either can make impossible a full encounter. For example, my web of theoretical beliefs would have to be surrendered if I embraced the religious ideals presented by a Korean shaman and my web of ethical beliefs if I embraced the religious ideals presented by a pre-Ch'in Taoist. In either case I would cease to be me.

Another more complex area involves cases where the fundamental choices a person has made within his or her general webs of theoretical and ethical beliefs have established enduring patterns that have basically changed the person. (Decisions to marry, have children, or commit to a profession can all be examples of such choices.) That is, I differ enough from what I would have become had another choice been made that I cannot really spiritually regret an option. In considering the alternative religious option, I am involved in a relationship that is not to myself but rather is to someone who closely resembles me, someone like an intimate friend.

Failures to see the inappropriateness of virtues like spiritual regret in either of these areas can be the result of intellectual mistakes. They can also, and more usually do, reflect the grip of vices like sentimentality or nostalgia. At worst the people involved manifest truly distorted human states. Unhappily, examples of this are all too evident both in people who have dabbled with powerful but alien religions and those who have ardently embraced them. At best these states manifest the counterfeits or perhaps semblances of the full virtue. Their state has only a few of the qualities the full virtue displays, and it is mixed with naive or even pathetic features.

Despite all this, there is also a range of other cases in which people face more subtle confrontations, and these are the places where virtues like spiritual regret ought to function. . . .

KEY TERMS AND CONCEPTS

apologetics The activity of offering a defense of one's religion.

insider's vs. outsider's perspectives Two different viewpoints from which the study of religion can be conducted. The insider's view is that of a religious participant who seeks understanding in order to increase faith. The outsider's perspective refers to the academic study of religion, which seeks understanding from a nonsectarian point of view.

meta, or second order, vs. first order *First order* refers to engagement in some primary activity like speaking a language or practicing a religion. *Second order* (meta) refers to reflection on some first-order activity. The academic study of religion is here characterized as a second-order activity.

spiritual regret According to Yearley, this is a new religious virtue appropriate for the study of religion in our age of religious pluralism that involves both joy at discovering a new spiritual view that attracts you and sadness that you cannot fully adopt such a view.

SUGGESTIONS FOR FURTHER READING

Carman, J., and S. Hopkins, eds. *Tracing Common Themes: Comparative Courses in the Study of Religion.* Atlanta, Ga.: Scholars Press, 1991. Essays on the value and importance of the academic study of religion.

Creel, Richard E. *Religion and Doubt: Toward a Faith of Your Own.* 2nd ed. Englewood Cliffs, N.J.: Prentice-Hall, 1991. Creel's first chapter addresses the issue of why one should study religion, and his fifth chapter details what he thinks are the traits of a healthy religious faith.

McCutcheon, Russell T., ed. *The Insider/Outsider Problem in the Study of Religion: A Reader.* London: Cassell, 1999. A useful collection of writings on issues relating to the academic study of religion.

Plantinga, Alvin. "A Defense of Religious Exclusivism." In *Philosophy of Religion: An Anthology*, 3rd ed., edited by Louis P. Pojman, pp. 517–530. Belmont, Calif.: Wadsworth, 1994. Plantinga argues that even in a pluralistic situation, religious exclusivism is neither morally wrong nor unreasonable—some exclusivism in belief is inevitable. However, he does believe we should seek knowledge of other religions, even if we risk lessening our own assurance.

Porter, Jean. "Virtue Ethics." In *A Companion to Philosophy of Religion*, edited by Phillip L. Quinn and Charles Taliaferro, pp. 466–472. Oxford: Blackwell, 1997. Provides a clear overview of recent developments in the thinking about virtue.

Reynolds, F., and S. Burkhalter, eds. *Beyond the Classics? Essays on Religious Studies and Liberal Education.* Atlanta, Ga.: Scholars Press, 1990. These essays take the reader deeper into the issues of how the study of religion relates to liberal education.

RESEARCH PROJECTS

1. Write a paper focusing on the insider/outsider distinction, and investigate whether the distinction is useful and whether it can be clearly articulated.

2. Write a paper on Yearley's notion of spiritual regret and investigate whether it truly is a virtue. This would involve pursuing the objections of sophisticated complacency and sophisticated parochialism in greater depth.
3. Consider this statement by Bruce Lincoln: "Reverence is a religious, and not a scholarly, virtue. When good manners and good conscience cannot be reconciled, the demands of the latter ought to prevail" ("Theses on Method," *Method and Theory in the Study of Religion* 1996). Write a brief paper exploring what you think Lincoln may mean, provide concrete examples, and evaluate Lincoln's thesis.

2

What Is Religion?

The question "What is religion?" is deceptively simple. Most people think they know what religion is. If I asked you to write a one-sentence definition, you could do so after a little thought. So, what is the problem with defining religion?

There are many problems for the student of religions, because not any sort of definition will do. In order to engage in the academic study of religion, we need a definition that is analytically useful. That means it should *be useful for the purposes at hand, be as precise as possible without being too narrow in scope, and be as free from bias as possible.*

USEFULNESS

Definitions are not true or false, but more or less useful. They tell us how to use words effectively depending on the situation and what we are trying to communicate. Historians who wish to study religious beliefs and practices that characterize people in China two thousand years ago may find one kind of definition useful for their purposes, but a sociologist who wishes to describe social influences on religious practices in contemporary England may find another kind of definition useful. Definitions are heuristic devices—they are an aid that stimulates further investigation and thought. Hence different academic disciplines (e.g., history, sociology, psychology, anthropology, literature, philosophy) find different definitions more or less useful, depending on the perspective of their discipline. Given these circumstances, the quest for one universal definition of religion that is useful for all academic disciplines seems hopeless.

You might be thinking that what I have just said does not sound quite right. What if the definition the historian uses and the definition the sociologist uses are totally different? How could we be sure that they were both studying religion rather than two very different phenomena?

PRECISION

That question leads directly into a discussion of precision. The purpose of definitions is to *draw boundaries* and thereby limit the field of study. If everything fell under the category of religion, then the study of religion would become the study of everything and thereby become impossible to manage. When drawing boundaries, however, we can be too precise and draw them so narrowly that we exclude some things that ought to be included. For example, if I defined religion as "belief in God," I would be leaving out too much of importance, such as religious practices. Religions are more than belief systems; they involve ritual practices, moral codes, various types of social organizations, and much more. Also, what about polytheistic religions that believe there is more than one god, religions that deny ultimate reality is divine (some types of Buddhism), or those that believe in totems and spirits? Is it reasonable to exclude them by definition?

The other side of the coin of drawing the boundaries too narrowly is drawing them too broadly. Some scholars have favored definitions that involve the use of words like *ultimate concern* or *sacred*. Unless carefully specified, these words are so vague that it seems practically anything can fit within their boundaries. Is the capitalist who devotes his life to the pursuit of wealth religious because money and the power it brings have become his ultimate concern? Is the socialist who devotes her life to the pursuit of social justice through the equal or near-equal distribution of wealth religious because economic justice is a sacred cause for the socialist?

The questions and problems associated with precision are closely tied to two very different theories of the nature of definition. For scholars who hold to a theory of essentialism, the purpose of definitions is to state the essence of something. The **essence** is a universal quality or set of qualities that make something *what it is* and *not something else.* For example, the fact that I have gray hair is not an essential quality. I could have black hair and still be who I am. However, it is hard to imagine me being who I am if I did not have the quality of being a human being. Being human seems to be more essential to who I am than my hair color.

However, an essence must be a quality or characteristic that not only makes something what it is but also makes it not something else. This means an essence must consist of both **necessary** and **sufficient** traits or characteristics. A quality might be necessary without being sufficient. I am human and that is necessary to my identity, but it is not sufficient to make me who I am because all other humans have that quality as well. A quality might also be sufficient, but not necessary. For example, a baseball striking a window is sufficient to break it, but it is not necessary since many other things besides baseballs break windows.

If you think good definitions must be **essential definitions,** then you need to find characteristics of religion that are both necessary and sufficient. This involves correctly identifying the genus and species. A **genus** is a class divisible into a smaller class called a **species.** For example, Aristotle's famous definition of a human being as a rational animal states the genus (animal) and within that genus a smaller class (rational beings). The smaller class or species is discovered by stating the differences (referred to as *differentia*) that distinguish one type of animal from another. This gives the definition greater precision because while all humans are animal, not all animals are human. There are other kinds of animals (like frogs), and what makes them different, if we follow Aristotle, is that they are not rational while humans are rational. If we take the two qualities (animal and rational) together, we have, if Aristotle is right, the necessary and sufficient characteristics of human beings.

Those who pursue essential definitions of religion usually favor either a **substantive definition** that states what religion is or a **functional definition** that states what religion does. Defining religion as belief in the supernatural is an example of a substantive type of essential definition. Defining religion as a be-

lief system that gives meaning and purpose to human life is an example of a functional type of essential definition. Both definitions identify the genus of religion as belief. The substantive example (belief in the supernatural) differentiates religious beliefs from other types of belief by stating what it is a belief in, namely, the supernatural. The functional example differentiates religious beliefs by stating what they do (provide meaning and purpose to human life).

Both of these types, substantive and functional, are problematic. Substantive types often turn out to be too narrow because of the vast diversity of religious beliefs and practices, and functional types often turn out to be too broad because different things can often function in the same way. For example, various types of political beliefs as well as religious beliefs can give meaning and purpose to human life.

A very different theory of definition rejects the idea of essences. According to this theory, we should look for a cluster of characteristics that makes something part of a certain family. **Cluster definitions** are based on an analogy with families. Families are made up of many members who have many different traits or qualities. Yet, despite these differences, they are all members of the same family. There may be no set of traits that are both necessary and sufficient, but there are traits that allow us to group them into the same family.

Perhaps religion is like a family. There are many members with many different characteristics but no set of characteristics that capture some essence. Those who favor cluster definitions of religion readily acknowledge that the boundaries between religion and other things are fuzzy. There is no sharp line of demarcation, but a kind of fading away until the cluster of qualities has become so thin that we best start talking about a different family.

BIAS

We said at the outset that good definitions of religion should be as free from bias as possible. As I said in the first chapter, none of us can totally escape our biases since we must necessarily study from various perspectives, but we can become aware of them. This awareness allows us to correct for bias when we formulate definitions. One common bias is what we might call the Western bias. It is very subtle (as many biases are), and to unmask it will take careful analysis.

The English word *religion* comes from the Latin word **religio**. Latin scholars are not certain whether *religio* comes from the Latin *relegere*, which refers to people who are careful in their ritual actions rather than neglectful, or *religare*, which means "to bind," that is, to be under an obligation. Early Latin Christians used the word *religio* to distinguish true religion from false. For them *religio* did not refer to the world religions as it does today, but rather to genuine or true worship. In the Middle Ages, *religio* was not widely used, but when it was, it often referred to "the religious," that is, those who choose the monastic life. Hence, *religio* distinguished the monastic life from the life of the laity.

With the dawn of the modern age, when knowledge of and encounters with religions different from Christianity increased, people began using the word *religion* to refer to the various religious traditions of the world. Today, *religion* and its cognates are also used to refer to different historical traditions with different beliefs and practices. In addition, the adjective form is used to refer to personal piety as in "She is a very religious person." Sometimes, *religion* is used in an ideal sense to refer to something that is desirable or valuable as in "Religion is a good thing." In the singular, the word can refer to religion in general.

Given this history, it is not surprising that some scholars have proposed dropping the use of the word *religion* for scholarly purposes because it is hopelessly abstract and tied too deeply to Western biases. Benson Saler, an anthropologist, summarizes this view when he writes, "The practitioners of a mostly Western profession (anthropology) employ a Western category (religion), conceptualized as a component of a larger Western category (culture), to achieve their professional goal of coming to understand what is meaningful and important for non-Western peoples" (*Conceptualizing Religion*, 1993:9).

Complicating this ethnocentric bias that seems to be built into the very word *religion* is a value bias. Definitions reflect how the people creating them value religion. If their attitude is positive, the definition will be positive. If their attitude is negative, the definition will be negative, and if their attitude is mixed or uncertain, their definition will reflect that too. For example, if I defined religion as "an illusory hope for a better future," you would immediately detect a negative attitude in my definition. We can check our value biases by adding qualifying words such as *allegedly*, *presumably*, or *maybe*. So I might revise my definition of religion to "the hope for a better future, a hope that may or may not prove to be an illusion."

Correcting for the very ethnicity of the word *religion* is much harder. If we do not use *religion*, what word should we use? Are *faith* or *tradition* any more free from a Western bias? Probably the best we can do is recognize that some ethnocentric words are starting points (we have to start from our own culture), but ethnocentrism should not be a stopping point. If it is, it shows we have not learned anything about our biases.

Every definition of religion is part of a more general theory of religion. It is "theory-laden" to use the technical term. Behind every definition is some theory about what religion means and how it functions. This is not a bad thing; indeed, it is unavoidable. However, one needs to be aware of the ways theory influences definition. For example, some theories hold that there is something irreducibly "religious" about religions—that religions are unique and can be understood only on their own ground. Other theories claim that religions are like any other human phenomenon and can be understood in cultural, historical, sociological, or psychological terms. According to these theories, there is nothing that is uniquely religious about religions. These two divergent types of theories generate very different definitions.

Still another subtle bias that slips into both theory and definition is gender bias. Since religions historically have been largely dominated by males, and since females often have been relegated to the back pews, so to speak, when we think about religion we often take as our implicit model traditional patriarchal religions. Our theories and definitions are then built up under the influence of these models and gender bias is the result. Even the word *God* implies for many a male figure. People may be inclined to define religion as "belief in God or gods," rather than "belief in gods and goddesses."

Another bias that slips into definitions is the confusion between spirituality and religion. Consider these two statements:

1. A person can belong to a religion and not be religious.

2. A person can be religious and not belong to a religion.

The key term is *belong to*. If *belong to* means being an official member of some organization, then the first statement seems obviously true. The term *religious hypocrite* would have little meaning if someone could not formally belong to a religious organization and fail to personally embody spirituality. The second statement is more problematic because one could make the case that the truly spiritual person will seek membership in some religious organization because religious organizations try to foster spirituality and provide an opportunity for spiritual fellowship. It is undoubtedly true that religious organizations present themselves as a path or way that fosters growth in spirituality, but there seems to be no good reason why someone could not foster spiritual growth in ways other than belonging to some religious organization.

Crucial to this debate about the relationship between **spirituality** and **religion** is a clear distinction between the two. Defining spirituality is even harder than defining religion. This is complicated by the fact that we sometimes use the adjective *religious* interchangeably with *spiritual*. To be spiritual is to be deeply and genuinely religious. But how can one be religious without religion?

There have, of course, been various attempts to define spirituality. The psychologist of religion William James (1842–1910) suggested that spirituality is a quest for a transformation from a state of perceived wrongness to a state of perceived rightness by making contact with some higher power or powers. The contemporary philosopher John Hick thinks of spirituality as a transformation from a selfish and egocentric state to an unselfish and caring state. However, all of these terms are vague and notoriously different to make precise. Nevertheless, it is important to not confuse religion and spirituality. When we do, we are tempted to transfer whatever negative qualities we may find in religious organizations to people who sincerely seek to make a better life for themselves and others.

The two statements I asked you to consider earlier presuppose that spirituality or religiosity is best thought of as a personal quality—a characteristic or set of characteristics that some people have. They also presuppose that religion refers to an organized group of people. This organized group presents itself as an effective way to nurture the personal quality of spirituality, but it is always possible that it fails to do so or, at least, fails to satisfy the spiritual desires of those who join. The problem of how religion and spirituality are related is itself a product of how we conceptualize religion.

I have discussed some of the many problems involved in the deceptively simple task of defining religion. Finding a useful definition that is analytically precise and free from bias is no easy task. There is another problem as well: Should we define religion before we study religions or only afterward? Some argue it is not fair to define one's subject matter before looking and seeing what is there. Others argue that without some idea of where to look (and a definition gives us an idea of where to look), we will be looking in vain. This is a variation of the chicken and the egg problem. But rather than being a problem about which came first (obviously, religion did), which *should* come first—definition or observation? I think this problem is not a real problem. Instead, definition and observation must go hand in hand. We need to start with working definitions that tell us where to look, and as we look we need to revise and refine our definitions.

2.1 DEFINING RELIGION

We discussed the differences between the concepts of essential definition and cluster definition earlier. Here we examine in greater detail the notion of a cluster definition and how it might be usefully applied to the problem of defining religion.

Rem B. Edwards, a professor of philosophy at the University of Tennessee, explores, in the following selection, the possibility of a cluster definition of religion. He discovers that the meaning of the English word *religion* is so influenced by Western theistic religions and Western culture that its cross-cultural usefulness is questionable. His discussion not only illuminates the notion of cluster definition but also illustrates how one might construct such a definition of religion. Edwards's analysis of the traits frequently associated with religion reveals some significant features of the way many of us think about religion.

REM B. EDWARDS

The Search for Family Resemblances of Religion

READING QUESTIONS

1. As you read, make a list of all the words and ideas you do not understand or are uncertain about. Discuss them with a classmate, look them up in a dictionary, or bring them up in class for discussion and clarification. (You should continue doing this for every selection in this book.)
2. What makes finding the essence of religion difficult?
3. All superior beings are not supernatural beings. Why?
4. Which family traits appear to be common or nearly common to all family members? What does this imply about the influence of Western religions on the search for family traits?
5. Edwards thinks that many of the family traits are sufficient, yet none of them is necessary. Do you agree? Why or why not?

The influential twentieth-century philosopher Ludwig Wittgenstein thought that there are many perfectly meaningful, useful words in our language that have no "common essence" of connotation. These words are not used to name some characteristic or set of characteristics common to and distinctive of all the objects to which we normally apply such words. Wittgenstein thought that the common-sense assumption that there has to be a common essence where there is a common name is exceedingly naive, and he recommended that instead of making this assumption uncritically we should "look and see" if it is so. He believed that we would not always find a common essence for many perfectly useful words, such as *game*, *language*, *knowledge*, and so on. That he was correct with respect to *all* the words he used to illustrate his point may be questioned, but his general idea that some words have only "family resemblances" instead of "common essences" is a very fruitful one to explore, especially in its application to the word *religion*. Wittgenstein him-

self did not apply it to *religion*, but others who have been influenced by him have made preliminary studies of its possible application in this area. We shall first discuss briefly what is meant by "the search for family resemblances," and then we shall see if the search throws any light on our understanding of *religion*.

Not all objects called by a common name have a common essence, but they are frequently related to one another by "a complicated network of similarities overlapping and criss-crossing: sometimes overall similarities, sometimes similarities of detail," according to Wittgenstein. He compared this web of resemblances to the complicated way in which members of a human family resemble one another and are recognizable as members of the same family. Suppose that there are five brothers and sisters who are easily recognizable as members of the same family, but among whom there is not a single family trait that each has in common with *all* the others, as illustrated by the following diagram. Their resemblance to one another may depend not on a common essence, but on a complicated web of traits shared with one or more, but not with all, of the other members of the family. (In the diagram, the presence of a family trait is indicated by P and the absence by A.)

| | FAMILY MEMBERS | | | | |
FAMILY TRAITS	Alex	Bill	Cathy	Dave	Enid
Over 6 feet tall	P	P	P	P	A
Blue eyes	P	P	P	A	P
Blond hair	P	P	A	P	P
Pug nose	P	A	P	P	P
Irritability	A	P	P	P	P

The obvious weakness of the family resemblance comparison is that if we were to add one additional family trait to our diagram, namely "Having the same parents," we would have a characteristic that was both common to and distinctive of each member of the family. But even this trait would not necessarily be common to all; suppose that Enid resembles all her brothers and sisters in all the respects indicated and yet is an adopted child! Nevertheless, there is always the possibility that such an additional family trait has been overlooked and will later turn up in any attempt to explore the meaning of a word in terms of family resemblances. When such a trait is discovered, this would seem to mean that our search for family resemblances has turned up a common essence as well and that the two approaches complement rather than conflict with each other. Perhaps this will turn out to be the case with the concept of "religion."

FAMILY TRAITS OF RELIGION

Many college students in the Western world who register for their first course in World Religions or Comparative Religions have some weird misconceptions about the non-Christian religions. They may think, for example, that in most of the non-Christian religions it is really the supernatural Christian God who is known and worshiped, but he is called by some other name such as the Buddha, the Brahman, or Allah, and that this knowledge is somewhat perversely distorted, since the devotees of these religions have not received all the benefits of the Christian revelation. Many students assume that most of the world religions teach that the individual human "soul" is created by God and is destined to everlasting existence in some place of reward or punishment, and that a program of "salvation" from the latter and for the former is invariably provided. Many students further assume that all world religions include a moral program —again somewhat distorted, of course—which contains the essentials of the Ten Commandments and the Sermon on the Mount and which is derived from and sanctioned by the Supreme Being. In short, it is typical for Westerners to assume at the outset of a study of the concept of "religion" or the phenomena of the world religions that the field of inquiry is considerably less diversified than it in fact turns out to be. Yet it is precisely this diversity that makes it so difficult to discover some common essence for "religion" and that has suggested that the search for family resemblances might be a more fruitful approach to the concept of "religion." Let us see how such a search can be conducted.

We shall now look at a selected list of family traits and family members for the concept of "religion." In the chart, . . . the family traits listed in the column on the left are all prominent characteristics of at least some of the things that we call religions, and the list of family members is a partial list of some of the things to which we apply the word with some degree of regularity. Neither list is in any way complete, especially the list of family members, and you can add to each list as you see fit. This chart and the discussion that follows are *not* to be construed as a survey of the field of comparative religion. The family members that are included were selected mainly because they permit us to introduce a preliminary discussion of the difficulties involved in discovering a common essence. The exercise as a whole is valuable because it allows us to make a place for the richness and concreteness of meaning that *religion* normally has. . . .

GENERAL CONCLUSIONS OF "THE SEARCH FOR FAMILY RESEMBLANCES"

1. The only family members in our chart that clearly exhibit all the family traits are Christianity, Judaism, and Islam, though Hinduism comes very close. This suggests that these Western religions have had a definitive influence on our very conception of religion. We do in fact take them as paradigms for the application of the concept, since they exhibit *all* the important traits that we ascribe to a "religion." We might conjecture that if we were making an ordinary-language analysis of religion in Ceylon we would have set up our list of family traits in such a way as to get a P in each case for Hinayana Buddhism, or in India a clear-cut P in each case for Hinduism—and in the languages of these countries it would be the Western religions that would be found wanting! If this is the case, then *religion* in English is only an approximate translation of any corresponding words in these other languages.

2. The family members on the chart are arranged in such a way that fewer and fewer P's appear as we move to the right in the direction of success, wealth, golf, and fishing, and get further and further away from our paradigms of Christianity, Judaism, and Islam. This suggests that as we Westerners become acquainted with other cultures and new developments in our own cultures, we are willing to extend the application of *religion* to those phenomena that bear some significant similarities to our own standard religions. It further suggests that as these similarities become fewer and fewer in particular cases, we come to have more and more reservations about the legitimacy of extending *religion* to cover these cases. This explains why we are uneasy about calling success, wealth, golf, and fishing religions—they are like Christianity *only* in that they involve deep, intense concern. We say that such "religions" are only "borderline cases," or that in speaking of them as religions we are only speaking metaphorically.

3. In deciding whether to call something a religion, it is not merely the *number* of respects in which it resembles our paradigms that guides us, it is also the *importance* of these traits. Other traits besides deep, intense concern, such as a complex world view interpreting the significance of human life or an account of the nature of, origin of, and cure for evil, are nearly universal in the religions, and this may be one clue that guides us in as-

SELECTED FAMILY TRAITS OF SOME RELIGIONS

FAMILY TRAITS	Christianity, Judaism, Islam	Vedanta Hindu Pantheism	Early Buddhism and Hinayana Buddhism	Early Greek Olympian Polytheism	Aristotle's Concept of Unmoved Mover	Communism	Moral Naturalistic Humanism	Spinozistic Pantheism	Success, Wealth, Golf, Fishing, etc.
1. Belief in a *supernatural* intelligent being or beings	P	A?	A	A	P	A	A	A	A
2. Belief in a *superior* intelligent being or beings	P	P	A	P	P	A	A	A?	A
3. Complex world view interpreting the significance of human life	P	P	P	P	P	P	P	P	A
4. Belief in experience after death	P	P	P	P?	A	A	A	A	A
5. Moral code	P	P	P	A	P	P	P	A	A
6. Belief that the moral code is sanctioned by a *superior* intelligent being or beings	P	P	A	A	A	A	A	A	A
7. An account of the nature of, origin of, and cure for evil	P	P	P	P?	P	P	P	P	A
8. Theodicy	P	P?	A	A	A	A	A	A	A
9. Prayer and ritual	P	P	P	P	A	P?	A	A?	A
10. Sacred objects and places	P	P	P	P	A	P	A	A	A?
11. Revealed truths or interpretations of revelatory events	P	P	P?	P	A	A	A	A	A
12. Religious experience—awe, mystical experience, revelations	P	P	P	P	A	A	A	A	P
13. Deep, intense concern	P	P	P	P	P?	P	P	P	P
14. Institutionalized social sharing of some of traits 1–13	P	P	P	P	A?	P	A?	A?	A?
15.									
16.									
17.									

Key: P = Present, A = Absent, ? = Unclear.

sessing their importance. What other traits are of crucial importance? To us Westerners belief in God and in experience after death weigh heavily, though even these are not deemed absolutely necessary. A typical Western atheist who passionately denies God and immortality, who never indulges in anything resembling prayer, ritual, or mysticism, and whose principles we regard as less than moral would not be called a religious man; but a dedicated Hinayana Buddhist who fails to affirm God and immortality and yet does engage in something resembling prayer, ritual, mysticism, and morality is called a religious man, mainly because his situation does exhibit a significant number of important resemblances to our paradigmatic religions.

4. The traits provide the differentia of "religion." We are willing to call a religion only a finite set of beliefs and practices through which we express our ultimate concerns. . . . The list of family traits on our chart represents the hard core of the traits that the "religions" must manifest, and although it is by no means complete, it nevertheless could not be indefinitely extended. Neither could the list of family members be indefinitely extended. There are many sufficient but no necessary conditions for calling something a religion if the Wittgensteinian approach is correct. So long as there are family resemblances, it is not necessary that there be common essences in order for there to be limits on the correct application of a concept and rules to guide us in

making those applications. However, is the contention that there are *only* family resemblances completely correct? What shall we say about the several nearly universal traits of religion that we have discovered? Would we call something a religion that completely failed to involve deep concern, answers to questions about the significance of human life, and perhaps even some account of the origin of, nature of, and cure for evil? Is the search for family resemblances completely at odds with the search for common essences? In looking to see, have we not found? In being nearly if not completely universal, these traits come as close to being necessary conditions for calling something a religion as we could expect to find for such a complex ordinary-language concept.

KEY TERMS AND CONCEPTS

cluster vs. essential definitions Cluster definitions list a set of family traits found in many members of the "family" religion. Essential definitions attempt to state the essence of religion.

essence That quality or qualities that make something what it is and not something else.

genus and species Genus is a class to which something belongs, and species is a subclass of the genus that distinguishes a particular member of the genus from other members.

necessary and sufficient qualities A necessary quality is any quality that X must have in order to be X, while a sufficient quality is any quality that X may have whose presence is enough to make X occur, but X could occur in its absence. Qualities may be necessary and not sufficient, or sufficient and not necessary, or both. A person searching for an essential definition seeks qualities that are both necessary and sufficient because these constitute the essences of the *diffiendum* (thing to be defined).

religio Latin word for religion that means either taking care in practicing rites like sacrifice or being under an obligation to practice rites. Combining both meanings, we get "the obligation to practice rites carefully."

spirituality vs. religion The development of spirituality is the goal of many religions, but it is not necessary to belong to a religious organization in order to pursue spiritual development.

substance vs. functional definitions Both are different types of essential definitions. The first focuses on the "what," or content, of religion; the second focuses on what religion *does*, that is, how it functions.

SUGGESTIONS FOR FURTHER READING

King, Winston L. "Religion." In *The Encyclopedia of Religion*, edited by Mircea Eliade, vol. 12, pp. 282–293. New York: Macmillan, 1987. A discussion of different definitions and some of the problems associated with defining religion along with different categories useful in comparing religions such as sacred actions, sacred times and places, sacred objects, myths, and symbols.

Smart, Ninian. *Worldviews: Crosscultural Explorations of Human Beliefs.* 2nd ed. Englewood Cliffs, N.J.: Prentice-Hall, 1995. Smart argues that we should subsume the category of religion under the even broader category of worldviews and that we should think of and compare worldviews in terms of six dimensions: doctrinal or philosophical, mythic or narrative, ethical or legal, ritual or practical, experiential or emotional, social or institutional.

Streng, Frederick J. *Understanding Religious Life.* 3rd ed. Belmont, Calif.: Wadsworth, 1985. The first chapter, "The Nature and Study of Religion," insightfully treats some of the themes and topics I have discussed in this chapter and in chapter 1.

RESEARCH PROJECTS

1. By yourself or with a study group of students, research some of the most influential definitions of religion in the past fifty years (your instructor can guide you). Then pick one definition and defend it as better than one or two other definitions you have selected.

2. Construct your own definition of religion and show how it is analytically useful (useful for the purpose at hand, as precise as possible without being too narrow in scope, and as free from bias as possible) for the comparative study of religions.

3. Write a one- or two-page critical précis of the selection by Edwards that consists of four elements: (1) a one-sentence statement of the thesis or main point of the reading; (2) a summary of the argument and evidence the author uses to establish the thesis; (3) a critique of the thesis *and* argument (critiques can be positive, negative, or a mixture of both); and (4) a statement of your own position with respect to the topic.

3

How Should We Study Religion?

The first chapter discussed some of the personal qualities useful in the study of religion: openness, honesty, critical intelligence, and careful reading and listening. This chapter is slightly more technical because we explore issues of methodology. How do we engage in the academic study of religion? That is, what are some of the methods we can employ?

THE FIELD OF RELIGIOUS STUDIES

Before I discuss method directly, let's look at a brief disciplinary outline of the field of religious studies as it is presently practiced in many colleges and universities in the United States and elsewhere:

   I. History of religions
      A. Developmental studies
      B. Comparative studies
  II. Social scientific study of religions
      A. Anthropology
      B. Sociology
      C. Psychology
 III. Philosophical study of religions
      A. Analytical
      B. Critical

This outline is incomplete because there are areas that cut across these divisions such as feminist studies, literary studies, biblical studies, and much more. However, it will do as a starting point.

Historical studies employ the theories and methods of history to study how a religion, religions, or part of a religion has developed through time. All religions change because nothing that survives can do so without adapting to its changing environment. Religions that are living traditions have changed and are changing. Those that have ceased to change are dead religions (although parts may have survived in other religious forms such as Easter and Christmas). The developmental historian is interested in how religions have changed and what factors are at work that cause change. A basic assumption of this approach is that religions are complex dynamic historical processes.

Comparative studies primarily focus on comparing different religious traditions. The concern is less with the changes religions undergo (although one could do a comparative study of changes) and more with structures or types. The comparativist often arrests time by taking snapshots, as it were, of different religious phenomena and then comparing them. The comparativist may select one of the many dimensions of religion such as ritual and do a comparative study of, for example, certain types of ritual activities in Islam and Judaism during the nineteenth century in Poland and Turkey. One basic assumption of comparative studies is that there are certain analytical categories (belief, ritual, morality, and so on) that are useful for cross-cultural comparison. Ideally the comparativist should be balanced in her or his description of similarities and differences, but this is sometimes difficult to do. Often, differences get submerged or overlooked in the rush to find similarities.

Social scientists use the current methods and theories of their fields to understand and explain religion within a larger setting. A basic assumption for social scientists is that insofar as religion is a human activity, it can be explained by cultural, social, or psychological factors just as any human phenomenon can. The anthropologist sees religion as an expression of and part of a wider culture. Religion is treated as a subclass of culture. For sociologists, the operative category is society: What are the social functions of religion? How do societies influence religions, and how do religions influence societies? Psychologists are usually more individually oriented than sociologists: How might religion express unconscious structures? How does religion affect character development? Does religious commitment have any bearing on deviant behavior, mental illness, or moral development?

I divide philosophy of religion into two categories: analytic and critical. However, this is somewhat artificial because in practice the categories are often combined. Elsewhere I have defined *philosophy of religion* as "the rational attempt to formulate, understand, and answer fundamental questions about religious matters" (*Philosophy of Religion: Toward a Global Perspective*, 1999:3). That definition requires quite a bit of detailed unpacking, but I will note here only that the philosophical quest for formulating, understanding, and answering fundamental questions demands both careful analysis of religious belief and action and a critical response (negative or positive) whose goal is a deeper rational understanding of religious matters. Exactly what is rational and what are fundamental questions are subjects of intense debate. A basic assumption of this field is that if there is such a thing as religious truth, careful philosophical criticism and analysis should be able to uncover it. So, philosophy of religion is characteristically concerned with arguments for God's existence, arguments for life after death, whether or not religious experiences provide evidence of some religious reality, and so on. Historians and social scientists usually refrain from offering judgments about the truth or falsity of the religious beliefs and actions they study, but philosophers often boldly go where others fear to tread. Philosophers want to know if religions are bearers of truth.

UNDERSTANDING AND EXPLANATION

As you might imagine, there is considerable professional rivalry among these various areas of religious studies and considerable debate about what is appropriate and what is not. One major debate centers on a distinction between understanding and explanation. These terms are vague and are often used in different ways (understanding can even be thought of as one type of explanation), but in this debate understanding usually means reconstructing meanings from the "agent's point of view." This is equivalent to a type of interpretation. Explanation amounts to a casual account that subsumes religion under a theory in the social sciences and treats it just like any other social phenomenon.

According to the camp (called **phenomenology of religion**) that seeks only understanding, religion is *sui generis*, which means that it is based on something irreducibly religious and hence cannot be explained in nonreligious terms. The phenomenologists (so called because they claim to focus on only what appears, or phenomena) maintain that the academic study of religion is properly made up of only one discipline, a discipline appropriate to the study of the *sui generis* nature of religion, sometimes referred to as "the sacred." The good student of religion is to describe and interpret what appears (religious phenomena), but should not explain or evaluate it by standards foreign to religion. Phenomenologists sometimes call what they do history of religions or comparative religions (remember, I said the terminology is vague and confusing). They shun social scientists as hopelessly prejudiced because they project their own nonreligious theories into religious phenomena. Phenomenologists accuse social scientists of being "reductionistic" because they explain religion in terms of social causes—economic, cultural, or psychological.

Social scientists and philosophers generally see the field of religious studies as multidisciplinary and multimethodological. There are many different ways of studying religion, and each has something of value to offer. There is no good reason to exclude nonreligious causes of religious events if in fact they were causes of that event, and, at least for the philosophers, there is no good reason to refrain from asking whether what some religions claim is true is in fact true.

Let us assume for now that the goal of religious studies, be it historical, social scientific, or philosophical, is very much like the general goal of all academic disciplines, namely, to describe, interpret, explain, and evaluate certain phenomena. Given the preceding discussion, it is clear that phenomenologists would disagree with the last two (explaining and evaluating), but having noted this, let us move on to distinguish these activities and say something about how they are done.

DESCRIPTION

There is no such thing as pure **description** because every description is already an interpretation, but if we might artificially isolate it for a minute, we can characterize it as gathering and stating the facts of the case. Much like in a court of law, a case cannot proceed without knowing the facts, so the study of religion cannot proceed with knowing the data. In the field of religious studies, there is an enormous amount of data in a variety of different languages and cultures ranging from archaeological artifacts, pictures, coins, statues, and the like to sacred scriptures, commentaries on sacred scriptures, and other writings. The range is great, and I have not yet mentioned rituals, rites, oral traditions, and extraordinary experiences of transformation and revelation. No one can hope to master all of this data, and this book includes only a very small amount of mostly textual data such as scriptures, commentaries, and interpretations.

Gathering the data requires mastering a variety of technical skills, and presenting the data fairly and accurately is sometimes quite difficult. Mistakes can easily creep in, especially when dealing with gestures, customs, games, and rites from a culture very different from one's own. In order to facilitate the collection and presentation of data, students of religion often resort to classification schemes. These schemes can be very general, often referring to religious traditions as a whole (e.g., Buddhism, Islam, Christianity, or they can be more specific, referring to aspects of different religious traditions (e.g., beliefs, myths, symbols, sacred scriptures, experiences, morality, rituals, organization). Whatever classification scheme is used, it is created by scholars based on reflection on data and then used to organize and interpret further data. That is one reason why I said pure description is not possible. It simply is not possible to describe without classifying, and every classification scheme reflects an interpretation.

INTERPRETATION

What do the described data mean? That is the central problem for **interpretation.** The first obvious question is "mean to whom?" If we are talking about meaning for the insider, then that meaning is part of the descriptive data. If we are talking about meaning for the outside observer, then that meaning reflects the best understanding an outsider can come to given the data, the methods of interpretation employed, and the theories available.

Methods of interpretation are often called hermeneutical. **Hermeneutics** is the "science of interpretation," although the word *science* is used here in a very broad sense. Theoretically, hermeneutical studies can focus on any aspect of religion (beliefs, rituals, or experiences), but I will focus on the interpretation of written texts. The first rule of hermeneutics

is that meaning is context dependent; that is, what a text means depends on a variety of contexts both immediate and remote. Just as words have different meanings in different contexts (the work bank can mean the shore beside a river, stream, or lake; a place where money is stored; a rebound off the side of a pool table; and so on), texts have different meanings in different contexts. If I said, "I am going to the bank," you would not know the exact meaning of the word *bank* until I went on to specify, "in order to fish." The context of fishing rather than the context of cashing a check lets you know what I mean. One way to get at the context is to discover what the Germans call the ***Sitz im Leben*** (situation in life) of a text. Where and when was it written? By whom and to whom was it written? What is its purpose or function? Knowing the situation in life will tell you much about the meaning of a text.

There are also certain formal features of a text that will tell you much about its meaning. These include what type of writing it is (a letter, poem, narrative, sacred scripture, commentary) and what its surface structure (organization, style, themes) is. There is also a deep structure that is more difficult to discern. Deep structures are the hidden rules governing what is said much like the structure of language is determined by the hidden rules of grammar. In order to get at this hidden structure, scholars often distinguish between the text (what the author writes) and the subtext (either explicit asides by the author about what he or she writes or indirect meanings such as irony). Scholars look at what is included in a text, but they must also be aware of what is excluded. Social rules about inclusion and exclusion determine, in part, what is said. For example, there are certain words I have excluded in my account of hermeneutics because they are deemed inappropriate in textbook writing or I have judged them to be misleading.

Fair **comparison** is an indispensable tool in determining meaning. The remote context of a religious phenomenon can be uncovered by comparing different examples and discerning their similarities and differences. Comparison is implicit in the activities of determining the type of text (or ritual or moral code or whatever) and in determining structure and function. A story of a saint in Christianity can be illuminated by comparison with a story of a saint in Buddhism even if the stories are very different and unrelated culturally and historically. F. Max Müller (1823–1900), an influential linguist and historian of religions, liked to apply to the study of religion what

Goethe applied to the study of language. "He who knows one . . . knows none" (*Lectures on the Science of Religion*, 1872:10–11).

No attempt should be made to determine if one example is "better than" another in the sense of truer or morally superior (the Christian saint is really a saint and the Buddhist saint is a fraud). One example might be judged more typical or less typical of the type under discussion (stories about saints), but even that judgment is tricky. As you can readily see, prejudice and unconscious bias can enter the selection process. Why is this story rather than "that" selected as "typical"? In fact, as the historian of religions Jonathan Z. Smith reminds us, the scholar's "primary skill is concentrated" in his or her choice of examples. Smith goes on to claim that three conditions are implicit in the scholar's effort to articulate her or his choices:

> First, that the exemplum [chosen example] has been well and fully understood. That requires a mastery of both the relevant primary material and the history and tradition of its interpretation. Second, that the exemplum be displayed in the service of some important theory, some paradigm, some fundamental question, some central element in the academic imagination of religion. Third, that there be some method for explicitly relating the exemplum to the theory, paradigm, or question and some method for evaluating each in terms of the other.
>
> *Imagining Religion: From Babylon to Jonestown*, 1982:xi–xii

EXPLANATION

Smith's mention of theory leads us directly to **explanation.** The study of religion seeks not only to collect and describe data and to interpret it by employing classificational, hermeneutical, and comparative methods, but also to explain what is going on. Phenomenologists, as I noted earlier, would insist the task is done once the data are described and understood, but other scholars would insist the most important work is yet to be done, namely, explanation.

The word *explanation* can mean several different things in the field of religious studies. Some mean by it no more than an understanding gained by discovering the meaning of religious phenomena. In other words, interpretation is one type of explanation. To others, explanation means finding and describing the cause(s) of some religious phenomenon. To do this, one must directly and explicitly appeal to some theory. Description and interpretation are influenced by theory, but explanation is more clearly theory-laden because it is by subsuming some activity under a theory that a causal explanation is found. In physics the event of a falling apple is explained by subsuming it (along with many other examples of falling things) under the theory of gravity. So, a religious event like a sacrifice might be explained by subsuming it under a general theory about violence and the role substitute victims play in bringing cycles of violent vengeance to a close (see René Girard's *Violence and the Sacred*, 1977).

EVALUATION

For an explanation to make sense, the theory that gives rise to it must be right. How can we find that out? Physical scientists can check their theories by conducting controlled experiments in a laboratory, but in religious studies such checking procedures are seldom possible. What is possible is to check the usefulness of a theory by measuring it against many different examples to see if it makes sense of all or most of them. Does a detailed and careful study of fifty examples of sacrifices selected at random from the world's religions make more sense when viewed from the violence theory rather than from some other theory?

Evaluation is difficult because there are so many different levels of it. You might be evaluating the accuracy of a description by checking it against your own reading of the original data, or evaluating an interpretation by checking on how rigorously the hermeneutical method was employed, or evaluating a theory and hence a causal explanation by checking its general fruitfulness against other possible theories. In this sense of evaluation, one scholar is evaluating the work of another against such criteria as logical consistency, strength of evidence and argument, compelling counterexamples, and alternative explanations.

What about evaluating religious claims themselves? Can this be done? Should it be done? Many scholars openly acknowledge that the methods of history, the social sciences, and philosophy are limited to natural explanations—that there is no human way to evaluate supernatural claims. Was Jesus truly the son of God, or did he and others just think so? That he made that claim or did not make it, that others made it, that it meant thus and so—these are things that are possible to check provided enough information survives. But the theological claim that Jesus is the son of God—how could we check that?

Some philosophers and theologians might think we can check this claim just like we check other metaphysical claims—that is, is it logically consistent with everything we know about all kinds of things? Given what we know about history, the physical universe, human behavior, other religions, and about the effects of believing Jesus is God's son on people's lives, is it plausible that Jesus is truly the son of God? You can imagine the arguments on both sides and also arguments claiming such questions fall outside the range of questions that can be asked (let alone answered) in the academic study of religion.

SUMMARY

The academic study of religion seeks to describe, interpret, explain, and evaluate religious data. It draws on the specific methods of different disciplines—history, social science, and philosophy—in order to do this. Some very general methods involve collecting and classifying data, applying hermeneutical tools, and using techniques of comparison. Phenomenologists generally want to limit religious studies to description and understanding the agent's interpretation because they think anything else involves projecting the bias of the scholar into the phenomena. They also believe that religion is *sui generis* and that its uniqueness will be overlooked if we treat it as we would any other human phenomenon. Other scholars claim explanation and/or evaluation are legitimate activities of the scholar. Whatever else it may be, religion is at least a human phenomenon and, like any other human phenomenon, understandable by the application of the normal methods of history, social science, and philosophy.

3.1 COMPARING RELIGIONS

William E. Paden, author of the next selection, teaches religious studies at the University of Vermont. He is particularly concerned with how best to do comparative studies of religion and with developing the concept of a plurality of worlds in order to better understand religion. He believes there is a uniquely "religious language," which he calls the "language of 'the sacred,'" and that the task of the student of religion is to learn how to understand that language.

Answer the reading questions and see whether Paden can convince you.

WILLIAM E. PADEN

Comparative Perspectives

READING QUESTIONS

1. As you read, make a list of all the words and ideas you do not understand or are uncertain about. Discuss them with a classmate, look them up in a dictionary, or bring them up in class for discussion and clarification.
2. What are the characteristics of what Paden calls the "comparative perspective"?
3. How does the comparative perspective differ from the activity of describing different religions?

In its elementary sense, comparative religion involves the study of the many religious traditions of the world. Such knowledge about "others" is deprovincializing. But it is one of the purposes of this book to show that the study of religion is not just limited to the description of various religious traditions, as if these were so many belief systems that posed alternatives to one's own or so many objects of intrinsic curiosity. Full comparative perspective involves more than simply describing side by side or serially the religions of the world, as though one were just sampling or judging various claims to truth.

There is also a second dimension of comparative investigation in religion: the study not just of different *religions* but of the structures of *religion*. What do we learn from the many species of religion about the genus itself? Religions do have things in common. They are in-

From *Religious Worlds* by William E. Paden, pp. 1–5. © 1988, 1994 by William E. Paden. Reprinted by permission of Beacon Press, Boston. References deleted.

stances of a human activity that has typical, expressive forms of its own. These religious structures constitute a subject matter in their own right. Like the study of music, which is not limited to examining a sequence of composers but also considers the special world of musical categories such as rhythm and harmony, so the study of religion is not limited to analyzing historical traditions such as Buddhism, Judaism, and Christianity but also investigates the religious "language" common to all traditions, the language of myth, gods, ritual, and sacrifice —in short, the language of "the sacred."

The general categories of religious behavior and the framework they provide for understanding particular religious systems are the primary subject matter of this book. This study therefore addresses the need to go beyond interpreting other religions simply in terms of their relationship to one's own.

Dissatisfied with the imposition of European and biblical classifications onto the interpretation of non-Western religious cultures, and eschewing grand, evolutionary hypotheses that simply reflected Western values, modern anthropology understandably abandoned attempts to find overarching patterns in religion and instead devoted itself to in-depth studies of individual cultures. Comparative typologies and concepts are still perceived by many scholars as a dangerously antihistorical endeavor that overlooks the important contexts and particularity of religious symbols and behavior. Certainly comparison has served as a vehicle for all kinds of distortions and apologetics.

Comparison has also been used as a polemical weapon by religions themselves to show the inferiority of other traditions and the superiority of one's own. It has been used to show that all religions are really the same. It has been used to show that all religions are false. Many people sense that the absoluteness of their own beliefs is threatened by the existence of parallels elsewhere. So there is a kind of politics of comparison.

In some ways comparison is simply unavoidable. We all employ comparison every day, and thinking itself is in large measure based on it. It is built into language and perception. What a thing "is" is determined by its similarity and difference with other things like or unlike it. Science would be impossible without it, and without it the realm of metaphor would vanish. The analogical process is part of the way every cultural system classifies its world.

Comparison can create error and distortion as well as insight and knowledge, and this is noticeably so in the area of religion. Religious phenomena have been compared for centuries, but not necessarily in the pursuit of fair description or accurate understanding. Comparison is most often a function of self-interest. It gets used to illustrate one's own ideology. It easily becomes an instrument of judgment, a device for approval or condemnation.

We all tend naturally to reduce areas of life to certain themes that fit our own worldview. As we thematize our world so we thematize religion. Everyone has summarizing ideas, usually positive or negative in connotation, about religion, and religious phenomena become occasions for all manner of precritical impressionistic generalizations. Thus, all religion is "about" love, money, God, social repression, escapism. All sects become "systems of brainwashing," oriental religions are "navel gazing." These approaches reduce religious phenomena to imagined stereotypes and ignore all evidence inconsistent with the type. It is as if the mind innately needs to reduce and typify experience in order to avoid the confusion and contradiction that might come with confronting religious diversity. The issue, then, is not *whether* to generalize and thematize about religion, but *how* to do so in appropriate and accurate ways.

In spite of the potential dangers of misuse, comparative perspective is a necessity for any field of study, and without it no real understanding of religion is possible. In this book I have tried to lay out a conceptual framework that avoids some of the past difficulties with comparative biases while still resolutely maintaining the importance and application of cross-cultural categories. Let us consider at the outset a summary of how the concept "comparative perspective" will be used.

1. First and most broadly, comparative perspective is not just a matter of juxtaposing one religion with another, but is the process of understanding any continuities and differences in the history of all types of religious phenomena. Comparative perspective is the knowledge of the whole in relation to the part, which are mutually informative. Every field of knowledge has its equivalent framework. Comparative literature, for example, studies not just writings other than English but themes, genres, and topics common to the whole history of literature as a human enterprise.

2. Comparative perspective is derived inductively from historical knowledge, not deductively from one's own philosophy. Comparative study presupposes history. It is not an alternative to historical perspective but an enrichment of it. Every religious expression has its own unique context of meaning, its own distinctive configuration that is different in some ways from others. Historical facts keep typologies honest, testing and challenging comparative generalizations at every point.

3. Comparative perspective involves different levels of specificity, different levels of part-to-whole relation-

ship. One can compare what a pilgrimage means to different people at one time and place, or one can compare that pilgrimage with all others within the same religion, or one can study pilgrimage as a theme that is manifest in all times and religions. Although this particular book makes a point of focusing on transcultural religious forms of the broadest generic scope, many "types" of religious expression—such as saviors, priests, or temples—are not found universally but within certain regions, periods, or types of religion. Much specific comparative work is best limited to studies of variations within a single religious culture or cluster of cultures. Each kind of phenomenon researched will have its own justifiable scope of comparative data and analysis.

4. Where comparative analysis deals with similarity, it deals with analogy rather than with identity, in which things, otherwise unlike, are similar in some respects. It is not just a matter of identifying what is "the same" everywhere. The *significance* of the analogies or parallels is a matter of judgment.

5. Comparative work is not only a process of establishing similarities or analogies. It is also the fundamental instrument for discerning differences. The point needs stressing because this double function has not been fully appreciated. Many people fear that comparative approaches lose sight of the richness of cultural diversity. But the study of continuity (or parallels) and the study of individuality cannot be separated. Only by seeing what is common between things can one see what is different or innovative about any one of them. A Christian or Jewish theology cannot fully understand its own uniqueness and its nuances, without knowing which of its features belong to religion in general and which are distinctively its own.

6. Finally, comparison is not an end in itself. It yields comparative *perspective*, the process by which overarching themes on the one hand and historical particulars on the other get enriched by the way they illumine each other. Because it is the central purpose of this book to illustrate this larger process, let us consider it a little further here.

There is a creative interplay between theme and example that enriches understanding of both. The variations develop, reveal, "work" the theme, as does a set of musical variations. Or, shifting the analogy, the species add to our understanding of the genus, just as the genus calls attention to common patterns present in a species. Many different creatures—such as fish, birds, mammals—amplify the theme "vertebrate." Dolphins, giraffes, armadillos, and humans are interestingly different versions of what a mammal can be. One could say the same

of any subject: bicycles and jets show what transportation can be, pianos and flutes demonstrate what musical instruments can be, Gandhi and Napoleon embody what leadership can be.

It is exactly the same with religious forms. Our understanding of what religious language and practice "can be" is diminished if we do not have the most complete awareness of its possible variations. By looking at all the gods in religious history, we see more fully what a god is. The variations make the theme stronger and more interesting. By seeing all the different things observed in various rites, we see more fully what ritual can be.

The Kaaba, the Muslim shrine at Mecca, the symbolic connecting point of heaven and earth for the Islamic world, is more fully comprehensible if we are familiar with the generic theme of "world centers." Without a sense of that theme and its prevalence, the Kaaba symbolism might be viewed merely as an odd or unintelligible belief. By the same token, the profound centering role of the Kaaba in the lives of Muslims provides an extraordinary living illustration and amplification of the world center motif.

The comparative process does not prejudge religious phenomena, as though they are there to be pinned and tagged like helpless specimens that must be made to conform by all means to our favorite taxonomies. Rather, religious expressions are facts—often living and articulate—that can continually instruct and illuminate our categories. In these ways, comparative perspective is a larger educational and interpretive process than any simple, straightforward act of describing or comparing different religions. . . .

3.2 EXPLAINING RELIGION

Wayne Proudfoot teaches religious studies at Columbia University. He is particularly interested in the psychology and philosophy of religion and has made important contributions to methodology. In the selection that follows, he considers the problems of **reductionism** and explanation, using some accounts of religious experiences as his primary examples. He argues that it is important to distinguish between descriptive and explanatory reduction. The first is inappropriate, but the second is both appropriate and essential for the student of religions. Note the ways in which the hermeneutical principle of context informs his readings of these accounts and the way he sees interaction between theory and explanation.

WAYNE PROUDFOOT

Explanation

READING QUESTIONS

1. As you read, make a list of all the words and ideas you do not understand or are uncertain about. Discuss them with a classmate, look them up in a dictionary, or bring them up in class for discussion and clarification.
2. According to Proudfoot's account of Mircea Eliade's views, what does Eliade think is wrong with reductionism?
3. What is **first-person privilege,** and how does it differ from the explanation offered by the analyst?
4. What is the difference between "descriptive reduction" and "explanatory reduction," and why is this distinction important?

Reductionism has become a derogatory epithet in the history and philosophy of religion. Scholars whose work is in other respects quite diverse have concurred in advocating approaches to the study of religion which are oriented around campaigns against reductionism. These campaigns are often linked to a defense of the autonomy of the study of religion. The distinctive subject matter of that study, it is argued, requires a distinctive method. In particular, religious experience cannot properly be studied by a method that reduces it to a cluster of phenomena that can be explained in historical, psychological, or sociological terms. Although it is difficult to establish exactly what is meant by the term, the label "reductionist" is deemed sufficient to warrant dismissal of any account of religious phenomena.

Questions have been raised about this wholesale rejection of reductive accounts and about the theological motivations that sometimes underlie it, but the issues in the discussion have not been sufficiently clarified. Penner and Yonan . . . , for example, take the problem to be crucial for the study of religion, survey the meaning of *reduction* in empiricist philosophy of science, and deplore the negative connotations that have been attached to the term. But they admit that they have found the issue difficult. They show no appreciation of why the at-

tack on reductionism has such an appeal, and thus they are unable to elucidate the discussion. The warnings against reductionism derive from a genuine insight, but that insight is often misconstrued to serve an apologetic purpose. I shall try to clarify the confusion surrounding the term *reduction* as it is applied to accounts of religious experience and to distinguish between the insight and misapplications that result in protective strategies. A recent essay in the philosophy of religion devoted to the exposure and critique of reductionism will serve to illustrate those misapplications and strategies.

THE PROBLEM

One of the most influential critics of reductionism in the study of religion has been Mircea Eliade. He has argued that the task of the historian of religion is a distinctive one and has contrasted it with what he takes to be the reductionist methods of the social sciences. . . . According to Eliade, a historical or sociological approach fails to grasp the meaning of religious phenomena. Like the literary critic interpreting a text, the historian of religion must attempt to understand religious data "on their own plane of reference." He or she should adopt a hermeneutic method. Just as literary works cannot be reduced to their origins, religious phenomena ought not to be reduced to their social, psychological, or historical origins or functions. Eliade . . . contends that "a religious datum reveals its deeper meaning when it is considered on its plane of reference, and not when it is reduced to one of its secondary aspects or its contexts." He cites Durkheim and Freud as examples of those who have adopted reductionist methods for the study of religion.

Two points are worthy of note: (1) Eliade thinks that what is lost by reductive approaches is the *meaning* of religious phenomena. He praises van der Leeuw for respecting the peculiar intentionality of religious data and thus the irreducibility of religious representations . . .; (2) his examples of reductionist approaches are drawn almost exclusively from history and the social sciences. Theories that purport to account for religious phenomena in terms of their origins or the functions they serve in a particular social context are *ipso facto* reductionist.

Eliade holds further that religious data represent the expression of religious experiences. Religion is "first of all, an experience *sui generis*, incited by man's encounter with the sacred . . . ." In order to understand religious data on their own plane of reference, the scholar must "'relive' a multitude of existential situations. . . ." Only through such a procedure can the meaning of the data be grasped. To reduce those data to their origins or social functions is to fail to understand them as expressions of

From Wayne Proudfoot, *Religious Experience* (Berkeley: University of California Press, 1985). Excerpts from chapter 5. Copyright © 1985 by The Regents of the University of California. Used by permission. References deleted.

religious experience. That understanding can come only from acquaintance. Since Eliade regards religious experience as experience of the sacred, he can summarize his antireductionist position by reference to "the irreducibility of the sacred."

Religious experience is the experience of something. It is intentional in that it cannot be described without reference to a grammatical object. Just as fear is always fear of something, and a perceptual act can only be described by reference to its object, a religious experience must be identified under a certain description, and that description must include a reference to the object of the experience. Eliade employs the term *sacred* to characterize the object of all religious experience. The notorious obscurity of that term need not concern us here, nor need we accept the suggestion that all religious experiences have the same object. The point is that when Eliade refers to the irreducibility of the sacred, he is claiming that it is the intentional object of the religious experience which must not be reduced. To do so is to lose the experience, or to attend to something else altogether.

This point is well taken. If someone is afraid of a bear, his fear cannot be accurately described without mentioning the bear. This remains true regardless of whether or not the bear actually exists outside his mind. He may mistakenly perceive a fallen tree trunk on the trail ahead of him as a bear, but his fear is properly described as fear of a bear. To describe it as fear of a log would be to misidentify his emotion and reduce it to something other than it is. In identifying the experience, emotion, or practice of another, I must restrict myself to concepts and beliefs that have informed his experience. I cannot ascribe to him concepts he would not recognize or beliefs he would not acknowledge. Though historical evidence might turn up to show that Socrates was dying of cancer, no evidence could show that he was afraid of dying of cancer. No such fear could be ascribed to him because he didn't possess the concept of cancer which is presupposed by that emotion.

Consider two examples cited by William James. The first is an experience reported by Stephen Bradley. . . .

> I thought I saw the Saviour, by faith, in human shape, for about one second in the room, with arms extended, appearing to say to me, Come. The next day I rejoiced with trembling; soon after my happiness was so great that I said that I wanted to die; this world had no place in my affections, as I knew of, and every day appeared to me as the Sabbath. I had an ardent desire that all mankind might feel as I did; I wanted to have them all love God supremely. . . .

The second is from Mrs. Jonathan Edwards.

> Part of the night I lay awake, sometimes asleep, and sometimes between sleeping and waking. But all night I continued in a constant, clear, and lively sense of the heavenly sweetness of Christ's excellent love, of his nearness to me, and of my dearness to him. I seemed to myself to perceive a glow of divine love come down from the heart of Christ in heaven into my heart in a constant stream, like a stream or pencil of sweet light. At the same time my heart and soul all flowed out in love to Christ, so that there seemed to be a constant flowing and reflowing of heavenly love, and I appeared to myself to float or swim, in these bright, sweet beams, like the motes swimming in the beams of the sun, or the streams of his light which come in at the window. . . .

Bradley tells of a vision in human shape, and Edwards reports a lively sense of Christ's love, which seemed to glow like a stream or pencil of light. Each of these experiences can only be properly described by reference to Christ and to Christian beliefs. One might try to separate the description of the core experience from its interpretation and to argue that only the interpretation is specifically Christian. But if the references to the Savior, the Sabbath, and God are eliminated from Bradley's report, we are left with something other than his experience. After deleting references to Christian concepts, we have a vision of a human shape with arms extended saying, "Come." Is this any less informed by Christian beliefs and doctrines than was the original experience? Surely the vision of a person with outstretched arms is not some universal archetype onto which Bradley has added an interpretation in Christian terms. Nor can his experience of comfort and salvation be abstracted from his Christian beliefs. Sarah Edwards's experience is not a vision, but it would be inaccurate to describe it exclusively in general terms and to characterize it only as a lively sense of sweetness, accompanied by the sensation of floating in streams of bright light. Her report cannot be purged of references to Christ and Christian beliefs and still remain an accurate description of the experience.

An emotion, practice, or experience must be described in terms that can plausibly be attributed to the subject on the basis of the available evidence. The subject's self-ascription is normative for describing the experience. This is a kind of first-person privilege that has nothing at all to do with immediate intuitive access to mental states versus mediated inferential reasoning. It is strictly a matter of intentionality. It is like the distinction between the words of a speaker and those of one who reports what he says. The speaker's meaning, and his choice of words to express that meaning, are normative for the reporter. The latter may choose to paraphrase or elaborate, but the words uttered by the speaker are authoritative for determining the message. Where it is the subject's experience which is the object of study, that experience must be identified under a description that can plausibly be attributed to him. In the cases cited above, the subject's own words constitute the description. If, however, an observer or analyst describes the experience of another, he must formulate it in terms that would be familiar to, incorporating beliefs that would be acknowledged by, the subject. If challenged, he must offer reasons in support of his ascription of those concepts and beliefs to the subject. He is not responsible for reasons offered in support of those beliefs.

The explanation the analyst offers of that same experience is another matter altogether. It need not be couched in terms familiar or acceptable to the subject. It must be an explanation of the experience as identified under the subject's description, but the subject's approval of the explanation is not required. Bradley's experience might be explained in terms of the conflicts of early adolescence and that of Sarah Edwards as a consequence of her life with Mr. Edwards. No reference need be made to God or Christ in the construction of these explanations. If the explanation is challenged, the one who proposed it is responsible for providing reasons to support it and for showing how it accounts for the evidence better than any of its rivals does. . . .

In the study of religion, considerable confusion has resulted from the failure to distinguish the requisite conditions for the identification of an experience under a certain description from those for explaining the experience. The analyst must cite, but need not endorse, the concepts, beliefs, and judgments that enter into the subject's identification of his experience. He must be prepared to give reasons for his ascription of those beliefs and judgments to the subject, but he need not defend the beliefs and judgments themselves. If he proposes an explanatory hypothesis to account for the experience, he need not restrict himself to the subject's concepts and beliefs, but he must be prepared to give reasons in support of his explanation.

DESCRIPTIVE AND
EXPLANATORY REDUCTION

We are now in a position to distinguish two different kinds of reduction. *Descriptive reduction* is the failure to identify an emotion, practice, or experience under the description by which the subject identifies it. This is indeed unacceptable. To describe an experience in non-

religious terms when the subject himself describes it in religious terms is to misidentify the experience, or to attend to another experience altogether. To describe Bradley's experience as simply a vision of a human shape, and that of Mrs. Edwards as a lively warm sense that seemed to glow like a pencil of light, is to lose the identifying characteristics of those experiences. To describe the experience of a mystic by reference only to alpha waves, altered heart rate, and changes in bodily temperature is to misdescribe it. To characterize the experience of a Hindu mystic in terms drawn from the Christian tradition is to misidentify it. In each of these instances, the subject's identifying experience has been reduced to something other than that experienced by the subject. This might properly be called reductionism. In any case, it precludes an accurate identification of the subject's experience.

Explanatory reduction consists in offering an explanation of an experience in terms that are not those of the subject and that might not meet with his approval. This is perfectly justifiable and is, in fact, normal procedure. The explanandum is set in a new context, whether that be one of covering laws and initial conditions, narrative structure, or some other explanatory model. The terms of the explanation need not be familiar or acceptable to the subject. Historians offer explanations of past events by employing such concepts as socialization, ideology, means of production, and feudal economy. Seldom can these concepts properly be ascribed to the people whose behavior is the object of the historian's study. But that poses no problem. The explanation stands or falls according to how well it can account for all the available evidence.

Failure to distinguish between these two kinds of reduction leads to the claim that any account of religious emotions, practices, or experience must be restricted to the perspective of the subject and must employ only terms, beliefs, and judgments that would meet with his approval. This claim derives its plausibility from examples of descriptive reduction but is then extended to preclude explanatory reduction. When so extended, it becomes a protective strategy. The subject's identifying description becomes normative for purposes of explanation, and inquiry is blocked to insure that the subject's own explanation of his experience is not contested. On this view, to entertain naturalistic explanations of the experiences of Bradley and Edwards is reductionist because these explanations conflict with the convictions of the subjects that their experiences were the result of divine activity in their lives.

Many of the warnings against reductionism in the study of religion conflate descriptive and explanatory reduction. Eliade exhorts the historian of religion to understand religious data on their own plane of reference and contrasts this understanding with the reductive accounts offered by social scientists. Wilfred Cantwell Smith . . . contends that a necessary requirement of the validity of any statement about a religion is that it be acknowledged and accepted by adherents of that religious tradition. This is appropriate if addressed to the problem of providing identifying descriptions of experiences in different traditions, but it is inappropriate if extended to include all statements about religion.

For some years Smith has waged a campaign against the use of the term *religion* in the study of what he calls faith and the historical traditions . . .. In criticizing this use of the term, he brings forth abundant evidence to show that it is of rather recent and parochial origin. According to his research, there is no concept in most of the world's cultures and traditions which can accurately be translated by our term *religion*. In other words, there is no evidence to support the ascription of that concept to people outside the modern West. From this evidence Smith concludes that the term ought to be avoided by scholars of the faiths of mankind. Even if the results of his philological researches were granted, however, there would be no more reason to reject *religion* than to reject *culture* and *economy*. The fact that it cannot accurately be ascribed to people in many societies does not require that it be excluded from the accounts we give of those societies. Smith's conclusion follows from his evidence only with the addition of the premise that any account of the religious life, including explanatory accounts, must be couched in terms that are familiar and acceptable to participants in that life. Smith accepts this premise and regards it as a requirement of the comparative study of religion, but we have seen that explanatory accounts are not subject to this restriction. . . .

first-person privilege The notion that the explanation offered by the subject is normative for anyone who wishes to accurately describe the phenomenon.

hermeneutics A method for interpreting data, particularly textual data, that pays close attention to the context and structure of the data or text.

interpretation A statement of what the data mean.

phenomenology of religion Sometimes used as equivalent to history of religions, but better thought of as a particular theory and comparative method that assumes religion and its history as the manifestations of the sacred and opposes all "reductionism" or causal explanations by social scientists on the grounds that religion is *sui generis* (literally, "of its own kind").

reductionism Often used by phenomenologists in a pejorative sense to refer to what they see as inappropriate explanations of religious phenomena. According to Proudfoot, there are two kinds: descriptive reduction, which results in a failure to accurately describe a situation by using ideas unacceptable to the subject; and explanatory reduction, which consists in offering a causal account of some phenomenon that is accurately described from the subject's viewpoint in terms that may not be acceptable to the subject but are acceptable to the analyst and are supported by good evidence and argument.

Sitz im Leben German, meaning "situation or place in life." Technically it refers to the establishment of the context of a text (where, when, by whom, to whom it was written, and its purpose or function) for purposes of interpretation.

KEY TERMS AND CONCEPTS

comparison A balanced description of the similarities and differences among examples of phenomena.

description A statement of facts of a case as objectively as possible. These facts can then serve as data for interpretation.

evaluation A value judgment about the quality of some description, interpretation, or explanation. It can also refer to a value judgment about the interpretation of the religious subject.

explanation Either an interpretation that deepens our understanding or a statement of a cause(s) that makes sense given some theory.

SUGGESTIONS FOR FURTHER READING

Benson, Thomas L. "Religious Studies as an Academic Discipline." In *The Encyclopedia of Religion*, edited by Mircea Eliade, vol. 14, pp. 88–92. New York: Macmillan, 1987. A brief history of the development of religious studies in the academy.

Capps, Walter H. *Ways of Understanding Religion.* New York: Macmillan, 1972. A somewhat dated but still useful collection of essays from a variety of disciplines (anthropology, history, psychology, philosophy, and others) on theories and methods.

Connolly, Peter, ed. *Approaches to the Study of Religion.* London: Cassell, 1999. A collection of essays discussing different ways of studying religions ranging from anthropological to theological approaches.

Penner, Hans H. "The Study of Religion." In *The HarperCollins Dictionary of Religion*, edited by Jonathan Z. Smith and William Scott Green, pp. 909–917. New York: HarperCollins, 1995. A clear and concise account of the nature of theory and basic approaches (sociological, phenomenological, psychological, historical, etc.) to the study of religion along with a critical discussion of functional theories and other types of theories.

Sharpe, Eric J. "Methodological Issues." In *The Encyclopedia of Religion*, edited by Mircea Eliade, vol. 14, pp. 83–88. New York: Macmillan, 1987. A discussion of different methodological issues such as value judgments, vocabulary translation, insider's and outsider's perspectives, and the like.

RESEARCH PROJECTS

1. Create a debate either in class between groups of students or in writing in which you present a position paper in favor of or against reductionism in the study of religions. If you write it, present a brief position paper on *both* sides of the issue.

2. Look at William James's *Varieties of Religious Experience: A Study in Human Nature* and select one of the first-person accounts of religious experience that James records. Describe the experience and then interpret it by applying the hermeneutical tools described in this chapter. (James's *Varieties* is available in many different editions but was first published in 1902 by Longmans, Green of New York.)

PART 2

WAYS OF BEING RELIGIOUS ORIGINATING IN ASIA

4

Hindu Ways of Being Religious

INTRODUCTION

There are many different ways of being religious in India. There are Jains, Sikhs, Muslims, Christians, Jews, Parses, Buddhists—to name only a few—who are practicing their own distinct religious ways. Here our focus will be on Hinduism. It should be noted, however, that Hinduism is found in other places besides India. While the majority of the estimated 700 to 800 million Hindus live in India, many live in such places as Bali, the Caribbean, South Africa, Europe, Canada, and the United States.

The word *Hinduism* is not an Indian word. It comes from an Arabic word originally used to refer to the people who lived in the Indus Valley. European scholars coined the word *Hinduism* as a collective term for the religious beliefs and practices of some of the people who live in India. The word is very misleading—so misleading that some scholars have argued we should abandon its use.

While it is doubtful whether we can or should abandon its use, we must be aware of why it is misleading. First, the word *Hinduism* implies that Hinduism is a separate and distinct religious tradition comparable to Christianity or Islam. However, Hinduism displays few of the characteristics generally associated with religion. There is no founder, no divinely revealed scriptures, no creed or dogmas, no ecclesiastical organization or "church," and, in many of its forms, the concept of a personal divinity is not of central importance. Given conventional understandings of the word *religion*, it is difficult to categorize all of Hinduism's forms as a "religion." Again the issue, discussed in chapter 2, of how best to define religion emerges as central to the problems involved in the academic study of Hinduism.

Second, Hinduism is extraordinarily diverse. On one end of the scale are small, local village cults focused on local gods and saints whose followers may encompass no more than two or three villages. At the other end of the scale are large religious movements with millions of adherents throughout India and elsewhere. In between are numerous movements, sects, **audience cults** (groups that gather to hear some **guru** teach but are otherwise unorganized), and **client cults** (people who visit practitioners for therapy, meditation instruction, or help with personal problems) such as astrology. Each of these, from the smallest to the largest, has its own mythologies, theologies, rituals, and moral codes. It is possible to find groups referred to by the umbrella term *Hinduism* that have little in common.

The diversity and the unity of a religious tradition are often in the eye of the beholder. If we wish to focus on the diversity of Hinduism in the hope of painting a more accurate picture of its richness and variety, we risk ignoring the fact that many Hindus affirm that it is, despite the diversity, a single religious tradition. This affirmation is based on a sense of a shared heritage and historical continuity as well as family resemblances among various groups. In this chapter, we sample a few of the rich religious and spiritual foods offered to us by the complexity and diversity of Hinduism.

4.1 AN OVERVIEW

David R. Kinsley is professor of medieval Hinduism at McMaster University in Hamilton, Canada. He studied at the University of Chicago (Ph.D. 1970) and in the following selection offers an introduction to and historical overview of Hinduism. He notes the complexity and diversity of this "religious tradition" and the difficulty that poses for introducing it to someone who knows little about it. His perspective is cultural and historical, offering insights into the ideas, folk beliefs, practices, social organizations,

GENERAL MAP OF INDIA

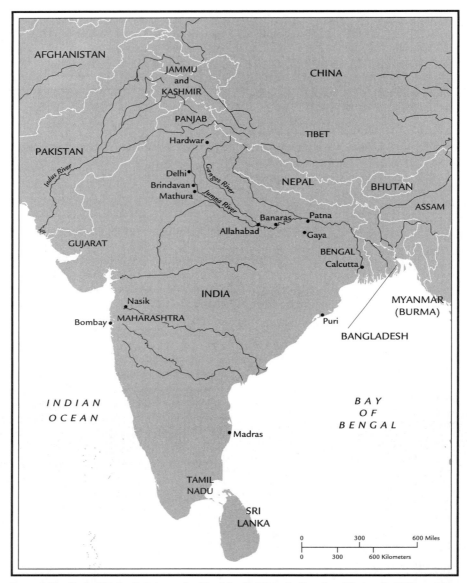

From *A Handbook of Living Religions*, edited by John R. Hinnells (London: Blackwell, 1997), p. 265, Fig. 5.1.

and historical dynamics that weave together to form the tapestry called Hinduism.

Like all complex religions, Hinduism teaches that human life has many different purposes because there are many different things that are good for humans and contribute to human flourishing. And, like all complex religions, Hinduism identifies those things

that prevent humans from realizing the variety of goods that contribute to human flourishing. This means that Hinduism is not *exclusively* concerned with such "spiritual" values as salvation (to use a Western term). However, it is definitely concerned with what is the highest good and what, among all the hindrances to good, is the worst. Hinduism understands ignorance (*avidya*) as primarily responsible for keeping humans from realizing the highest good, and hence knowledge (*vidya* or *jnana*) plays an important role in realizing complete human flourishing or freedom (*moksha*) from the ignorance and unhappiness that plagues human lives. However, precisely what is ignorance, what is knowledge, and what is *moksha*, the highest human good? Hinduism, like all religions, provides a variety of provocative answers.

DAVID R. KINSLEY

Hinduism

READING QUESTIONS

1. As you read, make a list of all the words and ideas you do not understand or are uncertain about. Discuss them with a classmate, look them up in a dictionary, or bring them up in class for discussion and clarification.
2. The author offers several generalizations about Hinduism. What are they?
3. What is a "very common definition" of Hinduism?
4. What do you think are the most important differences among the Vedic, devotional, ascetic, and popular traditions?
5. What is the tension reflected in the epics, and what are the three "solutions" to this tension? In your opinion, do these solutions relieve the tension? Why or why not?
6. Make a list of the things from the various historical periods you would like to know more about. Discuss them in class.

Even before the sun has risen, the streets and alleyways of Varanasi[1] leading to the Ganges River swirl with devout pilgrims making their way to the broad steps that lead down into the river. By the time the sun is up the steps teem with pilgrims and devout residents taking ritual baths in Mother Ganges' sacred waters, which are believed to cleanse one of all sins. Small shops specializing in religious paraphernalia crowd the area around the

From *Hinduism: A Cultural Perspective*, by David R. Kinsley © 1993 Prentice-Hall, Inc. Reprinted by permission of Prentice-Hall, Inc. Upper Saddle River, N.J. pp. 2–25. Footnotes omitted.
[1]Also known as Banaras or Benares.

steps and do a thriving business. Hundreds of priests whose task it is to aid pilgrims are setting up their large umbrellas against the heat of the sun, and by midday the steps leading to the river look as if they are overgrown with immense mushrooms.

Dawn also signals the beginning of activity in the hundreds of temples and shrines throughout the city dedicated to the many gods and goddesses of the Hindu pantheon. In the impressive Vishvanath temple of the ascetic god Shiva, hereditary priests prepare to do puja (worship by personally waiting upon a deity), and devotees crowd the temple precincts to have a view of the image of the deity, a sight that is held to be auspicious, and to watch the colorful ceremony. Throughout the day devotees stream to the hundreds of temples scattered all over Varanasi to worship their favorite god or goddess. The variety of images from which they can choose reflects the extraordinary richness through which the divine has revealed itself in the Hindu tradition.

Enshrined in these temples is a veritable kaleidoscope of divinity: Vishnu, the great heavenly king who descends to the world from time to time in various forms to maintain cosmic stability; Shiva, the ascetic god who dwells in yogic meditation in the Himalayas, storing up his energy so that he can release it periodically into the world to refresh its vigor; Krishna, the adorable cowherd god who frolics with his women companions in the idyllic forests of Vrindavana; Hanuman, the monkey god, who embodies strength, courage, and loyalty to the Lord Rama; Ganesha, the elephant-headed god who destroys all obstacles for his devotees; Durga, the warrior goddess who periodically defeats the forces of evil in order to protect the world; Kali, the black goddess who dwells in cremation grounds and is served with blood; and many more.

Dawn is a busy time at the cremation grounds on the Ganges too. A steady stream of funeral processions wends its way to a particular set of steps where several funeral pyres burn constantly. At the funeral grounds the stretcher-borne corpses are set down to await their turn in the purifying fires. The constant activity at this particular burning ground reflects the belief of pious Hindus that death in or near the Ganges at Varanasi results in moksha, the final liberation from the endless cycles of birth and rebirth that is the ultimate spiritual goal of most Hindus. Thousands of devout Hindus, in their old age, come to die in Varanasi, and many funeral processions seem joyous, reflecting the auspicious circumstances of the person's death. As one watches the crackling fires consume the corpse, the rising tendrils of smoke suggest the soul's final and longed-for liberation.

Varanasi is the center of several religious orders, and the city's population includes a great number of ascetics who have chosen to live in the holy city permanently or who are simply wandering through. It is not unusual to see several of these holy men or women sitting in meditation around the steps. The burning ground itself is an auspicious site to perform meditation, as the funeral pyres remind the ascetics of the transcience of the worldly life they have renounced. The appearance of these renouncers is striking. Ascetics often wear saffron-colored robes, a minimum of clothes, or perhaps are even naked. Their bodies may be smeared with ashes, sometimes taken from the cremation grounds. Their hair is long and matted, indicating their utter neglect of bodily appearance, or their heads may be shaven. Their only possessions are a water pot and a staff. In the midst of a bustling city like Varanasi, which like all cities caters to the inexhaustible worldly desires of its populace with markets, cinemas, shops, and so on, the ascetics look like wayfarers from another world. They are a common sight in Varanasi, however, and remind one of the importance of world renunciation and asceticism in the Hindu tradition.

Before the day is over, a visitor to Varanasi will have witnessed many scenes common to the Hindu tradition: Brahmins performing ancient Vedic rituals; devotees from Bengal performing communal worship to Lord Krishna with much singing and dancing; students at Banares Hindu University consulting an astrologer to determine if the day on which their exams will be held will be auspicious; a low-caste pilgrim making an offering at the shrine of a beloved saint who is little known outside the pilgrim's own caste; a traditional pundit, or teacher, expounding the ethereal subtleties of Hindu philosophy to students; a priest or storyteller telling stories from Hindu scriptures to groups of devotees in the precincts of a temple; a woman pouring sacred Ganges water on an image of Shiva; a pious person ritually worshiping a cow; and a woman performing a ritual for the well-being of her household.

By the end of the day the visitor to Varanasi seeking to discern the essential outlines of the Hindu religious tradition probably will be very confused and tempted to conclude that Varanasi, with all its diversity, is not the best place to look for the essential ingredients of Hinduism. Indeed, Hinduism itself, like Varanasi, tends to defy neat analysis and description and leaves the impression that what happens in the name of Hinduism is chaotic. Hinduism, it seems, eludes and frustrates attempts to summarize it neatly because it offers exceptions or even contradictions to what at first might seem essential or generally true.

For example, many Hindus in Varanasi say that ahimsa (noninjury) is essential to the Hindu vision of reality, and they will be able to cite countless texts to support that view. They will mention Mahatma Gandhi as a recent example of the centrality of this theme in Hinduism, and possibly also the Hindu respect for cows and the emphasis on vegetarianism. You may be convinced that here, indeed, is an essential aspect of Hinduism. Thanking your informant, you will go on your way, only to come upon a temple of Kali or Durga, where worshipers are beheading a goat in sacrifice to the goddess. Or you might happen upon a copy of the *Artha Shastra* of Kautiliya, an ancient and authoritative text on Hindu political philosophy from around the fourth century C.E. You will look in vain for Gandhian political principles in this book, because the *Artha Shastra* is consistently ruthless and cunning in its approach to seizing and holding power.

You might, on the other hand, be told by an ascetic in Varanasi that Hinduism involves essentially the renunciation of society and all egotistical desires and the achievement of liberation from the lures of the world. But before long you would find a group of orthodox Brahmins performing ancient rituals from the *Vedas*, also affirmed to be the essence of Hinduism, the explicit aim of which is the stability and welfare of the world, what the Hindus call *loka-samgraha*, one of the central teachings of Hinduism's most famous scripture, the **Bhagavad Gita**.

Who is right? The orthodox Brahmin who performs daily rituals prescribed by the ancient *Vedas?* The ascetic who performs no such rituals, who may even show disdain for them, and who denies any obligation to society? The low-caste farmer who daily praises the Lord Rama and celebrates his heroic exploits? The untouchable who makes a pilgrimage to Varanasi to honor a saint beloved by his or her entire caste but virtually unknown to most high-caste Hindus? Or the pious businessman who consults his astrologer before closing a deal? One must believe them all, it seems, for they are all Hindus undertaking common and acceptable Hindu practices. And this leads to our first generalizations about the Hindu religious tradition.

One cannot find the equivalent of a Hindu pope or an authoritative Hindu council in Varanasi. Historically, Hinduism has never insisted on the necessity of a supreme figure in religious matters and has never agreed on certain articles of belief as essential for all Hindus. Throughout its long history, Hinduism has been highly decentralized.

Another feature of Hinduism follows from this one, a feature reflected in both the caste system and the different paths one may take in the religious quest. Hinduism affirms in a variety of ways that people are different from one another and that these differences are both crucial and distinctive. People have different *adhikaras,* different aptitudes, predilections, and abilities. What is natural to one person is unnatural to another. So it is that different ways are made available to different types. Some may have an aptitude for philosophy, and a path centering on knowledge is available for them. Others may be of a devotional aptitude, and so a path of devotion is appropriate for them. Over the centuries, then, Hinduism has accepted a variety of paths, spiritual techniques, and views of the spiritual quest that all succeed in helping humans fulfill their religious destiny.

On the social level the Hindu emphasis on differences manifests itself in the caste system. Human differences are systematically arranged in hierarchical order, and people are segregated into specialized cohesive groups called castes. Social contact with other castes is carefully circumscribed in such a way that the religious beliefs and practices of a particular Hindu often reflects his or her caste tradition and differs markedly from the religious practices of other castes. The philosophical ideas underlying the caste system are karma, the moral law of cause and effect according to which a person reaps what he or she sows, and samsara, rebirth according to the nature of a person's karma. The basic idea is that what one is now is the result of all that one has done in the past, and what one will become in the future is being determined by all one's actions in the present. In effect, a person's present caste identity is only a brief scene in an endless drama of lives that will end only with moksha, liberation from this endless round of birth, death, and rebirth.

Hinduism also affirms that during one's life a person changes, and different kinds of activities are appropriate to various stages of life. Traditionally four stages have been described, with different obligations for each one. The ideal was designed primarily for men, and only very rarely did a woman follow the pattern. Ideally, a high-caste male is to pass through these stages in the following order: student, householder, forest recluse, and wandering holy man. As a student, a male's duty is to study his tradition, particularly the *Vedas* if he is a Brahmin. As a householder he is to foster a family, undertake an occupation appropriate to his caste, and perform rituals, usually Vedic rituals, that help insure the stability of the world. As a forest hermit, he is supposed to leave his home, retire to the forest with his wife, continue Vedic rituals, and meditate on those realities that will bring about liberation from the world and rebirth. Finally, he is to abandon even his wife, give up Vedic rituals, wander continually, begging his food, and strive for the knowledge that emancipates him from the cycles of rebirth. Although this pattern is not always followed, it affirms the tradition's liberality in permitting a variety of approaches in one's spiritual sojourn: study; support of the

world through rituals, work, and family life; meditation away from society; and renunciation of the world through extreme asceticism.

The Hindu insistence on differences between people, then, leads to the very common definition of Hinduism in sacred texts as varna-ashrama-dharma, which may be loosely translated as performing the duty (dharma) of one's stage of life (ashrama) and caste or social station (varna).

Hindus also have acknowledged that differences exist among the regional areas of the Indian subcontinent, and the Hindu Law Books accept regional customs and peculiarities as authoritative. These regional dissimilarities help us understand another aspect of the diversity of belief and practice among Hindus in Varanasi. Hindus from Tamilnad in the South have a cultural history that differs greatly from, say, Hindus from Bengal. Each region has its own vernacular tradition, its favorite gods and goddesses, its own distinctive customs and rituals. In Varanasi, where pilgrims from all over India congregate, these differences further complicate any attempt to discern common themes, patterns, and beliefs. The history of Hinduism is, to a great extent, the record of what has gone on in the regions of India and is therefore marked by much diversity in belief and practice.

On the other hand, a strong, articulate, and authoritative tradition, called the Great, Sanskrit, or Aryan tradition, has counterbalanced this diversity by imposing on it certain myths, beliefs, customs, and patterns of social organization. Dominated by a literate Brahmin elite, Hinduism over the centuries always has manifested a certain coherence because of the prestige of this tradition throughout India. Thus, today Hinduism is, as it always has been, the dynamic interaction of various regional traditions with an all-India tradition in which the particular beliefs and rituals of any given Hindu are a combination. For orthodox Varanasi Brahmins, very little if any of the regional traditions may affect their brand of Hinduism. For low-caste Bengali peasants, on the other hand, very little of the Sanskrit tradition may be a part of their religion.

All this adds up to what one might call a liberal tendency in Hinduism that permits and even encourages men and women to undertake their religious sojourns in a variety of ways. Some things, to be sure, are encouraged for all Hindus: caste purity (intermarriage between castes is discouraged strongly), respect for Brahmins, and life-cycle rituals, for example. Certain ethical precepts also are encouraged for all, and certain underlying beliefs are accepted by most Hindus, such as karma, samsara, and moksha. In Varanasi, then, we find very general parameters defining Hinduism that for the most part are provided by the Sanskrit tradition and that permit a great diversity of belief and practice. What goes on within these parameters, finally, may be summed up as representing four accents within the Hindu tradition.

1. *The Vedic Tradition.* Historically, the Aryans, who composed the *Vedas*, were foreigners who succeeded in superimposing on the indigenous peoples of India their language, culture, and religion. This Vedic religion is still dominant in living Hinduism and is best represented by the orthodox Brahmins. One of the central aims of this religion is the stability and welfare of the world, which is achieved through a great variety of rituals. In Varanasi today this accent is represented by those Brahmins who study the traditional Law Books and sponsor elaborate Vedic rituals.

2. *The Devotional Tradition.* The Hinduism of the majority of people in Varanasi is devotional, and this accent within the tradition goes all the way back to at least the time of the *Bhagavad Gita* (around 200 B.C.E.). Devotion is of varying types and is directed to a great variety of gods and goddesses, but generally we can speak of three strands within this tradition: (1) devotion to Shiva or to one of his family; (2) devotion to Vishnu or to one of his avatars (incarnations), the two most popular of which in the Varanasi area are Krishna and Rama; and (3) devotion to one of the many manifestations of the Great Goddess, the Mahadevi. It is primarily against the background of the devotional tradition that Hindus identify themselves as Shaiva (devotees of Shiva), Vaishnava (devotees of Vishnu), or Shakta (devotees of the Goddess). Devotion to all three manifestations of the divine is concerned with eternal proximity to the deity in his or her heaven or with liberation from the cycle of endless births (Moksha).

3. *The Ascetic Tradition.* The several thousand ascetics in Varanasi are the living representatives of a tradition that is probably as ancient as the *Vedas* and that has been highly honored in Hinduism for over twenty-five hundred years. The underlying assumptions of this tradition are that (1) life in the world is a hindrance to realizing one's spiritual destiny; (2) renunciation of society, including family ties, is necessary to realize one's spiritual essence; (3) various kinds of austerities are the necessary means of purifying oneself of both ignorance and attachments; and (4) the ultimate goal of this arduous path is complete liberation from the wheel of rebirth. There are various types of ascetics, ascetic orders, and spiritual exercises undertaken by ascetics. Generally, though, they all share these ideas and emphasize the importance of the individual's emancipation rather than one's obligations to the social order and its maintenance. In this respect there has often been a tension

between the Vedic tradition and the ascetic tradition, a tension we shall return to later.

4. *The Popular Tradition.* This tradition refers to all those other rites and beliefs of Varanasi Hindus that do not fit neatly under the other three traditions. The sanctity of Varanasi itself, and of the River Ganges that flows through it, points to the central importance of sacred places and pilgrimage in the Hindu tradition. For Hindus the entire subcontinent bubbles with sacred places where immediate access to sacred and purifying power is obtainable. Most prominent geographical features, such as mountains and rivers, are sacred and are the focal points of pilgrimage. Most cities contain famous temples and are also sacred centers. In addition to geographical sites and cities, some plants are held to be sacred. To the worshipers of Vishnu, the *tulasi* plant is particularly sacred, whereas to many devotees of the Goddess, it is the *bilva* tree. Time is punctuated by auspicious and inauspicious moments that are determined by the movements of the stars, the planets, the sun, and the moon. Many Hindus are extremely sensitive to these rhythms and will undertake nothing of significance unless they have been assured by their astrologer that the time is auspicious. Most Hindus know precisely at what time they were born, because they, and their parents, need that information to determine the compatibility of marriage partners. We also include under the popular tradition the preoccupation many Hindus have with diet. Many Hindu scriptures give lists of pure and impure foods and characterize the different properties of foods according to the physical and spiritual effects they produce. The preoccupation of many Hindus and many Hindu scriptures with signs and omens is also part of the popular tradition, as are rituals that have to do with gaining control over enemies and members of the opposite sex. In short, the popular tradition refers to things that we might call magical or superstitious simply because we do not understand them fully; we are unable to do so because those who practice them cannot articulate in ways we can understand what these practices and beliefs mean to them or meant to their ancestors.

By way of concluding this introductory portrait of Hinduism, let me suggest an image that might be useful in thinking about its diversity. We all know someone who is a collector, who rarely throws anything away, whose possessions include the exquisite treasure, the tackiest bauble, the unidentifiable photograph, the neglected and dusty item, and the latest flashy gadget. The Hindu religious tradition has shown itself to be an incurable collector, and it contains in the nooks and crannies of its house many different things. Today this great collector may hold one or another thing in fashion and seem to be utterly fascinated by it. But very few things are ever discarded altogether, and this is probably one of the most interesting and distinctive features of Hinduism. Like a big family, with its diversity, quarrels, eccentricities, and stubborn loyalty to tradition, Hinduism is a religion that expresses the ongoing history of a subcontinent of people for over thirty-five hundred years. The family album is too immense to describe in a single book, but I hope that what follows succeeds in at least suggesting the extraordinary wisdom, richness, and beauty of that particular family of humanity we call Hinduism.

HISTORICAL OUTLINE

The Formative Period
(2500–800 B.C.E.)

From the middle of the third millenniun B.C.E. to the second millennium B.C.E. there was a thriving city civilization in Northwest India, the Indus Valley civilization, which was centered in two cities, Harappa and Mohenjo-Daro. This civilization undertook extensive trade with the city civilizations of the ancient Near East, was based on an agricultural economy, and seems to have had a complex, hierarchical social structure. Writing was known, but it has not yet been deciphered by scholars.

It is difficult to say anything definite about the religion of the Indus Valley civilization. Many female figurines have been found, and it is probable that goddesses were worshiped in connection with the fertility of the crops. The bulls depicted on seals, the intriguing scenes depicted in the art, and a variety of stone objects are tantalizing in suggesting possible prototypes of later Indian religion, but until the script is deciphered most aspects of the religion of this ancient culture must remain unknown or at best vague.

The Indus Valley civilization came to an abrupt end around 1500 B.C.E. at about the time an energetic people known as the Indo-Aryans migrated into Northwest India. Although many aspects of later Hinduism may well have been inspired by the Indus Valley civilization or regional peasant cultures in India, it is the Indo-Aryans and their religion that Hinduism traditionally has looked to as its source and inspiration; the earliest scriptures of the Indo-Aryans, the *Vedas*, have been acknowledged for thousands of years to embody the primordial truths upon which Hinduism bases itself.

The *Vedas* represent a diversified and continuous tradition that extends from around 1200 B.C.E., the probable date of the *Rig Veda*, the earliest Vedic text, to around 400 B.C.E., the probable date of some of the late *Upanishads*. Generally, Vedic literature is of three types: (1) *Samhitas*, hymns in praise of various deities; (2) *Brahmanas*, sacrificial texts dealing with the meaning and technicalities of rituals; and (3) *Aranyakas* and *Upanishads*, philosophical and mystical texts dealing with the quest to realize ultimate reality.

The central figure of the *Samhita* texts is the rishi, a heroic visionary figure and poet who was able to experience directly the various gods and powers that pervaded the Vedic world. In the quest to commune with these sacred powers, the rishi does not seem to have employed ascetic techniques, as later Hindu visionaries were to do. The rishis did, however, employ a plant called *soma*, which was most likely a hallucinogenic mushroom. Drinking soma, the rishi was transported to the realm of the gods. Having experienced the gods, the rishis subsequently were inspired to compose hymns in their praise. The Vedic gods themselves are said to enjoy soma, and one of the most popular gods, Indra, a mighty warrior, is often described as drinking soma and experiencing its exhilarating effects. The centrality of the rishis' quest for an unmediated vision of the divine in the earliest Vedic literature has persisted in the Hindu tradition to this day, although the means of achieving this vision and the nature of the vision itself have changed over the centuries. In the later Hindu tradition, asceticism and devotion replaced the use of soma, and the polytheistic vision of the rishis has been replaced by visions emphasizing the underlying unity of reality.

Complementing the visionary dimension of the rishis in Vedic religion is a priestly, sacrificial cult centered on the great Vedic god Agni. Agni represents fire and heat. He is present at the sacrificial fire, at the domestic hearth, in the primordial fire of precreation, in the digestive fires of the stomach; he pervades all creatures as the fire of life. In addition, Agni is the intermediary between humans and gods because he transmits their offerings to the gods in the sacrificial fire. In general, nearly all Vedic sacrificial rituals aim at aiding, strengthening, or reinvigorating Agni so that the creative and vital powers of the world may remain fresh and strong.

At the daily and domestic level, the *agnihotra* ritual, performed by the head of most Vedic households three times each day, nourishes Agni in the form of the sun through simple offerings of clarified butter. At sunrise, midday, and twilight the householder makes offerings to Agni to help him in his perpetual and lifegiving round. On a much more elaborate scale, such as the ritual of building the fire altar, a similar aim is clear. The sacrificer, with the aid of Brahmin priests, builds an elaborate structure infused with elements and objects representing Agni in his many forms that have been collected over a year's period. The resulting fire altar in the form of a bird represents the rebuilt, distilled essence of Agni before he diffused himself throughout the created order. Agni is put back together again, as it were, so that he can regain the strength necessary to reinvigorate the world. This ritual, and others like it, then, is part of a cyclical pattern. Initially, Agni, representing the divine forces generally, diffused himself into the creation for the benefit of humans. Humans in turn sustain and reinvigorate Agni and the gods through rituals that enable Agni to redistribute himself periodically in the creation. In this ritual scheme the gods and humans are partners in maintaining the ongoing creative processes of the world.

The Speculative Period (800–400 B.C.E.)

The sacrificial texts concern themselves to a great extent with the underlying potency of the rituals they describe and as such are metaphysical in nature. However, philosophical and metaphysical concerns only come to dominate Vedic literature in the *Upanishads*, in which we find a third dimension of Vedic religion. This dimension may be described as the quest for redemptive knowledge, or the search for the truth that will make people free. The *Upanishads* are primarily dialogues between a teacher and a student, they usually take place away from society, and from time to time they criticize the performance of rituals as superfluous to the religious quest. Some of the texts extol the renunciation of society and the performance of austerities that in later Hinduism become increasingly important techniques for liberation.

Although the *Upanishads* are somewhat diverse in their teachings, all agree that underlying reality is a spiritual essence called Brahman. Brahman is One, is usually said to be without delimiting attributes, is impersonal, and is essentially present in all people in the form of the Atman, a person's inmost self, or soul. The religious quest in the *Upanishads* involves realizing the fundamental identity of Brahman and Atman and realizing that one's essential self transcends individuality, limitation, decay, and death. The realization of this truth wins the adept liberation or release (moksha) from the shifting world of constant flux and the endless cycle of rebirth (samsara), which is perpetuated and determined by all one's actions (karma).

Unlike earlier Vedic texts, then, the *Upanishads* do not associate the religious quest with the vitality of the physical world but rather aim at a goal that transcends or overcomes the world. In later Hinduism moksha comes to represent the highest religious goal in nearly all texts, and the *Upanishads* are therefore important in the history of Hinduism as the earliest scriptures to describe the religious quest for liberation from the world. The *Upanishads* are also important because they are the earliest texts to advocate withdrawal from society and the use of ascetic and meditational techniques in this quest. In the *Upanishads* it is clear that the Aryan-Vedic tradition has been influenced by one that was probably indigenous to India, the ascetic tradition.

The earliest systematic presentation of the ascetic tradition is found in the *Yoga Sutras*. Yoga is a technique of ascetic and meditational exercises that aims at isolating humans from the flux of the material world in order for them to recapture their original spiritual purity. Yoga seeks to disentangle the individual from involvement in prakriti (nature, matter, the phenomenal world generally) so that one may glimpse, and be liberated by, one's pure spiritual essence, purusha. Yoga represents an ancient Indian view of the world that emphasizes the transient nature of existence and seeks to overcome it by discovering and isolating one's eternal, unchanging, spiritual essence. Although this tendency is most clearly expressed in other Indian religions such as Jainism and Buddhism, it gains increasing importance in the Hindu tradition and remains central to that tradition to this day.

The Epic and Classical Periods (400 B.C.E.–600 C.E.)

The period from around 400 B.C.E. to 400 C.E. in Hinduism is known as the epic period. During this time the Indo-Aryans ceased to be a nomadic people. They settled into towns and cities, especially in the Gangetic plains of North India, and began to infuse their religion with elements of the religion of the indigenous peoples they had come to dominate. It was during this period that the two great Hindu epics were written, the *Mahabharata* and the *Ramayana*. Both epics concern themselves with royal rivalries, perhaps reflecting political turmoil during this period, and exhibit, in their rambling ways, a tension between a religion aimed at supporting and upholding the world order and one aimed at isolating a person from society in order to achieve individual liberation.

As both epics are explicitly concerned with royal heroes, they have much to say about the world-supporting aspects of Hinduism. Vedic rituals, the ideal social system, and the preservation of order are essential concerns of the ideal king in Hinduism, and the heroes in both epics grapple with the subtleties and complexities of these concerns in their kingly roles. Rama, the hero of the *Ramayana*, for example, must come to terms with a dilemma that contrasts the written law (in this case, that the eldest son should inherit his father's kingdom) with the unwritten law of obeying one's father (for complicated reasons Rama's father commands him to exile himself to the forest for fourteen years so that Rama's half-brother may inherit the kingdom). Both epics emphasize that the king is a crucial figure in maintaining the harmonious realm of dharma (social and moral obligation) and rarely question the ultimate good involved in the preservation and refinement of the social order and those rituals and religious practices that insure it.

In the background of the epics, however, a host of characters call into question the ultimate good of the order of dharma. Called by a variety of names, these individuals have usually renounced the world, live in forests or small settlements, and are said to possess extraordinary powers. The epic heroes almost always treat these world renouncers with great respect and are often their students or beneficiaries.

The epics, like Hinduism itself, manage in various ways to hold together the tension between the aims of the royal heroes, which have to do with worldly order, and the aims of the world renouncers, which have to do primarily with individual liberation. On the narrative plane, first of all, both sets of epic heroes must wander for many years in the forest away from civilization and the realm of dharmic order among those who have renounced the world before gaining world sovereignty. In the disorder of the forest and from the teachings and examples of the world renouncers, the royal heroes acquire the knowledge and means to become rulers.

The epics offer a second solution to the tension between supporting or renouncing the world by defining the stages of life each person passes through. When Yudhishthira, the eldest of the five brothers who are the heroes of the *Mahabharata*, wishes to renounce the world because he is depressed at the slaughter that has taken place as a result of his desire to become king, his brothers and wife argue against him by saying that it is not proper to renounce the world until one has fulfilled one's social obligations. Increasingly this becomes the Hindu tradition's official position in seeking to wed the world-supporting and world-renouncing traditions. First one must fulfill one's obligation to society, and in performing this obligation the religion of the *Vedas*, with its emphasis on refreshing and sustaining the world, is appropriate. Second, there is one's ultimate obligation to achieve final liberation, and this may be pursued when it is timely, preferably after one's grey hairs have appeared

and one has seen one's grandchildren. In performing this obligation, asceticism and renunciation of the world are appropriate.

A third solution to the tension between these two religious aims is found in the *Bhagavad Gita*, which forms a part of the *Mahabharata*. The *Gita*'s solution is philosophical, suggesting that true renunciation involves the renunciation of desires for the fruits of actions and that this renunciation may be undertaken in the world while fulfilling one's social duty. Selfless action without desire for reward, action as an end in itself, is true renunciation for the *Gita*, and as such no tension need exist between one's dual obligation to support the world and to seek individual liberation.

Roughly contemporary with the epics is a whole genre of literature concerned with the ideal nature of society, the Law Books. It is in this literature that the definition of the ideal society as varna-ashrama-dharma, the duty of acting according to one's stage of life (ashrama) and position in society (varna), is arrived at as most descriptive of Hindu society specifically and of Hinduism in general. The writers of these works have considerable respect for renouncing the world and seeking moksha in ascetic isolation, but they quite carefully relegate this aspect of the religious quest to old age. These works are concerned primarily with social stability, and underlying all the Law Books is the strong Hindu affirmation that an orderly, refined, stable society is to be cherished. Order, stability, and refinement have primarily and essentially to do with the proper functioning of the various castes and the proper observance of interaction among castes and among members of the same castes. Although the Law Books tolerate certain regional idiosyncrasies concerning social customs, all of them share a unified vision of society as hierarchically arranged according to caste. In the Law Books the social system has as its primary aim the support of Brahmins, who undertake Vedic rituals to maintain and renew the cosmic forces that periodically must be refreshed in order to keep the world bounteous and habitable. Beneath the Brahmins are the Kshatriyas (warriors) and Vaishyas (merchants). These three highest social groups (Brahmins, Kshatriyas, and Vaishyas) are called the twice-born classes, as they alone are permitted to perform the initiation ceremony of the sacred thread, which is believed to result in a second birth for the initiate. These groups alone, according to the Law Books, are qualified to study the *Vedas* and to undertake Vedic rituals. The serfs, or Shudras, are ranked below the twice-born classes, and their proper task is to support the higher castes by performing services for them. Beneath the Shudras, and barely even mentioned in the Law Books, are the untouchables, whose occupations are held to be highly polluting or who are so classed because they belong to tribal groups in India that are not yet acculturated.

Although the social ideal of the Law Books probably was never realized in the past, and although current Hindu society is quite different from this idealized model, the ideal society of the Law Books has had a great influence on Hindu thought and does succeed in capturing its underlying hierarchical assumptions and the preoccupation with ritual purity in Hindu religious practice and social intercourse.

The Medieval Period (600–1800 C.E.)

The medieval period in Hinduism is characterized by three developments: (1) the rise of devotional movements with a corresponding outburst in the construction of temples; (2) the systematization of Hindu philosophy into six schools dominated by the school of Advaita Vedanta (nondualistic Vedanta); and (3) the rise of Tantrism, a movement employing ritual techniques to achieve liberation.

Although devotion (called *bhakti* in Hinduism) enters the Hindu tradition as early as the *Bhagavad Gita* (around 200 B.C.E.), it was not until about the sixth century C.E. that devotion began to dominate the religious landscape of Hinduism. Beginning in the South with the Nayanars, devotional saints who praised Shiva, and the Alvars, devotional saints who worshiped Vishnu, an emotional, ecstatic kind of devotion became increasingly central to Hindu piety. By the seventeenth century, bhakti of this type had come to dominate the entire Hindu tradition. Devotion as described in the *Bhagavad Gita* was primarily a mental discipline aimed at controlling one's actions in the world in such a way that social obligations and religious fulfillment could be harmonized. In the later devotional movements, devotion is typically described as a love affair with God in which the devotee is willing to sacrifice anything in order to revel with the Lord in ecstatic bliss. The best example of this theme is the devotion to the cowherd Krishna, whose ideal devotees are married women who leave their husbands and homes to revel with Krishna in the woods. Unlike the *Bhagavad Gita*'s rather staid description of devotion, the later movements delight in describing the devotional experience as causing uncontrollable joy, fainting, frenzy, tears of anguish, madness, and sometimes social censure. Underlying most of these movements is the theological assumption that, although men and women may have differing inherited or ascribed duties and social positions, all creatures share the same inherent duty, which is to love and serve God. Although few devotional movements actually criticize the traditional social structure, it is sometimes the case that they are indifferent to traditional society, which they describe as confining when one undertakes the task of loving God. Two famous women devotees, Mahadeviyakka, a Virashaiva saint, and Mirabai, a Rajastani princess and devotee of Krishna, for example, both chafed under traditional marriages and eventually left their husbands to devote themselves entirely to their respective gods.

Contemporary with the rise and spread of devotional movements, and perhaps reflecting their importance, was the rise of temples as important religious centers in Hinduism. Hindu temples, as the earthly dwelling places of the gods, are usually patterned on the model of a divine mountain or palace. They are centers of worship, centers for religious instruction, and often the homes of devotees who have renounced the world to pursue their service to God. Traditionally some temples dominated by the high castes have excluded low-caste devotees, but Hindus of all castes take part in temple worship, either at grand temples famous throughout India or at village temples that may consist of nothing more than a mud hut.

At these temples a great variety of deities are worshiped. Generally, however, the deity belongs to one of three strands within the Hindu pantheon: the Shaivite strand, which includes Shiva and members of his family; the Vaishnavite strand, which includes Vishnu and his avatars (incarnations); and the Shakta strand, which includes Hindu goddesses. The worship may be elaborate or simple but usually consists of some form of puja, a type of ritual service to the deity. This rite is normally performed by a priest, who is usually a Brahmin in temples frequented by high-caste Hindus but who may be a low-caste non-Brahmin in humbler temples used by the low castes.

The mythology of the deities worshiped, which is often portrayed in temple artwork, became systematized during the medieval period in a genre of works known as the *Puranas*, or "stories of old." As elsewhere in the Hindu tradition, the tension between *loka-samgraha*, supporting the world, and moksha, striving for release from the world, is reflected in these texts. Dominating the *Puranas* are two quite different manifestations of the divine: Shiva and Vishnu.

Shiva is the ascetic god, the great yogi who meditates in isolation on Kailasa Mountain in the Himalayas, who burns the god of love to ashes with the fury from his middle eye when the god tries to distract him. He is often portrayed as an outsider with matted hair, his body smeared with ashes and clothed in animal skins, with snakes and a garland of skulls as ornaments. Although a good deal of Shiva's mythology concerns his eventual marriage to the goddess Parvati and his most typical emblem is the lingam, the phallus, Shiva clearly embodies the world-renouncing tendencies of Hinduism and as such provides a model for this aspect of the tradition.

Vishnu, on the other hand, is usually described as a cosmic king who lives in the heavenly splendor of his palace in Vaikuntha. His primary role in the divine economy is to supervise universal order and prosperity. As the cosmic policeman he descends from time to time in various forms to defeat enemies of world stability, and as such he provides a model for supporting the world.

Turning to the second major development of the medieval period, the systematization of Hindu philosophical thought, we find a considerable diversity tolerated. The six schools that eventually came to be accepted as orthodox emphasize very differing points of view and reveal again the underlying tension between dharma, supporting the world, and moksha, release from the world. The tension is best seen in the rivalry between the Purva Mimamsa and Uttara Mimamsa schools. Although both schools emphasize the *Vedas* as their source of inspiration, the former preoccupies itself with the ritual aspects of the *Vedas* and affirms the centrality of Vedic rituals as the key to realizing both religious duty and personal salvation. For this school, Vedic rituals are the most potent of all actions and are crucial in maintaining the world. One's ultimate duty, according to Purva Mimamsa, is continually to support the world by performing those rituals that are revealed in the *Vedas*.

The Uttara Mimamsa school, more commonly known as Vedanta, occupies itself with the *Upanishads*, which as we have noted emphasize individual release from the world by realizing the essential unity of Brahman, the Absolute, and Atman, the essential self in each person. The most brilliant and systematic exponent of this school was the eighth-century South Indian, Shankara, whose particular school of Vedanta is known as Advaita Vedanta (the Vedanta of no difference, or nondualism). For Shankara, actions per se, whether good or bad, are of no ultimate significance in achieving liberation because they arise from a false sense of individuality. Knowledge alone, a transforming, experiential knowledge of one's identity with Brahman, is the goal of the religious quest and is not dependent upon social obligations. However, Shankara's own life is often taken as a model for adepts of this path, and as Shankara himself was a world renouncer, most followers of his philosophy extol renunciation as helpful, if not necessary, in achieving liberating knowledge. Although Shankara did

not criticize traditional society and traditional religious practices that aim at supporting the world, he was clear that a person's ultimate spiritual goal is not achieved by or through them. Not surprisingly, Shankara is held by the Hindu tradition to have been an incarnation of the ascetic god Shiva.

The *Tantras*, the third major development of the medieval period, seem to have arisen outside the elite Brahmin tradition. The *Tantras*, of which there are hundreds, often criticize established religious practices and the upholders of those practices, the Brahmins. In many ways, however, the *Tantras* express central, traditional Hindu ideas and practices. Underlying Tantric practice, for example, is the assumption that an individual is a miniature or microcosm of the cosmos and that by learning the sacred geography of one's body one may, by means of various yogic techniques, bring about one's own spiritual fulfillment, which in most Tantric texts is the result of uniting various opposites within one's body/cosmos.

The *Tantras* claim to be appropriate to the present era, which is decadent and in which people are less spiritual and less inclined to perform the elaborate rituals prescribed in earlier ages. The *Tantras* claim to introduce techniques that lead directly to liberation without traditional practices and routines. Vedic study, Vedic rituals, pilgrimage, puja, and other traditional practices, although not always disregarded in the *Tantras*, are often held to be superfluous in the present age. The *Tantras*, then, offer a variety of rituals that employ mantras (sacred formulas), mandalas (schematic diagrams), and yogic techniques that are believed to achieve either complete liberation from the mundane world or extraordinary powers, such as omniscience and the ability to fly.

The *Tantras* themselves distinguish between a right-handed path and a left-handed path. The right-handed path is for all adepts and consists primarily in the use of mantras, mandalas, and ritual techniques based upon Tantric sacred bodily geography. The left-handed path, appropriate only for those of a special heroic temperament, centers on a particular ritual in which the adept partakes of five forbidden things, thereby transcending the tension between the sacred and the profane and gaining liberation. This left-handed aspect of Tantrism has been greatly criticized by the Brahmin establishment.

The Modern Period (1800 to the Present)

Increasing contact with the West, including the political and economic domination by England from the middle of the nineteenth century to the middle of the twentieth century, provides the background for three important developments in the modern period of the Hindu tradition: (1) the Hindu revival of the nineteenth century; (2) the independence movement of the nineteenth and twentieth centuries; and (3) the introduction of Hinduism in a variety of forms to the West, particularly to North America.

As early as the eighth century C.E. Muslims had entered India, and by the thirteenth century Islam had come to a position of political dominance in North India. Increasingly Hindus found themselves ruled by non-Hindus, and British domination, beginning in the eighteenth century, represented to Hindus a continuation of foreign rule. Although many Indians were attracted by the teaching of the equality of all believers in Islam and converted to that religion, the majority remained at least nominal Hindus and in various ways continued the traditions of the past. With the arrival of Western powers in the eighteenth century, however, both Westerners and Hindus began to articulate an increasingly vocal criticism of the Hindu tradition. Many aspects of traditional Hinduism were castigated, and in the nineteenth century Hindu reform movements arose that sought to meet these criticisms by distilling what was most central to the Hindu tradition and doing away with the rest. Two movements in particular gained all-India fame: the Brahmo Samaj, founded by Ram Mohan Roy, and the Arya Samaj, founded by Swami Dayananda.

Ram Mohan Roy (1774–1833) was a prominent citizen of Bengal, and before he founded the Brahmo Samaj (the Society of Brahman) he had considerable contact with Christian missionaries. He was acquainted with Western humanistic traditions and made a journey to England, where he became even more familiar with Western ideas. In 1828 he founded the Brahmo Samaj, which represented his vision of a reformed Hinduism. For Ram Mohan the essence of Hinduism was found in the *Upanishads*. There, he said, was revealed the One Nameless Absolute God of all people, who was to be worshiped through meditation and a pious life. Such Hindu customs as image worship, pilgrimage, festivals, and the rules of caste, he held, were superfluous in the service of this God. The Brahmo Samaj, then, instituted worship services and a type of piety that were rationalistic, humanistic, and devoid of distinctive Hindu symbols and customs. Many Westerners applauded this movement, but it never gained popularity among Hindus.

The Arya Samaj was founded in 1875 by Swami Dayananda (1824–1883) as another attempt to restore Hinduism to its original purity. Like Ram Mohan Roy, Dayananda found the essence of Hinduism in the *Vedas*, which he said taught monotheism and morality. Dayananda was particularly keen on abolishing image worship and

caste discrimination. His basis for criticizing the Hindu tradition as it existed in his own day was the *Vedas*. He was suspicious of Western ideas and insisted that a purified Hinduism must involve a return to the *Vedas*. Although the Arya Samaj had a wider appeal than the Brahmo Samaj, it did not succeed in gaining a very wide audience either. Both movements, however, were important in revitalizing Hindu pride and helped to lay the spiritual groundwork for the independence movement, with its championing of Indian traditions and criticisms of Western values and domination.

A third important religious phenomenon of this time was the Bengali saint, Ramakrishna. Ramakrishna (1836–1886) in most ways represented traditional Hindu beliefs and spiritual techniques. He was a temple priest of the goddess Kali, and though he found in this goddess his favorite object of devotion, he worshiped other deities as well in an attempt to discover the special blessing of each god. He also experimented with the different Hindu paths, such as Tantrism and the path of knowledge. His reaction to Western religions was simply to experiment with them in his own religious life. In these experiments he is said to have been successful, several times having visions of Muslim and Christian heroes. Ramakrishna sought, then, to incorporate Western ideas and religions into the expansive Hindu context and not to reform Hinduism by making it conform to Western ideas of monotheism or humanism. Unlike Ram Mohan Roy and Dayananda, Ramakrishna was widely considered a great saint by his fellow Hindus even before his death and probably represents the most typical Hindu response to foreign influence.

Ramakrishna's favorite disciple was Vivekananda (1863–1902), who is often considered the first successful Hindu missionary to the West. In 1893 he addressed the First World Parliament of Religions at Chicago and was enthusiastically received there and by many Americans in his subsequent travels throughout the United States. Returning to India a national hero, he instituted plans for fellow members of his movement to set up centers in the West to foster the teachings and practice of Hinduism. The Hinduism of Vivekananda was much less devotional than Ramakrishna's own piety and stressed the monistic teachings of the *Upanishads* and the Vedanta of Shankara. The Ramakrishna Mission was thus inaugurated in the West and became the first successful attempt to transplant Hinduism to that part of the world.

Both the persistence and modification of traditional Hindu themes are clear in the Indian independence movement, particularly in its two most famous leaders, Bal Gangadhar Tilak (1856–1920) and Mohandas Karamchand Gandhi (1869–1948). Both Tilak and Gandhi took the *Bhagavad Gita* and its teachings concerning *loka-samgraha*, supporting the world, as central to their positions, and both were considered karma-yogis, masters of disciplined action. However, the two differed considerably in their styles and provide a modern expression of the continuing tension between renunciation and support of the world.

Tilak's greatest work was his commentary on the *Bhagavad Gita*, the *Gita Rahasya*, in which he argued that the Hindu's primary responsibility is to work out his or her spiritual destiny while remaining in the world and acting without desire for the fruits of his or her actions. He systematically refuted all earlier commentaries on the *Gita* and saw in this most famous of Hindu scriptures the theoretical foundation of political activism. Tilak, opposing all Hindus who argued for gradual reform and eventual independence, advocated no compromise with foreign rulers. For Tilak the *Gita* was a manual for action that, given its context, the battlefield, permitted the use of violence in a just cause. Renunciation of the world was unpatriotic and a sign of weakness. In his many speeches and writings Tilak never tired of calling his fellow Hindus to responsible action in and for the world.

Gandhi, too, interpreted the *Gita* as teaching involvement in the world, and it was the *Gita* that provided the theoretical background for his teaching and technique of satyagraha, holding to the truth. Satyagraha for Gandhi was the task of expressing the truth in every action, no matter what the result, the task of acting without regard for rewards. Gandhi, however, chose to read the *Gita* as a nonviolent text and refused to permit violence in his various political campaigns; he urged restraint, negotiation, and self-sacrifice instead. His style of life also differed from Tilak's and is reminiscent of the ascetic tradition in Hinduism. Although a householder, Gandhi early in his career practiced strict poverty, restricting his possessions to a few necessities, and later in life took a vow of celibacy. He wore little clothing and lived on a very restricted diet. Gandhi added to the role of the classic Hindu world renouncer, however, the element of community service. His asceticism was aimed at harnessing energy and vitality that would be used to support India's poor and oppressed. His spiritual mission, in addition to personal liberation, was the liberation of his fellow Hindus from ignorance, caste hatred, economic and political domination by foreigners, and material poverty. Gandhi's quest represented the inextricable combination of personal purification with the purification of the world.

In recent years varied expressions of Hinduism have found their way to the West, in a continuation of the precedent set by Vivekananda in 1893. Although Hinduism had moved beyond its own borders before the modern period, it was primarily a result of Indian emigration to other countries and the resulting establishment of Hindu culture in such places as Sri Lanka and Indonesia. In the modern period, however, beginning with Vivekananda, various Hindus have self-consciously sought to spread Hinduism outside of India. These figures have been many and diverse in their interpretations of the Hindu religion.

Two recent gurus (spiritual masters) who have gained a degree of popularity in the West are Maharishi Mahesh Yogi (ca. 1911), founder of the Spiritual Regeneration Movement, or Transcendental Meditation, and Swami A. C. Bhaktivedanta (1896–1977), founder of the International Society for Krishna Consciousness. Although both movements have begun to take on certain pragmatic aspects suitable to the West, by emphasizing the scientific laws underlying their teachings and the practical or emotional benefits obtained from them, both movements, especially in their early phases, represent authentic Hindu traditions. Transcendental Meditation looks to Vedanta for its theoretical basis, emphasizing each person's inner divine essence and the liberating powers that may be harnessed when one's true identity is known. Maharishi is a typical modern exponent, then, of the ancient tradition in Hinduism that emphasizes the inward search for liberating knowledge. The International Society for Krishna Consciousness, on the other hand, emphasizes enthusiastic devotion to Lord Krishna and is a direct descendent of the Bengali devotionalism of Chaitanya (1485–1536). As such the movement expresses the kind of devotion to personal gods that has dominated Hinduism since the sixth century C.E.

SOURCES

I have organized the sources historically to provide an overview of some of the important religious literature of Hinduism. To facilitate readability, I have left out diacritical marks in my spelling of Sanskrit terms, but the translations I have used frequently include them. Diacritical marks indicate how sounds in a language other than English are to be made. See the Pronunciation Guide at the end of this chapter for more information.

4.2 THE VEDIC PERIOD

I am using the term *Vedic period* to designate the later part (ca. 1200–400 B.C.E.) of what Kinsley calls the formative and speculative periods. While there is much archaeological evidence surviving from pre-Vedic times (ca. 2500–1500 B.C.E.), the script has not yet been deciphered. As we learn more about this period, it is likely we will discover a greater influence on Vedic literature than presently imagined.

The **Vedas** are the earliest sacred writings of the Indo-Aryans who migrated into Northwest India from the North around 1500 B.C.E. The word *veda* means "knowledge" in Sanskrit (the language in which the *Vedas* are written) and in the *narrow* sense refers to the four *Vedas* (*Rig, Sama, Yajur,* and *Atharva*). In the *broad* sense, the *Vedas* also refer to a collection of three types of literature developed by the priestly specialists who produced the four *Vedas.* These three types are called the *Brahmanas* (ca. 1100–700 B.C.E.), the *Aranyakas* (ca. 800–600 B.C.E.), and the *Upanishads* (ca. 700–400 B.C.E.). This whole vast collection of literature is also called **shruti,** which literally means "that which is heard" and is sometimes translated as "revelation." Because these texts are religiously authoritative, they have been referred to as the Hindu scriptures. Both the words *revelation* and *scripture,* however, are misleading. There is no divine author of the *Vedas* (they are said to be "authorless"), and, while this collection constitutes sacred writing (scripture in the broad sense), it is not scripture in the narrow sense of a divinely inspired set of texts.

The claim that the *Vedas* are sacred yet without a divine author may strike you as odd if you have been raised in a Christian, Jewish, or Islamic tradition. However, according to later philosophical thought in India, one of the valid sources of knowledge is testimony. It is valid provided the person giving the testimony knows what she or he is talking about and testifies truthfully. If a testimony has no author, then its validity is difficult to doubt because there is no testifier to question. The doctrine that the *Vedas* are authorless is another way of saying that these writings have no human imperfection. Of course, there were "authors" in the conventional sense, some of whom were priests and poets called **rishis**—persons who have visions that they believe put them directly in touch with sacred powers and sources, including gods and goddesses. The *rishis,* it is said, *heard eternal truths,* and thus no stamp of these individual, historical "authors" is (presumably) found in the texts.

The gods of the Aryan religion referred to in the *Vedas* are, like the gods of the Greeks, in charge of various natural forces. Dyäus Pitr (whose name means "shining father") is, like his Greek counterpart Zeus Pater, father of the gods. Indra, the god of storm and war, receives great attention in the *Vedas,* suggesting that the early Aryan invaders were predominately from a warrior class. Agni, whose name is related to the English word *ignite,* is the fire god who carries the sacrifices to the gods in the sky. Ushas or Dawn is one of the few goddesses mentioned in the *Vedas.* Rudra is in charge of the wind, Varuna oversees justice, Vishnu is responsible for order, and Surya is the major sun god. Yama is the god of the dead, and the god Soma was able to give a foretaste of immortality even in this mortal life.

Many of these Aryan gods are no longer worshiped, but elements of this ancient Aryan religion live on in modern Hinduism especially in the lore and ritual activity. Fire, for example, still plays a major role in Hindu ritual life, and many of the ancient chants are still used.

4.2.1 *Rig Veda*

The *Rig Veda,* the oldest of the *Vedas,* consists of more than a thousand hymns composed and collected over hundreds of years. I include only four here. The first stands quite appropriately at the beginning of the *Rig Veda.* It is a prayer to **Agni,** the god of fire. The heart of Vedic religion is the performance of sacrifices to the gods. Fire transforms the sacrificed into smoke that ascends to the heavens and feeds the gods. Without sacrifice, the gods would go hungry and disorder rather than order would consume the universe.

The *Rig Veda* recognizes that, within the natural order, everything can be divided into food and the eaters of food. A vast food chain stretches from the gods to water. The gods feed on humans, symbolically represented by sacrificial victims. Humans feed on animals, animals on plants, and plants on water, the sustainer of life. Agni and the sacrifices connect this vast hierarchical food chain. Fire makes the world go round.

However, Agni is not the only means facilitating the divine-human relationship. **Soma,** the divine, sacrificial drink and the liquid (water) counterpart of fire, provides visions of the gods, goddesses, and the heavens. Scholars do not agree about which plant was used to make *Soma,* but it may have been a hallucinogenic mushroom. In any case, those who ritually drank it felt free of the bounds of mortality, as our second selection testifies.

The third selection, called the *Purusha-Sukta,* or "The Hymn of Man," celebrates the creation of the universe from the parts of a primal person called

Purusha (here translated as "Man"). Note that creation results from the sacrifice of Purusha, thus establishing the importance of ritual sacrifice for the maintenance of the world order.

The final hymn, usually called the "Creation Hymn," raises a skeptical note about how mere mortals can know anything about the absolute beginning of everything. Creation is a puzzle, challenging humans to raise what seem to be unanswerable questions.

TRANSLATED BY WENDY DONIGER O'FLAHERTY

Hymns from the Rig Veda

READING QUESTIONS

1. What is being prayed for in "I Pray to *Agni*"?
2. What benefits can *Soma* bestow?
3. How does the traditional organization of Hindu society into four general classes (*varnas*, sometimes translated as "castes") receive a cosmic sanction in this hymn?
4. What do you think the "Creation Hymn" means?

1.1 I PRAY TO AGNI

1 I pray to Agni, the household priest who is the god of the sacrifice, the one who chants and invokes and brings most treasure.

2 Agni earned the prayers of the ancient sages, and of those of the present, too; he will bring the gods here.

3 Through Agni one may win wealth, and growth from day to day, glorious and most abounding in heroic sons.

4 Agni, the sacrificial ritual that you encompass on all sides—only that one goes to the gods.

5 Agni, the priest with the sharp sight of a poet, the true and most brilliant, the god will come with the gods.

6 Whatever good you wish to do for the one who worships you, Agni, through you, O Angiras,[1] that comes true.

From *The Rig Veda: An Anthology*, translated by Wendy Doniger O'Flaherty (London: Penguin Books, Ltd., 1981), selections 1.1 (p. 99), 8.48 (pp. 134–135), 10.90 (pp. 30–31), and 10.129 (pp. 25–26). Copyright © 1981 Wendy Doniger O'Flaherty. Reprinted by permission of Penguin Books, Ltd. Footnotes edited.
[1] The Angirases were an ancient family of priests, often identified with Vedic gods such as Agni and Indra.

7 To you, Agni, who shine upon darkness, we come day after day, bringing our thoughts and homage

8 to you, the king over sacrifices, the shining guardian of the Order, growing in your own house.

9 Be easy for us to reach, like a father to his son. Abide with us, Agni, for our happiness.

8.48 WE HAVE DRUNK THE SOMA

1 I have tasted the sweet drink of life, knowing that it inspires good thoughts and joyous expansiveness to the extreme, that all the gods and mortals seek it together, calling it honey.

2 When you penetrate inside, you will know no limits, and you will avert the wrath of the gods. Enjoying Indra's friendship, O drop of Soma, bring riches as a docile cow brings the yoke.

3 We have drunk the Soma; we have become immortal; we have gone to the light; we have found the gods. What can hatred and the malice of a mortal do to us now, O immortal one?

4 When we have drunk you, O drop of Soma, be good to our heart, kind as a father to his son, thoughtful as a friend to a friend. Far-famed Soma, stretch out our life-span so that we may live.

5 The glorious drops that I have drunk set me free in wide space. You have bound me together in my limbs as thongs bind a chariot. Let the drops protect me from the foot that stumbles and keep lameness away from me.

6 Inflame me like a fire kindled by friction; make us see far; make us richer, better. For when I am intoxicated with you, Soma, I think myself rich. Draw near and make us thrive.

7 We would enjoy you, pressed with a fervent heart, like riches from a father. King Soma, stretch out our life-spans as the sun stretches the spring days.

8 King Soma, have mercy on us for our well-being. Know that we are devoted to your laws. Passion and fury are stirred up. O drop of Soma, do not hand us over to the pleasure of the enemy.

9 For you, Soma, are the guardian of our body; watching over men, you have settled down in every limb. If we break your laws, O god, have mercy on us like a good friend, to make us better.

10 Let me join closely with my compassionate friend so that he will not injure me when I have drunk him. O lord of bay horses, for the Soma that is lodged in us I approach Indra to stretch out our life-span.

11 Weaknesses and diseases have gone; the forces of darkness have fled in terror. Soma has climbed up in us, expanding. We have come to the place where they stretch out life-spans.

12 The drop that we have drunk has entered our hearts, an immortal inside mortals. O fathers, let us serve that

Soma with the oblations and abide in his mercy and kindness.

13 Uniting in agreement with the fathers, O drop of Soma, you have extended yourself through sky and earth. Let us serve him with an oblation; let us be masters of riches.

14 You protecting gods, speak out for us. Do not let sleep or harmful speech seize us. Let us, always dear to Soma, speak as men of power in the sacrificial gathering.

15 Soma, you give us the force of life on every side. Enter into us, finding the sunlight, watching over men. O drop of Soma, summon your helpers and protect us before and after.

10.90 PURUSA-SŪKTA, OR THE HYMN OF MAN

1 The Man has a thousand heads, a thousand eyes, a thousand feet. He pervaded the earth on all sides and extended beyond it as far as ten fingers.

2 It is the Man who is all this, whatever has been and whatever is to be. He is the ruler of immortality, when he grows beyond everything through food.

3 Such is his greatness, and the Man is yet more than this. All creatures are a quarter of him; three quarters are what is immortal in heaven.

4 With three quarters the Man rose upwards, and one quarter of him still remains here. From this he spread out in all directions, into that which eats and that which does not eat.

5 From him Virāj[1] was born, and from Virāj came the Man. When he was born, he ranged beyond the earth behind and before.

6 When the gods spread the sacrifice with the Man as the offering, spring was the clarified butter, summer the fuel, autumn the oblation.

7 They anointed the Man, the sacrifice born at the beginning, upon the sacred grass. With him the gods, Sādhyas, and sages sacrificed.

8 From that sacrifice in which everything was offered, the melted fat was collected, and he made it into those beasts who live in the air, in the forest, and in villages.

9 From that sacrifice in which everything was offered, the verses and chants were born, the metres were born from it, and from it the formulas were born.

10 Horses were born from it, and those other animals that have two rows of teeth; cows were born from it, and from it goats and sheep were born.

11 When they divided the Man, into how many parts did they apportion him? What do they call his mouth, his two arms and thighs and feet?

12 His mouth became the Brahmin; his arms were made into the Warrior, his thighs the People, and from his feet the Servants were born.

13 The moon was born from his mind; from his eye the sun was born. Indra and Agni came from his mouth, and from his vital breath the Wind was born.

14 From his navel the middle realm of space arose; from his head the sky evolved. From his two feet came the earth, and the quarters of the sky from his ear. Thus they set the worlds in order.

15 There were seven enclosing-sticks for him, and thrice seven fuel-sticks, when the gods, spreading the sacrifice, bound the Man as the sacrificial beast.

16 With the sacrifice the gods sacrificed to the sacrifice. These were the first ritual laws. These very powers reached the dome of the sky where dwell the Sādhyas, the ancient gods.

10.129 CREATION HYMN (NĀSADĪYA)

1 There was neither non-existence nor existence then; there was neither the realm of space nor the sky which is beyond. What stirred? Where? In whose protection? Was there water, bottomlessly deep?

2 There was neither death nor immortality then. There was no distinguishing sign of night nor of day. That one breathed, windless, by its own impulse. Other than that there was nothing beyond.

3 Darkness was hidden by darkness in the beginning; with no distinguishing sign, all this was water. The life force that was covered with emptiness, that one arose through the power of heat.

4 Desire came upon that one in the beginning; that was the first seed of mind. Poets seeking in their heart with wisdom found the bond of existence in non-existence.

5 Their cord was extended across. Was there below? Was there above? There were seed-placers; there were powers. There was impulse beneath; there was giving-forth above.

6 Who really knows? Who will here proclaim it? Whence was it produced? Whence is this creation? The gods came afterwards, with the creation of this universe. Who then knows whence it has arisen?

7 Whence this creation his arisen—perhaps it formed itself, or perhaps it did not—the one who looks down on it, in the highest heaven, only he knows—or perhaps he does not know.

---

[1] The active female creative principle, Virāj, is later replaced by Prakṛti, or material nature. . . .

4.2.2 Upanishads

The Upanishadic literature indicates that religious and philosophical reflection on the meaning and significance of sacrifice inspired many thinkers to explore questions about the nature of reality, the self, and life after death. Doubt arises about the effectiveness of ritual sacrifice since the law of *karma* represents a strict and universal cause-effect continuum. Any action (**karma**), including sacrifice, that is motivated by desire results in bondage to a universal round of reincarnations (**samsara**). The spiritual goal is to become liberated or released (*moksha* or *mukti*) from the cycle of *samsara*. It is ignorance about reality and the self that keeps us bound to *samsara*. Hence, genuine knowledge must replace ignorance if true freedom is to be achieved.

The ideas of *karma* and *samsara* are related. *Karma* is what determines one's rebirth in the samsaric cycle. Acting in any way at all produces *karma*, because *karma* is not only action but also the results of action. *Karma* is what you do and what happens to you. What happens to you in this life is a result of what you did in a previous life, and what will happen to you in the future is the result of what you do now. Your *jiva*, or individual soul, carries the imprints of your actions from one life to the next. Could one somehow leave the *jiva* behind and thereby break the samsaric cycle?

The idea of *moksha*, or release, indicates that it is possible to escape karmic results and gain liberation from the samsaric cycle. Just how best to do this became an intense religious debate in India, but that such release was possible is repeated many times in the *Upanishads*. The discipline (*yoga*) required to obtain *moksha* attracted much attention as religious ideas embedded deep in the *Upanishads* are explicated in later centuries.

Selections from two *Upanishads* follow. The *Brihadaranyaka Upanishad* is held in high esteem. Its first chapter revisits the theme of creation, and the second chapter reports a conversation about immortality between a sage named Yajnavalkya and his wife, Maitreyi. The *Chandogya Upanishad* contains a famous and influential conversation between a father and a son on the true nature of one's identity.

TRANSLATED BY PATRICK OLIVELLE

Brihadaranyaka and Chandogya Upanishads

READING QUESTIONS

1. How does the creative process start, and how are every male and female pair created?
2. What is *Brahman*'s super-creation?
3. Interpret verses 7 and 8 of chapter 1 of *Brihadaranyaka* in your own words. What do you think is the central message here? What evidence would you cite to support your views?
4. Why does Yajnavalkya say to Maitreyi, "by reflecting and concentrating on one's self, one gains the knowledge of this whole world"?
5. Yajnavalkya offers several analogies to illuminate his claim that "all that is nothing but this self." Explain how the analogies aid us in understanding this claim.
6. How does Yajnavalkya explain the meaning of his claim that "after death there is no awareness"?
7. What is the rule of substitution?
8. What do you think the phrase "that's how you are" means?

BRIHADARANYAKA

Chapter 1

4

In the beginning this world was just a single body (*ātman*) shaped like a man. He looked around and saw nothing but himself. The first thing he said was, "Here I am!" and from that the name "I" came into being. Therefore, even today when you call someone, he first says, "It's I," and then states whatever other name he may have. That first being received the name "man" (*puruṣa*), because ahead (*pūrva*) of all this he burnt up (*uṣ*) all evils.

From *Brihadaranyaka* 1.4.1–8, 2.4.1–14; *Chandogya* 6.1.1–7, 6.2.1–4, 6.10.1–3, 6.11.1–3; in *Upanishads*, translated by Patrick Olivelle (Oxford's World Classics, 1998), pp. 13–15, 28–30, 148–149, 153–154. Reprinted by permission of Oxford University Press.

When someone knows this, he burns up anyone who may try to get ahead of him.

[2] That first being became afraid; therefore, one becomes afraid when one is alone. Then he thought to himself: "Of what should I be afraid, when there is no one but me?" So his fear left him, for what was he going to be afraid of? One is, after all, afraid of another.

[3] He found no pleasure at all; so one finds no pleasure when one is alone. He wanted to have a companion. Now he was as large as a man and a woman in close embrace. So he split (*pat*) his body into two, giving rise to husband (*pati*) and wife (*patnī*). Surely this is why Yājñavalkya used to say: "The two of us are like two halves of a block." The space here, therefore, is completely filled by the woman.

He copulated with her, and from their union human beings were born. [4] She then thought to herself: "After begetting me from his own body (*ātman*), how could he copulate with me? I know—I'll hide myself." So she became a cow. But he became a bull and copulated with her. From their union cattle were born. Then she became a mare, and he a stallion; she became a female donkey, and he, a male donkey. And again he copulated with her, and from their union one-hoofed animals were born. Then she became a female goat, and he, a male goat; she became a ewe, and he, a ram. And again he copulated with her, and from their union goats and sheep were born. In this way he created every male and female pair that exists, down to the very ants.

[5] It then occurred to him: "I alone am the creation, for I created all this." From this "creation" came into being. Anyone who knows this prospers in this creation of his.

[6] Then he churned like this and, using his hands, produced fire from his mouth as from a vagina. As a result the inner sides of both these—the hands and the mouth —are without hair, for the inside of the vagina is without hair. "Sacrifice to this god. Sacrifice to that god"— people do say these things, but in reality each of these gods is his own creation, for he himself is all these gods. From his semen, then, he created all that is moist here, which is really Soma. Food and eater—that is the extent of this whole world. Food is simply Soma, and the eater is fire.

This is *brahman*'s super-creation. It is a super-creation because he created the gods, who are superior to him, and, being a mortal himself, he created the immortals. Anyone who knows this stands within this super-creation of his.

[7] At that time this world was without real distinctions; it was distinguished simply in terms of name and visible appearance—"He is so and so by name and has this sort of an appearance." So even today this world is distinguished simply in terms of name and visible appearance, as when we say, "He is so and so by name and has this sort of an appearance."

Penetrating this body up to the very nailtips, he remains there like a razor within a case or a termite within a termite-hill. People do not see him, for he is incomplete as he comes to be called breath when he is breathing, speech when he is speaking, sight when he is seeing, hearing when he is hearing, and mind when he is thinking. These are only the names of his various activities. A man who considers him to be any one of these does not understand him, for he is incomplete within any one of these. One should consider them as simply his self (*ātman*), for in it all these become one. This same self (*ātman*) is the trail to this entire world, for by following it one comes to know this entire world, just as by following their tracks one finds [the cattle]. Whoever knows this finds fame and glory.

[8] This innermost thing, this self (*ātman*)—it is dearer than a son, it is dearer than wealth, it is dearer than everything else. If a man claims that something other than his self is dear to him, and someone were to tell him that he will lose what he holds dear, that is liable to happen. So a man should regard only his self as dear to him. When a man regards only his self as dear to him, what he holds dear will never perish.

Chapter 2

4

"Maitreyī!" Yājñavalkya once said. "Look—I am about to depart from this place. So come, let me make a settlement between you and Kātyāyanī."

[2] Maitreyī asked in reply: "If I were to possess the entire world filled with wealth, sir, would it make me immortal?" "No," said Yājñavalkya, "it will only permit you to live the life of a wealthy person. Through wealth one cannot expect immortality."

[3] "What is the point in getting something that will not make me immortal?" retorted Maitreyī. "Tell me instead, sir, all that you know."

[4] Yājñavalkya said in reply: "You have always been very dear to me, and now you speak something very dear to me! Come and sit down. I will explain it to you. But while I am explaining, try to concentrate." [5] Then he spoke:

"One holds a husband dear, you see, not out of love for the husband; rather, it is out of love for oneself (*ātman*) that one holds a husband dear. One holds a wife dear not out of love for the wife; rather, it is out of love for oneself that one holds a wife dear. One holds children dear not out of love for the children; rather, it is out of love for oneself that one holds children dear. One holds wealth dear not out of love for wealth; rather, it is out of love for oneself that one holds wealth dear. One holds the priestly power dear not out of love for the priestly power; rather, it is out of love for oneself that one holds the priestly power dear. One holds the royal power dear not out of love for the royal power; rather, it is out of love for oneself that one holds the royal power dear. One holds the worlds dear not out of love for the worlds; rather, it is out of love for oneself that one holds the worlds dear. One holds the gods dear not out of love for the gods; rather, it is out of love for oneself that one holds the gods dear. One holds beings dear not out of love for beings; rather, it is out of love for oneself that one holds beings dear. One holds the Whole dear not out of love for the Whole; rather, it is out of love for oneself that one holds the Whole dear.

"You see, Maitreyī—it is one's self (*ātman*) which one should see and hear, and on which one should reflect and concentrate. For by seeing and hearing one's self, and by reflecting and concentrating on one's self, one gains the knowledge of this whole world.

[6] "May the priestly power forsake anyone who considers the priestly power to reside in something other than his self (*ātman*). May the royal power forsake anyone who considers the royal power to reside in something other than his self. May the gods forsake anyone who considers the gods to reside in something other than his self. May beings forsake anyone who considers beings to reside in something other than his self. May the Whole forsake anyone who considers the Whole to reside in something other than his self.

"All these—the priestly power, the royal power, worlds, gods, beings, the Whole—all that is nothing but this self.

[7] "It is like this. When a drum is being beaten, you cannot catch the external sounds; you catch them only by getting hold of the drum or the man beating that drum. [8] Or when a conch is being blown, you cannot catch the external sounds; you catch them only by getting hold of the conch or the man blowing that conch. [9] Or when a lute is being played, you cannot catch the external sounds; you catch them only by getting hold of the lute or the man playing that lute.

[10] "It is like this. As clouds of smoke billow from a fire lit with damp fuel, so indeed this Immense Being has exhaled all this: Ṛgveda, Yajurveda, Sāmaveda, the Atharva-Āṅgirasa, histories, ancient tales, sciences, hidden teachings (*upaniṣad*), verses, aphorisms, explanations, and glosses—it is that Immense Being who has exhaled all this.

[11] "It is like this. As the ocean is the point of convergence of all the waters, so the skin is the point of convergence of all sensations of touch; the nostrils, of all odours; the tongue, of all tastes; sight, of all visible appearances; hearing, of all sounds; the mind, of all thoughts; the heart, of all sciences; the hands, of all activities; the sexual organ, of all pleasures; the anus, of all excretions; the feet, of all travels; and speech, of all the Vedas.

[12] "It is like this. When a chunk of salt is thrown in water, it dissolves into that very water, and it cannot be picked up in any way. Yet, from whichever place one may take a sip, the salt is there! In the same way this Immense Being has no limit or boundary and is a single mass of perception. It arises out of and together with these beings and disappears after them—so I say, after death there is no awareness."

After Yājñavalkya said this, [13] Maitreyī exclaimed: "Now, sir, you have totally confused me by saying 'after death there is no awareness.'" He replied:

"Look, I haven't said anything confusing; this body, you see, has the capacity to perceive. [14] For when there is a duality of some kind, then the one can smell the other, the one can see the other, the one can hear the other, the one can greet the other, the one can think of the other, and the one can perceive the other. When, however, the Whole has become one's very self (*ātman*), then who is there for one to smell and by what means? Who is there for one to see and by what means? Who is there for one to hear and by what means? Who is there for one to greet and by what means? Who is there for one to think of and by what means? Who is there for one to perceive and by what means?

"By what means can one perceive him by means of whom one perceives this whole world? Look—by what means can one perceive the perceiver?"

CHANDOGYA

Chapter 6

1

There was one Śvetaketu, the son of Āruṇi. One day his father told him: "Śvetaketu, take up the celibate life of a student, for there is no one in our family, my son, who has not studied and is the kind of Brahmin who is so only because of birth."

[2] So he went away to become a student at the age of 12 and, after learning all the Vedas, returned when he was 24, swell-headed, thinking himself to be learned, and arrogant. [3] His father then said to him: Śvetaketu, here you are, my son, swell-headed, thinking yourself to be learned, and arrogant; so you must have surely asked

about that rule of substitution by which one hears what has not been heard of before, thinks of what has not been thought of before, and perceives what has not been perceived before?"

⁴"How indeed does that rule of substitution work, sir?"

"It is like this, son. By means of just one lump of clay one would perceive everything made of clay—the transformation is a verbal handle, a name—while the reality is just this: 'It's clay.'

⁵"It is like this, son. By means of just one copper trinket one would perceive everything made of copper—the transformation is a verbal handle, a name—while the reality is just this: 'It's copper.'

⁶"It is like this, son. By means of just one nail-cutter one would perceive everything made of iron—the transformation is a verbal handle, a name—while the reality is just this: 'It's iron.'

"That, son, is how this rule of substitution works."

⁷"Surely, those illustrious men did not know this, for had they known, how could they have not told it to me? So, why don't you, sir, tell me yourself?"

"All right, son," he replied.

2

"In the beginning, son, this world was simply what is existent—one only, without a second. Now, on this point some do say: In the beginning this world was simply what is non-existent—one only, without a second. And from what is non-existent was born what is existent.

²"But, son, how can that possibly be?" he continued. "How can what is existent be born from what is non-existent? On the contrary, son, in the beginning this world was simply what is existent—one only, without a second.

³"And it thought to itself: 'Let me become many. Let me propagate myself.' It emitted heat. The heat thought to itself: 'Let me become many. Let me propagate myself.' It emitted water. Whenever it is hot, therefore, a man surely perspires; and thus it is from heat that water is produced. ⁴The water thought to itself: 'Let me become many. Let me propagate myself.' It emitted food. Whenever it rains, therefore, food becomes abundant; and thus it is from water that foodstuffs are produced. . . .

10

"Now, take these rivers, son. The easterly ones flow towards the east, and the westerly ones flow towards the west. From the ocean, they merge into the very ocean;

they become just the ocean. In that state they are not aware that: 'I am that river,' and 'I am this river.' ²In exactly the same way, son, when all these creatures reach the existent, they are not aware that: 'We are reaching the existent.' No matter what they are in this world—whether it is a tiger, a lion, a wolf, a boar, a worm, a moth, a gnat, or a mosquito—they all merge into that.

³"The finest essence here—that constitutes the self of this whole world; that is the truth; that is the self (ātman). And that's how you are, Śvetaketu."

"Sir, teach me more."

"Very well, son.

11

"Now, take this huge tree here, son. If someone were to hack it at the bottom, its living sap would flow. Likewise, if someone were to hack it in the middle, its living sap would flow; and if someone were to hack it at the top, its living sap would flow. Pervaded by the living (jīva) essence (ātman), this tree stands here ceaselessly drinking water and flourishing. ²When, however, life (jīva) leaves one of its branches, that branch withers away. When it leaves a second branch, that likewise withers away, and when it leaves a third branch, that also withers away. When it leaves the entire tree, the whole tree withers away.

³"In exactly the same way," he continued, "know that this, of course, dies when it is bereft of life (jīva); but life itself does not die.

"The finest essence here—that constitutes the self of this whole world; that is the truth; that is the self (ātman). And that's how you are, Śvetaketu." . . .

4.3 THE CLASSICAL PERIOD

The classical period (ca. 500 B.C.E.–500) is often identified as one of "synthesis." During this period many of the beliefs and practices associated with orthodox Hinduism became solidified. It is sometimes called the epic period because the great Hindu epics, especially the *Mahabharata*, were composed at this time. However, the development of Hindu religious literature went far beyond the epics.

During this period the important distinction between **shruti** ("what is heard") and **smriti** ("what is remembered" or "tradition") develops. *Smriti* refers to all the literature that falls outside *shruti*, and, unlike *shruti*, which designates the eternal and author-less *Vedas*, *smriti* is historical and does have authors (some human and some divine). *Smriti* texts of this period proclaim the authority of the *Vedas* and thus declare their orthodoxy (right teaching). Hence any religious or philosophical ideas that developed in India and did not recognize the authority of the *Vedas* are heterodox ("other teaching") from the point of view of those religious movements (later called Hinduism) that did recognize the authority of the *Vedas*.

The **orthodox/heterodox** distinction arose because this was a time of political, social, and religious turbulence. Foreign peoples (Greeks, Scythians, Parthians, and others) encountered the Hindus, and Buddhist and Jainist groups (who rejected the authority of the *Vedas*) were beginning to gain followers. The need of Hindus to establish a religious and cultural identity grew as pluralism developed.

We will sample four of the most important *smriti* texts from this period. The first (*Laws of Manu*) represents developments in moral and legal ideas and the second and third (*Ramayana* and *Bhagavad Gita*) provide a look at the epic literature. Finally, the *Yoga Sutra* introduces us to a spiritual practice that was gaining widespread attention.

4.3.1 Laws of Manu

Tradition says that Manu, the author of the *Laws*, is the name of a king who is the ancestor of the human race. He is sometimes called the "Indian Adam," and his name means "wise one." Although he is said to be a king and hence a member of the *kshatriya*, or warrior class, clearly the priestly class, or **brahmins,** are portrayed as the superior class. Hence it seems safe to conclude that these *Laws* were written by priests to instruct other priests on what sort of law and morality they should teach. It should also be noted that they were written by males who were concerned with controlling the conduct of females.

I have referred to the priests and kings as **classes** (*varnas*) rather than **castes,** because there were many castes (*jatis*, meaning "birth") assigned to the four *varnas* (priests, warriors, merchant-farmers, and ser-

vants). Besides the four classes, the *Laws of Manu* detail the *ashramas*, or **four stages of life:** student, householder, forest dweller, and wandering-ascetic or world renouncer. The task of the priestly authors was to detail the **dharma** (a term that can be translated as duty, law, religion, right, justice, practice, teaching, and principle) appropriate for each class at each stage of life.

The duties outlined in the *Laws of Manu* codified and idealized a way of life. They established and reinforced a hierarchical structuring of society that concentrated social power and wealth in the hands of males who occupied the top rungs of the social ladder. The *Laws of Manu* (and similar texts from other religions) have provided fertile evidence for sociological theories of religion (see chapter 3) that seek to uncover the role religion plays in distributing power and maintaining social control.

We must, however, always keep in mind that written texts do not always reflect what is going on in society. Women and men do not necessarily act in the idealized ways the priests described in the *Laws of Manu*. Clearly, not every person between the ages of 8 and 20 fulfills the priestly ideal of a celibate student life devoted to learning religious texts. Nor, during the householder stage of marriage, does every wife accept without question the authority of her husband and live a life of complete domestic service. While many husbands may have tried in ancient times and are trying even today to "guard" their wives, their efforts have not always been appreciated. Likewise, after the householder stage of marriage and family, not every Hindu is able, when the grandchildren arrive, to retire to the forest and once again become devoted to the study of religious matters.

The final stage of world renouncer (*sannyasin*) allows one the freedom to wander homeless outside of caste or settle in a religious community (*ashram*). The purpose of this sort of life is to devote all one's energy to attaining *moksha*, but most people do not have either the opportunity or the luxury of complete abandonment of all worldly ties and responsibilities. Although many in India may admire a life of spiritual freedom, few are able to practice it.

TRANSLATED BY WENDY DONIGER WITH BRIAN K. SMITH

Laws of Manu

READING QUESTIONS

1. Where does the power of a king come from, what are the duties of a king, and what happens if the king fails to inflict just punishment?
2. How do you think the difference in duties for husbands and wives arose, and how does this codification of duties make it harder to deviate from expected social roles?
3. What are the duties of commoners (merchant-farmer class) during the householder stage of life?
4. What is the supreme good of the servant class?
5. How is the promise of rebirth into a higher class used to reinforce social control and order?

CHAPTER 7

[1] I will explain the duties of kings, how a king should behave, how he came to exist, and how (he may have) complete success. [2] A ruler who has undergone his transformative Vedic ritual in accordance with the rules should protect this entire (realm) properly. [3] For when this world was without a king and people ran about in all directions out of fear, the Lord emitted a king in order to guard this entire (realm), [4] taking lasting elements from Indra, the Wind, Yama, the Sun, Fire, Varuṇa, the Moon, and (Kubera) the Lord of Wealth. [5] Because a king is made from particles of these lords of the gods, therefore he surpasses all living beings in brilliant energy, [6] and, like the Sun, he burns eyes and hearts, and no one on earth is able even to look at him. [7] Through his special power he becomes Fire and Wind; he is the Sun and the Moon, and he is (Yama) the King of Justice, he is Kubera and he is Varuṇa, and he is great Indra. [8] Even a boy king should not be treated with disrespect, with the thought, "He is just a human being"; for this is a great deity standing there in the form of a man.

From *The Laws of Manu*, translated by Wendy Doniger with Brian K. Smith (London: Penguin Books, 1991), 7.1–24, 87–98 (pp. 128–130, 137–138); 9.1–19, 326–335 (pp. 197–199, 232–233). Copyright © 1991 Wendy Doniger and Brian K. Smith. Reprinted by permission from Penguin Books. Footnotes omitted.

[9] Fire burns just one man who approaches it wrongly, but the fire of a king burns the whole family, with its livestock and its heap of possessions. [10] In order to make justice succeed, he takes all forms again and again, taking into consideration realistically what is to be done, (his) power, and the time and place. [11] The lotus goddess of Good Fortune resides in his favour, victory in his aggression, and death in his anger; for he is made of the brilliant energy of all (the gods). [12] The man who is so deluded as to hate him will certainly be destroyed, for the king quickly makes up his mind to destroy him. [13] Therefore no one should violate the justice that the king dispenses for those that please him nor the unpleasant justice (that he dispenses) differently for those that displease him. [14] For (the king's) sake the Lord in ancient times emitted the Rod of Punishment, his own son, (the incarnation of) Justice, to be the protector of all living beings, made of the brilliant energy of ultimate reality. [15] Through fear of him all living beings, stationary and moving, allow themselves to be used and do not swerve from their own duty. [16] Upon men who persist in behaving unjustly he should inflict the punishment they deserve, taking into consideration realistically (the offender's) power and learning and the time and place. [17] The Rod is the king and the man, he is the inflicter and he is the chastiser, traditionally regarded as the guarantor for the duty of the four stages of life. [18] The Rod alone chastises all the subjects, the Rod protects them, the Rod stays awake while they sleep; wise men know that justice is the Rod. [19] Properly wielded, with due consideration, it makes all the subjects happy; but inflicted without due consideration, it destroys everything.

[20] If the king did not tirelessly inflict punishment on those who should be punished, the stronger would roast the weaker like fish on a spit. [21] The crow would eat the sacrificial cake and the dog would lick the oblation; there would be no ownership in anyone, and (everything) would be upside down. [22] The whole world is mastered by punishment, for an unpolluted man is hard to find. Through fear of punishment everything that moves allows itself to be used. [23] The gods, the titans, the centaurs, the ogres, the birds and the snakes, even they allow themselves to be used, but only when under pressure from punishment. [24] All the classes would be corrupted, and all barriers broken, all people would erupt in fury as a result of a serious error in punishment. . . .

[87] When a king who protects his subjects is challenged by kings who are his equal or stronger or weaker, he should remember the duties of rulers and not turn away from battle. [88] Not turning away from battle,

protecting subjects, and obedience to priests are the ultimate source of what is best for kings. [89] Kings who try to kill one another in battle and fight to their utmost ability, never averting their faces, go to heaven. [90] Fighting in a battle, he should not kill his enemies with weapons that are concealed, barbed, or smeared with poison or whose points blaze with fire. [91] He should not kill anyone who has climbed on a mound, or an impotent man, or a man who folds his hands in supplication, or whose hair is unbound, or anyone who is seated or who says, "I am yours"; [92] nor anyone asleep, without armour, naked, without a weapon, not fighting, looking on, or engaged with someone else; [93] nor anyone whose weapons have been broken, or who is in pain, badly wounded, terrified, or fleeing—for he should remember the duties of good men. [94] But if a man flees from a battle in terror and is killed by others, he takes upon himself all the evil deeds of his master, whatever they may be; [95] and whatever (credit for) good deeds a man has earned for the hereafter, if he is killed while fleeing, his master takes all that upon himself. [96] Horses and chariots, elephants, parasols, money, grain, livestock, women, all sorts of things and non-precious metals belong to the man who wins them. [97] But the revealed Vedic canon says, "They must give the king a special portion of the booty." And the king must distribute to all the fighters whatever has not been won individually.

[98] The unembellished, eternal duty of warriors has thus been explained; a ruler who kills his enemies in battle should not slip from this duty. . . .

CHAPTER 9

[1] I will tell the eternal duties of a man and wife who stay on the path of duty both in union and in separation. [2] Men must make their women dependent day and night, and keep under their own control those who are attached to sensory objects. [3] Her father guards her in childhood, her husband guards her in youth, and her sons guard her in old age. A woman is not fit for independence. [4] A father who does not give her away at the proper time should be blamed, and a husband who does not have sex with her at the proper time should be blamed; and the son who does not guard his mother when her husband is dead should be blamed.

[5] Women should especially be guarded against addictions, even trifling ones, for unguarded (women) would bring sorrow upon both families. [6] Regarding this as the supreme duty of all the classes, husbands, even

weak ones, try to guard their wives. [7] For by zealously guarding his wife he guards his own descendants, practices, family, and himself, as well as his own duty. [8] The husband enters the wife, becomes an embryo, and is born here on earth. That is why a wife is called a wife (*jāyā*), because he is born (*jāyate*) again in her. [9] The wife brings forth a son who is just like the man she makes love with; that is why he should guard his wife zealously, in order to keep his progeny clean.

[10] No man is able to guard women entirely by force, but they can be entirely guarded by using these means: [11] he should keep her busy amassing and spending money, engaging in purification, attending to her duty, cooking food, and looking after the furniture. [12] Women are not guarded when they are confined in a house by men who can be trusted to do their jobs well; but women who guard themselves by themselves are well guarded. [13] Drinking, associating with bad people, being separated from their husbands, wandering about, sleeping, and living in other people's houses are the six things that corrupt women. [14] Good looks do not matter to them, nor do they care about youth; "A man!" they say, and enjoy sex with him, whether he is good-looking or ugly. [15] By running after men like whores, by their fickle minds, and by their natural lack of affection these women are unfaithful to their husbands even when they are zealously guarded here. [16] Knowing that their very own nature is like this, as it was born at the creation by the Lord of Creatures, a man should make the utmost effort to guard them. [17] The bed and the seat, jewellery, lust, anger, crookedness, a malicious nature, and bad conduct are what Manu assigned to women. [18] There is no ritual with Vedic verses for women; this is a firmly established point of law. For women, who have no virile strength and no Vedic verses, are falsehood; this is well established.

[19] There are many revealed canonical texts to this effect that are sung even in treatises on the meaning of the Vedas, so that women's distinctive traits may be carefully inspected. . . .

[326] When a commoner has undergone the transformative rituals and has married a wife, he should constantly dedicate himself to making a living and tending livestock. [327] For when the Lord of Creatures emitted livestock he gave them over to the commoner, and he gave all creatures over to the priest and the king. [328] A commoner must never express the wish, "I would rather not tend livestock," nor should they ever be tended by anyone else when a commoner is willing. [329] He should know the high or low value of gems, pearls, coral, metals, woven cloth, perfumes, and spices. [330] He should know how to sow seeds, and recognize

the virtues and faults of a field, and he should know how to use all sorts of weights and measures; [331] and the worth or worthlessness of merchandise, the good and bad qualities of countries, the profit or loss from trades, and the way to raise livestock. [332] And he should know the wages of hired servants, the various languages of men, the way to preserve goods, and buying and selling. [333] He should make the utmost effort to increase his goods by means in keeping with his duty, and take pains to give food to all creatures.

[334] The servant's duty and supreme good is nothing but obedience to famous priestly householders who know the Veda. [335] If he is unpolluted, obedient to his superiors, gentle in his speech, without a sense of "I," and always dependent on the priests and the other (twice-born classes), he attains a superior birth (in the next life). . . .

4.3.2 Sita and Rama

During the classical, or epic, period, the *Ramayana* (ca. 400–200 B.C.E.) and the *Mahabharata* (ca. 500 B.C.E.– 400) were written. Like the *Laws of Manu*, these epics helped consolidate various strands of religious practices and ideas into a more integrated tradition. In particular, they gave renewed energy and recognition to the *bhakti*, or the devotional tradition.

The religious, moral, and intellectual activities celebrated in the *Vedas* and the law books like the *Laws of Manu* primarily express the religious concerns of the elite classes. The religious practices and concerns of the ordinary people were and are often very different from those of the elite. By focusing on texts written by the elite, we often overlook the unwritten beliefs and practices of the average villager. In many ways, the epics give written voice to the songs and stories told on the streets.

Devotion to various gods, goddesses, and saints is at the heart of the religious practices of the villagers. Incarnations (**avatara**) of the divine attract widespread devotion. The *Mahabharata* centers on **Krishna** and the *Ramayana* centers on **Rama,** both of whom are incarnations of the god Vishnu.

The *Vedas* refer to Vishnu, and, in later times, Vishnu is associated with the gods Brahma and Shiva. These three gods are the *trimurti,* or triple form of the divine. **Brahma** represents the creative power that makes the universe and is often depicted as a king with four faces that look in all four directions. **Vishnu** represents the power that preserves and sustains the created universe and is often depicted with four arms, which hold symbols of power. Ten major incarnations of Vishnu are commonly mentioned. Besides Rama and Krishna, Vishnu has incarnated as a fish, a boar, and a tortoise. Even the Buddha is an incarnation of Vishnu (an idea that helped reabsorb Indian Buddhism), and there is one incarnation yet to come, a savior figure on horseback who will judge the human race.

Shiva represents the power of destruction. The most familiar icon of Shiva is the Shiva Nataraja (ruler of the dance), which depicts Shiva with long yogi hair and dancing within a ring of fire, a drum in one hand symbolizing creation and fire in another hand symbolizing destruction. The universe, like everything else, is subject to cycles of rebirth. Before the creation of a new universe by Brahma, the old must be destroyed by Shiva. Destruction and death make way for new life. Death and life are parts of a single cycle. The fingers of a third arm point to Shiva's feet, inviting all of us to join the dance of life, and his fourth arm is extended in a blessing on all who do.

The *trimurti* (Brahma, Vishnu, and Shiva) is at the heart of much of the popular devotional, or *bhakti,* tradition of India. Temples, art, priests, and **puja** (the ritual offering of flowers, food, and incense to the images of these gods and their female consorts, the goddesses) sustain this tradition. It is also sustained by a rich storytelling tradition that celebrates the exploits of the divine incarnations. Sage-poets who went from village to village spreading the tales of gods and goddesses shaped and kept these traditions alive.

Valmiki was one of the most renowned sage-poets of ancient India and the author of the *Ramayana*. Book I of the epic opens with King Dasa-ratha of Ayodhya performing a sacrifice to get a son. At this time **Ravana,** a great and powerful demon, had conquered much of the world and the gods need a hero to fight and kill him. So Vishnu, the god who sustains the universe, becomes incarnate in the four sons— Rama, Bharat, Lakshmana, and Shatrughna—born to the three wives of King Dasa-ratha. He is most fully incarnate in Rama, who eventually wins the hand in marriage of **Sita,** the daughter of King Janaka in the neighboring kingdom of Videha. The wedding rite, included in the selection that follows, describes rites and vows that are still repeated in many Hindu weddings today.

Book II recounts how King Dasa-ratha intends to make Rama the heir to his kingdom, but he must relent and banish Rama from the kingdom for fourteen years in order to fulfill a vow made to his second queen, Kaikeyi. Kaikeyi wants her son, Bharat, to be king. Rama dutifully obeys his father and plans to leave without Sita but, as the account below indicates, she proves her devotion, love, and loyalty by accompanying Rama into exile. When King Dasa-ratha dies, Bharat, the new heir and divine brother of Rama, thinks it only just that Rama be king and tries to persuade him to return. However, as the following excerpt indicates, Rama holds fast to what he believes is the duty of a son to a father.

Books III through VI recount how Sita is kidnapped by the demon Ravana, how Rama and his brother Lakshmana enlist the aid of King Sugriva, the leader of a monkey tribe, whose chief minister is **Hanuman,** and how Rama and the monkey armies find Sita and rescue her after a series of pitched battles with the demons. Hanuman, the monkey general, becomes the foremost devotee and servant of Rama, and Ravana is finally slain by Rama, the hero of gods and humans. Because Rama questions Sita's virtue after having been a prisoner of Ravana, she must undergo an ordeal by fire in order to prove her faithfulness. Passing the test successfully, Sita and Rama return to Ayodhya to reign as king and queen.

Book VII, sometimes referred to as an epilogue, recounts how the people of Ayodhya spread rumors about Queen Sita's virtue and Rama banishes her to the forest. There she lives with the poet Valmiki and raises the two royal sons Kusha and Lava of whom Rama knows nothing. Finally discovering Sita and his sons, Rama asks for forgiveness and invites Sita to rule as his queen once more. She declines, as the last excerpt indicates, and returns to her mother earth, much to the sorrow of Rama. Rama eventually turns the kingdom over to his sons and ascends into heaven.

Throughout this story there are various subplots and exploits of one sort or another woven together in 48,000 lines of verse. Rama and Sita represent the ideal husband and wife. The geographic locations mentioned in the *Ramayana* have become holy pilgrimage sites. Legends and stories about Rama, Sita, and others are associated with brooks, hills, caverns, and glens in the region where the story is set. The wild fruits that grow there are "Sita-phal," being the reputed food of Rama and Sita in exile. It is said that one who recites the *Ramayana* in the morning, at noon, and at dusk, will never suffer adversity.

Ram Janmabhoomi, the reputed birthplace of Rama in Ayodhya, is today a focus of religious conflict between Muslims and Hindus. It is the symbolic battleground for those who claim to defend the Hindu tradition against the Muslim threat. The *Ramayana* still casts a long shadow over Indian devotion, culture, and politics.

There are many different translations of the *Ramayana.* The one used here is by Romesh C. Dutt (1848–1909), a Bengali poet, scholar, and divisional administrator. Although the language is dated in many ways, it still gives, unlike prose translations, the English reader some feeling for the poetic and epic qualities of the original.

VALMIKI

Ramayana

READING QUESTIONS

1. How does the wedding rite compare to others you know about?
2. What are Sita's primary virtues?
3. Whose point of view do you think this picture of Sita represents? Why?
4. Why does Rama reject Bharat's request that he return to Ayodhya and assume his rightful role as king?
5. What kind of ethical reasoning underlies Bharat's arguments and Rama's replies?
6. How do you interpret Sita's final departure?

BOOK I

VI THE WEDDING

Sage Vasishtha skilled in duty placed Videha's honoured king,
Viswa-mitra, Sata-nanda, all within the sacred ring,

And he raised the holy altar as the ancient writs ordain,
Decked and graced with scented garlands grateful unto gods and men,

And he set the golden ladles, vases pierced by artists skilled,

From *The Ramayana and The Mahabharata*, condensed into English verse by Romesh C. Dutt (London: J. M. Dent & Sons, 1910), pp. 9–10, 34, 57–59, 150–152. Selections from Books 1, III, IV, and XI.

Holy censers fresh and fragrant, cups with sacred
  honey filled,
Sanka bowls and shining salvers, *arghya* plates for
  honoured guest,
Parchéd rice arranged in dishes, corn unhusked that
  filled the rest,
And with careful hand Vasishtha grass around the altar
  flung,
Offered gift to lighted AGNI and the sacred *mantra* sung!

Softly came the sweet-eyed Sita,—bridal blush upon
  her brow,—
Rama in his manly beauty came to take the sacred vow,
Janak placed his beauteous daughter facing
  Dasa-ratha's son,
Spake with father's fond emotion and the holy rite
  was done:

"This is Sita child of Janak, dearer unto him than life,
Henceforth sharer of thy virtue, be she, prince, thy faithful
  wife,
Of thy weal and woe partaker, be she thine in every land,
Cherish her in joy and sorrow, clasp her hand within thy
  hand,
As the shadow to the substance, to her lord is faithful wife,
And my Sita best of women follows thee in death or life!"

Tears bedew his ancient bosom, gods and men his
  wishes share,
And he sprinkles holy water on the blest and wedded
  pair.

BOOK III [RAMA ADDRESSES SITA ON PARTING]

"Bharat's will with deep devotion and with faultless
  faith obey,
Truth and virtue on thy bosom èver hold their gentle
  away,
And to please each dear relation, gentle Sita, be it
  thine,
Part we love! for years of wand'ring in the pathless
  woods is mine!"

Rama spake, and soft-eyed Sita, ever sweet in speech
  and word,
Stirred by loving woman's passion boldly answered
  thus her lord:

"Do I hear my husband rightly, are these words my
  Rama spake,
And her banished lord and husband will the wedded
  wife forsake?

Lightly I dismiss the counsel which my lord hath lightly
  said,

For it ill beseems a warrior and my husband's princely
  grade!

For the faithful woman follows where her wedded lord may
  lead,
In the banishment of Rama, Sita's exile is decreed,
Sire nor son nor loving brother rules the wedded woman's
  state,
With her lord she falls or rises, with her consort courts her
  fate,
If the righteous son of Raghu wends to forests dark and drear,
Sita steps before her husband wild and thorny paths to clear!

Like the tasted refuse water cast thy timid thoughts
  aside,
Take me to the pathless jungle, bid me by my lord abide,
Car and steed and gilded palace, vain are these to
  woman's life,
Dearer is her husband's shadow to the loved and loving
  wife!

For my mother often taught me and my father often
  spake,
That her home the wedded woman doth beside her
  husband make,
As the shadow to the substance, to her lord is faithful
  wife,
And she parts not from her consort till she parts with
  fleeting life!

Therefore bid me seek the jungle and in pathless
  forests roam,
Where the wild deer freely ranges and the tiger makes
  his home,
Happier than in father's mansions in the woods will
  Sita rove,
Waste no thought on home or kindred, nestling in her
  husband's love!

World-renowned is Rama's valour, fearless by her
  Rama's side,
Sita will still live and wander with a faithful woman's
  pride,
And the wild fruit she will gather from the fresh and
  fragrant wood,
And the food by Rama tasted shall be Sita's cherished
  food!

BOOK IV

II BHARAT'S ENTREATY AND RAMA'S REPLY

"Speak, my true, my faithful Bharat," so the righteous
  Rama cried,

"Wherefore to this jungle dwelling hast thou from
 Ayodhya hied,

Speak, my fond and loving brother, if our father bade
 thee come,

Leaving throne and spacious empire in this wilderness
 to roam?

Heir and Regent of Kosala! Dost thou tend our father
 well,

And obey the lofty mandate from his royal lips that
 fell,

And the ancient Dasa-ratha, glorious still in regal
 might,

Doth he pass his bright life's evening in each pure and
 holy rite?

Doth my mother, Queen Kausalya, still for Rama wet
 her eye,

And the gentle Queen Sumitra for her banished
 Lakshman sigh,

Doth the peerless Queen Kaikeyi pass her days in
 duties fair,

Guard her Bharat's mighty empire, tend him with a
 mother's care?

Is each holy rite and homage to the Gods and Fathers
 done,

Is the honour due to elders rendered by each duteous
 son,

Do thy warriors guard thy kingdom as of yore with
 matchless skill,

And with counsel deep and duteous do thy min'sters
 serve thy will?

Rich thy fields in corn and produce fed by rivers broad
 and deep,

Rich thy green unending pastures with the kine and
 fattened sheep,

Tend the herdsman and his cattle, tend the tiller of
 the soil,

Watch and help with all thy bounty workmen in their
 peaceful toil,

For the monarch's highest duty is to serve his people's
 weal

And the ruler's richest glory is to labour and to heal!

Guard thy forts with sleepless caution with the engines
 of the war,

With the men who shoot the arrow and who drive the
 flying car,

Guard Kosala's royal treasure, make thy gifts of wealth
 and food,

Not to lords and proud retainers, but to worthy and
 the good!

Render justice pure and spotless as befits thy royal line,
And to save the good and guiltless, Bharat, be it ever
 thine,

For the tears of suffering virtue wither like the thunder
 levin,

And they slay our men and cattle like the wrath of
 righteous heaven,

Fruitful be thy lore of Veda, fruitful be each pious rite,
Be thy queen a fruitful mother, be thy empire full of
 might!"

Weeping, weeping, Bharat answered Dasa-ratha's
 eldest son,

"Dasa-ratha walks the bright sky, for his earthly task
 is done!

For impelled by Queen Kaikeyi to the woods he bade
 thee go,

And his spotless fame was clouded and his bosom sank
 in woe,

And my mother, late repenting, weeps her deed of
 deepest shame,

Weeps her wedded lord departed, and a woman's
 tarnished fame!

Thou alone canst wipe this insult by a deed of kindness
 done,—

Rule o'er Dasa-ratha's empire, Dasa-ratha's eldest son,

Weeping queens and loyal subjects supplicate thy
 noble grace,—

Rule o'er Raghu's ancient empire, son of Raghu's
 royal race!

For our ancient Law ordaineth and thy Duty makes
 it plain,

Eldest-born succeeds his father as the king of earth
 and main,

By the fair Earth loved and welcomed, Rama, be her
 wedded lord,

As by planet-jewelled Midnight is the radiant Moon
 adored!

And thy father's ancient min'sters and thy courtiers
 faithful still,

Wait to do thy righteous mandate and to serve thy
 royal will,

As a pupil, as a brother, as a slave, I seek thy grace,—
Come and rule thy father's empire, king of Raghu's
 royal race!"

Weeping, on the feet of Rama, Bharat placed his lowly
 head,

Weeping for his sire departed, tears of sorrow Rama
 shed,

Then he raised his loving brother with an elder's
    deathless love,
Sorrow wakes our deepest kindness and our holiest
    feelings prove!

"But I may not," answered Rama, "seek Ayodhya's
    ancient throne,
For a righteous father's mandate duteous son may not
    disown,

And I may not, gentle brother, break the word of
    promise given,
To a king and to a father who is now a saint in heaven!

Not on thee, nor on thy mother, rests the censure or
    the blame,
Faithful to his father's wishes Rama to the forest came,

For the son and duteous consort serve the father and
    the lord,
Higher than an empire's glory is a father's spoken word!

All inviolate is his mandate,— on Ayodhya's jewelled
    throne,
Or in pathless woods and jungle Rama shall his duty own,

All inviolate is the blessing by a loving mother given,
For she blessed my life in exile like a pitying saint of
    heaven!

*Thou shall rule the kingdom, Bharat, guard our loving
    people well,*
Clad in wild bark and in deer-skin I shall in the forests dwell,

So spake saintly Dasa-ratha in Ayodhya's palace hall,
*And a righteous father's mandate duteous son may not
    recall!"*

BOOK XI

V SITA LOST

Morning dawned; and with Valmiki, Sita to the
    gathering came,
Banished wife and weeping mother, sorrow-stricken,
    suffering dame,

Pure in thought and deed, Valmiki gave his troth and
    plighted word,—
Faithful still the banished Sita in her bosom held
    her lord!

"Mighty Saint," so Rama answered as he bowed his
    humble head,
"Listening world will hear thy mandate and the word
    that thou hast said,

Never in his bosom Rama questioned Sita's faithful
    love,
And the God of Fire incarnate did her stainless virtue
    prove!

Pardon, if the voice of rumour drove me to a deed of
    shame,
Bowing to my people's wishes I disowned my sinless
    dame,

Pardon, if to please my subjects I have bade my Sita
    roam,
Tore her from my throne and empire, tore her from
    my heart and home!

In the dark and dreary forest was my Sita left to mourn,
In the lone and gloomy jungle were my royal children
    born,

Help me, Gods, to wipe this error and this deed of
    sinful pride,
May my Sita prove her virtue, be again my loving
    bride!"

Gods and Spirits, bright Immortals to that royal *Yajna*
    came,
Men of every race and nation, kings and chiefs of
    righteous fame,

Softly through the halls of splendour cool and scented
    breezes blew,
Fragrance of celestial blossoms o'er the royal chambers
    flew.

Sita saw the bright Celestials, monarchs gathered
    from afar,
Saw her royal lord and husband bright as heaven-
    ascending star,

Saw her sons as hermit-minstrels beaming with a
    radiance high,
Milk of love suffused her bosom, tear of sorrow filled
    her eye!

Rama's queen and Janak's daughter, will she stoop her
    cause to plead,
Witness of her truth and virtue can a loving woman
    need?

Oh! her woman's heart is bursting, and her day on
    earth is done,
And she pressed her heaving bosom, slow and sadly
    thus begun:

*"If unstained in thought and action I have lived from day
    of birth,*
*Spare a daughter's shame and anguish and receive her,
    Mother Earth!*

If in duty and devotion I have laboured undefiled,
*Mother Earth! who bore this woman, once again receive thy
    child!*

If in truth unto my husband I have proved a faithful wife,
Mother Earth! relieve thy Sita from the burden of this life!"

Then the earth was rent and parted, and a golden
  throne arose,
Held aloft by jewelled *Nagas* as the leaves enfold
  the rose,
And the Mother in embraces held her spotless sinless
  Child,
Saintly Janak's saintly daughter, pure and true and
  undefiled,
Gods and men proclaim her virtue! But fair Sita is
  no more,
Lone is Rama's loveless bosom and his days of bliss
  are o'er!

4.3.3 Bhagavad Gita

The *Bhagavad Gita*, or *Song of God*, is part of the *Mahabharata* and recounts how Krishna comes to the aid of the Pandava brothers in a civil war with their cousins. The "song" is a dialogue between Krishna (posing as a chariot driver) and the warrior Arjuna, one of the five Pandava brothers.

Arjuna is caught in a dilemma. If he fulfills his duty (*dharma*) as a warrior and fights, he will be fighting and killing members of his own family (his cousins). To kill family members is to fail in one's duty. Arjuna is damned if he does fight and damned if he does not fight. Either way he fails to do his duty and hence gets bad *karma* leading to rebirth.

Here the logic of the law of *karma* and rebirth reaches a startling and disturbing impasse. As mentioned earlier, the word *karma* means both action and the consequences of action. Taking the law of *karma* to its logical extreme, then everything one does, good or bad, leads to rebirth because every action has consequences. There appears no way out of *samsara* (the cycle of suffering and rebirth) because even the paths to liberation (sacrifice, the pursuit of knowledge, doing one's duty) amount to actions. *Moksha*, liberation from rebirth, appears either forever out of reach or possible only if one renounces everything and does absolutely nothing!

Krishna teaches Arjuna the way out of this impasse. He acknowledges and reinforces three paths, or *yogas*, to liberation: action (*karmayoga*), knowledge (*jnanayoga*), and devotion (*bhaktiyoga*). The discipline of *karma* teaches us how to act without attachment to the consequences of our action; the discipline of knowledge teaches us the immortal nature of the true self; and devotion to the divine Krishna teaches us the true nature of sacrifice (surrendering all to the divine). Genuine ritual actions and genuine knowledge are, Krishna teaches, incomplete without genuine devotion to the divine.

As the battle is about to start, Dhritarashtra, the blind brother of Arjuna's father, is granted a boon by the sage Vyasa (the traditional author of the *Mahabharata*). Sanjaya, Dhritarashtra's personal bard and charioteer, is granted a "divine eye" so that he can see and report all the events of the battle directly. Sanjaya thus becomes the narrator of the unfolding events knowing, by virtue of his "divine eye," even the thoughts and feelings of Arjuna.

The first book describes Arjuna's dilemma. The second book, included in the selection, states some key assumptions of Krishna's teaching about the nature of the self and one's duty. The other sixteen books, or teachings, elaborate on the themes found in the second book. The proper relationship between sacrifice and action is discussed in books three and four. The fifth and sixth books examine the tension between a life of renunciation and a life of action. The final six books recapitulate basic teachings and integrate them with the need for religious devotion.

In the eleventh teaching, Krishna gives Arjuna a "divine eye" by which he can see the grandeur and majesty of Krishna's cosmic order. Krishna reveals his deadly destructiveness in an explosion of countless mouths, weapons, eyes, ornaments, and fangs that leaves Arjuna filled with amazement, "his hair bristling on his flesh" as the "god of gods" reveals the cosmic dance of destruction and creation *ad infinitum;* worlds upon worlds upon worlds.

The twelfth book, included in the selection, describes the result of this theophany (revelation of the divine), and, in the thirteenth teaching, Krishna shows that the true battlefield is the human body—the place where we all struggle to know ourselves, discipline our lives, and figure out our duties. The last words of Arjuna to Krishna as the *Gita* closes in book eighteen are "I stand here, my doubt dispelled, ready to act on your words."

TRANSLATED BY
BARBARA STOLER MILLER

Bhagavad Gita

READING QUESTIONS

1. Why does Krishna urge Arjuna to fight?
2. What type of spiritual discipline does Krishna recommend?
3. What is the person "deep in concentration" like?
4. What is the point of the twelfth teaching of the *Gita?*

THE SECOND TEACHING

Philosophy and Spiritual Discipline

Sanjaya
Arjuna sat dejected,
filled with pity,
his sad eyes blurred by tears.
Krishna gave him counsel.

Lord Krishna
Why this cowardice
in time of crisis, Arjuna?
The coward is ignoble, shameful,
foreign to the ways of heaven.

Don't yield to impotence!
it is unnatural in you!
Banish this petty weakness from your heart.
Rise to the fight, Arjuna!

Arjuna
Krishna, how can I fight
against Bhishma and Drona
with arrows
when they deserve my worship?

It is better in this world
to beg for scraps of food
than to eat meals
smeared with the blood

of elders I killed
at the height of their power
while their goals
were still desires.

We don't know which weight
is worse to bear—
our conquering them
or their conquering us.
We will not want to live
if we kill
the sons of Dhritarashtra
assembled before us.

The flaw of pity
blights my very being;
conflicting sacred duties
confound my reason.
I ask you to tell me
decisively—Which is better?
I am your pupil.
Teach me what I seek!

I see nothing
that could drive away
the grief
that withers my senses;
even if I won kingdoms
of unrivaled wealth
on earth
and sovereignty over gods.

Sanjaya
Arjuna told this
to Krishna—then saying,
"I shall not fight,"
he fell silent.

Mocking him gently,
Krishna gave this counsel
as Arjuna sat dejected,
between the two armies.

Lord Krishna
You grieve for those beyond grief;
and you speak words of insight;
but learned men do not grieve
for the dead or the living.

Never have I not existed,
nor you, nor these kings;
and never in the future
shall we cease to exist.

Just as the embodied self
enters childhood, youth, and old age,
so does it enter another body;
this does not confound a steadfast man.

Contacts with matter make us feel
heat and cold, pleasure and pain.
Arjuna, you must learn to endure
fleeting things—they come and go!

When these cannot torment a man,
when suffering and joy are equal
for him and he has courage,
he is fit for immortality.

Nothing of nonbeing comes to be,
nor does being cease to exist;
the boundary between these two
is seen by men who see reality.

Indestructible is the presence
that pervades all this;
no one can destroy
this unchanging reality.

Our bodies are known to end,
but the embodied self is enduring,
indestructible, and immeasurable;
therefore, Arjuna, fight the battle!

He who thinks this self a killer
and he who thinks it killed,
both fail to understand;
it does not kill, nor is it killed.

It is not born,
it does not die;
having been,
it will never not be;
unborn, enduring,
constant, and primordial,
it is not killed
when the body is killed.

Arjuna, when a man knows the self
to be indestructible, enduring, unborn,
unchanging, how does he kill
or cause anyone to kill?

As a man discards
worn-out clothes
to put on new
and different ones,
so the embodied self
discards
its worn-out bodies
to take on other new ones.

Weapons do not cut it,
fire does not burn it,
waters do not wet it,
wind does not wither it.

It cannot be cut or burned;
it cannot be wet or withered;

it is enduring, all-pervasive,
fixed, immovable, and timeless.

It is called unmanifest,
inconceivable, and immutable;
since you know that to be so,
you should not grieve!

If you think of its birth
and death as ever-recurring,
then too, Great Warrior,
you have no cause to grieve!

Death is certain for anyone born,
and birth is certain for the dead;
since the cycle is inevitable,
you have no cause to grieve!

Creatures are unmanifest in origin,
manifest in the midst of life,
and unmanifest again in the end.
Since this is so, why do you lament?

Rarely someone
sees it,
rarely another
speaks it,
rarely anyone
hears it—
even hearing it,
no one really knows it.

The self embodied in the body
of every being is indestructible;
you have no cause to grieve
for all these creatures, Arjuna!

Look to your own duty;
do not tremble before it;
nothing is better for a warrior
than a battle of sacred duty.

The doors of heaven open
for warriors who rejoice
to have a battle like this
thrust on them by chance.

If you fail to wage this war
of sacred duty,
you will abandon your own duty
and fame only to gain evil.

People will tell
of your undying shame,
and for a man of honor
shame is worse than death.

The great chariot warriors will think
you deserted in fear of battle;
you will be despised
by those who held you in esteem.

Your enemies will slander you,
scorning your skill
in so many unspeakable ways—
could any suffering be worse?

If you are killed, you win heaven;
if you triumph, you enjoy the earth;
therefore, Arjuna, stand up
and resolve to fight the battle!

Impartial to joy and suffering,
gain and loss, victory and defeat,
arm yourself for the battle,
lest you fall into evil.

Understanding is defined in terms of philosophy;
now hear it in spiritual discipline.
Armed with this understanding, Arjuna,
you will escape the bondage of action.

No effort in this world
is lost or wasted;
a fragment of sacred duty
saves you from great fear.

This understanding is unique
in its inner core of resolve;
diffuse and pointless are the ways
irresolute men understand.

Undiscerning men who delight
in the tenets of ritual lore
utter florid speech, proclaiming,
"There is nothing else!"

Driven by desire, they strive after heaven
and contrive to win powers and delights,
but their intricate ritual language
bears only the fruit of action in rebirth.

Obsessed with powers and delights,
their reason lost in words,
they do not find in contemplation
this understanding of inner resolve.

Arjuna, the realm of sacred lore
is nature—beyond its triad of qualities,
dualities, and mundane rewards,
be forever lucid, alive to your self.

For the discerning priest,
all of sacred lore
has no more value than a well
when water flows everywhere.

Be intent on action,
not on the fruits of action;
avoid attraction to the fruits
and attachment to inaction!

Perform actions, firm in discipline,
relinquishing attachment;

be impartial to failure and success—
this equanimity is called discipline.

Arjuna, action is far inferior
to the discipline of understanding,
so seek refuge in understanding—pitiful
are men drawn by fruits of action.

Disciplined by understanding,
one abandons both good and evil deeds;
so arm yourself for discipline—
discipline is skill in actions.

Wise men disciplined by understanding
relinquish the fruit born of action;
freed from these bonds of rebirth,
they reach a place beyond decay.

When your understanding passes beyond
the swamp of delusion,
you will be indifferent to all
that is heard in sacred lore.

When your understanding turns
from sacred lore to stand fixed,
immovable in contemplation,
then you will reach discipline.

Arjuna
Krishna, what defines a man
deep in contemplation whose insight
and thought are sure? How would he speak?
How would he sit? How would he move?

Lord Krishna
When he gives up desires in his mind,
is content with the self within himself,
then he is said to be a man
whose insight is sure, Arjuna.

When suffering does not disturb his mind,
when his craving for pleasures has vanished,
when attraction, fear, and anger are gone,
he is called a sage whose thought is sure.

When he shows no preference
in fortune or misfortune
and neither exults nor hates,
his insight is sure.

When, like a tortoise retracting
its limbs, he withdraws his senses
completely from sensuous objects,
his insight is sure.

Sensuous objects fade
when the embodied self abstains from food;
the taste lingers, but it too fades
in the vision of higher truth.

Even when a man of wisdom
tries to control them, Arjuna,

the bewildering senses
attack his mind with violence.

Controlling them all,
with discipline he should focus on me;
when his senses are under control,
his insight is sure.

Brooding about sensuous objects
makes attachment to them grow;
from attachment desire arises,
from desire anger is born.

From anger comes confusion;
from confusion memory lapses;
from broken memory understanding is lost;
from loss of understanding, he is ruined.

But a man of inner strength
whose senses experience objects
without attraction and hatred,
in self-control, finds serenity.

In serenity, all his sorrows
dissolve;
his reason becomes serene,
his understanding sure.

Without discipline,
he has no understanding or inner power
without inner power, he has no peace
and without peace where is joy?

If his mind submits to the play
of the senses,
they drive away insight,
as wind drives a ship on water.

So, Great Warrior, when withdrawal
of the senses
from sense objects is complete,
discernment is firm.

When it is night for all creatures,
a master of restraint is awake;
when they are awake, it is night
for the sage who sees reality.

As the mountainous depths
of the ocean
are unmoved when waters
rush into it,
so the man unmoved
when desires enter him
attains a peace that eludes
the man of many desires.

When he renounces all desires
and acts without craving,
possessiveness,
or individuality, he finds peace.

This is the place of the infinite spirit;
achieving it, one is freed from delusion;
abiding in it even at the time of death,
one finds the pure calm of infinity.

THE TWELFTH TEACHING

Devotion

Arjuna
Who best knows discipline:
men who worship you with devotion,
ever disciplined, or men who worship
the imperishable, unmanifest?

Lord Krishna
I deem most disciplined
men of enduring discipline
who worship me with true faith,
entrusting their minds to me.

Men reach me too who worship
what is imperishable, ineffable, unmanifest,
omnipresent, inconceivable,
immutable at the summit of existence.

Mastering their senses,
with equanimity toward everything,
they reach me, rejoining
in the welfare of all creatures.

It is more arduous when their reason
clings to my unmanifest nature;
for men constrained by bodies,
the unmanifest way is hard to attain.

But men intent on me
renounce all actions to me
and worship me, meditating
with singular discipline.

When they entrust reason to me,
Arjuna, I soon arise
to rescue them from the ocean
of death and rebirth.

Focus your mind on me,
let your understanding enter me;
then you will dwell
in me without doubt.

If you cannot concentrate
your thought firmly on me,
then seek to reach me, Arjuna,
by discipline in practice.

Even if you fail in practice,
dedicate yourself to action;

performing actions for my sake,
you will achieve success.

If you are powerless to do
even this, rely on my discipline,
be self-controlled,
and reject all fruit of action.

Knowledge is better than practice,
meditation better than knowledge,
rejecting fruits of action
is better still—it brings peace.

One who bears hate for no creature
is friendly, compassionate, unselfish,
free of individuality, patient,
the same in suffering and joy.

Content always, disciplined,
self-controlled, firm in his resolve,
his mind and understanding dedicated to me,
devoted to me, he is dear to me.

The world does not flee from him,
nor does he flee from the world;
free of delight, rage, fear,
and disgust, he is dear to me.

Disinterested, pure, skilled,
indifferent, untroubled,
relinquishing all involvements,
devoted to me, he is dear to me.

He does not rejoice or hate,
grieve or feel desire;
relinquishing fortune and misfortune,
the man of devotion is dear to me.

Impartial to foe and friend,
honor and contempt,
cold and heat, joy and suffering,
he is free from attachment.

Neutral to blame and praise,
silent, content with his fate,
unsheltered, firm in thought,
the man of devotion is dear to me.

Even more dear to me are devotees
who cherish this elixir of sacred duty
as I have taught it,
intent on me in their faith.

4.3.4 Yoga Sutra

The *Gita*, as we have seen, acknowledges that the way out of rebirth may be difficult because everything we do (*karma*) has the potential of keeping us bound to the cycle of *samsara*. Krishna suggests the practice of various *yogas* as the way to liberation. Arjuna is a war-rior and must act, so when Krishna defines *yoga* as equanimity, Arjuna protests by saying that such a state of mind is impossible. Krishna answers by claiming that practice and dispassion can quiet the mind. Here, Krishna hints at a radical type of *yoga* aimed at libera-tion through controlling the mind.

This type of **yoga** is the subject of a book called the *Yoga Sutra*. Although practice of a mind-stilling *yoga* is much older than the *Yoga Sutra*, this text is the earliest known systematic statement on the subject. The dating of the text varies by centuries, some plac-ing it as early as the third century B.C.E. and others around the third century C.E. According to legend, **Patanjali,** who is an incarnation of the serpent Ananta on whom the god Vishnu rests before the start of each new cycle of creation, is the author.

The *yoga* expounded by Patanjali is closely tied to a cosmological theory developed by the philosophi-cal school known as *Sankhya*. According to *Sankhya*, reality is structured dualistically in terms of the two fundamental principles of **purusha** (spirit or pure consciousness) and **prakriti** (nature or matter). In an ideal state, reality is a balance between *purusha* and *prakriti* in which *purusha* is completely isolated from *prakriti*. *Purusha* is eternally inactive while *prakriti* is active. From within *prakriti*, the worlds of creation and destruction evolve.

In the course of evolution, thought (*citta*), mind (*manas*), intelligence (*buddhi*), and ego (*ahamkara*) develop. These are material in nature, but through ignorance humans often confuse them with spirit or consciousness (*purusha*). Physical forces are gross manifestations of these subtle mental forces, and the "turnings of thought" sustain them. If these constant turnings of thought can be stopped, it is possible to realize one's true identity as *purusha* and hence be lib-erated from a false identification with aspects of *prak-riti*. For *Sankhya* and for Patanjali's *yoga*, the turnings of thought are fundamental to the confusion of *pu-rusha* with material nature. It follows that the way to extricate oneself is to still the movements of thought, thereby becoming invulnerable to the chaotic change of both mental and physical stimuli. Patanjali presents *yoga* as the way to gain this release and hence as the way to stop rebirth.

Patanjali's *yoga* is a complex system involving the development of a virtuous life, mastering difficult postures and breathing exercises, and gaining grad-ual control of the senses and the mind. Hatha yoga (force yoga), a set of physical exercises involving stretching and balancing, has gained much attention, especially in the West, because of its health benefits. It originally developed to make long periods of meditation physically easier. It is, however, only one small (although important) part of Patanjali's "eight-limbed" system.

TRANSLATED AND COMMENTED ON BY BARBARA STOLER MILLER

Yoga Sutra

READING QUESTIONS

1. Describe the eight limbs of *yoga* and state what you think each means.
2. What kind of logic do you see at work in the eight limbs of *yoga*?

PART TWO

THE PRACTICE OF YOGA

The Purpose of Yoga

The active performance of yoga involves ascetic practice, study of sacred lore, and dedication to the Lord of Yoga. (1)
Its purpose is to cultivate pure contemplation and attenuate the forces of corruption. (2)
The forces of corruption are ignorance, egoism, passion, hatred, and the will to live. (3)

Definition of the Forces of Corruption

Ignorance is the field where the other forces of corruption develop, whether dormant, attenuated, intermittent, or active. (4)
Ignorance is misperceiving permanence in transience, purity in impurity, pleasure in suffering, an essential self where there is no self. (5)

Egoism is ascribing a unified self to the organs and powers of perception, such as the eye and the power to see. (6)
Passion follows from attachment to pleasure. (7)
Hatred follows from attachment to suffering. (8)
The will to live is instinctive and overwhelming, even for a learned sage. (9)

Removing the Forces of Corruption

The subtle forces of corruption can be escaped by reversing their course. (10)
One can escape the effect of their turnings through meditation. (11)
Subliminal intention formed in actions, rooted in the forces of corruption, is realized in present or potential births. (12)
As long as this root exists, actions ripen into birth, a term of life, and experience in the world. (13)
These actions bear joyful or sorrowful fruits according to the actor's virtue or vice. (14)
All life is suffering for a man of discrimination, because of the sufferings inherent in change and its corrupting subliminal impressions, and because of the way qualities of material nature turn against themselves. (15)
Suffering that has not yet come can be escaped. (16)

Patanjali now calls on Sankhya philosophy to explain how evolution is the transformation of primary, undifferentiated material nature (*prakṛti*) into the constituents of existence, such as egoism, mind, reason, the senses, and the subtle and gross elements. "Reversing the course" of the subtle forces of corruption is a kind of involution, the opposite of the evolutionary process. . . .

. . . In Patanjali's analysis, the aggregate of impressions expresses itself in thought (*citta*) and action (*karma*), which account for subconscious predispositions that condition the character and behavior of an individual throughout many reincarnations. Thought and action then become involved in an endless round of reciprocal causality. Actions create memory traces, which fuel the mental processes and are stored in memory that endures through many rebirths. The store of subliminal impressions is obliterated only when the chain of causal relations is broken.

When the fruits of action (*karma*) and the seeds of thought are eliminated by means of meditation, thought no longer sustains the world, and what has evolved collapses into itself, like a black hole. The turnings (*vṛtti*) of the subtle forces of corruption can be eliminated, not by physical means, but through meditative insight, which cleans out the stock of invisible seeds that would otherwise germinate into new thoughts and actions.

The discriminating person knows that suffering is inherent in change, in the anxiety over change, and in the subliminal impressions left by this anxiety. The past and present are intertwined, and even pleasant experiences are tinged with pain. Suffering that is yet to come can be avoided, however, by relinquishing attachment to any desired outcome in the future, since such outcomes are illusory. Thus one eliminates the potential for suffering stored in subliminal impressions.

This section on the forces of corruption exhibits similarities with Buddhist discussions of methods by which defilements (kleśa) can be removed to eliminate suffering. Even though psychological modeling is crucial in both the yogic and Buddhist analyses, the objective is not merely a psychological shift but the actual removal of concrete defilements. This is the purificatory dimension of both yogic and Buddhist practice.

The Observer and the Phenomenal World

The cause of suffering, which can be escaped, is the connection between the observer and the phenomenal world. (17)
The phenomenal world consists of material elements and sense organs characterized by their clarity, activity, or stillness; this world can serve the goals of sensual experience or spiritual liberation. (18)
The qualities of material things are structured as specific, nonspecific, marked, and unmarked. (19)
The observer is simply the subject of observing— although pure, it sees itself in terms of conceptual categories. (20)
In its essence the phenomenal world exists only in relation to an observer. (21)
Even if the phenomenal world ceases to be relevant for an observer who has realized freedom, it continues to exist because it is common to other observers. (22)
The connection between the observer and the phenomenal world causes a misperceived identity between active power and its master. (23)
The cause of this connection is ignorance. (24)
When there is no ignorance, there is no such connection —the freedom of the observer lies in its absence. (25)
The way to eliminate ignorance is through steady, focused discrimination between the observer and the world. (26)
Wisdom is the final stage of the sevenfold way of the observer. (27)

In these aphorisms, Patanjali analyzes the misunderstanding that binds the observing spirit (puruṣa, also called "the observer," draṣṭṛ), to the phenomenal world (prakṛti). Ignorance of the true nature of this relation

misleads us into egoistically believing in a unified self and falsely identifying spirit with matter. Since worldly existence occurs in an environment of corruptive forces, the unliberated spirit tends to be attracted by the phenomenal world, and misidentifies itself with it. This misidentification, together with the attachment to that misidentification, is the source of pain—but the connection can be severed by discrimination, which comes about through the practice of yoga. When ignorance is dispelled, the spirit becomes an observer to the world, detached from the world's painful transience.

In order to effect this detachment, the yogi must understand the multidimensional structure of the world, in which everything is composed of the three qualities of material nature (guṇa). These qualities—lucidity (sattva), passion (rajas), and dark inertia (tamas)—are like energy existing in potential form. Among them, Patanjali is mainly concerned with lucidity, which he contrasts with spirit. . . .

The qualities of material nature are structured into gross elements that can be particular or specific, subtle elements that can be universal or nonspecific, subtle matter that is differentiated or marked, and gross matter that is undifferentiated or unmarked. The misidentification of the power to act in the world (śakti) with its master, the spirit (puruṣa), is brought about by the false attribution of the qualities of material nature to the nature of the spirit itself.

The reference to a "sevenfold way" is somewhat obscure, since Patanjali does not elaborate on it. Commentators have proposed several versions of the sevenfold way and how its stages relate to the eight limbs of yogic practice described in the following sections.

The Limbs of Yogic Practice

When impurity is destroyed by practicing the limbs of yoga, the light of knowledge shines in focused discrimination. (28)
The eight limbs of yoga are moral principles, observances, posture, breath control, withdrawal of the senses, concentration, meditation, and pure contemplation. (29)

Patanjali's eight-limbed practice includes moral principles (yama), observances (niyama), posture (āsana), breath control (prāṇāyāma), withdrawal of the senses (pratyāhāra), concentration (dhāraṇā), meditation (dhyāna), and pure contemplation (samādhi). The eight limbs are essentially eight stages in the cumulative acquisition of yogic power. The first five will be elaborated in the remaining aphorisms of Part Two and the last three, which constitute the final stage of yoga, will be addressed in Part Three.

Patanjali's set of practices is parallel to the eight-limbed path of early Buddhism. In both yoga and Buddhism, this set of practices is crucial to the realization of spiritual freedom. The Buddhist eight-limbed path comprises right views, right speech, right conduct, right livelihood, right effort, right mindfulness, and right contemplation. Several of these are also central elements in Patanjali's practice: right conduct encompasses moral principles and observances, right mindfulness includes breath control and withdrawal of the senses, and right contemplation is equivalent to pure contemplation (*samādhi*).

The Moral Principles and Observances

The moral principles are nonviolence, truthfulness, abjuration of stealing, celibacy, and absence of greed. (30)
These universal moral principles, unrestricted by conditions of birth, place, time, or circumstance, are the great vow of yoga. (31)
The observances are bodily purification, contentment, ascetic practice, study of sacred lore, and dedication to the Lord of Yoga. (32)
When one is plagued by ideas that pervert the moral principles and observances, one can counter them by cultivating the opposite. (33)
Cultivating the opposite is realizing that perverse ideas, such as the idea of violence, result in endless suffering and ignorance—whether the ideas are acted out, instigated, or sanctioned, whether motivated by greed, anger, or delusion, whether mild, moderate, or extreme. (34)

A commitment to live according to the five universal moral principles (*yama*), without restrictions, constitutes the great vow (*mahāvrata*), which is the first step in undertaking yogic practice. In distinct contrast to the relativity of values that characterizes caste Hinduism, where moral obligations and relations are relative to one's birth, for Patanjali social status is irrelevant to moral behavior. . . .

The Moral Principles

When one perseveres in nonviolence, hostility vanishes in its presence. (35)
When one abides in truthfulness, activity and its fruition are grounded in the truth. (36)
When one abjures stealing, jewels shower down. (37)
When one observes celibacy, heroic energy accrues. (38)
When one is without greed, the riddle of rebirth is revealed. (39)

The Observances

Aversion to one's own body and avoidance of contact with others comes from bodily purification. (40)
Also purity of intelligence, mental satisfaction, psychic focus, victory over the sense organs, and a vision of one's inner being. (41)
Perfect happiness is attained through contentment. (42)
Perfection of the body and senses comes from ascetic practice, which destroys impurities. (43)
Communion with one's chosen deity comes from the study of sacred lore. (44)
The perfection of pure contemplation comes from dedication to the Lord of Yoga. (45)

Posture

The posture of yoga is steady and easy. (46)
It is realized by relaxing one's effort and resting like the cosmic serpent on the waters of infinity. (47)
Then one is unconstrained by opposing dualities. (48)

Breath Control

When the posture of yoga is steady, then breath is controlled by regulation of the course of exhalation and inhalation. (49)
The modification of breath in exhalation, inhalation, and retention is perceptible as deep and shallow breathing regulated by where the breath is held, for how long, and for how many cycles. (50)
A fourth type of breath control goes beyond the range of exhalation and inhalation. (51)
Then the cover over the light of truth dissolves. (52)
And the mind is fit for concentration. (53)

Withdrawal of the Senses

When each sense organ severs contact with its objects, withdrawal of the senses corresponds to the intrinsic form of thought. (54)
From this comes complete control of the senses. (55)

PART THREE

Perfect Discipline

Concentration is binding thought in one place. (1)
Meditation is focusing on a single conceptual flow. (2)
Pure contemplation is meditation that illumines the object alone, as if the subject were devoid of intrinsic form. (3)

Concentration, meditation, and pure contemplation focused on a single object constitute perfect discipline. (4)

The light of wisdom comes from mastery of perfect discipline. (5)

The practice of perfect discipline is achieved in stages. (6)

In contrast with the prior limbs of yoga, the final triad is internal. (7)

Yet it is only an external limb of seedless contemplation. (8)

This section defines the final three limbs of the eight-fold way, collectively the hyperconscious state known as "perfect discipline" (*samyama*). Concentration, meditation, and pure contemplation are the internal limbs of yoga, which concentrate the yogi's energy and free his thought of constraints, allowing it to experience limitless knowledge and powers, such as the ability to know past and future, enter into other bodies, and understand the languages of animals and birds.

Each of the three limbs of perfect discipline is a stage in the process of achieving spiritual freedom. Concentration (*dhāraṇā*) involves focusing attention on a particular spot, such as the navel, the heart, the tip of the nose, or an internally visualized image. Meditation (*dhyāna*) is unwavering attention to a single object—a continuous flow of attention that, like the flow of oil, is uninterrupted by any extraneous idea. Pure contemplation (*samādhi*) is achieved when the meditative subject is so absorbed in the object of meditation that the distinction between subject and object disappears. The observer, transcending all awareness of a separate personal identity, takes the form of the object contemplated, attains complete control over it, and is absorbed in it—obliterating the artificial, conceptual separation between the observer and object.

Patanjali closes his account of the limbs of perfect discipline by reminding us that even pure contemplation (*samādhi*) is not the deepest level in the process of spiritual transformation. Beyond it, at the culmination of yogic practice, is seedless contemplation (*nirbīja-samādhi*). . . .

4.4 MEDIEVAL PERIOD

Kinsley (Reading 4.1) speaks of three major developments during the medieval period (ca. 600–1800). The first is the spread and growing popularity of **bhakti,** or devotion to one of the incarnations of the divine such as Krishna. The second is the resur-

gence of a philosophical school popularly known as Vedanta because of its concern with interpreting the *Upanishads.* The third is the development of a tradition known as **tantra** that criticized established religious rituals and the priests who supported such practices.

Advocates of these three traditions produced a vast amount of very important literature. What follows is a small sample.

4.4.1 Mirabai

We have seen in the *Laws of Manu* (Reading 4.3.1) that the duties and rights of women in Hindu society were very different from those of men. Many women suffered because their actions, rights, and choices were so much more restricted than men's. One consequence of this was the development of female *bhakti*-saints who became known for their ardent religious devotion and achieved significant influence as role models for those who would strive to be the perfect devotee.

Typically, these female saints leave unhappy marriages and male religious authorities reject them, but nonetheless they triumph by the example of their lives. Mirabai (ca. 1500–1550) was one of these saints. She was born in Rajasthan in northern India, but her reputation spread throughout India. Her arranged marriage was to a local prince, but she came to regard her true husband as Krishna. Running away from her marriage, she joined a group of Krishna devotees in Brindavan. At first the male leader of the group refused even to speak with her because he had made a vow never to speak to a woman. However, she made the point that there was really only one male at Brindavan, Hari (Lord) Krishna, because *all true devotees* are *females* in relation to him.

Mirabai is no dependent female guarded by men. She is not a passive agent, but actively takes charge of her life. However, she uses the traditional image of the passive and dependent female as a symbol for both male and female devotion to Krishna. Just as all females are to be devoted to their husbands (which she is not), all people (male and female) are to be totally devoted to Krishna (which she is). Indeed, it is Mirabai's devotion to Krishna that justifies her lack of devotion to her husband. Here is a good example of the complex functions religious symbols and ideas can play in social life. We should not too quickly conclude that religious ideals of female devotion necessarily reinforce traditional ideas of social control.

Here are three of Mirabai's songs to her Lord. They express a spiritual longing in erotic imagery focusing on Krishna's beautiful dark skin, handsome face, and great power.

MIRA

Songs

READING QUESTIONS

1. How does the first poem begin and end?
2. What images come to mind as you read aloud the second poem?
3. What value do you think might be found in complete and intense devotion to the divine?

Life without Hari is no life, friend,
And though my mother-in-law fights,
  my sister-in-law teases,
  the *rana* is angered,
A guard is stationed on a stool outside,
  and a lock is mounted on the door,
How can I abandon the love I have loved
  in life after life?
Mira's Lord is the clever Mountain Lifter:
  Why would I want anyone else?

                  [Caturvedi, no. 42]

I saw the dark clouds burst,
  dark Lord,
Saw the clouds and tumbling down
In black and yellow streams
  they thicken,
Rain and rain two hours long.
See—
  my eyes see only rain and water,
  watering the thirsty earth green.
Me—
  my love's in a distant land
  and wet, I stubbornly stand at the door,

For Hari is indelibly green,
  Mira's Lord,
And he has invited a standing,
  stubborn love.

                  [Caturvedi, no. 82]

I have talked to you, talked,
  dark Lifter of Mountains,
About this old love,
  from birth after birth.
Don't go, don't,
  Lifter of Mountains,
Let me offer a sacrifice—myself—
  beloved,
    to your beautiful face.
Come, here in the courtyard,
  dark Lord,
The women are singing auspicious wedding songs;
My eyes have fashioned
  an altar of pearl tears,
And here is my sacrifice:
  the body and mind
Of Mira,
  the servant who clings to your feet,
    through life after life,
      a virginal harvest for you to reap.

                  [Caturvedi, no. 51]

4.4.2 Birth of Kali

Goddess worship became increasingly popular from around the fourth century C.E. in India and continues into the present. As the goddess in her many forms gained increased popularity, an elaborate mythology developed around the goddess's exploits. One very well known story occurs in the *Markandeya Devi-Mahatmya Purana*. It tells about the goddess **Durga** slaying a buffalo demon. This demon threatens to upset the order of the cosmos, and the male gods, who fear it, call on Durga to save them. In some versions, the male gods create Durga specifically to fight the buffalo demon (Chanda). During the heat of battle, Durga gives birth to Kali, who battles the demons (*asuras*) who make up the Daitya (demon) army. Durga and Kali are often interchangeable in popular devotion.

    In this account, Durga is called Ambika and the Kali she gives birth to is portrayed in her fierce warrior aspect. **Kali** is a being who dwells on the boundary of society, threatening to subvert the status quo. She is a bloodthirsty warrior goddess in revolt. We often see her wearing a necklace of human skulls, her

From *Songs of the Saints of India*, edited by John Stratton Hawley, translated by John Stratton Hawley and M. Juergensmeyer, pp. 134–135, 138. Translation copyright © 1988 by Oxford University Press, Inc. Used by permission of Oxford University Press, Inc.

fanged teeth dripping blood and her many arms full of fearsome weapons. These weapons destroy her enemies but protect her children. Kali, like Shiva, embodies what some consider an eternal truth: Destruction is necessary for new order to emerge. Creation and destruction are two sides of the same coin. Life and death belong together. Those who know Kali, know this truth.

Devi-Mahatmya

READING QUESTIONS

1. Retell this story in your own words.
2. Why do you think this story is so popular?
3. Since the story of Kali's birth and battle with the demons ends by emphasizing the positive side of the goddess (a side more commonly emphasized in contemporary Hindu worship of Kali), why must Kali have a destructive side and appear so terrifying?

As they had been commanded, the Daityas, led by Caṇḍa and Muṇḍa, formed a four-fold army and sallied forth, their weapons raised aloft. They saw the goddess, smiling slightly, positioned on her lion atop the great golden peak of a mighty mountain. When they saw her, they made zealous efforts to seize her, while other demons from the battle approached her with bows and swords drawn. Then Ambikā became violently angry with her enemies, her face growing black as ink with rage. Suddenly there issued forth from between her eyebrows Kālī, with protruding fangs, carrying a sword and a noose, with a mottled, skull-topped staff, adorned with a necklace of human skulls, covered with a tiger-skin, gruesome with shriveled flesh. Her mouth gaping wide, her lolling tongue terrifying, her eyes red and sunken, she filled the whole of space with her howling. Attacking and killing the mighty demons, she devoured the armed force of the enemies of the gods. Seizing with

From *Classical Hindu Mythology: A Reader in the Sanskrit Puranas*, edited and translated by Cornelia Dimmitt and J. A. B. van Buitenen, pp. 238–240. Reprinted by permission of Temple University Press. © 1978 by Temple University. All Rights Reserved.

one hand the elephants with their back-riders, drivers, warriors and bells, she hurled them into her maw. In the same way she chewed up warriors with their horses, chariots and charioteers, grinding them up most horribly with her teeth. One she grabbed by the hair of the head, another by the nape of the neck, another she trod underfoot while another she crushed against her chest. The mighty striking and throwing weapons loosed by those demons she caught in her mouth and pulverised in fury. She ravaged the entire army of powerful evil-souled Asuras; some she devoured while others she trampled; some were slain by the sword, others bashed by her skull-topped club, while other demons went to perdition crushed by the sharp points of her teeth.

Seeing the sudden demise of the whole Daitya army, Caṇḍa rushed to attack that most horrendous goddess Kālī. The great demon covered the terrible-eyed goddess with a shower of arrows while Muṇḍa hurled discuses by the thousands. Caught in her mouth, those weapons shone like myriad orbs of the sun entering the belly of the clouds. Then howling horribly, Kālī laughed aloud malevolently, her maw gaping wide, her fangs glittering, awful to behold. Astride her huge lion, the goddess rushed against Caṇḍa; grabbing his head by the hair, she decapitated him with her sword. When he saw Caṇḍa dead, Muṇḍa attacked, but she threw him too to the ground, stabbing him with her sword in rage. Seeing both Caṇḍa and the mighty Muṇḍa felled, the remains of the army fled in all directions, overcome with fear.

Grabbing the heads of the two demons, Kālī approached Caṇḍikā and shrieked, cackling with fierce, demoniac laughter, "I offer you Caṇḍa and Muṇḍa as the grand victims in the sacrifice of battle. Now you yourself will kill Śumbha and Niśumbha!" Witnessing this presentation of the two great Asuras, the eminent Caṇḍikā spoke graciously to Kālī, "Since you have captured Caṇḍa and Muṇḍa and have brought them to me, O goddess, you will be known as Cāmuṇḍā!" . . .

So speaking, the honorable goddess Caṇḍikā of fierce mettle vanished on the spot before the eyes of the gods. And all the gods, their enemies felled, performed their tasks without harassment and enjoyed their shares of the sacrifices. When Śumbha, enemy of the gods, world-destroyer, of mighty power and valor, had been slain in battle and the most valiant Niśumbha had been crushed, the rest of the Daityas went to the netherworld.

In such a way, then, does the divine goddess, although eternal, take birth again and again to protect creation. This world is deluded by her; it is begotten by her; it is she who gives knowledge when prayed to and prosperity when pleased. By Mahākālī is this entire egg of Brahmā pervaded, lord of men. At the awful time of dissolution she takes on the form of Mahāmārī, the great destructress of the world. She is also its unborn source; eternal, she sustains creatures in time. As Lakṣmī, or Good Fortune, she bestows wealth on men's homes in times of prosperity. In times of disaster she appears as Misfortune for their annihilation. When the goddess is praised and worshiped with flowers, incense, perfume and other gifts, she gives wealth, sons, a mind set upon Dharma, and happiness to all mankind.

4.4.3 Vedanta

Who are you? You might reasonably respond to that question by giving your name. What if I persisted and asked, "Who are you really?" Perhaps I challenge you a little: "Does your name designate who you really are? Could you have a different name and still be you?" Abandoning the use of a name, you might point to your body. You are your body. However, again I might ask, "Are you identical with your body? Could you be you even in a different body? What about the breath that keeps you alive? Are you that? Maybe you are your mind that thinks and receives sensations or the intellect that reasons?" It seems you are many things. However, is there any one thing you might be?

"I am none of these many things," you might say, "I am myself, me, my ego." Shankara (ca. 788–820), the great Hindu philosopher and teacher of **Advaita** (nondualistic) Vedanta, might say you were an "almost" good student if you said that. According to Shankara, we are all victims of *maya* (illusion), which causes us to missidentify our true selves. We are not the "five coverings" (body, vital energy, mind, intellect, ego) even though we often think we are. Indeed, you may have stopped with the ego, that sense of "I" we all have, because it is so natural to say "I am I." That is why Shankara would find you an "almost" good student. Shankara would demand that you go beyond even your sense of ego to the *Atman,* or true self. However, even when you got there, you would need to go further.

But how much further? In the following selection, Shankara, or one of his students (this text is attributed to Shankara, but there is some doubt he is its author), tells us. This text is a philosophical meditation on the Upanishadic claim *"Tat tvam asi"* ("that art thou") found in the *Chandogya Upanishad* (Reading 4.2.2). The "that" is not just the *Atman* understood as consciousness purified of all its erroneous identifications, but it is also ***Brahman***, the essence of all that is real.

Just as we can imagine stripping away all the layers that we think of as our self until we come to consciousness itself (*Atman*), we can imagine stripping away all the layers of what we think of as an external world until we get to what is fundamentally real. The real itself, or *Brahman*, is that permanent, unchanging essence at the heart of all things. So, according to Shankara, the deeper awareness or higher knowledge of self and universe leads us to the realization that *Atman* (Pure Consciousness) is Brahman (Pure Being). That is what you truly are and what everything truly is. To realize this experientially is to experience bliss. Hence, ultimate reality may be characterized as Satchitanandu; Being (*sat*), Consciousness (*chit*), and Bliss (*ananda*).

Other members of the Vedanta school of philosophy disagreed with Shankara's interpretation of the *Upanishads.* Ramanuja (eleventh century) was an exponent of devotionalism who rejected Shankara's nondualistic interpretation, in part, because it would make devotion absurd. If Shankara was right, both the worshiper and the worshiped would be *maya* (illusion). It makes no sense, Ramanuja thought, to worship oneself. Religious devotion, or *bhakti*, becomes, on Shankara's account, an activity caught in the realm of illusion and make-believe.

Therefore, instead of nondualism, Ramanuja offered a theory called **qualified nondualism**. *Brahman* has two aspects: selves and matter. While these aspects are dependent on *Brahman*, they are not reducible to *Brahman*. Your life is dependent on *Brahman*, but you are not the same as *Brahman*. Thus, genuine devotion is preserved along with the authority of the *Upanishadic* phrase "that art thou," which indicates, given Ramanuja's interpretation, that our life depends on the divine reality. This provides one more good reason why worship of and devotion to God is the right way to live.

For many religions that have written sacred texts, in time controversies erupt about the proper interpretation of those texts. Such controversies lead to different schools of thought and often different religious movements, yet they also energize religious traditions and restore their vitality. Here we listen in on one such controversy in Hinduism. Although Advaita Vedanta seems to have won the day among intellectuals in modern India, the devotionalism of Ramanuja is still very much alive.

SHANKARA

Crest-Jewel of Discrimination (Viveka-Chudamani)

READING QUESTIONS

1. What arguments and analogies does Shankara use to convince the reader that *Atman* is *Brahman?*
2. How does Shankara characterize *Brahman?*
3. How does Ramanuja analyze the meaning of "thou" and "that," and what arguments does he present to support his analysis?
4. Why, according to Ramanuja, can ignorance not be ended by the act of knowing *Brahman* as the Universal Self?

THAT ART THOU

The scriptures establish the absolute identity of Atman and Brahman by declaring repeatedly: "That art Thou." The terms "Brahman" and "Atman," in their true meaning, refer to "That" and "Thou" respectively.

In their literal, superficial meaning, "Brahman" and "Atman" have opposite attributes, like the sun and the glow-worm, the king and his servant, the ocean and the well, or Mount Meru and the atom. Their identity is established only when they are understood in their true significance, and not in a superficial sense.

"Brahman" may refer to God, the ruler of Maya and creator of the universe. The "Atman" may refer to the individual soul, associated with the five coverings which are effects of Maya. Thus regarded, they possess opposite attributes. But this apparent opposition is caused by Maya and her effects. It is not real, therefore, but superimposed.

These attributes caused by Maya and her effects are superimposed upon God and upon the individual soul. When they have been completely eliminated, neither soul nor God remains. If you take the kingdom from a king and the weapons from a soldier, there is neither soldier nor king.

From *Shankara's Crest-Jewel of Discrimination: Viveka-Chudamani*, translated by Swami Prabhavananda and Christopher Isherwood (Hollywood, Calif.: Vedanta Press, 1947, 1975), pp. 72–76. Reprinted by permisson.

The scriptures repudiate any idea of a duality in Brahman. Let a man seek illumination in the knowledge of Brahman, as the scriptures direct. Then those attributes, which our ignorance has superimposed upon Brahman, will disappear.

"Brahman is neither the gross nor the subtle universe. The apparent world is caused by our imagination, in its ignorance. It is not real. It is like seeing the snake in the rope. It is like a passing dream"—that is how a man should practice spiritual discrimination, and free himself from his consciousness of this objective world. Then let him meditate upon the identity of Brahman and Atman, and so realize the truth.

Through spiritual discrimination, let him understand the true inner meaning of the terms "Brahman" and "Atman," thus realizing their absolute identity. See the reality in both, and you will find that there is but one.

When we say: "This man is that same Devadatta whom I have previously met," we establish a person's identity by disregarding those attributes superimposed upon him by the circumstances of our former meeting. In just the same way, when we consider the scriptural teaching "That art Thou," we must disregard those attributes which have been superimposed upon "That" and "Thou."

The wise men of true discrimination understand that the essence of both Brahman and Atman is Pure Consciousness, and thus realize their absolute identity. The identity of Brahman and Atman is declared in hundreds of holy texts.

Give up the false notion that the Atman is this body, this phantom. Meditate upon the truth that the Atman is "neither gross nor subtle, neither short nor tall," that it is self-existent, free as the sky, beyond the grasp of thought. Purify the heart until you know that "I am Brahman." Realize your own Atman, the pure and infinite consciousness.

Just as a clay jar or vessel is understood to be nothing but clay, so this whole universe, born of Brahman, essentially Brahman, is Brahman only—for there is nothing else but Brahman, nothing beyond That. That is the reality. That is our Atman. Therefore, "That art Thou" —pure, blissful, supreme Brahman, the one without a second.

You may dream of place, time, objects, individuals, and so forth. But they are unreal. In your waking state, you experience this world, but that experience arises from your ignorance. It is a prolonged dream, and therefore unreal. Unreal also are this body, these organs, this life-breath, this sense of ego. Therefore, "That art Thou"—pure, blissful, supreme Brahman, the one without a second.

Because of delusion, you may mistake one thing for another. But, when you know its real nature, then that nature alone exists, there is nothing else but that. When the dream breaks, the dream-universe has vanished. Does it appear, when you wake, that you are other than yourself?

Caste, creed, family and lineage do not exist in Brahman. Brahman has neither name nor form; it transcends merit and demerit; it is beyond time, space and the objects of sense-experience. Such is Brahman, and "That art Thou." Meditate upon this truth.

It is supreme. It is beyond the expression of speech; but it is known by the eye of pure illumination. It is pure, absolute consciousness, the eternal reality. Such is Brahman, and "That art Thou." Meditate upon this truth.

It is untouched by those six waves—hunger, thirst, grief, delusion, decay and death—which sweep the ocean of worldliness. He who seeks union with it must meditate upon it within the shrine of the heart. It is beyond the grasp of the senses. The intellect cannot understand it. It is out of the reach of thought. Such is Brahman, and "That art Thou." Meditate upon this truth.

It is the ground upon which this manifold universe, the creation of ignorance, appears to rest. It is its own support. It is neither the gross nor the subtle universe. It is indivisible. It is beyond comparison. Such is Brahman, and "That art Thou." Meditate upon this truth.

It is free from birth, growth, change, decline, sickness and death. It is eternal. It is the cause of the evolution of the universe, its preservation and its dissolution. Such is Brahman, and "That art Thou." Meditate upon this truth.

It knows no differentiation or death. It is calm, like a vast, waveless expanse of water. It is eternally free and indivisible. Such is Brahman, and "That art Thou." Meditate upon this truth.

Though one, it is the cause of the many. It is the one and only cause, no other beside it. It has no cause but itself. It is independent, also, of the law of causation. It stands alone. Such is Brahman, and "That art Thou." Meditate upon this truth.

It is unchangeable, infinite, imperishable. It is beyond Maya and her effects. It is eternal, undying bliss. It is pure. Such is Brahman, and "That art Thou." Meditate upon this truth.

It is that one Reality which appears to our ignorance as a manifold universe of names and forms and changes. Like the gold of which many ornaments are made, it remains in itself unchanged. Such is Brahman, and "That art Thou." Meditate upon this truth.

There is nothing beyond it. It is greater than the greatest. It is the innermost self, the ceaseless joy within us. It is absolute existence, knowledge and bliss. It is endless, eternal. Such is Brahman, and "That art Thou." Meditate upon this truth.

Meditate upon this truth, following the arguments of the scriptures by the aid of reason and intellect. Thus you will be freed from doubt and confusion, and realize the truth of Brahman. This truth will become as plain to you as water held in the palm of your hand.

RAMANUJA

Vedanta Sutra Commentary (Shri-Bhashya)

Scripture does not teach that release is due to knowledge of a non-qualified Brahman

Nor can we admit the assertion that scripture teaches the cessation of ignorance to spring only from the cognition of a *Brahman* devoid of all difference. . . . For the reason that *Brahman* is characterised by difference all Vedic texts declare that final release results from the cognition of a qualified *Brahman*. And that even those texts which describe *Brahman* by means of negations really aim at setting forth a *Brahman* possessing attributes, we have already shown above.

In texts, again, such as "Thou art that," the co-ordination of the constituent parts is not meant to convey the idea of the absolute unity of a non-differenced substance; on the contrary, the words "that" and "thou" denote a *Brahman* distinguished by difference. The word "that" refers to *Brahman* omniscient, etc., which had been introduced as the general topic of consideration in previous passages of the same section, such as "It thought, may I be many"; the word "thou," which stands in co-ordination to "that," conveys the idea of *Brahman* in so far as having for its body the individual selves connected with non-intelligent matter. This is in accordance with the

From *The Vedanta Sutras with the Commentary of Ramanuja*, translated by George Thibaut, *Sacred Books of the East*, vol. XLVII (Oxford, England: Clarendon Press, 1904), pp. 129–132, 134.

general principle that co-ordination is meant to express one thing subsisting in a twofold form. If such doubleness of form (or character) were abandoned, there could be no difference of aspects giving rise to the application of different terms, and the entire principle of co-ordination would thus be given up. . . . If the text "Thou art that" were meant to express absolute oneness, it would, moreover, conflict with a previous statement in the same section, viz. "It thought, may I be many"; and, further, the promise (also made in the same section) that by the knowledge of one thing all things are to be known could not be considered as fulfilled. It, moreover, is not possible (while, however, it would result from the absolute oneness of "*tat*" and "*tvam*") that *Brahman*, whose essential nature is knowledge, which is free from all imperfections, omniscient, comprising within itself all auspicious qualities, there should belong ignorance; and that it should be the substrate of all those defects and afflictions which spring from ignorance. . . . If . . . the text is understood to refer to *Brahman* as having the individual selves for its body, both words ("that" and "thou") keep their primary denotation; and, the text thus making a declaration about one substance distinguished by two aspects, the fundamental principle of "co-ordination" is preserved. On this interpretation the text further intimates that *Brahman*—free from all imperfection and comprising within itself all auspicious qualities—is the internal ruler of the individual selves and possesses lordly power. It moreover satisfies the demand of agreement with the teaching of the previous part of the section, and it also fulfils the promise as to all things being known through one thing, viz. in so far as *Brahman* having for its body all intelligent and non-intelligent beings in their gross state is the effect of *Brahman* having for its body the same things in their subtle state. . . .

. . . From all this it follows that the entire aggregate of things, intelligent and non-intelligent, has its Self in *Brahman* in so far as it constitutes *Brahman*'s body. And as, thus, the whole world different from *Brahman* derives its substantial being only from constituting *Brahman*'s body, any term denoting the world or something in it conveys a meaning which has its proper consummation in *Brahman* only: in other words all terms whatsoever denote *Brahman* in so far as distinguished by the different things which we associate with those terms on the basis of ordinary use of speech and etymology.—The text "that art thou" we therefore understand merely as a special expression of the truth already propounded in the clause "in that all this has its Self."

Ignorance cannot be terminated by the simple act of cognising Brahman as the Universal Self

The doctrine, again, that ignorance is put an end to by the cognition of *Brahman* being the Self of all can in no way be upheld, for as bondage is something real it cannot be put an end to by knowledge. How, we ask, can any one assert that bondage—which consists in the experience of pleasure and pain caused by the connexion of selves with bodies of various kind, a connexion springing from good or evil actions—is something false, unreal? . . . the cessation of such bondage is to be obtained only through the grace of the highest Self pleased by the devout meditation of the worshipper, . . .

i.ii.12. And on account of distinctive qualities.

. . . Those, however, who understand the Vedānta, teach as follows: There is a highest *Brahman* which is the sole cause of the entire universe, which is antagonistic to all evil, whose essential nature is infinite knowledge and blessedness, which comprises within itself numberless auspicious qualities of supreme excellence, which is different in nature from all other beings, and which constitutes the inner Self of all. Of this *Brahman*, the individual selves—whose true nature is unlimited knowledge, and whose only essential attribute is the intuition of the supreme Self—are modes, in so far, namely, as they constitute its body. The true nature of these selves is, however, obscured by ignorance, i.e., the influence of the beginningless chain of works; and by release then we have to understand that intuition of the highest Self, which is the natural state of the individual selves, and which follows on the destruction of ignorance. . . .

4.4.4 Tantra of the Great Liberation

Tantric Hinduism developed in the fourth to sixth centuries C.E. in areas where Brahmanic influence was weakest. It sought to extend (*tantra* literally means "what extends") Vedic practices and the implications of *bhakti* Hinduism. Tantric beliefs and practices seek to balance and integrate the usually male-centered *bhakti* by emphasizing the goddess as **shakti** (power or energy). Tantric practice (sadhana) promotes the experience of the unity of *purusha* (understood as both soul and male deity) with *prakriti* (understood as both matter and goddess). The gendered material body itself becomes the vehicle for liberation.

Tantric Hinduism intentionally criticizes Brahmanic Hinduism, which is controlled by a male priesthood. Adepts come from all castes and use different types of yogic techniques, the most famous being *kundaliniyoga*, which is designed to awaken the dormant *shakti* power (imaged as a coiled serpent resting between the genitals and the anus). Once awake *shakti* transforms the various *chakras* (energy centers, usually six in number) by rising through the body's channels (**nadis**) to unite with Shiva in the "thousand petaled *chakra*" in the brain.

The practice of *kundaliniyoga* is common to the two main strands of Tantrism—the right-handed path and the left-handed path. However, the left-handed path goes further by engaging in the practice of the "five m's": eating fish (*matsya*), eating meat (*mamsa*), eating parched grain (*mudra*), drinking wine (*madya*), and engaging in ritualized sexual intercourse (*maithuna*). The uniting of male and female can be the means for uniting the energies of the universe and the divine into a harmonious whole. The spiritual goal of the unification of opposites becomes concretely symbolized and realized in tantric practice.

Excerpts from the *Mahanirvana Tantra* (*Tantra of the Great Liberation*) are presented in the selection. This translation was done by Arthur Avalon in 1913, and I have made some changes primarily to update the language and explain technical terminology. Arthur Avalon is a pseudonym for Sir John Woodroffe, an eminent jurist and professor at the University of Calcutta during colonial rule.

This *Tantra* is a series of conversations between the god *Shiva* and *shakti* (consort-energy) in which *Shiva* gives instructions for meditation exercises and rituals involving shaktic worship. In Indian devotional religion, female consorts accompany male deities and are so much a part of the male god that the god cannot be active without them. These female consorts are thus called *shaktis*, or energies, because they are essential for the power of the male gods.

The *Mahanirvana Tantra* presents itself as the teaching most appropriate for the *Kali* age. In classical devotional Hinduism, time is structured in three main rhythms. The longest is a *mahakalpa* (311,040 billion human years), which is made up of *kalpas*. Each *kalpa* is made up of a thousand *mahayugas* (4,320 million human years), which in turn is made up of four *yugas*. A full four-yuga cycle lasts 12,000 years, or one *mahayuga* (great yuga).

The *yugas* are not just time periods, but outline a progressive religious and moral decline from an age of perfection (*kritayuga*) to an imperfect and degenerate age (*kaliyuga*). Each age has teachings and teachers most appropriate to it. These teachings become more important and more urgent as degeneration sets in. We here sample part of a teaching meant to aid us in these terrible *kaliyuga* times.

Mahanirvana Tantra

READING QUESTIONS

1. What do you think is the significance of establishing that Shiva reveals a truth appropriate for each age?
2. What is the truth that Shiva reveals?
3. While tantric rituals and teachings refer to the complementary nature of the sexes and the need to unite female-male energy to achieve liberation, do you detect any elements in this account that might signal gender inequality? If so, what are they and why do you think they show gender inequality?

Shri Parvati [Shiva's spouse] said: "O God of the Gods, Lord of the World, Jewel of Mercy, my husband, you are my Lord on whom I am ever dependent and to whom I am ever obedient. Nor can I say ought without your word. If you have affection for me, I desire to lay before you that which passes in my mind. Who else but you, O Great Lord, in the three worlds is able to solve these doubts of mine. You who know all and all the scriptures."

Shri Sadashiva responded: "What is that you say, O You Great Wise One and Beloved of My Heart, I will tell you anything, be it ever so bound in mystery, even that which should not be spoken of before **Ganesha** [elephant-headed god and son of Shiva and Shakti] and Skanda [another son], Commander of the hosts of heaven. What is there in all the three worlds which should be concealed from you? For you, O Goddess, are my very self. There is no difference between me and you. You too are omnipresent. What is it then that you do not know and question like one who knows nothing?"

Shri Adaya [Primordial Shakti, another title for Shiva's wife] said: "O Lord of All and Greatest Among Those Versed in Dharma, you in former ages in your mercy did through Brahma [creator god] reveal the four Vedas which are the propagators of all dharmas and which ordain the rules of life for all the varying castes of humans and for the different stages of their lives. In the First Age, people by the practice of yoga . . . were virtuous and pleasing to gods and ancestors. By the study of the Vedas, meditation, asceticism, and the conquest of the senses, by acts of mercy and charity people were of

From *Tantra of The Great Liberation* (*Mahanirvana Tantra*), translated by Arthur Avalon (London: Luzac & Company, 1913), pp. 4–9, 13–17, 103–104.

exceeding power and courage, strength and vigor, adherents of the true Dharma, wise and truthful and of firm resolve, and mortals though they were, they were yet like gods and went to the abode of gods. . . . After the Krita Age had passed, you in Treta Age, perceived the Dharma was in disorder and people were no longer able by Vedic rites to get what they desired . . . and you made known on earth the scripture in the form of Smriti which explains the meaning of the Vedas.

. . . Then in the Dvapara Age, when humans abandoned the good works prescribed in the Smritis, and were deprived of one half of Dharma and were afflicted by the ills of mind and body, they were yet again saved by you, through the instructions of the Sanghita and other religious lore. Now the sinful Kalic Age is upon them, when dharma is destroyed, an Age full of evil customs and deceit. People pursue evil ways. The *Vedas* have lost their power, the Smritis are forgotten, and many of the Puranas, which contain stories of the past, and show the many ways (which lead to liberation), will O Lord! be destroyed. People will become averse from religious rites, without restraint, maddened with pride, ever given over to sinful acts, lustful, gluttonous, cruel, heartless, harsh of speech, deceitful, short-lived, poverty-stricken, harassed by sickness and sorrow, ugly, feeble, low, stupid, mean and addicted to mean habits. . . . Say, O Lord of all the distressed in your mercy, how, without great pains, men may obtain longevity, health, and energy, increase of strength and courage, learning, intelligence, and happiness; and how they may become great in strength and valor, pure of heart, obedient to parents, not seeking the love of others' wives but devoted to their own, mindful of the good of their neighbors, reverent to the gods and to their gurus, cherishers of their children and kinsmen, possessing the knowledge of the Brahman, learned in the lore of and ever meditating on the Brahman. Say, O Lord for the good of the world, what people should and should not do according to their different castes and states of life. For who but you is their protector in all the three worlds?" . . .

[Shiva speaks]: "Truly, truly and yet again truly I say to you that in this Age there is no way to liberation but that proclaimed by the Tantra. I, O Blissful One, have already foretold in the *Vedas*, Smritis, and Puranas, that in this Age the wise shall worship after the doctrine of the Tantra. Truly, truly, and beyond all doubt, I say to you that there is no liberation for him who in this Age, heedless of such doctrine, follows another. There is no Lord but I in this world, and I alone am He who is spoken of in the *Vedas*, Puranas, and Smritis and Sanghitas. . . . In this Age the **mantras** [holy sounds] of the Tantras are efficacious, yield immediate fruit, and are auspicious for Japa (recitation), Yajna (sacrificial rites)

and all such practices and ceremonies. The Vedic rites and mantras which were efficacious in the First Age have ceased to be so in this."

[The rest of the text describes in detail various meditations, mantras, purifications, rituals, duties, and the like appropriate for the pious in this the Kali age. I include below the beginning of chapter VI, which describes the rites of the Pancha-tattvas, or five elements of worship—wine, meat, fish, parched food, and *maithuna* (ritualized sexual intercourse)—Ed.]

Shri Devi [goddess] said: "As you have kindness for me, pray tell me, O Lord, more particularly about the Pancha-tattvas and the other observances of which you have spoken."

Shri Sadashiva said: "There are three kinds of wine which are excellent, namely, that which is made from molasses, rice, or the Madhuka flower. . . . Howsoever it may have been produced, and by whomsoever it is brought, the wine, when purified, gives to the worshipper all siddhi (supernormal powers). There are no distinctions of caste in the taking of wine so sanctified. Meat, again, is of three kinds, that of animals of the waters, of the earth, and of the sky. From wheresoever it may be brought, and by whomsoever it may have been killed, it gives, without doubt, pleasure to the gods. Let the desire of the disciple determine what should be offered to the gods. Whatsoever he himself likes, the offering of that conduces to his well-being. Only male animals should be decapitated in sacrifice. It is the command of Shambhu that female animals should not be slain. There are three superior kinds of fish . . . there are also three kinds of parched food, superior, middle, and inferior. . . . O Great Goddess when the weakness of the Kali Age becomes great, one's own shakti or wife should alone be known as the fifth tattva [element]. This is devoid of all defect. . . ."

4.5 MODERN PERIOD

Since the eighteenth century, India and the Hindu tradition have undergone profound and far-reaching changes, first under the impact of British colonialism and then under the impact of independence. There are two intertwined directions of change: first, developments stemming from the revival and renewal within the Hindu tradition and, second, the emergence of a Neo-Hinduism. The first involves a restatement of the tradition referred to as *Sanatana Dharma* (roughly, "old-style religion"). Many local associations were created to protect the tradition and, in many cases, to re-create it in light of the colonial experience and the impact of modernization. The second strand (Neo-Hinduism) is a representation of the Hindu tradition created by English-speaking, educated elite Hindus.

4.5.1 Adherence to Truth

The leaders and the accomplishments of the Hindu revival are too numerous to recount here. We will look at one example, perhaps the most famous, the work of Mohandas Karamchand Gandhi (1869–1948). Gandhi combined what he considered the best in all religions including Hinduism into a social philosophy designed to win independence for India and, eventually, justice for all oppressed peoples. While he won fame as a political leader, he was first a religious leader.

In his teachings he combined three central ideas: adherence to the truth (*satyagraha*), nonviolence (*ahimsa*), and increasing the welfare of all or universal uplift (*sarvodaya*). In the selection from his autobiography that follows, Gandhi speaks of some of his deepest convictions—convictions that reveal the power of the Hindu tradition to inspire the human effort toward understanding and peace.

GANDHI

Experiments with Truth

READING QUESTION

1. What elements of traditional Hinduism do you find in Gandhi's experiments with truth?

This time has come to bring these chapters to a close. My life from this point onward has been so public that there is hardly anything about it that people do not know. Moreover, since 1921 I have worked in such association with the Congress leaders that I can hardly describe any episode in my life since then without referring

From M. K. Gandhi, *An Autobiography or The Story of My Experiments with Truth* (London: Penguin, 1927), pp. 452–454. Reprinted by permission of the Navajivan trust.

to my relations with them. For though Shraddhanandji, the Deshabandhu, Hakim Saheb and Llalji are no more with us today, we have the good luck to have a host of other veteran Congress leaders still living and working in our midst. The history of the Congress, since the great changes in it that I have described above, is still in the making. And my principal experiments during the past seven years have all been made through the Congress. A reference to my relations with the leaders would therefore be unavoidable, if I set about describing my experiments further. And this I may do, at any rate for the present, if only from a sense of propriety. Lastly, my conclusions from my current experiments can hardly as yet be decisive. It therefore seems to me to be my plain duty to close this narrative here. In fact my pen instinctively refuses to proceed further.

It is not without a wrench that I have to take leave of the reader. I set high value on my experiments. I do not know whether I have been able to do justice to them. I can only say that I have spared no pains to give a faithful narrative. To describe truth, as it has appeared to me, and in the exact manner in which I have arrived at it, has been my ceaseless effort. The exercise has given me ineffable mental peace, because it has been my fond hope that it might bring faith in Truth and *Ahimsa* to waverers. My uniform experience has convinced me that there is no other God than Truth. And if every page of these chapters does not proclaim to the reader that the only means for the realization of Truth is *Ahimsa*, I shall deem all my labour in writing these chapters to have been in vain. And, even though my efforts in this behalf may prove fruitless, let the readers know that the vehicle, not the great principle, is at fault. After all, however sincere my strivings after *Ahimsa* may have been, they have still been imperfect and inadequate. The little fleeting glimpses, therefore, that I have been able to have of Truth can hardly convey an idea of the indescribable lustre of Truth, a million times more intense than that of the sun we daily see with our eyes. In fact what I have caught is only the faintest glimmer of that mighty effulgence. But this much I can say with assurance, as a result of all my experiments, that a perfect vision of Truth can only follow a complete realization of *Ahimsa*.

To see the universal and all-pervading Spirit Truth face to face one must be able to love the meanest of creation as oneself. And a man who aspires after that cannot afford to keep out of any field of life. That is why my devotion to Truth has drawn me into the field of politics; and I can say without the slightest hesitation, and yet in all humility, that those who say that religion has nothing to do with politics do not know what religion means.

Identification with everything that lives is impossible without self-purification; the observance of the law of *Ahimsa* must remain an empty dream; God can never be realized by one who is not pure of heart. Self-purification therefore must mean purification in all the walks of life. And purification being highly infectious, purification of oneself necessarily leads to the purification of one's surroundings.

But the path of self-purification is hard and steep. To attain to perfect purity one has to become absolutely passion-free in thought, speech and action; to rise above the opposing currents of love and hatred, attachment and repulsion. I know that I have not in me as yet that triple purity, in spite of constant ceaseless striving for it. That is why the world's praise fails to move me, indeed it very often stings me. To conquer the subtle passions seems to me to be harder far than the physical conquest of the world by the force of arms. Ever since my return to India I have had experiences of the dormant passions lying hidden within me. The knowledge of them has made me feel humiliated though not defeated. The experiences and experiments have sustained me and given me great joy. But I know that I have still before me a difficult path to traverse. I must reduce myself to zero. So long as a man does not of his own free will put himself last among his fellow creatures, there is no salvation for him. *Ahimsa* is the farthest limit of humility.

In bidding farewell to the reader, for the time being at any rate, I ask him to join with me in prayer to the God of Truth that He may grant me the boon of *Ahimsa* in mind, word and deed.

4.5.2 Religion and Politics

Hindu myths, legends, and moral literature often celebrate the subordination of women to men. Sita, the perfect wife of the *Ramayana*, is loyal to her husband, Rama, even when he mistreats her (Reading 4.3.2). The rights and responsibilities afforded women by Manu, the First Man, are not at all equal to men (Reading 4.3.1). The practices of seclusion and *sati* (or *suttee*, meaning "good wife" and referring to the self-immolation of widows on their husband's funeral pyre) promote negative stereotypes of the treatment of women in traditional India. Although *suttee* is now illegal, many suspect that the view of women it represents is far from dead.

However, the Hindu tradition also has its goddesses who destroy demons, women who actively fight for justice, and female saints whose devotion is often portrayed as greater than men's piety (Readings 4.4.1 and 4.4.2). In

today's India these two views of women—one as passive and obedient, the other as active and independent—often clash and mix as modern Indian governments seek to accommodate the civil and domestic laws of different religious groups with the equality guaranteed by the constitution.

In the selection that follows, Katherine K. Young, who teaches Hinduism at McGill University and is an editor of the *Annual Review of Women in World Religions*, reports on an interview with Uma Bharati, who is not only an activist in promoting the cause of women in India but also a member of the Bharatiya Janata Party (BJP), which is often labeled "fundamentalist." The BJP supports more political power for Hindus and the promotion of traditional religious ideals and practices. There is a growing polarization between the secularists and the religiously conservative political parties like the BJP. Religious minorities prefer the present secular state because India is eighty-two percent Hindu, and they fear they would lose their religious freedom in a state based on Hindu tradition and law. Leaders of the movement for more rights for women also fear a religious state because of the traditional teachings about the role of women found in some Hindu literature.

Uma Bharati reveals that the situation in present-day India is more complex than this distinction between secularists and conservative Hindus indicates. Although a member of the BJP and a religious traditionalist, she nevertheless is a supporter of women's rights and is a political activist.

KATHERINE K. YOUNG

The Case of Uma Bharati

READING QUESTIONS

1. How do you think Uma Bharati harmonizes her support of more rights for women and her traditional religious commitments?
2. How does Bharati use traditional religious language for political purposes?

A different style of activism on women's issues is represented by Ms. Uma Bharati. She has been a BJP member of Parliament from Khajuraho. When she was interviewed in December, 1989, for *Times of India News*, she described her life in the style of a sacred biography. She recalled, for instance, her early, extraordinary religious experiences:

> I began having unusual experiences. At the age of six, I found myself giving discourses on the scriptures to the villagers. As far back as I can remember I have had this feeling of two existences within me—dual voices—one of a philosopher-scholar, the other of a child. It was almost an organic phenomenon; I can't explain it. It was as natural as breathing, to orate on religious matters or on the need for a spiritual revolution.

The interviewer then asked how she was discovered as a religious prodigy. Bharati answered:

> Well, one day some professors from a Tikamgarh degree college came to the village as part of a *baraat* (marriage party). When they heard me, they were so amazed, they did not even wait for the *bidaai* (nuptials). They bundled me into a car and I was admitted to a school in the town. Then followed years of participation at religious *sammelans*. I travelled abroad, toured in private planes, was feted and banqueted, nearly drowned in flowers from admirers. When the initial glamour of the adulation wore off, I began to feel caged in the worship. I wanted to appear ordinary, not the image of a *devi* or *avatar*, or live up to a created image.

Bharati remarks that she was once engaged but broke off the relationship because of her "religious commitments." She thought of becoming a *brahmacāriṇī* until her mentor told her that being a *brahmacāriṇī* meant total renunciation—that is, complete withdrawal from the world. Because she wanted to serve the people and work for the welfare of the world (*lokasaṅgraha*), she decided against total renunciation (hence her sporadic wearing of the ochre robe). Working for the "welfare of the world" has meant working with outcastes and women in her native village and in Khajuraho. Of women, she said:

> Women are inherently superior as a created species. Men are not such noble beings that women should fight for equality. Instead they should fight to be treated with respect. . . .
>
> If Indian women combine the *madhurya* (sweetness), their femininity, with self-pride and political awareness, they can teach the whole world the path of liberation. . . .

You cannot sacrifice either aspect—sword in the hand and child on the back. Our women have to combine the heroism of Draupadi, Gargi, Savitri, Jabala, and Kunti. It is self-respect that will free us, not legislation. I don't eat in houses where, as per the tradition, women eat after men and observe *purdah* . . . for crimes like rape, I feel there should be [the] death sentence.

When the interviewer asked her whether she has ever experienced sexual discrimination in political life, she replied, "No, because I am well known in my area. And in the BJP we give the woman a very exalted status." Then, with a twinkle in her eye, she told the reporter, "my religious image has helped women overcome their prejudices." Folding her ochre robes, she added "I have faith in myself. . . . And may God give me some of the reformist energy of my idols—Rani Laxmi Bai and Swami Vivekananda."

Uma Bharati sees no contradiction between working for the cause of women and being a member of the BJP Party, usually portrayed in the press as the Hindu fundamentalist or militant party, and stereotyped as a regressive force on women's issues. Bharati is a Hindu liberal, at least on women's issues. But like many other Hindus she is disturbed at the loss of Hindu values and perceives secularism under leaders such as Rajiv Gandhi negatively. When defending Indian voters, she remarks: "maybe they didn't like Rajiv's foreign wife . . . or his elite coterie of friends . . . or his mania for computerisation and breakneck modernisation in certain sectors when so many lakhs [100,000] were denied basic amenities."

Her remedy for conflict brought on by communalism and religious extremism is to make room for moderate religion in the public square:

> The fact is the Indians can only understand religion. We are an instinctively religious people. The police, law, science—these are external controls; even our communists are "astiks" (theists) in their heart of hearts. The best methods of controlling communalism is to get moderate religious leaders on public forums to address the masses, spiced with examples from the scriptures. Those who are inflamed by religion can only be calmed down by religion, not by a slick or rational explanation.

Bharati told the interviewer that all parties exploit religious sentiment: "But the BJP believe in Hindutva ("Hinduness") and are proud of it and just because of this we are branded communal." More recently, Bharati has become much more militant and vociferous against the Muslims. Prior to the projected showdown (regarding the rebuilding of a Hindu temple to Lord Rāma at the site of a mosque) at Ayodhya on October 30, 1990, she made speeches in Hindi that were later made into cassettes and sold. The message was virulent:

> On October 30, by beginning the construction of the temple, our holy men will be laying the foundations of making Hindustan a Hindu [state]. Bharat Mata Ki jai . . . Glory to Mahadev [the Great Deity]. Destroy the tyrant in the same way that Ravana was vanquished. Do not display any love (nij preet). This is the order of Ram. Announce it boldly to the world that anyone who opposes Ram cannot be an Indian. Muslims, remember Rahim who longed for the dust of Lord Ram's feet. . . . Songs of Hindu Muslim brotherhood were sung by Mahatma Gandhi. We got ready to hear the Azaan along with the temple bells, but they can't do this, nor does their heritage permit them to do so. . . . The two cultures are polar opposites. But still we preached brotherhood. . . . We could not teach them with words, now let us teach them with kicks. . . . Let there be bloodshed once and for all. . . . Leftists and communists ask me if we desire to turn this land into a Hindu rashtra. I say it was declared one at the time of Partition in 1947—Hindustan, a nation of Hindus and Pakistan, a nation of the Muslims. Those Muslims who stayed behind could do so because of the tolerance and large-heartedness of the Hindus. . . . Declare without hesitation that this is a Hindu rashtra, a nation of Hindus.

Uma Bharati finally took saṁnyāsa (formal renunciation) in 1992. It was prompted, some say, to clear her reputation after she was accused by the opposition parties of having an affair. Be that as it may, she shaved her head, was renamed Uma Shri Bharati, and began to wear only ochre robes. As the opposition was quick to point out, she did not give up her status as a member of parliament. She also continued to support the cause of rebuilding the Rām Janmabhoomi temple. . . .

CONTEMPORARY SCHOLARSHIP

Reading about Hinduism has, perhaps, left you with more questions than it has answered. If so, that is good. The more we learn, the more questions we

have, and the more questions we have the more likely we are to keep on learning. There is always more to discover and understand.

We turn here to two historians of religion who seek to deepen their own understanding and, by sharing their scholarship, our understanding as well about issues relating to gender complementarity in cosmogonic myths (stories about the origin of the universe) and the use of images in Hindu worship. The references to the roles of male and female divinities on the mythological level have sometimes been praised as a refreshing escape from the male-centeredness of Western religions and, at the same time, have been found incongruent with the treatment of females in India society. The use of images has often struck the Christian, Jew, and Muslim as little more than idol worship. Perhaps your reading of this material has raised similar issues in your own mind.

4.6 PURANIC ACCOUNTS OF CREATION

Purana, which means "belonging to ancient times," is the name of a class of Hindu writings containing stories about creation, gods, goddesses, demons, ancestors, rituals, and much more. These stories have had widespread appeal to the peoples of India and, in some cases, are the primary means by which they learn Hinduism, just as the stories in the Bible and Qur'an are the means by which Jews, Christians, and Muslims learn about their religions.

Creation stories are of particular importance because, by recounting how everything got started, they provide models of how everything should be. The meanings conveyed by stories, especially those thought to be sacred and telling us the way things were meant to be, can be enormously influential in shaping people's values, attitudes, and practices. Often such stories mask things such as gender inequality and thereby give it a divine sanction, even when official teachings tell us all humans are equal in the sight of the divine.

Tracy Pintchman is an assistant professor of Hindu studies at Loyola University in Chicago. Her Ph.D. is from the University of California, Santa Barbara. In the following selection she probes the hidden gender inequality embedded in Hindu stories that, on the surface, support gender complementarity.

TRACY PINTCHMAN

Gender Complementarity and Hierarchy

READING QUESTION

1. Summarize Pintchman's argument in your own words. Do you think she is right? Why or why not?

In his impressive study, *Classifying the Universe: The Ancient Indian Varṇa System and the Origins of Caste*, Brian K. Smith notes the role that cosmogonies recorded in Vedic texts play in supporting, legitimating, and perpetuating caste divisions in Hindu society. Vedic cosmogonies portray the *varṇas*, the broad classes comprising Indian society on which caste divisions are based, as being created, "in the beginning" in conjunction with the creation of all other things, beings, and worlds; hence the division of people into *varṇas* is "represented as aboriginal, as hard-wired into the essence of reality, as the 'way things are' because they were created that way." This is significant because as sources of legitimation, Smith notes, cosmogonic myths carry weight: "Cosmogony legitimizes the present insofar as it conforms to what things were like 'in the beginning.' Creation stories ensure that departures from a status quo appear as deviations from a god-given norm, as degenerations vis-à-vis a pristine time of original perfection. To pronounce on how things were at the dawn of time is to describe how things really are—or at least how they really should be. Religions have always depended on myths of origins to validate the dictates of particular human beings living in particular historical eras. Both Vedic and Hindu religions bestowed such cosmogonic legitimations on the social system they advocated and instituted in India. . . .

Smith further argues that the portrayal of the *varṇa* system in Vedic cosmogonies as primordial, "natural," and "the way things are" (instead of human in origin) serves well the interests of the Brahmin authors of the Vedic texts. By affirming the validity of *varṇa* divisions,

Excerpts from Tracy Pintchman, "Gender Complementarity and Gender Hierarchy in Puranic Accounts of Creation," *Journal of the American Academy of Religion* 66 (Summer 1998): 257–261, 274–275, 277–279. Reprinted by permission. References and notes omitted.

Vedic cosmogonies implicitly affirm the superiority of the Brahmins. The Vedas consistently portray the Brahmin class as the highest of the *varṇas*, the "hierarchically superior social entity" that is "invariably found in the top spot in any taxonomy; in the classification of society, the Brahmins are also and always given the highest position." . . . But the Brahmin authors of the Vedic texts conceal their own authorship and achieve the "illusion of objectivity necessary for authority" by portraying Vedic texts as authorless, eternal, and embodying absolute truth. . . .

Since Smith is concerned primarily with *varṇa* and caste (*jāti*), he does not engage questions regarding the role that Brahmanical cosmogonic myths might play in supporting the other powerful and pervasive hierarchy in Brahmanical Hinduism—that of gender. But the authors of Brahmanical scriptures, after all, were not just Brahmin, but also male, and it was in their interest to perpetuate an ideology of superiority that encompasses both of these dimensions of their identity. Vedic and post-Vedic Brahmanical texts do in fact tend to favor both Brahminhood and maleness, and caste and gender tend to function in similar ways in determining social hierarchy. In Brahmanical scriptures high-caste males are usually privileged over their subordinates, who comprise both low-caste individuals and all females. In the ancient Brahmanical law book, the Laws of Manu, for example, both women and Shudras (the lowest of the four *varṇas*) are often portrayed as inherently inferior beings and are excluded, at least theoretically, from studying the Veda, reciting the Veda, and performing sacrifices. . . .

There is, of course, an important distinction between caste and gender as markers of difference: there is no empirically verifiable biological basis for caste differentiation, whereas the biological realities of gender difference are obvious to all. But caste and gender tend to function socially in similar ways. Like caste, gender plays an important role in structuring social hierarchy in contemporary Indian culture, and both caste and gender have been invoked to legitimate inequitable distributions of wealth and power, differences in status, discrepancies in rights, divisions of labor, and hierarchical notions of inherent worth. Gender may in fact be even more fundamental than caste as a principle of hierarchy. In his study of Newars in Nepal, for example, Steven M. Parish notes that for some Newars, "not the opposition of pure and impure, or of Brahman and untouchable, but the opposition of male and female seems to be the most basic prototype of hierarchy. God, they say, originally made only two castes—male and female. All the rest came later—as surplus difference, the mere construction of kings, history, society. The original difference of male and female is the key to order; the caste hierarchy can go, but the gender hierarchy is natural and necessary." . . .

The most elaborate Brahmanical cosmogonies and the richest portrayals of gender and gender dynamics in cosmogonic processes are found in the Purāṇas, which are post-Vedic. Smith focuses his concerns with *varṇa* and caste on Vedism and the world of Vedic texts and hence does not venture into the world of post-Vedic Brahmanical scripture, but post-Vedic Brahmanical texts are equally part of the Brahmanical Hindu tradition, and cosmogonies found in these texts are equally "weighty." Furthermore, in matters concerning the ideology of gender Purāṇic cosmogonies are richer than their earlier Vedic counterparts and tend to be more consistent in their descriptions of gender dynamics in accounts of creation. During the Vedic period religious and social values and practices were probably less affected by gender difference than in later Hinduism; . . . the increased attention given to gender dynamics in Purāṇic cosmogonies and the way in which these dynamics are portrayed may reflect increased attention to gender and gender roles in the social realm.

One finds numerous accounts of creation scattered throughout different Brahmanical scriptures, and they represent a variety of divergent views regarding cosmogony. But there are predominant patterns and tendencies in these narratives. Purāṇic cosmogonies tend to portray male and female cosmogonic principles and actors as complementary, and processes associated with creation are driven by their mutual interaction. Many of the numerous creation narratives in the Mahā-Purāṇas maintain the need for balanced and fruitful interaction between female and male principles on different levels and at different stages of cosmogony in order for the process to succeed and for creation to be maintained.

What might the portrayal of gender and the complementary nature of gender roles in these narratives suggest about underlying gender ideologies? First, Purāṇic cosmogonies repeatedly acknowledge female contributions to the process of creation. In this regard they affirm the importance of the feminine principle in cosmogony. It is also important to note that an emphasis on gender complementarity reflects the biological realities of procreation, which, of course, requires both male and female participation. Beyond the basic biological facts, these descriptions of creation also have a good deal in common with Brahmanical ideologies regarding procreation, as we shall see. Finally, however, I believe there is another overriding agenda here that is rooted neither in the affirmation of female creativity nor in the biological facts of reproduction.

Many scholars have noted that assertions of gender complementarity frequently move beyond the biological and are invoked to support androcentric social biases. In her discussion of complementarity with respect to male-female roles in Jewish law, for example, Rebecca Alpert notes underlying gender prejudice, remarking, "Because of the essential androcentric bias of Jewish law, men are the central category. . . . All issues related to women are delineated in terms of their relationship to men." Gender biases are especially effective when they are concealed and give the impression of being natural or divine, not social, in origin. The account of the creation of Eve from Adam's rib in Genesis 2:18–25, for example, has often been invoked as evidence that women are inferior to men by nature and by divine decree. Gerda Lerner notes that the creation of woman from Adam's rib "has been interpreted in the most literal sense for thousands of years to denote the God-given inferiority of woman. Whether that interpretation has rested upon the rib as being one of Adam's 'lower' parts, and therefore denoting inferiority, or on the fact that Eve was created from Adam's flesh and bone, while he was created from earth, the passage has historically had profoundly patriarchal symbolic meaning." . . . I am reminded also of a passage from Dennis Covington's *Salvation on Sand Mountain*, a book about snake handling in Southern Appalachia. Covington describes a church service he attended led by Brother Carl, who launches into a diatribe about the need for women to stay in their place: " 'It's not godly for a woman to do a man's job!' he said. 'To wear a man's pants! Or cut her hair like a man does his! It doesn't please God to go on like that, acting like Adam was made out of Eve's rib instead of the other way around! . . . A woman's got to stay in her place!' Carl shouted. 'God made her for a helpmate to man! It wasn't intended for her to have a life of her own! If God had wanted to give her a life of her own, he'd have made her first instead of Adam, and then where would we be!' "

In the creation narratives of the Purāṇas models of gender complementarity tend to mask underlying androcentric biases even though they also acknowledge female contributions to cosmogony. Just as Vedic accounts of creation portray distinctions among the *varṇas* and the consequent inherent superiority of the Brahmins over everybody else as part of the natural order of things—the "way things are"—Purāṇic cosmogonies similarly communicate notions concerning the "inherent" attributes of maleness and femaleness that move beyond the biological to support Brahmanical notions concerning the "natural" dominance of maleness over femaleness. Throughout the Purāṇas at various stages of the cosmogonic process the dynamics between male and female suggest that male hegemony is built into "the way things are" from the very beginning and hence is "natural," although such evaluations are not made explicit in the accounts of creation themselves. . . .

GENDER COMPLEMENTARITY
AS GENDER HIERARCHY?
AN ASSESSMENT

In the patterns described above interaction between male and female elements provides the energy that drives and sustains the creative process. In these narratives cosmogony could not take place without the abiding presence of the feminine, and the roles that females play at different stages of creation are different from but no less essential than those played by males. This emphasis on the necessity of not only the male principle but also the female principle—especially at the "crisis point" in secondary creation when the female temporarily drops out and the process threatens to come to a standstill—might tempt one to see these myths as generally supportive of women in their stance toward gender. These narratives do, in fact, imply that creation is not a uniquely male activity and convey the importance of the female contribution to the cosmogonic process. In this regard the Purāṇic creation narratives detailed above stand in contradistinction to creation narratives like the biblical accounts of creation found in the first two chapters of Genesis, where the participation of a female agent in cosmogony is so remarkably absent.

Ultimately, however, these cosmogonies seem to reflect gender biases in Brahmanical Hinduism that favor the dominance of males over females. These biases have to do with the relative status ascribed to male and female principles and roles during the different stages of cosmogony. The male is consistently portrayed as an autonomous agent that takes charge and directs the process, whereas the female is portrayed as lacking autonomy and submissive to male command. In the descriptions of primary creation detailed above, for example, the ultimate source of creation, Brahman, may be best described as a formless androgyne. Brahman is understood to be *nirguṇa* on the highest level, so Brahman transcends both male and female dimensions. But since this formless Brahman is also understood to be the ultimate identity of an essentially male god—in the Mahā-Purāṇas Śiva, Viṣṇu, or one of the forms of Viṣṇu—how androgynous can Brahman really be? As [Wendy] O'Flaherty has observed, not all androgynes are equal; while there are true mythological androgynes, many are

either primarily male or primarily female. . . . This Purāṇic image of androgyny, which is really a male androgyny, is carried over from earlier Brahmanical scriptures. In her discussion of late Vedic texts, for example, O'Flaherty notes the presence of "the image of the pregnant male, the truly androgynous figure, though it is usually a *male* androgyne . . . Most ancient Indian androgynes are primarily male—men who can have babies as women do. . . . On the other hand, it does not happen that some woman or goddess suddenly finds herself endowed with a phallus or, to her surprise and ours, becomes able to produce children all by herself." . . . In the Mahā-Purāṇas Brahman tends to be this type of male androgyne. Femaleness is portrayed as a power (*śakti*) of the male with no autonomous ontological status. . . .

In telling the story of creation in the ways that they do, Purāṇic cosmogonies suggest notions about how at the time of creation male and female emerged and established patterns of relating to one another; "how things were at the dawn of time," as Smith puts it, and therefore "how they really should be" in the present—whatever that present may be—with respect to the proper dynamics between males and females. Males contain, females are contained; males are active creative agents, females are submissive ones; male seed is the source of new life, the female womb is merely an incubator; males are allied with spiritual processes, females are allied with material—especially sexual—processes. While there is a stress on complementarity of roles in these dynamics—both male and female have a part to play—the ways in which their mutual roles are constructed and the relative status of male and female principles at each stage of creation suggest the dominance of male over female and the primacy of the male contribution to creative processes. Brahmanical values would hold those activities associated in these cosmogonies with male creativity to be allied with "higher" human functions engaging the spiritual faculties, and therefore inherently better than those associated with femaleness, which tend to be allied with material and bodily functions.

Ideology underlying these portrayals of gender in Purāṇic cosmogonies is echoed in notions regarding the biology of conception and reproduction found both in Brahmanical teachings and in popular Hinduism. The Laws of Manu establishes the metaphor of the female as the "field" that acts as passive recipient of the male seed; while both contribute to the process of procreation, the seed is said to be superior (*utkṛṣṭa*), with the offspring of all beings marked with the characteristics of the seed. . . . The likening of a female to a vessel or field and a male to a seed or plower of the field is also fairly common in

Hindu culture, as in other cultures. . . . There is, of course, an ideological agenda here. In commenting upon how this metaphor operates among the Newars of Nepal, Parish notes that "there is a tacit rhetoric here, an implicit ideology that validates patriarchal patterns in the Newar family. The essential qualities of personhood—thought, knowledge, judgment—are constituted by the active male principle of 'seed.' Life and spirit reside in the seed." . . .

The gender ideology detailed above is also mirrored both in social teachings expounded in Brahmanical texts and in the realm of contemporary Hindu culture in notions concerning the complementary relationship of husband and wife. The Laws of Manu, for example, suggests that a woman who marries becomes a part of her husband and takes on his qualities, like a river that merges into an ocean. . . . The ocean, of course, does not mutually flow toward the river. Hence, the married couple, like the cosmogonic male androgyne, represents a complementary balance of male and female, but the female is the lesser of the two and must conform to her male counterpart. In her study of marriage in Bengal, Lina Fruzzetti notes that, when a woman becomes a wife, she becomes encompassed by the male lineage of her husband . . . just as *śakti* is encompassed; in many parts of India when a woman gets married, she loses her separate identity and becomes the "half-body" of her husband. . . . Vanaja Dhruvarajan notes in her study of women's lives in a village in south-central India that a wife refers to her husband as "my lord" or by using the formal third person "they," whereas a husband refers to his wife as "she who is mine" or "she who shares half of my being." . . . While it would be naive, of course, to draw a direct line from Purāṇic cosmogonies to Brahmanical ideology to related dimensions of contemporary Hindu social thought and practice, a similar ideology of gender appears to inform all three.

Such biases are not, of course, unique to the Hindu tradition, although different texts and traditions frame gender ideologies differently in accordance with their own particular emphases. The creation of Eve from Adam's rib in Genesis 2.21–22, for example, echoes the male-as-container, female-as-contained imagery that we find in the Purāṇas. As Rosemary Radford Ruether notes, in the story of Adam's rib the male gives "birth" to the female—the reverse of normal, everyday experience. . . . Lerner notes an emphasis on the male seed as the sole source of life, such as we find in the Hindu tradition, at work in Genesis 15–17, where God blesses Abraham's seed "as though it were self-generating." . . . Aristotle proclaimed a similar understanding of procreation, as Ruether points out, portraying the female womb as "merely the passive incubators of the male seed" that is the real source of life. . . . Ruether also observes that in much of Greek thought male gender is associated with human consciousness and the transcendent realm of spirit, whereas female gender is associated with the body and its passions or appetites. . . . Hence, gender associations at play in Purāṇic cosmogonies and more generally in Hindu culture are not unique but exemplify much more widespread biases.

There are, of course, other ways to tell the story of creation and other ways of portraying gender roles in cosmogony than what we find in the Purāṇas. William Sax has recorded a Garhwali song, for example, that portrays the primary creator as the goddess Ādiśakti, who produces offspring from blood that flows from her womb. . . . Similarly, Ann Gold has recorded a cosmogonic narrative in Rajasthan in which a goddess is accorded pride of place. . . . Accounts of creation narrated in some Tantric texts, such as the Lakṣmī Tantra, also ascribe more independence and active agency to female participants. But this is not the way the Mahā-Purāṇas tend to tell it. While they do not explicitly assert that females should be subordinate to males, Purāṇic cosmogonies like those above imply that in the "order of things" males are in charge. . . .

4.7 DARSAN

Darsan means "to see" and can refer to the act of seeing an image of the divine. However, what is "seen" (understood) when images are seen? Is the image simply an idol? What do the images *mean* to the devotee?

Diana L. Eck, a professor of comparative religion and Indian studies at Harvard University, explores, in the next selection, the meaning of what we might call "sacred seeing." She was first attracted to the study of Hinduism by seeing the arts, images, and landscapes of India. In the preface to the book from which this selection is taken, she indicates that she wrote this "for those who want to 'see' something of India, in the hope that what catches the eye may change our minds."

DIANA L. ECK

Seeing the Divine

READING QUESTIONS

1. Why, according to Eck, is the Hindu use of images not idolatry?
2. How does the ritual use of images help us to understand their meaning to the Hindu?

THE IMAGE OF GOD

The vivid variety of Hindu deities is visible everywhere in India. Rural India is filled with countless wayside shrines. In every town of some size there are many temples, and every major temple will contain its own panoply of shrines and images. One can see the silver mask of the goddess Durgā, or the stone shaft of the Śiva *liṅga*, or the four-armed form of the god Viṣṇu. Over the doorway of a temple or a home sits the plump, orange, elephant-headed Gaṇeśa or the benign and auspicious Lakṣmī. Moreover, it is not only in temples and homes that one sees the images of the deities. Small icons are mounted at the front of taxis and buses. They decorate the walls of tea stalls, sweet shops, tailors, and movie theatres. They are painted on public buildings and homes by local folk artists. They are carried through the streets in great festival processions.

It is visibly apparent to anyone who visits India or who sees something of India through the medium of film that this is a culture in which the mythic imagination has been very generative. The images and myths of the Hindu imagination constitute a basic cultural vocabulary and a common idiom of discourse. Since India has "written" prolifically in its images, learning to read its mythology and iconography is a primary task for the student of Hinduism. In learning about Hinduism, it might be argued that perhaps it makes more sense to begin with Gaṇeśa, the elephant-headed god who sits at the thresholds of space and time and who blesses all

Republished with permission of the Columbia University Press, 562 W 113th St., New York, NY 10025. *Darsan: Seeing the Divine Image in India* (excerpts), Diana L. Eck, Anima Publications, 1981. Reproduced by permission of the publisher via Copyright Clearance Center, Inc. Pp. 12, 14–17, 33–36. Notes omitted.

beginnings, and then proceed through the deities of the Hindu pantheon, rather than to begin with the Indus Valley civilization and proceed through the ages of Hindu history. Certainly for a student who wishes to visit India, the development of a basic iconographic vocabulary is essential, for deities such as the monkey Hanumān or the fierce Kālī confront one at every turn.

When the first European traders and travelers visited India, they were astonished at the multitude of images of the various deities which they saw there. They called them "idols" and described them with combined fascination and repugnance. For example, Ralph Fitch, who traveled as a merchant through north India in the 1500s, writes of the images of deities in Vārāṇasī (Benares): "Their chiefe idols bee blacke and evill favoured, their mouths monstrous, their eares gilded and full of jewels, their teeth and eyes of gold, silver and glasse, some having one thing in their hands and some another."

Fitch had no interpretive categories, save those of a very general Western Christian background, with which to make sense of what he saw. Three hundred years did little to aid interpretation. When M.A. Sherring lived in Benares in the middle of the 1800s he could still write, after studying the city for a long time, of "the worship of uncouth idols, of monsters, of the liṅga and other indecent figures, and of a multitude of grotesque, ill-shapen, and hideous objects." When Mark Twain traveled through India in the last decade of the nineteenth century, he brought a certain imaginative humor to the array of "idols" in Benares, but he remained without what Arnheim would call "manageable models" for placing the visible data of India in a recognizable context. Of the "idols" he wrote, "And what a swarm of them there is! The town is a vast museum of idols—and all of them crude, misshapen, and ugly. They flock through one's dreams at night, a wild mob of nightmares."

Without some interpretation, some visual hermeneutic, icons and images can be alienating rather than enlightening. Instead of being keys to understanding, they can kindle xenophobia and pose barriers to understanding by appearing as a "wild mob of nightmares," utterly foreign to and unassimilable by our minds. To understand India, we need to raise our eyes from the book to the image, but we also need some means of interpreting and comprehending the images we see.

The bafflement of many who first behold the array of Hindu images springs from the deep-rooted Western antagonism to imaging the divine at all. The Hebraic hostility to "graven images" expressed in the Commandments is echoed repeatedly in the Hebrew Bible: "You shall not make for yourself a graven image, or any likeness of anything that is in heaven above, or that is in the earth beneath, or that is in the water under the earth."

The Hebraic resistance to imaging the divine has combined with a certain distrust of the senses in the world of the Greek tradition as well. While the Greeks were famous for their anthropomorphic images of the gods, the prevalent suspicion in the philosophies of classical Greece was that "what the eyes reported was not true." Like those of dim vision in Plato's cave, it was thought that people generally accept the mere shadows of reality as "true." Nevertheless, if dim vision described human perception of the ordinary world, the Greeks continued to use the notion of true vision to describe wisdom, that which is seen directly in the full light of day rather than obliquely in the shadowy light of the cave. Arnheim writes, "The Greeks learned to distrust the senses, but they never forgot that direct vision is the first and final source of wisdom. They refined the techniques of reasoning, but they also believed that, in the words of Aristotle, 'the soul never thinks without an image.'"

On the whole, it would be fair to say that the Western traditions, especially the religious traditions of the "Book"—Judaism, Christianity, and Islam—have trusted the Word more than the Image as a mediator of the divine truth. The Qur'ān and the Hebrew Bible are filled with injunctions to "proclaim" and to "hear" the word. The ears were somehow more trustworthy than the eyes. In the Christian tradition this suspicion of the eyes and the image has been a particularly Protestant position.

And yet the visible image has not been without some force in the religious thinking of the West. The verbal icon of God as "Father" or "King" has had considerable power in shaping the Judeo-Christian religious imagination. The Orthodox Christian traditions, after much debate in the eighth and ninth centuries, granted an important place to the honoring of icons as those "windows" through which one might look toward God. They were careful, however, to say that the icon should not be "realistic" and should be only two-dimensional. In the Catholic tradition as well, the art and iconography, especially of Mary and the saints, has had a long and rich history. And all three traditions of the "Book" have developed the art of embellishing the word into a virtual icon in the elaboration of calligraphic and decorative arts. Finally, it should be said that there is a great diversity within each of these traditions. The Mexican villager who comes on his knees to the Virgin of Guadalupe, leaves a bundle of beans, and lights a candle, would no doubt feel more at home in a Hindu temple than in a stark, white New England Protestant church. Similarly,

the Moroccan Muslim woman who visits the shrines of Muslim saints, would find India less foreign than did the eleventh century Muslim scholar Alberuni, who wrote that "the Hindus entirely differ from us in every respect."

Worshiping as God those "things" which are not God has been despised in the Western traditions as "idolatry," a mere bowing down to "sticks and stones." The difficulty with such a view of idolatry, however, is that anyone who bows down to such things clearly does not understand them to be sticks and stones. No people would identify themselves as "idolators," by faith. Thus, idolatry can be only an outsider's term for the symbols and visual images of some other culture. Theodore Roszak, writing in *Where the Wasteland Ends*, locates the "sin of idolatry" precisely where it belongs: in the eye of the beholder.

In beginning to understand the consciousness of the Hindu worshiper who bows to "sticks and stones," an anecdote of the Indian novelist U. R. Anantha Murthy is provocative. He tells of an artist friend who was studying folk art in rural north India. Looking into one hut, he saw a stone daubed with red *kunkum* powder, and he asked the villager if he might bring the stone outside to photograph it. The villager agreed, and after the artist had photographed the stone he realized that he might have polluted this sacred object by moving it outside. Horrified, he apologized to the villager, who replied, "It doesn't matter. I will have to bring another stone and anoint *kunkum* on it." Anantha Murthy comments, "Any piece of stone on which he put *kunkum* became God for the peasant. What mattered was his faith, not the stone." We might add that, of course, the stone matters too. If it did not, the peasant would not bother with a stone at all.

Unlike the zealous Protestant missionaries of a century ago, we are not much given to the use of the term "idolatry" to condemn what "other people" do. Yet those who misunderstood have still left us with the task of understanding, and they have raised an important and subtle issue in the comparative study of religion: What is the nature of the divine image? Is it considered to be intrinsically sacred? Is it a symbol of the sacred? A mediator of the sacred? How are images made, consecrated, and used, and what does this tell us about the way they are understood? But still another question remains to be addressed before we take up these topics. That is the question of the multitude of images. Why are there so many gods?

The Ritual Uses of the Image

How is the divine image regarded by Hindus? And how is it used in a ritual context? Pursuing these questions is important to our understanding of the nature of the divine image which Hindus "see."

Two principal attitudes may be discerned in the treatment of images. The first is that the image is primarily a focus for concentration, and the second is that the image is the embodiment of the divine.

In the first view, the image is a kind of *yantra*, literally a "device" for harnessing the eye and the mind so that the one-pointedness of thought (*ekāgrata*) which is fundamental to meditation can be attained. The image is a support for meditation. As the *Viṣṇu Saṁhitā*, a ritual *āgama* text, puts it:

Without a form, how can God be mediated upon?
If (He is) without any form, where will the mind
fix itself? When there is nothing for the mind to
attach itself to, it will slip away from meditation
or will glide into a state of slumber. Therefore the
wise will meditate on some form, remembering,
however, that the form is a superimposition and
not a reality.

The Jābāla Upaniṣad goes even a step further, intimating that such an image, while it may be a support for the beginner, is of absolutely no use to the yogi. "Yogins see Śiva in the soul and not in images. Images are meant for the imagination of the ignorant."

It is the second attitude toward images that most concerns us in the context of this essay. That is, that the image is the real embodiment of the deity. It is not just a device for the focusing of human vision, but is charged with the presence of the god. This stance toward images emerged primarily from the devotional *bhakti* movement, which cherished the personal Lord "with qualities" (*saguṇa*) and which saw the image as one of the many ways in which the Lord becomes accessible to men and women, evoking their affections.

In the early theistic traditions of the Bhāgavatas or Pāñcarātras, who emphasized devotional worship (*pūjā*) rather than the Vedic sacrifice (*yajña*), the image was considered to be one of the five forms of the Lord. The five are the Supreme form (*para*), the emanations or powers of the Supreme (*vyūha*), the immanence of the Supreme in the heart of the individual and in the heart of the universe (*antaryāmin*), the incarnations of the Supreme (*vibhava*), and, finally, the presence of the Supreme Lord in a properly consecrated image (*arcā*). Later, the Śrī Vaiṣṇavas used the term *arcāvatāra* to re-

fer to the "image-incarnation" of the Lord: the form Viṣṇu graciously takes so that he may be worshiped by his devotees. Indeed, the very theology of the Śrī Vaiṣṇava community, as articulated by Rāmānuja in the 11th century, is based on the faith that the Lord is characterized both by his utter Supremacy (*paratva*) and his gracious Accessibility (*saulabhya*).

God has become accessible not only in incarnations, but also in images. In the *Bhagavad Gītā* (4.11), Kṛṣṇa tells Arjuna, "In whatever way people approach me, in that way do I show them favor." The word *bhajāmi* translated here as "I show favor," is from the same root as *bhakti*. It could equally be translated "in that way do I love them," or "in that way do I share myself with them." Rāmānuja, in commenting on this passage, says that it means "in that way do I make myself visible (*darśayāmi*) to them." He goes on to comment, "God does not only rescue those, who resort to him in the shape of one of his *avatāras*, by descending into that shape alone, but He reveals himself to all who resort to him, whatever the shape in which they represent him."

Following Rāmānuja, another theologian of the Śrī Vaiṣṇava movement, Piḷḷai Lokācārya, writes of the grace by which the Lord enters and dwells in the image for the sake of the devotee:

This is the greatest grace of the Lord, that being
free He becomes bound, being independent He
becomes dependent for all His service on His
devotee. . . . In other forms the man belonged to
God but behold the supreme sacrifice of Isvara,
here the Almighty becomes the property of the
devotee. . . . He carries Him about, fans Him, feeds
Him, plays with Him—yea, the Infinite has become
finite, that the child soul may grasp, understand and
love Him."

The image, which may be seen, bathed, adorned, touched, and honored does not stand *between* the worshiper and the Lord, somehow receiving the honor properly due to the Supreme Lord. Rather, because the image is a form of the Supreme Lord, it is precisely the image that facilitates and enhances the close relationship of the worshiper and God and makes possible the deepest outpouring of emotions in worship.

In observing Hindu worship, in the home or in the temple, many Western students are baffled by the sense in which it appears to be an elaborate form of "playing house" with God. The image is wakened in the morning, honored with incense and song, dressed, and fed. Throughout the day, other such rites appropriate to the time of day are performed until, finally, the deity is put to bed in the evening.

How is one to honor God? What human acts and gestures most directly convey the devotion of *bhakti*? For Hindus and for people of many religious traditions, they are the gestures of humility, with which a servant approaches his master, or a host his guest—gestures such as bowing, kneeling, prostrating, and, in the Hindu world, touching the feet of a revered superior. In addition to such servant-master gestures, however, the Hindus utilize the entire range of intimate and ordinary domestic acts as an important part of ritual. These are common, affectionate activities, family activities, which are symbolically powerful because of their very simplicity and their domestic nature: cooking, eating, serving, washing, dressing, waking, and putting to sleep. These are precisely the acts which ordinary people have most carefully refined through daily practice with loved ones in the home. In summary, Hindu worship reveals not only an attitude of honor but also an attitude of affection in the range of ritual act and gesture utilized in the treatment of the image.

The general term for rites of worship and honor is *pūjā*. The simple lay rites of making offerings of flowers and water, and receiving both *darśan*, the "sight" of the deity, and *prasād*, the sanctified food offerings, may be called *pūjā*. More specifically, however, *pūjā* consists of elaborate forms of worship performed in the home by the householder and in the temple by special priests called *pūjārīs* who are designated for that purpose. These rites involved the presentation of a number of articles of worship, called *upacāras*, "honor offerings," to the deity. The number of *upacāras* presented may vary, but sixteen is considered a proper number for a complete *pūjā*. The *upacāras* include food, water, fresh leaves, sandalwood perfume, incense, betel nuts, and cloth. They are the type of hospitality offerings with which one would honor a guest, or a revered elder, or a king. In addition to such tangible offerings, the waving of the fan and the fly-whisk are considered *upacāras*, since they are pleasing to the deity, and the rite of circumambulation is an *upacāra*, since it shows honor to the deity.

An important *upacāra* is the honoring of the deity with light. The priest or the householder slowly circles a five-wicked oil lamp or camphor lamp before the deity, often to the accompaniment of the ringing of handbells and the singing of hymns. This lamp-offering is called *āratī*, and the rite is so central to Hindu worship that *arati* has become the common general name for the daily rites of honoring the deity, often replacing the term *pūjā* completely. In a temple there will ordinarily be several *āratīs* during the day and into the evening....

PRONUNCIATION GUIDE

Vowels

1. *e, ai, o,* and *au* are long and are pronounced as in *gray, aisle, open,* and *cow*.
2. *ā, ī, ū,* with lines over them (macrons) are long and are pronounced as in *father, machine,* and *rude*.
3. The same vowels without macrons are short as in *but, tin,* and *full*.
4. *ṛ* is sounded as in *rill* and is lightly trilled.

Consonants

5. *c* as in *church, j* as in *jungle, ṣ* as in *ship, ś* as in *sun,* and *jn* as in *gyana*.
6. Aspirated consonants should be pronounced distinctly: thus, *bh* as in *caB-House, dh* as in *maD-House, gh* as in *doG-House, jh* as in *fudGE-House, kh* as in *rocK-House, ph* as in *toP-Hat,* and *th* as in *goaT-Herd*.

Accent

7. Words of two syllables are accented on the first syllable: *VEda*.
8. Words of more than two syllables are accented on the penult (second syllable from end) when the penult is long or has a short vowel followed by two or more consonants: *veDANta*.
9. Words of more than two syllables are accented on the antepenult (third syllable from the end) in cases where the penult is short and *not* followed by two consonants: *UpaniSHAD*.

KEY TERMS AND CONCEPTS

Advaita Vedanta Nondualistic interpretation of the books at the end of the **Vedas** called the **Upanishads**. Shankara was a leading exponent of this philosophy/theology.

agni Primordial fire of creation. Also a god.

ahimsa Nonviolence or noninjury.

atman Usually translated as Self or Soul if referring to the universal Self or as self (soul) if referring to the individual.

audience cults Religious groups consisting primarily of people who temporarily assemble to hear teachings.

avatara Incarnations or appearances of the divine in material forms.

avidya Ignorance.

Bhagavad Gita *The Song of God,* known in India as *Gita.* It is about Krishna's advice to Arjuna on how to avoid *karma.* Part of the epic poem *Mahabharata.*

bhakti Devotion to the divine.

Brahma The creator god.

Brahman Usually used to refer to absolute or ultimate reality.

brahmin A priest or priestly class.

caste (*jatis*) A grouping of people according to birth. Castes usually have no social mobility.

chakra Literally "wheel." In Tantric Buddhism, refers to centers of energy within the human body.

class In classical India, a grouping of people according to occupation. In India classes are called *varnas* and there are four main groups: **brahmins** (priests), **kshatriyas** (warriors or kings), **vaishyas** (merchants), and **shudras** (laborers). These classes are assigned specific duties, are arranged hierarchically, and within each are various castes (*jatis*).

client cults Groups of people who go to religious practitioners for various specific services such as therapy or spiritual advice.

dharma Can mean law, teaching, and duty. Sometimes translated as "religion."

Durga A warrior goddess.

four stages of life (*ashramas*) Student, householder, forest recluse or hermit, wandering ascetic. These four stages present an ideal picture of human spiritual development.

Ganesha The elephant-headed god.

guru A religious teacher often thought to be a representative if not a manifestation of the divine or, at least, a perfected soul.

Hanuman The monkey god.

jnana In general, means knowledge and is usually contrasted with ignorance (*avidya*). Hence it is one important key to liberation (*moksha*).

Kali Known as the Black Goddess and usually identified with **Durga.** She has both fierce and gentle aspects.

karma Means action or the law of action, viz., that every act produces a result. Usually tied to the idea of reincarnation or rebirth. The *karma* accumulated in this life determines one's birth in the next life.

Krishna Incarnation of the god **Vishnu.** See *Bhagavad Gita.* A devotee of Krishna is called a Vaishnava.

kundalini A latent power to be awakened in the practice of *kundaliniyoga.*

laws of Manu (**Manu Dharma Shastra**) A law book attributed to the ancestor of the human race, Manu, detailing the rules and duties for each *varna,* or class.

mantra Sacred sounds recited in worship and meditation. The most famous mantra is "OM."

moksha Release or liberation from suffering, ignorance, and the seemingly endless round of reincarnation, or *samsara.*

nadi A system of channels connecting the various *chakras* through which *kundalini* is to travel.

orthodox/heterodox Literally, "correct" or "right" teaching in contrast to "other than correct" teaching. In Hinduism, orthodoxy is determined by acknowledging the authority of the **Vedas.**

Patanjali Alleged author of the *Yoga Sutra,* which is a manual for yogic instruction.

puja Service or worship by personally attending the image of a god or goddess.

purusha/prakriti Usually translated as "consciousness" and "material nature," respectively. These concepts play a major role in *Sankhya* philosophy whose goal is to help people recognize the radical difference between spirit and matter.

qualified nondualism A rival of Shankara's interpretation of the **Upanishads** taught by Ramanuja. It claims that while individual souls and the material universe are attributes or qualities of the single substance **Brahman,** they are not identical to it.

Rama An incarnation of the divine whose exploits are recounted in the epic *Ramayana.*

Ravana The great demon of the *Ramayana* who kidnaps **Sita** and is killed by **Rama.**

rishi A visionary or seer who "saw" or "heard" the truths recorded in the **Vedas.**

samsara A word used for the world of change and rebirth.

sarvodaya A word used by Gandhi to refer to our obligation to increase the welfare of all people.

satyagraha Gandhi's principle of holding to the truth.

shakta Derived from *shakti* meaning creative energy or power and a general designation for the goddess.

Shaivas Devotees of the god *Shiva.*

Shiva The divine power of destruction that makes way for new life.

shruti Literally that which is heard. Sometimes translated as "revelation" and used to refer to *Vedas.*

Sita The wife of **Rama** who is presented as the ideal

wife in the *Ramayana* and must be rescued by **Rama** from the demon **Ravana.**

smriti Usually translated as "tradition" or "memory." It refers to all religiously authoritative writings that are not *shruti* such as **laws of Manu.**

soma A god and a drink (probably hallucinogenic) used in Vedic times.

Tantras A group of writings setting forth the ideas of Tantrism, a religious movement critical of the priestly dominated traditions.

trimurti The name for the three forms of the divine: **Brahma** the creator, **Vishnu** the preserver, and **Shiva** the destroyer/renewer.

Upanishads A collection of writings at the end of the *Vedas* recording philosophical ideas about the nature of the divine, human beings, and immortality.

Vedas A collection of writings considered **shruti,** consisting of hymns, sacrificial texts, and philosophical texts.

vidya Knowledge.

Vishnu A Hindu god who sustains the universe and appears as an *avatar* (incarnation) such as **Rama** and **Krishna** from time to time to save the world.

yoga Usually used to refer to a spiritual discipline leading to **moksha** such as *bhaktiyoga, jnanayoga, karmayoga,* and the like.

SUGGESTIONS FOR FURTHER READING

Basham, A. L. *The Wonder That Was India.* London: Sidgwick & Jackson, 1954, 3rd rev. ed. 1967; New York: Taplinger, 1968; London: Fontana, 1971. A classic study still widely cited as an authoritative historical study of Indian culture and civilization.

De Bary, W. T., et al., ed. *Sources of Indian Tradition.* New York: Columbia University Press, 1958, repr. 1969. An excellent collection of important and representative source material with introductions.

Flood, Gavin. *An Introduction to Hinduism.* New York: Cambridge University Press, 1996. An overview of Hinduism, utilizing the latest research, that is both clearly written and well organized.

Fuller, C. J. *The Camphor Flame: Popular Hinduism and Society in India.* Princeton: Princeton University Press, 1992. A very good introduction to Hinduism taking into account recent scholarship with a useful annotated bibliography.

Klostermaier, Klaus K. *A Survey of Hinduism.* 2nd ed. Albany: State University of New York Press, 1994. A topical approach that emphasizes the diversity of the Hindu tradition.

O'Flaherty, W. E. ed. *Hindu Myths: A Sourcebook: Translated from the Sanskrit.* Harmondsworth, England: Penguin, 1975. Mythological source materials arranged by topics in a very readable translation.

Shattuck, Cybelle. *Hinduism.* Upper Saddle River, N.J.: Prentice-Hall, 1999. This little book presents a clear and accurate historical survey including a list of holy days and festivals along with a peek at the possible future of Hinduism in the modern world.

RESEARCH PROJECTS

1. If there is a Hindu temple near you, visit it and speak with the priest about the temple and its activities. Write a report on your visit for the class.

2. View the video *Gandhi* and write down your observations on how religion influenced Gandhi's political career.

3. Collect or make some slides of Indian art and/or some recordings of Indian music. Present them to the class, and describe their religious symbolism. (Mira's songs are available by M. S. Subbalaxmi, *Meera Bhajans,* serial number EALP 1297 [Dum Dum: Gramophone Company of India, 1965]. Also, over ten films have been made about her life —see Kusum Gokarn, "Popularity of Devotional Films [Hindi]," *National Film Archive of India Research Project* 689/5/84.)

4. Many Indian "comic books" are about religious heroes, saints, and gods. See if you can locate some of these, analyze their religious message, and share them with the class.

5. Gather news accounts of the clashes between Hindus and Muslims at Rama's birthplace that resulted in the destruction of the Babri Masjid in 1992. Indicate, in a written report, the sequence of events and the role traditional religious symbolism played in the events. A brief summary can be found in Shattuck's *Hinduism,* pp. 97–101.

5

Buddhist Ways of Being Religious

INTRODUCTION

Are most people you know happy and content? Have you been emotionally upset or hurt in a deep way? Have you experienced the death of loved one's or seen people suffer from disease? What is suffering and what causes it? Why is there so much suffering in life? Would it not be good to live without suffering? Are we hopelessly trapped in a world of suffering?

If you have thought about these questions and wondered about the answers, you have been concerned about some of the same questions that pressed themselves on an Indian prince named Siddhartha **Gautama** 2,500 years ago. Siddhartha became so deeply concerned about the suffering that characterizes so much of life that he devoted his life to finding out the causes of suffering and how suffering might be overcome and helping others to find release from suffering. When he found the answers he became known as a **Buddha,** that is, as someone who has gained enlightenment. To this day, millions of people all over the world still listen to his teachings and follow the practices that he and his followers recommended in the hope that they too might learn how to live happy and contented lives.

For 2,500 years, there has existed a complex and bewildering variety of beliefs, practices, rituals, arts, philosophies, sects, cults, politics, gods, goddesses, demons, saints, buddhas, cultures, and more associated with Siddhartha, the Buddha of this age. When Westerners first began traveling to Asian countries like Sri Lanka, China, Korea, Thailand, Tibet, and Japan, they observed this wonderful variety and richness. At first it was just thought of as a kind of "Orientalism"—an idea invented by Europeans to refer rather vaguely to an Asian cultural mix of exotic creatures, romance, strange religions, and remarkable experiences. Eventually, about 300 years ago, Western

scholars settled on the term *Buddhism* in order to distinguish what they saw in some Asian countries from what they encountered in India.

What is it that is being named by the term *Buddhism?* Is it a religion? If religion must involve a belief in the divine, then some of what is called Buddhism might count and some might not because, for some Buddhists, divinities of one kind or another play an important role in their stories and practices and for other Buddhists the divine is essentially unimportant when it comes to understanding life, suffering, and the way to overcome suffering. Is Buddhism a culture? It certainly has inspired great cultural achievements in politics, language, art, literature, philosophy, and architecture. However, it clearly is not a single culture since it has equally inspired the lavish ornamentalism of the Tibetan tradition and the austere simplicity of Japanese Zen.

The recent academic study of Buddhism tends to treat it as a "total social phenomenon" to use the words of Stanley Tambiah, an anthropologist. Buddhism is a name for a religion (if it names religion at all) and much more. Space does not permit introducing Buddhism as a political, artistic, economic, cultural, and social phenomenon here. Since our concern is primarily with religious traditions, we will focus on the more typically religious aspects of Buddhism. However, we need to remind ourselves that Buddhism is much more than a religion. It is, in the fullest sense, a way of life.

5.1 AN OVERVIEW

It is uncertain precisely when Prince Siddhartha, the Sage of the Sakya Clan (**Sakyamuni**) lived. Western and Indian scholars suggest either 566–486 B.C.E. or 563–483 B.C.E., whereas Sri Lankan and Southeast

Asian Buddhists believe he lived earlier, around 624–544 B.C.E. Japanese scholars, using Chinese and Tibetan texts, put the dates at 448–368 B.C.E.

Although there is disagreement about precisely when the Buddha lived, there is little disagreement about where he lived. He lived in a region of the Ganges river basin in northeastern India. A great civilization had existed in this region starting around 2000 B.C.E. However, around 1500 B.C.E. it was replaced by nomadic peoples probably migrating from eastern Turkey, northern Iran, and southern Russia. Their religion centered on the myths, gods, and sacrifices described in the *Vedas* (see chapter 4).

Central to this Vedic religion was a Brahmin, or priestly, caste. Many Brahmins hoped to attain immortality by studying the *Vedas,* performing sacrifices, and living in accord with a priestly code of duties, or **dharmas.** During the seventh and sixth centuries B.C.E., the region where the Buddha lived underwent political, economic, and cultural transformation. Small kingdoms and clan-based communities were united into four large kingdoms, economy and trade flourished, a banking and money system was begun (perhaps the first in world history), populations grew and settled in large cities, and many in the priestly and warrior classes became very rich. While some Brahmins enjoyed the worldly fruits of these changes, others felt them to be spiritually corrupting.

Along with the prosperity came spiritual discontent. Religious camps were set up along the Ganges where spiritual teachers discussed religious and philosophical questions with interested students. *Samanas,* wandering priests and philosophers, dissatisfied with Vedic practices and ideas, expounded and debated a variety of views in such camps. Many came to believe that renouncing violence was the only way to attain lasting peace and happiness. Violence and the suffering associated with it were such a pronounced feature of everyday life that one could not even go to worship without seeing bloody sacrifices of animals. Surely violent sacrifice was not the way to alleviate suffering. All it did was to increase suffering.

One of the major *samana* groups was the Jains, led by Vardhamana the Mahavira, or Great Hero. Mahavira taught that all things are alive, each containing a *jiva*, or life principle. The goal of human life and hence the goal of Jainism, the religion he founded, is to liberate the *jiva* from the round of rebirths by destroying the results of previous **karma** (actions or deeds) through the practice of such austerities as fasting, going unwashed, pulling out one's hair, practic-

ing self-restraint, and vegetarianism. Most important of all is to live a life of complete nonviolence, or *ahimsa,* so that new, bad *karma* will not be created. Jainism today still teaches nonviolence, an idea that has profound political consequences in the hands of such leaders as Mohandas (Mahatma) Gandhi in India and Martin Luther King Jr. in the United States.

In origin, Buddhism is another one of these *samana* groups. While Prince Siddhartha found the Jain emphasis on nonviolence laudable, he opposed its asceticism as too extreme. He also did not think that there are individually distinct *jivas* or souls, that pass from one life to the next until released from the round of reincarnation (although he did believe in rebirth and karmic continuity). Nevertheless, he did come to believe, with many other *samanas* of his day, that a life of luxury, lavish consumption, meat eating, and bloody sacrifices to gods was spiritually corrupting.

In the following selection, Donald S. Lopez Jr., who is a professor of Buddhist and Tibetan studies at the University of Michigan, introduces us to the Buddha, the Buddha's teachings, and the community he founded. The foreign words will seem strange at first but, after a while, will seem less strange. You can refer to the Pronunciation Guide for Sanskrit in chapter 4 since many of these words are either Sanskrit or Pali (a language closely associated with Sanskrit). The Key Terms and Concepts at the end of this chapter will also provide a quick and convenient reference.

DONALD S. LOPEZ JR.

Buddhism: An Overview

READING QUESTIONS

1. As you read, make a list of all the words and ideas you do not understand or are uncertain about. Discuss them with a classmate, look them up in a dictionary, or bring them up in class for discussion and clarification.
2. What is the point of the story about Siddhartha's early life before enlightenment?

From the "Introduction" to *Buddhism in Practice,* edited by Donald S. Lopez Jr. (Princeton, N.J.: Princeton University Press, 1995), pp. 16–35. Copyright © 1995 Princeton University Press. Reprinted by permission of Princeton University Press.

3. What does the word *noble* signify in the phrase "the Four Noble Truths"?
4. Explain each of the Four Noble Truths in your own words.
5. What is one factor that accounts for the variety of practices described as "Buddhist"?
6. What is a **stupa**, and what role does it, along with icons, play in Buddhism?
7. What is the three-body doctrine, and why is it important?
8. What impact has the "absence" of the Buddha had on the development of Buddhist practice and teaching?
9. How did the goal of the religious life shift from the early tradition to the Mahayana, and how did this affect the length of time it took to become enlightened as well as the concept of the *bodhisattva*?
10. What are the two kinds of "tantric **sadhanas**"?
11. What is the meaning of *dharma*?
12. What were some of the objections of the Hinayana tradition to the Mahayana, and how did the doctrine of skillful means figure in this debate?
13. What role have texts played in the development of Buddhism?
14. What is the *sangha* and **vinaya?**
15. Why do you think there are different rules for monks and nuns?

THE BUDDHA

Scholars are increasingly reluctant to make unqualified claims about the historical facts of the Buddha's life and teachings. There is even a difference of opinion concerning the years of his birth and death. The long accepted dates of 563–483 B.C.E. have recently been called into question with the suggestion that the Buddha may have lived and died as much as a century later.

The traditional accounts of the Buddha's life are largely hagiographic and tend to include the following narrative. It tells of the miraculous birth of a prince of the warrior (*kṣatriya*) caste in a kingdom in what is today southern Nepal. Astrologers predict that the prince, named Siddhārtha ("He Who Achieves His Goal") will be either a great king or a great religious teacher. His father the king, apparently convinced that dissatisfaction with the world is what causes one's mind to turn to existential questions and the spiritual quest, is determined to protect his son from all that is unpleasant, and keeps him in a palace where he is surrounded by beauty and all forms of sport and delight. Only at the age of twenty-nine does the prince become sufficiently curious about the world beyond the palace walls to venture forth on four chariot rides. During the first he sees an old person for the first time in his life, and is informed by his charioteer that this is not the only old man in the world, but

that old age eventually befalls everyone. On the next tour he sees a sick person, on the next a corpse. It is only then that he learns of the existence of sickness and death. On his final chariot ride he sees a religious mendicant, who has renounced the world in search of freedom from birth and death. He decides to follow a similar path and, against his father's orders and leaving behind his wife and infant son, goes forth from the life of a householder in search of liberation from suffering.

Over a period of six years he engages in a number of the yogic disciplines current in India at the time, including severe asceticism, and concludes that mortification of the flesh is not conducive to progress toward his goal of freedom from birth, aging, sickness, and death. He eventually sits beneath a tree and meditates all night. After repulsing an attack by the evil deity Māra and his armies, at dawn he comes to a realization that makes him the Buddha ("Awakened One"), forever free from future rebirth. Exactly what it was that he understood on that full-moon night has remained a source of both inspiration and contention throughout the history of Buddhism. Some accounts say that the content of the enlightenment was so profound that the Buddha was initially reluctant to try to teach it to others, and decided otherwise only after being beseeched by the great god Brahmā, himself subject to rebirth and hence desirous of liberation. . . .

The Buddha was one of an infinite series of buddhas, all of whom reached their exalted state in the same manner, at exactly the same spot in India under one or another species of bodhi tree. When the Buddha gained enlightenment (*bodhi*), he did so all at once, in an instant, and his realization of the truth was perfect. He also made his momentous discovery by himself, without the aid of a teacher. It was this fact above all that distinguished the Buddha from his enlightened disciples, called *arhats*, in the early tradition. The disciples had to rely on his teachings to realize nirvāṇa, and typically did so only in stages. The Buddha was able to reach his enlightenment on his own and in a single night of meditation because he had previously devoted himself to the practice of virtues such as generosity, patience, and effort over countless previous lifetimes. In one of his previous lives, in the presence of a previous buddha, he had made the firm resolution to become a buddha himself at a future time when the path to liberation had been lost; he had dedicated his practice of virtue over the next eons of rebirth to that goal.

Seven weeks after his enlightenment, the Buddha is said to have walked to the city of Varanasi (Banaras) and to a deer park on its outskirts, where he encountered five renunciates with whom he had previously practiced asceticism. To them he gave his first teaching, usually referred to as the "four noble truths." However, it is not the truths that are noble. The term is perhaps less euphoniously but more accurately rendered as the "four truths for nobles." The term "noble" or "superior" in Sanskrit is *āryan*, the term with which the Indo-European invaders of India had described themselves and which Buddhism appropriated to mean one who is spiritually superior, that is, who has had a vision of a state beyond birth and death. The four things that the Buddha set forth to the five ascetics are known to be true by such people, not by others. Although some Mahāyāna texts dispute that this was the Buddha's very first teaching after his enlightenment, all agree that the teaching of the four truths was of great importance. Over the centuries it has received numerous renditions, the general contours of which follow.

The first truth is that life is inherently unsatisfactory, qualified as it inevitably is by birth, aging, sickness, and death. Various forms of suffering are delineated in Buddhist texts, including the fact that beings must separate from friends and meet with enemies, that they encounter what they do not want, and do not find what they want. The fundamental problem is presented as one of a lack of control over future events; a person wanders constantly from situation to situation, from rebirth to rebirth without companions, discarding one body to take on another, with no certainty or satisfaction, sometimes exalted and sometimes debased. Briefly stated, the problem is change or, as more commonly rendered, impermanence (*anitya*). Because suffering can occur at any moment without warning, even pleasure is in a sense a form of pain, because it will eventually be replaced by pain; there is no activity in which one can engage that will not, in the short or long term, become either physically or mentally painful.

The second truth is the cause of this suffering, identified as action (*karma*), specifically nonvirtuous action, and the negative mental states that motivate such action. As described above, the experience of pleasure and pain is the direct result of actions performed in the past. These actions are motivated by states of mind called *kleśas* (often translated as "afflictions" or "defilements"), the most important of which are desire, hatred, and ignorance. The exact content of this ignorance is again the subject of extensive discussion in Buddhist literature, but it is represented as an active misconception of the nature of reality, usually described as a belief in self (*ātman*). There is, in fact, no permanent and autonomous self in the mind or the body, and to believe otherwise is the root cause of all suffering. It is this imagined self that is inflamed by desire and defended by hatred. As long as one believes in the illusion of self, one will continue to engage in deeds and accumulate karma, and will remain

in the cycle of rebirth. This belief in self, in short, is not merely a philosophical problem, but is the cause of the egotism and selfishness that harm others now and oneself in the future through the negative karma they create. . . .

The third truth is the truth of cessation, the postulation of a state beyond suffering. If suffering is caused by negative karma, and karma is caused by desire and hatred, and desire and hatred are caused by ignorance, it follows that if one could destroy ignorance then everything caused by ignorance, directly or indirectly, would also be destroyed. There would be a cessation of suffering. This state of cessation is called *nirvāṇa* ("passing away") and, again, a remarkable range of opinion has been expressed concerning the precise nature of this state beyond suffering—whether it is the cessation also of mind and body or whether the person persists in nirvāṇa.

The postulation of a state beyond suffering would be of little interest if there were not some means to achieve it. The fourth truth, then, is the path, the technique for putting an end to ignorance. Diverse renditions of this path are represented. . . . One useful way to approach the topic is through the traditional triad of ethics, meditation, and wisdom. Ethics refers to the conscious restraint of nonvirtuous deeds of body and speech, usually through observing some form of vows. Meditation (*dhyāna*), in this context, refers to developing a sufficient level of concentration (through a wide variety of techniques) to make the mind a suitable tool for breaking through the illusion of self to the vision of nirvāṇa. Wisdom is insight, at a deep level of concentration, into the fact that there is no self. Such wisdom is said not only to prevent the accumulation of future karma but eventually to destroy all past karma so that upon death one is not reborn but passes into nirvāṇa. A person who has achieved that state is called an *arhat* ("worthy one"). Two paths to becoming an arhat were set forth. The first was that of the *śrāvaka* ("listener"), who hears the Buddha's teachings and then puts them into practice The second was the *pratyekabuddha* ("privately awakened one") who becomes an arhat in solitude.

It is important to reiterate that although many Buddhists throughout history have known the teaching of the four truths in more or less detail, not very many have actively set out to destroy the ignorance of self and achieve nirvāṇa through the practice of meditation. Lay people tended to see this as the business of monks, and most monks tended to see it as the business of the relatively few among them who seriously practiced meditation. Even for such monks, the practice of meditation should be understood as a ritual act in a ritual setting. . . .

If the Buddha taught the four truths, he also must have taught many other things over the course of the four decades that followed his enlightenment. He is renowned for his ability to teach what was appropriate for a particular person, for adapting his message to the situation. Indeed, in the more spectacular descriptions of his pedagogical powers it was said that the Buddha could sit before an audience and simply utter the letter *a* and each person in the audience would hear a discourse designed specifically to meet his or her needs and capacities, in his or her native language. What he taught was represented as a truth that he had not invented but discovered, a truth that had been discovered by other buddhas in the past and would be discovered by buddhas in the future. Importantly, this truth, whatever it may be, was portrayed as something that could be taught, that could be passed on from one person to another, in a variety of languages. It is in this sense that we may speak of a Buddhist tradition. At the same time, the emphasis on the flexibility of the Buddha's teaching helps to account for the remarkable range of practices described as "Buddhist."

According to traditional accounts, at the age of eighty the Buddha died, or passed into nirvāṇa. He is said to have instructed his followers to cremate his body and distribute the relics that remained among various groups of his followers, who were to enshrine them in hemispherical reliquaries called stūpas. For all Buddhist schools, the stūpa became a reference point denoting the Buddha's presence in the landscape. Early texts and the archeological records link stūpa worship with the Buddha's life and especially the key sites in his career, such as the site of his birth, enlightenment, first teaching, and death. A standard list of eight shrines is recommended for pilgrimage and veneration. However, stūpas are also found at places that were sacred for other reasons, often associated with a local deity. Stūpas were constructed for past buddhas and for prominent disciples of the Buddha. Indeed, . . . stūpas dedicated to disciples of the Buddha may have been especially popular because the monastic rules stipulate that donations to such stūpas became the property of the monastery, whereas donations to stūpas of the Buddha remained the property of the Buddha, who continued to function as a legal resident of most monasteries in what was called "the perfumed chamber."

The Mahāyāna stūpa later became a symbol of buddhahood's omnipresence, a center of text revelation, a place guaranteeing rebirth in a pure land. By the seventh century, the practice of enshrining the physical relics of the Buddha ceases to appear in the archaeological record. Instead, one finds stūpas filled with small clay tablets that have been stamped or engraved with a four-line verse that was regarded as the essence of the Buddha's teaching: "The Tathāgata has explained the cause of all things that arise from a cause. The great renunciate has

also explained their cessation." Although this pithy statement is subject to wide interpretation, we can see here an intimation of the four truths: the Buddha has identified that suffering arises from the cause of ignorance and he has also identified nirvāṇa, the cessation of suffering. It is said that the wisest of the disciples, Śāriputra, decided to become the Buddha's follower upon simply hearing these words spoken by a monk, in the absence of the Buddha. But of perhaps greater importance in this context is the fact that this statement functions as a slogan, a mantra, and as a substitute for the relics of the Buddha to be enshrined in a stūpa. The teaching has become the teacher. . . .

Stūpas were pivotal in the social history of Buddhism: these monuments became magnets attracting monastery building and votive construction, as well as local ritual traditions and regional pilgrimage. The economics of Buddhist devotionalism at these centers generated income for local monasteries, artisans, and merchants, an alliance basic to Buddhism throughout its history. At these geographical centers arrayed around the symbolic monument, diverse devotional exertions, textual studies, and devotees' mercantile pursuits could all prosper. The great stūpa complexes—monasteries with endowed lands, a pilgrimage center, a market, and support from the state—represent central points in the Buddhist polities of Central, South, and Southeast Asia. . . .

The Buddha was also worshiped in paintings and statues. The production and worship of Buddhist icons —whether images of buddhas such as Śākyamuni and Amitābha, or bodhisattvas such as Avalokiteśvara and Maitreya—has been a central feature of Buddhist religious life throughout Asian history. . . . The worship of Buddhist icons was promoted by sūtras, and sponsoring the production of an icon was considered an act of great merit, as was bathing an image, a practice that continues in Southeast Asia, China, and Japan. A common goal of both devotional and ascetic Buddhist practice was to recollect the good qualities of the Buddha, which sometimes led to seeing the Buddha "face to face." Images of the Buddha seem to have been important aids in such practices, in part because, far from being a "symbol" of the departed master, images of the Buddha were ritually animated in consecration ceremonies intended to transform an inanimate image into a living deity. . . . Icons thus empowered were treated as spiritual beings possessed of magical powers, to be worshiped with regular offerings of incense, flowers, food, money, and other associated valuables. Buddhist literature from all over Asia is replete with tales of miraculous occurrences associated with such images.

The Buddha was thus the object of elaborate ritual devotions, often accompanied by recitations of his myriad

virtues and powers. . . . These devotions were later incorporated into a larger liturgy that included the visualization of vast offerings and the confession of misdeeds.
. . . But not all buddhas were so extraordinary. Indeed,
the Japanese Zen master Dōgen went to some lengths to
explain why the extraordinary telepathic powers that
were supposedly a standard byproduct of enlightenment
were not necessarily possessed by enlightened Zen masters in China. The true Zen master is utterly beyond all
such categories of Buddhist doctrine. . . .

The question arose early as to the object of devotion
in the universal practice of taking refuge in the three
jewels: the Buddha, the dharma, and the sangha. In some
formulations, the Buddha was regarded as having a physical body that was the result of past karma; it consisted
of his contaminated aggregates (skandha), the final resi-
due of the ignorance that had bound him in samsāra until his last lifetime. Because that body was the product
of ignorance and subject to disintegration, it was not
considered suitable as an object of veneration, as the
Buddha-jewel. The Buddha was at the same time said to
possess certain qualities (also called dharma) that are uncontaminated by ignorance, such as his pure ethics, his
deep concentration, his wisdom, his knowledge that he
has destroyed all afflictions, and his knowledge that the
afflictions will not recur. The qualities were later categorized as the eighteen unshared qualities of a buddha's uncontaminated wisdom. . . . This "body of [uncontami-
nated] qualities" was deemed the true object of the
practice of refuge. Thus, the term "body" came to shift
its meaning from the physical form of the Buddha, corporeal extension in space and over time, to a collection
of timeless abstract virtues. In addition, the early community had to account for those fantastic elements in the
Buddha's hagiography such as his visit to his mother, who
had died shortly after his birth and been reborn in the
Heaven of the Thirty-Three. The Buddha is said to have
made use of a "mind-made body" for his celestial journey. These notions were later systematized into a three-
body theory encompassing the physical body (rūpakāya),
the body of uncontaminated qualities (dharmakāya), and
the mind-made or emanation body (nirmāṇakāya).

In Mahāyāna literature also there is a doctrine of the
three bodies of the Buddha. There we find references
to the dharmakāya as almost a cosmic principle, an ultimate reality in which all buddhas partake through their
omniscient minds. After the dharmakāya comes the enjoyment body (saṃbhogakāya), a fantastic form of a buddha that resides only in the highest pure lands, adorned
with thirty-two major and eighty minor physical marks,
eternally teaching the Mahāyāna to highly advanced bodhisattvas; the enjoyment body does not appear to ordinary beings. The third body is the emanation body

(nirmāṇakāya). It is this body that appears in the world
to teach the dharma. Thus we can discern an important change in the development of the conception of
the Buddha in India: whereas in the earlier tradition, the
nirmāṇakāya had been that specialized body employed
by the Buddha for the performance of occasional supernormal excursions, in the Mahāyāna there is no buddha
that ever appears in the world other than the nirmāṇakāya. All of the deeds of the Buddha are permutations of
the emanation body—they are all magical creations, the
reflexive functions of the dharmakāya. These functions
are by no means random. Indeed, the biography of the
Buddha is transformed from the linear narration of a
unique event into a paradigm, reduplicated precisely by
all the buddhas of the past, present, and future in twelve
deeds: descent from the Joyous Pure land, entry into
his mother's womb, being born, becoming skilled in arts
and sports as a youth, keeping a harem, taking four trips
outside the city that cause him to renounce the world,
practicing austerities for six years, sitting under the
bodhi tree, defeating Māra and his hosts, attaining enlightenment, turning the wheel of doctrine, and passing
into nirvāṇa.

The effects of this final deed have long been felt by
Buddhist communities. Their sense of loss was not limited to the direct disciples of the Buddha but has been
expressed by generations of future followers, often in
the form of the lament that one's negative karma caused
one to be reborn someplace other than northern India
during the lifetime of the Buddha, that one's misdeeds
prevented one from joining the audience of the Buddha's
teaching. A standard part of Buddhist rituals became the
request that other buddhas not pass into nirvāṇa but
remain in the world for an eon, which they could do if
they wished. . . .

The absence of the Buddha has remained a powerful motif in Buddhist history, and remedies have taken
a wide variety of forms. In Burma, secret societies, with
possible antecedents in tantric traditions, concentrate
their energies on kinds of supernormal power that the
mainstream tradition regards with some suspicion. Specifically, they engage in longevity practices to allow them
to live until the coming of the next buddha, Maitreya. . . .
In China and Japan, rituals constructed around the
chanting of the name of the buddha Amitābha offer a
means of being delivered at death into the presence of a
buddha who is not present here but is present now, elsewhere, in the western paradise of Sukhāvatī. . . .

With the absence of the historical Buddha, a variety
of substitutes were conceived to take his place. One such
substitute was the icon, as we already noted. Another was
the written text of his teaching, the sūtra, described below. In the absence of the Buddha, the transcendent

principle of his enlightenment, sometimes called the buddha nature, became the subject of a wide range of doctrinal speculation, devotion, and practice. This impersonal principle, which made possible the transformation of Prince Siddhārtha from an ignorant and suffering human being into an omniscient and blissful buddha, was most commonly referred to as the *tathāgatagarbha*. *Tathāgata*, "One Who Has Thus Come [or Gone]" is one of the standard epithets of the Buddha. *Garbha* has a wide range of meanings, including "essence" and "womb," which were exploited in works like the *Tathāgatagarbha Sūtra* . . . , a popular and influential Mahāyāna work which declared that this seed or potential for buddhahood resides equally in all beings, and it needs only to be developed. A related work . . . states that everything in the universe contains in itself the entire universe, and that, therefore, the wisdom of a buddha is fully present in each and every being. Such an impersonal principle was not only an important point of doctrine but could also be the object of devotion and praise, prompting the Japanese monk Myōe to address an island as the Buddha. In so doing, Myōe, who had desired to go to India, was able to find the Buddha in Japan. . . .

There is a vacillation in the metaphors and similes employed in these texts as if between two models of the means of making manifest the buddha nature, of achieving enlightenment. One model regards the buddha nature as something pure that has been polluted. The process of the path, therefore, is a gradual process of purification, removing defilements through a variety of practices until the utter transformation from afflicted sentient being to perfect buddha has been effected. Other tropes in these texts, however, do not suggest a developmental model but employ instead a rhetoric of discovery: buddhahood is always already fully present in each being. It need only be recognized. It was this latter model that exercised particular influence in the Chan and Zen schools of China and Japan, which were at least rhetorically dismissive of standard doctrinal categories and traditional practices. . . .

One of the earliest substitutes for the Buddha was the wisdom by which he became enlightened and, by extension, the texts that contained that wisdom. This wisdom was called the "perfection of wisdom" (*prajñāpāramitā*). In part because it was this wisdom that metaphorically gave birth to the Buddha and, in part, because the word *prajñāpāramitā* is in the feminine gender in Sanskrit, this wisdom was anthropomorphized and worshiped as a goddess, referred to sometimes as Prajñāpāramitā, sometimes as "the Great Mother." But not all of the important female figures in Buddhism have been anthropomorphized principles. . . . The eighth-century queen of Tibet is identified as a female buddha, and the tantric

symbolism of her vagina as the source of enlightenment is set forth. . . . Gotamī, not the Buddha's metaphorical mother, but his aunt and foster-mother (his own mother died shortly after his birth), was instrumental in convincing the Buddha to establish the order of nuns, and her life story has served as a female parallel to the life of the Buddha. The account of her passage into nirvāṇa . . . clearly mimics the story of the Buddha's death.

Perhaps the most popular substitute for the absent Buddha, however, was the bodhisattva. The Buddha is said to have been able to remember all of his past lives, and he is said to have employed his prodigious memory to recount events from those lives. The Buddha's remarkable memory provided a scriptural justification for the appropriation of a diverse body of folklore into the canon. The **Jātakas** ("Birth Stories"), of which there are over five hundred, were transformed from an Indian version of Aesop's Fables into the word of the Buddha by a conclusion appended to each story, in which the Buddha represents the tale as the recollection of one of his former lives and inevitably identifies himself as the protagonist ("in that existence the otter was Ānanda, the jackal was Maudgalyāyana, the monkey was Śāriputra, and I was the wise hare"). In these tales, the Buddha is referred to as the *bodhisattva*, a term widely etymologized in later literature, but which generally means a person who is intent on the attainment of bodhi, enlightenment. If very few Buddhists felt that they could emulate the Buddha in his last life by leaving their families, living the life of an ascetic, and practicing meditation, the stories of the Buddha's previous lives provided a more accessible model. Stories of the Bodhisattva's deeds of generosity, morality, patience, and perseverance against great odds have remained among the most popular forms of Buddhist literature, both written and oral, and both in the Jātaka tales and in another genre called Avadāna. . . .

In the early Mahāyāna sūtras, the bodhisattva's deeds were represented not merely as an inspiration but as a model to be scrupulously emulated. Earlier in the tradition, the goal had been to follow the path set forth by the Buddha and become liberated from rebirth as an arhat. But in the Mahāyāna, the goal became to do not what the Buddha said but what he did: to follow a much, much longer path to become a buddha oneself. It seems that, at least in the time of the Buddha, it had been possible to become an arhat in one lifetime. Later Mahāyāna exegetes would calculate that, from the time that one made buddhahood one's goal until buddhahood was achieved, a minimum of 384×10^{58} years was required. This amount of time was needed to accumulate the vast stores of merit and wisdom that would result in the omniscience of a buddha, who was able to teach the path to liberation more effectively than any other because of his telepathic knowledge of the capacities and interests of his disciples. It was not the case, then, that bodhisattvas were postponing their enlightenment as buddhas; instead, they would forego the lesser enlightenment of the arhat, which offered freedom from suffering for oneself alone, in favor of the greater enlightenment of a buddha, whereby others could also be liberated.

Formal ceremonies were designed for taking the vow to become a bodhisattva and then follow the long bodhisattva path to buddhahood in order to liberate others from saṃsāra. This included the promise to follow a specific code of conduct. . . . At those ceremonies, the officiant, speaking as the Buddha, would declare that a particular disciple, at a point several eons in the future, would complete the long bodhisattva path and become a buddha of such and such a name, presiding over such and such a pure land. So, with the rise of the Mahāyāna we see the goal of enlightenment recede to a point beyond the horizon, but with the millions of intervening lives, beginning with this one, consecrated by the Buddha's prophecy that these present lives are a future buddha's former lives, part of a buddha's story and thus sacred history.

But the bodhisattva was not simply an object of emulation; the bodhisattva was also an object of devotion, for if the bodhisattva had vowed to liberate all beings in the universe from suffering, all beings were the object of the bodhisattva's compassionate deeds. The bodhisattvas mentioned in the Mahāyāna sūtras were worshiped for the varieties of mundane and supramundane succor they could bestow—bodhisattvas such as Mañjuśrī, the bodhisattva of wisdom; Kṣitigarbha, who as Jizō in Japan rescues children, both born and unborn; Maitreya, the bodhisattva who will become the next buddha; and most of all, Avalokiteśvara, the most widely worshiped bodhisattva, who takes a female form as Guanyin in China . . . and Kannon in Japan, and who in Tibet takes human form in the succession of Dalai Lamas. . . .

Yet another substitute for the absent Buddha is to be found in the Vajrayāna, in which rituals (called *sādhana*, literally, "means of achievement") are set forth in which the practitioner, through a practice of visualization, petitions a buddha or bodhisattva to come into the practitioner's presence. Much of the practice described in tantric sādhanas involves the enactment of a world—the fantastic jewel-encrusted world of the Mahāyāna sūtras or the horrific world of the charnel ground. In the sūtras, these worlds appear before the audience of the sūtra at the command of the Buddha, as in the *Lotus Sūtra*, or are described by him, as in the Pure Land sūtras. In the tantric sādhana, the practitioner manifests that world through visualization, through a process of invitation, descent, and identification, evoking the world that the

sūtras declare to be immanent, yet only describe. The tantric sādhana is, in this sense, the making of the world of the Mahāyāna sūtras here and now. Tantric sādhanas usually take one of two forms. In the first, the buddha or bodhisattva is requested to appear before the meditator and is then worshiped in the hope of receiving blessings. . . . In the other type of tantric sādhana, the meditator imagines himself or herself to be a fully enlightened buddha or bodhisattva now, to have the exalted body, speech, and mind of an enlightened being. Those who become particularly skillful at this practice, it is said, gain the ability to appear in this form to others. . . .

DHARMA

Before the Buddha passed away, it is said that he was asked who would succeed him as leader of the community. He answered that his teaching should be the teacher. That teaching is most commonly referred to with the name *dharma*, a word derived from the root *dhṛ*, "to hold," a term with a wide range of meanings. Indeed, ten meanings of *dharma*, including "path," "virtue," "quality," "vow," and "nirvāṇa" were enumerated by a fifth-century scholar. Nineteenth-century translators often rendered *dharma* as "the law." But two meanings predominate. The first is the teaching of the Buddha, creatively etymologized from *dhṛ* to mean "that which holds one back from falling into suffering." The second meaning of dharma, appearing particularly in philosophical contexts, is often rendered in English as "phenomenon" or "thing," as in "all dharmas lack self."

The ambiguities encountered in translating the term are emblematic of a wide range of practices that have been regarded as the teaching of the Buddha. And because the Buddha adapted his teachings to the situation and because (at least according to the Mahāyāna), the Buddha did not actually disappear into nirvāṇa but remains forever present, works that represented themselves as his teaching (which begin with the standard formula, "Thus did I hear") have continued to be composed throughout the history of Buddhism. The term "Buddhist apocrypha" has generally been used to describe those texts composed outside of India (in China, for example) which represent themselves as being of Indian origin. Yet strictly speaking all Buddhist texts, even those composed in Indian languages, are apocryphal because none can be identified with complete certainty as a record of the teaching of the historical Buddha. This has, on the one hand, led to a certain tolerance for accepting diverse doctrines and practices as Buddhist. Sometimes new texts were written as ways of summarizing what was most important from an unwieldy and overwhelming canon. In some cases, these new texts represented themselves as the words of the historical Buddha . . . ; in other cases, essays were composed in poetry and prose with the purpose of explicating for a newly converted society the most essential teachings from a bewildering scriptural tradition. . . .

The absence of the Buddha did not merely occasion the creation of substitutes for him. Over the course of the history of Buddhism in Asia, it also portended crisis, notably in a variety of texts that responded to the notion of the decline of the dharma. Within a century or two after the Buddha's death, there were predictions of the eventual disappearance of the dharma from the world. Various reasons were given for its demise, ranging from a general deterioration in human virtue to the fact that the Buddha had agreed to admit women into the order. These texts, like most Buddhist sūtras, are set at the time of the Buddha, and the dire circumstances that signal the demise of the dharma are expressed in terms of prophecies by the Buddha of what will happen in the future. We can assume that the authors of the sūtras were in fact describing the events of their own day, usually including the corrupt and greedy behavior of monks, the persecution of Buddhism by the state, or the threat posed by foreign invaders. Some works of this genre not only prophesied decline of the dharma but offered prescriptions so that decline could be averted. . . .

When works such as these were composed to respond to a particular historical circumstance, it was sometimes necessary to account for the fact that there had been no previous record of such a text. It was explained that [some] texts . . . had been found locked inside an iron stūpa, having been placed there long ago to be discovered at the appropriate time. The fact that the version which eventually reached China seemed little more than an outline was the result of an unfortunate circumstance: the larger and more comprehensive version of the work had inadvertently been thrown overboard on the sea journey from India to China. Likewise, the Tibetan ritual text of the Great Bliss Queen . . . is an example of a Tibetan genre of texts known as *gter ma* (treasures). It is believed that the Indian tantric master who visited Tibet in the late eighth century, Padmasambhava, and his followers buried texts all over Tibet, knowing that they would be uncovered at an appropriate time in the future.

As one might imagine, there were those who found such claims fantastic, and the Mahāyāna was challenged by the foundational schools for fabricating new sūtras and distorting the Buddhist teaching. A sixth-century Mahāyāna author, Bhāvaviveka, summarizes the Hīnayāna argument that the Mahāyāna is not the word of the Buddha: the Mahāyāna sūtras were not included in ei-

ther the original or subsequent compilations of the word of the Buddha; by teaching that the Buddha is permanent, the Mahāyāna contradicts the dictum that all conditioned phenomena are impermanent; because the Mahāyāna teaches that the buddha nature is all-pervasive, it does not relinquish the belief in self; because the Mahāyāna teaches that the Buddha did not pass into nirvāṇa, it suggests that nirvāṇa is not the final state of peace; the Mahāyāna contains prophecies that the great early disciples will become buddhas; the Mahāyāna belittles the arhats, the Mahāyāna praises bodhisattvas above the Buddha; the Mahāyāna perverts the entire teaching by claiming that the historical Buddha was an emanation; the statement in the Mahāyāna sūtras that the Buddha was constantly in meditative absorption is unfeasible; by teaching that great sins can be completely absolved, the Mahāyāna teaches that actions have no effects, contradicting the law of karma. Therefore, the opponents of the Mahāyāna claim, the Buddha did not set forth the Mahāyāna; it was created by beings who were demonic in order to deceive the obtuse and those with evil minds.

Centuries earlier we find implied responses to these criticisms in the Mahāyāna sūtras themselves, side by side with the assertions that the Hīnayāna found so heretical. The most influential defense of new sūtras as authoritative teachings of the Buddha is found in the *Lotus Sūtra*, with its doctrine of skillful means (*upāya*). In that work the validity of the Mahāyāna and the Mahāyāna vision of buddhahood is defended by the use of parables. Because the *Lotus* is the most influential of Buddhist texts in all of East Asia, it is worthwhile to consider some of these.

The *Lotus Sūtra* must somehow account for the fact that the Mahāyāna has appeared late, after the Buddha had taught a path to nirvāṇa that had already been successfully followed to its terminus by his original disciples, the great arhats such as Śāriputra, Maudgalyāyana, and Kāśyapa. If the Mahāyāna is the superior teaching, why had it not been evident earlier? Several of the parables place the fault with the disciples themselves. Thus, in the parable of the hidden jewel, a man falls asleep drunk in the house of a friend who, unbeknownst to him, sews a jewel into the hem of his garment. The man awakes and goes on his way, only to suffer great poverty and hardship. He encounters his friend, who reveals the jewel, showing him that he had been endowed with great wealth all the while. In the same way, the disciples of the Buddha have constant access to the path to supreme enlightenment but are unaware of it; they are bodhisattvas unaware of their true identity. Again, the Buddha compares his teaching to the rainfall that descends without discrimination on the earth. That this rain causes some seeds to grow into flowers and some into great trees implies no differentiation in the rain but rather is due to the capacities of the seeds that it nurtures. Thus, the teaching of the Buddha is of a single flavor but benefits beings in a variety of ways according to their capacity. The Buddha knows the abilities and dispositions of his disciples and causes them to hear his dharma in a way most suitable to them.

Other parables employ a more radical strategy of authorization, suggesting that the Hīnayāna nirvāṇa is but a fiction. The oft-cited parable of the burning house tells of a father distraught as his children blithely play, unaware that the house is ablaze. Knowing of their respective predilections for playthings, he lures them from the inferno with the promise that he has a cart for each waiting outside, a deer-drawn cart for one, a goat-drawn cart for another, and so on. When they emerge from the conflagration, they find only one cart, a magnificent conveyance drawn by a great white ox, something that they had never even dreamed of. The burning house is saṃsāra, the children are ignorant sentient beings, unaware of the dangers of their abode, the father is the Buddha, who lures them out of saṃsāra with the teaching of a variety of vehicles—the vehicle of the śrāvaka, the vehicle of the pratyekabuddha, the vehicle of the bodhisattva—knowing that in fact there is but one vehicle, the buddha vehicle whereby all beings will be conveyed to unsurpassed enlightenment. And the Buddha tells the parable of the conjured city, in which a skillful guide leads a group of travelers on a long journey in search of a cache of jewels. Along the way, the travelers become exhausted and discouraged and decide to turn back. The guide magically conjures a great city in the near distance, where the travelers can rest before continuing toward their ultimate goal. The travelers enter the city where they regain their strength, at which point the guide dissolves the city and announces that the jewel cache is near. The travelers are those sentient beings who are weak and cowardly, intimidated by the thought of traversing the long Mahāyāna path to buddhahood. For their benefit, the Buddha creates the Hīnayāna nirvāṇa, more easily attained, which they mistakenly believe to be their final goal. He then announces to them that they have not reached their ultimate destination and exhorts them on to buddhahood, revealing that the nirvāṇa they had attained was but an illusion.

Thus, the claim to legitimacy of the earlier tradition is usurped by the Mahāyāna through the explanation that what the Buddha had taught before was in fact a lie, that there is no such thing as the path of the arhat, no such thing as nirvāṇa. There is only the Mahāyāna (also called the *ekayāna*, the "one vehicle"), which the Buddha intentionally misrepresents out of his compassionate understanding that there are many among his disciples who are incapable of assimilating so far-reaching a vision. But what of those disciples of the Buddha who are reported in the early sūtras to have become arhats, to have passed into nirvāṇa—what of their attainment? In an ingenious device (found also in other Mahāyāna sūtras) the great heroes of the Hīnayāna are drafted into the Mahāyāna by the Buddha's prophecies that even they will surpass the trifling goal of nirvāṇa and go on to follow the Mahāyāna path to eventual buddhahood. The first such prophecy is for the monk Śāriputra, renowned in the works of the foundational tradition as the wisest of the Buddha's disciples, who is transformed into a stock character in the Mahāyāna sūtras as one who is oblivious of the higher teaching. When his ignorance is revealed to him, he desires to learn more, coming to denounce as parochial the wisdom that he had once deemed supreme. The champion of the Hīnayāna is shown to reject it and embrace that which many adherents of the foundational tradition judged to be spurious. Thus the early history of the movement, already highly mythologized into a sacred history, was fictionalized further in the Mahāyāna sūtras, and another sacred history was eventually created. To legitimate these newly appearing texts, their authors claimed the principal figures of the earlier tradition, indeed its very codifiers, as converts to the Buddha's true teaching and central characters in its drama. The early story of Gautama Buddha and his disciples, preserved in the Pāli canon and already accepted as an historical account by the "pre-Mahāyāna" traditions, is radically rewritten in the *Lotus* in such a way as to glorify the *Lotus* itself as the record of what really happened. Such rewriting recurs throughout the history of the Buddhist traditions in the perpetual attempt to recount "what the Buddha taught."

And who is this Buddha that the *Lotus Sūtra* represents? In the fifteenth chapter, billions of bodhisattvas well up out of the earth and make offerings to the Buddha. The Buddha declares that all of these bodhisattvas who have been practicing the path for innumerable eons are in fact his own disciples, that he had set each of them on the long path to buddhahood. The bodhisattva Maitreya, who has witnessed this fantastic scene, asks the obvious question. He reckons that it had only been some forty years since the Buddha had achieved enlightenment under the tree at Bodhgayā. He finds it incredible that in that short period of time the Buddha could have trained so many bodhisattvas who had progressed so far on the path. "It is as if there were a man, his natural color fair and his hair black, twenty-five years of age, who pointed to men a hundred years of age and said, 'These are my sons!'" Maitreya, representing the self-doubt of the early Mahāyāna and reflecting the Hīnayāna critique, is deeply troubled by this inconsistency, fearing that people who hear of this after the Buddha's passing will doubt the truth of the Buddha's words and attack his teaching.

It is at this point that the Buddha reveals another lie. He explains that even though he is widely believed to have left the palace of his father in search of freedom from suffering and to have found that freedom six years later under a tree near Gayā, in fact, that is not the case. He achieved enlightenment innumerable billions of eons ago and has been preaching the dharma in this world and simultaneously in myriad other worlds ever since. Yet he recognizes the meager intelligence of many beings, and out of his wish to benefit them resorts to the use of skillful methods (upāya), recounting how he renounced his princely life and attained unsurpassed enlightenment. And, further recognizing that his continued presence in the world might cause those of little virtue to become complacent and not ardently seek to put his teaching into practice, he declares that he is soon to pass into nirvāṇa. But this also is a lie, because his lifespan will not be exhausted for many innumerable billions of eons.

Thus, the prince's deep anxiety at being confronted with the facts of sickness, aging, and death, his difficult decision to abandon his wife and child and go forth into the forest in search of a state beyond sorrow, his ardent practice of meditation and asceticism for six years, his triumphant attainment of the liberation and his imminent passage into the extinction of nirvāṇa—all are a pretense. He was enlightened all the time, yet feigned these deeds to inspire the world.

But we should not conclude that once the Lotus and other Mahāyāna sūtras declared the superiority of the bodhisattva path, the supremacy and authority of the Mahāyāna was finally and unequivocally established. Defenses of the Mahāyāna as the word of the Buddha remained the preoccupation of Mahāyāna scholastics throughout the history of Buddhism in India. . . . Nor should we assume that teachings were ranked only as Hīnayāna and Mahāyāna. Even sects that exalted the Lotus Sūtra above all others, for example, could disagree about whether there was more than one true practice, one true sūtra, one true buddha. In Japan, a dispute over the meaning of "original enlightenment" in what is called the Matsumoto Debate led to a bloody conflict in 1536 that involved thousands of troops on each side. . . . In China, the promotion and control of sacred scripture was the prerogative of the highest imperial offices. A sect that came into conflict with this authority, the "Teaching of the Three Stages," had its texts de-

clared heretical and banned from the official collection of Buddhist texts. . . .

. . . The significance of Buddhist texts does not lie simply in their doctrinal or philosophical content but in the uses to which they have been put. We find, for example, . . . that the Abhidharma (literally, "higher dharma," sometimes rendered as "phenomenology"), a class of Buddhist scriptures concerned with minute analyses of mental states, is chanted at Thai funerals. Contained in virtually every Mahāyāna sūtra was a proclamation of the marvelous benefits that would accrue to those who piously handled, recited, worshiped, copied, or circulated the text itself—again, the teaching had become the teacher. Ritual enshrinement and devotion to the sūtra as a vital embodiment of the dharma and, in a certain sense, as a substitute for the Buddha himself was instrumental to the rise of the disparate collections of cults of the book that came to be known as the Mahāyāna. In China, no text was more venerated than the Lotus, and tales were told of the miracles that attended its worship. . . .

The importance of texts in Buddhism derives in part from the fact that the tradition represents the Buddha as being eventually persuaded to teach others after his enlightenment. This suggests that the dharma is something that can be passed on, something that is transmittable, transferable. The Buddha is said to have spoken not in Sanskrit, the formal language of the priests of his day, but in the vernacular, and he is said to have forbidden monks from composing his teachings in formal verses for chanting. The implication was that the content was more important than the form. This led to the notion that the dharma could be translated from one language to another, and the act of translation (and the sponsorship of translation) has been regarded throughout Asia as one of the most pious and meritorious acts that could be performed. It was therefore common for Buddhist kings and emperors to sponsor the translation of texts from one language into another: from Sanskrit into Chinese, from Sanskrit into Tibetan, from Tibetan into Manchu, from Pāli into Burmese, and so on. Adding to this notion of translatability was the fact that the primary objects of Buddhist devotion—texts, relics, icons—were all portable; stories of the transportation and enshrinement of a particularly potent image of the Buddha figure in the histories of almost all Buddhist cultures. We should not conclude, however, as Buddhist sometimes do, that the dharma is something self-identical and transcendent, that showers over the cultures of Asia, transforming and pacifying them. . . . For example, Buddhism is portrayed [in one instance] as a Korean possession that can be offered in tribute to the Japanese court as a means of protecting the state. It is this universalism of the Buddhist dharma with its plastic pantheon into which any local deity could easily be enlisted, its doctrine of the Buddha's skillful methods for accommodating conflicting views, and its claims about the pervasive nature of reality that have made it a sometimes useful ideology for rulership and empire.

Buddhism has indeed transformed Asia, but it has been transformed in the process. We may consider even whether there ever was some entity called "Buddhism" to be transformed in the first place. What cannot be disputed is that if Buddhism exists, it is impossible to understand it outside the lives of Buddhists, outside the saṅgha.

SAṄGHA

The last of the three jewels is the saṅgha, "the community." Technically taken to mean the assembly of enlightened disciples of the Buddha, the term more commonly connotes the community of Buddhist monks and nuns. In the rules governing the ordination ceremony, the saṅgha is said to be present when four fully ordained monks are in attendance. However, in its broadest sense the saṅgha is the whole body of Buddhist faithful. . . .

As mentioned earlier, Buddhist practice was traditionally subsumed under three headings: ethics (śīla), meditation (dhyāna), and wisdom (prajñā). Ethics, which in this context refers to refraining from nonvirtue through the conscious control of body and speech, was regarded as the essential prerequisite for progress in meditation and wisdom. It was the element of the triad most widely practiced both by lay people and monks and nuns, and this practice generally took the form of the observance of vows. Since in Buddhist ethical theory karma, both good and bad, depended not on the deed but on the intention, if one could make a promise not to kill humans, for example, and maintain that promise, the good karma accumulated by such restraint would be far greater than had one simply not had the occasion to commit murder. From the early days of the tradition, therefore, elaborate systems of rules for living one's life, called vinaya, were established, along with ceremonies for their conferral and maintenance. Laypeople could take vows not to kill humans, not to steal, not to commit sexual misconduct, not to lie about spiritual attainments (for example, not to claim to be telepathic when one actually was not), and not to use intoxicants. Novice monks and nuns took these five vows, plus vows not to eat after the noon meal (a rule widely transgressed in some Buddhist cultures through recourse to the evening "medicinal meal"), not to handle gold or silver, not to adorn their bodies, not to sleep in high beds, and not to attend musical performances. Fully ordained monks (bhikṣu) and nuns (bhikṣunī) took many more vows, which covered the entire range of personal and public decorum, and regulated physical movements, social intercourse, and property. Monks and nuns convened twice monthly to confess their transgressions of the rules in a ceremony and reaffirm their commitment to the code, with transgressions carrying punishments of various weights. The gravest misdeeds entailed expulsion from the order, whereas others could be expiated simply by confessing them aloud. In Buddhist traditions across Asia, ritual maintenance of these monastic codes has served as the mark of orthodoxy, much more than adherence to a particular belief or doctrine. Indeed, it is said that the teaching of the Buddha will endure only as long as the vinaya endures.

The Buddha and his followers were probably originally a group of wandering ascetics. However, they adopted the practice of other ascetic groups in India of remaining in one place during the rainy season. Wealthy patrons had shelters built for their use, and these shelters evolved into monasteries that were inhabited throughout the year. It seems that early in the tradition, the saṅgha became largely sedentary, although the tradition of the wandering monk continued. Still, the saṅgha was by no means a homogeneous community. The vinaya texts describe monks from a wide variety of social backgrounds. Mention is made of monks from all four of India's social castes. There were also a wide variety of monastic specialties. The vinaya texts describe monks who are skilled in speech, those who memorize and recite the sūtras, those who memorize and recite the vinaya, and those who memorize and recite lists of technical terms. There are monks who live in the forest, who wear robes of felt, who wear robes made from discarded rags, who live only on the alms they have begged for, who live at the foot of a tree, who live in a cemetery, who live in the open air, who sleep sitting up, and so on. There were also monks who specialized in meditation, monks who served as advisors to kings, and monks responsible for the administration of the monastery and its property. One of the tasks of this administrator was to insure that the wandering monks were not given mundane work, that meditating monks not be disturbed by noise, and that monks who begged for alms received good food. Whether they wandered without a fixed abode or lived in monasteries, monks and nuns that lived in a designated region, called a sīmā, were to gather twice a month to confess and affirm their vows communally, a ceremony that laypeople also attended.

Throughout the Buddhist world, monks and laypeople have lived in a symbiotic relationship: the laity provide material support for monks while monks provide a locus for the layperson's accumulation of merit (by supporting monks who maintained their vows). The rules and regulations in the vinaya texts were meant to govern the lives of Buddhist monks and to structure their relations with the laity. Monks in the vinaya literature are caught in a web of social and ritual obligations, are fully and elaborately housed and permanently settled, and are preoccupied not with nirvāṇa, but with bowls and robes, bathrooms and buckets, and proper behavior in public. . . . The saṅgha was also a community where disputes arose and had to be settled. Because it is said that the Buddha only prescribed a rule in response to a specific misdeed, the vinaya texts often provide the story of that first offense and the Buddha's pronouncement of a rule against such behavior in the future. . . .

There were also rules for nuns, although these receive much less attention in the vinaya literature. According to several traditions, the Buddha was approached early in his career by his aunt and step-mother, Mahāpajāpatī . . . , at the head of a delegation of women who wished him to institute a Buddhist order of nuns. The Buddha initially declined to institute such an order. But when the Buddha's cousin and personal attendant, Ānanda, asked him whether women were able to attain the fruits of the practice of the dharma, the Buddha unhesitatingly answered in the affirmative and agreed to establish an order for women. However, the same text states that if the Buddha had not agreed to establish an order for nuns, his teaching would not disappear from the world so quickly. The rules for nuns are both more numerous and stricter than those for monks, and placed nuns in a position of clear subordination to monks. For example, seniority in the order of monks and nuns is measured by the length of time one has been ordained, such that someone who has been a monk for five years must pay respect to a monk of six years, even if the first monk is chronologically older. However, the rules for nuns state that a woman who has been a nun for one hundred years must pay respect to a man who was ordained as a monk for one day. The difficulties entailed in maintaining the strict nuns' vows and a lack of institutional support led to the decline and eventual disappearance of the order of nuns in India, Sri Lanka, and Southeast Asia, and to an order of novices alone (rather than fully ordained nuns) in Tibet. The tradition of full ordination for women was maintained only in China.

Throughout the development of the Mahāyāna and the Vajrayāna, the rules for monks and nuns seems to have remained fairly uniform and the adherents of the new vehicles seem to have seen no contradiction between the monastic life and the practices of the Mahāyāna and the Vajrayāna. But if we understand the vinaya not as that which restricts individuals and their actions but as that which creates them, we will not be surprised that additional vows were formulated for the bodhisattva and the tantric practitioner, and that rituals which mimicked the monastic confession ceremony were designed for their administration. The vows of a bodhisattva included not only the vow to liberate all beings in the universe from suffering but also to act compassionately by always accepting an apology, not to praise oneself and belittle others, to give gifts and teachings upon request, and so on. Those who took the bodhisattva vows also promised never to claim that the Mahāyāna sūtras were not the word of the Buddha. . . .

Vajrayāna practice also entailed extensive sets of vows. . . . As mentioned above, it was common for Buddhist monks, especially in late Indian Buddhism and in Tibet, to hold bodhisattva and tantric vows in addition to their monk's vows. In the case of the more advanced tantric initiations, which involved sexual union with a consort, this presented problems, for monks were bound by the rule of celibacy. Whether or not monks were permitted to participate in such initiations became a question of some gravity when Buddhism was being established in Tibet. . . .

. . . Because of the portability of relics, texts, and icons, sacred sites were established across the Buddhist world and pilgrimages to those sites was a popular form of buddhist practice throughout Asia. Pilgrimage was sometimes to a stūpa associated with the life of the Buddha; Bodhgayā, the site of the Buddha's enlightenment, has drawn pilgrims from the outer reaches of the Buddhist world for centuries. Particularly powerful buddha images also attracted pilgrims; it was not uncommon for pilgrims from as far east as Manchuria and as far west as the Mongol regions of Russia to travel to Lhasa, the capital of Tibet, to visit the statue of the Buddha there. They would travel on foot or on horseback; the most pious would proceed by prostration—bowing and then stretching their bodies on the ground before rising, taking one step forward and prostrating again, along the entire route. In China, mountains believed to be the abodes of munificent bodhisattvas were (and are) popular destinations of communal pilgrimages. . . . But we should not assume that Buddhist travel was always directed from the periphery to the center. [There is a] story of a renowned Buddhist scholar who left one of the great monastic universities of India on a perilous sea voyage to Sumatra, where the preeminent teacher of the practice of compassion was said to reside. Nor was the travel always so concerned with what or who was to be found at the end of the journey; the Japanese monk Ippen saw travel itself as essential to his practice of devotion to Amitābha. . . .

WORLD DISTRIBUTION OF BUDDHISTS

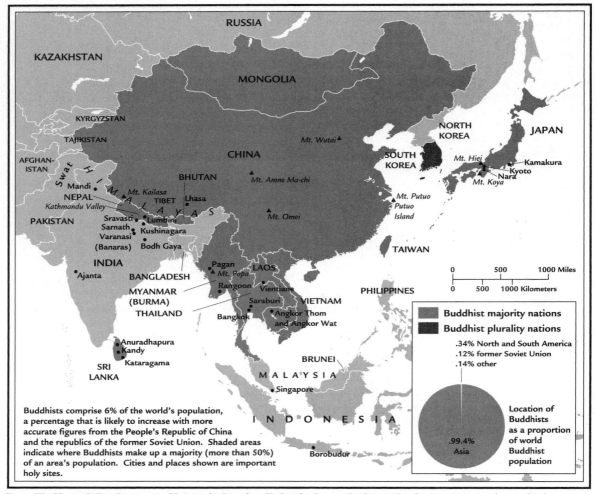

Buddhists comprise 6% of the world's population, a percentage that is likely to increase with more accurate figures from the People's Republic of China and the republics of the former Soviet Union. Shaded areas indicate where Buddhists make up a majority (more than 50%) of an area's population. Cities and places shown are important holy sites.

Buddhist majority nations

Buddhist plurality nations

.34% North and South America
.12% former Soviet Union
.14% other

.99.4% Asia

Location of Buddhists as a proportion of world Buddhist population

From *The HarperCollins Dictionary of Religion* by Jonathan Z. Smith. Copyright © 1995 by the American Academy of Religion. Reprinted by permission of HarperCollins Publishers, Inc.

SOURCES

I have organized the sources historically and by traditions (vehicles) in order to provide a developmental overview of some of the important religious literature of Buddhism. However, one should not assume that this structure indicates that one vehicle somehow stopped developing when our attention shifts to another vehicle. Neither does this sequence—Nikaya (Hinayana), Mahayana, and Vajrayana—imply a value judgment about which is the "original" form or which is the "best" tradition.

I have selected material that has been particularly important in the development of Buddhism. However, we must remember that this literature was created by a small religious elite, most of whom were monks or nuns as well as scholars and much of it was not well known or even read by the vast majority of Buddhist practitioners. I have included descriptions of practices, such as meditation and pilgrimage, that will give you an idea of what these practices are like. Buddhism, like many religions, lives, for most of its followers, more in what is done than in what is known about the fine points of doctrines or philosophical/theological arguments.

Nothing was written down for 400 to 500 years after the Buddha's *parinirvana* (final release from rebirth and suffering after death). Hence it is extremely difficult to recover the original teachings of the historical Buddha. Monks orally preserved material for centuries. During this time other material dating from after the time of the Buddha was added as problems arose in the monasteries, there were divisions among Buddhists into different groups, and questions needed to be clarified and answered. Add to this popular stories circulating among the laity and you have a vast mix of materials dealing with a wide variety of issues and topics. Only when the oral traditions were in danger of being lost did the task of recording them begin.

Over time, as Buddhism spread from one culture to another, new materials were added from local traditions. As encounters intensified with new indigenous traditions, new ideas, interpretations, and writings were added. For example, as Buddhism moved into China, it encountered the Confucian and Taoist traditions. It adapted, adopted, and disputed in reaction to this experience.

Buddhism has shown a remarkable flexibility. It both transforms and is transformed by the religions and cultures it comes into contact with. Hence the literature has, over the centuries, become both immense and complex. Thich Nhat Hanh, a Vietnamese Buddhist monk who has helped bring Buddhism to America, has expressed the situation well:

> Buddhism is not one. The teachings of Buddhism are many. When Buddhism enters a country, that country always acquires a new form of Buddhism. . . . The teaching of Buddhism in this country [America] will be different from other countries. Buddhism, in order to be Buddhism, must be suitable, appropriate to the psychology and the culture of the society that it serves. (*The Heart of Understanding*, Berkeley: Parallax Press, 1988, p. viii)

5.2 ENLIGHTENMENT

Enlightenment is that for which every Buddhist ultimately hopes although most will settle for rebirth in a better place than this world of suffering and pain. With enlightenment come wisdom, serenity, and release from suffering. Sakyamuni's own enlightenment is the model. Before enlightenment a person who has

taken the appropriate vows is called a **bodhisattva,** or *buddha to be*. To walk the *bodhisattva* path is to aim at enlightenment or buddhahood if not in this life, then in some future life.

We do not have a psychological description of Sakyamuni's enlightenment from his own mouth. What we do have is a pious reconstruction written sometime in the first and second centuries c.e. in a document, attributed to a poet named Ashvaghosha, called *The Deeds of the Buddha* (*Buddhacarita*). The author presents what he considers to be the basic moral and spiritual teachings of the Buddha. Even when writing about events such as the enlightenment experience, Ashvaghosha's primary concern is to instruct his readers rather than simply describe an event.

Ashvaghosha's text gained wide popularity not only among the Mahayana Buddhists in East Asia but also throughout India and South Asia. Enlightenment is a concern of Buddhists everywhere and of all schools of Buddhism. The story of the Buddha's enlightenment belongs to the whole of Buddhism.

ASHVAGHOSHA

Enlightenment (Buddhacarita)

READING QUESTION

1. Write a brief commentary on two or three of the most important parts of this account. Why are these significant in your view? What do they mean? What spiritual insight do they show?

THE DEFEAT OF MARA

Because the great Sage, the scion of a line of royal seers, had made his vow to win emancipation, and had seated himself in the effort to carry it out, the whole world rejoiced—but Mara, the inveterate foe of the true Dharma, shook with fright. People address him gladly as the God of Love, the one who shoots with flower-arrows, and yet they dread this Mara as the one who

From *Buddhist Scriptures*, translated by Edward Conze (Middlesex, England: Penguin Books, Ltd., 1959), pp. 48–53. Copyright © 1959 Edward Conze. Reprinted by permission of Penguin Books, Ltd.

rules events connected with a life of passion, as the one who hates the very thought of freedom. He had with him his three sons—Flurry, Gaiety, and Sullen Pride—and his three daughters—Discontent, Delight, and Thirst. These asked him why he was so disconcerted in his mind. And he replied to them with these words: "Look over there at that sage, clad in the armour of determination, with truth and spiritual virtue as his weapons, the arrows of his intellect drawn ready to shoot! He has sat down with the firm intention of conquering my realm. No wonder that my mind is plunged in deep despondency! If he should succeed in overcoming me, and could proclaim to the world the way to final beatitude, then my realm would be empty today, like that of the king of Videha of whom we hear in the Epics that he lost his kingdom because he misconducted himself by carrying off a Brahmin's daughter. But so far he has not yet won the eye of full knowledge. He is still within my sphere of influence. While there is time I therefore will attempt to break his solemn purpose, and throw myself against him like the rush of a swollen river breaking against the embankment!"

But Mara could achieve nothing against the Bodhisattva, and he and his army were defeated, and fled in all directions—their elation gone, their toil rendered fruitless, their rocks, logs, and trees scattered everywhere. They behaved like a hostile army whose commander had been slain in battle. So Mara, defeated, ran away together with his followers. The great seer, free from the dust of passion, victorious over darkness' gloom, had vanquished him. And the moon, like a maiden's gentle smile, lit up the heavens, while a rain of sweet-scented flowers, filled with moisture, fell down on the earth from above.

THE ENLIGHTENMENT

Now that he had defeated Mara's violence by his firmness and calm, the Bodhisattva, possessed of great skill in Transic meditation, put himself into trance, intent on discerning both the ultimate reality of things and the final goal of existence. After he had gained complete mastery over all the degrees and kinds of trance:

1. In the first watch of the night he recollected the successive series of his former births. "There was I so and so; that was my name; deceased from there I came here"—in this way he remembered thousands of births, as though living them over again. When he had recalled his own births and deaths in all these various lives of his, the Sage, full of pity, turned his compassionate mind towards other living beings, and he thought to himself: "Again and again they must leave the people they regard as their own, and must go on elsewhere, and that without ever stopping. Surely this world is unprotected and helpless, and like a wheel it turns round and round." As he continued steadily to recollect the past thus, he came to the definite conviction that this world of Samsara is as unsubstantial as the pith of a plantain tree.

2. Second to none in valour, he then, in the second watch of the night, acquired the supreme heavenly eye, for he himself was the best of all those who have sight. Thereupon with the perfectly pure heavenly eye he looked upon the entire world, which appeared to him as though reflected in a spotless mirror. He saw that the decease and rebirth of beings depend on whether they have done superior or inferior deeds. And his compassionateness grew still further. It became clear to him that no security can be found in this flood of Samsaric existence, and that the threat of death is ever-present. Beset on all sides, creatures can find no resting place. In this way he surveyed the five places of rebirth with his heavenly eye. And he found nothing substantial in the world of becoming, just as no core of heartwood is found in a plantain tree when its layers are peeled off one by one.

3. Then, as the third watch of that night drew on, the supreme master of trance turned his meditation to the real and essential nature of this world: "Alas, living beings wear themselves out in vain! Over and over again they are born, they age, die, pass on to a new life, and are reborn! What is more, greed and dark delusion obscure their sight, and they are blind from birth. Greatly apprehensive, they yet do not know how to get out of this great mass of ill." He then surveyed the twelve links of conditioned co-production, and saw that, beginning with ignorance, they lead to old age and death, and, beginning with the cessation of ignorance, they lead to the cessation of birth, old age, death, and all kinds of ill.

When the great seer had comprehended that where there is no ignorance whatever, there also the karma-formations are stopped—then he had achieved a correct knowledge of all there is to be known, and he stood out in the world as a Buddha. He passed through the eight stages of Transic insight, and quickly reached their highest point. From the summit of the world downwards he could detect no self anywhere. Like the fire, when its fuel is burnt up, he became tranquil. He had reached perfection, and he thought to himself: "This is the authentic Way on which in the past so many great seers, who also knew all higher and all lower things, have travelled on to ultimate and real truth. And now I obtained it!"

4. At that moment, in the fourth watch of the night, when dawn broke and all the ghosts that move and those that move not went to rest, the great seer took up the position which knows no more alteration, and the leader of all reached the state of all-knowledge. When, through his Buddhahood, he had cognized this fact, the earth swayed like a woman drunken with wine, the sky shone bright with the Siddhas who appeared in crowds in all the directions, and the mighty drums of thunder resounded through the air. Pleasant breezes blew softly, rain fell from a cloudless sky, flowers and fruits dropped from the trees out of season—in an effort, as it were, to show reverence for him. Mandarava flowers and lotus blossoms, and also water lillies made of gold and beryl, fell from the sky on to the ground near the Shakya sage, so that it looked like a place in the world of the gods. At the moment no one anywhere was angry, ill, or sad; no one did evil, none was proud; the world became quite quiet, as though it had reached full perfection. Joy spread through the ranks of those gods who longed for salvation; joy also spread among those who lived in the regions below. Everywhere the virtuous were strengthened, the influence of Dharma increased, and the world rose from the dirt of the passions and the darkness of ignorance. Filled with joy and wonder at the Sage's work, the seers of the solar race who had been protectors of men, who had been royal seers, who had been great seers, stood in their mansions in the heavens and showed him their reverence. The great seers among the hosts of invisible beings could be heard widely proclaiming his fame. All living things rejoiced and sensed that things went well. Mara alone felt deep displeasure, as though subjected to a sudden fall.

For seven days He dwelt there—his body gave him no trouble, his eyes never closed, and he looked into his own mind. He thought: "Here I have found freedom," and he knew that the longings of his heart had at last come to fulfillment. Now that he had grasped the principle of causation, and finally convinced himself of the lack of self in all that is, he roused himself again from his deep trance, and in his great compassion he surveyed the world with his Buddha-eye, intent on giving it peace. When, however, he saw on the one side the world lost in low views and confused efforts, thickly covered with the dirt of the passions, and saw on the other side the exceeding subtlety of the Dharma of emancipation, he felt inclined to take no action. But when he weighed up the significance of the pledge to enlighten all things he had

taken in the past, he became again more favourable to the idea of proclaiming the path to Peace. Reflecting in his mind on this question, he also considered that, while some people have a great deal of passion, others have but little. As soon as Indra and Brahma, the two chiefs of those who dwell in the heavens, had grasped the Sugata's intention to proclaim the path to Peace, they shone brightly and came up to him, the weal of the world their concern. He remained there on his seat, free from all evil and successful in his aim. The most excellent Dharma which he had seen was his most excellent companion. His two visitors gently and reverently spoke to him these words, which were meant for the weal of the world: "Please do not condemn all those that live as unworthy of such treasure! Oh, please engender pity in your heart for beings in this world! So varied is their endowment, and while some have much passion, others have only very little. Now that you, O Sage, have yourself crossed the ocean of the world of becoming, please rescue also the other living beings who have sunk so deep into suffering! As a generous lord shares his wealth, so may also you bestow your own virtues on others! Most of those who know what for them is good in this world and the next, act only for their own advantage. In the world of men and in heaven it is hard to find anyone who is impelled by concern for the weal of the world's." Having made this request to the great seer, the two gods returned to their celestial abode by the way they had come. And the sage pondered over their words. In consequence he was confirmed in his decision to set the world free.

Then came the time for the alms-round, and the World-Guardians of the four quarters presented the seer with begging-bowls. Gautama accepted the four, but for the sake of his Dharma he turned them into one. At that time two merchants of a passing caravan came that way. Instigated by a friendly deity, they joyfully saluted the seer, and, elated in their hearts, gave him alms. They were the first to do so. After that the sage saw that Arada and Udraka Ramaputra were the two people best equipped to grasp the Dharma. But then he saw that both had gone to live among the gods in heaven. His mind thereupon turned to the five mendicants. In order to proclaim the path to Peace, thereby dispelling the darkness of ignorance, just as the rising sun conquers the darkness of night, Gautama betook himself to the blessed city of Kashi, to which Bhimaratha gave his love, and which is adorned with the Varanasi river and with many splendid forests. Then, before he carried out his wish to go into the region of Kashi, the Sage, whose eyes were like those of a bull, and whose gait like that of an elephant in rut, once more fixed his steady gaze on the root of the Bodhi tree, after he had turned his entire body like an elephant.

5.3 NIKAYA, OR HINAYANA, BUDDHISM

In the third century B.C.E., there were eighteen sects of Buddhism. These were given the pejorative name **Hinayana** ("Little Vehicle") by later Mahayana (Great Vehicle) Buddhists because the Mahayanists argued that the Hinayana tradition, concentrating as it did on the life of monks, carried fewer people to enlightenment. Of these eighteen sects only the **Theravada** (Way of the Elders) survives today, mostly in Sri Lanka and Southeast Asia. Hence, sometimes this whole tradition is called Theravada.

I have used the term **Nikaya** in order to avoid the pejorative term Hinayana and the misleading term Theravada, but Nikaya (often used to refer to a textual collection of discourses attributed to the Buddha or to an ordination lineage of the *sangha*) is not yet in widespread use in the textbooks. Nikaya Buddhism (Buddhism of the Schools) is not without its own problems, but it is sometimes used by Buddhists themselves and is increasingly being adopted by scholars.

We know little about the early history of the Theravada school in India, but we do know it was and is a conservative tradition and considers itself as preserving the original form of Buddhism. It refuses to deify the Buddha as some later traditions have and rejects any scriptures written after the formation of the *Tripitika* ("The Three Baskets," a term for the Buddhist canon). It tends to be individualistic in the sense that each individual is responsible for treading the path to enlightenment relying primarily on his or her own efforts. Of course, the Buddhist community (*sangha*) provides support in general, and those who can become monks and nuns live and practice in a community of like-minded individuals.

5.3.1 The Evolution of the World

There is no creation myth in early Buddhism because there is no creation or creator god. The universe or world is eternal. However, it does go through a cycle of beginning, evolving, and decaying and, then, repeats itself endlessly. The standard cosmology divides the universe into three realms, or worlds—the realm of desire, of form, and of the formless.

The realm of desire is inhabited by humans and organized into four islands surrounding a central mountain, **Mount Meru** (or Sumeru). On the lower elevation of Mount Meru live a class of beings called *asuras,* often translated as "demigods" or "titans." *Asuras* are often depicted as mean-spirited and causing harm to humans. At a higher elevation and above Mount Meru live six classes of gods. These gods, while living a long time, are not immortal and they too eventually die and are reborn. These gods are usually honored for the benefits they bestow. *Pretas,* or hungry ghosts, also inhabit the realm of desire. Monks and nuns have a special responsibility of feeding these ghosts, who have enormous stomachs and throats the size of the eye of a needle and hence are always hungry and thirsty.

Still in the realm of desire, but below the Southern Island on which humans live, are numerous hells, some burning hot and others freezing cold. It is desirable not to be reborn here, since beings here undergo a variety of tortures. These hells, however, are more like purgatories because it is possible to be reborn out of them.

The realm of form is situated above the realm of desire. Gods who experience the pleasures of sight, sound, and touch (but not taste and smell) live here. These gods have great powers of concentration that provide them with mental bliss.

Even more sublime than the realm of form is the formless realm. Here, gods exist in states of pure consciousness without bodies and sense organs of any kind. This is the most blissful of abodes and one of the most desirable places to be reborn.

The following story tells about the beginning of a new cycle of the universe and is referred to as the *Sutra on Knowing the Beginning (Aganna sutta)*. At the start of a new cycle, humans live in a paradise, in which there is no need for food and their life span is immeasurable. But things change for the worse. Unfortunately, it seems, they always do.

Sutra on Knowing the Beginning (Agganna Sutta)

READING QUESTIONS

1. What are the beings like who fall from the Realm of the Radiant Gods, and why do they fall?
2. Why does one of these beings begin to eat the earth-essence and why do others follow suit? What effect does this activity have on the beings?
3. What is the sequence of events after the earth-essence disappears?
4. What is the point of this story?

O monks, eventually there comes a time when, after a long period, this world starts to wind down. And as the world is winding down, beings for the most part are re-born out of it, in the Realm of the Radiant Gods. Eventually, after another long period, it happens that this world that has ended begins to reevolve. And as it is re-evolving, settling, and becoming established, certain beings, in order to work out their karma, fall from the Realm of the Radiant Gods and come to be once again in this world. These beings by nature are self-luminescent and move through the air. They are made of mind, feed on joy, dwell in bliss, and go where they will.

When at first they reappear, there is no knowledge in the world of the sun and the moon. And likewise there is no knowledge of the forms of the stars, of the paths of the constellations, of night and day, month and fort-night, seasons and years. . . .

Eventually, this Great Earth appears; it is like a pool of water. It is pretty and savory and tastes just like pure sweet honey, and in physical appearance it is like the scum on milk or ghee.

Now, monks, it happens that a certain being, fickle and greedy by nature, tastes some of this earth-essence with his finger. He enjoys its color, its smell, and its sa-vor. Then other beings, seeing what he has done, imi-tate him. They also taste some of the earth-essence with their fingers, and they too take pleasure in its color, its smell, its savor.

Then, on another occasion, that being takes a morsel of earth-essence and eats it, and the other beings too,

seeing what he has done, imitate him. . . . And because they take morsels of earth-essence and eat them, in due course their bodies become heavy, solid, and hard, and their former qualities—of being self-luminescent, of moving through the air, being made of mind, feeding on joy, dwelling in bliss, and going where they will—dis-appear. And when this happens, the sun and the moon and likewise the forms of the stars, the paths of the con-stellations, night and day, month and fortnight, seasons and years come to be known in the world.

Now, monks, for a very long time these beings con-tinue to consume this earth-essence. It is their food, what they eat, and it shapes them. Those who eat a lot of it take on an ugly appearance, whereas those who con-sume only a little of it become good looking. And the ones who are good looking become contemptuous of those who are ugly. "We are handsome," they declare, "and you look bad." While they go in this way, con-vinced of their own superior beauty, proud and arro-gant, the earth-essence disappears. . . .

Now monks, when those beings eat the rice that is huskless, polished, and sweet smelling, bodily features of femininity appear in those who are women, and bod-ily features of masculinity appear in those who are men. Then, overflowing thoughts of passion for each other arise in their minds; they are pleased with each other, consumed by passion for each other, and have illicit sex together.

Then, other beings see them having illicit sex to-gether and throw sticks and clods of dirt and dust at them. . . . Nowadays, when a girl is carried off to be mar-ried, people throw sticks and clods of dirt. In this way, they repeat an ancient primeval custom without realiz-ing the meaning of it. In former times, it was thought to be immoral, profane, and undisciplined, but nowadays it is deemed moral, sacred, and disciplined. . . .

Then, it occurs to a certain being who has gone out to gather rice that he is needlessly wearying himself. "Why," he reflects, "should I go on tiring myself by get-ting rice for supper in the evening and rice for breakfast in the morning, when I could be gathering it for both evening and morning meals just once a day?" And that is what he begins to do.

Then, one evening, some other being says to him: "Come, my friend, let's go get some rice."

But the first being replies: "You go, friend. I already brought back rice for both evening and morning meals."

Then it occurs to that second being: "This is a won-derful way of doing things! Why, I could be gathering rice all at once for two or three days!" And that is what he begins to do.

Then, monks, it happens that a third being says to him: "Come, my friend, let's go get some rice."

And he replies: "You go, my friend. I already brought back rice for two or three days."

Then it occurs to that third being: "Now this is a wonderful way of doing things! Why, I could be gathering rice all at once for four or five days!" And that is what he begins to do.

But because these beings are now hoarding and consuming that rice that is huskless, polished, and sweet smelling, husks and reddish coatings begin to appear on it. And if it is reaped in the evening, by daybreak it has not sprouted, ripened, or grown back, and it is clear that it has been cut.

Then, those beings quickly assemble together and take counsel with one another. . . . "Now what if we were to divide the rice fields and draw boundaries between them?"

And that, monks, is what those beings do, declaring, "This field is yours, and this field is mine."

Then it occurs to one of those beings who has gone to gather rice: "How will I get my livelihood if my allotment of rice is destroyed? Why don't I now go and steal someone else's rice?"

And so that being, while guarding his own share of rice, goes and steals somebody else's portion. But another being happens to see him stealing that other person's portion, and he goes up to him and says, "Ho, my friend, you have taken someone else's rice!"

To which he replies: "Yes, my friend, but it will not happen again."

Nonetheless, it occurs a second time . . . and a third time. He goes and steals somebody else's portion, and another being sees him. But this time, that other being goes up to him and beats him with a stick, and says: "This is the third time, friend, that you have taken someone else's rice!"

Then that being holds up his arms, wails, and cries out: "Friends, immorality has appeared in the world! Irreligion has appeared in the world, for the taking up of sticks is now known!" But, the first being throws his stick on the ground, holds up his arms, wails, and cries out: "Friends, immorality and irreligion have appeared in the world, because stealing and lying are now known!"

In this way, monks, these three evil and demeritorious things first come to be known in the world: theft, lying, and violence. . . .

5.3.2 The Three Marks of Existence

If I asked you to name three things that characterize human existence, what would you name? You might say that while humans are happy and satisfied some of the time, they also suffer to one degree or another.

You also might notice a link between human suffering and change or impermanence. We have desires for things that please us and want to avoid pain and experience as much pleasure as is reasonably possible. When we find something that gives us pleasure, we become attached to it and do not want it to change. However, sooner or later it does change. We cannot avoid the passage of time, and inevitably the pleasures of childhood will give way to adulthood, old age, and eventually death. It makes us sad to lose the pleasures and innocence of childhood, and the thought of death often scares us.

Who is, however, being scared? Who is it that desires pleasure, becomes attached, experiences change, and then suffers? The answer seems obvious: I do. But who is this I? "Your self," you might reply. Quite so, but who is this self? Is it your soul? Probably many of us would answer yes, because the idea of a soul is so deeply rooted in Western culture and tradition. But what exactly is the soul? Is it a thing, a spiritual substance of some sort? How long does it live? Is it also impermanent?

In the Buddha's India, some Brahmins and others taught that the self (*atman* in Sanskrit) is an eternal, permanent substance (see previous chapter on Hinduism). The Buddha disagreed. Careful introspection showed there is no such self or soul (**anatman** in Sanskrit, **anatta** in Pali). The Buddha thought that this lack of a permanent self, along with suffering and impermanence, constitute the three main marks of existence. He also thought that if there is no such thing as a substantial soul or self, then the problem of attachment and suffering takes on a new light. It becomes possible to experience a freedom from suffering and attachment once one is free from a false view of the self. All this talk of suffering seems pointless if there is no self to suffer, no self to become attached, no self to cling to the momentary but passing existence of things.

Even if this idea of no self can help us see the problem of suffering and attachment in a new light, it seems to undercut both moral responsibility and the idea of rebirth. If there is no self, one would not be able to say that a particular individual had made merit or attained enlightenment. And what would pass from one life to the next? How could my *karma*, good or bad, get passed along?

This denial of a permanent self (the no-self doctrine) startled and puzzled many people in Buddha's day, and today many find it a rather strange idea. In fact, some Buddhists, called the Personalists, while admitting that there is no universal self or *atman* as the Hindus taught, argue that there is something they call the person (*pudgala* in Sanskrit, *puggala* in Pali). If there is a person, then moral responsibility and rebirth make sense. But other Buddhists disagree, arguing that the mark of impermanence applies to everything, including person.

Below are three brief selections dealing with the three marks of existence. The first, from the *Samyutta-Nikaya*, deals with suffering and co-dependent origination. The second, from the *Anityatasutra*, claims that impermanence extends to the Triple World of desire, form, and formlessness. In the final selection, also from the *Samyutta-Nikaya*, a Buddhist nun Vajira encounters **Mara,** the Evil One, who tempted the Buddha himself just before his enlightenment, and she sets him straight about "this Being" called "the self."

Suffering, Co-Dependent Arising, Impermanence, and No-Self (Samyutta-Nikaya and Anityatasutra)

READING QUESTIONS

1. What is the "**Middle Way**" between eternalism and annihilationism, and how does it answer the question about what causes suffering?
2. What does impermanence mean?
3. What, according to Vajira, is the meaning of no-self?

SUFFERING

Thus have I heard. Once, when the Blessed One was dwelling in Rājagaha, . . . he got dressed early in the morning, took his bowl and his robe, and went into town

From *Experience of Buddhism*, 1st ed., by J. S. Strong, pp. 90, 94–95, 100–101. Copyright © 1995 Wadsworth Publishing. Reprinted by permission of Wadsworth Publishing, a division of International Thomson Publishing. Fax 800-730-2215.

for alms. Kassapa, the naked ascetic, saw his coming from a distance. He approached him, they exchanged greetings, and Kassapa, standing to one side, said: "If it is all right, good Gotama, I would like to ask you to explain something."

"Kassapa," the Buddha replied, "this is not a good time for questions; I am visiting houses. . . ."

But Kassapa repeated his request, and added: "I do not have many things to ask, good Gotama."

"Then go ahead and ask if you wish to, Kassapa."

"Good Gotama," Kassapa began, "is the suffering that one suffers caused by oneself?"

"No, it is not, Kassapa," replied the Blessed One.

"Then is the suffering that one suffers caused by someone else?"

"No, it is not Kassapa."

"Well, then, is it caused both by oneself and by someone else?"

"No, it is not, Kassapa."

"Well, then, . . . does it arise spontaneously?"

"No, it does not."

"Then suffering is nonexistent, good Gotama."

"No, Kassapa, it is not nonexistent; there *is* suffering."

"But you do not know it, nor do you see it?"

"Not so, Kassapa, I both know it and see it."

"Good Gotama, to all these questions that I have asked you . . . you have answered no. So please tell me, please teach me about suffering."

"Kassapa, if you say, 'The same individual who does a deed experiences its results'—what you called 'suffering caused by oneself'—then you fall into the view of eternalism. But if you say, 'One individual does a deed and another experiences its results'—what a sufferer would call 'suffering caused by another'—then you fall into the view of annihilationism. Kassapa, avoiding these two extremes, the Tathāgata teaches the Dharma in the manner of a Middle Way:

"Conditioned by ignorance are karmic constituents; conditioned by karmic constituents is consciousness; conditioned by consciousness is individuality (name and form); conditioned by individuality are the six senses; conditioned by the six senses is contact; conditioned by contact is feeling; conditioned by feeling is desire; conditioned by desire is clinging; conditioned by clinging is becoming; conditioned by becoming is rebirth; conditioned by rebirth are old age, death, sorrow, lamentation, suffering, depression, and dismay. In this way, this whole great heap of suffering originates.

"But from the complete cessation and dissipation of ignorance comes the cessation of karmic constituents; and from the complete cessation and dissipation of karmic constituents comes the cessation of consciousness;

and from the complete cessation and dissipation of consciousness comes the cessation of individuality; and from the complete cessation of individuality . . . [and so forth until]: from the complete cessation and dissipation of rebirth comes the cessation of old age, death, sorrow, lamentation, suffering, depression, and dismay. In this way, this whole great heap of suffering ceases."

IMPERMANENCE

Thus have I heard: Once the Blessed One was dwelling in Śrāvastī at the Jetavana monastery together with a great company of monks. And he said: "O monks, all karmically constituted things are impermanent; they are not fixed, not comforting, and are characterized by constant change. . . . For all beings, all creatures, all living things, life is limited by death; for them there is no termination of death and rebirth.

"And, monks, those who are householders from prominent families, brahmins, nobles, rich people . . .— their lives too are limited by death; for them there is no termination of death and rebirth.

"And, monks, nobles who have been annointed king, who have attained power and sovereignty over the people, and who have conquered the whole earth—their lives too are limited by death; for them there is no termination of death and rebirth.

"And, monks, brahmanical ascetics who dwell in the forest, who grasp for the fruit of liberation, who enjoy the fruit of liberation, who live by the fruit of liberation—their lives too are limited by death; for them there is no termination of death and rebirth.

"And, monks, those gods of the realm of desire, the four great guardian kings, the gods of the Trāyastriṃśa, Yama, Tuṣita, and other heavens—their lives too are limited by death; for them there is no termination of death and rebirth.

"And, monks, those gods of the realm of form—those who have attained the first, the second, the third, or the fourth trance levels—their lives too are limited by death; for them there is no termination of death and rebirth.

"And, monks, those gods of the formless realm, those who dwell in the contemplation of endless space, those who dwell in the contemplation of endless consciousness, those who dwell in the contemplation of nothingness, and those who dwell in the contemplation of neither perception nor nonperception—their lives too are limited by death; for them there is no termination of death and rebirth. Thus it is for the Triple World. . . .

NO-SELF

One morning, the nun Vajirā got dressed in her robes, and, taking her bowl, she entered the city of Sāvatthi for alms and went about the town on her begging round. On her way back, after her noonday meal, she entered into the Andhavana woods and seated herself at the foot of a tree to take her midday rest.

Then Māra, the Evil One, wishing to engender fear, shock, and dread in the nun Vajirā and hoping to disturb her meditation, approached her and spoke these verses:

Vajirā, who created this Being?
Where is Being's maker?
Where did Being come from?
Where will it disappear to?

But the nun Vajirā replied:

Māra, why do you keep coming back to Being?
You are resorting to false views.
There is no Being to be found here—
only a heap of karmic constituents.
Just as the word *chariot* is used,
when we come across a combination of parts,
so we speak conventionally of a Being
when the five skandhas are present.
But, truly, it is only suffering that arises,
suffering that persists and passes away,
nothing other than suffering that arises,
nothing else than suffering that ceases to be.

5.3.3 The Path to Enlightenment

The **Eightfold Path** or Way (the Fourth Noble Truth) is often divided into three parts: wisdom, moral conduct, and mental discipline or meditation. The Buddhist, seeking the middle way between extremes, must develop a right understanding of the **Four Noble Truths** and realize the truth of the three marks of existence. Right understanding or wisdom, however, cannot be developed in isolation from moral conduct and the practice of meditation.

The two selections that follow deal with moral conduct in relation to the life of a monk and the practice of meditation. Buddhist texts have much to say about meditation—how to do it, what to meditate on, what trance states to expect. They also contain practical advice for beginners, who inevitably will face difficulties. The second selection (from the *Saundarananda of Ashvaghosha*) recounts advice the Buddha reputedly gave to his half-brother, Nanda. Nanda was happily married and reluctant to join the *sangha* and leave his family. When he does leave, the Buddha instructs him in his meditation practice in order to help him concentrate on his new life on the path to *nirvana.*

Moral Conduct and Meditation

READING QUESTIONS

1. How do you respond to these moral ideals? In your view, what is positive about them and what is negative?
2. How do you think disciplining the mind by meditation practice helps one attain liberation?

MORAL CONDUCT

"Life in a household is confining and polluting; the monastic life is like open air. Living in a home, it is not easy to lead an utterly fulfilling, pure, chaste, and studious life, polished like mother of pearl. Why don't I, therefore, cut off my hair and beard, put on a yellow robe, leave home, and adopt the homeless life?"

Thus thinking, a householder or his son . . . abandons his accumulated wealth, whether great or small, and leaves behind the circle of his relations, whether many or few. And once he has wandered forth, he lives . . . endowed with good conduct, careful of the slightest transgressions, undertaking to observe the precepts, doing meritorious deeds of body, speech, and mind and leading a pure life, perfect in morality. . . .

In what ways . . . is a monk perfect in morality? Forsaking the taking of life, he abstains from killing. Having laid down his stick and his sword, he lives in modesty, showing kindness, compassion, and concern for the welfare of all living beings. Such is his moral conduct.

Forsaking the taking of what is not given, he abstains from theft. He lives, openly accepting and ex-

pecting gifts, keeping himself pure. Such is his moral conduct.

Forsaking unchastity, he leads a chaste life, aloof, abstaining from the vulgar practice of sex. Such is his moral conduct.

Forsaking uttering falsehoods, he abstains from lying. He . . . speaks the truth and is reliable, open, and trustworthy, not deceiving the world. Such is his moral conduct.

Forsaking malicious speech, he abstains from slander. What he hears here he does not repeat there so as to create factions; and what he hears there he does not repeat here for the same reason. In this way, he reconciles those who are at odds, he encourages those who are united, and he rejoices, delights, and takes pleasure in concord and promotes it when he speaks. Such is his moral conduct.

Forsaking harsh speech, he abstains from rudeness. Instead, he speaks words that are blameless, pleasing to the ear, kind, heart-warming, polite, delightful, and charming to many people. Such is his moral conduct.

Forsaking frivolous talk, he abstains from trivial conversations. His speech is timely, factual, and to the point, dealing with Dharma and the Vinaya. At the right time, he speaks words that are worth treasuring, that are reasonable, well defined, and purposeful. Such is his moral conduct.

He refrains from harvesting seeds or plants. He takes one meal a day and refrains from eating after noon or at night. He avoids watching shows that involve dancing, singing, and music. He abstains from bodily ornaments or jewelry and from wearing garlands, perfumes, or cosmetics. He does not use high or large beds. He refuses to accept gold or silver. . . .

MEDITATION

. . . Sit down cross-legged in some solitary place, hold your back straight, and direct your mindfulness in front of you, to the tip of your nose, your forehead, or the space between your eyebrows. Make your wandering mind focus entirely on one thing. Now if that mental affliction—a lustful imagination—should rear its head, do not abide it but brush it off as though it were dust on your clothes. For even if you have consciously rid yourself of desires, . . . there remains an innate proclivity toward them, like a fire hidden in the ashes. This, my friend, must be extinguished by meditation, like a fire put out by water. Otherwise, from that innate proclivity, desires will grow back again, as plants do from a seed. Only by its destruction will they cease to be, as plants whose roots are destroyed. . . .

Now if malice or thoughts of violence should unsettle your mind, you should use their antidotes to make it calm, the way a jewel settles muddied water. Know that their antidotes are love and compassion, for the opposition between them is eternal, like that between light and darkness. Those who have controlled wickedness but still harbor malicious thoughts throw dirt onto themselves, the way an elephant does after a bath. What noble, compassionate person could wish to impose further suffering on mortals who are already afflicted by sickness, death, old age, and so forth? . . . Therefore, abandon what is demeritorious, and meditate on what is meritorious, for that will cause you to attain your goals in this world, as well as the ultimate goal. . . .

Now if your thoughts should turn to the prosperity or lack thereof of your own family members, you should examine the inherent nature of the world of living beings in order to suppress them. Among beings who are being dragged along through saṃsāra by the force of karma, who is a stranger, who is a relative? It is due to delusion that one person seems attached to another. Your relative in a past life has become a stranger, and in a future life a stranger may become a relative. Just as birds assemble here and there in the evening to roost, so it is with the closeness of relatives and strangers from one birth to the next. . . . He who was your beloved relative in another existence—what is he to you now, or you to him? Therefore, you should not let your mind dwell on thoughts of your family; in saṃsāra there is no steady distinction between relatives and nonrelatives. . . .

Now if thoughts should arise in your mind that this country or that country is peaceful or fortunate or that alms are easy to get there, discard them, my friend, and do not dwell on them in any way whatsoever. For you know that the whole world everywhere is plagued by one problem or another. . . . Whether by cold, heat, disease, or danger, people are always being oppressed; nowhere in this world is there a refuge. There is no country where fear does not exist, where the people are not in terror of old age, sickness, and death. . . .

Now if you should have any thoughts that assume that there is no death, make efforts to ward them off, as though they were an illness you had come down with. Not even for a moment should you trust in the continuity of life. Like a tiger lying in wait, death can strike down the unsuspecting at any time. Do not think "I am strong, I am young." Death does not consider age but kills in all circumstances. Realizing the world to be insubstantial and ephemeral like a bubble, what sane person could ever fail to take death into consideration?

In summation then, my friend, in order to avoid having all of these thoughts, you should become a master of mindfulness. . . . In order to obtain gold, one must wash away the dirt—first the big clods and then, to cleanse it further, the smaller ones, until finally one retains pure particles of gold. Just so, in order to obtain liberation, one must discipline the mind and wash away from it first the big clods of one's faults and then, to purify it further, the smaller ones until finally one retains pure particles of Dharma.

5.3.4 The Goal

Nirvana (*nibbana* in Pali), or release from suffering, is the Buddhist equivalent of salvation. Buddhism usually distinguishes between two kinds of *nirvana*: *nirvana* with remaining *karma* and *nirvana* without remaining *karma* (*parinirvana*). The first is possible in this physical world and is what the Buddha experienced at enlightenment. The second is possible after death. To enter *parinirvana* is never to return again to this physical world of sorrow and rebirth (*samsara*).

What exactly is *nirvana*? Although it is, according to Buddhists, a bliss ultimately beyond the ability of human language to describe, much is said about it. The selections that follow deal with some aspects of it. The first selection, from the *Udana*, recounts what the Buddha presumably said about *nirvana* to his monks and discusses the sense in which *nirvana* is the end of suffering. The second selection, from the *Therigatha* (*Songs of Nuns*), was written by Patacara after she became an **arhati** (a female **arhat** or saint who has attained *nirvana* with remaining *karma*).

Patacara lived a tragic life. Her entire family is killed one by one, and she was almost driven mad with suffering. While in a state of despair, she meets the Buddha, who counsels her and allows her to become a nun. After years of meditative practice, she severs all attachments to worldly things.

The third selection, also from the *Therigatha*, was written by the mother of a monk who became an *arhat*. She left her unhappy home and became a nun. When she becomes an *arhati*, she celebrates her freedom.

Nirvana, The Cessation of Suffering (by Patacara), and The Joy of Release

READING QUESTIONS

1. What terms would you use to describe *nirvana?*
2. Would you like to experience *nirvana?* Why or why not?
3. What notion of freedom is found in these selections?

NIRVANA

Monks, there exists something in which there is neither earth nor water, fire nor air. It is not the sphere of infinite space, nor the sphere of infinite consciousness, nor the sphere of nothingness, nor the sphere of neither perception nor non-perception. It is neither this world nor another world, nor both, neither sun nor moon.

Monks, I do not state that it comes nor that it goes. It neither abides nor passes away. It is not caused, established, arisen, supported. It is the end of suffering. . . .

What I call the selfless is difficult to perceive, for it is not easy to perceive the truth. But one who knows it cuts through craving, and for one who knows it, there is nothing to hold onto. . . .

Monks, there exists something that is unborn, unmade, uncreated, unconditioned. Monks, if there were not an unborn, unmade, uncreated, unconditioned, then there would be no way to indicate how to escape from the born, made, created, and conditioned. However, monks, since there exists something that is unborn, unmade, uncreated, and unconditioned, it is known that there is an escape from that which is born, made, created, and conditioned. . . .

There is wandering for those who are attached, but there is no wandering for those who are unattached. There is serenity when there is no wandering, and when there is serenity, there is no desire. When there is no desire, there is neither coming nor going, and when there

is no coming nor going there is neither death nor rebirth. When there is neither death nor rebirth, there is neither this life nor the next life, nor anything in between. It is the end of suffering.

[*Udana*, ch. 8.1–4]

THE CESSATION OF SUFFERING

Ploughing their fields, sowing seeds in the ground,
Men care for their wives and children and prosper.
Why is it that I, endowed with morality and adhering to the teachings,
Do not attain nirvana? I am neither lazy nor conceited.
After washing my feet, I observed the water; watching the water flow downwards,
I focused my mind as one [trains] a noble thoroughbred horse.
Then I took a lamp and entered my cell. After observing the bed, I sat on the couch.
Holding a pin, I pulled out the wick.
The lamp goes out: nirvana. My mind is free!

[*Therigatha*, psalm 47]

THE JOY OF RELEASE

Free, I am free!
I am completely free from my kitchen pestle!
[I am free from] my worthless husband and even his sun umbrella!
And my pot that smells like a water snake!
I have eliminated all desire and hatred,
Going to the base of a tree, [I think,] "What happiness!"
And contemplate this happiness.

[*Therigatha*, psalm 22]

From *Scriptures of the World's Religions*, by James Fieser and John Powers (Boston: McGraw-Hill, 1998), pp. 86–87, 94–95. Translation by John Powers from the 1948 edition of *Udana*, edited by Paul Steinthal (London: Geoffrey Cumberlege), pp. 80–81, and the 1883 edition of *Therigatha*, edited by Hermann Oldenberg and Richard Pischel (London: Pali Text Society), pp. 134–135. Reprinted by permission of John Powers.

5.4 MAHAYANA BUDDHISM

Mahayana (Great Vehicle) Buddhism probably emerged in India five hundred years after the Buddha's death, although its proponents claim that its teachings go back to the Buddha himself. Mahayana lived side by side with Nikaya Buddhism for several centuries, but by the third or fourth century C.E. there were ordination lineages that distinguished themselves from earlier forms of Buddhism. As the Theravada sect of Nikaya moved south, Mahayana moved east and north, eventually becoming the dominant form of Buddhism in China, Vietnam, Korea, and Japan. However, elements of both can be found in southern as well as northern Asia.

Exactly what factors led to Mahayana formation we do not know. Possibly one or more of the eighteen sects of early Buddhism developed the ideas and practices that eventually became characteristic of Mahayana. Perhaps it arose out of a new movement in southern India and spread across several early Buddhist sects. One thing is clear, however: Mahayanists wanted to give a greater role to lay disciples. In early Buddhism, the monks were the full-time religious professionals and the laity gave them material support (food, clothing, land, buildings, and the like) in exchange for merit. However, if a layperson wanted to make serious spiritual progress toward enlightenment in this lifetime, he or she would have to "depart of the world" and become a monk or nun. Mahayanists, in contrast, gave the laity a greater religious role and held it was possible to make serious spiritual progress, even gain enlightenment, without becoming a monk or nun.

The greater role afforded the laity by Mahayanists slowly changed the *sangha* and Buddhism itself. For one thing, it increased the religious importance of the laity. It also led to greater emphasis on the Buddha's compassion and his role as a savior figure who could dispense grace to those whose faith and worship is sincere. Pilgrimages to stupas enshrining holy relics had been a part of early Buddhism, but now became more popular and widespread. Merit that could change one's karmic future could be made by participating in such pilgrimages and even transferred to others (such as dead relatives). Veneration of *bodhisattvas* who now, unlike the *arhat* ideal of Theravada, dedicated themselves primarily to the salvation of all living beings also became increasingly popular. And, as we shall shortly see, distinctive teachings arose claiming to convey a perfect wisdom.

5.4.1 Parable of the Lost Son

Do you think it is sometimes necessary to trick people for their own good? Does a good teacher tailor her or his message for the level the students can understand? Perhaps religious teachers say things that appear contradictory because they are tailoring their message for the abilities of their audience. Maybe they employ "skillful means" (**upaya**) in their words and deeds in order to bring people of different capacities to the truth.

The *Saddharma-Pundarika* (*The Lotus of the True Law*), better known as the *Lotus Sutra*, is a Mahayana text that treats many Buddhist teachings (particularly the Nikaya teachings) as provisionally expedient. They are steps toward the true teaching, the true law revealed in the *Lotus Sutra*. The situation is like a father who cannot get his children to come out of a burning house. Finally, he promises them toys if they will come out. It is a deceptive lure, but it leads to an expedient rescue. Is the father justified in deceiving his children? Is his lie a noble one? Is all well that ends well?

This story is a brief summary of the famous "Parable of the Burning House" found in the *Lotus Sutra*. However, it is not the only parable dealing with the issue of *upaya*, or skillful means. There is also the "Parable of the Lost Son." Although this story reminds many readers of the "Parable of the Prodigal Son" found in the Christian New Testament, there are important differences. For one thing, Mahayana Buddhism uses the story of the "Lost Son" along with the story of the "Burning House" to emphasize that teachings are like rafts. The purpose of the raft is to get you from one shore to another. Once you are successfully on the other side, do you need the raft anymore? So the Buddha's teachings are like rafts or vehicles intended to get you to enlightenment. Their value is in where they take you. They are not ends in themselves.

The Lost Son

READING QUESTIONS

1. Why does the poor son run away when he sees the rich man?
2. How does the rich father get his poor son to come back and work for him?
3. What did the poor son think when his father revealed his identity and gave him his inheritance?
4. State what you take to be the point of the parable.
5. Read the "Parable of the Prodigal Son" in the New Testament (Luke 15:11–32), and compare the Bud-

From *Saddharma-Pundarika, or The Lotus of the True Law*, translated by Hendrik Kern. Volume XXI of *The Sacred Books of the East*, edited by F. Max Mueller (Oxford, England: Clarendon Press, 1884), pp. 99–108.

dhist story of the Lost Son with the story of the Prodigal Son. How are they alike and how are they different?

It is a case, O Lord, as if a certain man went away from his father and betook himself to some other place. He lives there in foreign parts for many years, twenty or thirty or forty or fifty. In course of time the one (the father) becomes a great man; the other (the son) is poor; in seeking a livelihood for the sake of food and clothing he roams in all directions and goes to some place, whereas his father removes to another country. . . .

In course of time, Lord, that poor man, in quest of food and clothing, roaming through villages, towns, boroughs, provinces, kingdoms, and royal capitals, reaches the place where his father, the owner of much wealth and gold, treasures and granaries, is residing. Now the poor man's father, Lord, the owner of much wealth and gold, treasures and granaries, who was residing in that town, had always and ever been thinking of the son he had lost fifty years ago, but he gave no utterance to his thoughts before others, and was only pining in himself and thinking: I am old, aged, advanced in years, and possess abundance of bullion, gold, money and corn, treasures and granaries, but have no son. It is to be feared lest death shall overtake me and all this perish unused. Repeatedly he was thinking of that son: O how happy should I be, were my son to enjoy this mass of wealth!

Meanwhile, Lord, the poor man in search of food and clothing was gradually approaching the house of the rich man, the owner of abundant bullion, gold, money and corn, treasures and granaries. And the father of the poor man happened to sit at the door of his house, surrounded and waited upon by a great crowd of Brâhmans, Kshatriyas, Vaisyas, and Sûdras; he was sitting on a magnificent throne with a footstool decorated with gold and silver, while dealing with hundred thousands of kotis of gold-pieces, and fanned with a chowrie, on a spot under an extended awning inlaid with pearls and flowers and adorned with hanging garlands of jewels; sitting (in short) in great pomp. The poor man, Lord, saw his own father in such pomp sitting at the door of the house, surrounded with a great crowd of people and doing a householder's business. The poor man frightened, terrified, alarmed, seized with a feeling of horripilation all over the body, and agitated in mind, reflects thus: Unexpectedly have I here fallen in with a king or grandee. People like me have nothing to do here; let me go; in the street of the poor I am likely to find food and clothing without much difficulty. Let me no longer tarry at this place, lest I be taken to do forced labour or incur some other injury.

Thereupon, Lord, the poor man quickly departs, runs off, does not tarry from fear of a series of supposed dangers. But the rich man, sitting on the throne at the door of his mansion, has recognised his son at first sight, in consequence whereof he is content, in high spirits, charmed, delighted, filled with joy and cheerfulness. He thinks: Wonderful! he who is to enjoy this plenty of bullion, gold, money and corn, treasures and granaries, has been found! He of whom I have been thinking again and again, is here now that I am old, aged, advanced in years.

At the same time, moment, and instant, Lord, he despatches couriers, to whom he says: Go, sirs, and quickly fetch me that man. The fellows thereon all run forth in full speed and overtake the poor man, who, frightened, terrified, alarmed, seized with a feeling of horripilation all over his body, agitated in mind, utters a lamentable cry of distress, screams, and exclaims: I have given you no offence. But the fellows drag the poor man, however lamenting, violently with them. He, frightened, terrified, alarmed, seized with a feeling of horripilation all over his body, and agitated in mind, thinks by himself: I fear lest I shall be punished with capital punishment; I am lost. He faints away, and falls on the earth. His father dismayed and near despondency says to those fellows: Do not carry the man in that manner. With these words he sprinkles him with cold water without addressing him any further. For that householder knows the poor man's humble disposition and his own elevated position; yet he feels that the man is his son.

The householder, Lord, skilfully conceals from every one that it is his son. He calls one of his servants and says to him: Go, sirrah, and tell that poor man: Go, sirrah, whither thou likest; thou art free. The servant obeys, approaches the poor man and tells him: Go, sirrah, whither thou likest; thou art free. The poor man is astonished and amazed at hearing these words; he leaves that spot and wanders to the street of the poor in search of food and clothing. In order to attract him the householder practises an able device. He employs for it two men ill-favoured and of little splendour. Go, says he, go to the man you saw in this place; hire him in your own name for a double daily fee, and order him to do work here in my house. And if he asks: What work shall I have to do? tell him: Help us in clearing the heap of dirt. The two fellows go and seek the poor man and engage him for such work as mentioned. . . .

Then the householder descends from his mansion, lays off his wreath and ornaments, parts with his soft, clean, and gorgeous attire, puts on dirty raiment, takes a basket in his right hand, smears his body with dust, and goes to his son, whom he greets from afar, and thus addresses: Please, take the baskets and without delay remove the dust. By this device he manages to speak to his son, to have a talk with him and say: Do, sirrah, remain here in my service; do not go again to another place; I will give thee extra pay, and whatever thou wantest thou mayst confidently ask me, be it the price of a pot, a smaller pot, a boiler or wood, or be it the price of salt, food, or clothing. . . . Be at ease, fellow; look upon me as if I were thy father, for I am older and thou art younger, and thou hast rendered me much service by clearing this heap of dirt, and as long as thou hast been in my service thou hast never shown nor art showing wickedness, crookedness, arrogance, or hypocrisy; I have discovered in thee no vice at all of such as are commonly seen in other man-servants. From henceforward thou art to me like my own son. . . .

After a while, Lord, the householder falls sick, and feels that the time of his death is near at hand. He says to the poor man: Come hither, man, I possess abundant bullion, gold, money and corn, treasures and granaries. I am very sick, and wish to have one upon whom to bestow (my wealth); by whom it is to be received, and with whom it is to be deposited. Accept it. For in the same manner as I am the owner of it, so art thou, but thou shalt not suffer anything of it to be wasted. . . .

After a while, Lord, the householder perceives that his son is able to save, mature and mentally developed; that in the consciousness of his nobility he feels abashed, ashamed, disgusted, when thinking of his former poverty. The time of his death approaching, he sends for the poor man, presents him to a gathering of his relations, and before the king or king's peer and in the presence of citizens and country-people makes the following speech: Hear, gentlemen! this is my own son, by me begotten. It is now fifty years that he disappeared from such and such a town. He is called so and so, and myself am called so and so. In searching after him I have from that town come hither. He is my son, I am his father. To him I leave all my revenues, and all my personal (or private) wealth shall he acknowledge (his own).

The poor man, Lord, hearing this speech was astonished and amazed; he thought by himself: Unexpectedly have I obtained this bullion, gold, money and corn, treasures and granaries.

Even so, O Lord, do we represent the sons of the Tathâgata, and the Tathâgata says to us: Ye are my sons, as the householder did. We were oppressed, O Lord, with three difficulties, viz. the difficulty of pain, the difficulty of conceptions, the difficulty of transition (or evolution); and in the worldly whirl we were disposed to what is low. Then have we been prompted by the Lord to ponder on the numerous inferior laws (or conditions, things) that are similar to a heap of dirt. Once directed to them we have been practising, making efforts, and seek-

ing for nothing but Nirvâna as our fee. We were content, O Lord, with the Nirvâna obtained, and thought to have gained much at the hands of the Tathâgata because of our having applied ourselves to these laws, practised, and made efforts. But the Lord takes no notice of us, does not mix with us, nor tell us that this treasure of the Tathâgata's knowledge shall belong to us, though the Lord skilfully appoints us as heirs to this treasure of the knowledge of the Tathâgata. And we, O Lord, are not (impatiently) longing to enjoy it, because we deem it a great gain already to receive from the Lord Nirvâna as our fee. We preach to the Bodhisattvas Mahâsattvas a sublime sermon about the knowledge of the Tathâgata; we explain, show, demonstrate the knowledge of the Tathâgata, O Lord, without longing. For the Tathâgata by his skilfulness knows our disposition, whereas we ourselves do not know, nor apprehend. It is for this very reason that the Lord just now tells us that we are to him as sons, and that he reminds us of being heirs to the Tathâgata. For the case stands thus: we are as sons to the Tathâgata, but low (or humble) of disposition; the Lord perceives the strength of our disposition and applies to us the denomination of Bodhisattvas; we are, however, charged with a double office in so far as in presence of Bodhisattvas we are called persons of low disposition and at the same time have to rouse them to Buddha-enlightenment. Knowing the strength of our disposition the Lord has thus spoken, and in this way, O Lord, do we say that we have obtained unexpectedly and without longing the jewel of omniscience, which we did not desire, nor seek, nor search after, nor expect, nor require; and that inasmuch as we are the sons of the Tathâgata. . . .

5.4.2 Perfection of Wisdom

A voluminous literature starts to appear around the beginning of the common era known as *Prajnaparamita*, usually translated as the "perfection of wisdom," but literally it means the "wisdom gone beyond." To enter the world created by this literature is something like accompanying Alice in her trip to wonderland in that it carries you beyond ordinary ways of thinking and speaking.

One of the best-known *Prajnaparamita* texts is the *Heart Sutra*. It is recited by monks and laity throughout East Asia, Tibet, and, most recently, Europe and the United States. The **sutra** is put in the mouth of **Avalokiteshvara,** one of the most important *bodhisattvas* of the Mahayana tradition. He instructs Sariputra, a disciple of the Buddha. There is a polemical intent in the text. Sariputra represents Nikaya Buddhism. Hence his instruction by a Mahayana *bodhisattva* in a wisdom that "goes beyond" clearly proclaims the superiority of Mahayana teachings.

At the heart of the text is the concept of emptiness. The **Abhidharma** (advanced doctrine) section of the Theravada scripture discusses the self-existence (**svabhava**), or essence, of *dharmas*. The *dharmas* here name elements of existence, and Avalokiteshvara, in the *Heart Sutra*, proclaims all such *dharmas* to be "empty of any inherent self-existence." This is a logical extension of the doctrines of impermanence and No-Self (see 5.3.2). However, calling the *dharmas* empty does not mean that they do not exist. It just means that their nature is not what the Abhidharmists said it was, namely, self-existence (*svabhava*). In other words, things have no abiding essence or substantial self-identity.

The *Heart Sutra* ends with a **mantra,** or formula, that not only sums up the *sutra* but also presumably is effective in saving people from suffering through its sincere repetition. As you say it, it carries you to a wisdom beyond conventional thought and into a wonderland of new insight into the insubstantial fluidity of reality providing you with an opportunity to awaken beyond this present dream. I recommend that you read this short *sutra* aloud and, at first, with enough speed to allow your mind to be disoriented by the negations that tumble over one another undermining any stable place to stand.

Heart Sutra

READING QUESTIONS

1. How did reading this sutra make you feel, and what did it make you think?
2. Why is the *mantra* of the perfection of wisdom the *mantra* of great knowledge?

From *Scriptures of the World's Religions,* by James Fieser and John Powers (Boston: McGraw-Hill, 1998), pp. 98–101. Translation by John Powers from the 1960 edition of *Samyutta,* edited by Leon Feer (London: Pali Text Society), pp. 134–135. Reprinted by permission of John Powers.

Thus have I heard: At one time the Exalted One was dwelling on the Vulture Peak in Rajagriha together with a great assembly of monks and a great assembly of bodhisattvas. At that time, the Exalted One was immersed in a meditative absorption (*samadhi*) on the enumerations of phenomena called "perception of the profound." Also at that time, the bodhisattva, the great being, the superior Avalokiteshvara was considering the meaning of the profound perfection of wisdom, and he saw that the five aggregates (*skandha*) are empty of inherent existence. Then, due to the inspiration of the Buddha, the venerable Shariputra spoke thus to the bodhisattva, the great being, the superior Avalokiteshvara: "How should a son of good lineage train if he wants to practice the profound perfection of wisdom?"

The bodhisattva, the great being, the superior Avalokiteshvara spoke thus to the venerable Shariputra: "Shariputra, sons of good lineage or daughters of good lineage who want to practice the profound perfection of wisdom should perceive [reality] in this way: They should correctly perceive the five aggregates also as empty of inherent existence. Form is emptiness; emptiness is form. Emptiness is not other than form; form is not other than emptiness. In the same way, feelings, discriminations, compositional factors, and consciousness are empty. Shariputra, in that way, all phenomena are empty, without characteristics, unproduced, unceasing, undefiled, not undefiled, not decreasing, not increasing. Therefore, Shariputra, in emptiness there is no form, no feelings, no discriminations, no compositional factors, no consciousness, no eye, no ear, no nose, no tongue, no body, no mind, no form, no sound, no odor, no taste, no object of touch, no phenomenon. There is no eye constituent, no mental constituent, up to and including no mental consciousness constituent. There is no ignorance, no existence of ignorance, up to and including no aging and death and no extinction of aging and death. In the same way, there is no suffering, no source [of suffering], no cessation [of suffering], no path, no exalted wisdom, no attainment, and also no non-attainment.

"Therefore, Shariputra, because bodhisattvas have no attainment, they depend on and abide in the perfection of wisdom. Because their minds are unobstructed, they are without fear. Having completely passed beyond all error, they go to the fulfillment of nirvana. All the buddhas who live in the three times [past, present, and future] have been completely awakened into unsurpassable, complete, perfect awakening through relying on the perfection of wisdom.

"Therefore, the *mantra* of the perfection of wisdom is the *mantra* of great knowledge, the unsurpassable *mantra*, the *mantra* that is equal to the unequaled, the *mantra* that thoroughly pacifies all suffering. Because it is not false, it should be known to be true. The *mantra* of the perfection wisdom is as follows:

> *Om gate gate paragate parasamgate bodhir svaha* [*Om* gone, gone, gone beyond, gone completely beyond; praise to awakening.]

"Shariputra, bodhisattvas, great beings, should train in the profound perfection of wisdom in that way."

Then the Exalted One arose from that meditative absorption and said to the bodhisattva, the great being, the superior Avalokiteshvara: "Well done! Well done, well done, son of good lineage, it is just so. Son of good lineage, it is like that; the profound perfection of wisdom should be practiced just as you have indicated. Even the Tathagatas admire this." When the Exalted One had spoken thus, the venerable Shariputra, the bodhisattva, the great being, the superior Avalokiteshvara, and all those around them, and those of the world, the gods, humans, demigods, and *gandharvas* were filled with admiration and praised the words of the Exalted One.

5.4.3 Mahayana Philosophy

Most adherents of religious traditions probably know little about the theological and philosophical controversies that develop within their traditions. For most people, religion consists of devotional practices like prayer and worship, pilgrimages to sacred sites, participation in charitable activities, and listening to the stories told and teachings given by their priests, pastors, gurus, or other religious leaders.

However, any full appreciation of a religious tradition requires some familiarity with its theological and philosophical literature. Therefore, the student of religion cannot ignore the intellectual developments of religious traditions even though such developments are often difficult to comprehend and may appear far removed from the life of devotion that concerns most adherents.

Below we will sample the thoughts of two influential Buddhist philosophers: Nagarjuna (first or second century C.E.?), founder of the Madhyamika school of Mahayana Buddhism, and Vasubandhu (320–400), a representative of the Yogacara philosophical school of Mahayana Buddhism.

Nagarjuna detects an apparent inconsistency in the early philosophical interpretations of Nikaya Buddhism. According to Nikaya, the Buddha taught both the no-self (*anatman*) and *dharma* doctrines.

Dharma here refers to the notion that things are made up of basic indivisible elements or essences (*svabhava*). Some Hindu scholars taught that with respect to human beings the self (*atman*) is the essence. Nikaya Buddhism denied that *atman* is the essence (*anatman*), yet affirmed that there are essences. Nagarjuna argues that consistency requires the extension of the *anatman* doctrine to all things (*dharmas*).

This philosophical expansion of the no-self doctrine is equivalent, Nagarjuna believes, to applying the concept of emptiness or **shunyata** of the Perfection of Wisdom literature to all *dharmas* (see Reading 5.4.2, especially that section of the *Heart Sutra* which reads, "Form is emptiness; emptiness is form"). Things are empty of essences. *Shunyata* is, for Nagarjuna, simply the logical development of the Buddha's teaching about co-dependent origination. If things (*dharmas*) have an inherent nature (*svabhava*) that makes them separate and independent, then true interdependency is impossible. If change truly characterizes the nature of *all* existence, and everything is interdependent, then reality must be empty of those things that make for independence and separateness.

Is the claim that things are empty of essences the same as claiming that there are no essences? The answer, according to Nagarjuna, is no. Nagarjuna develops the tetralemma (1. X is; 2. X is not; 3. X is both X and not X; 4. X is neither X nor not X) in order to make his teaching about emptiness clear. The tetralemma confounds those who would make Nagarjuna's doctrine of emptiness into a metaphysical category that is equivalent to claiming there are no essences. Nagarjuna makes no claims at all. According to the tetralemma, Nagarjuna does not assert that (1) essences exist, and he does not assert that (2) essences do not exist. Further, he does not assert that (3) essences both exist and do not exist. However, do not be fooled. Even the fourth logical possibility, (4) essences neither exist nor do they not exist, is not asserted by Nagarjuna.

The tetralemma pulls the logical rug out from under our feet. Nagarjuna refuses to assert anything at all about essences. If Nagarjuna did assert anything about essences, his very assertion would be empty because it would be a form and "form is emptiness; emptiness is form" according to the "wisdom that goes beyond."

In our first selection, Nagarjuna applies the tetralemma to *nirvana* thereby confounding those who would make *nirvana* a kind of heaven or place where the faithful go after death. Emptiness, as used by Nagarjuna, means that all of our basic concepts such as self, essence, and nirvana cannot convey the true nature of reality. According to Nagarjuna, when it comes to dealing with the true nature of reality all human concepts are inadequate. This is one of the most profound and least understood philosophical implications of what the Buddha taught.

Nagarjuna's ideas about emptiness may strike you as a negative philosophical viewpoint. What are we to make of a philosophy that does not tell us about the nature of reality (shouldn't philosophies do that sort of thing?) but, rather, tells us that we cannot conceptually grasp the nature of reality? Some Mahayana philosophers thought more can be said than Nagarjuna allows. Vasubandhu, author of our second selection, is one of those philosophers.

Vasubandhu represents a Yogacara philosophical approach to the issue of reality. This philosophical school is often called "Mind-Only" or "Consciousness-Only" because of what appear to be its idealistic tendencies. Vasubandhu seeks to deny the conventional dualistic distinction between subject (my consciousness or awareness) and object (some object of my consciousness) that pervades so much of our ordinary thinking. Just as Nagarjuna and the Madhyamika school developed the idea of emptiness (*shunyata*) to counter the idea of essences (*svabhava*), so Vasubandhu develops the idea of consciousness-only to counter subject/object dualism.

According to Vasubandhu, the problem of the nature of things (*dharmas*) is really a problem about consciousness or awareness. There are eight different types of consciousness. The first five types result from the activities of the five senses: seeing, hearing, smelling, tasting, and touching. The "sixth sense" is associated with the brain and involves thinking. These six types were recognized and analyzed by Nikaya thinkers, but they missed two more types. The seventh is the mind (*manas*) which, through reflection, falsely attributes individuality to ourselves and other things. The eighth Vasubandhu calls the "granary consciousness" or "storehouse consciousness." In this storehouse, seeds for what become conscious moments or events are stored.

In this selection, Vasubandhu begins with the granary consciousness and moves on to the other types. All things (*dharmas*) can be seen as a part of or associated with a type of consciousness. Does this mean that the true nature of reality is perception? Does it mean that the objects of awareness are themselves made up of seeds of awareness? Vasubandhu

warns that if we think like this, then we have reestablished the subject/object dualism he has worked so hard to dispel. The notion that "all this is merely perception" should *not* be construed as some sort of external object of perception.

It is time to turn to the words of Nagarjuna and Vasubandhu themselves. Both philosophers express a viewpoint that goes beyond most of our conventional wisdom. Our conventional thought relies on the concept of essence and presupposes a subject/object dualism. Nagarjuna and Vasubandhu articulate a wisdom that goes beyond conventional modes of thinking and thereby challenge us to rethink some of our fundamental views about the nature of reality.

NAGARJUNA AND VASUBANDHU

Nirvana and *Consciousness-Only*

READING QUESTIONS

1. Restate in your own words the argument Nagarjuna presents that supports the conclusion that *nirvana* is "not a thing and not a nothing."
2. Why, according to Nagarjuna, should we *not* assert that *nirvana* is "both a thing and a nothing" and that *nirvana* is "neither a thing nor a nothing"?
3. What do you think Nagarjuna means when he says, "There is no distinction whatsoever between *samsara* and *nirvana*"? Why does he say this? If there is no distinction, why follow the Buddhist path?
4. What is "consciousness-only," and what would it be like to experience such a state?
5. Do you think nondualistic consciousness is possible? Why or why not?

NIRVANA

An opponent argues:

1. If everything is empty, there can be no arising or passing away; therefore, by what abandonment, by what cessation can nirvāna be expected?

Nāgārjuna replies:

2. [It is only] if everything is *not* empty that there can be no arising or passing away [and that one can ask]: by what abandonment, by what cessation can nirvāṇa be expected?

3. This is said about nirvāṇa: no abandonment, no attainment, no annihilation, no eternality, no cessation, no arising.

4. Nirvāṇa is not a thing, for then it would follow that it would be characterized by old age and death, for no thing is free from old age and death.

5. And if nirvāṇa were a thing, it would be karmically constituted, for no thing anywhere has ever been found not to be karmically constituted.

6. And if nirvāṇa were a thing, how could it not be dependent on other things, for no independent thing has ever been found.

7. If nirvāṇa is not a thing, can it be that it is a "nonthing"? [No, because] wherever there is no thing, neither can there be a nonthing.

8. And if nirvāṇa were a nonthing, how could it not be dependent on other things, for no independent nonthing has ever been found.

9. The state of moving restlessly to and fro [in saṃsāra] is dependent and conditioned; independent and unconditioned, it is said to be nirvāṇa.

10. The Buddha said that both existence and freedom from existence are abandoned. Therefore it is fitting to say that nirvāṇa is not a thing and not a nonthing.

11. If nirvāṇa were *both* a thing and a nonthing, liberation would also be *both* a thing and a nonthing, but that does not make sense.

12. If nirvāṇa were *both* a thing and a nonthing, it would not be independent [of other things], for both [things and nonthings] are dependent.

13. And how could nirvāṇa be both a thing and a nonthing? Nirvāṇa is not karmically constituted, but things and nonthings are.

14. [And anyhow,] how could nirvāṇa be both a thing and a nonthing? Like light and darkness, these two are opposites and cannot both exist at the same place.

15. Only if things and nonthings are established can the proposition "Nirvāṇa is *neither* a thing nor a nonthing" be established.

16. But how could it be asserted that nirvāṇa was found to be "neither a thing nor a nonthing"?

17. It is not asserted that the Blessed One exists after his passing away; nor is it asserted that he does not exist, that he both exists and does not exist, or that he neither exists nor does not exist.

18. Even while he is living, it is not asserted that the Blessed One exists; nor is it asserted that he does not exist, both exists and does not exist, or neither exists nor does not exist.

19. There is no distinction whatsoever between saṃsāra and nirvāṇa; and there is no distinction whatsoever between nirvāṇa and saṃsāra.

20. The limit of nirvāṇa and the limit of saṃsāra: one cannot find even the slightest difference between them.

21. Views about such things as the finitude or infinitude of the state coming after death, are related to the issue of nirvāṇa having beginning and ending limits.

22. Given that all elements of reality are empty, what is infinite? What is finite? What is both finite and infinite? What is neither finite nor infinite?

23. What is just this? What is that other? What is eternal? What is noneternal? What is both eternal and noneternal? What is neither eternal nor noneternal?

24. Ceasing to fancy everything and falsely to imagine it as real is good; nowhere did the Buddha ever teach any such element of reality.

CONSCIOUSNESS-ONLY

Vasubandhu

. . . The transformation of consciousness is of three kinds: coming to fruition, intellectualizing, and perceiving sense-objects.

The consciousness that is called "coming to fruition" is the granary consciousness (ālayna-vijñāna); it comprises all of the seeds (bīja). Its substratum, its disposition, its perceptions cannot be discerned, but it is always accompanied by the following factors: linkage to sense objects, attention, feeling, conceptualization, and volition. Its feelings are [neither pleasant nor unpleasant but] neutral, and it is undefiled and karmically indeterminate. . . . Its behavior is like the current of a stream. At arhatship, there occurs in it a fundamental revolution.

The intellectualizing consciousness is called "the mind" [manas]. As it develops, it is dependent on the granary consciousness and takes it as its object. It is karmically indeterminate but obstructed by four defilements to which it is always connected. These are called false view of the Self, delusion about the Self, pride of the Self, and love of the Self. Whenever the mind comes into being, it is accompanied by linkage to sense objects and by the other mental factors: attention, feeling, conceptualization, and volition. It ceases to exist at arhatship, or in the trance of cessation, or on the supramundane path. That is the second transformation of consciousness.

The third transformation concerns the consciousnesses dependent on the six senses: [the visual, auditory, olfactory, gustatory, tactile, and mental consciousnesses]. They are meritorious and/or demeritorious. They are accompanied by the three kinds of feeling [that is, pleasant, unpleasant, and neutral sensations], and they are connected to the following mental factors: the five mental factors that accompany them everywhere; the five special [mental factors which are not always present]; the meritorious mental states; the defilements, which are demeritorious; and the secondary defilements, which are also demeritorious.

First, the five mental factors that accompany the sense consciousnesses everywhere are: linkage to sense objects, attention, feeling, conceptualization, and volition.

The special mental factors are; zeal, resolve, mindfulness, concentration, and wisdom.

The meritorious mental states are: faith, modesty, fear of blame, lack of desire, lack of hatred, lack of delusion, striving, serenity, carefulness, and noninjury.

The defilements are: greed, hatred, confusion, pride, false views, and doubt.

The secondary defilements are: anger, enmity, disparaging others, irritation, envy, selfishness, deception, guile, assault, immodesty, nonfear of blame, sluggishness, excitability, lack of faith, sloth, carelessness, loss of mindfulness, distraction, and nondiscernment; there are also remorse and sleepiness, reflection and investigation, two pairs which are double factors [that can be either defiled or undefiled].

The first five sense consciousnesses [that is, the visual, auditory, olfactory, gustatory, and tactile consciousnesses] arise in the granary consciousness, either together or not, depending on conditions. They are like waves on the water. The sixth sense consciousness, the mental consciousness, always arises with them except in a situation where there is no recognition; in the two trance states where there is no mental consciousness; in dreamless sleep; in fainting; or in unconsciousness.

The whole transformation of consciousness is itself ultimately a false discrimination, and because it is a false discrimination, it does not exist. Therefore, all this is merely perception.

The granary consciousness contains all the seeds; its transformation takes place according to a process of give and take between it and the false discriminations to which it gives rise [and which in turn affect it. This process leaves in the granary consciousness] residual impressions [vāsanā] of actions, which along with the residual impressions of dualistic grasping give rise to a new "coming to fruition" when the former "fruition" has died out. [...]

As long as consciousness is not content with being perception only, there will continue to be a tendency toward dualistic grasping. This is so even with the thought "All this is perception only." If you come to apprehend this and set it up in front of you, you are not being content with "this only." But when consciousness truly no longer apprehends any object of consciousness, it abides as consciousness only; for when what it grasps does not exist, there is no grasping. It is then free of thought, nondependent, transcendent knowledge. This is the fundamental revolution of all consciousness, the destruction of the double depravity. This element is also free from evil attachments, unimaginable, meritorious, constant, blissful. It is the liberation body, which is called the Dharma body of the Buddha.

5.4.4 The Bodhisattva Vow

As mentioned earlier, *bodhisattva* is a being headed for buddhahood. In Nikaya Buddhism the title is used primarily for Siddhartha prior to his enlightenment. In Mahayana Buddhism the idea is broadened to include, potentially, every being. We are all potentially headed for enlightenment, and the first step toward actualizing that is to take the *bodhisattva* vow.

In its simplest form, this vow is a solemn commitment to sincerely walk the path to enlightenment. Central to the vow is the idea of compassion. You should not tread the path for selfish reasons. If you do, you shall never reach the goal. Rather, you undertake this journey motivated by compassion. The true *bodhisattva*, even after enlightenment, postpones final *nirvana* (*nirvana* without remainder, or *parinirvana*) in order to help others.

Taking the *bodhisattva* vow can be a simple act of promising to pursue enlightenment and postpone one's own *parinirvana* to help others, or it can be a ritualized event beginning with the worship of Buddhas, reaffirming refuge, confessing sins, expressing thanksgiving for merit, asking the Buddhas for help, and making a declaration to lead an altruistic life.

The following selection is from the *Bodhicaryavatara* (*Entering the Path of Enlightenment*), written by the eighth-century poet Shantideva. Shantideva gives eloquent expression to the ideal *bodhisattva* mindset.

SHANTIDEVA

Entering the Path

READING QUESTIONS

1. How would you characterize the attitude expressed in the section "Worship and Devotion"?
2. What sorts of things are confessed?
3. What connection do you see between the sections on rejoicing at the merit of others and altruistic intent?
4. What sort of outlook on beings and reality motivates a *bodhisattva* to take such a vow?

WORSHIP AND DEVOTION

So as to obtain this gem of the mind set on enlightenment, I make devotional offerings to the Tathāgatas, to the immaculate jewel of the good Dharma, and to the Sangha, consisting of the sons of the Buddha, who are oceans of virtue.

However many flowers and fruits, medicinal plants, and previous gems there are in the world, as well as clear delightful waters;

and mountains made of jewels, and forest retreats where solitude is pleasant, where the creepers are resplendent with blossoms and the trees laden with fruit;

and sweet-smelling incenses from, among other places, the worlds of the gods; and wish-granting trees, and trees made of gems, and ponds bedecked with lotuses, made enchanting by the loud cries of wild geese;

and cultivated and uncultivated crops, and other things to honor those deserving devotional offerings; everything stretching as far as the limits of space, even those things that cannot be grasped—

All this I mentally give to the most eminent sages and their sons. . . .

REFUGE AND CONFESSION

And I sing the praises of these oceans of virtue, with verses, with a flood of utterances. May the clouds of my hymns reach them without fail.

I go to the Buddha for refuge, taking enlightenment as my highest aim; and I go to the Dharma for refuge, as well as to the troop of bodhisattvas.

With folded hands, I make this confession to the Buddhas, spread out in all directions, as well as to the greatly compassionate bodhisattvas:

"Consumed by remorse, I hereby confess the evil deeds that I, no better than a beast, have committed or caused others to commit, either here in this life or throughout beginningless saṃsāra; and I confess the things that I deludedly took pleasure in and that led to self-destruction.

"And I confess all the wrongs that I have done with my body, speech, and mind, lacking respect for the Three Jewels, my parents, my teachers, and others; and the cruel evil deeds that I, guilty of many faults, have committed.

"Lords, how can I be rid of this burden? Help me quickly, lest death arrive soon while my pile of evil is still undiminished. . . .

"Lords, accept the sins I have committed. What was not good, I will not do again. . . ."

REJOICING AT THE MERIT OF OTHERS AND SUPPLICATING THE BUDDHAS

And I joyously applaud the good done by all beings that results in the cessation of the suffering of rebirth in the lower realms. May all those who suffer be happy!

And I applaud the liberation of embodied beings from the sufferings of saṃsāra, and I applaud the bodhisattvahood and Buddhahood of those so liberated.

And I applaud the Teachers, who are oceans of resolution, who bring happiness and welfare to all beings.

And with folded hands, I request the Buddhas in all directions to be a lamp of Dharma for those who have fallen into suffering because of their delusion.

With folded hands, I ask the Victorious Ones, who desire cessation, to stay in this world for endless aeons lest it remain blind.

ALTRUISTIC INTENT

May I too, through whatever good I have accomplished by doing all this, become one who works for the complete alleviation of the sufferings of all beings.

May I be medicine for the sick; may I also be their physician and attend to them until their disease no longer recurs.

With showers of food and water, may I eliminate the pain of hunger and thirst, and during the intermediate periods of great famine between aeons, may I *be* food and drink.

And may I be an inexhaustible storehouse for the poor, and may I always be first in being ready to serve them in various ways.

So that all beings may achieve their aims, may I sacrifice, without regret, the bodies, as well as the pleasures that I have had, and the merit of all the good that I have accomplished and will accomplish in the past, present, and future.

Nirvāṇa means to renounce everything. My mind is set on nirvāṇa, so because I am to renounce everything, it is best for me to give it to others.

I therefore dedicate this self of mine to the happiness of all beings. Let them smite me, constantly mock me, or throw dirt at me.

Let them make sport with my body, laugh, and make fun of me! I have given my body away to them: what could its misfortune mean to me?

Let them do to me whatever pleases them, but let no one suffer any mishap on my account.

Whether they direct toward me thoughts that are angry or kindly, may those very thoughts be a constant cause for their achieving all their aims.

Those who accuse me falsely, others who do me wrong, and still others who deride me—may they attain enlightenment!

May I be a protector of the unprotected, a guide for travelers on the way, a boat, a bridge, a means of crossing for those who seek the other shore.

For all creatures, may I be a light for those who need a light, a bed for those who need a bed, and a slave for those who need a slave.

For all creatures, may I be a wish-fulfilling gem, a vase of fortune, a spell that works, a true panacea, a wish-granting tree, a cow of plenty. . . .

Just as the Buddhas of the past grasped the mind set on enlightenment and went on to follow the bodhisattva-training,

so too will I give rise to the mind set on enlightenment for the well-being of the world, and so will I train in the stages of the bodhisattva discipline.

5.4.5 Savior *Bodhisattvas* and Buddhas

Mahayana Buddhism, unlike Theravada Buddhism, has given rise to devotional cults centered on the saving power of buddhas and *bodhisattvas* living in celestial realms. These savior figures are available not only to aid you along the path to enlightenment, but to help you out in other ways as well.

Avalokiteshvara, whose mercy and compassion was celebrated in the *Lotus Sutra*, became particularly popular in China and Japan where he took the female form of the Goddess of Mercy (Kuan-yin in Chinese and Kannon in Japanese). In Tibet his mantra *"Om Mani Padme Hum"* is used to call upon his compassion, and his devotional following became so great that Avalokiteshvara became the guardian deity of Tibet.

Also popular in Tibet and elsewhere is the Goddess **Tara,** who sometimes is paired with Avalokiteshvara. She is both compassionate, tirelessly providing aid to the oppressed, and ferocious in fiercely destroying the enemies of sentient beings.

Somewhere to "the West," where the sun sets and the dead travel, there is a **Pure Land,** a land of bliss, called *Sukhavati.* There lives the **Tathagata Amitabha,** a celestial buddha who long ago was the Bodhisattva Dharmakara. When Dharmakara took his *bodhisattva* vows, he guaranteed that when he became a buddha he would give entry into his Pure Land to anyone who repeats his name ten times with sincere faith.

The description of the Pure Land included below is from a Sanskrit text called *Smaller Description of the Land of Bliss*, and it gives you some idea of why entry into the Pure Land is so desirable to Buddhists. Although beginning in India, Pure Land Buddhism became particularly popular in China and Japan. In Japan, Amitabha is known as Amida, and chanting the phrase *"Namu Amida Butsu"* ("Praise to the Buddha Amitabha") with sincere faith can become your ticket into the Pure Land. Although some celestial buddhas in Pure Lands to the East would allow entry of women as women, *Sukhavati* was different because Dharmakara had vowed (vow #33) that those who entered his Pure Land to the West would be "freed from being women."

Avalokiteshvara, Tara, and Amitabha

READING QUESTIONS

1. Why do you think beliefs in savior *bodhisattvas* and in Pure Land buddhas became important as Buddhism developed?
2. What possible tensions do you see among the concepts merit, grace, faith, and a life of true compassion? Explain.

AVALOKITESHVARA

Listen to the conduct of Avalokiteśvara.

3. Hear from my indication how for numerous, inconceivable Æons he has accomplished his vows under many thousand *kotis* [millions] of Buddhas.

4. Hearing, seeing, regularly and constantly thinking will infallibly destroy all suffering, (mundane) existence, and grief of living beings here on earth.

5. If one be thrown into a pit of fire, by a wicked enemy with the object of killing him, he has but to think of Avalokiteśvara, and the fire shall be quenched as if sprinkled with water.

Selection on Avalokiteshvara from *Saddharma-Pundarika, or the Lotus of the True Law*, translated by Hendrik Kern. Volume XXI of *The Sacred Books of the East*, edited by F. Max Mueller (Oxford, England: Clarendon Press, 1884), pp. 413–417. Selections on Tara and Amitabha from *Experience of Buddhism*, 1st ed., by J. S. Strong, pp. 184–185, 189–190. Copyright © 1995 Wadsworth Publishing. Reprinted by permission of Wadsworth Publishing, a division of International Thomson Publishing. Fax 800-730-2215.

6. If one happens to fall into the dreadful ocean, the abode of Nâgas, marine monsters, and demons, he has but to think of Avalokiteśvara, and he shall never sink down in the king of waters.

7. If a man happens to be hurled down from the brink of the Meru, by some wicked person with the object of killing him, he has but to think of Avalokiteśvara, and he shall, sunlike, stand firm in the sky.

8. If rocks of thunderstone and thunderbolts are thrown at a man's head to kill him, he has but to think of Avalokiteśvara, and they shall not be able to hurt one hair of the body.

9. If a man be surrounded by a host of enemies armed with swords, who have the intention of killing him, he has but to think of Avalokiteśvara, and they shall instantaneously become kind-hearted.

10. If a man, delivered to the power of the executioners, is already standing at the place of execution, he has but to think of Avalokiteśvara, and their swords shall go to pieces.

11. If a person happens to be fettered in shackles of wood or iron, he has but to think of Avalokiteśvara, and the bonds shall be speedily loosened.

12. Mighty spells, witchcraft, herbs, ghosts, and spectres, pernicious to life, revert thither whence they come, when one thinks of Avalokiteśvara.

13. If a man is surrounded by goblins, Nâgas, demons, ghosts, or giants, who are in the habit of taking away bodily vigour, he has but to think of Avalokiteśvara, and they shall not be able to hurt one hair of his body. . . .

[Then Akshayamati in the joy of his heart uttered the following stanzas:]

20. O thou whose eyes are clear, whose eyes are kind, distinguished by wisdom and knowledge, whose eyes are full of pity and benevolence; thou so lovely by thy beautiful face and beautiful eyes!

21. Pure one, whose shine is spotless bright, whose knowledge is free from darkness, thou shining as the sun, not to be beaten away, radiant as the blaze of fire, thou spreadest in thy flying course thy lustre in the world. . . .

25. Think, O think with tranquil mood of Avalokiteśvara, that pure being; he is a protector, a refuge, a recourse in death, disaster, and calamity.

26. He who possesses the perfection of all virtues, and beholds all beings with compassion and benevolence, he, an ocean of virtues, Virtue itself, he, Avalokiteśvara, is worthy of adoration.

27. He, so compassionate for the world, shall once become a Buddha, destroying all dangers and sorrows; I humbly bow to Avalokiteśvara.

28. This universal Lord, chief of kings, who is a [rich] mine of monastic virtues, he, universally worshipped, has reached pure, supreme enlightenment, after plying his course (of duty) during many hundreds of Æons. . . .

TARA

Oṃ! Praise to the Blessed Noble Tārā! [. . .]

Your compassion truly extends equally to all beings on the pathways of rebirth; therefore, I am surely among those whom it embraces.

Your unequaled capacity to save beings shines like the sun on the dark passions, the impurities of the whole world; and I too suffer and am tormented! Oh! The impure misdeeds that I have committed!

Woe! Woe! Ill-fated am I! I am blind, even in the light of the sun! I am thirsty even on the banks of a refreshing icy mountain stream! I am poor even with access to abundant jewels in the mines of the Isle of Gems! Being without refuge, I make you my protector, Blessed Lady, you who are the support of the whole world.

Even a mother gets tired of a baby who constantly cries for milk. Even a father gets angry at a son who daily asks for things he does not have. But you, like a great wish-granting tree, fulfill the desires of this Triple World. You never fail to grant the requests of all those who reverence you. [. . .]

When those who are injured—whose limbs are being fed on by vermin that have attached themselves to their oozing open wounds, smelling of flesh, flowing with blood, suppurating with stinking pus, filled with impurities due to their past evil deeds—devote themselves . . . to service at your feet, their physical bodies become beautiful like gold, and their eyes like lotuses.

Those in whose ear the gurus have not repeated the sacred texts (as though they were putting alms in a bowl) and those who, lacking a wealth of knowledge, become mute in the fellowship of the learned—they will become the Lord of Speech as a result of devotion to you. . . .

Those whose loins are covered with rags that are torn and dark with dirt from lying on the ground; who pick lice and seek food from others in a broken pot— they will gain universal sovereignty over the earth by propitiating you. . . .

Those who are tired of seeking ways in which to make a living by bartering, by carrying out a trade, or by being employed in the service of others and who fail to get money even though they have amassed merit in previous lives—by turning to you who surpass the gods, Mother of the destitute, they . . . will obtain a treasure of gold spewed forth from the earth. [. . .]

Some see you in your fierce form, striking out with bright weapons uplifted and swinging, breaking and pervading the sky, your arms entwined with bracelets that are hooded serpents. Taking on this frightful aspect, you scare enemies away, your laughter causes great tumult, like the rolling and striking of a great drum. . . .

But for others, in each of your hairs is visible the expanse of heaven and earth wherein dwell in bliss the gods Brahmā, Indra, and Rudra as well as humans, maruts, siddhas, gandharvas, and nāgas. And all directions are pervaded by hundreds of Buddhas without end, which you have magically fashioned. Worthy of worship by the Triple World, in your own being, you contain all creatures. . . .

Some see you red like the sun whose rays are redder than red lacquer or vermillion. Others see you blue like dust made of the pulverized fragments of a magnificent precious sapphire. And some see you white, more dazzling than the churned ocean of milk and brighter than gold. Your form, like a crystal, takes on various aspects, changing according to the different things that are placed near it.

AMITABHA

Then the Blessed One spoke to the Venerable Śāriputra: "Śāriputra, over a hundred thousand billion Buddha fields to the west of here, there is a Buddha field called the world of Sukhāvatī. And there dwells a Tathāgata, an altogether enlightened Buddha named Amitāyus [Amitābha]. . . . Now what do you think, Śāriputra, why do they call that world the land of bliss? Because, Śāriputra, in that world, Sukhāvatī, beings do not experience suffering [duḥkha], neither with their body nor with their mind, and the things causing happiness are innumerable. . . .

"Śāriputra, Sukhāvatī is adorned and enclosed by seven railings, seven rows of palm trees and strings of bells. And it is beautiful and embellished with four kinds of precious materials: gold, silver, lapis lazuli, and crystal. . . . And, Śāriputra, there are lotus pools there made of seven precious materials: gold, silver, lapis lazuli, crystal, red pearls, diamonds, and coral. They are filled with water endowed with eight good qualities . . . and they are strewn with sand of gold. And going down into those lotus pools, from all four sides, are four flights of steps, beautiful, and embellished with four precious materials, . . . and all around the lotus pools jewel-trees are growing, beautiful, and embellished with seven precious materials. . . . And in those lotus pools, lotuses are growing: various kinds of blue ones, and various kinds of yellow ones, and various kinds of red ones, and various kinds of white ones, beautiful, beautifully colored, beautifully resplendent, beautiful to look at, and as big around as the wheel of a cart. . . .

"Furthermore, Śāriputra, in that Buddha field, divine musical instruments are always playing, and the earth is pleasant and golden colored. And in that Buddha field, three times each night and three times each day, showers of blossoms fall, divine mandārava blossoms. And the beings there, during the time it takes to eat one morning meal, can pay homage to a hundred thousand billion Buddhas, by going to other universes. And after showering each Tathāgata with a hundred thousand billion flowers, they return to their own world in time for a nap. . . .

"Furthermore, Śāriputra, in that Buddha field, there are geese, snipe, and peacocks. Three times each night and three times each day, they come and sing together, each uttering its own cries. . . . And when the people there hear that sound, they become mindful of the Buddha, mindful of the Dharma, and mindful of the Sangha. Now, Śāriputra, [because of these birds] are you thinking that there are beings who have been reborn in that Buddha land as animals? That is not the way you should see it. Why? Because, in that Buddha field, Śāriputra, no one is born as a hell being, an animal, or a hungry ghost in the dominion of Yama the god of the dead. These birds were magically fashioned by the Tathāgata Amitāyus, and their cries are the sound of the Dharma. With such marvelous Buddha-field qualities, Śāriputra, is that Buddha field Sukhāvatī arrayed."

5.5 MAHAYANA BUDDHISM IN CHINA AND JAPAN

Mahayana Buddhism began to move into China sometime around the first century and reached Korea and Japan by the sixth century. Buddhist monks tell a more dramatic story than present-day historians do. According to a widely circulated story among Chinese Buddhists, the Emperor Ming (58–75) dreamed about a golden deity flying near his palace in Loyang,

the capital of China at that time. Emperor Ming's ministers of state informed him that the deity he dreamt about was named Buddha, who lived in India. Immediately the Emperor sent ambassadors to India, and they returned with monks and scriptures, which were translated into Chinese.

Chinese indigenous religions such as Taoism and Confucianism had their impact on Buddhism, and, as a result of this creative encounter, there were new Buddhist developments. However, at first, the various schools of Mahayana Buddhism in India made converts and established religious centers. Both the *Madhyamika* (*San-lun* in Chinese) and the *Yogacara* (*Fa-hsiang* in Chinese) schools made a significant impact along with Pure Land Buddhism.

For comments on translation and pronunciation of Chinese words, see the Pronunciation Guide at the end of chapter 6.

5.5.1 The Goddess

The Indian Buddhist stories of *bodhisattvas* and celestial buddhas made a strong impression on the Chinese. Particularly popular were stories of Vimalakirti, a kind of rogue Indian *bodhisattva* often portrayed as upsetting the disciples of the Buddha and his fellow *bodhisattvas* by his unorthodox teaching methods and life style. He was not a monk but a layperson, and this added to his popularity in China.

Stories about Vimalakirti are recounted in *The Holy Teaching of Vimalakirti*, probably written sometime in the first century B.C.E. The stories elaborate on the Perfect Wisdom (*Prajnaparamita*) tradition, often in a playful way. In one story, Vimalakirti invites Shariputra, a direct disciple of the Buddha, to his home. Shariputra represents the "old" Buddhism (perhaps the Theravadan perspective), having mastered only the "outer" (exoteric) teachings of the Buddha, not their "inner" (esoteric) meaning. At one point Shariputra encounters a goddess in Vimalakirti's home, and, believing in the inferiority of women and their need to be reborn as males in order to attain spiritual enlightenment, asks her why she does not use her supernatural powers to become a man. Her answer is surprising, especially to Shariputra.

The Goddess

READING QUESTION

1. What do you think the quotation "In all things, there is neither male nor female," attributed to the Buddha by the goddess, means?

Śāriputra:

Goddess, what prevents you from transforming yourself out of your female state?

Goddess:

Although I have sought my "female state" for these twelve years, I have not yet found it. Reverend Śāriputra, if a magician were to incarnate a woman by magic, would you ask her, "What prevents you from transforming yourself out of your female state?"

Śāriputra:

No! Such a woman would not really exist, so what would there be to transform?

Goddess:

Just so, reverend Śāriputra, all things do not really exist. Now, would you think, "What prevents one whose nature is that of a magical incarnation from transforming herself out of her female state?"

Thereupon, the goddess employed her magical power to cause the elder Śāriputra to appear in her form and to cause herself to appear in his form. Then the goddess, transformed into Śāriputra, said to Śāriputra, transformed into a goddess, "Reverend Śāriputra, what prevents you from transforming yourself out of your female state?"

And Śāriputra, transformed into the goddess, replied, "I no longer appear in the form of a male! My body has changed into the body of a woman! I do not know what to transform!"

The goddess continued, "If the elder could again change out of the female state, then all women could also change out of their female states. All women appear in the form of women in just the same way as the elder appears in the form of a woman. While they are not women in reality, they appear in the form of women. With this in mind, the Buddha said, 'In all things, there is neither male nor female.'"

Then, the goddess released her magical power and each returned to his ordinary form. She then said to him, "Reverend Śāriputra, what have you done with your female form?"

Śāriputra:

I neither made it nor did I change it.

Goddess:

Just so, all things are neither made nor changed, and that they are not made and not changed, that is the teaching of the Buddha.

Śāriputra:

Goddess, where will you be born when you transmigrate after death?

Goddess:

I will be born where all the magical incarnations of the Tathāgata are born.

Śāriputra:

But the emanated incarnations of the Tathāgata do not transmigrate nor are they born.

Goddess:

All things and living beings are just the same; they do not transmigrate nor are they born!

Śāriputra:

Goddess, how soon will you attain the perfect enlightenment of Buddhahood?

Goddess:

At such time as you, elder, become endowed once more with the qualities of an ordinary individual, then will I attain the perfect enlightenment of Buddhahood.

Śāriputra:

Goddess, it is impossible that I should become endowed once more with the qualities of an ordinary individual.

Goddess:

Just so, reverend Śāriputra, it is impossible that I should attain the perfect enlightenment of Buddhahood! Why? Because perfect enlightenment stands upon the impossible. Because it is impossible, no one attains the perfect enlightenment of Buddhahood.

Śāriputra:

But the Tathāgata has declared: "The Tathāgatas, who are as numerous as the sands of the Ganges, have attained perfect Buddhahood, are attaining perfect Buddhahood, and will go on attaining perfect Buddhahood."

Goddess:

Reverend Śāriputra, the expression, "the Buddhas of the past, present and future," is a conventional expression made up of a certain number of syllables. The Buddhas are neither past, nor present, nor future. Their enlightenment transcends the three times! But tell me, elder, have you attained sainthood?

Śāriputra:

It is attained, because there is no attainment.

Goddess:

Just so, there is perfect enlightenment because there is no attainment of perfect enlightenment.

Then the Licchavi Vimalakīrti said to the venerable elder Śāriputra, "Reverend Śāriputra, this goddess has already served ninety-two million billion Buddhas. She plays with the superknowledges. She has truly succeeded in all her vows. She has gained the tolerance of the birthlessness of things. She has actually attained irreversibility. She can live wherever she wishes on the strength of her vow to develop living beings."

5.5.2 Buddha Nature

There is a common saying in Chinese Buddhism, "Hua-yen and T'ien-t'ai for doctrines and Ch'an and Pure Land for practice." We have already discussed Pure Land Buddhism in the Indian tradition, and in the next section we will discuss Ch'an Buddhism (Zen in Japanese). Here we will get a glimpse of teaching common to Hua-yen and T'ien-t'ai.

The T'ien-t'ai school is also called the Lotus School because it claims the *Lotus Sutra* (see Readings 5.4.1 and 5.4.5) represents the culmination of the Buddha's teaching. Chih-yi (538–597), its greatest systematic thinker, was concerned with reconciling what appeared to be very different teachings of the Buddha. His answer was to develop the notion of skillful means. The Buddha, employing skillful means, teaches different things at different times depending on the level of understanding of his audience.

The Hua-yen, or Flower Garland School, was also concerned with reconciling the different teachings of the Buddha. In addition, it sought to harmonize Buddhism with both Confucianism and Taoism. While the Hua-yen had Indian roots, no similar school existed in India, so its development is essentially Chinese.

Fa-tsang (643–712) is the founder of the Flower Garland School, and his *Treatise on the Golden Lion* is an influential work that uses a statue of a golden lion to teach that one thing is in all things and all things are in one thing. This teaching allowed the Hua-yen school to argue that the Buddha said essentially the same thing in different ways, to synthesize the teachings of various Buddhist schools with Confucianism and Taoism, and to argue that all things contain the Buddha Nature. However, it still claims that Buddhism, especially as understood by Hua-yen, is the most complete spiritual teaching.

The author of the following selection is Tsung-mi (780–841), the fifth patriarch of the Hua-yen school. This treatise is not a basic scripture nor particularly well known, but it applies the philosophical teachings about unity, characteristic of the Hua-yen, to the religious life.

TSUNG-MI

An Inquiry on Man

READING QUESTIONS

1. What is meant by **Tathagatagarbha**?
2. What advice for living the religious life does Tsung-mi find in the teaching of the *Tathagatagarbha*?

DIRECTLY MANIFESTING THE TRUE SOURCE

The Doctrine of the Manifestation of Dharma-nature in the One Vehicle (of the T'ien-t'ai and Hua-yen Schools) preaches that all sentient beings possess the true mind of natural enlightenment, which from time immemorial has always been there, clear and pure, shining and not obscured, understanding and always know-

From *The Great Asian Religions: An Anthology*, edited by Wing-tsit Chan, Isma'il Ragi al Fārāgui, Joseph M. Kitagawa, and P. T. R. Raju (New York: Macmillan Publishing Co., Inc., 1969), p. 209. © Copyright 1969, Macmillan Publishing Co., Inc. Reprinted by permission. Endnotes omitted.

ing. It is also called Buddha-nature and Tathāgatagarbha (Store of the Thus-come). From the beginning of time, it has been obscured by erroneous ideas without knowing its own (Buddha-nature), but only recognizing its ordinary nature, loving it and being attached to it, accumulating action-influence, and suffering from the pain of life and death. The Buddha pitied these sentient beings. He preached to them that all things are empty. He also revealed to them that the true mind of spiritual enlightenment, being clear and pure, is completely identical with that of the Buddhas. Therefore the *Flower Splendor Scripture* says, "Among the Buddhas-sons (all sentient beings), none is without the wisdom of the Tathāgata complete in him. Only because of their erroneous ideas and clinging have they not realized it. If they are freed from erroneous ideas, the knowledge of all that exists, the knowledge naturally present from the beginning, and the knowledge without obstacle will immediately come to the fore." The scripture forthwith gives the analogy of one speck of dust containing a great scripture whose quantity is equivalent to the world system of 1,000 million worlds, equating the dust to the sentient beings and the great scripture to the Buddha-wisdom. Following this, it also says, "At that time the Tathāgata surveyed all sentient beings in the realm of dharmas and said these words: How strange! How strange! Why are the sentient beings deceived and deluded and do not see the wisdom of the Tathāgata complete in them? I must teach them the Holy Path to enable them to be free forever from erroneous thoughts and see the great and vast Tathāgata-wisdom in their own persons, making them the same as the Buddha."

Comment: For many aeons we have not encountered the True Doctrine. We have not learned how to reflect on our own bodies, but have merely clung to false characters and willingly admit that we are ordinary or inferior—perhaps we are animals or perhaps we are men. Only now that we make the inquiry in accordance with the perfect doctrine do we realize that we are originally Buddhas. Therefore our deeds must be in accordance with those of the Buddha, and our minds must be harmonious with the mind of the Buddha. We must revert to the foundation and return to the source, and cut off the habits of an ordinary man. "Decrease and further decrease until one reaches the point of taking no action." One will then naturally respond and function in as many ways as the number of sand grains in the Ganges River, and will be called a Buddha. We should know that both the deluded and the awakened share the same true mind. Great is this wonderful gate. This is the point to which our inquiry on man has come. (*Taishō daizōkyō* [Taishō edition of the Buddhist Canon], 45:710)

5.5.3 Ch'an Buddhism

"Point directly to the human mind." This is one of the mottos of Ch'an Buddhism (Son in Korea, Zen in Japan). Ch'an Buddhism began as a reformation movement in Buddhism. As the other schools of Chinese Buddhism translated Indian scriptures, argued over their interpretation, discussed which rituals brought the most merit, and asserted their own superiority over the other schools, Ch'an Buddhists started a "get back to basics" movement.

Why do we revere the Buddha? "Because he is enlightened," the Ch'an replied. And under what circumstances did his enlightenment happen? "While he was meditating under the Bodhi tree," the Ch'an replied. It is a very short step from these answers to the view that the heart of Buddhist practice should be meditation. Indeed, *Ch'an* is the way the Chinese say the Sanskrit word for meditation, *dhyana*. Ch'an Buddhism is meditation Buddhism.

Bodhidarma (460–534?) is the Indian monk credited with bringing meditation Buddhism to China. He is a semilegendary figure who arrived at the Shao-lin monastery where he sat in silent meditation in front of a wall for several years. Needless to say, this strange behavior attracted attention, and when he broke silence and began to teach, he had a ready following. The first Chinese patriarch of the school was one of his disciples. However, according to the Ch'an school, their teachings go back to the Buddha himself and constitute a "special transmission outside the scriptures."

In China, Ch'an eventually split between two major schools, the Northern School that stressed gradual enlightenment and the Southern School that stressed sudden enlightenment. Both schools agreed that *nirvana* is identical to the Buddha-mind and therefore is the Buddha-Nature in all sentient beings. However, the Northern School believed that you could realize your own Buddha-Nature only by gradually, through the practice of *samadhi* (concentration), removing the erroneous and impure thoughts that have obscured that nature. The practice of *samadhi* will eventually lead you to wisdom (*prajna*) buried within.

The Southern School, which eventually became the most dominant, insisted that all mental activities are functions of suchness. There are not two minds, a true original Buddha-mind and a false mind that obscures it. There is one mind, the Buddha-mind, and it is everywhere. Anything can be an occasion for its realization. It can happen at any moment and in any way. It can happen to a monk or a layperson, to someone early on in the transmigration cycle or someone who has lived millions of lives.

It follows from this that, although reading scriptures, debating fine philosophical points about the no-self, making offerings to the Buddha, reciting his name, joining monastic orders, and the like may be occasions for enlightenment, they are not necessary. Enlightenment could happen to a child at the sound of a bell.

Clearly these ideas are reforming, if not revolutionary, because the whole Buddhist organization is threatened by the claim that the heart of true Buddhism is to be concerned about truly getting in touch with your mind and that this can be done immediately and "in this very body." And so another Ch'an motto, "See one's nature and become a Buddha," struck Chinese Buddhism like a bomb.

Like many religious reformations, however, Ch'an Buddhism developed organizations, teachings, and rituals—the very things it maintained were not necessary for enlightenment! The most important teachings are found in the *Platform Sutra* (*Liu-tsu*), written by the sixth patriarch, Hui-neng (638–713). A selection follows.

HUI-NENG

Platform Sutra

READING QUESTIONS

1. Why do you think the teachings contained in this selection of the *Platform Sutra* would become so popular? Be specific.
2. Can you think of any parallels to the movement of Ch'an Buddhism in other religions? If so, what are the parallels?

13. "Good and learned friends, calmness (*samādhi*) and wisdom (*prajñā*) are the foundations of my method.

From Chan, Wing-tsit, *A Source Book in Chinese Philosophy*, pp. 433–436. Copyright © 1963, renewed 1991 by Princeton University Press. Reprinted by permission of Princeton University Press. Footnotes and comments omitted.

First of all, do not be deceived into thinking that the two are different. They are one substance and not two. Calmness is the substance of wisdom and wisdom is the function of calmness. Whenever wisdom is at work, calmness is within it. Whenever calmness is at work, wisdom is within it. Good and learned friends, the meaning here is that [calmness and] wisdom are identified. Seekers of the Way, arouse your minds. Do not say that wisdom follows calmness or vice versa, or that the two are different. To hold such a view [would imply that] the dharmas (elements of existence) possess two different characters. In the case of those whose words are good but whose hearts are not good, wisdom and calmness are not identified. But in the case of those whose hearts and words are both good and in whom the internal and the external are one, calmness and wisdom are identified. Self-enlightenment and practice do not consist in argument. If one is concerned about which comes first, he is a [deluded] person. If he is not freed from the consideration of victory or defeat, he will produce the dharmas as real entities and cannot be free from the Four Characters [of coming into existence, remaining in the same state, change, and going out of existence]." . . .

16. "Good and learned friends, in method there is no distinction between sudden enlightenment and gradual enlightenment. Among men, however, some are intelligent and others are stupid. Those who are deluded understand gradually, while the enlightened achieve understanding suddenly. But when they know their own minds, then they see their own nature, and there is no difference in their enlightenment. Without enlightenment, they remain forever bound in transmigration."

17. "Good and learned friends, in this method of mine, from the very beginning, whether in the sudden-enlightenment or gradual-enlightenment tradition, absence-of-thought has been instituted as the main doctrine, absence-of-characters as the substance, and nonattachment as the foundation. What is meant by absence-of-characters? Absence-of-characters means to be free from characters while in the midst of them. Absence-of-thought means not to be carried away by thought in the process of thought. Nonattachment is man's original nature. Thought after thought goes on without remaining. Past, present, and future thoughts continue without termination. But if we cut off and terminate thought one instant, the dharma-body (Law-body or spiritual body) is freed from the physical body. At no time should a single instant of thought be attached to any dharma. If one single instant of thought is attached to anything, then every thought will be attached. That is bondage. But if in regard to dharmas no thought is attached to anything, that is freedom.

[This is] the meaning of having nonattachment as the foundation.

"Good and learned friends, to be free from all characters means the absence of characters. Only if we can be free from characters will the substance of our nature be pure. That is the meaning of taking the absence-of-character as the substance.

"Absence-of-thought means not to be defiled by external objects. It is to free our thoughts from external objects and not to have thoughts arise over dharmas. But do not stop thinking about everything and eliminate all thought. As soon as thought stops, one dies and is reborn elsewhere. Take heed of this, followers of the Way. If one does not think over the meaning of the Law and becomes mistaken himself, that is excusable. How much worse is it to encourage others to be [mistaken]! Deluded, he does not realize that he is so, and he even blasphemes the scripture and the Law! That is the reason why absence-of-thought is instituted as the doctrine. Because people who are deluded have thoughts about the spheres of objects, perverse views arise in them, and all sorts of afflictions resulting from passions and erroneous thoughts are produced. . . .

"However, this school has instituted absence-of-thought as the doctrine. When people of the world are free from erroneous views, no thoughts will arise. If there are no thoughts, there will not even be an 'absence-of-thought.' Absence means absence of what? Thought means thought of what? Absence-of-thought means freedom from the character of the duality (existence or nonexistence of characters) and from all afflictions resulting from passions. [Thought means thought of the true nature of True Thusness (True Reality).] True Thusness is the substance of thought and thought is the function of True Thusness. It is the self-nature that gives rise to thought. Therefore in spite of the functioning of seeing, hearing, sensing, and knowing, self-nature is not defiled by the many spheres of objects and always remains free and at ease. As the *Wei-mo-chieh [so-shuo] ching* (Scripture Spoken by Vimalakīrti) says, "Externally it skillfully differentiates the various dharma-characters while internally it abides immovably in the First Principle."

18. "Good and learned friends, according to this method sitting in meditation is at bottom neither looking at the mind nor looking at purity. Nor do we say that there should be imperturbability. Suppose we say to look at the mind. The mind is at bottom false. Since being false is the same as being illusory, there is nothing to look at. Suppose we say to look at purity. Man's nature is originally pure. It is by false thoughts that True Thusness is obscured. Our original nature is pure as long as it is free from false thoughts. If one does not realize that his own nature is originally pure and makes up his mind to look at purity, he is creating a false purity. Such purity has no objective existence. Hence we know that what is looked at is false. Purity has neither physical form nor character, but some people set up characters of purity and say that this is the object of our task. People who take this view hinder their own original nature and become bound by purity. If those who cultivate imperturbability would ignore people's mistakes and defeats, their nature would not be perturbed. Deluded people may not be perturbed physically themselves, but whenever they speak, they criticize others and thus violate the Way. Thus looking at the mind or at purity causes a hindrance to the Way."

19. "Now, this being the case, in this method, what is meant by sitting in meditation? In this method, to sit means to be free from all obstacles, and externally not to allow thoughts to rise from the mind over any sphere of objects. To meditate means to realize the imperturbability of one's original nature. What is meant by meditation and calmness? Meditation means to be free from all characters externally; calmness means to be unperturbed internally. If there are characters outside and the inner mind is not disturbed, one's original nature is naturally pure and calm. It is only because of the spheres of objects that there is contact, and contact leads to perturbation. There is calmness when one is free from characters and is not perturbed. There is meditation when one is externally free from characters, and there is calmness when one is internally undisturbed. Meditation and calmness mean that external meditation is attained and internal calmness is achieved. The *Wei-mo-chieh [so-shuo] ching* says, 'Immediately we become completely clear and recover our original mind.' The *P'u-sa chieh ching* (Scripture of Disciplines for Bodhisattvahood) says, 'We are originally pure in our self-nature.' Good and learned friends, realize that your self-nature is naturally pure. Cultivate and achieve for yourselves the Law-body of your self-nature. Follow the Way of the Buddha yourselves. Act and achieve Buddhahood for yourselves." . . .

5.5.4 Zen Buddhism

It took six hundred years for Mahayana Buddhism to spread across China, into Korea and then to Japan. According to legend, Prince Shotoku (574–622) welcomed Buddhist missionary monks and formulated the *Seventeen-Article Constitution*, which urged reverence for the Three Gems or Refuges: the Buddha, the *Dharma* (teachings), and the *sangha* (community). It also counseled harmony with the indigenous religion of Shinto. Today, Japan presents the broadest surviving range of the rich variety of Mahayana Buddhist schools and practices.

Among the various schools that came to Japan from China, *Ch'an* Buddhism, now known as **Zen,** left a deep and lasting impression on Japanese art, literature, architecture, military training, and general life style from the tea ceremony to bathing.

Both the Northern and Southern schools of Ch'an that had developed in China were established in Japan. The Rinzai school (*Lin-chi* in China) was introduced by Eisai (1141–1215) in 1191, and the Soto school (*Ts'ao-tung* in China) was established in 1227 by Dogen (1200–1253). Rinzai, with its emphasis on sudden enlightenment, emphasized the use of the *koan* (Chinese: *kung-an*; Korean: *kongan*) in meditation. *Koans* are enigmatic sayings or questions such as "What is the sound of one hand clapping?" that are given to students who are instructed to wrestle with them with all their strength until they reach a sudden insight called *satori*. The first *koan* often given to meditators is "Joshu's Mu." "Mu" means "no" and is said to have been the answer that the Chinese Ch'an master Chao Chou (Joshu in Japanese) gave to a monk who asked whether a dog had the Buddha-Nature.

Soto Zen placed more emphasis on gradual enlightenment, and thus monks were taught a more traditional type of meditation called **zazen,** or seated meditation. The following selection is a translation of three passages from the teachings of Dogen (*Shobogenzo Zuimonki,* or *Eye and Treasure of the True Law*) as recorded by his disciple Ejo. Note that in the first passage Dogen criticizes other Buddhist schools and in the last passage he answers a charge leveled against Buddhists, first by the Confucianists in China and then by those in Japan who believed that reverence and loyalty to one's parents and ancestors was of central importance to the moral life and the stability of society. Since Buddhism advocated the life of a monk or a nun, such a life appeared to lead to the abandonment of an important moral standard in both Chinese and Japanese society.

DOGEN

Eye and Treasure of the True Law

READING QUESTIONS

1. Why is *zazen* important?
2. How does Dogen answer the question about indebtedness to one's parents?
3. If you are a member of a religious tradition, and someone asked you what is the one thing in your tradition that everyone should practice, what would you say? How does your answer compare to Dogen's?

Once Dōgen taught, "One must remember how quickly the wind of transitoriness blows our life away, and how important are life and death. If one wishes to do and study something worthwhile during his short life, he ought to practice Buddhist disciplines and study the Law. It goes without saying that one should discard literary composition and writing poems inasmuch as they are of no value. One should not attempt to cover to many subjects even in his study and practice of Buddhism. Moreover, one should have nothing to do with those schools of Buddhism such as all the exoteric and esoteric sects, which unlike Zen build their doctrines based on scriptures and commentaries. Even the Buddha's own sayings should not be studied indiscriminately. Most people with limited abilities can hardly concentrate even on one thing. It is not desirable, therefore, for them to indulge in many things simultaneously, for in so doing their minds will lose control. . . .

Once, Ejō inquired, "What is the one thing in the Buddhist Law which we should practice?" The Master said, "What you should practice depends on your own abilities. However, the one practice which has been handed down in the tradition of Bodhidharma is *zazen* (meditation). This practice is suited for all people, regardless of differences of innate ability. When I learned this principle under the tutelage of the late master (Ju-ching,

From *The Great Asian Religions: An Anthology,* edited by Wing-tsit Chan et al. (New York: Macmillan Publishing Co., Inc., 1969), pp. 284–285. © Copyright 1969, Macmillan Publishing Co., Inc. Reprinted by permission. Endnotes omitted.

1163–1268) of the T'ien-t'ung Monastery [in China], I started practicing *zazen* day and night and continued it even when some other monks gave it up in the extremely hot and cold days. I then said to myself, 'I should practice *zazen* even if I should become ill or die on account of it. What good would it do if I, who am not sick, failed to do so! If I should die in following the practice of *zazen* before attaining enlightenment, I might at least create a cause to be born in future life as a follower of the Buddha. After all, it is useless simply to live long without undergoing Buddhist disciplines. Even if I take great care of my health, I might drown or encounter unexpected death, and then I will surely have cause to regret.' I, therefore, urge all of you to practice *zazen* most intensely. All of you without exception will find the true path. Such was the teaching of my late master [Ju-ching]." . . .

During one of the evening conversations Ejō asked, "What shall we do to repay our indebtedness to our parents?" Dōgen replied, "One should observe filial piety, of course. However, there is a difference between the filial piety of the monk and that of the layman. In the case of the layman, he should, as taught in the *Classic of Filial Piety*, serve his parents during their lifetime and engage in acts of repaying gratitude to them after their death. On the other hand, the monk who has entered the Buddhist life—which is characterized by inactivity, [by forsaking the indebtedness toward his parents]—should not try to repay gratitude only toward his physical parents. His sense of indebtedness toward all living beings must be considered as deep as his sense of indebtedness toward his parents of this lifetime, so that the latter should not be singled out as special objects of filial piety. This attitude is in keeping with the Buddhist principle of inactivity. To follow the path of the Buddha in one's daily disciplines and in one's study of the Law is the true filial piety. Holding a memorial service on the memorial days of the parents or doing charitable deeds for the repose of the parents during the forty-nine days following their death are examples of the way of the laity, [and not the way of the monks]. . . .

5.5.5 Nichiren Buddhism

Ch'an was only one of many forms of Mahayana Buddhism imported from China. T'ien-t'ai became Tendai in Japan. It was brought by the Japanese monk Saicho (766–822) and established on Mount Hiei, which became a Buddhist stronghold. Another Japanese monk, named Kukai (774–835), established

Shingon (True Word) in Japan after studying Chen-yen Buddhism in China. Kukai, who became known as Kobo Daishi after his death, made Mount Koya (near Osaka) his home base and taught the mystery of the three rituals: body **mudras,** or hand gestures, speech (*mantras*, or mystical sounds), and mind (contemplation of celestial *buddhas* and *bodhisattvas*). However, one of the most popular schools was Pure Land Buddhism (*Jodo* in Japanese, *Ching-t'u* in Chinese), also called Amida Buddhism (from the Japanese name Amitabha).

Honen (1133–1212) taught Amida devotion, advocating that we need to rely on the grace of Amida for enlightenment. Devotion consisted of the recitation of Amida's name called the **nembutsu.** Honen's disciple, Shinran (1173–1262), contrasted "other power" (*tariki*) with self-power (*jiriki*). We live, Shinran thought, in a degenerate age called *mappo* in which the self-power taught by Zen is not sufficient for enlightenment. Only the "other power" of Amida can save us. Thus it might appear that the rallying cry of Martin Luther's Protestant Reformation in Germany—salvation by faith alone—had already been heard in Japan some three centuries earlier. However, the faith Luther advocated was faith in Jesus Christ's loving grace while the faith Honen and Shinran advocated was faith in the loving grace of Amida.

The path of faith became far more popular than Zen in Japan, in part because it did not require one to enter a monastery, practice *zazen*, and struggle with *koans*. A sincere recitation of *nembutsu* was enough to guarantee a place with Amida in the Pure Land to the West. However, even as Shinran preached, another Japanese Buddhist named Nichiren (1222–1282) proclaimed that these evil times of the *mappo*—the end of all decency, morality, and true teaching of the *Dharma*—required more drastic measures than silly chants. In order to save Japan and Buddhism, the people had to abandon their heretical beliefs in things like the *nembutsu*, repent of their sins, and turn in faith to the power of the *Lotus Sutra* (Japanese *Myoho-horengekyo*, or, in its abbreviated form, *Hokekyo*). According to Nichiren, the *Lotus Sutra* is the only *sutra* containing the true teachings of the Buddha for these degenerate times. He did not hesitate to call the followers of Zen devils, to claim that the three Shingon rituals would destroy the land, and to declare that the Pure Land *nembutsu* chanters would go to hell. He called on the Japanese government to outlaw all Buddhist sects but his own.

As you might expect, this got him into a lot of trouble. He was attacked by a mob, arrested, exiled twice, and nearly executed, but, persecution only made his convictions and the convictions of his followers stronger. His movement grew strong and inspired intense patriotism to the ideal of a glorious Japan in which the power of the Buddha and the *kamis* (traditional gods and spirits of the indigenous Shinto religion) would save the nation from corruption and destruction. Today, new religious groups in Japan such as Reiyukai (1925), Soka Gakkai (1937), and Rossho Koseikai (1938) have been inspired by Nichiren's teachings.

The following is a summary translation of *The Establishment of Righteousness and the Security of the Nation (Rissho ankoku ron)*, written in 1260.

NICHIREN

Righteousness and Security

READING QUESTIONS

1. List the main points of this summary. Do you notice any parallels between what is said here and other religious teachings that you have heard or heard about? If so, what are they?
2. Why do you think some religious groups are led to denounce other groups within their own religious traditions?

A visitor came and lamented, saying, "In recent years there have been strange phenomena in heaven, while famines and plagues have occurred all over the earth, so that it is not uncommon to find not only dead animals but also human corpses on the streets. I rather fancy that death has claimed over half of our population, and every family without exception has been in grief. In this situation, people have been prompted to seek various forms of superhuman help, such as uttering the holy name of the Buddha of the Western Pure Land [Amida], or offer-

From *The Great Asian Religions: An Anthology*, edited by Wing-tsit Chan et al. (New York: Macmillan Publishing Co., Inc., 1969), pp. 281–283. © Copyright 1969, Macmillan Publishing Co., Inc. Reprinted by permission. Endnotes omitted.

ing the incantations of esoteric Buddhism to avoid calamities, or practicing Zen meditation to attain liberation from worldly cares, or worshiping the Shintō kami of heaven and earth at various places to avoid pestilence. The rulers, too, are concerned with the plight of peasants and people, and they have remitted taxes. In spite of such kindness to the people, the famine and the plague are more oppressing, there are beggars everywhere, the dead can be seen everywhere, and more corpses are piled up each day. The sun, moon, and five stars follow their proper courses, Buddhism is respected, and the influence of the ruler is still great, and yet the life has gone out of the world, and religion too is losing its [spiritual] vitality. What is the cause of all this, I wonder?"

The Master of the house said, "I too have been anxious about these things and feel very indignant. Now that we share the same concerns, let us exchange our views on the subject. As far as I can ascertain, on the basis of my reflections and reading of the scriptures, all kinds of calamities have descended on us because the people have violated righteousness and turned to evil. That is why good kami have left the land, and sages have not returned, and thus demons and evil spirits have come."

The visitor said, "I have learned for the first time from you [that our troubles were caused by the departure of good kami and holy men and by the arrival of demons and evil spirits]. I would like to know the scriptural evidences for your view, though."

The Master replied, "Scriptural passages and their evidences are extensive. Among them, let me mention the *Scripture of the Golden Light (Konkōmyō kyō)*, *Mahā-sannipāta sūtra (Daishū kyō* or Scripture of great assembly), the *Scripture of the Divine Healer (Yakushi kyō)*, and the *Scripture of the Benevolent Kings (Ninnō kyō)*. The contents of these four scriptures are so clear that no one can question their meaning. However, those whose eyes have been blinded and those whose minds have been misguided would rather believe in the false teaching, not realizing the true doctrine. This accounts for the fact that people are discarding the Buddhas and scriptures instead of protecting them. And, since good kami and sages have left this country, evil spirits and heretical teachings are causing various kinds of troubles and calamities."

The visitor, who was now angered by the foregoing answer, stated, "Emperor Ming (r. 58–75) of the Eastern Han dynasty (25–220) was guided by a dream of a golden image and opened the door for the introduction of Buddhism to China. . . . [In our own country, since the time of the noble Prince Shōtoku, 573–621] . . . the sovereign as well as all his subjects have venerated Buddhist statues and scriptures. Our country is dotted with great temples, and scriptures are found in every corner of the land. Seeing all this, on what ground do you say that Buddhism is being neglected and discarded in our country?"

The Master explained to the guest, saying, "You are right in stating that there are many temples, many storehouses for scriptures, and many monks, and that Buddhism has for a long time been venerated and is still venerated. However, the monks are so degraded and lead people astray with flattery, whereas the sovereign as well as his subjects cannot tell good from evil because of their ignorance. . . . [Our present tragic situation is exactly like what was prophesied in the *Scripture of Benevolent Kings*, the *Nirvāṇa Scripture*, and the *Lotus Scripture*.] In this situation, righteousness cannot be restored unless we first remonstrate and correct the evil monks."

The guest, now angrier than ever, asked, "Isn't it the duty of the monarch to influence the nation according to the [great way of] heaven and earth, while the sages bring order by distinguishing right and wrong? Now, the monks of the world are highly respected by the people, [and that implies that these monks are not evil]. Otherwise, why does the wise monarch trust them? Why do you speak so disparagingly of the venerable clergy? Tell me, for instance, who is an evil monk?"

The Master replied, "I shall tell you. During the reign of Emperor Go-Toba (r. 1184–1198) there was a certain monk called Hōnen who wrote a book entitled "Collection of passages" [on the original vow of Amida in which the *nembutsu* is chosen above all ways of achieving rebirth]. In this "Collection," following the false interpretations by Donran (Tan-luan in Chinese, 476–542), Dōshaku (Tao-ch'o, d. 645), and Zendō (Shen-tao, d. 681), which divided Buddhism into the Gate of the Holy Path or the Path of Difficult Practice and the Gate of Pure Land or the Path of Easy Practice, [Hōnen classified all teachings except that of Pure Land into the former category.] Thus, he urged people to give up, close, discard, or destroy 637 scriptures, 2,883 sections in all, including those of the Lotus, the esoteric, and all the Mahāyāna teachings taught during the life of the Buddha, all other Buddhas and bodhisattvas and heavenly beings. . . . Hōnen's teaching is counter to the [original] vow of Amida, who pledged to save all beings except those who commit the Five Great Sins and those who falsely accuse the True Law, as clearly stated in the three Pure Land Scriptures from which Hōnen presumably derived his own views. However, in this period of Latter End of Law there is no holy man; rather, [many clergy] have forgotten the right path and lead others to distorted faith instead of helping them to see things clearly. [Under the influence of Hōnen's writing, people] venerate only Amida, the Buddha of the Western Pure Land, for-

getting even the supreme Buddha Śākyamuni. No wonder temples other than those of Amida are neglected, and offerings are given only to the priests of the *nembutsu* sect. Since the main traditions of Buddhism, such as the most comprehensive and central vehicle of the Lotus (the Tendai School), are neglected in favor of the Pure Land teaching, which lies at the border of historic Buddhism, it is understandable that the good kami are angry and evil spirits take advantage of the situation. Thus, the foremost task before us is not to offer various kinds of prayers to ward off famine and pestilence, but to forbid the very evil which is the cause of all these troubles."

The visitor, now looking a little more pleasant, said, "I now realize [Hōnen's mistakes in renouncing all other scriptures, and you have explained how Hōnen's writing has been the cause of all our troubles]. Now, everyone, from the sovereign to all his subjects, are concerned with the peace of the land. If the nation declines and the people vanish, who will be left to venerate Buddha and his Law? Thus, I feel that we must first pray for the security of the nation before thinking about Buddhism, and would like to know the means of eliminating the troubles which are now confronting the nation."

The Master replied, "Being stupid by nature, I cannot offer any clever solution of my own. However, based on the scriptures, I am convinced that the nation will attain peace and prosperity if those who slander the True Law are rejected and those who preach the true doctrine are given important positions. Concretely, if we want the security of the nation, we must first eliminate the false teaching [of Hōnen]. All the scriptures consider the act of slandering the Law a grave sin. Is it not foolish for one to be caught by the net of this grave sin and eventually descend into the flame of hell? Let me exhort you to be converted straightway to the true teaching of the Lotus, and when people follow the teaching of the Lotus, the Three Worlds and the ten regions will be transformed into the Buddha Land, and be it noted that the Buddha Land will never be destroyed by any calamity or trouble. When the nation thus attains security, we will all attain the safety of the body and peace of mind. You should believe and respect this statement." (*Nihon Bukkyō shisō shiryōshū* [Collection of source materials on the history of Japanese Buddhist thought], pp. 537–52)

5.6 VAJRAYANA OR TANTRIC BUDDHISM IN TIBET

Tantric Buddhism is based on a group of texts called **tantras** as distinguished from *sutras*. It began in India and is sometimes treated as an outgrowth of the Mahayana tradition. However, it is sufficiently distinct to be regarded as a "vehicle" in itself along with Nikaya (Hinayana) and Mahayana. As such it is often called the **Vajrayana,** or "Diamond Vehicle." Introduced to Tibet in the seventh century, it transformed Tibetan culture and political life. According to legend, the Tibetan king was converted to Buddhism by two princesses—one from China and one from Nepal—whom he married as the result of political treaties.

Tantric Buddhism took seriously the Madhyamika teaching of the identity of *nirvana* and *samsara* (see Reading 5.4.3). If *samsara* is truly *nirvana*, then at least two important things follow. First, polar opposites in thought are, in reality, unified; second, anything could become a means to enlightenment. Followers of "left-handed" tantrism engaged in meat-eating, wine-drinking, and ritualized sexual intercourse along with other behaviors forbidden to monks in order to symbolize the union of opposites and the freedom that enlightenment brings. Tantrism of the "right-handed" form took a less transgressive approach.

In general, Vajrayana urged people to identify with the Buddha in body, speech, and mind. If one could do so successfully, enlightenment was possible in this lifetime. One did not have to live for eons through thousands of reincarnations seeking *nirvana*. The Vajrayana commonly came to be known as the "shortcut" to enlightenment and developed elaborate visualization techniques that employ *mandalas* (elaborate structures symbolizing the unity of opposites) and figures of *buddhas* and *bodhisattvas*. During *mandala* meditation, one can merge with the sacred symbols and thereby realize one's Buddha-Nature.

5.6.1 The Tibetan Book of the Dead

In addition to the story of princesses from China and Nepal converting the king to Buddhism, there is the story that Vajrayana Buddhism was brought to Tibet by an Indian monk named Padmasambhava, now revered as the Guru Rimpoche ("precious teacher"). The indigenous religion of Tibet is known as Bon ("truth"), and one of its main ritual objectives was the safe conduct of the souls of the dead to an afterlife. Bon religion combined and interacted with Buddhism leaving its imprint in various ways. Among them are Buddhist shamanistic practices, including trance dances, oracular utterances, possession by gods and goddesses, and healing.

Another influence of the Bon concern with life after death is found in a special body of literature containing instructions to both the dead and the living about afterlife states. These instructions are the *Bardo Thodal (Liberation by Hearing on the After-Death Plane)*, better known as the *Tibetan Book of the Dead*. These instructions are read aloud to the dying in order to help them achieve liberation during the three stages of the *bardo* state between death and rebirth.

During the first stage (*chikhai bardo*), after a period of unconsciousness, one sees a colorless bright light. If this light is recognized as the Dharma Body of the Buddha, one will experience *nirvana*. If not (and most of us do not because of our bad *karma*), one enters the *chonyid bardo* (second stage) where both kind and wrathful deities are met. Once again there is a chance for *nirvana*, but if it is missed, the *sidpa bardo* (third stage) is entered during which one experiences judgment according to one's *karma* followed by rebirth.

Bardo Thodal

READING QUESTIONS

1. How should one conceive the spirit of enlightenment at death?
2. What is the clear light?
3. Why do you think there are different instructions about the clear light for a spiritual teacher?
4. What are the six kinds of "between"?
5. What causes one to miss the chances at liberation?
6. Why is it important to recognize the "sounds, lights, and rays" as one's own perceptions?

Hey, noble one! Now you have arrived at so-called "death," so you should conduct yourself according to your conception of the spirit of enlightenment. You should conceive your spirit of enlightenment thus: "Alas! I have arrived at the time of death. From now, relying on this death, I will develop my spirit only by contemplating the conception of the spirit of enlightenment of love and compassion. For the sake of the whole space-full of beings, I must attain perfect Buddhahood." And especially you should think, "Now for the sake of all beings, I will recognize the death clear light as the Body of Truth. Within its experience, I will attain the supreme accomplishment of the Great Seal, and I will accomplish the purposes of all beings. If I don't attain that, then in the time of the between, I will recognize it as the between. I will realize that between as the Great Seal Body of Integration, and I will accomplish the purposes of all the infinite space-full of beings by manifesting whatsoever is needed to tame whomsoever." Thus never losing the willpower of that spiritual conception, you should remember the experience of whatever instructions you have previously practiced.

This should be clearly enunciated with the lips near the ear. In this way, not allowing even an instant's distraction, you should pray for the deceased to accomplish this practice.

Then, when the outer breath has ceased, you should press the sleep channels (at the neck) forcefully and say the following; first, to a spiritual teacher or spiritual superior:

Venerable teacher! Right now the objective clear light dawns for you. Recognize it! Please incorporate it within your experience.

You should describe it to all others as follows:

Hey, noble one, you named So-and-so, listen here! Now the pure clear light of reality dawns for you. Recognize it! Hey, noble one, this, your present conscious natural clear void awareness, this presence in clear voidness without any objectivity of substance, sign, of color—just this is the reality, the Mother, Buddha All-around Goodness! And this, your conscious awareness natural voidness, not succumbing to a false annihilative voidness, just your own conscious awareness, unceasing, bright, distinct, and vibrant—just this awareness is the Father, Buddha All-around Goodness! Just this presence of the indivisibility of your awareness's natural insubstantial voidness and the vibrant bright presence of your conscious awareness—just this is the Buddha Body of Truth. Your awareness thus abides in this vast mass of light of clarity-void indivisible. You are free of birth or death—just this is the Buddha Changeless Light. It is enough just to recognize this. Recognizing this your own conscious awareness's purity nature as the Buddha, yourself beholding your own awareness—that is to dwell in the inner realization of all Buddhas. . . .

THE MILD DEITY REALITY BETWEEN

. . . If the deceased is still not liberated, it is then called the "third between phase." The reality between dawns. This becomes the third between, in which the evolutionary hallucinations dawn. Therefore it is crucial to read this great orientation to the reality between at that time, with its very great power and benefits. At that time, her loved ones will weep and wail, her share of food is no longer served, her clothes are stripped off, her bed is broken. She can see them, but they cannot see her. She can hear them calling her, but they cannot hear when she calls them. So she must depart, her heart sinking in despair. Perceptions arise of sounds, lights, and rays, and she feels faint with fear, terror, and panic. Then you must use this great description of the reality between. You should call the deceased by name, and clearly and distinctly say as follows:

Hey, noble one! Listen unwavering with intense concentration! There are six kinds of between: the natural life between, the dream between, the contemplation between, the death-point between, the reality between, and the emergent existence between.

Hey, noble one, three betweens will dawn for you: the death-point between, the reality between, and the existence between will dawn. Until yesterday, in the death-point between, the reality clear light dawned. But you did not recognize it, so you had to wander here. Now the reality between and the existence between will dawn for you. As I describe them, you must recognize them without fail.

Hey, noble one! Now you have arrived at what is called "death." You are going from this world to the beyond. You are not alone; it happens to everyone. You must not indulge in attachment and insistence on this life. Though you are attached and you insist, you have no power to stay, you will not avoid wandering in the life cycle. Do not lust! Do not cling! Be mindful of the Three Jewels!

Hey, noble child! Whatever terrifying visions of the reality between may dawn upon you, you should not forget the following words. You must proceed remembering in your mind the meaning of these words. Therein lies the key of recognition.

Hey! Now when the reality between dawns upon me,
I will let go of the hallucinations of instinctive terror,
Enter the recognition of all objects as my mind's own
*   visions,*
and understand this as the pattern of perception in the
*   between;*

Come to this moment, arrived at this most critical
  cessation,
I will not fear my own visions of deities mild and
  fierce! . . .

You should proceed clearly saying this verse aloud and remembering its meaning. Do not forget this, as it is the key to recognizing whatever terrifying visions dawn as certainly being your own perceptions.

Hey, noble one! At this time when your mind and body are parting ways, pure reality manifests in subtle, dazzling visions, vividly experienced, naturally frightening and worrisome, shimmering like a mirage on the plains in autumn. Do not fear them. Do not be terrified! Do not panic! You have what is called an "instinctual mental body," not a material, flesh and blood body. Thus whatever sounds, lights, and rays may come at you, they cannot hurt you. You cannot die. It is enough just for you to recognize them as your own perceptions. Understand that this is the between.

Hey, noble one! If you don't recognize them as your own perceptions in this way—whatever other meditations and achievements you may have experienced in the human world, if you did not meet this particular instruction—the lights will frighten you, the sounds will panic you, the rays will terrify you. If you don't know the key of this instruction, you will not recognize the sounds, lights, and rays, and you will wander in the life cycle. . . .

5.6.2 Pilgrimage to Mount Kailasa

Going on pilgrimages to sacred sites is a common practice in many religions including Buddhism. From Sri Lanka to Japan, Buddhist sacred sites dot the landscape and attract pilgrims. Pilgrimage is widely regarded as a meritorious practice as well as an act of devotion that will contribute to one's spiritual development.

In Tibet, Mount Kailasa, a peak in the western Himalayas that some Tibetans believe is at the center of the world, is a sacred pilgrimage site second only to Lhasa, the holy city of Tibet. Mount Kailasa is called Gang Rimpoche and is associated with Milarepa, an eleventh-century saint. Pilgrims journey hundreds of miles, many on foot, to reach this mountain. Once there, the devotees go around Gang Rimpoche in a clockwise direction, called circumambulation, which is a common act of veneration. They also engage in prostration (placing one's body full length on the ground), and some use successive grand prostrations to travel all the way around Gang Rimpoche, body length by body length.

The following description is by a Japanese sociologist, Kazuhiko Tamamura, who visited Gang Rimpoche in 1985.

KAZUHIKO TAMAMURA

Seizan Junrei

READING QUESTIONS

1. Make a list of as many different factors as you can think of that would motivate people to undertake this pilgrimage.
2. How might such pilgrimages contribute to the development of spiritual qualities?

What is known as the Gang Rimpoche [Mount Kailāsa] pilgrimage involves circumambulating the circumference of the sacred peak any number of times. . . . The pilgrims, coming from various directions, "appear" in Tarchen, the village near the base of the mountain [which serves as the takeoff point for the circumambulation path]. The word "appear" is entirely appropriate, for these people pay no attention to existing roads and simply take the shortest route. Some of them arrive, driving several dozen sheep on which they have loaded their baggage; some ride on horseback or in trucks or tractors; but the vast majority of them come on foot, their belongings on their back neatly packed in panniers made of willow branches. They carry staffs or tent poles in their hands in order to drive off ferocious dogs.

Except for those pilgrims travelling alone or in very small groups, most of the parties bring with them tents of white cotton cloth. As soon as they arrive in Tarchen, they set up these tents . . . and begin searching for fuel, yak dung, which they collect and carry in the folds of their aprons or shepherds' robes.

The fatigue of the long journey they have made to reach Tarchen is great [some have come on foot from Eastern Tibet as much as three thousand kilometers away], but the very next day after their arrival, they set out on the Gang Rimpoche pilgrimage circuit with eager anticipation. Their fervent desire to make the circuit of the holy mountain as soon as possible prompts them to take to the road again. . . .

The pilgrimage route around Gang Rimpoche is 52 kilometers long. If you were to extend your arms in front of you to make a circle corresponding to the route, Tarchen would be where your head is, and Gang Rimpoche itself would tower majestically from a spot just inside of the place where the tips of your fingers meet. The pilgrimage route thus leaves from Tarchen, at an altitude of 4,700 meters, follows the La Chu River upstream (corresponding to your left arm), crosses the Dorma Pass at 5,600 meters [located roughly where your right hand would be], and returns to Tarchen along a course that follows the Son Chu River (your right arm).

Tibetans make this circumambulation in one fourteen-hour day. If they were to spend the night on the road, they would require a good deal of baggage including their tents, so they choose to go all out and make the circuit in a day. It is also considered to be more meritorious to make the trip in a single day. . . . They make the circumambulation with the same joy and high spirits that we associate with going on a picnic, and return to Tarchen in the evening. Then, after resting in Tarchen for a day or two, they once again make the circuit. In this way, they go around the sacred mountain many times [13 and 26 times are popular numbers], and so end up staying in Tarchen for quite a long while. . . .

A NOTE ON GRAND PROSTRATIONS

The special feature of the Tibetan Buddhists' grand prostration is the repetition with which it is performed. In front of a temple, around a temple, facing holy ground, around holy ground, and, at times, on the way to temples and holy areas, the grand prostration is repeated constantly time and again. I could not help feeling a sense of awe at the rigorous and strenuous nature of the practice of Tibetan Buddhists which involved completing the 52 kilometer circuit around Gang Rimpoche by making grand prostrations. . . .

In Tibetan, this type of practice is called "kyang chak." "Kyang" means "to extend the body," and "chak" means "to worship." First, one holds one's two hands together on top of one's head, and one prays: "May the sins that I have committed up until now with this body be cleansed." Then one lowers the hands cupping them in front of one's face, and one says: "May the sins that

I have committed up until now with this mouth be cleansed." Then one lowers one's hands further to chest level and says: "May the sins that I have committed up until now with this mind be cleansed." Then one falls to one's knees, forcefully extends the body forward, reaching the hands out as far as possible and bringing the palms together while flat on one's face. Then, getting up, one advances to the point to which one's hands extended, and one repeats the whole thing again. Each time, one can only move the distance one has measured out with one's body. Thus the ground that can be covered in a day is not very great. They say that it takes two weeks to cover the 52 kilometers around Gang Rimpoche by this method. . . . In the course of the circuit, any number of fords across rivers need to be made, but the pilgrims keep up their grand prostrations right across the stones in the stream. . . .

5.6.3 The White Lotus

Vajrayana Buddhism in Tibet is divided into four major groups: Karma-pa, Kagyu-pa, Sakya-pa, and Geluga-pa. The Karma-pa (the ancients) trace their line back to Padmasambhava and base their doctrines on tantric texts. There are strong Bon elements in this line, and other schools do not always accept them.

The Kagyu-pa began in the eleventh century with Marpa (1012–1096), who presumably learned from the Indian master Naropa (956–1040). The Kagyu-pa place emphasis on certain yogic practices such as *tum-mo* (generating inner body heat) and the quick path to enlightenment. Milarepa, one of the great saints of Tibet, is one of Marpa's disciples.

The Sakya-pa are most closely associated with the principality of Sakya and emphasize tantric practices that focus attention on the universal consciousness within.

Perhaps the best-known tradition, the Geluga-pa began as a reform movement started by the great scholar Tsongkha-pa (1357–1419), who emphasized learning, discipline, and celibacy (in contrast to the Karma-pa and Kagyu-pa, who allow monks to marry). In the seventeenth century, the head of the Geluga-pa, the fifth **Dalai Lama,** was able to consolidate political power and a succession of Dalai Lamas or their regents continued to rule Tibet until 1959.

Since the 1959 takeover of Tibet by the Chinese, the present Dalai Lama, who was born in 1935, has lived in exile. He has traveled the world teaching, supporting his people, and seeking freedom for Tibet. He was awarded the Nobel Peace Prize in 1989. He is, as he likes to say, "a simple Buddhist monk" whose love of peace and deep spirituality have impressed many. Among his many books is *Freedom in Exile*, from which the following selection is taken.

THE DALAI LAMA

Freedom in Exile

READING QUESTIONS

1. According to the Dalai Lama, what is the fundamental precept of Buddhism, and how do the theories of consciousness and rebirth derive from this precept?
2. Who is this Dalai Lama, and how was he found?
3. How do you think the Dalai Lama's Buddhism influenced his impressions of the West?
4. While the Dalai Lama is traveling abroad, what approach does he take when addressing groups of people?
5. What is the Dalai Lama's attitude toward religions other than Buddhism?
6. How does the Dalai Lama answer the question "What is religion?"?
7. What impresses you most about the Dalai Lama's religious practice? Why?

Before going on to tell about my discovery as Dalai Lama, I must first say something about Buddhism and its history in Tibet. The founder of Buddhism was an historical figure, Siddhartha, who came to be recognized as the Buddha Shakyamuni. He was born more than 2,500 years ago. His teachings, now known as the *Dharma*, or Buddhism, were introduced to Tibet during the fourth century A.D. They took several centuries to supplant the native Bon religion and become fully established, but eventually the country was so thoroughly converted that Buddhist principles governed all society, at every level. And whilst Tibetans are by nature quite aggressive people and quite warlike, their increasing interest in religious practice was a major factor in bringing about the country's isolation. Before then, Tibet

possessed a vast empire, which dominated Central Asia with territories covering large parts of northern India, Nepal and Bhutan in the south. It also included much Chinese territory. In 763 A.D., Tibetan forces actually captured the Chinese capital, where they extracted promises of tribute and other concessions. However, as Tibetans' enthusiasm for Buddhism increased, so Tibet's relations with her neighbours became of a spiritual rather than a political nature. This was especially true of China, where a "priest-patron" relationship developed. The Manchu Emperors, who were Buddhists, referred to the Dalai Lama as "King of Expounding Buddhism."

The fundamental precept of Buddhism is Interdependence or the Law of Cause and Effect. This simply states that everything which an individual being experiences is derived through action from motivation. Motivation is thus the root of both action and experience. From this understanding are derived the Buddhist theories of consciousness and rebirth.

The first holds that, because cause gives rise to effect which in turn becomes the cause of further effect, consciousness must be continual. It flows on and on, gathering experiences and impressions from one moment to the next. At the point of physical death, it follows that a being's consciousness contains an imprint of all these past experiences and impressions, and the actions which preceded them. This is known as *karma*, which means "action." It is thus consciousness, with its attendant *karma*, which then becomes "reborn" in a new body—animal, human or divine.

So, to give a simple example, a person who has spent his or her life mistreating animals could quite easily be reborn in the next life as a dog belonging to someone who is unkind to animals. Similarly, meritorious conduct in this life will assist in a favourable rebirth in the next.

Buddhists further believe that because the basic nature of consciousness is neutral, it is possible to escape from the unending cycle of birth, suffering, death and rebirth that life inevitably entails, but only when all negative *karma* has been eliminated along with all worldly attachments. When this point is reached, the consciousness in question is believed to attain first liberation and then ultimately Buddhahood. However, according to Buddhism in the Tibetan tradition, a being that achieves Buddhahood, although freed from *Samsara*, the "wheel of suffering," as the phenomenon of existence is known, will continue to return to work for the benefit of all other sentient beings until such time as each one is similarly liberated.

Now in my own case, I am held to be the reincarnation of each of the previous thirteen Dalai Lamas of Tibet (the first having been born in 1351 A.D.), who are in turn considered to be manifestations of Avalokiteshvara, or Chenrezig, Bodhisattva of Compassion, holder of the White Lotus. Thus I am believed also to be a manifestation of Chenrezig, in fact the seventy-fourth in a lineage that can be traced back to a Brahmin boy who lived in the time of Buddha Shakyamuni. I am often asked whether I truly believe this. The answer is not simple to give. But as a fifty-six year old, when I consider my experiences during this present life, and given my Buddhist beliefs, I have no difficulty accepting that I am spiritually connected both to the thirteen previous Dalai Lamas, to Chenrezig and to the Buddha himself.

When I was not quite three years old, a search party that had been sent out by the Government to find the new incarnation of the Dalai Lama arrived at Kumbum monastery. It had been led there by a number of signs. One of these concerned the embalmed body of my predecessor, Thupten Gyatso, the Thirteenth Dalai Lama, who had died aged fifty-seven in 1933. During its period of sitting in state, the head was discovered to have turned from facing south to north-east. Shortly after that the Regent, himself a senior lama, had a vision. Looking into the waters of the sacred lake, Lhamoi Lhatso, in southern Tibet, he clearly saw the Tibetan letters *Ah*, *Ka* and *Ma* float into view. These were followed by the image of a three-storeyed monastery with a turquoise and gold roof and a path running from it to a hill. Finally, he saw a small house with strangely shaped guttering. He was sure that the letter *Ah* referred to Amdo, the north-eastern province, so it was there that the search party was sent.

By the time they reached Kumbum, the members of the search party felt that they were on the right track. It seemed likely that if the letter *Ah* referred to Amdo, then *Ka* must indicate the monastery at Kumbum—which was indeed three storeyed and turquoise roofed. They now only needed to locate a hill and a house with peculiar guttering. So they began to search the neighbouring villages. When they saw the gnarled branches of juniper wood on the roof of my parents' house, they were certain that the new Dalai Lama would not be far away. Nevertheless, rather than reveal the purpose of their visit, the group asked only to stay the night. The leader of the party, Kewtsang Rinpoché, then pretended to be a servant and spent much of the evening observing and playing with the youngest child in the house.

The child recognised him and called out "Sera Lama, Sera Lama." Sera was Kewtsang Rinpoché's monastery. Next day they left—only to return a few days later as a formal deputation. This time they brought with them a number of things that had belonged to my predecessor, together with several similar items that did not. In every case, the infant correctly identified those belonging to

the Thirteenth Dalai Lama saying, "It's mine. It's mine." This more or less convinced the search party that they had found the new incarnation. However, there was another candidate to be seen before a final decision could be reached. But it was not long before the boy from Taktser was acknowledged to be the new Dalai Lama. I was that child.

Needless to say, I do not remember very much of these events. I was too small. My only real recollection is of a man with piercing eyes. These turned out to belong to a man named Kenrap Tenzin, who became my Master of the Robes and later taught me to write.

As soon as the search party had concluded that the child from Taktser was the true incarnation of the Dalai Lama, word was sent back to Lhasa informing the Regent. It would be several months before official confirmation was received. Until then, I was to remain at home. In the meantime, Ma Pu-feng, the local Governor, began to make trouble. But eventually I was taken by my parents to Kumbum monastery, where I was installed in a ceremony that took place at dawn. I remember this fact particularly as I was surprised to be woken and dressed before the sun had risen. I also remember being seated on a throne. . . .

Overall I have found much that is impressive about western society. In particular, I admire its energy and creativity and hunger for knowledge. On the other hand, a number of things about the western way of life cause me concern. One thing I have noticed is an inclination for people to think in terms of "black and white" and "either, or," which ignores the fact of interdependence and relativity. They have a tendency to lose sight of the grey areas which inevitably exist between two points of view.

Another observation is that there are a lot of people in the West who live very comfortably in large cities, but virtually isolated from the broad mass of humanity. I find this very strange—that under the circumstance of such material well-being and with thousands of brothers and sisters for neighbours, so many people appear able to show their true feelings only to their cats and dogs. This indicates a lack of spiritual values, I feel. Part of the problem here is perhaps the intense competitiveness of life in these countries, which seems to breed fear and a deep sense of insecurity.

For me, this sense of alienation is symbolised by something I once saw at the home of a very rich man whose guest I was on one of my trips abroad. It was a very large private house, obviously designed expressly for convenience and comfort, and fitted with every kind of appliance. However, when I went into the bathroom, I could not help noticing two large bottles of pills on the shelf above the hand basin. One contained tranquillisers, the other sleeping pills. This was proof, too, that material prosperity alone cannot bring about lasting happiness.

As I have already said, I usually go abroad at the invitation of others. Very often, I am also asked to address groups of people. When this happens, my approach is threefold. Firstly, as a human being, I talk about what I have termed Universal Responsibility. By this I mean the responsibility that we all have for each other and for all sentient beings and also for all of Nature.

Secondly, as a Buddhist monk I try to contribute what I can towards better harmony and understanding between different religions. As I have said, it is my firm belief that all religions aim at making people better human beings and that, despite philosophical differences, some of them fundamental, they all aim at helping humanity to find happiness. This does not mean that I advocate any sort of world religion or "super religion." Rather, I look on religion as medicine. For different complaints, doctors will prescribe different remedies. Therefore, because not everyone's spiritual "illness" is the same, different spiritual medicines are required.

Finally, as a Tibetan, and furthermore as the Dalai Lama, I talk about my own country, people and culture whenever anyone shows interest in these matters. However, although I am greatly encouraged when people do show concern for my homeland and my suffering fellow countrymen and women in occupied Tibet, and although it gives fuel to my determination to continue the fight for justice, I do not consider those who support our cause to be "pro-Tibet." Instead, I consider them to be pro-Justice.

One of the things that I have noticed whilst travelling is the amount of interest shown by young people in the things that I talk about. This enthusiasm could, I suppose, be due to the fact that my insistence on absolute informality appeals to them. For my own part, I greatly value exchanges with younger audiences. They ask all sorts of questions concerning everything from the Buddhist theory of Emptiness, through my ideas about cosmology and modern physics, to sex and morality. Those questions which are unexpected and complicated are the ones I appreciate most. They can help me a great deal as I am compelled to take an interest in something that might not otherwise have occurred to me. It becomes a bit like debating.

Another observation is that many of the people I talk to, especially in the West, have a highly sceptical cast of mind. This can be very positive, I feel, but with the proviso that it is used as the basis for further enquiry. . . .

Whenever I go abroad, I try to contact as many other religious practitioners as possible, with a view to fostering inter-faith dialogue. On one of my foreign visits, I met some Christians with a similar desire. This led to a monastic exchange whereby for a few weeks some Tibetan monks went to a Christian monastery, while a similar number of Christian monks came out to India. It proved to be an extremely useful exercise for both parties. In particular, it enabled us to gain a deeper understanding of other people's way of thinking.

Amongst the many religious personalities that I have met, I will single out a few notable Christians (though I should add that I have been fortunate enough to meet wonderful people from a great variety of different religious backgrounds). The present Pope is a man I hold in high regard. To begin with, our somewhat similar backgrounds give us an immediate common ground. The first time we met, he struck me as a very practical sort of person, very broad-minded and open. I have no doubt that he is a great spiritual leader. Any man who can call out "Brother" to his would-be assassin, as Pope John Paul did, must be a highly evolved spiritual practitioner.

Mother Teresa, whom I met at Delhi airport on my way back from a conference at Oxford, England, during 1988 (which she had also attended), is someone for whom I have the deepest respect. I was at once struck by her demeanour of absolute humility. From the Buddhist point of view she could be considered to be a Bodhisattva.

Another person whom I think of as a highly evolved spiritual master is a Catholic monk I met at his hermitage near Monserrat in Spain. He had spent a great many years there, just like an eastern sage, surviving off nothing more than bread and water and a little tea. He spoke very little English—even less than me—but from his eyes I could see that I was in the presence of an extraordinary person, a true practitioner of religion. When I asked him what his meditations were about, he answered simply, "Love." Since then, I have always thought of him as a modern Milarepa, after the Tibetan master of that name who spent much of his life hidden away in a cave, meditating and composing spiritual verses.

One religious leader with whom I have had several good conversations is the outgoing Archbishop of Canterbury, Dr. Robert Runcie (whose courageous emissary, Terry Waite, I always remember in my prayers). We share the view that religion and politics do mix and both agree that it is the clear duty of religion to serve humanity, that it must not ignore reality. It is not sufficient for religious people to be involved with prayer. Rather, they are morally obliged to contribute all they can to solving the world's problems. . . .

Religion should never become a source of conflict, a further factor of division within the human community.

For my own part, I have even, on the basis of my deep respect for the contribution that other faiths can make towards human happiness, participated in the ceremonies of other religions. And, following the example of a great many Tibetan lamas both ancient and modern, I continue to take teachings from as many different traditions as possible. For whilst it is true that some schools of thought felt it desirable for a practitioner to stay within his or her own tradition, people have always been free to do as they think fit. Furthermore, Tibetan society has always been highly tolerant of other people's beliefs. Not only was there a flourishing Muslim community in Tibet, but also there were a number of Christian missions which were admitted without hindrance. I am therefore firmly in favour of a liberal approach. Sectarianism is poison. . . .

What is religion? As far as I am concerned, any deed done with good motivation is a religious act. On the other hand, a gathering of people in a temple or church who do not have good motivation are not performing a religious act when they pray together. . . .

As for my own religious practice, I try to live my life pursuing what I call the Bodhisattva ideal. According to Buddhist thought, a Bodhisattva is someone on the path to Buddhahood who dedicates themselves entirely to helping all other sentient beings towards release from suffering. The word Bodhisattva can best be understood by translating the *Bodhi* and *Sattva* separately: *Bodhi* means the understanding or wisdom of the ultimate nature of reality, and a *Sattva* is someone who is motivated by universal compassion. The Bodhisattva ideal is thus the aspiration to practise infinite compassion with infinite wisdom. As a means of helping myself in this quest, I choose to be a Buddhist monk. There are 253 rules of Tibetan monasticism (364 for nuns) and by observing them as closely as I can, I free myself from many of the distractions and worries of life. Some of these rules mainly deal with etiquette, such as the physical distance a monk should walk behind the abbot of his monastery; others are concerned with behaviour. The four root vows concern simple prohibitions: namely that a monk must not kill, steal, or lie about his spiritual attainment. He must also be celibate. If he breaks any one of these, he is no longer a monk.

I am sometimes asked whether this vow of celibacy is really desirable and indeed whether it is really possible. Suffice to say that its practice is not simply a matter of suppressing sexual desires. On the contrary, it is necessary fully to accept the existence of these desires and to transcend them by the power of reasoning. When suc-

cessful, the result on the mind can be very beneficial. The trouble with sexual desire is that it is a blind desire. To say "I want to have sex with this person" is to express a desire which is not intellectually directed in the way that "I want to eradicate poverty in the world" is an intellectually directed desire. Furthermore, the gratification of sexual desire can only ever give temporary satisfaction. Thus as Nagarjuna, the great Indian scholar, said:

When you have an itch, you scratch.
But not to itch at all
Is better than any amount of scratching.

Regarding my actual daily practice, I spend, at the very least, five and a half hours per day in prayer, meditation, and study. On top of this, I also pray whenever I can during odd moments of the day, for example over meals and whilst travelling. In this last case, I have three main reasons for doing so: firstly, it contributes towards fulfilment of my daily duty; secondly, it helps to pass the time productively; thirdly, it assuages fear! More seriously though, as a Buddhist, I see no distinction between religious practice and daily life. Religious practice is a twenty-four-hour occupation. In fact, there are prayers prescribed for every activity from waking to washing, eating and even sleeping. For Tantric practitioners, those exercises which are undertaken during deep sleep and in the dream state are the most important preparation for death.

However, for myself, early morning is the best time for practice. The mind is at its freshest and sharpest then. I therefore get up at around four o'clock. On waking, I begin the day with the recitation of *mantras*. I then drink hot water and take my medicine before making prostrations in salutation of the Buddhas for about half an hour. The purpose of this is twofold. Firstly, it increases one's own merit (assuming proper motivation) and secondly, it is good exercise. After my prostrations, I wash—saying prayers as I do so. Then I generally go outside for a walk, during which I make further recitations, until breakfast at around 5:15 A.M. I allow about half an hour for this meal (which is quite substantial) and whilst eating read scriptures.

From 5:45 A.M. until around 8:00 A.M., I meditate, pausing only to listen to the 6:30 news bulletin of the BBC World Service. Then, from 8:00 A.M. until noon, I study Buddhist philosophy. Between then and lunch at 12:30, I might read either official papers or newspapers, but during the meal itself I again read scripture. At 1:00 P.M., I go to my office, where I deal with government and other matters and give audiences until 5:00 P.M. This is followed by another short period of prayer and meditation as soon as I get back home. If there is anything worthwhile on television, I watch it now before having tea at 6:00 P.M. Finally, after tea, during which I read scripture once more, I say prayers until 8:30 or 9:00 P.M., when I go to bed. Then follows very sound sleep.

Of course, there are variations to this routine. Sometimes during the morning I will participate in a *puja* or, in the afternoon, I will deliver a teaching. But, all the same, I very rarely have to modify my daily practice—that is my morning and evening prayers and meditation.

The rationale behind this practice is quite simple. During the first part of it when I make prostrations, I am "taking refuge" in the Buddha, the *Dharma*, and the *Sangha*. The next stage is to develop *Bodhichitta* or a Good Heart. This is done firstly by recognising the impermanence of all things and secondly by realising the true nature of being which is suffering. On the basis of these two considerations, it is possible to generate altruism.

To engender altruism, or compassion, in myself, I practise certain mental exercises which promote love towards all sentient beings, including especially my so-called enemies. For example, I remind myself that it is the actions of human beings rather than human beings themselves that make them my enemy. Given a change of behaviour, that same person could easily become a good friend.

The remainder of my meditation is concerned with *Sunya* or Emptiness, during which I concentrate on the most subtle meaning of Interdependence. Part of this practice involves what is termed "deity yoga," *lhāi naljor*, during which I use different *mandalas* to visualise myself as a succession of different "deities." (This should not, however, be taken to imply belief in independent external beings.) In so doing, I focus my mind to the point where it is no longer preoccupied with the data produced by the senses. This is not a trance, as my mind remains fully alert; rather it is an exercise in pure consciousness. What exactly I mean by this is hard to explain: just as it is difficult for a scientist to explain in words what is meant by the term "space-time." Neither language nor every-day experience can really communicate the meaning experience of "pure mind." Suffice to say that it is not an easy practice. It takes many years to master.

One important aspect of my daily practice is its concern with the idea of death. To my mind, there are two things that, in life, you can do about death. Either you can choose to ignore it, in which case you may have some success in making the idea of it go away for a limited period of time, or you can confront the prospect of your own death and try to analyse it and, in so doing, try to minimise some of the inevitable suffering that it causes. Neither way can you actually overcome it. However, as a Buddhist, I view death as a normal process of life. I accept it as a reality that will occur while I am in *Samsara*. Knowing that I cannot escape it, I see no point in worrying about it. I hold the view that death is rather like changing one's clothes when they are torn and old. It is not an end in itself. Yet death is unpredictable—you do not know when and how it will take place. So it is only sensible to take certain precautions before it actually happens. . . .

CONTEMPORARY SCHOLARSHIP

The contemporary scholarship on Buddhism by Buddhists and non-Buddhists alike is immense. Scholarship by Buddhists has sometimes been questioned on the grounds that it reflects too much of a sympathetic bias. It compromises, some claim, that critical distance that only an outsider can bring.

It is necessary to recognize that both the insider and the outsider bring perspectives (and in that sense biases) to their scholarship. Perspectives cannot be avoided, but they can be acknowledged and their distinct advantages (and disadvantages) recognized. If one automatically questions the quality of all scholarship done from an insider's viewpoint, then one should also automatically question the quality of all scholarship done from an outsider's viewpoint.

What follows are two selections written by scholars who are also followers of Buddhist traditions. Both combine the insider's understanding with the rigors of scholarly distance. The first selection is by D. T. Suzuki, a Japanese scholar and follower of Zen Buddhism, who helped make that type of Buddhism popular in the United States and Europe. The second selection is by Rita M. Gross, an American scholar of comparative religions, a feminist, and a follower of Vajrayana Buddhism.

5.7 SATORI

In 1927, Daisetz Teitaro Suzuki (1870–1966), author of the next selection, awakened the interest of Americans and Europeans to the world of Zen Buddhism with his book *Essays in Zen Buddhism*. D. T. Suzuki was a professor of Buddhist philosophy at Otani University in Kyoto, Japan, and he took his training in Zen meditation at the Zen monastery in Kamakura. He was also a visiting professor at many universities, including Columbia University in New York where he became particularly interested in the comparative study of mystical experiences.

Suzuki believed that there are deep similarities between the Zen experience of *satori* (sudden awakening) and the experiences of other mystics, in particular, the German Roman Catholic Meister Eckhart (1260–1328). However, he also found that one of the major differences between Christian mystical experiences and Zen *satori* is the characterization of the experience as "union with God." While this characterization appears to be a central part of Christian mysticism, it is not found among Zen Buddhist characterizations of *satori*.

D. T. SUZUKI

The Essence of Zen

READING QUESTIONS

1. According to Suzuki, what is the essence of Zen Buddhism?
2. Suzuki defines *satori* as "an intuitive looking into the nature of things." What does he mean by this?
3. How is *satori* similar to and different from the "eureka!" experience sometimes involved in solving a mathematical or scientific problem?

The essence of Zen Buddhism consists in acquiring a new viewpoint on life and things generally. By this I mean that if we want to get into the inmost life of Zen, we must forgo all our ordinary habits of thinking which control our everyday life, we must try to see if there is any other way of judging things, or rather if our ordinary way is always sufficient to give us the ultimate satisfac-

Excerpts from D. T. Suzuki, "Satori or Enlightenment," in *Zen Buddhism: Selected Writings of D. T. Suzuki*, edited by William Barrett (New York: Doubleday & Company, 1956), pp. 83–85. Copyright © 1956 by William Barrett. Reprinted by permission of Susan Barrett. Footnotes omitted.

tion of our spiritual needs. If we feel dissatisfied somehow with this life, if there is something in our ordinary way of living that deprives us of freedom in its most sanctified sense, we must endeavour to find a way somewhere which gives us a sense of finality and contentment. Zen proposes to do this for us and assures us of the acquirement of a new point of view in which life assumes a fresher, deeper, and more satisfying aspect. This acquirement, however, is really and naturally the greatest mental cataclysm one can go through with in life. It is no easy task, it is a kind of fiery baptism, and one has to go through the story, the earthquake, the overthrowing of the mountains, and the breaking in pieces of the rocks.

This acquiring of a new point of view in our dealings with life and the world is popularly called by Japanese Zen students "satori" (*wu* in Chinese). It is really another name for Enlightenment (*anuttara-samyak-sambodhi*), which is the word used by the Buddha and his Indian followers ever since his realization under the Bodhi-tree by the River Nairanjana. There are several other phrases in Chinese designating this spiritual experience, each of which has a special connotation, showing tentatively how this phenomenon is interpreted. At all events there is no Zen without satori, which is indeed the Alpha and Omega of Zen Buddhism. Zen devoid of satori is like a sun without its light and heat. Zen may lose all its literature, all its monasteries, and all its paraphernalia; but as long as there is satori in it, it will survive to eternity. I want to emphasize this most fundamental fact concerning the very life of Zen; for there are some even among the students of Zen themselves who are blind to this central fact and are apt to think when Zen has been explained away logically or psychologically, or as one of the Buddhist philosophies which can be summed up by using highly technical and conceptual Buddhist phrases, Zen is exhausted, and there remains nothing in it that makes it what it is. But my contention is, the life of Zen begins with the opening of satori (*kai wu* in Chinese).

Satori may be defined as an intuitive looking into the nature of things in contradistinction to the analytical or logical understanding of it. Practically, it means the unfolding of a new world hitherto unperceived in the confusion of a dualistically-trained mind. Or we may say that with satori our entire surroundings are viewed from quite an unexpected angle of perception. Whatever this is, the world for those who have gained a satori is no more the old world as it used to be; even with all its flowing streams and burning fires, it is never the same one again. Logically stated, all its opposites and contradictions are united and harmonized into a consistent organic whole. This is a mystery and a miracle, but according to the Zen masters such is being performed every day. Satori can thus be had only through our once personally experiencing it.

Its semblance or analogy in a more or less feeble and fragmentary way is gained when a difficult mathematical problem is solved, or when a great discovery is made, or when a sudden means of escape is realized in the midst of most desperate complications; in short, when one exclaims "Eureka! Eureka!" But this refers only to the intellectual aspect of satori, which is therefore necessarily partial and incomplete and does not touch the very foundations of life considered one indivisible whole. Satori as the Zen experience must be concerned with the entirety of life. For what Zen proposes to do is the revolution, and the revaluation as well, of oneself as a spiritual unity. The solving of a mathematical problem ends with the solution, it does not affect one's whole life. So with all other particular questions, practical or scientific, they do not enter the basic life-tone of the individual concerned. But the opening of satori is the remaking of life itself. When it is genuine—for there are many simulacra of it—its effects on one's moral and spiritual life are revolutionary, and they are so enhancing, purifying, as well as exacting. When a master was asked what constituted Buddhahood, he answered, "The bottom of a pail is broken through." From this we can see what a complete revolution is produced by this spiritual experience. The birth of a new man is really cataclysmic.

In the psychology of religion this spiritual enhancement of one's whole life is called "conversion." But as the term is generally used by Christian converts, it cannot be applied in its strict sense to the Buddhist experience, especially to that of the Zen followers; the term has too affective or emotional a shade to take the place of satori, which is above all noetic. The general tendency of Buddhism is, as we know, more intellectual than emotional, and its doctrine of Enlightenment distinguishes it sharply from the Christian view of salvation; Zen as one of the Mahayana schools naturally shares a large amount of what we may call transcendental intellectualism, which does not issue in logical dualism. When poetically or figuratively expressed, satori is "the opening of the mind-flower," or "the removing of the bar," or "the brightening up of the mind-works." . . .

5.8 GENDER AND EMPTINESS

Rita M. Gross teaches comparative religions at the University of Wisconsin–Eau Claire. She is an author and editor of numerous articles, essays, and books. Dr. Gross studied the history of religions at the University of Chicago and the practice of Bud-

dhism with teachers from the Vajrayana tradition. She characterizes herself as an "engaged historian of religions" because she is simultaneously engaged in what she calls the "practice of theology and of the history of religions."

Many scholars take an "either/or" stance with respect to theology and history of religions: *Either* one engages in a "constructive-theological-normative" study of religion from an insider's viewpoint *or* one engages in a historical-comparative study from an outsider's viewpoint. Dr. Gross rejects this dichotomy and, instead, practices a "method of inseparability" that combines both of these approaches. She believes that the student of religions must not only practice objectivity and empathy but also has an obligation to promote genuine religious pluralism and criticize dysfunctional traditional religious values.

RITA M. GROSS

Feminist Comments on the Mahayana

READING QUESTIONS

1. According to Gross, what are two common misunderstandings of emptiness?
2. How can the "two levels of truth" teaching be applied to gender issues? When so applied, what does it show?
3. Why are concepts of sex neutrality never sufficient as a corrective to androcentrism?

The earliest, best-known, and most widespread Mahayana teachings are a philosophical concept—*shunyata*—and an ethical precept—the Bodhisattva path. Here we are considering them as teachings of the second turning, following the system that sees some of the later Mahayana concepts as yet another complete revolution of the wheel of *dharma*, a classification scheme not agreed

From Rita M. Gross, *Buddhism After Patriarchy: A Feminist History, Analysis, and Reconstruction of Buddhism* (Albany, N.Y.: State University of New York Press, 1993), pp. 173–178. Copyright © 1993 State University of New York. Reprinted by permission. All rights reserved. Notes omitted.

upon even by all Mahayanists. Mythically, the Buddha himself taught the doctrine of emptiness at Rajagriha on Vulture Peak Mountain to a congregation of both Bodhisattvas and *arahants*, as narrated in Prajnaparamita literature, especially the Heart Sutra, the most famous and widely used succinct summary of Mahayana teachings. In the "three turnings" organizational framework, the second-turning teachings are particularly associated with the Madyamika school of Mahayana philosophy, while the third-turning teachings are particularly associated with the school often called the Yogacara school. However, the concepts of emptiness and the Bodhisattva path are also centrally important to all Mahayanists.

The second-turning refers especially to a specific emphasis on and interpretation of emptiness. The interpretation of emptiness to be discussed in this chapter emphasizes "what *shunyata* is *not*." This interpretation is the foundation for understanding that "*shunyata is not nothing*" in subsequent sections of this feminist analysis of key Buddhist concepts. Furthermore, in the context of this chapter, the philosophical outlook and the ethical precept are interdependent with each other: because emptiness is, the bodhisattva path is possible.

SHUNYATA, TWO TRUTHS, AND GENDER: THE CLASSIC BUDDHIST ARGUMENT

Even more than the term "egolessness," the term *shunyata*, "emptiness," confuses both outsider and insider. Buddhist texts themselves warn of the ease with which the concept can be misunderstood and of the extremely serious consequences of such misunderstanding. Like many another Buddhist concept that posits what is not, rather than what is, non-Buddhists have persistently attributed to it a negativity that is foreign to the concept itself. The concept has proved interesting and elusive to Westerners, especially those who look to Buddhism as a possible source of philosophical and spiritual inspiration for dealing with certain difficult issues in Western thought. Perhaps no other Buddhist concept has attracted similar attention or proved more interesting to such seekers.

As we have seen, the concept of emptiness has already been directly and explicitly connected with the issue of gender by Buddhists. It is the only Buddhist concept to have been used in classical Buddhist texts to criticize Buddhist practices of gender discrimination. Buddhists long ago saw that, logically, the fact of emptiness makes gender discriminations, like all other discriminations, inappropriate.

Though arguments and analyses regarding *shunyata* can become incredibly complex and, therefore, confusing, if one keeps returning to the basics, much of the complexity and confusion can be defused. It is simplest to see that, from the Mahayana perspective, *shunyata* is the logical outcome of thoroughly understanding egolessness and interdependent co-arising. When things are said to be empty, the important question is "empty of what?" The answer is that they are empty of, or lack "own-being," inherent existence. They do not exist in and of themselves, but only relative to their matrix, dependent on causes and conditions. For Mahayana Buddhism, such emptiness is thoroughgoing and pervasive. Nothing escapes it to exist inherently, in its own right, independent of its matrix, not subject to causes and conditions. There is no exempted, privileged corner somewhere, whether a Supreme Being or an eternal Soul, or even Buddhist *nirvana*, that is not completely and thoroughly characterized by *shunyata*.

Mahayanists have always emphasized that emptiness is nothing but thoroughgoing egolessness. The early Buddhist analysis primarily focused on the first object of reification, the thing most likely to be taken as really existing, substantially, inherently, and eternally by those who absolutize conventional psychological reactions—the Self or Soul. That reified ego was examined, broken down into its component parts, and found to be lacking any metaphysical glue that held those parts together, which means that ego does not exist. Instead of focusing only on ego itself, Mahayana analysis also focuses on the constituents of ego, which in the Mahayana analysis, are comprised of just basic space, openness, all-pervasive egolessness, *shunyata*. Mahayanists claim that earlier Buddhist analysis stopped too soon; it understood clearly the egolessness of ego, but did not thoroughly comprehend the egolessness of the components of ego; instead it reified them. The Mahayanists claim that even at the subtle level of analysis involved in discerning the component parts of ego, we do not find "ultimate realities at all but only mental constructions." One finds no fixed reference points, but only empty, interdependent, relatively existing fluidity.

Mahayanists claim that fully understanding the doctrine of interdependent co-arising, which can be seen as the central doctrine of early Buddhism, compels one to the conclusion of all-pervading emptiness. "To be dependent means to be devoid of self-nature or own-being (*svabhava*). What is devoid of self-nature is said to be empty (*sunya*). Conditionality and emptiness are the same thing." Therefore, the most famous line of Nagarjuna's root text on the Madyamika: "*Pratityasamutpada* is *shunyata*." According to Mahayana analysis, *nothing*, including the unconditioned elements posited by earlier

Buddhist analysis, escapes this verdict. They exist only as mental constructs and only in relation to the conditioned elements; they do not exist as ultimate realities, since they are imaginable or thinkable only in relation to the conditioned elements. The unconditioned elements, including *nirvana*, are unthinkable by themselves; they are thinkable only in relation to, and therefore dependent upon, conditioned elements. Therefore, such asserted unconditioned elements cannot exist as genuinely unconditioned, but only as empty, conditioned interdependent, relative elements. This is the logic behind the assertions that so often baffle students of Buddhism and that so infuriated advocates of the earlier Buddhist systems—that *samsara* and *nirvana* can be equated, and that the Four Noble Truths are not absolutes.

Mahayanists see this analysis as the Middle Way, so important to all Buddhist endeavors, between eternalism and nihilism, between granting ultimacy either to assertions or to negations. But they also see this middle way as a razor's edge, from which it is easy to fall into either extreme. Falling into the extreme of nihilism was always considered to be the more dangerous pitfall. To emphasize this point, Mahayanists warned of the "poison of *shunyata*," which they compare to a snake seized by the wrong end; it can easily wound a person fatally. Probably the most common version of the poison of *shunyata* is belief that, since, everything is relative rather than ultimate, nothing really matters and one can do anything one wants. To see emptiness, however, cuts only one's habitual tendency towards fixated attachment to things as if they were ultimate, not their existence in relative terms. Some things are still more or less helpful or satisfying than other things, even in a world devoid of ultimates.

The other way of retreating from the razor's edge is probably more abstract and less likely, though it is a way of understanding emptiness that often allures Westerners. It is often assumed that emptiness is what everything is made of, that it is a kind of negative substance underlying the appearance of things. Such assumptions sometimes underlie the equation of God and emptiness that is so popular in some comparisons of Buddhism and Christianity. But Mahayanists are careful to point out that emptiness should not itself be reified. *Everything* lacks own-being, including emptiness, which is a tool used to cut conceptual fixation, not an alternative concept out of which to build a worldview. It is important to realize not just emptiness, but the emptiness of emptiness.

Because this understanding of emptiness would undercut all assertions, Mahayanists also developed a tool, already known to early Indian Buddhism, for using and evaluating language more effectively. It was recognized that there are two levels of language, or more accurately, two levels of truth—absolute truth and relative truth. It was always conceded by Buddhists that conventional ways of speaking about persons and things are convenient and useful, relatively speaking. That all things are empty of own-being does not obviate their relative existence and the need to operate in the world of relative things. To believe otherwise would be to fall into the poison of *shunyata*. It also must be conceded that within the realm of relative truth, some analyses are more cogent and some actions more appropriate than others. The temptation is to fixate and reify. The constant reminder that relative truth is only relative truth, not absolute or ultimate, cuts that temptation. The level of absolute truth transcends verbalization or conceptualization. To say anything at all about it is already to return to the level of relative truth, according to Buddhism, which does not mean that one should never speak of Absolute Reality, but only that one should regard one's words as nothing more than tools and pointers. The difficulty of speaking about Truth accurately does not, for Buddhists, undercut the expectation that it is possible to experience intuition into Things-As-They-Are (*tathata*).

Fortunately, some implications of these concepts to the problem of gender are found in classic Buddhist texts. . . .

The application is quite simple. "Male" and "female," like all other labels and designations, are empty and lack substantial reality. Therefore, they cannot be used in a rigid and fixed way to delimit people. In the classic Mahayana texts, this argument is used against those who hold to a belief that high levels of spiritual attainment and Buddhist understanding cannot be combined with a female body. As we have seen, girls and women demonstrate by their skill in presenting complex Buddhist concepts that women can attain high levels of accomplishment. They also demonstrate how fluid sexual identity can be, as they change their sex into the male sex, and sometimes back again. All this can happen because maleness and femaleness do not exist as fixed, inherently existing forms, but only as convenient designations and mere tokens. And finally, they argue decisively that gender traits cannot really be found; therefore, they cannot be used as a basis for discrimination or challenges to change one's body into a male body in order to prove that one's understanding is as deep as it appears to be.

The goddess of the *Vimalakirtinirdesa Sutra* says it best, in words that could be echoed by many a contemporary liberal or equal-rights feminist. After being taunted to change her sex, as genuine proof of the depth of her understanding of emptiness (as if having a penis helped one understand abstract concepts), she says: "I have been here for twelve years and have looked for the innate characteristics of the female sex and haven't been able to find them." Many a woman, held back from her life choices and unable to find comfort or relevance in the female gender role, has made similar statements about the lack of inherent, essential traits of femininity, supposedly possessed by all women, by virtue of their female anatomy. These traits simply cannot be found, even in the quantified research of contemporary psychology. Furthermore, the attempt to limit and classify people on the basis of sex, to say that women can't do something or that men should behave in a certain way, is to make absolute determinations and discriminations on the basis of a relative, empty trait. Or one could say that such judgments and limitations absolutize the relative. In either case, conventional social arrangements, including those common to Buddhist institutions contradict the essential Mahayana teaching of emptiness.

Though not explicitly citing the theory of the two truths, these texts also utilize that concept. After changing herself into a man and her interlocutor into a woman, the goddess says to him (who is now temporarily "her"), "Just as you are not really a woman but appear to be female in form, all women also only appear to be female in form but are not really women. Therefore, the Buddha said all are not really men or women." In terms of the two truths, the level of convention and appearance is the level of gender roles and stereotypes, but at the level of absolute truth, "all are not really men or women." Notice that, consonant with the unspeakability of absolute truth, the text does not try to say what people really are beyond maleness and femaleness, but it does state clearly that they are not *really*, but only apparently, men or women.

The conclusions to be drawn are obvious and were drawn in theory in the Buddhist texts, though the practical applications of those conclusions have never been integrated into Buddhist institutions and everyday life. You cannot predict, on the basis of gender, who is likely to be able to comprehend and practice "the dharma which is neither male nor female." The whole apparatus of preselecting people for roles on the basis of their gender, of forcing people to fit gender roles, and of limiting their options on the basis of gender would become inadmissible if the emptiness and relativity of maleness and femaleness were to be taken seriously.

Strong as these traditional arguments from emptiness, the assertions that the "*dharma* is neither male nor female" and that maleness and femaleness do not really exist, may be, they are not sufficient to undercut patriarchal conventions. These assertions are certainly useful and accurate. But they do not really break free of the androcentrism that so pervades Buddhist thought. The Buddhist statement that "the *dharma* is neither male nor female" is strikingly similar to the Christian Pauline statement that "in Christ there is neither male nor female," a statement that, however often quoted, has not kept Christianity from developing male dominance, any more than its Buddhist parallel has been effective in ridding Buddhism of male dominance. It is important to ascertain why.

In both cases, the statement about the irrelevance of gender is made in an androcentric context. Given that context, those statements are only superficially gender neutral. In fact, they always mean, "You can make it, even if you are female." They never mean, "You can make it even if you are male." Often the sex-neutral language hides the fact that women become acceptable only by transcending their femaleness and becoming "manly." They are supposedly given the opportunity to match the human norm, but that human norm is collapsed into the male ideal. Men are rarely, if ever, expected to become "unmanly" to the extent that women are expected to become "unfeminine" in order to achieve the same level of spiritual attainment, though, to be fair, it must be admitted that men must transcend their culture's version of the macho male. The point is, however, that the ideal "spiritual person," for both Buddhism and Christianity, is not androgynous or neutral, and certainly is not feminine; it is male, and the qualities that make a person spiritual are conflated with the qualities that make a person male, while the qualities that make a person overtly female are shunned as spiritual ideals by both traditions. Therefore, concepts of sex-neutrality as a corrective to androcentrism are never sufficient because the neutral ideal is in fact much more male than female. As a result, both Buddhism and Christianity waver between a male-defined sex neutrality that a few women might be able to achieve and an outright favoring of biological males. Clearly, these two options are not sufficient. . . .

KEY TERMS AND CONCEPTS

Abhidharma (Pali: ***Abhidhamma***) One of the principal divisions of the ***Tripitika*** containing elaboration on the teachings of the Buddha.

Amitabha (Japanese: **Amida**) Savior Buddha of the **Pure Land** in the West and the Buddha of central importance to the **Pure Land** movement. Also named Amitayus (Buddha of Infinite Life).

anatman (Pali: *anatta*) Denial of the existence of a permanent, unchanging self.

Anitya (Pali: **anicca**) Impermanence. Along with *anatman* and *duhkha* (suffering), one of the "Three Marks" of existence.

arhat (female: *arhati*) A term used in Theravada Buddhism for a saint or one who has attained enlightenment.

asura One of a class of extraordinary beings. Sometimes translated as "titans" and pictured as waging war with the gods (*devas*).

Avalokiteshvara (Chinese: *Kuan-yin;* Japanese: *Kannon;* Tibetan: *Chenrezik*) Compassionate savior *bodhisattva* and protector of Tibet.

bodhisattva (Pali: *bodhisatta*) Any person who has taken a vow to become a buddha and lives a life of compassion intent on the goal of his or her own enlightenment and the enlightenment of others.

Buddha The title for someone who is enlightened. When capitalized, it usually refers to the Buddha **Sakyamuni.**

Ch'an (Korean: *Son;* Japanese: *Zen*) A school of Buddhism that emphasizes meditation as the heart of Buddhist practice.

Dalai Lama Temporal and spiritual leader of Tibet thought to be one of a line of successive reincarnations of **Avalokiteshvara.**

dharma (Pali: *dhamma*) The word has many meanings most of which refer to what is true or real. Often used specifically to refer to the teachings of the Buddha **Sakyamuni** and philosophically to refer to basic elements of reality. Also translated as Truth, Doctrine, and Law.

dhyana (Pali: *Jhana;* Chinese: *Ch'an;* Korean: *Son;* Japanese: *Zen*) In general, it refers to meditation and specifically to one of the levels of trance.

Duhkha (Pali: *dukkha*) The first of the **Four Noble Truths** usually translated as suffering or unsatisfactoriness.

Eightfold Path The development of wisdom, moral purity, and mental discipline leading to *nirvana.* Usually listed as right view, right thought, right speech, right conduct, right livelihood, right effort, right mindfulness, and right meditation. Also known as the **Middle Way.**

Four Noble Truths These Aryan (Noble) truths are considered by many to be the heart of the Buddha's teaching. They are (1) suffering, (2) cause of suffering, (3) cessation of suffering, and (4) **Eightfold Path,** or **Middle Way.**

Gautama (Pali: *Gotama*) The family name of the historical **buddha** of this age, Buddha **Sakyamuni,** whose personal name is Siddhartha.

Hinayana *Yana* means "vehicle," and *hina* can be translated as "smaller, lesser, baser." A pejorative name given by Mahayana Buddhists to some of the other schools.

Jātaka Stories of the past lives of the Buddha **Sakyamuni** that are very popular and well known among many Buddhists.

karma In general it refers to action or deed, specifically, to any intentional deed (often ritualistic or moral) that will cause effects in this life or the next. Also refers to the Law of Karma, which is the principle of cause and effect in general and specifically the principle that good deeds bring good results and bad deeds bring bad results.

koan A riddle used for meditation in **Zen** Buddhism.

Mahayana Sanskrit term meaning Great Vehicle used by one of the three main branches of Buddhism.

Maitreya (Pali: **Metteyya**) The next **buddha** due to come at some point in the future.

mandala A Sanskrit word meaning circle and used to refer to structured space symbolically depicting various levels of the universe and different **buddhas** and **bodhisattvas.** Widely used in Tantric Buddhism for purposes of visualization meditations.

mantra A set of sounds that have spiritual potency. They are frequently chanted in worship and as a focus for meditation.

Mappo A Japanese word that refers to a time near the end of the *Dharma* when following the path to enlightenment becomes very difficult.

Mara The tempter of Buddha and others who is concerned with keeping people living in the realm of desire over which he rules.

Middle Way A term used broadly to refer to the Buddha's teachings as a whole as a moderate way to release from suffering that avoids the extremes of asceticism and indulgence. More narrowly it refers to the **Eightfold Path.**

Mount Meru The mythic mountain at the center of the Buddhist cosmos and the dwelling place of *asuras* and *devas.*

mudra Symbolic hand gestures widely used in *Vajrayana* ritual.

nembutsu Japanese term for calling on Amida Buddha involving the recitation of the **mantra** "*Namu Amida Butsu.*"

Nikaya A section of the Pali canon and sometimes used as a nonderogatory term for **Hinayana** Buddhism.

nirvana (Pali: *nibbana*) The third **Noble Truth** and the soteriological goal of Buddhism—release from desire, ignorance, hatred, and, in general, suffering. Sometimes used to refer to enlightenment and also used to refer to *parinirvana.*

parinirvana nirvana without remainder.

prajna (Pali: *panna*) Wisdom or a true understanding of the nature of reality.

Pure Land A paradise like heaven where devotees may be reborn after death. Often used specifically of the Western Pure Land of *Amitabha* and the Pure Land school centering on his worship.

sadhana A Vajrayana visualization meditation used to invoke and identify with a deity or **buddha.**

Sakyamuni Means the Sage of the Sakya Clan and is an honorific title frequently used for the Buddha, Siddhartha **Gautama.**

samadhi Meditative concentration and the trance state attained by yogic meditation.

sangha The Buddhist community in general (lay and monastic) and, more narrowly, the monastic community of monks and nuns.

satori Zen Buddhist term for a sudden awakening or insight.

shunyata Usually translated as "emptiness." It refers specifically to the lack of any inherent self-existence (*svabhava*) in things.

Skandha (Pali: *khandha*) Means "aggregate" and usually refers to the five aggregates of individual existence: form, feelings, perceptions, dispositions or karmic constituents, and consciousness.

stupa A moundlike structure usually containing a relic of the Buddha **Sakyamuni** and a place for pilgrimage and worship.

sutra (Pali: *sutta*) Any discourse attributed to the Buddha and one of the principal divisions of the Buddhist canon.

svabhava The substance of a thing understood as independently existing. Usually translated as "self-existent."

tantras A group of writings setting forth the ideas and practices of Tantric Buddhism, which some consider a shortcut to enlightenment. These practices often involve violating the traditional norms of society and traditional monastic vows (such as drinking and sexuality) in order to show that the truly enlightened are free from ordinary rules.

Tara (Tibetan: *Drolma*) Female savior *bodhisattva* often associated with **Avalokiteshvara** and popular in Tibet.

Tathagata Literally the "Thus-Come One" and a title used for the Buddha.

Tathagatagarbha Literally the "embryo or womb of the **Tathagata**" and refers to the potential for enlightenment within all beings.

Theravada A sect or school within **Nikaya** Buddhism meaning the "Teachings of the Elders."

Tripitika (Pali: *Tipitaka*) The Buddhist canon consisting of the *Vinaya, Sutra,* and *Abhidharma.*

Triple Gem The "Three Jewels" or "Three refuges": the Buddha, the *Dharma,* and the *Sangha.*

upaya The employment of "skillful means" in teaching.

Vajrayana Refers to the "Diamond (or Thunderbolt) Vehicle" that is one of the three main branches of Buddhism.

vinaya The code of conduct for monks and nuns as well as a name for one of the principal divisions of **Tripitika.**

zazen Seated meditation, a practice common in **Zen.**

Zen See *Ch'an.*

SUGGESTIONS FOR FURTHER READINGS

Buddhist Scriptures, selected and translated by Edward Conze. London: Penguin Books, 1959. A collection of sources arranged in three parts: The Teacher, Doctrines, and Other Worlds and Future Worlds.

Harvey, P. *An Introduction to Buddhism: Teaching, History and Practices.* Cambridge: Cambridge University Press, 1990. A clear and informative introduction to Buddhism.

Kitagawa, Joseph M., et al. eds. *Buddhism and Asian History.* New York: Macmillan, 1987, 1989. Articles on religion, history, and culture taken from *The Encyclopedia of Religion.*

Lopez Jr., Donald S. ed. *Buddhism in Practice.* Princeton: Princeton University Press, 1995. A good collection of difficult-to-locate source material with excellent introductions and interpretations.

Strong, John S. *The Experience of Buddhism: Sources and Interpretations.* Belmont, Calif.: Wadsworth, 1995. A good collection of sources with commentary.

RESEARCH PROJECTS

1. If you are interested in the possible influences of Buddhist stories on the Christian scriptures and the parallels between them, read Roy C.

Amore's *Two Masters, One Message* (Nashville, Tenn.: Abingdon, 1978) and write a critical review.

2. If you are interested in pursuing the topic of women and Buddhism, read Diana Y. Paul's *Women in Buddhism: Images of the Feminine in the Mahayana Tradition* (Berkeley: University of California Press, 1985) and write a critical review.

3. Locate and interview a local Buddhist about the things most important to her or him about Buddhism and why the person is a Buddhist. Analyze the results of your interview and write a report.

4. Do a Web search on some aspect of Buddhism, take notes on the information available, analyze it, and write a report that includes an annotated list of sources.

5. Get a copy of *The Teaching of Buddha* (Tokyo: Buddyo Dendo Kyokai, 1966), which, like the Gideon Bible, is a collection of Buddhist scripture placed in many hotel rooms and hospitals throughout Asia and Europe. Analyze how it presents information about Buddhism and the Buddha's teaching. You may order a copy from the Buddhist Promoting Foundation, c/o MTI Corporation, 18 Essex Road, Paramus, NJ 07652.

Confucian Ways of Being Religious

INTRODUCTION

When I was visiting the Temple of Heaven in Beijing, China, I got into a discussion with a Chinese guide about Chinese religion. Quoting a popular Chinese saying, he spoke of the "three teachings" and ended by saying that the three are fundamentally the same. These three teachings are what Western scholars call Confucianism, Taoism, and Buddhism.

Like all sayings, the claim that Chinese religion consists of "three teachings that are one" both reveals and conceals. There are indeed three relatively distinct teachings or religious traditions in China, but Chinese religion is more diverse and varied than the term "three teachings" reveals. While these three traditions have profoundly influenced one another and, over the centuries, blended somewhat, they have also been at odds and in conflict with one another.

Here our focus will be on Confucianism, but we must be aware that abstracting this teaching from the other two is misleading. In the previous chapter we discussed Chinese Buddhism, and in the next we shall look at Taoism, but this division is for convenience only. In reality the three are blended like threads in a tapestry.

This tapestry contains more than three threads. One of these other threads is called Chinese popular religion. The designation "popular religion" is usually used in two senses. In the first sense, it refers to the type of religion practiced by almost all Chinese people, regardless of explicit religious identification. These practices involve certain funeral rituals, consultation with fortune-tellers, health and medical routines, offerings to the ancestors, New Year's rites, seeking advice from spirit mediums, exorcism of ghosts, and the like. In another sense, the term "popular religion" is used to designate the religion of the masses or lower classes as distinguished from the religion of the elite. Although both groups may engage in the same or very similar religious practices, their understandings are very different. For the elite, such cults as those devoted to the veneration of ancestors are important for promoting morality, social order, and a venerable cultural tradition. The elite are more likely to be somewhat skeptical about the existence of ghosts and demons than the general populace.

Confucianism appears to have begun as a loose collection of moral, ritual, political, aesthetic, and historical teachings of the elite. Indeed, many have claimed that it is not really a religion, but, rather, a kind of humanistic philosophy largely attractive to scholars or the literati, as they are sometimes called. Others have claimed that there is no such thing as Confucianism, but that a number of different literary writings and figures have been lumped together into a school of thought labeled Confucian.

These issues will come up for further discussion below. For now it is sufficient to note two things. First, when we study any putative religious tradition, it is important to raise questions of social class. Who writes the literature and performs the rituals? What kind of people is their audience? Who participates? Second, although Confucianism is an elite movement, the Chinese family system and the Chinese form of bureaucracy have been deeply shaped by it, and hence Confucianism touches the lives of practically all Chinese regardless of social class.

Although I focus on China below, we need to be aware that Confucianism has spread outside of China to such places as Vietnam, Japan, and Korea. Immigration has brought it to the West, and, after a period of decline in China, aspects of it may now be entering a new phase of creativity sometimes referred to as New Confucianism.

6.1 AN OVERVIEW

Imagine that you are interested in the art of government, that you believe good government can improve the lives of people, that in the past there were great rulers who benefited the people they governed, and that, at the present time, when you live, social chaos reigns. Imagine that the present political leaders are corrupt, government officials take bribes, many are mean and some cruel, families are disintegrating, and injustice rather than justice is abroad in the land. What would you do? What would you say?

One thing you might do is seek some kind of governmental position of influence. One thing you might say is that there are important lessons to be learned from the great rulers of the past. You might start studying the past with a view to applying what you learn to the present. You might teach others what you are learning and try to get them to find positions of influence so that social conditions can be improved. You might try to restore "family values" and to figure out ways to get educated people of good moral character into office. You might, in short, do the sorts of things that Confucius (551–479 B.C.E.) seems to have done.

Julia Ching, Professor of Religious Studies at the University of Toronto and Fellow of the Royal Society of Canada, describes the origins and development of Confucianism in our first selection. She begins by asking the question "What do I mean by 'Confucianism'?" This is an important question because there is considerable doubt about our ability to neatly define what it is.

When Western scholars first encountered Confucianism, they wondered what they had found. Was it a religion, a form of Asian wisdom literature, a kind of philosophy, or a form of social ethics? Interestingly, the early Christian missionary-scholars called the most important Confucian texts "classics" rather than "scriptures." This indicates that they felt some uncertainty about how Confucian literature might be categorized in Western terms. "Classic literature" might be religious, ethical, political, philosophical, or all of these.

You will notice that Professor Ching gives two different spellings for Chinese terms. A word is first spelled according to the Wade-Giles system of rendering Chinese sounds. After the slash mark ("/"), the word is rendered according to the pinyin system. For more information on these spelling systems and pronunciation of Chinese terms, see the Pronunciation Guide at the end of this chapter.

As you read Professor Ching's overview, answer the reading questions. They will help you highlight key ideas.

JULIA CHING

Confucianism as Religious Humanism

READING QUESTIONS

1. As you read, make a list of all the words and ideas you do not understand or are uncertain about. Discuss them with a classmate, look them up in a dictionary, or bring them up in class for discussion and clarification.
2. Why are the Five Classics important?
3. What is the "negative Golden Rule"? What is the difference between the negative and positive formulation?
4. What are the Five Relationships, and why are they significant?
5. How is *jen* related to *li*?
6. Describe the cult of Heaven and the cult of ancestors.
7. What is the Mandate of Heaven, and when is the removal of the Mandate justified?
8. Why is the Han period important in the religious history of China?
9. What is Neo-Confucianism, and how is it related to the Four Books?
10. How are *T'ai-chi*, *li*, and *ch'i* related?

What do I mean by "Confucianism"? A Western designation of a Chinese tradition, the term itself is ambiguous, representing an ideology developed by a man of the name Confucius (552?–479 B.C.). The Chinese themselves have usually preferred *Ju-chia/Rujia* or *Ju-chiao/Rujiao*, the school or teachings of the scholars. Etymologically, it has been claimed that the word *ju/ru* is related to the word for "weaklings" or "cowards," and referred originally to those dispossessed aristocrats of an-

From Julia Ching, *Chinese Religions* (Maryknoll, N.Y.: Orbis Books, 1993), pp. 53–65, 72–75, 77–80, 153–160, 165–167. © 1993 Julia Ching. Reprinted by permission of the publisher. Footnotes omitted.

tiquity who were no longer warriors, but lived off their knowledge of rituals or history, music, numbers or archery. It is a case of a pejorative term becoming eventually a designation of honour, as also with the Christians. Eventually, the school of *Ju* came to refer to the ethical wisdom of the past that Confucius transmitted to later ages, as well as the entire development of the tradition after his time. . . .

THE HISTORICAL CONFUCIUS

In recent history, the *questioning* into Chinese tradition as such and Confucianism in particular involved also a *quest*—that for the historical Confucius, as distinct from the Confucius-image of popular veneration. The development in the 1920s and 1930s of a more scientifically critical historical method facilitated this task to a certain extent. It might be studied in terms parallel to the quest for the historical Jesus. But it is a much more difficult quest, since the oldest extant source, the *Analects*, was compiled at least a century after the Master's death, whereas the oldest document in the New Testament came from within a generation of Jesus' death.

First of all, *Confucius* is the Latin rendering by seventeenth-century Jesuit missionaries of K'ung Fu-tzu, or Master K'ung, whose name was K'ung Ch'iu, also styled K'ung Chung-ni. He was a native of the small state of Lu, whose birthplace is near modern Ch'ü-fu (Qufu, Shantung). As with the life of Jesus or even more, little can be established about his life, including the exact year of birth, and about his forebears and immediate family. However, legends (including very early ones) are abundant. He is sometimes said to be a direct descendant of the Shang royal house. However, at the time of his parents, the family's circumstances were far from comfortable. The highest public office he occupied at the age of fifty was as a kind of police commissioner in his home state, and only for about a year. In over ten years of travel, K'ung visited many feudal states, seeking, but never finding, a ruler who would use his advice. In old age, he devoted more time to teaching disciples, while also occupying himself with music and poetry, occasionally conversing with rulers or ministers.

Were we to judge him on the basis of his attainments in public office, we would not even give him a footnote in history. This is despite the praises sung about the good order he set up for the state of Lu, where the people allegedly could go to sleep without locking their house doors, and also despite the allegation from some sources that he had his deputy executed on dubious grounds—an allegation that fuelled the Anti-Confucius campaign in 1973–74. Like many great personages, K'ung was to be remembered for reasons other than those goals to which he had oriented his life. Without doubt, he had a correct sense of his own mission to regenerate the culture of his time, without fully realising how that was to come about. Like Jesus, K'ung became historically influential only after his death, which was at around the age of seventy, from natural causes. Like Jesus, K'ung did not develop any systematic doctrinal structure in which manners, morals, law, philosophy and theology were clearly separated. In K'ung's case, the teachings were systematised only with Mencius (c. 371–289) and Hsün-tzu (c. 298–238).

The following passage gives us some insight into K'ung's own self-consciousness. His profound sense of reverence for the will of Heaven should help us appreciate the basically religious orientation of his life and character.

> At fifteen I set my heart on learning [to be a sage].
> At thirty I became firm.
> At forty I had no more doubts.
> At fifty I understood Heaven's Will.
> At sixty my ears were attuned [to this Will].
> At seventy I could follow my heart's desires, without overstepping the line.
>
> (*Analects* 2:4)

It is interesting to dwell on how his ears were attuned, presumably to Heaven's will. After all, the word *sage* was originally the graph for a large ear and a small mouth. But K'ung was a modest man who said, "How dare I rank myself with sages . . . ? I prefer to say of myself, that I strive without cease [for sageliness] and teach others without weariness." But then, what is sagehood, if not this constant striving—as his disciples recognised? They responded: "This is just what we, your disciples, have been unable to learn from you" (*Analects* 7:33).

It might also be inferred that K'ung was a believer in Heaven as personal deity, as higher power, order and law, displacing the many "gestalts" of the old gods. "He who sins against Heaven, has no one to whom he can pray" (*Analects* 3:13). K'ung lived in an age of turmoil, during which the ancient religious beliefs were questioned, and he contributed to the rationalist atmosphere of philosophical reflection. But why shouldn't he question them, knowing what we do of ancient religion, with its emphasis on divination and sacrifice, including human sacrifice? Understandably, K'ung distanced himself from this. Interestingly, he heralded in a new age of ethical wisdom, by appealing to the legacy of the ancients. Was he a conservative or a reformer, or perhaps a revolutionary? We may already have some clues to answering this question.

THE CONFUCIAN CLASSICS

While Confucius' teachings are best found in the *Analects*—the record of his conversations with his disciples—early Confucianism regards as its special texts the Five Classics. This group of books includes various genres. Let us take another look at this text and the others in proper focus:

- The *Book of Changes* or the *I-ching* probably existed at the time of Confucius, and was attributed to the sages of old. The manual centres upon short oracles arranged under sixty-four hexagrams, symbols made up of combinations of broken and unbroken lines in groups of six. Commentaries were later added to the oracles. The longest one is the *Hsi-tz'u* or Appended Remarks, which offer early cosmological and metaphysical speculation in a cryptic language. The text is reaching a wide audience in our own times, especially since the psychoanalyst Carl Jung introduced the notion of "synchronicity" to replace that of chance in evaluating the validity of divination.
- The *Book of History*, also called the *Book of Documents* (*Shang-shu*, literally, ancient documents), is allegedly a collection organised and introduced by Confucius. It is mainly an assortment of speeches from royalty and chief ministers, as well as certain narrative accounts of royal achievements and principles of government, arranged chronologically. While the materials describing early Chou times are more credible, some of the allegedly older chapters have been called forgeries.
- The *Book of Poetry*, also called the *Book of Songs*, or the *Odes* (*Shih-ching*) is basically a collection of three hundred and five songs. Probably compiled around 600 B.C., even if the materials could be much older, it includes four sections, with various genres, such as folk songs of love, courtship and desertion, as well as about hunts and dances. There are also banquet songs, or state hymns. Allegedly, Confucius compiled them from an ancient repertory of three thousand.
- The *Classic of Rites* is an entire corpus. This includes the *Ceremonials* (*I-li*), an early manual of etiquette for the nobility, detailing such occasions as marriages and funerals, sacrifices and archery contests. There is also the *Book of Rites* (*Li-chi*), with its forty-nine sections of ritual and government regulations, as well as treatises on education, the rites, music and philosophy. Then there is the *Institutes of Chou* (*Chou-li*), apparently an idealised description of offices of government in early Chou times. It is believed that these texts were compiled in the early first century B.C., on the basis of somewhat earlier materials.
- The *Spring-Autumn Annals* (*Ch'un-ch'iu*) is basically a didactically and laconically written chronicle of the state of Lu, the Master's native state, which purports to explain the decline of the ancient political and moral code. The Annals cover the period dating from 722 to 481 B.C., and from this we have derived the "Spring-Autumn Period." It was attributed to Confucius as author, but this is no longer acceptable. It is usually associated with three commentaries, or rather appendages: the vividly narrative *Tso-chuan* or Tso Commentary, the catechetical (question-and-answer) Kung-yang Commentary and Ku-liang Commentary.

A sixth classic, the *Book of Music*, is no longer extant.

In the past, Confucius has been considered the author of the classics, or at least, as their editor. Contemporary scholarship no longer takes this seriously. True, the core of many of these classical texts goes back to Confucius, and even to the time preceding him, which shows the ancient lineage of the school of *Ju*. But each of them underwent a long period of evolution, receiving accretions postdating Confucius. . . .

THE MORALITY OF HUMAN RELATIONSHIPS

It has sometimes been said that Confucius' great merit is his discovery of the moral character of human relationships. He taught a doctrine of reciprocity and neighbourliness.

> To regard every one as a very important guest, to manage the people as one would assist at a sacrifice, *not to do to others what you would not have them do to you.* (*Analects* 15:23)

For its resemblance to Christian teachings, the last part of this quotation (my italics) has come to be called the *negative* Golden Rule.

Within Confucianism, the well-known "Five Relationships" include the ruler–minister, father–son, husband–wife, elder and younger brother, and friend and friend. Three of these are family relationships, while the other two are usually conceived in terms of the family models. For example, the ruler–minister relationship resembles the father–son, while friendship resembles brotherliness. For this reason, the Confucian society regards itself as a large family: "Within the four seas all men are brothers" (*Analects* 12:5).

The responsibilities ensuing from these relationships are mutual and reciprocal. A minister owes loyalty to his ruler, and a child filial respect to the parent. But the ruler must also care for his subjects, and the parent for the child. All the same, the Five Relationships emphasise the vertical sense of hierarchy. Even with the horizontal relationship between friends, seniority of age demands a certain respect; and if the conjugal relationship bears more natural resemblance to that between older and younger brothers, it is more usually compared to the ruler–minister relationship. Indeed, the duty of filial piety, the need for procuring progeny for the sake of assuring the continuance of the ancestral cult, has been for centuries the ethical justification for polygamy.

Confucius' main legacy is the teaching on *jen/ren*. Etymologically, it is written with the radical "human" and the word for "two," or, if one wishes, for a sign that might also be interpreted as "above." It is pronounced the same as the word for human being. Understandably, *jen* is always concerned with human relationship, with relating to others. It may also be explained as the virtue of the "superior man," the gentleman. It is associated with loyalty (*chung/zhong*)—referring basically to loyalty to one's own heart and conscience, rather than to a narrower political loyalty—and reciprocity (*shu*)—respect of, and consideration for others (*Analects* 4:15).

Jen is also related to *li* (propriety or ritual). But the latter refers more to social behavior, and the former, to the inner orientation of the person. *Jen* is translated variously as goodness, benevolence, humanity and humanheartedness. It was formerly a particular virtue, the kindness which distinguished the gentleman in his behaviour toward his inferiors. He transformed it into a universal virtue, that which *makes* the perfect human being, the sage. The later importance of his teachings gave this a social importance—that moral character and merit should replace birth as the criterion for a gentleman. . . .

If the natural feelings underlying kinship call for special consideration, the natural feelings aroused by the neighbour's—*any* neighbour's—need for help are also recognised. This is especially underlined by Mencius, who gives the example of a man witnessing a child falling into a well (Mencius 2A:6). The *natural* first impulse is to rescue the child, and this comes before any desire for praise or fear of blame. The following of this impulse is an act of commiseration, or love of neighbour. This example serves as a kind of Confucian parable of the Good Samaritan, illustrating the meaning of universal love. And natural feelings serve also as an experiential guide. For the follower of Confucius, parental love

for children can be extended to cover other people's children, just as filial respect for the aged can be extended to cover other people's parents and elders, so that the natural order serves as a starting point and an experiential guide in achieving universal love.

Familial relations provide a model for social behaviour. Respect your own elders, as well as others' elders; be kind to your own children and juniors, as well as those of others. These are the instructions of Mencius (1A:7), and have provided inspiration for generations of Confucians. They have been the reason for the strong sense of solidarity not only in the Chinese family, but also in Confucian social organisations even among overseas communities.

CONFUCIANISM AS RITUAL RELIGION

Rituals are an essential dimension of religious life, giving expression to communal beliefs. . . . The Chinese word for ritual (*li*) is related etymologically to the words "worship" and "sacrificial vessel" with a definite religious overtone. But, in fact, the term has a much broader range of meanings in the Chinese context, straddling the sacred and the profane spheres. Somewhat like the contemporary English term, it came to include social practices, partaking even of the nature of law, as a means of training in virtue and of avoiding evil. And going beyond the English term, it refers also to propriety, that is, proper behaviour.

Ritual is a very important part of Confucius' teachings, and has been understood as such by his disciples, who were also teachers of rituals. Thus, Confucianism also became known as the ritual religion *li-chiao/lijiao*, with its emphases upon the doctrinal as well as ritual prescriptions for "proper behaviour" in family and society. Confucian teachings helped to keep alive the older cult of veneration for ancestors, and the worship of Heaven, a formal cult practised by China's imperial rulers, who regarded themselves as the keepers of Heaven's Mandate of government, a kind of High Priest, a mediator figure between the human order and the divine order. With the official establishment of Confucianism, its classical texts were inscribed in stone, and collected a corpus of commentaries and sub-commentaries, establishing various traditions of textual exegesis. This took place during the period of time spanning the Han (B.C. 206–220 A.D.) and the T'ang (618–906 A.D.) dynasties. Among these texts, the *Spring-Autumn Annals* in particular gave rise to allegorical interpretations that drew in *yin-yang* metaphysics offering a new cosmological and historical vision, while the *Book of Rites*, with its elaborate instructions for correct deportment, especially regarding mourning and funerals, became the backbone of Chinese society.

Confucius also emphasised the need to have the right inner dispositions, without which ritual propriety becomes hypocrisy (*Analects* 15:17). He insisted that sacrifice is to be performed, with the consciousness of the presence of the spirits (3:12). Besides, "what can rites do for a person lacking in the virtue of humanity (*jen*)? What can music do for a person lacking in humanity?" (3:3). . . .

The Cult of Heaven

We made mention of the worship of Heaven. The phrase refers to the annual sacrifices offered by the emperor to heaven and earth. Today we may still visit the sites on which these rituals took place in Peking (Beijing). The Temple of Heaven, which goes back to the Ming dynasty (1368–1661), is situated in a wide park outside the former "forbidden city." There are several old structures there, including the well-known circular prayer hall for good harvests, with its blue tiles (blue being the colour of Heaven). What is even more impressive are the three circular open-air marble terraces, under the sky itself. Here is the altar for the cult of Heaven. The middle of the topmost terrace is the place where the emperor used to make sacrifices to the Lord-on-high at the time of the winter solstice.

To what religion does the Temple of Heaven belong? This is a question often posed by visitors. The correct answer is: to Chinese religion. But exactly what is Chinese religion? Tradition has transmitted a plurality including Confucianism and Taoism. We would have to say more specifically: that Chinese religion includes a dimension of nature worship which was transformed by Confucianism and Taoism and incorporated into each system in a different way. And, to the extent that the cult of Heaven has been approved by the Confucian tradition, one might even designate the Temple of Heaven as a *Confucian* temple. Indeed, the *Book of Rites* contains precise instructions for the performance of this cult to Heaven. This ritual surrounding the cult of Heaven developed very early, existing already at the time of Confucius, and remaining in many respects the main feature of Chinese religion until the twentieth century.

The cult to Heaven was a sacrifice of burnt offerings. . . . Attendance was strictly limited, as the population in general was not admitted, and individual citizens would be guilty of high treason should they attempt to perform it. Rather, the performance was the privilege as well as sacred duty of the Son of Heaven, the emperor.

This itself was not only proof that there was no separation between political and religious powers, between the *imperium* and the *sacerdotium*, but also that the office of the emperor was basically a continuation of the ancient office of the priest-shaman-king. . . .

In speaking of the cult to Heaven, one should not neglect the other cult, offered to Earth. The dual cults give an impression that Heaven and Earth are equals, each accepting a sacrifice. But the reality is not quite so. While the sacrifices of Heaven and Earth both belonged to the category of "great" sacrifices, performed by the emperor himself as Son of Heaven, Heaven takes on greater importance and is addressed as Lord-on-high. It would appear that these cults represented a mixture of beliefs, which came down with the interaction of Shang and Chou religions. Sacrifices were thus offered both to Heaven and Earth as cosmic forces, and to Heaven in particular as a supreme deity.

The Other State Cults

Starting from the time of the Han dynasty, an elaborate state cult was evolved, which has been, rightly or wrongly, attributed to Confucian teachings. They include expressions of very ancient beliefs, not just in a supreme deity, and in natural powers as deity symbols, as well as in the intercessory powers of deceased worthies or heroes. We mentioned the great rituals performed by the emperor himself, not only for the worship of Heaven but also for that of Earth, and of his imperial ancestors. There were also intermediate rituals, for the worship of the sun and the moon, and numerous spirits of earth and sky. There were the lesser sacrifices to minor gods, including those of mountains, lakes, and rivers as well as those well-known historical figures—in particular wise and incorrupt magistrates—honoured as "city gods." Besides, surrounded by his disciples, and also by later worthies, Confucius himself became the centre of an elaborate cult which possibly would have been most repugnant to him. While not deified, he received official sacrifices as the teacher *par excellence*, and was especially venerated by the scholarly class. The Confucian emphasis on rituals assured a continuity with the past, and offered also a ritual as well as a moral education for the would-be gentleman.

With the establishment of a republic in China (1912) the cult of Heaven, as well as the other state cults, came to an end. But their memory remains as witness to a theistic belief (be this monotheism or polytheism, depending on one's interpretations) present at the heart of traditional Chinese religion, and persisting throughout the ages, in spite of the changes in the philosophical interpretation of this belief.

The Cult of Ancestors

Any religion that focuses so much on ancestors presupposes some belief in the hereafter. The Confucian belief was that the human being is compounded of two "souls," an upper, or intellectual soul, called the *hun*, which becomes the spirit (*shen*), and ascends to the world above, and a lower, or animal soul, called the *p'o/po*, which becomes the ghost (*kuei*) and descends with the body into the grave. These ideas are especially found in the *Tso Commentary* (*Tso-chuan*), in a recording of a conversation dated 534 B.C., where these "souls" are also presumed to be possessed by everyone, not just nobility. Such ideas are confirmed by archaeological findings of tomb paintings of a heavenly realm, as in Ma-wang-tui, the Han site. They were also accepted by the Taoist religion, which greatly elaborated them. The Taoist cult of immortality, involving physical immortality or the ascent to Heaven as immortals, developed from these beliefs, especially regarding the *hun*.

The ancestral cult was a memorial service, held previously at ancestral temples, and after that at gravesides or at home. Wine and food libations were usually offered, with silent prostrations in front of the tablets. The ancestors were alleged to have tasted the food, before the whole family partook of the meal. Conversion to Christianity frequently represented a rupture with this tradition, since the converts were either forbidden, or no longer expected, to continue the cult.

Much better known than the cult of Heaven, the cult of ancestors goes back to the dawn of Chinese history, although originally it was the exclusive privilege of the nobility. It became associated with the state orthodoxy, while remaining very much a family practice—an expression of a community of both the living and the beloved deceased. While the ancestral cult may be regarded as a religion in itself, its persistence has also been considered as another indication of the religious character of Confucianism. Until today, in many Chinese houses in Hong Kong, Taiwan and Southeast Asia—as well as in Korea and Japan—the ancestral shrine is maintained. . . .

The Family Rituals

There are, of course, other rituals as well, recorded in the *Book of Rites* and practised during many centuries. I am referring especially to those ceremonies surrounding a person's growth and maturity, the affirmation of the family principle by marriage, and the mourning and funerary rites. These are the so-called Family Rituals, and they have been singled out for special attention by the great Neo-Confucian thinker Chu Hsi (1130–1200), who has helped to promote their influence not only in China itself, but also in traditional Korea and beyond. While many of these rituals are no longer observed, they offer useful evidence of the religious character of Confucianism.

The rituals include the male adolescent's "Capping," some time between the ages of fifteen and twenty, when he receives his formal hat and ceremonial gown, as well as his formal name. In addition, a wine libation is made and the young man is presented formally to his ancestors. . . . After that comes marriage, also a union of families, which begins with the announcement of the event to the ancestors in the temple, accompanied by a wine libation. . . .

The family rituals are obviously part and parcel of an ancestral cult. The invisible ancestors receive reports from the living members of the family regarding births and weddings, as well as during those occasions that mark the adolescent's entry into adult society. There are also other rituals dedicated more directly to the deceased, such as mourning and funerary rites, and the anniversaries attached to the memories of the deceased members of the family. These occupy much attention in the *Book of Rites;* one might say the entire classical text is preoccupied especially with these occasions and how such rituals should be enacted. . . .

HUMAN NATURE AND THE RITES: MENCIUS AND HSÜN-TZU

As we have described it, Confucianism was an ancient teaching, which Confucius himself preferred to attribute to the sages of old, even if we find in it facets that are new and distinct against the perspective of ancient religion. With time, the disciples of the school, called *Ju* or scholars, achieved greater social recognition. Etymologically, as we have mentioned, the word refers to a coward or weakling, and it became associated with these people probably because they preferred attention to ritual matters and the learning of the ancients rather than to the sword at a time when aristocrats were mostly fighting men. Eventually, the term would also achieve respectability, and the entire culture became tilted to scholarly rather than military virtues, even if conquests continued to be made by the sword.

The Confucian school was further developed by its later followers, including Mencius and Hsün-tzu. These differed not merely with Confucius himself on certain issues, but even more among themselves. Yet they share enough to contribute together to the building up of the Confucian tradition. On the other hand, Mo-tzu, who was once a follower of the Confucian school, moved away from it to begin a distinctive school of thought, and was much criticised, especially by Mencius, for ideas like universal love, as being subversive of family values.

The word Mencius, like the word Confucius, is the Latinised form for Master Meng (Meng-tzu), whose name was Meng Ko (372–289 B.C.), a native of a small state adjacent to Confucius' Lu. From the stories that have come down to us, Meng is described as having been an orphan boy, quite difficult when very young, and brought up by a wise and virtuous mother. Like Confucius, he travelled from one feudal state to another, looking for a ruler who would accept his advice. Unlike Confucius, his advise was often given bluntly, and of course, his time (the "Warring States") was in much greater turmoil than the earlier times (the "Spring and Autumn period"). It appears that the feuding lords regarded him as hopelessly impractical for preaching benevolence and righteousness when might was making right in the struggle for political survival. More than the *Analects*, the *Book of Mencius* possesses real eloquence, with passages of lofty idealism and even mysticism.

Hsün-tzu was no contemporary of Mencius. Master Hsün, called Hsün K'uang or Hsün Ch'ing (312?–238 B.C.), a native of the state of Chao, also in North China, from which came virtually all early Confucians and even Mohists. He was appointed magistrate of Lan-ling, in the powerful state of Ch'i, and served as such for a short period. He left behind a work of the same name (*Hsün-tzu*) with thirty-two sections. The extant version appears to include sections coming from his own hand as well as from his disciples. The work is organised around definite topics, such as the nature of Heaven, and the wickedness of human nature. The thinking is developed much more logically than in the other Confucian works.

Some of Hsün-tzu's teachings were diametrically opposed to those of Mencius. Besides, by career as well as by orientation of thinking, he has been associated with some Legalists. He is said to have had as disciples both Li Ssu, the chief minister of Ch'in who helped to propel the state to pre-eminence and became prime minister of the First Emperor of the Ch'in dynasty, and Han Fei, the aristocrat whose teachings on political power have come down in the work, *Han Fei Tzu*.

The Rites: Sacred or Secular?

In the *Book of Mencius*, we find a clear evolution in the meaning of the term Heaven. Where Confucius only makes infrequent mention of the personal deity, Mencius speaks much more of Heaven—but not always as personal deity. According to Mencius, Heaven is present within man's heart, so that he who knows his own heart and nature, knows Heaven (*Mencius* 7A:1). It represents,

therefore, a greater immanence. It also refers more and more to the source and principle of ethical laws and values. Nevertheless, Mencius continues to hold in esteem the practice of offering sacrifices to the Lord-on-high and to ancestors: "Though a man may be wicked, if he adjusts his thoughts, fasts and bathes, he may sacrifice to the Lord-on-high" (*Mencius* 4B:25).

Hsün-tzu sees a difference between a *gentleman* of education, who uses his rationality, and the common people, who believe in fortune and misfortune. Where we had earlier found divination in the royal ancestral temples of the Shang dynasty, and rain dances sponsored by the state, we find in *Hsün-tzu* the movement away from such religious practices, on the part of the higher classes, and the identification of such with the "superstitious" commoners. It is the beginning of the separation between Confucianism as an élite tradition, and so-called popular religion, at a grass-roots level. . . .

As an education, the rites are supported by music. In the *Book of Rites*, a text which manifests Hsün-tzu's influence, the chapter on music also extols it as a help in gaining inner equilibrium and tranquility—the equilibrium is the reflection of the harmony of elegant music. Together, music and the rites maintain or restore an inner harmony, which is or ought to be, a reflection of the harmony between Heaven and earth. This reflects the teachings of the Doctrine of the Mean, also a chapter from the same ritual text. The philosophical assumption here is the correlation between the microcosm and the macrocosm, between the inner workings of man's mind and heart and the creative processes of the universe. Here, we touch upon the heart of the Chinese meaning of harmony, with its obvious mystical dimension. . . .

Human Nature: Good or Evil?

The Chinese word for human nature is *hsing/xing*, a compound including the term for mind or heart, and life or offspring. Philological scholarship demonstrates the association between etymology and early religious worship. The human being is he or she who has received from Heaven the gift of life and all the innate endowments of human nature, especially the shared faculty of moral discernment. Thus the meaning of *hsin* as mind and heart is closer to the biblical Hebrew notion of *lev*, the seat of both reason and emotions, than it is to the somewhat more intellectual Greek *nous* or Latin *mens*, to which English "mind" is related. Mencius says that the sense of right and wrong is common to all (2A:6), distinguishing the human from the beast. From this flows another belief, that of the natural equality of all, which exists in spite of social hierarchy, or any distinction between the "civilised" and the "barbarian."

The Confucian tradition has sometimes been criticised for its inability to explain the place of evil in human existence. While the Shang dynasty's King T'ang publicly begged the Lord-on-high for forgiveness for his sins . . . , Confucian philosophy was not to develop a theory of sin as offence against God. Rather, it affirms the presence of evil, explaining this as either the product of contact between an originally good nature and its wicked environment, as Mencius tends to say, or as inherent in human nature itself, which is the position of Hsün-tzu. . . .

POLITICS: CONFUCIANISM AS "CIVIL RELIGION"

The term "civil religion" comes from the American sociologist Robert Bellah, who is also a Japan specialist. It refers to the religious or quasi-religious regard for civic values and traditions marked by feasts, rituals, dogmas and creeds. He applied the term especially to the American situation, with the coexistence of several faiths like Protestant and Roman Catholic Christianity and Judaism, sharing a common belief in one God and in a set of religious values, as well as in a religion of nationalism with its creed, catechism and dogma reflected in symbols of civil unity like the flag, and in documents like the Declaration of Independence and the Constitution. Certain addresses like Washington's Farewell and Lincoln's Second Inaugural took on religious overtones, while the Pledge of Allegiance became a standard rite for school children much as morning prayers had been.

We make use of the term here in the Chinese context, because we find certain parallels in the cases of a modern society like that of the United States and traditional Chinese society. Although not usually regarded as a high priest, the American President is expected to adhere to, and articulate, certain common tenets of the religious beliefs of the people, and does this in a near-ritual form on certain state occasions. In the Chinese case, state religion, which overlaps with Confucianism as the state ideology, actually embraces the tenets and practices of Taoism. Aside from the sacrifice to Heaven and the ancestral cult, which are not found in American civil religion, traditional China adhered to certain political principles with implicit religious sanctions. These bear similarity to some of the principles enshrined in the American Declaration of Independence, which offers the justification for the people's revolution against British rule. We refer here to the Chinese belief in Heaven's bestowing a mandate to govern to the rulers, who forfeit it if they become tyrants.

The Politics of Heaven's Mandate

Much more than Christianity, Confucian teachings are oriented to improving the political order, as a means of achieving human-heartedness. The teaching of *jen* is extended to the political order, where it is defined as benevolent government, a government of moral persuasion, in which the leader gives the example of personal integrity, and selfless devotion to the people. Confucian teaching prompted generations of scholars to strive for participation in government. For the human is never regarded as dualistic, as matter and mind, body and soul. It is always accepted as *one*, as existing in society, as striving as well for physical well-being, for social harmony, and for moral and spiritual perfection. The Confucian sage has been described as possessing the qualities of "sageliness within and kingliness without." In other words, he should have the heart of the sage, and the wisdom of the king. We have here what may be called "philosopher kings" as in Plato's *Republic*.

But while Confucian teachings were originally aimed at advising the rulers, they became increasingly applied to the training of those who would act as the rulers' advisors. The problem for the minister or would-be minister is: what should one do were the ruler not only less than sage, as most rulers turned out to be, but even despotic and tyrannical, as some of them definitely were? Confucius himself offers a doctrine of Rectification of Names, which has sometimes been misunderstood. In eight cryptic words, he says: "Ruler, ruler; minister, minister; father, father; son, son" (*Analects* 13:3). These have been misinterpreted as representing a caste system where the ruler is always ruler, the minister always minister. However, this is obviously a mistake, since every son is expected to become a father. The correct interpretation is that the ruler should be a *good* ruler, the minister a *good* minister, the father a *good* father, and the son a *good* son. Names should represent realities, but in Plato's sense of ideal forms. . . .

. . . And Mencius also offered a clear formulation of the doctrine of rebellion or revolution, known popularly as the "removal of the Mandate" (*ko-ming/geming*). It was Mencius who said that killing a tyrant was not regicide, since the tyrant no longer deserved to rule (1B:8); it was Mencius who declared: "The people come first; the altars of the earth and grain come afterwards; the ruler comes last" (7B:14). . . .

The Confucian tradition was to include political conservatives as well as moderate and radical reformers; there were those whose priority was to serve the state; there were also those who remained independent of the state, while seeking to change or transform it. Confucian scholars were usually activists, either serving the government, advising and admonishing the ruler or engaging in reforms, or even protesting against tyranny through passive or active resistance. . . .

COMPROMISES WITH OTHER SCHOOLS: HAN CONFUCIANISM

The Han period is important in religious history because during that time Confucianism became a state orthodoxy (some would say, the state religion), Taoism became an institutional religion, and Buddhism was introduced into the country. Han China represents an epoch when all under Heaven was unified under one emperor ruling by Heaven's mandate with the help of Confucian orthodoxy. . . .

Kingship: Real and Ideal

The Han scholar reputed to be the most influential in consolidating Confucian gains was the "political theologian" Tung Chung-shu (179–104 B.C.), who sought with metaphysical arguments to persuade the ruler to exercise benevolent government. Systematising traditional thought, he established Heaven, Earth and Man as a horizontal triad or trinity, with kingship as the vertical link between them:

> Those who in ancient times invented writing drew three lines and connected them through the middle, calling the character "king." The three lines are Heaven, earth and man, and that which passes through the middle joins the principles of all three. . . . Thus the king is but the executor of Heaven. He regulates its seasons and brings them to completion. . . .

Cosmology: Yin-Yang and the Five Agents

Tung Chung-shu and Han Confucians also incorporated ideas from the Yin-Yang and **Five Agents** schools. These were independent and ancient schools, but their ideas gradually fused with one another and were absorbed into both Taoism and Confucianism. We are here referring to cosmological ideas of two opposing yet complementary forces, *yin* and *yang*, as well as to a system of thinking focused on five primal elements that were also viewed as active cosmic agents always engaged in a process of mutual interaction and change. These five agents are water, fire, wood, metal and earth. Each has power over the other; that is, water is over fire, fire over earth, earth over metal, metal over wood, wood over water.

These five agents thus differ from the Greek or Hindu "Four Elements" of earth, air, fire and water. Not only does the Chinese group include an organic substance, wood, but it appears to exclude the very important and all-pervasive air. Actually, air or *ch'i* had always been regarded as fundamental and indeed, all-pervasive. The Five Agents, however, served another purpose. Together with *yin* and *yang*, they formed a system of correlation which integrated life and the universe.

Han Confucianism was tolerant of exaggerations and superstitions. Together with the reconstructed Five Classics, many apocryphal texts were also accepted; indeed, each classic had at least one apocryphal text associated with it. We hear of Confucius' alleged miraculous birth and many other legends. There were also widespread beliefs in omens and portents, supported by a wide array of prognostication and divination texts. Eventually, scholarly consensus would subordinate the non-rational and non-historical materials to stricter scrutiny. But the Chinese belief in omens and portents continued until our own times. During centuries of history, eclipses of the sun and moon were carefully predicted and studied for their values as portents or omens. Natural disasters, whether flood or droughts, were also regarded as signs from Heaven of displeasure of misrule. The earthquake in Tangshan, North China, that just preceded Mao Zedong's death in 1976, was widely seen as an omen, predicting drastic change.

NEO-CONFUCIANISM AS A RESPONSE TO BUDDHISM

As a term, "Neo-Confucianism" is also a Western coinage. The usual Chinese usage is to refer to the later development of Confucianism as the "Metaphysical Thought" (*Li-hsüeh*, literally "the learning of principle"). This was a *new* expression of Confucian thought, based on a smaller corpus of classical texts, reinterpreted in response to Buddhist challenges. In this respect, the Neo-Confucian movement parallels scholastic philosophy in the West, which sought to reinterpret Christian teachings with the assistance of Greek philosophical concepts. Ironically, since the rise of Neo-Confucianism signalled the decline of Buddhism, Buddhist influences on Chinese thought are best discerned afterwards in the structure of Neo-Confucian thinking.

During the Han dynasty and the later T'ang dynasty (when Buddhism became prominent), many commentaries and subcommentaries were written on the classical texts themselves, which also became the core of the examination curriculum. But all this was largely the work of philologists. The Neo-Confucian philosophers made a different kind of contribution, as they developed their new thinking in response to Taoist and Buddhist influences. These thinkers also turned away from Han philology and superstitions. They looked for the spiritual legacy of Confucianism itself—the "legacy of the mind and heart" that we may call spirituality. It was a new development, quite different from the direction of Han Confucianism, which oscillated between the rationalism of Hsün-tzu and the superstitions of signs and omens. It also marked all later Chinese thinking, drawing the wealth of spiritual doctrine into mainstream philosophy. While Western spirituality has its rightful place in ascetical and mystical theology, it remains the domain of the monks rather than the laity, and has never been part and parcel of Western philosophical heritage. In the Chinese context, the spirituality of Confucius and Mencius, and even of Lao-tzu and Chuang-tzu, became strengthened through the Buddhist experience and the Neo-Confucian response to this experience, which was primarily the response of lay teachers and thinkers on a quest for sageliness.

The Neo-Confucian movement also strengthened a new understanding of lineage, so central to Chinese religious as well as philosophical thought. According to Chu Hsi (1130–1200), the true understanding of Confucius' teachings was lost after Mencius, and only rediscovered by his own intellectual predecessors—the eleventh-century thinkers Chou Tun-yi, Chang Tsai and the Ch'eng brothers.

The Four Books as a New Canon

The Five Classics had stimulated philological exegesis, but had not promoted sufficient philosophical and religious commentaries. The Sung dynasty Neo-Confucian philosophers reformulated Confucian philosophy on the basis of a smaller corpus of texts, the **Four Books**. They contained the following texts:

- The *Analects* of Confucius (*Lun-yü*) includes twenty chapters, divided into nearly fifty sections, some of which are very brief. The earliest text with any historical information about Confucius, it goes back to about one century after the Master's death and gives the conversations between Confucius and his disciples. The chapters are not organised systematically, and the dialogues they offer are fragmentary.

- The *Book of Mencius*, a work in seven chapters, each subdivided into two parts, presents the conversations between Mencius and his disciples. Probably compiled after Mencius' death, although perhaps not that much later, it too is not systematically organised. But the passages are longer and the contents livelier, and include many anecdotes.

- The *Great Learning* is a brief chapter taken from the *Book of Rites*. Its concern is less ritual, but rather moral and spiritual cultivation, considered the beginning of good rulership.

- The *Doctrine of the Mean* is a slightly longer text, also taken from the *Book of Rites*. Its spiritual and philosophical content focuses on the inner life of psychic equilibrium and harmony.

In giving these texts pre-eminence, Chu Hsi and the other Neo-Confucian philosophers oriented Confucian scholarship increasingly to metaphysical and spiritual questions, at a time when Buddhism had made great inroads. In fact, their own thinking shows signs of Buddhist and Taoist philosophical influence. The result is a new synthesis, a *Weltanschauung* that builds on the old moralist answers to questions about life and the world, with a clearer metaphysical framework and spiritual profundity. The basic Neo-Confucian quest, while it has its scholastic roots, is definitely oriented to self-transcendence in the achievement of sagehood, rather than to rising on the bureaucratic ladder simply by passing official examinations. The synthesis took shape especially during the Sung (960–1279) and Ming (1368–1661) dynasties.

Chu Hsi on the Absolute: T'ai-chi *and* Li

Chu Hsi's philosophy represents a conscious synthesis of previous philosophies, combining as it does the "naturalist" legacy of the Taoists and Buddhists, and the psychist and culturalist legacy of the Confucians themselves, modified also by an undercurrent of Buddhist influences. His theory of human nature draws from both sides. For Chu Hsi, as for the mainstream of Chinese philosophy, the human being and the cosmos are each paradigms, one of the other, so that evil loses its significance in the affirmation of human perfectibility, as expressed through the doctrine of sagehood.

A terse expression of the world regarded as an ontological paradigm is given in the philosophy of the Great Ultimate (*T'ai-chi*), which Chu Hsi took over from Chou Tun-yi. This is a symbolic expression of cosmology which emphasises the interrelatedness of the world and man in macrocosm/microcosm terms; it also hides within itself a secret Taoist formula for alchemy and yoga. And it points possibly to early Chinese beliefs in a supreme deity under symbols of astral bodies.

Chu Hsi interprets the *T'ai-chi* with the help of the concept of *li*, those "principles" which constitute all things, and which had been given prominence by the Ch'eng brothers, especially Ch'eng Yi. *Li* may be defined as forms of essences, as organising and normative principles, belonging to the realm "above shapes." It is prior—although not in a temporal sense—to its co-ordinate, *ch'i*, translated sometimes as "ether," or "matter-energy," which belongs to the realm "within shapes." All things are constituted of both *li* and *ch'i*, somewhat as with Aristotelian form and matter, with the difference that *li* is passive and *ch'i* is dynamic.

The Great Ultimate is the most perfect *li*, a kind of primal archetype. It is also the *totality* of all the principles (*li*) of the myriad things, as brought together into a single whole. It serves in Chinese philosophy the function of the Form of the Good in Platonism, and that of God in Aristotelianism.

In place of a personal deity, Chu Hsi was speaking about an absolute which he clearly identified with both Heaven and the Lord-on-high. He asserted that it is not correct to speak about "a man in Heaven" who is lord of the world, but that it is equally wrong to say that "there is no such Ruler." He was removing the anthropomorphic overtones of these terms while affirming the presence of a higher power, a metaphysical more than a personal Absolute.

> The Book of Poetry and the Book of History speak as though there is a human being there above, commanding things to come to pass, as in [passages] where they mention the Lord (*Ti*) as being filled with wrath, etc. But even here what they refer to is [the action of] *Li*. There is nothing more eminent under Heaven [i.e., in the universe] than *Li*. Hence it is called Ruler. "The august Lord-on-high has conferred even upon the inferior people a moral sense." [The word] "conferred" conveys the idea of a ruler. . . .

Chu Hsi was probably the greatest mind, and the most prolific author among the Neo-Confucian giants. Though he was not accepted as an orthodox thinker during his own life, his commentaries on the Four Books were eventually integrated into the curriculum of the civil service examinations (1313), making his philosophy the new state orthodoxy for six centuries to come. The history of Chinese philosophy after Chu Hsi may be described as a debate between those who, like him, wished to give more importance to *li*, and others who wished to give more emphasis to *ch'i*. The protagonists of *li* tended to presuppose a pre-established pattern of harmony in the universe and in human nature, to be recaptured and maintained by a proper balance of reason and the emotions. The protagonists of *ch'i*, on the other hand, were inclined to minimise the opposition between reason and

the emotions. In other words, the tendency was toward either idealism, in the first case, or materialism, in the second. It is interesting to note that Chinese Marxist scholars have consistently sought to discover in *ch'i* a materialist ancestry for Chinese Marxism. . . .

NEO-CONFUCIANISM IN MODERN TIMES

During most of the last thousand years, Neo-Confucianism has been the official philosophy for China. But the Jesuit missionaries, including especially Matteo Ricci, preferred classical Confucianism to the later development. They opposed the metaphysical dimensions of Neo-Confucian philosophy, which bore a pantheistic imprint of Buddhist influence. Actually, it has become impossible to separate Neo-Confucianism from earlier Confucianism, so that an onslaught on one meant the same on the other. In the late nineteenth century, Chinese intellectuals began a soul-searching questioning of the cultural heritage, particularly Confucianism. It was regarded by many of them as a weight and a burden —an intellectual shackle on the mind, preventing the country from modernisation. Its strongest critic was probably the early-twentieth-century writer Lu Hsün, whose short stories attacked the "cannibalistic" ritual religion that stifled human freedom and individual initiative in the name of passive, conformist virtues. These critiques satirised the dehumanising elements in a fossilised tradition until then inextricably bound up with the social-political establishment. They were also expressive of the newly awakened nationalism, desirous of asserting independence against the coming of the Western Powers and Japan. It was in the midst of these anti-traditionalist, anti-Confucian voices of the May Fourth Movement (1919) that the Chinese Communist Party was born (1921). What began as a search for intellectual freedom entailed finally a repudiation of the monopoly of tradition, with the Communist takeover of the mainland (1949).

Mainland scholars have sought as well to point out for the sake of attack the *religious* character of the Neo-Confucian movement, including Chu Hsi's teachings on meditation and spiritual cultivation and Wang Yang-ming's penchant for mysticism. However, Liu Shaoqi, former head of state in Communist China, had lauded both Confucian and Neo-Confucian ideas in his address, *How to Be a Good Communist*:

> The Chinese scholars of the Confucian school had a number of methods for the cultivation of their body and mind. Every religion has various

methods and forms of cultivation of its own. The "investigation of things, the extension of knowledge, sincerity of thought, the rectification of the heart, the cultivation of the person, the regulation of the family, the ordering well of the state and the making tranquil of the whole kingdom" as set forth in the Great Learning also means the same. All this shows that in achieving one's progress one must make serious and energetic efforts to carry on self-cultivation and study.

During the Cultural Revolution (1966–76), the Anti-Confucius movement entered a new phase, with diatribes in 1973–74 linking the fallen Defence chief Lin Piao with Confucius. This was the most vehement attack ever mounted. Long before that, Liu Shaoqi had become "enemy number one" to Chairman Mao. His writings were banned, and the Confucian and Neo-Confucian ideas he had praised also came under heavy attack.

While Marxist scholars were vigorously criticising the entire traditional legacy, a group of philosophers and scholars in Taiwan and Hong Kong expressed their concern for the survival of Chinese culture, which they identified especially with Neo-Confucianism. I refer here to the plea for a return to Neo-Confucian sources, in "A Manifesto for the Reappraisal of Sinology and Reconstruction of Chinese Culture," made public by a group of Chinese philosophers in Taipei in 1958. This statement speaks of the harmony of the "way of Heaven" (*t'ien-tao/tiandao*) and the "way of man" (*jen-tao/rendao*) as the central legacy of Confucianism. It also challenges Western Sinologists to give greater attention to Confucian spirituality as the core of Chinese culture, which it claims was not properly understood by the missionaries of the sixteenth and seventeenth centuries. In saying this, these scholars interestingly concurred with mainland scholars in the judgement that Neo-Confucianism in particular possesses an undeniably spiritual and religious character. . . .

SOURCES

I have organized the sources chronologically into six different periods in order to provide a developmental overview of the significant literature of Confucianism. A historical arrangement is particularly important in the case of Confucianism because so much of the later literature comments on and presupposes a knowledge of the earlier materials.

A wide variety of topics are discussed in this literature including rituals, the origin of the universe, the nature of morality, good government, how one should conduct one's life, and much more. Much of what you will find is instruction on how to become a sage, or wise person. This goal is of central importance in Confucianism and is as important to a Confucian as enlightenment is to a Buddhist.

6.2 THE CLASSICAL PERIOD (ca. 700–221 B.C.E.)

From the classical period stems the classical texts of Confucianism that have had a formative impact on the subsequent tradition. The texts attributed to the three most important Confucian thinkers, Confucius (551–479 B.C.E.), Mencius (371–289 B.C.E.), and Hsün Tzu (298–238 B.C.E.), come from this period. Also, the **Five Classics,** although containing material from a previous period, took shape during this period.

6.2.1 Book of Rites

The Confucian tradition does not begin with Confucius. Even though Confucius is respectfully called the First Teacher, he explicitly states that he is a transmitter of a tradition much older than he is. According to the Confucian tradition, he preserved, edited, transmitted, and commented on a wisdom he inherited from antiquity.

As do many religious traditions, Confucianism views innovation and newness suspiciously. Even when something radically new emerges, it is often claimed to be nothing more than a return to the classical teachings. Being faithful to the tradition is what counts. Religions, and Confucianism is no exception here, tend to view themselves as conserving a revered past. However, they also change, adapt, and give rise to innovative geniuses that keep the tradition alive and growing. Confucius was one of those innovative geniuses who both transmitted and changed a tradition.

The *Book of Rites* is part of the *Classic of Rites* (one of the Five Classics) Confucius supposedly edited and transmitted. It is a collection of discourses compiled during the Former or Western Han dynasty (206 B.C.E.–8 C.E.) from earlier materials. The Chinese word here translated as "rites" is *li. Li* encompasses all kinds of behavior, both public and private, ranging across such activities as seasonal festivals, table manners, rites of passage, and governmental functions.

According to some social scientists, ritual actions, like many actions, have both a manifest function and a latent function. The manifest function of some action is the conscious or intended function, and the latent, or hidden, function is unconscious or unintended. A function is what any belief or activity does to satisfy some social need. For example, beliefs and rituals surrounding death may manifestly (be intended to) reduce anxiety over death. However, these same beliefs may also unintentionally increase anxiety by reminding people of their own deaths (latent function).

In most activities, the manifest function is the same as the purpose of an action. So, for example, the manifest function of an economic activity like spending money is the same as its purpose, to gain something. However, in religious activities (only in religious activities?), the manifest function may not be the same as the purpose. A prayer for a safe fishing trip may manifestly reduce anxiety over traveling on the ocean, but its purpose may be to appease the anger of some storm deity or spirit thereby ensuring a safe trip. In order to discover the manifest functions of some activity, ask what *social needs* it may be intended to satisfy. Discovering the latent function is more difficult and requires a sensitivity to possible unintended consequences of human action.

The selections that follow come from three important chapters of the *Book of Rites:* "The Principles of Sacrifice," "The Mean," and "The Great Learning." A later Confucian scholar named Chu Hsi (1130–1200) excerpted both "The Mean" and "The Great Learning" and made them independent texts. These two books, along with the *Analects* and the *Mencius*, are known as the **Four Books,** and in the fourteenth century they became required reading for the civil service examination—a system of study and examination that lasted into the early twentieth century. Given their use, it seems appropriate that Chu Hsi rearranged the eight steps of "The Great Learning" to begin with "the investigation of things" rather than "making thoughts sincere," the latter being the original first step. Chu Hsi's arrangement has become standard and is followed in the translation below.

The Principles of Sacrifice, The Mean, and The Great Learning

READING QUESTIONS

1. What attitude is expressed through ritual, and what does "completion" (blessings) mean?
2. What is filial behavior?
3. What are the manifest and latent (hidden) functions of sacrifices in honor of the ancestors?
4. What does sacrifice teach?
5. What are centrality and harmony, and why are they important?
6. What does sincerity have to do with the trinity of heaven, earth, and humans?
7. What is the great learning, and what makes it "great"?

THE PRINCIPLES OF SACRIFICE

Of all the ways of governing human beings well, none is more compelling than ritual; of the five categories of rites, none is more important than sacrificial offerings. Sacrifice does not enter from without: it issues from within, in the mind. When the mind is in awe, it is expressed through ritual. Only worthies are able to plumb the meaning of sacrifice.

The sacrifices of worthy persons receive their blessings, but these are not what the world ordinarily calls blessings. The term "blessings" here means "completion," an expression that means complete accord. When everything is in accord, there is completion. This is to say that internally, there is full completion of the self; externally, there is complete accord with the Way. When loyal ministers serve their sovereigns and filial children serve their parents, they act from this same fundamental basis. When this happens, then on high there is complete accord with ghosts and spiritual beings; outside the family sphere, there is accord with sovereigns and seniors; inside the family sphere, there is filiality toward parents. This then is completion. Only worthy people can attain to this completion, and when they do they may then sacrifice. The sacrifices of worthy people may be described thus: the sacrificers perfect their sincerity and good faith with loyalty and reverence and then offer

From *Chinese Religion: An Anthology of Sources*, edited by Deborah Sommer, pp. 35–39. Copyright © 1995 by Oxford University Press. Used by permission of Oxford University Press, Inc.

their votive gifts following the way of ritual, accompanying the rites with music and performing them openly, without seeking anything. This then is the attitude of the filial child.

By sacrificing, one continues to care for one's parents and act with filiality. Filiality means "to care for," and caring means according with the Way and not transgressing proper conventions of behavior. Filial people serve their parents in three ways: in life, they care for them; in death, they mourn them; when mourning is over, they sacrifice to them. Caring for parents expresses accord; mourning expresses sorrow; sacrifice expresses reverence and timely attentiveness. Filial behavior lies in fulfilling these three criteria.

Upon fulfilling one's responsibilities within the family, one then seeks a helpmate from outside, and for this there are the rites of marriage. When a ruler seeks a wife, he says, "I ask from you this jadelike maiden to share with my humble self this poor state, to serve at the ancestral temple and at the altars of the land and grain." This is essentially how one seeks a helpmate. Husbands and wives must conduct sacrifices together, and each has his or her own respective duties, without and within. Only when these responsibilities are performed is there completion. Everything, of lesser and greater importance, must be prepared: minces and pickles made from the products of land and water, stands for the meats of the three sacrificial animals, condiments for the eight dishes, rare animals and plants—all the things of the yin and the yang forces. Everything, whether generated by heaven or grown upon the earth, is set forth. Outwardly, there is a complete profusion of things, and inwardly, there is a complete perfection of the will. This is the attitude appropriate to sacrificing.

Hence the Son of Heaven himself plows south of the city to provide grain for the sacrificial cauldrons, and the empress tends silkworms north of the city to supply ritual attire. The enfeoffed lords also plow east of the city to supply grain, and their wives likewise practice sericulture north of the city to supply caps and attire. It is not that the Son of Heaven and feudal lords have no one to do the plowing for them, or that the empress and the lords' wives have no one to do sericulture for them: it is just that they themselves want to express their sincerity and good faith. Such qualities are what is meant by perfection, and perfection means reverence; only when reverence is perfected can one serve the spiritual and the numinous. This is the way of sacrifice. . . .

Three aspects of sacrifice are especially important: of offerings, libations; of music, the high songs; and of dance performances, the "Night of the Battle of King Wu." These are the ways of the Chou, and they give outward expression to the will of the honorable person

and enhance it. One's will is expressed in the advancing and retreating motion of one's steps, lighter and heavier, proportionate to the sentiment behind them. Even a sage cannot be inwardly lighthearted and outwardly serious. Honorable people conduct sacrifices in person to clarify what is important, and they follow the way of ritual. Emphasizing the three important aspects of sacrificing, they present offerings to the august personator of the dead. This is the way of the sage.

After sacrificing there are foodstuffs left over, and even though these are the most peripheral aspects of rites, one must still know what to do with them. As the ancient saying goes, the ending must be as fine as the beginning, and leftovers must be considered in the same vein. As a gentleman of antiquity once said, "The personator of the dead eats what the ghosts and spirits leave behind." This is a kind practice that illustrates the workings of governance. When the personator arises after eating, the ruler and three great ministers eat, and when the ruler arises, the six great officers eat, consuming what the ruler has left over. The great officers get up, and then the eight officers eat, those of lower rank eating what their superiors have left. Then the officers get up, and taking what is left, go out, placing it in the hall below. Finally the lesser officials come in and take it away, and the subordinate officials eat what their superiors have left. At each change there are more people, illustrating the degrees of higher and lower rank. Everyone shares in this beneficent custom, and this is what happens to the contents of the four vessels of millet in the ancestral temple. The ancestral temple is itself symbolic of the whole land.

Sacrifice is a great benefaction. When superiors receive some benefit, they then bestow it on those below them. It is just that superiors receive the beneficence first and subordinates receive it later; it is not that superiors accumulate excess while subordinates suffer from cold and hunger. When people of higher rank receive some boon, those below wait for it to flow down to them, knowing that beneficence will reach them. One can see all this by considering the distribution of leftovers from sacrifice, and hence it is said that this practice illustrates the workings of governance.

Sacrifice is the greatest of things when all its preparations are complete. What do such preparations teach? Through them the ruler can teach respect for rulers and ministers in the sphere outside of the family, and within the family sphere he can teach people to be filial. So if the sovereign is enlightened, the ministers will follow him. When he discharges his duties in the ancestral temple and to the altars of the land and grain, then his sons and grandsons will be filial. His teaching is brought forth because he perfects this Way and perfects this kind of deportment. Honorable people should act this way themselves in serving the ruler. Misunderstandings that occur between higher-ranking people should not be taken out on their subordinates, and subordinates should not direct their own animosities toward their superiors. Criticizing the actions of others but then doing the same thing oneself goes contrary to this teaching. So these are the fundamentals of the instruction of the honorable person. Is this not truly the epitome of concord? Is this not truly what is meant by sacrificing? So it is said that sacrifice is the basis of instruction.

In sacrifice there are ten proper norms: the ways appropriate to serving ghosts and spirits, the proper comportment of rulers and ministers, the relationships between parent and child, the distinctions between those of higher and lower rank, the degrees of intimacy between close and distant relatives, the distributions of rank and emolument, the differences between husband and wife, fairness in the affairs of governance, the order of priorities between senior and junior, and the boundaries between higher and lower. These are the ten norms.

THE MEAN

What heaven has mandated is called the nature. According with this nature is called the Way (*Tao*). Cultivating the Way is called instruction.

This Way cannot be departed from for even an instant, and if it can be, then it is not really the Way. Hence the honorable person is cautious about things as yet unseen and apprehensive about things as yet unheard.

Nothing is more visible than what is darkly hidden, and nothing is more evident than what can be barely detected. So the honorable person is cautious even when alone.

The condition when pleasure, anger, sorrow, and joy have not yet arisen is called centrality; the condition when these do arise and all reach a measured expression is called harmony. Centrality is the fundamental basis of the world, and harmony is the attainment of the Way throughout the world.

When centrality and harmony are perfected, everything in heaven and earth finds its place and all things flourish.

[1.1–5]

Spirits

The master said, "The virtue of ghosts and spirits is truly marvelous. One looks for them but they cannot be seen; one listens for them but they cannot be heard. They are at the marrow of things but they cannot be

detected. They cause everyone in the world to observe vigils and purify themselves, dress in their richest attire, and present sacrificial offerings. Then the spirits seem to float just above the heads of the sacrifiers, all around them. As it is said in the *Book of Odes*, 'The approaches of spirits are unfathomable. How could one be unmoved by this?' So it is said that what can barely be detected becomes evident, and that sincerity cannot be kept concealed."

[16.1–5]

The Five Relationships

So that the Way may be attained throughout the land, people must consider five things, and for enacting the Way, one must consider three. The five are the relationships between ruler and minister, parent and child, husband and wife, elder and younger brother, and friend and friend. These five constitute the attainment of the Way throughout the land. Understanding, humanity, and fortitude are the three aspects of attaining to virtue throughout the land, and one enacts them with a single-minded oneness. Some people understand all this from birth, others understand it through study, and still others understand it only through painful experience; nevertheless, once they understand it, those people are all the same. Some are able to enact all this with ease; others, with some effort; still others, with strenuous effort. Nevertheless, once they succeed, they are all the same.

[20.8–9]

Sincerity

Sincerity is the Way of heaven, and the attainment of sincerity is the Way of human beings. A person who is possessed of sincerity, who achieves things effortlessly and apprehends things without excessive deliberation, who goes along with things and attains the Way, is a sage. Those possessed of sincerity embrace what is good and hold fast to it.

They study widely and inquire extensively, ponder things carefully and make clear deliberations; they act with earnestness.

They do not rest lest there be something they have not studied or studied but not yet grasped, or lest there be something they have not inquired about or have inquired about but do not yet understand. Nor do they rest lest there be something they have not yet pondered or have pondered but not yet apprehended, or lest there be something they have not yet deliberated, or have deliberated but have not yet clarified. They do not rest lest there be something they have not done or have done but without earnestness. If someone else accomplishes things after only one try, they will try a hundred times; if someone else accomplishes things after only ten attempts, they will try a thousand times.

If people are able to proceed in this way, then even if they are stupid they will become bright and intelligent, and even if they are weak they will become strong.

That this intelligence comes from sincerity is human nature itself. The fact that sincerity comes from intelligence is due to instruction. If there is sincerity there will be intelligence, and where there is intelligence there will be sincerity.

[20.18–20]

A Trinity with Heaven and Earth

In this world only those who have attained the epitome of sincerity can perfect their natures, and when they have perfected their own natures, they can then perfect the natures of other people. When they have perfected the natures of other people, they can then perfect the natures of things. When they have perfected the natures of things, they can then participate in the transforming and sustaining forces of heaven and earth and form a trinity with heaven and earth.

Next below these people are those who first develop themselves in small ways. When they are able to do that, they can attain to sincerity, and when they are sincere, they begin to take shape. Shape becomes lustrous and luster becomes brightness; brightness becomes vibrancy, vibrancy becomes change, and change becomes transformation. In this world when one attains sincerity, one can transform things.

Such is the Way of the perfection of sincerity that one can have foreknowledge of things before they happen. When a state is about to prosper, auspicious omens will appear, and when a state is about to perish, baneful prodigies become manifest. These can be seen in the milfoil stalks and the tortoiseshell, and they will vibrate within one's four limbs. When either misfortune or prosperity is about to happen, both the good and the bad will be foreknown. To perfect sincerity, then, is to become like a spirit.

[22–24]

Heaven and Earth

The ways of heaven and earth can be completely explained in one phrase: they are impartial to all things. How they generate things is unfathomable. The way of heaven and earth is expansive and generous, lofty and bright, far-reaching and enduring. Heaven seems to be but a glow of brightness, but if one gazes into its inexhaustible reaches, one will see the sun, moon, stars, and celestial bodies all suspended from it. It covers all things. The earth seems to be but a mass of soil, but if one looks farther into its breadth and depth, one will see that it effortlessly bears the weight of even the Hua peaks and carries the rivers and seas without their leaking away. It holds up all things. Mountains seem to be but lumps of rock, but looking at their breadth and height one sees plants and trees flourishing and birds and beasts thriving in their midst. Many treasures lie within them. Consider a spoonful of water, but then look at water's unfathomable depths where great turtles, sea tortoises, scaly creatures, dragons, fishes, and green turtles live. Precious things abound there.

[26.7–9]

THE GREAT LEARNING

The Way of the great learning lies in clarifying bright virtue, loving the people, and abiding in the highest good.

Only if one knows where to abide can one develop resolve, and only with resolve can one become tranquil. Only tranquility allows one to be restfully secure, and only with this security can one be reflective. Only by reflecting on things can one apprehend them.

Things have their roots and their branches, and affairs have their beginnings and their ends. If one knows what should be first and what should be last, then one can draw near the Way.

In antiquity, those who wanted to clarify their bright virtue throughout the entire realm first had to govern their states well. Those who wanted to govern their states well first had to manage their own families, and those who wanted to manage their families first had to develop their own selves. Those who wanted to develop themselves first rectified their own minds, and those who wanted to rectify their minds first made their thoughts sincere. Those who wanted to make their thoughts sincere first extended their knowledge. Those who wanted to extend their knowledge first had to investigate things.

Once things are investigated, knowledge can be extended. When knowledge is extended, thoughts can be made sincere; when thoughts are sincere, the mind can be rectified. When the mind is rectified, one can develop the self; once the self is developed, the family can be managed. When the family is managed, the state can be governed well; when the state is governed well, peace can prevail throughout the land.

From the Son of Heaven to the common people, everyone must consider developing the self to be the fundamental root of things. If the roots are confused, then the branches cannot be well governed. It should never happen that important things are trifled with, or that trifles are considered important.

6.2.2 Analects

The **Analects** (literally, "Sayings") are a collection of aphoristic sayings recorded and collected by Confucius's students. Some of his students are mentioned by name, and he is often referred to by the title "Master." It contains material that probably dates to Confucius himself mixed with other material.

Confucius claims that people who genuinely seek to cultivate their humanity in a social context of appropriate relationships can become a *chün-tzu,* a word sometimes translated as "honorable person," "superior man," "noble man," or "gentleman." Literally, *chün-tzu* means "scion of a ruling family." In Confucius's day, it was widely believed that one is a *chün-tzu* by birth, but Confucius lays the groundwork for a new and radical idea: A person can become noble and honorable by effort. In particular, one can achieve this status by cultivating such virtues as kindness (*jen*), mutual consideration (*shu*), loyalty (*chung*), and understanding (*chih*). The *tao,* or way to live properly, is not to retreat from society as some kind of recluse, but, rather, to engage society properly and live one's life as an example for others. This is particularly important for government officials and rulers: If peace, harmony, and good will are to arise in a state, the rulers must set good examples for the people to follow.

CONFUCIUS

Selected Sayings

READING QUESTIONS

1. What is the honorable person like?
2. How are humanity, virtue, and consideration related?

3. What seems to be Confucius's attitude toward ritual, sacrifice, spirits, and praying?
4. What is the point of the two stories about "recluses"?

CONFUCIUS'S CHARACTER

The master said, "How delightful it is to study and to review from time to time what one has studied! How pleasant to have friends visit from afar!"

[1.1.1–2]

The master said, "One can still find happiness if one has only simple food to eat, water to drink, and a bent arm for a pillow. Wealth and high rank attained unrighteously are to me but floating clouds."

[7.15]

Tzu-kung said, "The master is congenial, pleasant, courteous, good tempered, and complaisant. Thus does he engage the world, and his way of engaging it is quite different from that of other people."

[1.10.2]

There were four things he was completely free of. He never showed a lack of forethought, he was not opinionated, he was not hidebound, and he was not egoistic.

[9.4]

The master offered instruction concerning four things: cultural refinement, proper conduct, loyalty, and good faith.

[7.24]

When the master was eating next to someone who was in mourning, he never ate to the full. He never sang on a day in which earlier he had been crying.

[7.9]

The master fished, but not with a net. When hunting he did not shoot at roosting birds.

[7.26]

HUMAN NATURE

Tzu-kung said, "One can apprehend the master's disquisitions on culture and refinement, but not his discussions of human nature or the way of heaven."

[5.12]

The master said, "In terms of human nature, people are much alike. But in terms of practice and effort, they are quite different."

[17.2]

Confucius said, "Those who are possessed of understanding from birth are the highest type of people. Those who understand things only after studying them are of the next lower type, and those who learn things from painful experience are yet the next. Those who have painful experiences but do not learn from them are the lowest type of people."

[16.9]

THE HONORABLE PERSON

The master said, "Isn't one truly an honorable person if one is not acknowledged by others yet still does not resent it!"

[1.1.3]

The master said, "Honorable people are modest in what they say but surpassing in what they do."

[14.29]

The master said, "There are three aspects to the way of the honorable person, but I am incapable of them: to be possessed of humanity and have no anxieties, to be wise and have no doubts, and to be strong and have no fears." Tzu-kung said, "Master, those are your ways."

[14.30]

The master said, "Honorable persons seek things within themselves. Small-minded people, on the other hand, seek things from others."

[15.20]

Confucius said, "There are three things of which the honorable person is in awe: the mandate of heaven, great people, and the words of the sages. Small-minded people do not understand the mandate of heaven and are not in awe of it; they are insolent toward great people and ridicule sages."

[16.8]

HUMANITY, VIRTUE, AND CONSIDERATION

The master rarely spoke of profit, of one's mandated fate, or of humanity.

[9.1]

The master said, "Persons possessed of humanity are like this: wanting to develop themselves, they also develop others; wanting to achieve things themselves, they also allow others to achieve what they want. This is the direction humanity takes: to use what is close to oneself as an analogy to be extended to others."

[6.28.2–3]

Chung-kung asked about humanity. The master said, "In your social affairs behave as if you are meeting with important guests, and treat people as if you were participating in a great sacrificial offering. Do not impose on other people anything you yourself dislike. Let there be no animosity either in the state or in the family." Chung-kung said, "Even though I am not gifted, I will try to practice what you have just said."

[12.2]

Fan Ch'ih asked about humanity. The master said, "Be solicitous of others." Fan Ch'ih asked about understanding. The master said, "Be understanding toward others."

[12.22]

The master said, "Only persons possessed of humanity can truly like other people or truly dislike them."

[4.3]

The master said, "Is humanity something far away? If I want to be humane, then humanity has already been attained."

[7.29]

Someone asked, "What of repaying animosity with virtue?" The master said, "How could one repay that with virtue? Repay animosity with directness, and repay virtue with virtue."

[14.36]

Tzu-kung asked, "Is there one word by which one may live one's entire life?" The master said, "Isn't that word 'consideration'? Do not impose on other people anything you yourself dislike."

[15.23]

THE WAY

The master said, "It is enough that someone who dies in the evening has heard of the Way only that morning."

[4.8]

The master said, "Tseng-tzu, my way has only one theme that holds it all together." Tseng-tzu replied, "That is so." When the master went out, the other disciples asked Tseng-tzu what Confucius had meant. Tseng-tzu replied, "The master's way is simply loyalty and consideration."

[4.15]

It is that human beings glorify the Way, not that the Way glorifies human beings.

[15.28]

GOVERNANCE

The master said, "Someone who governs with virtue is like the northern polar star, which stays in one place while all the other stars pay their respects to it."

[2.1]

Chi-k'ang Tzu asked Confucius about governance. Confucius replied, "To govern means to rectify. If you start by rectifying yourself, how would anyone else not do the same?"

[12.17]

The master said, "If you rectify your own self, then even if you give no orders they will still be carried out. If you don't rectify yourself, then even if you do give orders they will still not be followed."

[13.6]

The master said, "If one adopts administrative measures and implements punishments in a consistent fashion, the people will comply with them but will have no shame. But if one follows the Way of virtue and implements ritual consistently, the people will have a sense of shame and moreover will correct themselves."

[2.3]

Fan Ch'ih asked to study farming with him. The master said, "Better to ask an old farmer about it." He then asked to study gardening. "Better to ask an old gardener." When Fan Ch'ih left, the master said, "Fan Chih is such a small-minded person. If a superior loves ritual, then the people will be reverent. If a superior loves righteousness, the people will oblige him, and if he loves good faith, the people will respond to him. If he can be like this, then people from all directions will come to him, bearing their children on their backs. Why should he need to study farming?"

[13.4]

HEAVEN

The master said, "No one understands me." Tzu-kung said, "How can you say that no one understands you?" The master said, "I bear no animosity toward heaven and no ill-will toward human beings. My studies, while lowly, attain certain heights. It is heaven that understands me."

[14.37]

The master said, "I don't want to say anything." Tzu-kung said, "If you don't say anything, then what should we write down?" The master said, "Does heaven say anything? The four seasons proceed and all things are generated, but does heaven say anything?"

[17.19]

The master said, "Heaven has generated the virtue within me. What can Huan T'ui do to me?"

[7.22]

A great minister asked Tzu-kung, saying, "Can't your master be considered a sage? He is a man of many different abilities." Tzu-kung replied, "Heaven has granted that he has very nearly become a sage, and, moreover, he is a man of many skills." The master heard this, and said, "The great minister understands me. When I was young, I was of very humble background, and hence I am capable at many different but nevertheless common things. But does the honorable person need this diversity? No."

[9.6]

Ssu-ma Niu lamented, "All people have brothers, but only I do not." Tzu-hsia said, "I have heard it said that 'Death and life are mandated, and wealth and high honor lie with heaven.' If the honorable person is reverential and well mannered, is respectful of others and follows ritual, then within the four seas all people will be brothers. How could the honorable person be worried that he have no brothers?"

[12.5]

RITUAL

The master said, "People say 'ritual this' and 'ritual that.' But is ritual just jades and silks? They say 'music this' and 'music that.' But is music just bells and drums?"

[17.11]

When Fan Ch'ih was Confucius's charioteer, the master said, "Meng-sun asked me what filiality was and I said, 'Not being disobedient.'" Fan Ch'ih asked, "What did you mean by that?" The master replied, "I meant to serve one's parents with ritual when they are alive, to bury them with ritual when they die, and thereafter to sacrifice to them with ritual."

[2.5.2–3]

Tzu-kung wanted to eliminate the offering of the sacrificial sheep at the beginning of the lunar month. The master said, "Tzu-kung, you are concerned about the sheep, but I am concerned about the ritual."

[3.17]

The master said, "Honorable people, widely studied in cultural things and guided by ritual, will not overstep themselves."

[6.25]

The master said, "Respect without ritual becomes tiresome, circumspection without ritual becomes timidity, bold fortitude without ritual becomes unruly, and directness without ritual becomes twisted."

[8.2.1]

SACRIFICE

Someone asked about the meaning of the great Ti sacrifice. The master said, "I do not know. Someone who knew how to explain it would find the whole realm in the palm of his hand."

[3.11]

The master was very circumspect about observing the vigils before sacrificing, about warfare, and about illness.

[7.12]

When observing the vigils before sacrifice, Confucius wore immaculately clean clothing. He altered his diet, and he moved from the place where he commonly sat.

[10.7]

The food was spare, with only soup and vegetables, but when sacrificing that was how he observed the vigils.

[10.8.10]

SPIRITS

The master said, "To sacrifice to a spirit with which one has no proper association is merely to curry favor with it."

[2.24]

When he sacrificed to the ancestral spirits, he did so as if they were actually present; when he sacrificed to other spirits, he did so as if they were actually present. The master said, "If I do not really take part in the sacrifice, it is as if I did not sacrifice at all."

[3.12]

Fan Ch'ih asked about wisdom. The master said, "To perform the obligations properly due to the people; and to pay reverence to ghosts and spirits, while keeping a distance from them—this may be called wisdom."

[6.20]

The master did not talk about strange marvels, the use of force, chaos and disorder, or spirits.

[7.20]

PRAYER

When the master became very ill, Tzu-lu asked to be allowed to pray for him. The master asked, "Is this usually done?" and Tzu-lu replied, "It is. It is said in the eulogies that one prays to the spirits above and to the terrestrial divinities below." The master remarked, "Then I have been praying for a long time."

[7.34]

Wang-sun Chia asked, "What is meant by the expression 'Rather than supplicate the tutelary powers of the southwest corner of the house, supplicate those of the stove'?" The master replied, "That is not the case at all. Those who offend heaven have nothing to whom they might pray."

[3.13]

SHAMANISM, DIVINATION, AND EXORCISM

The master said, "The people of the south say that unless someone is a steady person, they cannot become either a shaman or a healer. That is an excellent saying! Unless one is of steady virtue, one will invite disgrace. This would come simply from not divining properly."

[13.22]

When the villagers were performing the Nuo exorcism, he donned court dress and stood on the eastern steps.

[10.10.2]

RECLUSES

Once when Ch'ang Chü and Chieh Ni were out plowing their fields together, Confucius passed by and had Tzu-lu ask them where the ford was. Ch'ang Chü asked, "Who is that there in the carriage?"

"Confucius."

"Confucius from Lu?"

"Yes," Tzu-lu replied.

"Well, if that's who it is," Ch'ang added, "then he knows where the ford is."

Tzu-lu then asked Chieh Ni, who said, "Who are you?"

"I am Tzu-lu."

"You're a disciple of Confucius from Lu?"

"That is so."

"The whole world is flooded," Chieh stated, without interrupting his raking, "and who can change it? It's better to be a follower of someone who withdraws from the whole world than of someone who withdraws only from certain people."

When Tzu-lu got back he told Confucius what they said. Surprised, the master said, "One cannot flock together with birds and beasts. If I do not associate with human beings, then with whom should I associate? If the Way prevailed within the world, then I would not try to change it."

[18.6]

Tzu-lu, following at some distance behind the master, encountered an elderly man carrying a bamboo basket slung over his shoulder on a pole. Tzu-lu asked, "Have you seen my master?" The old man replied, "You don't look too hard-working, and you probably can't even tell one kind of grain from another. Just who might your master be?" The man stuck his staff in the ground and started weeding, but Tzu-lu just stood there respectfully with his hands clasped in front of his chest. In the end the old man invited Tzu-lu to stay over; he killed a chicken and prepared some millet to feed him, and he introduced him to his two children. The next day, Tzu-lu went on his way, and when he caught

up with the master he told him what had happened. The master said, "He is a recluse." He had Tzu-lu go back so that he might meet him, but when they arrived, he had already gone out. Tzu-lu said, "Not to serve in office is not right. The proper customs between old and young cannot be set aside, but how much less can one set aside the righteousness between ruler and minister? By wanting to make himself pure, this man has thrown greater human relationships into disarray. When honorable persons serve in office, they enact this righteousness. When the Way is not enacted, they also know it of themselves."

[18.7]

6.2.3 Is Human Nature Good or Evil?

Do you think human beings are morally good or bad by nature? Do you think strong governments with strictly enforced laws and severe punishments are necessary for a good social order? Or do you think that the less government there is the better?

What role does education play in making people good? Can virtue be taught? Should our schools engage in moral education? Should education impart knowledge only, or should it also build character?

What exactly is the human potential? If people are uneducated and controlled by few laws, will they become more humane and civil or will they become more antisocial and uncivil? Can education and strict laws guarantee civility?

These questions and others like them arose as the Confucian tradition developed. Like many religions, Confucianism found society falling far short of its ideal. Societies were often riddled with crime, people did evil and cruel things, and rulers were corrupt. Why did evil and imperfection exist? If things were not wrong, there would be no need to set them right. However, why are they wrong in the first place? Could it be that humans are evil by nature?

Confucius had little to say directly about human nature, but he appears to have been optimistic about the human potential. According to Confucius, if people who are not honorable by birth can become so through the cultivation of virtue, then, given the proper education, most people, even those lowly born, should be able to become honorable and wise.

Mencius (371–289 B.C.E.), the author of the first selection, was taught, according to tradition, by the grandson of Confucius. Mencius believed that Confucius's teachings implied that humans are good by nature. However, if they are good by nature, whence comes evil? Mencius believed that evil comes from society: Bad societies corrupt humans who are *originally* good. Hence, he argued that education must center on recovering the innate knowledge of the good and the innate tendency to do the good thereby countering the effects of a corrupting culture.

Mencius's views represent the idealistic wing of Confucian philosophy. Hsün Tzu, the author of the second selection, was born sometime around 312 B.C.E., and his views represent the naturalistic wing. Whereas Mencius argued for the goodness of human nature, Hsün Tzu disputed Mencius's views and argued that humans are evil by nature.

Both Mencius and Hsün Tzu believed that heaven generates human nature. However, Mencius thought heaven is good and hence that humans have an inherent tendency to do good. Hsün Tzu thought heaven is neutral with respect to good and evil and that humans are generated by heaven to be what they are, creatures born with conflicting desires and an innate tendency to be selfish.

Although Hsün Tzu develops his views in opposition to Mencius, the difference between them is not as great as it might first appear. Both were strong supporters of education, but for different reasons. For Mencius proper education is essential to allowing our originally good nature to flourish, whereas for Hsün Tzu it can make "straight" an originally "crooked" nature.

Readers of this debate who are familiar with Christianity should not read Christian ideas into it. In Christian theology, the debate about human nature takes place in the context of the notion of an "original sin." According to Christianity, humans are created good by a good god, but they sin by rebelling against the divine. This sin of rebellion is prefigured by a cosmic rebellion led by Lucifer or Satan, who is an angel and who, in the form of a serpent, tempts the first humans to sin. Just as Satan is cast out of heaven because of his sin, so the first humans "fall" from an original goodness. This first sin has infected the whole human race. Such, according to Christianity, is the story of how evil came to be.

There is no "fall" for either Mencius or Hsün Tzu. Indeed, there is neither a personal creator god nor any Satan figure. For them the issue of good and evil centers on whether original human nature prior to social influences has an innate tendency to do good or whether it lacks the ability to control its many conflicting desires.

The selection from Mencius recounts part of a debate he had with Kao Tzu. Kao Tzu holds the view that there is neither good nor evil in human nature. Human nature, according to Kao Tzu, is morally neutral. The selection opens with a discussion of whether Kao Tzu's analogies are correct and moves on to Mencius's criticism of Kao Tzu's claim that "nature" means the same as "inborn." In the second selection, Hsün Tzu explains his view that humans are evil by nature and provides a refutation of Mencius's views.

Much argument in ancient Chinese philosophy took place by using analogies to support or refute ideas. This use of analogy will be illustrated in the selections that follow. One question to keep in mind as you read is, How strong and compelling are the analogies? Do they persuade you or not?

MENCIUS

Human Nature Is Good

READING QUESTIONS

1. According to Mencius, why is the native endowment of humans not the cause of evil?
2. What reason does Mencius give to support the claim that no human lacks a heart sensitive to the suffering of others? Do you think he is right about this? Why?
3. According to Hsün Tzu, why is Mencius wrong when he says, "Man learns because his nature is good"?
4. According to Hsün Tzu, from where do propriety and righteousness come?
5. How does Hsün Tzu define good and evil?
6. In your view, who is right about human nature, Mencius or Hsün Tzu, and why?

BOOK VI • PART A

1. Kao Tzu said, "Human nature is like the *ch'i* willow. Dutifulness is like cups and bowls. To make morality out of human nature is like making cups and bowls out of the willow."

From *Mencius*, translated by D. C. Lau, volume 2. Copyright © 1970 D. C. Lau. Reprinted by permission of Penguin Books, Ltd. Footnotes omitted.

"Can you," said Mencius, "make cups and bowls by following the nature of the willow? Or must you mutilate the willow before you can make it into cups and bowls? If you have to mutilate the willow to make it into cups and bowls, must you, then, also mutilate a man to make him moral? Surely it will be these words of yours men in the world will follow in bringing disaster upon morality."

2. Kao Tzu said, "Human nature is like whirling water. Give it an outlet in the east and it will flow east; give it an outlet in the west and it will flow west. Human nature does not show any preference for either good or bad just as water does not show any preference for either east or west."

"It certainly is the case," said Mencius, "that water does not show any preference for either east or west, but does it show the same indifference to high and low? Human nature is good just as water seeks low ground. There is no man who is not good; there is no water that does not flow downwards.

"Now in the case of water, by splashing it one can make it shoot up higher than one's forehead, and by forcing it one can make it stay on a hill. How can that be the nature of water? It is the circumstances being what they are. That man can be made bad shows that his nature is no different from that of water in this respect."

3. Kao Tzu said, "The inborn is what is meant by 'nature.'"

"Is that," said Mencius, "the same as 'white is what is meant by "white"'?"

"Yes."

"Is the whiteness of white feathers the same as the whiteness of white snow and the whiteness of white snow the same as the whiteness of white jade?"

"Yes."

"In that case, is the nature of a hound the same as the nature of an ox and the nature of an ox the same as the nature of a man?"

6. Kung-tu Tzu said, "Kao Tzu said, 'There is neither good nor bad in human nature,' but others say, 'Human nature can become good or it can become bad, and that is why with the rise of King Wen and King Wu, the people were given to goodness, while with the rise of King Yu and King Li, they were given to cruelty.' Then there are others who say, 'There are those who are good by nature, and there are those who are bad by nature.' For this reason, Hsiang could have Yao as prince, and Shun could have the Blind Man as father, and Ch'i, Viscount of Wei and Prince Pi Kan could have Chou as nephew as well as sovereign.' Now you say human nature is good. Does this mean that all the others are mistaken?"

"As far as what is genuinely in him is concerned, a man is capable of becoming good," said Mencius. "That is what I mean by good. As for his becoming bad, that is not the fault of his native endowment. The heart of compassion is possessed by all men alike; likewise the heart of shame, the heart of respect, and the heart of right and wrong. The heart of compassion pertains to benevolence, the heart of shame to dutifulness, the heart of respect to the observance of the rites, and the heart of right and wrong to wisdom. Benevolence, dutifulness, observance of the rites, and wisdom do not give me a lustre from the outside, they are in me originally. Only this has never dawned on me. That is why it is said, 'Seek and you will find it; let go and you will lose it.' There are cases where one man is twice, five times or countless times better than another man, but this is only because there are people who fail to make the best of their native endowment. The *Odes* say,

Heaven produces the teeming masses,
And where there is a thing there is a norm.
If the people held on to their constant nature,
They would be drawn to superior virtue.

Confucius commented, 'The author of this poem must have had knowledge of the Way.' Thus where there is a thing there is a norm, and because the people hold on to their constant nature they are drawn to superior virtue."

8. Mencius said, "There was a time when the trees were luxuriant on the Ox Mountain, but as it is on the outskirts of a great metropolis, the trees are constantly lopped by axes. Is it any wonder that they are no longer fine? With the respite they get in the day and in the night, and the moistening by the rain and dew, there is certainly no lack of new shoots coming out, but then the cattle and sheep come to graze upon the mountain. That is why it is as bald as it is. People, seeing only its baldness, tend to think that it never had any trees. But can this possibly be the nature of a mountain? Can what is in man be completely lacking in moral inclinations? A man's letting go of his true heart is like the case of the trees and the axes. When the trees are lopped day after day, is it any wonder that they are no longer fine? If, in spite of the respite a man gets in the day and in the night and of the effect of the morning air on him, scarcely any of his likes and dislikes resembles those of other men, it is because what he does in the course of the day once again dissipates what he has gained. If this dissipation happens repeatedly, then the influence of the air in the night will no longer able to preserve what was originally in him, and when that happens, the man is not far removed from an animal. Others, seeing his resemblance to an animal, will be led to think that he never had any

native endowment. But can that be what a man is genuinely like? Hence, given the right nourishment there is nothing that will not grow, while deprived of it there is nothing that will not wither away. Confucius said, 'Hold on to it and it will remain; let go of it and it will disappear. One never knows the time it comes or goes, neither does one know the direction.' It is perhaps to the heart this refers."

15. Kung-tu Tzu asked, "Though equally human, why are some men greater than others?"

"He who is guided by the interests of the parts of his person that are of greater importance is a great man; he who is guided by the interests of the parts of his person that are of smaller importance is a small man."

"Though equally human, why are some men guided one way and others guided another way?"

"The organs of hearing and sight are unable to think and can be misled by external things. When one thing acts on another, all it does is to attract it. The organ of the heart can think. But it will find the answer only if it does think; otherwise, it will not find the answer. This is what Heaven has given me. If one makes one's stand on what is of greater importance in the first instance, what is of smaller importance cannot displace it. In this way, one cannot but be a great man."

16. Mencius said, "No man is devoid of a heart sensitive to the suffering of others. Such a sensitive heart was possessed by the Former Kings and this manifested itself in compassionate government. With such a sensitive heart behind compassionate government, it was as easy to rule the Empire as rolling it on your palm.

"My reason for saying that no man is devoid of a heart sensitive to the suffering of others is this. Suppose a man were, all of a sudden, to see a young child on the verge of falling into a well. He would certainly be moved to compassion, not because he wanted to get in the good graces of the parents, nor because he wished to win the praise of his fellow villagers or friends, nor yet because he disliked the cry of the child. From this it can be seen that whoever is devoid of the heart of compassion is not human, whoever is devoid of the heart of shame is not human, whoever is devoid of the heart of courtesy and modesty is not human, and whoever is devoid of the heart of right and wrong is not human. The heart of compassion is the germ of benevolence; the heart of shame, of dutifulness; the heart of courtesy and modesty, of observance of the rites; the heart of right and wrong, of wisdom. Man has these four germs just as he has four limbs. For a man possessing these four germs to deny his own potentialities is for him to cripple himself; for him to deny the potentialities of his prince is for him to cripple his prince. If a man is able to develop all these four germs that he possesses, it will be like a fire starting up or a spring coming through. When these are fully developed, he can tend the whole realm within the Four Seas, but if he fails to develop them, he will not be able even to serve his parents."

HSÜN TZU

Human Nature Is Evil

The nature of man is evil; his goodness is the result of his activity.[1] Now man's inborn nature is to seek for gain. If this tendency is followed, strife and rapacity result and deference and compliance disappear. By inborn nature one is envious and hates others. If these tendencies are followed, injury and destruction result and loyalty and faithfulness disappear. By inborn nature one possesses the desires of ear and eye and likes sound and beauty. If these tendencies are followed, lewdness and licentiousness result, and the pattern and order of propriety and righteousness disappear. Therefore to follow man's nature and his feelings will inevitably result in strife and rapacity, combine with rebellion and disorder, and end in violence. Therefore there must be the civilizing influence of teachers and laws and the guidance of propriety and righteousness, and then it will result in deference and compliance, combine with pattern and order, and end in discipline. From this point of view, it is clear that the nature of man is evil and that his goodness is the result of activity.

Crooked wood must be heated and bent before it becomes straight. Blunt metal must be ground and whetted before it becomes sharp. Now the nature of man is evil. It must depend on teachers and laws to become correct and achieve propriety and righteousness and then it becomes disciplined. Without teachers and laws, man is unbalanced, off the track, and incorrect. Without pro-

From Chang, Wing-tsit, *A Source Book in Chinese Philosophy*, pp. 128–132. Copyright © 1963, renewed 1991 by Princeton University Press. Reprinted by permission of Princeton University Press. Footnotes edited.

[1]According to Yang Liang, *wei* (artificial) is "man's activity." It means what is created by man and not a result of natural conditions. This is accepted by most commentators, including Hao I-hsing, who has pointed out that in ancient times *wei* (ordinally meaning false or artificial) and *wei* (activity) were interchangeable.

priety and righteousness, there will be rebellion, disorder, and chaos. The sage-kings of antiquity, knowing that the nature of man is evil, and that it is unbalanced, off the track, incorrect, rebellious, disorderly, and undisciplined, created the rules of propriety and righteousness and instituted laws and systems in order to correct man's feelings, transform them, and direct them so that they all may become disciplined and conform with the Way (Tao). Now people who are influenced by teachers and laws, accumulate literature and knowledge, and follow propriety and righteousness are superior men, whereas those who give rein to their feelings, enjoy indulgence, and violate propriety and righteousness are inferior men. From this point of view, it is clear that the nature of man is evil and that his goodness is the result of his activity. . . .

Mencius said, "Man learns because his nature is good." This is not true. He did not know the nature of man and did not understand the distinction between man's nature and his effort. Man's nature is the product of Nature; it cannot be learned and cannot be worked for. Propriety and righteousness are produced by the sage. They can be learned by men and can be accomplished through work. What is in man but cannot be learned or worked for is his nature. What is in him and can be learned or accomplished through work is what can be achieved through activity. This is the difference between human nature and human activity. Now by nature man's eye can see and his ear can hear. But the clarity of vision is not outside his eye and the distinctness of hearing is not outside his ear. It is clear that clear vision and distinct hearing cannot be learned. Mencius said, "The nature of man is good; it [becomes evil] because man destroys his original nature." This is a mistake. By nature man departs from his primitive character and capacity as soon as he is born, and he is bound to destroy it. From this point of view, it is clear that man's nature is evil.

By the original goodness of human nature is meant [by Mencius] that man does not depart from his primitive character but makes it beautiful, and does not depart from his original capacity but utilizes it, so that beauty being [inherent] in his primitive character and goodness being [inherent] in his will are like clear vision being inherent in the eye and distinct hearing being inherent in the ear. Hence we say that the eye is clear and the ear is sharp. Now by nature man desires repletion when hungry, desires warmth when cold, and desires rest when tired. This is man's natural feeling. But now when a man is hungry and sees some elders before him, he does not eat ahead of them but yields to them. When he is tired, he dares not seek rest because he wants to take over the work [of elders]. The son yielding to or taking over the work of his father, and the younger brother yielding to or taking over the work of his older brother—these two lines of action are contrary to original nature and violate natural feeling. Nevertheless, the way of filial piety is the pattern and order of propriety and righteousness. If one follows his natural feeling, he will have no deference or compliance. Deference and compliance are opposed to his natural feelings. From this point of view, it is clear that man's nature is evil and that his goodness is the result of his activity.

Someone may ask, "If man's nature is evil, whence come propriety and righteousness?" I answer that all propriety and righteousness are results of the activity of sages and not originally produced from man's nature. The potter pounds the clay and makes the vessel. This being the case, the vessel is the product of the artisan's activity and not the original product of man's nature. The artisan hews a piece of wood and makes a vessel. This being the case, the vessel is the product of the artisan's activity and not the original product of man's nature. The sages gathered together their ideas and thoughts and became familiar with activity, facts, and principles, and thus produced propriety and righteousness and instituted laws and systems. This being the case, propriety and righteousness, and laws and systems are the products of the activity of the sages and not the original products of man's nature.

As to the eye desiring color, the ear desiring sound, the mouth desiring flavor, the heart desiring gain, and the body desiring pleasure and ease—all these are products of man's original nature and feelings. They are natural reactions to stimuli and do not require any work to be produced. But if the reaction is not naturally produced by the stimulus but requires work before it can be produced, then it is the result of activity. Here lies the evidence of the difference between what is produced by man's nature and what is produced by his effort. Therefore the sages transformed man's nature and aroused him to activity. As activity was aroused, propriety and righteousness were produced, and as propriety and righteousness were produced, laws and systems were instituted. This being the case, propriety, righteousness, laws, and systems are all products of the sages. In his nature, the sage is common with and not different from ordinary people. It is in his effort that he is different from and superior to them.

It is the original nature and feelings of man to love profit and seek gain. Suppose some brothers are to divide their property. If they follow their natural feelings, they will love profit and seek gain, and thus will do violence to each other and grab the property. But if they are transformed by the civilizing influence of the pattern and order of propriety and righteousness, they will even yield to outsiders. Therefore, brothers will quarrel if they follow their original nature and feeling but, if they are transformed by righteousness and propriety, they will yield to outsiders.

People desire to be good because their nature is evil. If one has little, he wants abundance. If he is ugly, he wants good looks. If his circumstances are narrow, he wants them to be broad. If poor, he wants to be rich. And if he is in a low position, he wants a high position. If he does not have it himself, he will seek it outside. If he is rich, he does not desire more wealth, and if he is in a high position, he does not desire more power. If he has it himself, he will not seek it outside. From this point of view, [it is clear that] people desire to be good because their nature is evil. . . .

Mencius said, "The nature of man is good." I say that this is not true. By goodness at any time in any place is meant true principles and peaceful order, and by evil is meant imbalance, violence, and disorder. This is the distinction between good and evil. Now do we honestly regard man's nature as characterized by true principles and peaceful order? If so, why are sages necessary and why are propriety and righteousness necessary? What possible improvement can sages make on true principles and peaceful order?

Now this is not the case. Man's nature is evil. Therefore the sages of antiquity, knowing that man's nature is evil, that it is unbalanced and incorrect, and that it is violent, disorderly, and undisciplined, established the authority of rulers to govern the people, set forth clearly propriety and righteousness to transform them, instituted laws and governmental measures to rule them, and made punishment severe to restrain them, so that all will result in good order and be in accord with goodness. Such is the government of sage-kings and the transforming influence of propriety and righteousness.

But suppose we try to remove the authority of the ruler, do away with the transforming influence of propriety and righteousness, discard the rule of laws and governmental measure, do away with the restraint of punishment, and stand and see how people of the world deal with one another. In this situation, the strong would injure the weak and rob them, and the many would do violence to the few and shout them down. The whole world would be in violence and disorder and all would perish in an instant. From this point of view, it is clear that man's nature is evil and that his goodness is the result of his activity. . . .

6.3 HAN ORTHODOXY (206 B.C.E.–220 C.E.)

During the Han dynasty, scholars spent countless hours collecting, preserving, and editing the literature they had inherited from the past. One problem the Han scholars faced was that the transition from individual states to an empire had been destructive. Archives and written records, not to mention disfavored scholars, were burned by the first Ch'in emperor of a unified China. The demise of the Ch'in led to a protracted civil war before the Han were able to reestablish order and unity. In a society where books were hand-copied and rare, such political turmoil and destruction severely reduced the sources available for understanding and reconstructing the past.

An anti-Confucian school of political philosophy known as Legalism had gained power under the Ch'in. Advocating the use of strong and harsh laws to control the people, the Legalists helped the Ch'in replace the feudal domains with a system of provinces that still exists today. The Ch'in also standardized the Chinese written language, expanded military power, and finished the Great Wall. For the first hundred years of the Han dynasty, Taoism became more influential in government circles than Legalism. However, Confucians slowly came back into power and eventually their philosophy became the official ideology of the Han empire. Confucianism now became a state cult, and Confucius was elevated to a semidivine status. Temples were built in his honor, and sacrifices were offered to him as the supreme teacher of wisdom.

6.3.1 Correlative Thinking

Tung Chung-shu (176–104 B.C.E.), a Confucian scholar, was summoned, along with a hundred-odd scholars, to the Han court of Emperor Wu-ti (ruled 140–87 B.C.E.) in order to advise him. Tung Chung-shu told the emperor to practice the teachings of Confucius and to patronize only Confucianism. He advocated a Confucian system of education and government officials educated in the Six Classics. Emperor Wu was so impressed with Tung's ideas that he made Tung a chief minister and, in 125 B.C.E., founded a national academy based on the study of the Confucian classics. This school lasted until the twentieth century.

According to Tung's interpretation of the Confucian literature, there is a correspondence among

Heaven, Earth, and humans. Humans are a microcosm of the universe, and events in society are correlated with events in the natural order. The emperor ruled by Heaven's mandate and represented all humans before Heaven.

If there is, as Tung taught, an organic and dynamic correlation among Heaven, Earth, and humans, then a number of important inferences can be drawn. First, signs of Heaven's mandate can be gleaned from the study of natural events. Floods, eclipses, drought, and the like are omens and portents that must be carefully interpreted. Second, humans, especially the ruler, must act appropriately and cultivate virtue or risk disturbing the harmony of the universe. Third, there are "Three Bonds," the bonds between ruler and ruled, between father and son, and between husband and wife, which must be informed by righteousness and humaneness lest the natural order be upset and Heaven's mandate lost.

What follows are excerpts from Tung Chung-shu's book *Luxuriant Gems of the Spring and Autumn Annals (Ch'un-ch'iu fan-lu)*. As you read, you should be able to see how correlative thinking informs Tung's ideas. Joseph Needham, a scholar of Chinese science and thought, has described the correlative system as something like a huge Victorian roll-top desk with many small drawers inside: Order is created out of potential disorder by finding a place for everything *in relation* to everything else.

TUNG CHUNG-SHU

Luxuriant Gems

READING QUESTIONS

1. In what sense are Heaven, Earth, and humans the basis of all creatures?
2. What are the threefold obligations of the ruler?
3. How do Tung's teachings on human nature compare to the teachings of Mencius and Hsün Tzu?

4. What is the theory of portents, and how can this theory function as a justification of Heaven even though Heaven causes "evil" events like drought and famine?
5. Do you believe in omens and portents? Why or why not?

THE THREEFOLD OBLIGATIONS OF THE RULER

The ruler is the basis of the state. In administering the state, nothing is more effective for educating the people than reverence for the basis. If the basis is revered then the ruler may transform the people as though by supernatural power, but if the basis is not revered then the ruler will have nothing by which to lead his people. Then though he employ harsh penalties and severe punishments the people will not follow him. This is to drive the state to ruin, and there is no greater disaster. What do we mean by the basis? Heaven, earth, and man are the basis of all creatures. Heaven gives them birth, earth nourishes them, and man brings them to completion. Heaven provides them at birth with a sense of filial and brotherly love, earth nourishes them with clothing and food, and man completes them with rites and music. The three act together as hands and feet join to complete the body and none can be dispensed with. . . . If all three are lacking, then the people will become like deer, each person following his own desires, each family possessing its own ways. Fathers cannot employ their sons nor rulers their ministers, and though there be walls and battlements they will be called an "empty city." Then will the ruler lie down with a clod of earth for a pillow. No one menacing him, he will endanger himself; no one destroying him, he will destroy himself. This is called a spontaneous punishment, and when it descends, though he hide in halls of encircling stone or barricade himself behind steep defiles, he can never escape. But the enlightened and worthy ruler, being of good faith, is strictly attentive to the three bases. His sacrifices are conducted with utmost reverence; he makes offerings to and serves his ancestors; he advances brotherly affection and encourages filial conduct. In this way he serves the basis of Heaven. He personally grasps the plow handle and plows a furrow, plucks the mulberry himself and feeds the silkworms, breaks new ground to increase the grain supply and opens the way for a sufficiency of clothing and food. In this way he serves the basis of earth. He sets up schools for the nobles and in the towns and villages to teach filial piety and brotherly affection, reverence and humility. He enlightens the people with education and moves them with rites and music. Thus he serves the basis of man. If he rightly serves these three, then the people will be like sons and brothers, not daring to be unsubmissive. They will regard their country as a father or a mother, not waiting for favors to love it nor for coercion to serve it, and though they dwell in fields and camp beneath the sky they will count themselves more fortunate than if they lived in palaces. Then will the ruler go to rest on a secure pillow. Though none aid him he will grow mighty of himself, though none pacify his kingdom peace will come of its own. This is called a spontaneous reward, and when it comes, though he relinquish his throne, give up his kingdom and depart, the people will take up their children on their backs, follow him, and keep him as their lord, so that he can never leave them.

[From *Ch'un-ch'iu fan-lu*, Sec. 19, 6:7a–8a]

HUMAN NATURE AND EDUCATION

For discovering the truth about things there is no better way than to begin with names. Names show up truth and falsehood as a measuring-line shows up crooked and straight. If one inquires into the truth of a name and observes whether it is appropriate or not, then there will be no deception over the disposition of truth. Nowadays there is considerable ignorance on the question of human nature and theorists fail to agree. Why do they not try returning to the word "nature" itself? Does not the word "nature" (*hsing*) mean "birth" (*sheng*), that which one is born with?[1] The properties endowed spontaneously at birth are called the nature. The nature is the basic substance. Can the word "good," we inquire, be applied to the basic substance of the nature? No, it cannot. . . . Therefore the nature may be compared to growing rice, and goodness to refined rice. Refined rice is produced from raw rice, yet unrefined rice does not necessarily all become refined. Goodness comes from the nature of man, yet all natures do not necessarily become good. Goodness, like the refined rice, is the result of man's activities in continuing and completing Heaven's work; it is not actually existent in what Heaven itself has produced. Heaven acts to a certain degree and then ceases, and what has been created thus far is called the heavenly nature; beyond this point is called the work of man. This work lies outside of the nature, and yet by

it the nature is inevitably brought to the practice of virtue. The word "people" (*min*) is taken from the word "sleep" (*ming*). . . .

The nature may be compared to the eyes. In sleep the eyes are shut and there is darkness; they must await the wakening before they can see. At this time it may be said that they have the potential disposition to see, but it cannot be said that they see. Now the nature of all people has this potential disposition, but it is not yet awakened; it is as though it were asleep and awaiting the wakening. If it receives education, it may afterwards become good. In this condition of being not yet awakened, it can be said to have the potential disposition for goodness, but it cannot be said to be good. . . . Heaven begets the people; their nature is that of potential good, but has not yet become actual good. For this reason it sets up the king to make real their goodness. This is the will of Heaven. From Heaven the people receive their potentially good nature, and from the king the education which completes it. It is the duty and function of the king to submit to the will of Heaven, and thus to bring to completion the nature of the people.

[From *Ch'un-ch'iu fan-lu*, Sec. 35, 10:3a–5b]

THE THEORY OF PORTENTS

The creatures of Heaven and earth at times display unusual changes and these are called wonders. Lesser ones are called ominous portents. The portents always come first and are followed by wonders. Portents are Heaven's warnings, wonders are Heaven's threats. Heaven first sends warnings, and if men do not understand, then it sends wonders to awe them. This is what the *Book of Odes* means when it says: "We tremble at the awe and fearfulness of Heaven!" The genesis of all such portents and wonders is a direct result of errors in the state. When the first indications of error begin to appear in the state, Heaven sends forth ominous portents and calamities to warn men and announce the fact. If, in spite of these warnings and announcements, men still do not realize how they have gone wrong, then Heaven sends prodigies and wonders to terrify them. If, after these terrors, men still know no awe or fear, then calamity and misfortune will visit them. From this we may see that the will of Heaven is benevolent, for its has no desire to trap or betray mankind.

If we examine these wonders and portents carefully, we may discern the will of Heaven. The will of Heaven desires us to do certain things, and not to do others. As to those things which Heaven wishes and does not wish, if a man searches within himself, he will surely find

---

[1]Tung is using a favorite Chinese type of argument, that based upon the supposed affinities between characters of similar pronunciation. Such "puns," as we should call them, are intended to be taken in all seriousness.

warnings of them in his own heart, and if he looks about him at daily affairs, he will find verification of these warnings in the state. Thus we can discern the will of Heaven in these portents and wonders. We should not hate such signs, but stand in awe of them, considering that Heaven wishes to repair our faults and save us from our errors. Therefore it takes this way to warn us.

According to the principles used in writing the *Spring and Autumn Annals*, if when the ruler changed the ancient ways or departed from what was right Heaven responded and sent portents, then the country was called fortunate. . . . Because Heaven sent no portents and earth brought forth no calamities in his kingdom, King Chuang of Ch'u prayed to the mountains and streams, saying: "Will Heaven destroy me? It does not announce my faults nor show me my sins." Thus we can see how the portents of Heaven come about as a response to errors, and how wonders make these faults clear and fill us with awe. This is because of Heaven's desire to save us. Only those who receive such portents are called fortunate in the *Spring and Autumn Annals*. This is the reason why King Chuang prayed and beseeched Heaven. Now if a sage ruler or a wise lord delights in receiving remonstrances from his faithful ministers, how much more should he delight in receiving the warnings of Heaven!

[From *Ch'un-ch'iu fan-lu*, Sec. 30, 8:13b–14b]

6.3.2 The Perfect Confucian Woman

The principle of correlation, so highly valued by Han Confucianists like Tung Chung-shu, had important implications for women. One of the Three Bonds is the bond between husband and wife. Just as there are cosmological correlations between the ruler and the ruled, so too there are cosmological correspondences between husband and wife. The husband must be strong, firm, and dominant like Heaven, and the wife must be weak, pliant, and subservient like Earth. The husband's duty is to support and protect his wife, and the wife's duty is to serve her husband.

Traditional Chinese marriage practices require a daughter to leave her birth family and household upon marriage and live in her husband's house. Her husband's father and mother become her new parents, and her filial duty transfers from her birth parents to her parents-in-law. This practice places considerable stress on the new wife. It requires of women the practice of selfless virtue well beyond any demands placed on males. It is clear that women need some preparation for the demanding role of wife, es-

pecially because Confucians believe that the family is the foundation of the social order.

Pan Chao (ca. 48–ca. 112) provided that preparation in a short work called "Lessons for Women." From a prominent scholarly family, she was well educated and widely recognized for her scholarship and intellect. She became one of the foremost historians of the Han period. According to a fifth-century biography, Pan Chao worked at one of the imperial libraries editing treatises on astronomy and chronological tables of nobility. She served as court tutor for the women in the imperial family, but she wrote this particular text for the unmarried women of her own family, her daughters and nieces.

Pan Chao's "Lessons for Women" exerted considerable influence on the lives of Chinese women. This work became the model for all subsequent instructional texts for preparing women to accept the responsibilities of wives. It is something of an irony that a woman educated in the same way as a man and holding a position normally given to men should write an instructional manual admonishing women to fulfill traditional roles.

PAN CHAO

Lessons for Women

READING QUESTIONS

1. What does Pan Chao mean by "humility"?
2. What is the proper relationship between husband and wife? What makes it proper?
3. What is the main point of the chapter titled "Respect and Caution"?
4. What are the "womanly qualifications"?
5. What must a wife do to gain the love of her husband?
6. What role do the concepts of *yin* and *yang* play in Pan Chao's advice?
7. Does the advice of Pan Chao reinforce the moral, religious, and social conventions of her age, or does it subvert them? If you think it does some of both, what is subversive about her advice?

From Nancy Lee Swann, *Pan Chao: Foremost Woman Scholar of China* (New York: Russell & Russell, 1932), pp. 82–90. Copyright © 1968 by Russell & Russell. Reprinted by permission. Footnotes omitted.

INTRODUCTION

I, the unworthy writer, am unsophisticated, unenlight-ened, and by nature unintelligent, but I am fortunate both to have received not a little favor from my schol-arly father, and to have had a (cultured) mother and in-structresses upon whom to rely for a literary education as well as for training in good manners. More than forty years have passed since at the age of fourteen I took up the dustpan and the broom in the Ts'ao family. Dur-ing this time with trembling heart I feared constantly that I might disgrace my parents, and that I might mul-tiply difficulties for both the women and the men (of my husband's family). Day and night I was distressed in heart, (but) I labored without confessing weariness. Now and hereafter, however, I know how to escape (from such fears).

Being careless, and by nature stupid, I taught and trained (my children) without system. Consequently I fear that my son Ku may bring disgrace upon the Impe-rial Dynasty by whose Holy Grace he has unprecedent-edly received the extraordinary privilege of wearing the Gold and the Purple, a privilege for the attainment of which (by my son, I) a humble subject never even hoped. Nevertheless, now that he is a man and able to plan his own life, I need not again have concern for him. But I do grieve that you, my daughters, just now at the age for marriage, have not at this time had gradual training and advice; that you still have not learned the proper cus-toms for married women. I fear that by failure in good manners in other families you will humiliate both your ancestors and your clan. I am now seriously ill, life is un-certain. As I have thought of you all in so untrained a state, I have been uneasy many a time for you. At hours of leisure I have composed in seven chapters these in-structions under the title, "Lessons for Women." In or-der that you have something wherewith to benefit your persons, I wish every one of you, my daughters, each to write out a copy for yourself.

From this time on every one of you strive to practise these (lessons).

CHAPTER I HUMILITY

On the third day after the birth of a girl the ancients ob-served three customs: (first) to place the baby below the bed; (second) to give her a potsherd with which to play; and (third) to announce her birth to her ancestors by an offering. Now to lay the baby below the bed plainly in-dicated that she is lowly and weak, and should regard it as her primary duty to humble herself before others. To give her potsherds with which to play indubitably signi-fied that she should practise labor and consider it her primary duty to be industrious. To announce her birth before her ancestors clearly meant that she ought to es-teem as her primary duty the continuation of the obser-vance of worship in the home.

These three ancient customs epitomize a woman's ordinary way of life and the teachings of the traditional ceremonial rites and regulations. Let a woman modestly yield to others; let her respect others; let her put others first, herself last. Should she do something good, let her not mention it; should she do something bad, let her not deny it. Let her bear disgrace; let her even endure when others speak or do evil to her. Always let her seem to tremble and to fear. (When a woman follows such max-ims as these,) then she may be said to humble herself be-fore others.

Let a woman retire late to bed, but rise early to duties; let her not dread tasks by day or by night. Let her not re-fuse to perform domestic duties whether easy or diffi-cult. That which must be done, let her finish completely, tidily, and systematically. (When a woman follows such rules as these,) then she may be said to be industrious.

Let a woman be correct in manner and upright in character in order to serve her husband. Let her live in purity and quietness (of spirit), and attend to her own affairs. Let her love not gossip and silly laughter. Let her cleanse and purify and arrange in order the wine and the food for the offerings to the ancestors. (When a woman observes such principles as these,) then she may be said to continue ancestral worship.

No woman who observes these three (fundamentals of life) has ever had a bad reputation or fallen into dis-grace. If a woman fail to observe them, how can her name be honored; how can she but bring disgrace upon herself?

CHAPTER II HUSBAND AND WIFE

The Way of husband and wife is intimately connected with *Yin* and *Yang*, and relates the individual to gods and ancestors. Truly it is the great principle of Heaven and Earth, and the great basis of human relationships. Therefore the "Rites" honor union of man and woman; and in the "Book of Poetry" the "First Ode" manifests the principle of marriage. For these reasons the rela-tionship cannot but be an important one.

If a husband be unworthy, then he possesses nothing by which to control his wife. If a wife be unworthy, then she possesses nothing with which to serve her husband. If a husband does not control his wife, then the rules of conduct manifesting his authority are abandoned and broken. If a wife does not serve her husband, then the proper relationship (between men and women) and the natural order of things are neglected and destroyed. As a matter of fact the purpose of these two (the controlling of women by men, and the serving of men by women) is the same.

Now examine the gentlemen of the present age. They only know that wives must be controlled, and that the husband's rules of conduct manifesting his authority must be established. They therefore teach their boys to read books and (study) histories. But they do not in the least understand that husbands and masters must (also) be served, and that the proper relationship and the rites should be maintained.

Yet only to teach men and not to teach women,—is that not ignoring the essential relation between them? According to the "Rites," it is the rule to begin to teach children to read at the age of eight years, and by the age of fifteen years they ought then to be ready for cultural training. Only why should it not be (that girls' education as well as boys' be) according to this principle?

to licentiousness. Out of licentiousness will be born a heart of disrespect to the husband. Such a result comes from not knowing that one should stay in one's proper place.

Furthermore, affairs may be either crooked or straight; words may be either right or wrong. Straightforwardness cannot but lead to quarreling; crookedness cannot but lead to accusation. If there are really accusations and quarrels, then undoubtedly there will be angry affairs. Such a result comes from not esteeming others, and not honoring and serving (them).

(If wives) suppress not contempt for husbands, then it follows (that such wives) rebuke and scold (their husbands). (If husbands) stop not short of anger, then they are certain to beat (their wives). The correct relationship between husband and wife is based upon harmony and intimacy, and (conjugal) love is grounded in proper union. Should actual blows be dealt, how could matrimonial relationship be preserved? Should sharp words be spoken, how could (conjugal) love exist? If love and proper relationship both be destroyed, then husband and wife are divided.

CHAPTER III RESPECT AND CAUTION

As *Yin* and *Yang* are not of the same nature, so man and woman have different characteristics. The distinctive quality of the *Yang* is rigidity; the function of the *Yin* is yielding. Man is honored for strength; a woman is beautiful on account of her gentleness. Hence there arose the common saying: "A man though born like a wolf may, it is feared, become a weak monstrosity; a woman though born like a mouse may, it is feared, become a tiger."

Now for self-culture nothing equals respect for others. To counteract firmness nothing equals compliance. Consequently it can be said that the Way of respect and acquiescence is woman's most important principle of conduct. So respect may be defined as nothing other than holding on to that which is permanent; and acquiescence nothing other than being liberal and generous. Those who are steadfast in devotion know that they should stay in their proper places; those who are liberal and generous esteem others, and honor and serve (them).

If husband and wife have the habit of staying together, never leaving one another, and following each other around within the limited space of their own rooms, then they will lust after and take liberties with one another. From such action improper language will arise between the two. This kind of discussion may lead

CHAPTER IV WOMANLY QUALIFICATIONS

A woman (ought to) have four qualifications: (1) womanly virtue; (2) womanly words; (3) womanly bearing; and (4) womanly work. Now what is called womanly virtue need not be brilliant ability, exceptionally different from others. Womanly words need be neither clever in debate nor keen in conversation. Womanly appearance requires neither a pretty nor a perfect face and form. Womanly work need not be work done more skillfully than that of others.

To guard carefully her chastity; to control circumspectly her behavior; in every motion to exhibit modesty; and to model each act on the best usage, this is womanly virtue.

To choose her words with care; to avoid vulgar language; to speak at appropriate times; and not to weary others (with much conversation), may be called the characteristics of womanly words.

To wash and scrub filth away; to keep clothes and ornaments fresh and clean; to wash the head and bathe the body regularly, and to keep the person free from disgraceful filth, may be called the characteristics of womanly bearing.

With whole-hearted devotion to sew and to weave; to love not gossip and silly laughter; in cleanliness and order (to prepare) the wine and food for serving guests, may be called the characteristics of womanly work.

These four qualifications characterize the greatest virtue of a woman. No woman can afford to be without them. In fact they are very easy to possess if a woman only treasure them in her heart. The ancients had a saying: "Is Love afar off? If I desire love, then love is at hand!" So can it be said of these qualifications.

CHAPTER V
WHOLE-HEARTED DEVOTION

Now in the "Rites" is written the principle that a husband may marry again, but there is no Canon that authorizes a woman to be married the second time. Therefore it is said of husbands as of Heaven, that as certainly as people cannot run away from Heaven, so surely a wife cannot leave (a husband's home).

If people in action or character disobey the spirits of Heaven and of Earth, then Heaven punishes them. Likewise if a woman errs in the rites and in the proper mode of conduct, then her husband esteems her lightly. The ancient book, "A Pattern for Women" (*Nü Hsien*), says: "To obtain the love of one man is the crown of a woman's life; to lose the love of one man is to miss the aim in woman's life." For these reasons a woman cannot but seek to win her husband's heart. Nevertheless, the beseeching wife need not use flattery, coaxing words, and cheap methods to gain intimacy.

Decidedly nothing is better (to gain the heart of a husband) than whole-hearted devotion and correct manners. In accordance with the rites and the proper mode of conduct, (let a woman) live a pure life. Let her have ears that hear not licentiousness; and eyes that see not depravity. When she goes outside her own home, let her not be conspicuous in dress and manners. When at home let her not neglect her dress. Women should not assemble in groups, nor gather together, (for gossip and silly laughter). They should not stand watching in the gateways. (If a woman follows) these rules, she may be said to have whole-hearted devotion and correct manners.

If, in all her actions, she is frivolous, she sees and hears (only) that which pleases herself. At home her hair is dishevelled, and her dress is slovenly. Outside the home she emphasizes her femininity to attract attention; she says what ought not to be said; and she looks at what ought not to be seen. (If a woman does such as) these, (she may be) said to be without whole-hearted devotion and correct manners.

CHAPTER VI IMPLICIT OBEDIENCE

Now "to win the love of one man is the crown of a woman's life; to lose the love of one man is her eternal disgrace." This saying advises a fixed will and a whole-hearted devotion for a woman. Ought she then to lose the hearts of her father- and mother-in-law?

There are times when love may lead to differences of opinion (between individuals); there are times when duty may lead to disagreement. Even should the husband say that he loves something, when the parents-in-law say "no," this is called a case of duty leading to disagreement. This being so, then what about the hearts of the parents-in-law? Nothing is better than an obedience which sacrifices personal opinion.

Whenever the mother-in-law says, "Do not do that," and if what she says is right, unquestionably the daughter-in-law obeys. Whenever the mother-in-law says, "Do that," even if what she says is wrong, still the daughter-in-law submits unfailingly to the command.

Let a woman not act contrary to the wishes and the opinions of parents-in-law about right and wrong; let her not dispute with them what is straight and what is crooked. Such (docility) may be called obedience which sacrifices personal opinion. Therefore the ancient book, "A Pattern for Women," says: "If a daughter-in-law (who follows the wishes of her parents-in-law) is like an echo and a shadow, how could she not be praised?"

CHAPTER VII HARMONY
WITH YOUNGER BROTHERS-
AND SISTERS-IN-LAW

In order for a wife to gain the love of her husband, she must win for herself the love of her parents-in-law. To win for herself the love of her parents-in-law, she must secure for herself the good will of younger brothers- and sisters-in-law. For these reasons the right and the wrong, the praise and the blame of a woman alike depend upon younger brothers- and sisters-in-law. Consequently it will not do for a woman to lose their affection.

They are stupid both who know not that they must not lose (the hearts of) younger brothers- and sisters-in-law, and who cannot be in harmony with them in order to be intimate with them. Excepting only the Holy Men, few are able to be faultless. Now Yen Tzû's greatest virtue was that he was able to reform. Confucius praised him (for not committing a misdeed) the second time. (In comparison with him) a woman is the more likely (to make mistakes).

Although a woman possesses a worthy woman's qualifications, and is wise and discerning by nature, is she able to be perfect? Yet if a woman live in harmony with her immediate family, unfavorable criticism will be silenced (within the home. But) if a man and woman disagree, then this evil will be noised abroad. Such consequences are inevitable. The "Book of Changes" says:

> Should two hearts harmonize,
> The united strength can cut gold,
> Words from hearts which agree,
> Give forth fragrance like the orchid.

This saying may be applied to (harmony in the home).

Though a daughter-in-law and her younger sisters-in-law are equal in rank, nevertheless (they should) respect (each other); though love (between them may be) sparse, their proper relationship should be intimate. Only the virtuous, the beautiful, the modest, and the respectful (young women) can accordingly rely upon the sense of duty to make their affection sincere, and magnify love to bind their relationships firmly.

Then the excellence and the beauty of such a daughter-in-law becomes generally known. Moreover, any flaws and mistakes are hidden and unrevealed. Parents-in-law boast of her good deeds; her husband is satisfied with her. Praise of her radiates, making her illustrious in district and in neighborhood; and her brightness reaches to her own father and mother.

But a stupid and foolish person as an elder sister-in-law uses her rank to exalt herself; as a younger sister-in-law, because of parents' favor, she becomes filled with arrogance. If arrogant, how can a woman live in harmony with others? If love and proper relationships be perverted, how can praise be secured? In such instances the wife's good is hidden, and her faults are declared. The mother-in-law will be angry, and the husband will be indignant. Blame will reverberate and spread in and outside the home. Disgrace will gather upon the daughter-in-law's person, on the one hand to add humiliation to her own father and mother, and on the other to increase the difficulties of her husband.

Such then is the basis for both honor and disgrace; the foundation for reputation or for ill-repute. Can a woman be too cautious? Consequently to seek the hearts of young brothers- and sisters-in-law decidedly nothing can be esteemed better than modesty and Acquiescence.

Modesty is virtue's handle; acquiescence is the wife's (most refined) characteristic. All who possess these two have sufficient for harmony with others. In the "Book of Poetry" it is written that "here is no evil; there is no dart." So it may be said of (these two, modesty and acquiescence).

6.4 THE DEFENSE OF THE CONFUCIAN WAY (220–907)

From the fall of the Han dynasty in 220 to the end of the T'ang dynasty in 907, state-sponsored Confucianism lost some of its previous influence. This is the golden era of Chinese Buddhism, and, along with Taoism, it attracted imperial favor, the attention of the intellectual elite, and a widespread following among the masses.

When Confucianism became the officially recognized state cult under the Han, it enjoyed considerable imperial patronage. Temples, libraries, and a university were built. Artworks were commissioned, scholars were employed, Confucian music and dance flourished, and there were elaborate public rites, sacrifices, and seasonal rituals. However, there is always a price to pay for state favors. That price is independence.

Confucianism had become dependent on the state, and when imperial favoritism waned, so did the fortunes of Confucianism. The conquest of Northern China by people from Central Asia introduced Buddhism into China. At first Buddhism was considered a relative of Taoism, but in time it spread and broadened its appeal, thereby establishing its autonomy with respect to both Confucianism and Taoism. During this Confucian winter, Confucians found themselves in fierce competition with Buddhism and Taoism for the emperor's patronage, the intellectuals' minds, and the loyalty of the masses.

6.4.1 The True Way

Han Yü (768–829) was one Confucian among others who championed the Confucian cause. In his famous *An Inquiry on Human Nature* (*Yüan-hsing*), he revived the debate about human nature and offered his theory of the "Three Grades." According to this theory, human nature has three grades: superior, medium, and inferior. The superior grade is the only good grade because at this level the Five Virtues of humanity (*jen*), righteousness (*i*), propriety (*li*), wisdom (*chih*), and loyalty (*chung*) are practiced in their purity. At the other end of the scale, the inferior grade, a person rebels against at least one of these virtues and is out of harmony with the others. The medium grade, in between the superior and the inferior, tends toward one or the other end of the scale depending on how many of the Five Virtues are sincerely practiced.

Beyond reviving Confucian interest in the debate over human nature, Han Yü waged a campaign against both Buddhism and Taoism. He asserted the superiority of Confucianism and advised the emperor to favor Confucianism alone.

Confucianists had never been happy with the reclusive tendencies of Taoism and Buddhism. Buddhism, in particular, counseled sons and daughters to leave home and become monks or nuns. They should forsake the world, not marry, and thus not produce children. This violated the norms of Confucianism at its deepest level because if monastic lifestyles should prevail, the sacred ancestral line would stop. This would undermine the family and, eventually, according to Confucian thought, undermine humanity.

Below are two selections from Yan Yü, in which he attacks Buddhism and argues that Confucianism represents the true way. Han Yü did not find many adherents in his own day because the view of Taoism and Buddhism as complementary to Confucianism had become well entrenched. However, Han Yü was rediscovered later by one of the first leaders of the Confucian revival. He became a virtual patron saint of Neo-Confucianism.

HAN YÜ

Memorial on the Bone of Buddha and What Is the True Way?

READING QUESTIONS

1. What are Han Yü's objections to Buddhism in general and to the emperor's participation in a ceremony honoring a relic of the Buddha in particular?
2. How do you think Han Yü reconciled his commitment to the Confucian principle of benevolence (*jen*) and his attack on Taoism and Buddhism?

Republished with permission of Columbia University Press, 562 W. 113th St., New York, NY 10025. *Sources of the Chinese Tradition*, compiled by Wm. Theodore De Bary, Wing-tsit Chan, and Burton Watson, 1960. Reproduced by permission of the publisher via Copyright Clearance Center, Inc. pp. 372–374, 376–379. Footnotes edited.

3. Some advocates of different religious today also preach both love of humanity and hatred toward those seen as religiously different. Why do you think this is the case?

MEMORIAL ON THE BONE OF BUDDHA

Your servant begs leave to say that Buddhism is no more than a cult of the barbarian peoples which spread to China in the time of the Latter Han. It did not exist here in ancient times. . . . When Emperor Kao-tsu [founder of the T'ang] received the throne from the House of Sui, he deliberated upon the suppression of Buddhism. But at that time the various officials, being of small worth and knowledge, were unable fully to comprehend the ways of the ancient kings and the exigencies of past and present, and so could not implement the wisdom of the emperor and rescue the age from corruption. Thus the matter came to nought, to your servant's constant regret.

Now Your Majesty, wise in the arts of peace and war, unparalleled in divine glory from countless ages past, upon your accession prohibited men and women from taking Buddhist orders and forbade the erection of temples and monasteries, and your servant believed that at Your Majesty's hand the will of Kao-tsu would be carried out. Even if the suppression of Buddhism should be as yet impossible, your servant hardly thought that Your Majesty would encourage it and on the contrary cause it to spread. Yet now your servant hears that Your Majesty has ordered the community of monks to go to Feng-hsiang to greet the bone of Buddha, that Your Majesty will ascend a tower to watch as it is brought into the palace, and that the various temples have been commanded to welcome and worship it in turn. Though your servant is abundantly ignorant, he understands that Your Majesty is not so misled by Buddhism as to honor it thus in hopes of receiving some blessing or reward, but only that, the year being one of plenty and the people joyful, Your Majesty would accord with the hearts of the multitude in setting forth for the officials and citizens of the capital some curious show and toy for their amusement. How could it be, indeed, that with such sagely wisdom Your Majesty should in truth give credence to these affairs? But the common people are ignorant and dull, easily misled and hard to enlighten, and should they see their emperor do these things, they might say that Your Majesty was serving Buddhism with a true heart. "The Son of Heaven is a Great Sage," they would cry, "and yet he reverences and believes with all his heart! How should we, the common people, then begrudge our bodies and our lives?" Then would they set about singeing their heads and scorching their fingers,[1] binding together in groups of ten and a hundred, doffing their common clothes and scattering their money, from morning to evening urging each other on lest one be slow, till old and young alike had abandoned their occupations to follow [Buddhism]. If this is not checked and the bone is carried from one temple to another, there will be those who will cut off their arms and mutilate their flesh in offering [to the Buddha]. Then will our old ways be corrupted, our customs violated, and the tale will spread to make us the mockery of the world. This is no trifling matter!

Now Buddha was a man of the barbarians who did not speak the language of China and wore clothes of a different fashion. His sayings did not concern the ways of our ancient kings, nor did his manner of dress conform to their laws. He understood neither the duties that bind sovereign and subject, nor the affections of father and son. If he were still alive today and came to our court by order of his ruler, Your Majesty might condescend to receive him, but it would amount to no more than one audience in the Hsüan-cheng Hall, a banquet by the Office for Receiving Guests, the presentation of a suit of clothes, and he would then be escorted to the borders of the nation, dismissed, and not allowed to delude the masses. How then, when he has long been dead, could his rotten bones, the foul and unlucky remains of his body, be rightly admitted to the palace? Confucius said: "Respect ghosts and spirits, but keep them at a distance!" So when the princes of ancient times went to pay their condolences at a funeral within the state, they sent exorcists in advance with peach wands to drive out evil, and only then would they advance. Now without reason Your Majesty has caused this loathsome thing to be brought in and would personally go to view it. No exorcists have been sent ahead, no peach wands employed. The host of officials have not spoken out against this wrong, and the censors have failed to note its impropriety. Your servant is deeply shamed and begs that this bone be given to the proper authorities to be cast into fire and water, that this evil may be rooted out, the world freed from its error, and later generations spared this delusion. Then may all men know how the acts of their wise sovereign transcend the commonplace a thousandfold. Would this not be glorious? Would it not be joyful?

Should the Buddha indeed have supernatural power to send down curses and calamities, may they fall only upon the person of your servant, who calls upon High Heaven to witness that he does not regret his words.

With all gratitude and sincerity your servant presents this memorial for consideration, being filled with respect and awe.

[From *Ch'ang-li hsien-sheng wen-chi*, SPTK ed., 39:2b–4b]

WHAT IS THE TRUE WAY? (YÜAN TAO)

. . . To love universally is called humanity (*jen*); to apply this in a proper manner is called righteousness (*i*). The operation of these is the Way (*Tao*), and its inner power (*te*) is that it is self-sufficient, requiring nothing from outside itself. Humanity and righteousness are fixed principles, but the Way and its inner power are speculative concepts. Thus we have the way of the gentleman and the way of the small man, and both good and evil power. Lao Tzu made light of humanity and righteousness, but he did not thereby abolish them. His view was narrow like that of a man who sits at the bottom of a well and looks up at the sky, saying, "The sky is small." This does not mean that the sky is really small. Lao Tzu understood humanity and righteousness in only a very limited sense, and therefore it is natural that he belittled them. What he called the Way was only the Way as he saw it, and not what I call the Way; what he called inner power was only power as he saw it, and not what I call inner power. What I call the Way and power are a combination of humanity and righteousness and this is the definition accepted by the world at large. But what Lao Tzu called the Way and power are stripped of humanity and righteousness, and represent only the private view of one individual.

After the decline of the Chou and the death of Confucius, in the time of Ch'in's book burnings, the Taoism of the Han, and the Buddhism of the Wei, the Chin, the Liang, and the Sui, when men spoke of the Way and power, of humanity and righteousness, they were approaching them either as followers of Yang Chu or of Mo Tzu, of Lao Tzu or of Buddha. Being followers of these doctrines, they naturally rejected Confucianism. Acknowledging these men as their masters, they made of Confucius an outcast, adhering to new teachings and vilifying the old. Alas, though men of later ages long to know of humanity and righteousness, the Way and inner power, from whom may they hear of them? . . .

In ancient times there were only four classes of people, but now there are six.[2] There was only one teach-

---

[1] Acts symbolic of a person's renunciation of the world upon entering Buddhist orders.

[2] The four classes of traditional Chinese society—official, farmer, artisan, and merchant—to which were added the Taoist and the Buddhist clergy.

ing, where now there are three.[3] For each family growing grain, there are now six consuming it; for each family producing utensils, there are six using them; for one family engaged in trade, six others take their profits. Is it surprising then that the people are reduced to poverty and driven to theft?

In ancient times men faced many perils, but sages arose who taught them how to protect and nourish their lives, acting as their rulers and teachers. They drove away the harmful insects and reptiles, birds and beasts, and led men to settle in the center of the earth. The people were cold and they made them clothes, hungry and they gave them food. Because men had dwelt in danger in the tops of trees or grown sick sleeping on the ground, they built them halls and dwellings. They taught them handicrafts that they might have utensils to use, trades so that they could supply their wants, medicine to save them from early death, proper burial and sacrifices to enhance their sense of love and gratitude, rites to order the rules of precedence, music to express their repressed feelings, government to lead the indolent, and punishments to suppress the overbearing. Because men cheated each other, they made tallies and seals, measures and scales to insure confidence; because men plundered they made walls and fortifications, armor and weapons to protect them. Thus they taught men how to prepare against danger and prevent injury to their lives.

Now the Taoists tell us that "until the sages die off, robbers will never disappear," or that "if we destroy our measures and break our scales then the people will cease their contention." Alas, how thoughtless are such sayings! If there had been no sages in ancient times, then mankind would have perished, for men have no feathers or fur, no scales or shells to protect them from cold and heat, no claws and teeth to contend for food. Therefore those who are rulers give commands which are carried out by their officials and made known to the people, and the people produce grain, rice, hemp, and silk, make utensils and exchange commodities for the support of the superiors. If the ruler fails to issue commands, then he ceases to be a ruler, while if his subordinates do not carry them out and extend them to the people, and if the people do not produce goods for the support of their superiors, they must be punished. Yet the Way [of the Taoists and Buddhists] teaches men to reject the ideas of ruler and subject and of father and son, to cease from activities which sustain life and seek for some so-called purity and Nirvāna. Alas, it is fortunate for such doctrines that they appeared only after the time of the Three Reigns and thus escaped suppression at the hands of Yü

and T'ang, kings Wen and Wu, the Duke of Chou and Confucius, but unfortunate for us what they did not appear before the Three Reigns so that they could have been rectified by those sages. . . .

The *Book of Rites* says: "The ancients who wished to illustrate illustrious virtue throughout the kingdom first ordered well their own states. Wishing to order well their states, they first regulated their families. Wishing to regulate their families, they first cultivated their persons. Wishing to cultivate their persons, they first rectified their hearts. Wishing to rectify their hearts, they first sought to be sincere in their thoughts" [*Great Learning*, I]. Thus when the ancients spoke of rectifying the heart and being sincere in their thoughts, they had this purpose in mind. But now [the Taoists and Buddhists] seek to govern their hearts by escaping from the world, the state and the family. They violate the natural law, so that the son does not regard his father as a father, the subject does not look upon his ruler as a ruler, and the people do not serve those whom they must serve.

When Confucius wrote in the *Spring and Autumn Annals*, he treated as barbarians those feudal lords who observed barbarian customs, and as Chinese those who had advanced to the use of Chinese ways. The *Analects* [III, 5] says: "The barbarians with rulers are not the equal of the Chinese without rulers." The *Book of Odes* [Odes of Lu, 4] says: "Fight against the barbarians of the west and north, punish those of Ching and Shu." Yet now [the Buddhists] come with their barbarian ways and put them ahead of the teachings of our ancient kings. Are they not become practically barbarians themselves?

What were these teachings of our ancient kings? To love universally, which is called humanity; to apply this in the proper manner, which is called righteousness; to proceed from these to the Way and to be self-sufficient without seeking anything outside, which is called [inner] power. The *Odes* and the *History*, the *Changes* and the *Spring and Autumn Annals*, are their writings; rites and music, punishments and government, their methods. Their people were the four classes of officials, farmers, artisans, and merchants; their relationships were those of sovereign and subject, father and son, teacher and friend, guest and host, elder and younger brother, and husband and wife. Their clothing was hemp and silk; their dwelling halls and houses; their food grain and rice, fruit and vegetables, fish and meat. Their ways were easy to understand; their teachings simple to follow. Applied to oneself, they brought harmony and blessing; applied to others, love and fairness. To the mind they gave peace; to the state and the family all that was just and fitting. Thus in life men were able to satisfy their emotions, and at death the obligations due them were fulfilled. Men sacrificed to Heaven and the gods were

---

[3] Confucianism, to which was added Taoism and Buddhism.

pleased; to the spirits of their ancestors and the ancestors received their offerings. What Way is this? It is
what *I* call the Way, and not what the Taoists and Buddhists call the Way. Yao taught it to Shun, Shun to Yü,
Yü to T'ang, and T'ang to kings Wen and Wu and the
Duke of Chou. These men taught it to Confucius and
Confucius to Mencius, but when Mencius died it was no
longer handed down. Hsün Tzu and Yang Hsiung understood elements of it, but their understanding lacked
depth; they spoke of it but incompletely. In the days before the Duke of Chou, the sages were rulers and so they
could put the Way into practice, but after the time of
the Duke of Chou they were only officials and so they
wrote at length about the Way.

What should be done now? I say that unless [Taoism
and Buddhism] are suppressed, the Way will not prevail; unless these men are stopped, the Way will not be
practiced. Let their priests be turned into ordinary men
again, let their books be burned and their temples converted into homes. Let the Way of our former kings
be made clear to lead them, and let the widower and the
widow, the orphan and the lonely, the crippled and the
sick be nourished. Then all will be well.

[From *Ch'ang-li hsien-sheng wen-chi*,
SPTK ed., 11:1a–3b]

6.5 NEO-CONFUCIANISM (960–1644)

Some of the Chinese literati who had embraced Buddhism begin, in the eleventh century, to question it
for a variety of reasons. Among them was the growing belief that Buddhism was a foreign religion, fit
for "barbarians" who taught doctrines destructive of
Chinese family traditions. These intellectuals began
to embrace Confucianism once more and revived the
tradition among the elite after the long Confucian
winter that had begun with the fall of the Han dynasty in 220 and the state-supported cult of Confucius. This revival is known in China as the "Study
of Nature and Propriety" and in the West as Neo-
Confucianism.

Buddhist philosophical speculation on the nature
of ultimate reality and the intellectual rigor of Buddhist metaphysical debates had appealed to the Chinese literati. In light of this, it is not surprising to find
the renewal of Confucianism concerning itself with
cosmological and ontological questions.

6.5.1 The Great Ultimate

One of the philosophers responsible for the Con-
fucian revival is Chou Tun-i (1017–1073), who
is sometimes referred to as the pioneer of Neo-
Confucianism. He discussed what were to become
some of its principal themes in two short treatises:
An Explanation of the Diagram of the Great Ultimate
(*T'ai-chi-t'u shuo*) and *Penetrating the Book of Changes*
(*T'ung-shu*).

The *Book of Changes* (*I-Ching*) is one of the *Five
Classics* and had long been used for purposes of divination as well as a source for understanding how nature operates. The book shows sixty-four abstract
symbols made of solid (*yang*) and broken (*yin*) lines.
Yang lines represent all strong, active, creative, dominate, male, bright, high, and other associated forces in
the universe, whereas **yin** lines represent all the weak,
passive, receptive, submissive, female, dark, low, and
other associated forces. For example, the first hexagram (an image of six lines) is called the Creative
Principle and the second is called the Receptive, or
Passive, Principle.

The Creative	The Receptive
——————	—— ——
——————	—— ——
——————	—— ——
——————	—— ——
——————	—— ——
——————	—— ——

Each hexagram is made up of three trigrams (units
of three lines). The remaining sixty-two hexagrams
are made up of different combinations of *yang* and *yin*
lines. If you faced a problem and wished advice, you
could ask a question and throw some coins or sticks
that yield a *yang/yin* pattern leading you to one of
the hexagrams. That hexagram, rightly interpreted, is
thought to contain the answer to your question. Over
the centuries, various commentaries were written on
the hexagrams in the belief that the secret workings
of nature as a dynamic interaction of *yang/yin* forces
were inscribed in the *Book of Changes*.

Chou Tun-i's comments on the *I-Ching* brought
the book into the forefront of Confucian thought and
thus made metaphysical speculation more prominent
in Confucianism than it had been before. Likewise,
his writing on the Great Ultimate, or **T'ai-chi**, reinforced the newfound interest in metaphysics and
thereby made Confucianism more intellectually com-

petitive with both Taoism and Buddhism. It is possible to see both Taoist and Buddhist metaphysical speculation in Chou Tun-i's claim that *T'ai-chi* is equal to the "Ultimate of Non-being" (*wu-chi*). The movement of *T'ai-chi* generates *yang* forces, and its rest generates *yin* forces. As these two forces interact, the "five elements" that make up the world as it appears to us are generated.

YIN/YANG

Yin-Yang

CHOU TUN-I

An Explanation of the Diagram of the Great Ultimate and Penetrating the Book of Changes

READING QUESTIONS

1. Some scholars have characterized the cosmology presupposed by Chou Tun-i's explanation of the diagram of the Great Ultimate as one of "organic harmony." Do you agree? Why or why not?
2. What do you think is meant by the claim that fundamentally the Great Ultimate is the Non-ultimate? (See "Comment" by the translator, Wing-tsit Chan.)
3. How does this cosmological explanation of the universe differ from creation stories you have read?

From Chan, Wing-tsit, *A Source Book in Chinese Philosophy*, pp. 463–467, 473–474, Copyright © 1963, renewed 1991 by Princeton University Press. Reprinted by permission of Princeton University Press. Footnotes edited.

4. What is sincerity, and how does it relate to "sagehood"?
5. How can sincerity be said to give rise to both "good and evil"? What exactly is "evil" in this context?
6. What are the marks of a sage, and how does one become a sage?

AN EXPLANATION OF THE DIAGRAM OF THE GREAT ULTIMATE

The Ultimate of Non-being and also the Great Ultimate (*T'ai-chi*)! The Great Ultimate through movement generates yang. When its activity reaches its limit, it becomes tranquil. Through tranquility the Great Ultimate generates yin. When tranquility reaches its limit, activity begins again. So movement and tranquility alternate and become the root of each other, giving rise to the distinction of yin and yang, and the two modes are thus established.

By the transformation of yang and its union with yin, the Five Agents of Water, Fire, Wood, Metal, and Earth arise. When these five material forces (*ch'i*) are distributed in harmonious order, the four seasons run their course.

The Five Agents constitute one system of yin and yang, and yin and yang constitute one Great Ultimate. The Great Ultimate is fundamentally the Non-ultimate. The Five Agents arise, each with its specific nature.

When the reality of the Ultimate of Non-being and the essence of yin, yang, and the Five Agents come into mysterious union, integration ensues. *Ch'ien* (Heaven) constitutes the male element, and *k'un* (Earth) constitutes the female element. The interaction of these two material forces engenders and transforms the myriad things. The myriad things produce and reproduce, resulting in an unending transformation.

It is man alone who receives (the Five Agents) in their highest excellence, and therefore he is most intelligent. His physical form appears, and his spirit develops consciousness. The five moral principles of his nature (humanity or *jen*, righteousness, propriety, wisdom, and faithfulness) are aroused by, and react to, the external world and engage in activity; good and evil are distinguished; and human affairs take place.

The sage settles these affairs by the principles of the Mean, correctness, humanity, and righteousness (for the way of the sage is none other than these four), regarding tranquility as fundamental. (Having no desire, there will therefore be tranquility.) Thus he establishes himself as the ultimate standard for man. Hence the character of the sage is "identical with that of Heaven and Earth; his brilliancy is identical with that of the sun and moon; his order is identical with that of the four seasons; and his good and evil fortunes are identical with those of spiritual beings." The superior man cultivates these moral qualities and enjoys good fortune, whereas the inferior man violates them and suffers evil fortune.

Therefore it is said that "yin and yang are established as the way of Heaven, the weak and the strong as the way of Earth, and humanity and righteousness as the way of man." It is also said that "if we investigate the cycle of things, we shall understand the concepts of life and death." Great is the *Book of Changes!* Herein lies its excellence! (*Chou Tzu ch'üan-shu*, chs. 1–2, pp. 4–32)

Comment. This *Explanation* has provided the essential outline of Neo-Confucian metaphysics and cosmology in the last eight hundred years. Few short Chinese treatises like this have exerted so much influence. Although the whole concept owes much to the *Book of Changes*, it is to be noted that it rejected the idea of the Eight Trigrams of the *Book of Changes* and used the Five Agents instead, thus showing that the system was the product of Chou Tun-i's own speculation.

A great amount of literature has grown up on the history of the diagram and on the concept of the Great Ultimate. So far as philosophy is concerned, most Neo-Confucianists have followed Chou although they have differed in many details. However, two of Chou's ideas have aroused considerable criticism. One is the idea of the Non-ultimate. One of the famous debates between Chu Hsi and Lu Hsiang-shan (Lu Chiu-yüan, 1139–1193) was over this idea. The word *erh* in the opening sentence means "and also" or "in turn." But it can be interpreted in the sense of "and then," in which case, the Non-ultimate and the Great Ultimate would be two separate entities. This was precisely what Lu Hsiang-shan was objecting to, as he saw in Chou Tun-i a bifurcation of reality as two. On the other hand, Chu Hsi claimed that Chou never meant that there is a Non-ultimate outside of the Great Ultimate, that the Non-ultimate is the state of reality before the appearance of forms whereas the Great Ultimate is the state after the appearance of forms, and that the two form a unity. This interpretation has been accepted by most Neo-Confucianists. . . .

PENETRATING THE BOOK OF CHANGES

Ch. 1. Sincerity, Pt. 1

Sincerity (*ch'eng*)[1] is the foundation of the sage. "Great is the *ch'ien*, the originator! All things, obtain their beginning from it." It is the source of sincerity. "The way of *ch'ien* is to change and transform so that everything will obtain its correct nature and destiny." In this way sincerity is established. It is pure and perfectly good. Therefore "the successive movement of yin and yang constitutes the Way (Tao). What issues from the Way is good, and that which realizes it is the individual nature." Origination and flourish characterize the penetration of sincerity, and advantage and firmness are its completion (or recovery). Great is the Change, the source of nature and destiny!

Ch. 2. Sincerity, Pt. 2

Sagehood is nothing but sincerity. It is the foundation of the Five Constant Virtues (humanity, righteousness, propriety, wisdom, and faithfulness) and the source of all activities. When tranquil, it is in the state of non-being, and when active, it is in the state of being. It is perfectly correct and clearly penetrating. Without sincerity, the Five Constant Virtues and all activities will be wrong. They will be depraved and obstructed. Therefore with sincerity very little effort is needed [to achieve the Mean]. [In itself] it is perfectly easy but it is difficult to put into practice. But with determination and firmness, there will be no difficulty. Therefore it is said, "If a man can for one day master himself and return to propriety, all under heaven will return to humanity."

Ch. 3. Sincerity Is the Subtle, Incipient, Activating Force (Chi) of Virtue

Sincerity [in its original substance] engages in no activity, but is the subtle, incipient, activating force giving rise to good and evil. The virtue of loving is called humanity, that of doing what is proper is called righteousness, that of putting things in order is called propriety, that of penetration is called wisdom, and that of abiding by one's commitments is called faithfulness. One who is in accord with his nature and acts with ease is a sage. One who returns to his nature and adheres to it is a wor-

---

[1]This word means not only sincerity in the narrow sense, but also honesty, absence of fault, seriousness, being true to one's true self, being true to the nature of being, actuality, realness.

thy. And one whose subtle emanation cannot be seen and whose [goodness] is abundant and all-pervasive without limit is a man of the spirit.

Comment. The first sentence of this chapter occasioned a great deal of discussion among Neo-Confucianists. Chou seems to contradict himself, for sincerity, being the original state of man's moral nature, is perfectly good and yet it gives rise to both good and evil. Actually the problem of evil had bothered Confucianists right along and there was no solution until Chang Tsai (Chang Heng-ch'ü, 1020–1077). Chou adheres to the traditional Confucian position that human nature is inherently good but as one's nature comes into contact with external things, good and evil appear. Whereas both Taoism and Buddhism maintain that this external influence corrupts. Confucianism puts the responsibility on man himself by holding that evil appears when man fails to adhere to the Mean. Thus the good moral nature is substance, and good and evil appear only in its function. This doctrine was upheld throughout the history of Neo-Confucianism. As Sun Ch'i-feng (1584–1675) has observed in commenting on this chapter, Chou teaches that good results from one's being correct and evil from one's being one-sided, a theory quite different from that of Hu Hung (Hu Wu-feng, 1100–1155), who said that both good and evil proceed from nature. Chou Tzu's important contribution in this connection is his idea of subtle, incipient activation. It is also found in chapters four and nine and, according to Chu Hsi, is implicit in chapter twenty-seven.

The word *chi* means an originating power, an inward spring of activity, an emergence not yet visible, a critical point at which one's direction toward good or evil is set. It is here and now that one must be absolutely sincere and true to his moral nature so he will not deviate from it either in going too far or not going far enough. Thus Chou turns a quietistic state into a dynamic one.

Ch. 4. Sagehood

"The state of absolute quiet and inactivity" is sincerity. The spirit is that which, "when acted on, immediately penetrates all things." And the state of subtle incipient activation is the undifferentiated state between existence and nonexistence when activity has started but has not manifested itself in physical form. Sincerity is infinitely pure and hence evident. The spirit is responsive and hence works wonders. And incipient activation is subtle and hence abstruse. The sage is the one who is in the state of sincerity, spirit, and subtle incipient activation.

Ch. 20. Learning to Be a Sage

"Can one become a sage through learning?"
"Yes."
"Is there any essential way?"
"Yes."
"Please explain it to me."
"The essential way is to [concentrate on] one thing. By [concentrating on] one thing is meant having no desire. Having no desire, one is vacuous (*hsü*, being absolutely pure and peaceful) while tranquil, and straightforward while in action. Being vacuous while tranquil, one becomes intelligent and hence penetrating. Being straightforward while active, one becomes impartial and hence all-embracing. Being intelligent, penetrating, impartial, and all-embracing, one is almost a sage."

Comment. Confucianists had never advocated having no desire. Mencius merely advocated having few desires. The Taoist influence here is obvious. Hitherto, it was only a Taoist and Buddhist method of moral cultivation, but from now on, it became a Confucian method too. But as Chu Hsi said, Chou went too far, and as the prerequisite for concentrating on one thing, Ch'eng had to substitute seriousness (*ching*) for desirelessness, evidently in order to eliminate this Taoist influence.

6.5.2 Spiritual Beings

In Reading 6.1, Julia Ching provided an overview of Chu Hsi's ideas about the Great Ultimate, principle (*li*), and material energy (*ch'i*) as well as his important place in the development of Confucianism. Here I present a brief selection on spiritual beings from the *Complete Works of Chu Hsi (Chu Tzu ch'üan-shu)*.

It is helpful to remember that, according to some Confucians, human beings have two souls: an upper soul (*hun*) and a lower soul (*p'o*). At death the upper soul becomes a spirit (*shen*) and the lower soul a ghost (*kuei*). Because of the cult of the ancestors and the widespread belief in ghosts, considerable debate arose about the existence of spirits and ghosts. Sometimes the question of whether the dead are conscious and know what is happening was treated as a theme for wit. For example, a Queen who commanded that her lover be buried alive with her when she died was presumably dissuaded, as the following dialogue indicates.

"Do you think the dead have knowledge?"

"They do not," said the Queen.

"If Your Majesty's divine intelligence plainly knows that the dead lack knowledge, why uselessly bury the man you loved in life beside an unknowing corpse? But if the dead do have knowledge, his late Majesty's wrath has been mounting for a long time."

Wang Ch'ung (ca. 27–100) wrote a treatise on death in which he argued that people become neither ghosts nor spiritual beings at death. It was quite natural then that Chu Hsi should be asked about spiritual beings. His reply follows.

CHU HSI

Spiritual Beings and Forces

READING QUESTIONS

1. Make a list of all the ideas you do not understand and discuss them in class. First, state what you think they mean. Second, formulate as precise a question as you can about what you do not understand.
2. How does Chu Hsi relate his views on principle (*li*) and material energy (*ch'i*) to the issue of spiritual beings?
3. What is Chu Hsi's objection to Buddhist ideas of rebirth? Do you agree with this objection? Why or why not?

Someone asked whether there are spiritual beings (*kuei-shen*)?

Answer: How can this matter be quickly explained? Even if it could, would you believe it? You must look into all principles of things and gradually understand, and then this puzzling problem will be solved by itself. When Fan Ch'ih asked about wisdom, Confucius said, "Devote oneself earnestly to the duties due to men, and

From Chan, Wing-tsit, *A Source Book in Chinese Philosophy*, pp. 643–646. Copyright © 1963, renewed 1991 by Princeton University Press. Reprinted by permission of Princeton University Press. Footnotes edited.

respect spiritual beings but keep them at a distance. This may be called wisdom." Let us attend to those things that should be attended to. Those that cannot be attended to, let us set aside. By the time we have attended thoroughly to ordinary daily matters, the principles governing spiritual beings will naturally be understood. This is the way to wisdom. [When Confucius said], "If we are not yet able to serve man, how can we serve spiritual beings?" he expresses the same idea. (51:2a)

Is expansion positive spiritual force (*shen*) and contraction negative spiritual force (*kuei*)?

The Teacher drew a circle on the desk with his hand and pointed to its center and said: Principle is like a circle. Within it there is differentiation like this. All cases of material force which is coming forth belong to yang and are positive spiritual force. All cases of material force which is returning to its origin belong to yin and are the negative spiritual force. In the day, forenoon is the positive spiritual force, afternoon is the negative spiritual force. In the month, from the third day onward is the positive spiritual force; after the sixteenth day, it is the negative spiritual force.

T'ung Po-yü *asked:* Is it correct when speaking of the sun and moon as opposites, to say that the sun is the positive spiritual force and the moon is the negative spiritual force?

Answer: Yes, it is. Plants growing are the positive spiritual force, plants declining are the negative spiritual force. A person from childhood to maturity is the positive spiritual force, while a man in his declining years and old age is the negative spiritual force. In breathing, breath going out is the positive spiritual force, breath coming in is the negative spiritual force. (51:6b)

The positive and negative spiritual forces are so-called with respect to function. Spirit is so-called with respect to the wonderful functioning. In the cases of positive and negative spiritual forces, like yin and yang, contraction and expansion, going and coming, and diminution and augmentation, there are rough traces that can be seen. In the case of spirit which is so-called because of the mysterious functioning, it happens all of a sudden and is unfathomable. It suddenly comes, suddenly goes; it is suddenly here, suddenly there. (51:7b)

Question about the principles of life and death and spiritual beings. (*Question:* Although we know that spiritual beings and life and death are governed by one and the same principle, we do not understand the exact point. *Answer:* "Essence and material force are combined to be things. The wandering away of the spirit becomes change." This is the principle of life and death. The questioner did not understand. *Further remark:* Essence and material force consolidate to become man, and as they disintegrate, they become a spiritual being.

Further question: When essence and material force consolidate, is this principle attached to material force?)

Answer: As the Way of Heaven operates, the myriad things develop and grow. There is (logically) principle first and then material force. Although they coexist at the same time, in the final analysis principle is basic. Man receives it and thus possesses life. (But material force may be clear or turbid.) The clear part of material force becomes his vital force (*ch'i*), while the turbid part becomes his physical nature. (The clear part belongs to yang while the turbid part belongs to yin.) Consciousness and movement are due to yang, while physical form and body (bones and flesh, skin and hair) are due to yin. The vital force belongs to the heavenly aspect of the soul (*hun*) and the body is governed by the earthly aspect of the soul (*p'o*). In his commentary on the *Huai-nan Tzu*, Kao Yu . . . said, "*Hun* is the spirit of yang and *p'o* is the spirit of yin." By spirit is meant the master of the body and the vital force. Man is born as a result of integration of essence and material force. He possesses this material force only in a certain amount, which in time necessarily becomes exhausted. (This is what is meant by physicians when they say that yin or yang no longer rises or falls.) When exhaustion takes place, the heavenly aspect of the soul and the vital force return to Heaven, and the earthly aspect of the soul and the body return to the Earth, and the man dies. When a man is about to die, the warm material force leaves him and rises. This is called the *hun* rising. The lower part of his body gradually becomes cold. This is called the *p'o* falling. Thus as there is life, there is necessarily death, and as there is beginning, there must be an end. What integrates and disintegrates is material force. As to principle, it merely attaches itself to material force, but from the beginning it does not consolidate into a separate thing by itself. However, whatever in one's functioning that is correct is principle. It need not be spoken of in terms of integration and disintegration. When a man dies, his material force necessarily disintegrates. However, it does not disintegrate completely at once. Therefore in religious sacrifices we have the principle of spiritual influence and response. Whether the material force (or vital force) of ancestors of many generations ago is still there or not cannot be known. Nevertheless, since those who perform the sacrificial rites are their descendants, the material force between them is after all the same. Hence there is the principle by which they can penetrate and respond. But the material force that has disintegrated cannot again be integrated. And yet the Buddhists say that man after death becomes a spiritual being and the spiritual being again becomes a man. If so, then in the universe there would always be the same number of people coming and going, with no need of the creative process of production and reproduction. This is decidedly absurd. (51:18b–19b)

6.5.3 Why Does Great Learning Manifest Clear Character?

Wang Yang-ming (1472–1529) is the main representative of the idealistic wing of Neo-Confucianism. He argued against the rationalism of Chu Hsi that placed "the investigation of things" prior to "making thoughts sincere" in "The Great Learning," (Reading 6.2.1). According to Wang Yang-ming, the study of mind, not things, should be primary. Understanding the truth comes from within and not from externals.

WANG YANG-MING

Inquiry on the Great Learning

READING QUESTIONS

1. What does Master Wang mean by "one body"?
2. What are the differences between the "great man" and the "small man"?
3. Why does the learning of the "great man" consist in loving the people?
4. What is "clear character," and how is it related to "abiding in the highest good"?

Question: The *Great Learning* was considered by a former scholar [Chu Hsi] as the learning of the great man. I venture to ask why the learning of the great man should consist in "manifesting the clear character"?

Master Wang said: The great man regards Heaven and Earth and the myriad things as one body. He regards the world as one family and the country as one person. As to those who make a cleavage between objects and distinguish between the self and others, they are small men. That the great man can regard Heaven, Earth, and the myriad things as one body is not because he deliberately wants to do so, but because it is natural to the hu-

From Chan, Wing-tsit, *A Source Book in Chinese Philosophy*, pp. 659–663. Copyright © 1963, renewed 1991 by Princeton University Press. Reprinted by permission of Princeton University Press. Footnotes edited.

mane nature of his mind that he do so. Forming one body with Heaven, Earth, and the myriad things is not only true of the great man. Even the mind of the small man is no different. Only he himself makes it small. Therefore when he sees a child about to fall into a well, he cannot help a feeling of alarm and commiseration. This shows that his humanity (*jen*) forms one body with the child. It may be objected that the child belongs to the same species. Again, when he observes the pitiful cries and frightened appearance of birds and animals about to be slaughtered, he cannot help feeling an "inability to bear" their suffering. This shows that his humanity forms one body with birds and animals. It may be objected that birds and animals are sentient beings as he is. But when he sees plants broken and destroyed, he cannot help a feeling of pity. This shows that his humanity forms one body with plants. It may be said that plants are living things as he is. Yet even when he sees tiles and stones shattered and crushed, he cannot help a feeling of regret. This shows that his humanity forms one body with tiles and stones. This means that even the mind of the small man necessarily has the humanity that forms one body with all. Such a mind is rooted in his Heaven-endowed nature, and is naturally intelligent, clear, and not beclouded. For this reason it is called the "clear character." Although the mind of the small man is divided and narrow, yet his humanity that forms one body can remain free from darkness to this degree. This is due to the fact that his mind has not yet been aroused by desires and obscured by selfishness. When it is aroused by desires and obscured by selfishness, compelled by greed for gain and fear of harm, and stirred by anger, he will destroy things, kill members of his own species, and will do everything. In extreme cases he will even slaughter his own brothers, and the humanity that forms one body will disappear completely. Hence, if it is not obscured by selfish desires, even the mind of the small man has the humanity that forms one body with all as does the mind of the great man. As soon as it is obscured by selfish desires, even the mind of the great man will be divided and narrow like that of the small man. Thus the learning of the great man consists entirely in getting rid of the obscuration of selfish desires in order by his own efforts to make manifest his clear character, so as to restore the condition of forming one body with Heaven, Earth, and the myriad things, a condition that is originally so, that is all. It is not that outside of the original substance something can be added.

Question: Why, then, does the learning of the great man consist in loving the people?

Answer: To manifest the clear character is to bring about the substance of the state of forming one body with Heaven, Earth, and the myriad things, whereas loving the people is to put into universal operation the function of the state of forming one body. Hence manifesting the clear character consists in loving the people, and loving the people is the way to manifest the clear character. Therefore, only when I love my father, the fathers of others, and the fathers of all men can my humanity really form one body with my father, the fathers of others, and the fathers of all men. When it truly forms one body with them, then the clear character of filial piety will be manifested. Only when I love my brother, the brothers of others, and the brothers of all men can my humanity really form one body with my brother, the brothers of others, and the brothers of all men. When it truly forms one body with them, then the clear character of brotherly respect will be manifested. Everything from ruler, minister, husband, wife, and friends to mountains, rivers, spiritual beings, birds, animals, and plants should be truly loved in order to realize my humanity that forms one body with them, and then my clear character will be completely manifested, and I will really form one body with Heaven, Earth, and the myriad things. This is what is meant by "manifesting the clear character throughout the empire." This is what is meant by "regulation of the family," "ordering the state," and "bringing peace to the world." This is what is meant by "full development of one's nature."

Question: Then why does the learning of the great man consist in "abiding in the highest good"?

Answer: The highest good is the ultimate principle of manifesting character and loving people. The nature endowed in us by Heaven is pure and perfect. The fact that it is intelligent, clear, and not beclouded is evidence of the emanation and revelation of the highest good. It is the original substance of the clear character which is called innate knowledge of the good. As the highest good emanates and reveals itself, we will consider right as right and wrong as wrong. Things of greater or less importance and situations of grave or light character will be responded to as they act upon us. In all our changes and movements, we will stick to no particular point, but possess in ourselves the Mean that is perfectly natural. This is the ultimate of the normal nature of man and the principle of things. There can be no consideration of adding to or subtracting from it. If there is any, it means selfish ideas and shallow cunning, and cannot be said to be the highest good. Naturally, how can anyone who does not watch over himself carefully when alone, and who has no refinement and singleness of mind, attain to such a state of perfection? Later generations fail to realize that the highest good is inherent in their own minds, but exercise their selfish ideas and cunning and grope for it outside their minds, believing that every event and every object has its own peculiar definite principle. For this reason the law of right and wrong is obscured; the mind becomes concerned with fragmentary and isolated details and broken pieces; the selfish desires of man become rampant and the Principle of Nature is at an end. And thus the learning of manifesting character and loving people is everywhere thrown into confusion. In the past there have, of course, been people who wanted to manifest their clear character. But simply because they did not know how to abide in the highest good, but instead drove their own minds toward something too lofty, they thereby lost them in illusions, emptiness, and quietness, having nothing to do with the work of the family, the state, and the world. Such are the followers of Buddhism and Taoism. There have, of course, been those who wanted to love their people. Yet simply because they did not know how to abide in the highest good, but instead sank their own minds in base and trifling things, they thereby lost them in scheming strategy and cunning techniques, having neither the sincerity of humanity nor that of commiseration. Such are the followers of the Five Despots and the pursuers of success and profit. All of these defects are due to a failure to know how to abide in the highest good. Therefore abiding in the highest good is to manifesting character and loving people as the carpenter's square and compass are to the square and the circle, or rule and measure to length, or balances and scales to weight. If the square and the circle do not abide by the compass and the carpenter's square, their standard will be wrong; if length does not abide by the rule and measure, its adjustment will be lost; if weight does not abide by the balances, its exactness will be gone; and if manifesting clear character and loving people do not abide by the highest good, their foundation will disappear. Therefore, abiding in the highest good so as to love people and manifest the clear character is what is meant by the learning of the great man.

Question: "Only after knowing what to abide in can one be calm. Only after having been calm can one be tranquil. Only after having achieved tranquility can one have peaceful repose. Only after having peaceful repose can one begin to deliberate. Only after deliberation can the end be attained." How do you explain this?

Answer: People fail to realize that the highest good is in their minds and seek it outside. As they believe that everything or every event has its own definite principle, they search for the highest good in individual things. Consequently, the mind becomes fragmentary, isolated, broken into pieces; mixed and confused, it has no definite direction. Once it is realized that the highest good is in the mind and does not depend on any search outside,

then the mind will have definite direction and there will be no danger of its becoming fragmentary, isolated, broken into pieces, mixed, or confused. When there is no such danger, the mind will not be erroneously perturbed but will be tranquil. Not being erroneously perturbed but being tranquil, it will be leisurely and at ease in its daily functioning and will attain peaceful repose. Being in peaceful repose, whenever a thought arises or an event acts upon it, the mind with its innate knowledge will thoroughly sift and carefully examine whether or not the thought or event is in accord with the highest good, and thus the mind can deliberate. With deliberation, every decision will be excellent and every act will be proper, and in this way the highest good will be attained.

Question: "Things have their roots and their branches." A former scholar [Chu Hsi] considered manifesting the clear character as the root (or fundamental) and renovating the people as the branch (or secondary), and that they are two things opposing each other as internal and external. "Affairs have their beginnings and their ends." The former scholar considered knowing what to abide in as the beginning and the attainment of the highest good as the end, both being one thing in harmonious continuity. According to you, "renovating the people" (*hsin-min*) should be read as "loving the people" (*ch'in-min*). If so, isn't the theory of root and branches in some respect incorrect?

Answer: The theory of beginnings and ends is in general right. Even if we read "renovating the people" as "loving the people" and say that manifesting the character is the root and loving the people is the branches, it is not incorrect. The main thing is that root and branches should not be distinguished as two different things. The trunk of the tree is called the root (or essential part), and the twigs are called the branches. It is precisely because the tree is one that its parts can be called roots and branches. If they are said to be two different things, then since they are two distinct objects, how can we speak of them as root and branches of the same thing? Since the idea of renovating the people is different from that of loving the people, obviously the task of manifesting the character and that of loving the people are two different things. If it is realized that manifesting the clear character is to love the people and loving the people is to manifest the clear character, how can they be split in two? What the former scholar said is due to his failure to realize that manifesting the character and loving the people are basically one thing. Instead, he believed them to be two different things and consequently, although he knew that root and branches should be one, yet he could not help splitting them in two. . . .

6.6 CH'ING CONFUCIANISM (1644–1911)

During the Ch'ing dynasty, a critical reaction to the Neo-Confucian metaphysical emphasis on transcendence developed in the School of Evidential Research. The School of Evidential Research wanted to return to a more solid, concrete, and practical emphasis than was found in Neo-Confucianism. Although the work of Chu Hsi continued to be the basis for the civil service examinations, many Confucians believed his emphasis on nonphysical principle (*li*) and material energy (*ch'i*) moved dangerously close to dualism, thereby introducing an element of disharmony.

We shall look at one example below of how the potential bifurcation and disharmony of Chu Hsi's distinction between *li* and *ch'i* might be overcome.

6.6.1 The Harmony of Nature

Passions and desires are powerful sorts of things that drive us to eat, drink, sleep, and have sex. They move our bodies in ways that are natural, yet in ways that seem to take the control of our bodies away from us.

Many religious thinkers have had problems with passions and desires. They want to turn our minds toward heaven, not earth. They want us to contemplate the spiritual, not the bodily. Some Confucianists want us to restrain and always control our bodies, and Buddhists find human desires the cause of suffering. Indeed, both morality and salvation appear to depend, for many deeply religious people, on the suppression, if not the rejection, of the body and its desires.

If we learn that an antagonistic relationship exists between the bodily and the spiritual, then we may experience tension between what seems natural to us as humans and what seems appropriate for our spiritual development. Disharmony rather than harmony characterizes our lives as we strive to transcend the desires of our earthly bodies and focus on our heavenly homes. Maybe there is a better way to live.

Wang Fu-chih (1619–1692) did not like the dualistic tendency of Chu Hsi's rationalism. However, he also found Wang Yang-ming's idealistic emphasis on mind too subjective. Wang Fu-chih sought to reconstruct Confucianism in ways that avoided the twin pitfalls of dualism and subjectivism.

Wang Fu-chih believed that Chang Tsai (1020–1077), author of the *Western Inscription*, provided a fruitful starting point for recovering both the emphasis on harmony and the emphasis on moral practice. The opening lines of the *Western Inscription* read:

> Heaven is my father and Earth is my mother, and even such a small creature as I finds an intimate place in their midst. Therefore that which fills the universe I regard as my body and that which directs the universe I consider as my nature. All people are my brothers and sisters, and all things are my companions.

Wang Fu-chih thought the emphasis on a reality that transcends the world of space and time that is found among metaphysical Confucianists as well as Taoists and Buddhists takes our attention away from the world in which we live. In our world, both material and immaterial elements are aspects of a creative process of change. Wang Fu-chih wanted to emphasize a synthesis of principle (*li*) and material energy (*ch'i*) without positing something beyond the universe in which we live. Thus he finds a positive place for the passions (in opposition to much Buddhist and some Confucianist thinking) as natural human forces with which we need to learn how to live by developing a harmony between passion and proper restraint. He argues that the rules of ritual are themselves natural expressions, which must be embodied in human desires. There can, Wang claims, never be a "Heaven distinct from man."

WANG FU-CHIH

The Principle of Nature and Human Desires

READING QUESTIONS

1. Create your own set of reading questions for this selection and answer them. Focus on what you think are the most important ideas.

From Chan, Wing-tsit, *A Source Book in Chinese Philosophy*, pp. 700–701. Copyright © 1963, renewed 1991 by Princeton University Press. Reprinted by permission of Princeton University Press. Footnotes edited.

2. According to Wang Fu-chih, what is wrong with Taoism and Buddhism?

Although rules of propriety are purely detailed expressions of the Principle of Nature, they must be embodied in human desires to be seen. Principle is a latent principle for activities, but its function will become prominent if it varies and conforms to them. It is precisely for this reason that there can never be a Heaven distinct from man or a principle distinct from desires. It is only with the Buddhists that principle and desires can be separated. . . . Take fondness for wealth and for sex. Heaven, working unseen, has provided all creatures with it, and with it man puts the great virtue of Heaven and Earth into operation. They all regard wealth and sex as preserved resources. Therefore the *Book of Changes* says, "The great characteristic of Heaven and Earth is to produce. The most precious thing for the sage is [the highest] position. To keep his position depends on humanity. How to collect a large population depends on wealth." Thus in sound, color, flavor, and fragrance we can broadly see the open desires of all creatures, and at the same time they also constitute the impartial principle for all of them. Let us be broad and greatly impartial, respond to things as they come, look at them, and listen to them, and follow this way in words and action without seeking anything outside. And let us be unlike Lao Tzu, who said that the five colors blind one's eyes and the five tones deafen one's ears, or the Buddha, who despised them as dust and hated them as robbers. . . . If we do not understand the Principle of Nature from human desires that go with it, then although there may be a principle that can be a basis, nevertheless, it will not have anything to do with the correct activities of our seeing, hearing, speech, and action. They thereupon cut off the universal operation of human life, and wipe it out completely. Aside from one meal a day, they would have nothing to do with material wealth and aside from one sleep under a tree, they would have nothing to do with sex. They exterminate the great character of Heaven and Earth and ruin the great treasure of the sage. They destroy institutions and eliminate culture. Their selfishness is ablaze while principles of humanity are destroyed. It is like the fire of thunder or a dragon. The more one tries to overcome it, the more it goes on. Mencius continued the teaching of Confucius which is that wherever human desires are found, the Principle of Nature is found. (*Tu Ssu-shu ta-ch'üan shuo*, 8:10b–11a)

6.7 NEW CONFUCIANISM (1911–PRESENT)

Confucianism suffered many setbacks as Asia in general and China in particular went through the turmoil that greeted the dawn of the twentieth century. Two world wars, the spread of communism, and the rise of secularization stressed traditional Confucianism almost to the breaking point. Many predicted that the tradition was dying and soon would be dead.

However, the creativity of Confucianism proved more durable than the pundits had imagined. Slowly a new Confucianism took shape among scholars dedicated to the reform and renewal of the tradition from a critical perspective. They have tried to identify the themes that a genuine Confucianism must be concerned with from *jen* (humaneness) and *li* (ritual action/civility) to *ch'i* (energy). At the same time, they tried to reform the elitist tendencies of the tradition, its subservience to government authority, and its patriarchal denigration and oppression of women, and they tried to demonstrate its spiritual resources.

6.7.1 Does Confucianism Have a Religious Element?

When Christian missionaries entered China in the seventeenth century, they brought with them the concept of religion and tried to identify a Chinese religion. They asked, "Is Confucianism a religion?" The Chinese did not have a Western conception of religion, so this question had not bothered them. It was only during the nineteenth century, when the Western idea of a religion had become a part of Chinese thinking, that Chinese scholars began to debate whether or not Confucianism is a religion.

The Christian missionaries observed, when they came to China, both popular and elite traditions. Most classified the popular veneration of ancestors, the worship of various spirits and deities, and the ritual activities associated with temples as "mere superstition" and hence not genuine religion. The elite tradition they regarded as a kind of secular humanism and political theory designed to support imperial rule. The Neo-Confucianism they encountered was not organized or institutionalized in any way that resembled a "church." There were no clergy preaching to any laity, no revealed scriptures, and no liturgical worship. In short, there was nothing that looked like religion as the missionaries had come to define the term under the influence of Christianity.

If there is no Confucian church, how can there be a Confucian religion? The answer rests, in part, on how one thinks of religion. If religion equals an institutionalized form like Christian churches, then there is no Confucian religion. But if religion is a quest for transforming humans so that they live more in accord with the "way of Heaven," then there is a deep and profound religious aspect to Confucianism.

Once again the theoretical issue of how one defines religion (see chapter 2) takes center stage. This illustrates not only the way in which theory and definition influence interpretations of facts but also the way in which our thinking can be so strongly influenced by one tradition that neutral cross-cultural comparison becomes very difficult to achieve. However, these problems do not deter Tu Wei-ming from explicating the religious dimension of Confucianism as he understands it.

Tu Wei-ming is a professor of Chinese history and philosophy at Harvard University and one of the exponents of New Confucianism. In the following selection, he addresses the question of whether or not Confucianism is a religion. Earlier in the chapter from which this selection is taken, he defined the Confucian way of being religious as "ultimate self-transformation as a communal act and as a faithful dialogical response to the transcendent."

One of the profound Confucian insights into the human situation is that the process by which we become fully human is a process that must be carried out, according to Tu Wei-ming, in "a constant dialogical relationship with Heaven." But what does this mean? What is Heaven? Is Heaven something like God and, if so, does it exist independently of the world? Read and see how Tu Wei-ming answers these questions.

TU WEI-MING

On Confucian Religiousness

READING QUESTIONS

1. What does "ultimate self-transformation" imply?
2. What is the difference between the "great body" and the "small body," and why is this difference important?
3. What is *hsin*, and what does it have to do with religiousness?

In our examination of Confucian religiosity, we need to address the intriguing issue of transcendence. We must ask ourselves whether or not the idea of the theistic God, which features so prominently in Judaism, Christianity and Islam, is at all relevant to the Confucian mode of being religious. Such a line of questioning does not grow out of the Confucian tradition itself, but if we raise the issue here we can sharpen the contours of Confucian religiosity by defining the kind of transcendence that is most appropriate to Confucian self-understanding. Certainly the idea of theistic God, not to mention the "wholly other," is totally absent from the symbolic resources of the Confucian tradition. In exploring the issue of transcendence in Confucian religiosity, we must be careful not to impose an alien explanatory model or to introduce problems that are only peripheral to its central concerns.

Confucian religiousness begins with the phrase "ultimate self-transformation," which implies a critical moment in a person's life as well as a continuous process of spiritual cultivation. For us to be actively involved in ultimate self-transformation, we must make a conscious decision to do so. Since being religious is tantamount to learning to be fully human, we are not religious by default but by choice. This does not necessarily contradict the idea of *homo religiosus*, which is an ontological assertion about human nature. We are by nature religious, but we must make an existential decision to initiate our ultimate self-transformation.

Actually, the conscious choice or the existential decision can be understood in terms of the "either-or" dichotomy of Kierkegaard. Specifically, two kinds of "either-or" decisions are necessary. First, one must decide that learning to be human, which is a conventional Confucian way of denoting the process of ultimate self-transformation, is either "for the sake of others" (*wei-jen*) or "for the sake of the self" (*wei-chi*). Theoretically, learning to be human can be both "for the sake of others" and "for the sake of the self." Indeed, this preference for the inclusive "both-and" rather than the exclusive "either-or" solution to conflicts between self and society is a distinctive feature of Confucian ethics. Yet, in practice, the difference between learning for the sake of the self and learning for the sake of others is fundamental and crucial.

Learning for the sake of others may appear to be altruistic, but Confucius criticized it as inauthentic since it is often motivated by considerations other than a genuine desire to improve oneself. Strictly speaking, even though the demands of society and the urgings of parents are important for prompting us to become aware of our duty, they are secondary reasons for learning to become fully human. The primary reason is simply that learning is for our own good. A decision to turn our attention inward to come to terms with our inner self, the true self, is the precondition for embarking on the spiritual journey of ultimate self-transformation. Learning for the sake of the self is the authentic way of learning to be fully human.

However, inward reflection involves not only the choice of the self over others as the primary focus for learning but also a critical sense of developing the true self rather than the private ego. Another "either-or" decision is required: either the realization of the true self, which creatively establishes and enlarges itself as an open system by entering into fruitful communication with an ever-expanding network of human-relatedness; or the dominance of the private ego, which is encapsulated in its own "opinionatedness, dogmatism, inflexibility, and egoism." This inner decision to realize the true self does not lead to self-centeredness (nor does it lead to individualism), for it is never meant to be an isolated quest for spirituality devoid of social relevance. Yet we must also bear in mind that, despite its social relevance, it does not function primarily as a mechanism in social ethics and cannot be reduced to a choice in social relations.

In Mencian terms, the purpose of the inner decision to know our true self is to "recognize the great body" in us. The "great body" (*ta-t'i*) is contrasted with the "small body" (*hsiao-t'i*); it refers to the true self that can form a unity with Heaven, Earth, and the myriad things.

Mencius singled out sympathy-and-empathy ("the heart that cannot bear the suffering of others") as the unique and defining characteristic of our nature. Although he also accepted instinctive demands for food and sex as legitimately human (the "small body"), he noted that they are common to other animals as well. He acknowledged that since instinctive demands constitute much of what we naturally are, the difference between us and the birds and the beasts is not at all pronounced and studying birds and beasts can be immensely helpful in understanding humans on the biological level. However, Mencius was primarily interested in that difference that, in his view, makes humans unique. The slight difference between humans beings and the other animals, therefore, became the focus of his attention. For Mencius, the "great body" is both the basis for and the natural result of cultivating that which makes us uniquely human. This subtle point is vitally important for understanding how the Mencian project works.

The characterization of the "slight difference" between human beings and other animals as the "great body" implies that the uniqueness of being human is not a static quality but a dynamic process. Since sympathetic and empathic feeling is the source of our humanity, so it is also the basis of our ultimate self-transformation. By increasing our supply of sympathetic and empathic feeling, we can enrich our humanity; in this way we can become fully human. To employ the metaphor of the stream again, unless the supply from the source is sufficient, our humanity will not flow very far.

The Mencian idea of "recognizing the great body" is synonymous with the more common Confucian expression "establishing the will" (*li-chih*). As Mencius noted, when we acknowledge the slight difference that makes human beings unique, we recognize the great body inherent in our nature, take self-cultivation seriously, and aspire to become profound persons. A profound person preserves and increases what is common to us all. Yet we are not merely acknowledging and recognizing the principle that each of us is capable of sympathetic and empathic feelings. We are also asserting that we will be guided by these feelings in our conduct. "Establishing the will" can thus be interpreted as making the decision to act in accordance with the "great body," specifically with the sympathetic and empathic feelings that characterize the nature of the "great body."

Because the "great body" is not a static structure but a dynamic unfolding of human care, the decision to act in accord with it cannot be made once for all. Nor can the will be established by one momentous act. It can only be established by an infinite process of firm and continuous resolve. The decision so conceived is not a "function" of something else; it does not assume a finite form. It is a "substance" signifying the ontological reality of the "great body."

This decision can be seen as a self-illumination of the "great body"; it is, therefore, always enlightening as an autonomous center of creativity. Neither the loving care of our parents nor the inspiring guidance of our teachers can establish our will; we must self-consciously transcend the limitations of learning for the sake of others in order to learn for ourselves. Yet as soon as we are *willing* to learn ourselves, we have an inexhaustible supply of inner resources for self-transformation.

This decision is the necessary and sufficient condition for establishing the will. Here and only here can we be absolutely certain that willing entails having. Confucius assured us that if we desire humanity, it will automatically come. Mencius reiterated the confidence that only in this unique case, seeking implies getting. If we get it ourselves, we are truly "self-possessed" (*tzu-te*). This sense of being "self-possessed" is what Mencius recommended as the authentic way of learning to be human:

> The profound person steeps himself in the Way because he wishes to "get it" himself. When he gets it himself, he will be at ease with it. When he is at ease with it he can trust it deeply, and when he can trust it deeply, he can find its source wherever he turns. This is why the profound person wishes to take it himself.

The Way that the profound person wishes to get himself is not somewhere else, to be appropriated by departing from where we are here and now. On the contrary, it is right here, near at hand and inseparable from the existential conditions that underlie our daily lives. Paradoxically, once we get the Way by assuming full responsibility for our self-education, we can benefit from virtually every human encounter, including the loving care of our parents and the inspiring guidance of our teachers. In nurturing our human way, we can benefit from nature and the world beyond.

Our decision to establish the will signifies, then, the presence of the heart-and-mind (*hsin*), not only as an empirical entity but also, in the ontological sense, as an absolute, transcendental reality. This reading of the Confucian project may give the impression that it is yet another version of the "God talk" that has generated much controversy in theological circles recently. If the reference to an absolute, transcendental reality carries a particular theological flavor, it is not the result of a conscious design to think theologically about Confucian religiousness but the natural outcome of an attempt to understand Confucian humanism religiously.

The *hsin* (heart-and-mind) that enables us to make our inner decision to cultivate our sensitivity (humanity) is what Mencius referred to as the "great body." It is also the ultimate ground for "establishing the will." Yet it is not an objective reality separable from and independent of our lived concreteness. The temptation to reify *hsin* is mitigated by a strong preference for understanding it as an infinite being and as continuous creativity. *Hsin* manifests itself through a ceaseless process of internal illumination. It constantly transcends itself by fundamentally transforming the particular forms that crystallize its existence. No finite form, no matter how spectacular, can fully realize its inexhaustible possibilities. The multiplicity of forms that the heart-and-mind assumes demonstrates that its creativity cannot be incarnated fully in any given moment, place or person, even though it only manifests itself through the concrete in given moments, places, and persons.

Hsin can never maintain a pure objectivity as the absolute transcendental Mind by according itself the status of the wholly other. For its own realization, it must work through the subjectivity of a person in time and space. *Hsin* is omnipresent but not omnipotent. It cannot detach itself from the arena in which its creativity resides. Its true nature lies not in radical transcendence but in immanence with a transcendent dimension. In the last analysis, Confucian transcendence is an integral part of its inclusive humanism.

CONTEMPORARY SCHOLARSHIP

Contemporary scholarship on Chinese religions in general and Confucianism in particular is undergoing a renaissance. More students are learning Chinese, traveling to China, and discovering beneath the surface of older scholarship new and exciting information. We will sample only a small part of this renewed scholarship here, but I trust it will whet your appetite for more.

6.8 THE SECULAR AS SACRED

Many scholars, especially modern philosophers, find Confucius a parochial moralizer whose ideas are largely irrelevant to modern society and the larger world. From the modern philosophical view, Confucius barely qualifies as a philosopher and his level of ethical thinking seems archaic.

In 1972 an American philosopher, Herbert Fingarette, wrote a penetrating study of Confucius that transformed the conventional thinking about Confucius. Fingarette, a professor of philosophy at the University of California in Santa Barbara, found insights in Confucius's *Analects* that convinced him (and many others) that Confucius can be a "teacher to us today." In many ways, Fingarette, who is the author of the next selection, found Confucius "ahead of our times," especially with respect to his understanding of ritual.

HERBERT FINGARETTE

Human Community as Holy Rite

READING QUESTIONS

1. What does Fingarette mean by magic?
2. What, according to Fingarette, is Confucius's creative insight, and how does it relate to *li?*
3. In what sense is *li* characteristic of "human relationships at their most human" level?
4. What has Fingarette's interpretation of Confucius taught you about Confucius and about being human?

The remarks which follow are aimed at revealing the magic power which Confucius saw, quite correctly, as the very essence of human virtue. It is finally by way of the magical that we can also arrive at the best vantage point for seeing the holiness in human existence which Confucius saw as central. In the twentieth century this central role of the holy in Confucius's teaching has been largely ignored because we have failed to grasp the existential point of that teaching.

Specifically, what is needed (and is here proposed) is a reinterpretation which makes use of contemporary philosophical understanding. In fact such a reinterpretation casts, by reflection as it were, illumination into dimensions of our own philosophical thought, which have remained in shadow.

The distinctive philosophical insight in the *Analects*, or at least in its more authentic "core," was quickly obscured as the ideas of rival schools infected Confucius's teaching. It is not surprising that this insight, requiring as it does a certain emphasis on the magical and religious dimensions of the *Analects*, is absent from the usual Western-influenced interpretations of modern times. Today the *Analects* is read, in its main drift, either as an empirical, humanist, this-worldly teaching or as a parallel to Platonist-rationalist doctrines. Indeed, the teaching of the *Analects* is often viewed as a major step toward the explicit rejection of superstition or heavy reliance on "supernatural forces."

There is no doubt that the world of the *Analects* is profoundly different in its quality from that of Moses, Aeschylus, Jesus, Gautama Buddha, Lao-tzu or the Upanishadic teachers. In certain obvious respects the *Analects* does indeed represent the world of a humanist and a traditionalist, one who is, however, sufficiently traditional to render a kind of pragmatic homage, when necessary, to the spirits.

"Devote yourself to man's duties," says the Master; "respect spiritual beings but keep distance." (6:20) He suited the deed to the precept and himself, "never talked of prodigies, feats of strength, disorders, or spirits." (7:20) In response to direct questions about the transcendental and supernatural he said: "Until you are able to serve men, how can you serve spiritual being? Until you know about life, how can you know about death?" (11:11)

If we examine the substance of the *Analects* text, it is quickly evident that the topics and the chief concepts pertain primarily to our human nature, comportment and relationships. Merely to list some of the constantly recurring themes suffices for our present purposes: Rite (*li*), Humaneness (*jen*), Reciprocity (*shu*), Loyalty (*chung*), Learning (*hsueh*), Music (*yüeh*), and the concepts by which are defined the familial-social relationships and obligations (prince, father, etc.).

The this-worldly, practical humanism of the *Analects* is further deepened by the teaching that the moral and spiritual achievements of man do not depend on tricks or luck or on esoteric spells or on any purely external agency. One's spiritual condition depends on the "stuff" one has to begin with, on the amount and quality of study and good hard work one puts into "shaping" it. Spiritual nobility calls for persistence and effort. "First the difficult. . . ." (6:20) "His burden is heavy and his course is long. He has taken *jen* as his burden—is that not heavy?" (8:7) What disquieted Confucius was "leaving virtue untended and learning unperfected, hearing about what is right but not managing either to turn toward it or to reform what is evil." (7:3) The disciple of Confucius was surely all too aware that his task was one calling not for amazement and miracle but for constant "cutting, filing, carving, polishing" (1:15) in order to become a fully and truly human being, a worthy participant in society. All this seems the very essence of the antimagical in outlook. Nor does it have the aura of the Divine.

Yet, in spite of this dedicated and apparently secular prosaic moralism, we also find occasional comments in the *Analects* which seem to reveal a belief in magical powers of profound importance. By "magic" I mean the power of a specific person to accomplish his will directly and effortlessly through ritual, gesture and incantation. The user of magic does not work by strategies and devices as a means toward an end; he does not use coercion or physical forces. There are no pragmatically developed and tested strategies or tactics. He simply wills the end in the proper ritual setting and with the proper ritual gesture and word; without further effort on his part, the deed is accomplished. Confucius's words at times strongly suggest some fundamental magical power as central to this way. (In the following citations, the Chinese terms all are central to Confucius's thought, and they designate powers, states and forms of action of fundamental value. Insofar as necessary, they will be discussed later.)

"Is *jen* far away? As soon as I want it, it is here." (7:29)

"Self-disciplined and ever turning to *li*—everyone in the world will respond to his *jen*." (12:1)

Shun, the great sage-ruler, "merely placed himself gravely and reverently with his face due South (the ruler's ritual posture); that was all" (i.e., and the affairs of his reign proceeded without flaw). (15:4)

The magical element always involves great effects produced effortlessly, marvelously, with an irresistible power that is itself intangible, invisible, unmanifest. "With correct comportment, no commands are necessary, yet affairs proceed." (13:6) "The character of a noble man is like wind, that of ordinary men like grass; when the wind blows the grass must bend." (12:19) "To govern by *te* is to be like the North Polar Star; it remains in place while all the other stars revolve in homage about it." (2:1)

Such comments can be taken in various ways. One may simply note that, as Duyvendak remarks, the "original magical meaning" of 2:1 is "unmistakable," or that the ritual posture of Shun in 15:4 is "a state of the highest magical potency." In short, one may admit that these are genuine residues of "superstition" in the *Analects*.

However, many modern interpreters of the *Analects* have wished to read Confucius more "sympathetically," that is, as one whose philosophic claims would have maximum validity for us in our own familiar and accepted terms. To do this, these commentators have generally tried to minimize to the irreducible the magical claims in the *Analects*. For it is accepted as an axiom in our times that the goal of direct action by incantation and ritual gesture cannot be taken as a serious possibility. (The important exception to this general acceptance of the axiom . . . is contemporary "linguistic analysis." But the import of this work has as yet hardly extended beyond the world of professional philosophy.)

The suggestion of magic and marvel so uncongenial to the contemporary taste may be dissipated in various ways: only one of the sayings I have quoted comes from the portion of the *Analects*—Books 3 to 8—that has been most widely of all accepted as "authentic" in the main. The other sayings might be among the many interpolations, often alien in spirit to Confucius, which are known to be in the received text. Or one might hold that the magical element is quite restricted in scope, applying only to the ruler or even the perfect ruler alone. Still another possible method of "interpreting away" the "magical" statements is to suppose that Confucius was merely emphasizing and dramatizing the otherwise familiar power of setting a good example. In short, on this view we must take the "magical" sayings as being poetic statements of a prosaic truth. Finally, one might simply argue that Confucius was not consistent on the issue—perhaps that he was mainly and characteristically antimagic, but, as might well be expected, he had not entirely freed himself of deep-rooted traditional beliefs.

All of these interpretations take the teaching of a magical dimension to human virtue as an obstacle to acceptance by the sophisticated citizen of the twentieth century. The magic must be interpreted away or else treated as a historically understandable failure on Confucius's part. I prefer to think we can still learn from Confucius on this issue if we do not begin by supposing the obvious meaning of his words as unacceptable.

Rather than engage in polemics regarding these other interpretations, I shall devote the remainder of my remarks to a positive exposition of what I take to be the genuine and sound magical view of man in Confucius's teaching. I do not hold that my interpretation is correct to the exclusion of all others. There is no reason to suppose that an innovator such as Confucius distinguishes all possible meanings of what he says and consciously intends only one of these meanings to the exclusion of all others. One should assume the contrary. Of the various meanings of the Confucian magical teaching, I believe the one to be elaborated in the following remarks is authentic, central and still unappreciated.

Confucius saw, and tried to call to our attention, that the truly, distinctively human powers have, characteristically, a magical quality. His task, therefore, required, in effect, that he reveal what is already so familiar and universal as to be unnoticed. What is necessary in such cases is that one come upon this "obvious" dimension of our existence in a new way, in the right way. Where can one find such a new path to this familiar area, one which provides a new and revealing perspective? Confucius found the path: we go by way of the notion of *li*.

One has to labor long and hard to learn *li*. The word in its root meaning is close to "holy ritual," "sacred ceremony." Characteristic of Confucius's teaching is the use of the language and imagery of *li* as a medium within which to talk about the entire body of the *mores*, or more precisely, of the authentic tradition and reasonable conventions of society. Confucius taught that the ability to act according to *li* and the will to submit to *li* are essential to that perfect and peculiarly human virtue or power which can be man's. Confucius thus does two things here: he calls our attention to the entire body of tradition and convention, and he calls upon us to see all this by means of a metaphor, through the imagery of sacred ceremony, holy rite.

The (spiritually) noble man is one who has labored at the alchemy of fusing social forms (*li*) and raw personal existence in such a way that they transmitted into a way of being which realizes *te*, the distinctively human virtue of power.

Te is realized in concrete acts of human intercourse, the acts being of a pattern. These patterns have certain general features, features common to all such patterns of *li*: they are all expressive of "man-to-man-ness," of reciprocal loyalty and respect. But the patterns are also specific: they differentiate and they define in detail the ritual performance-repertoires which constitute civilized, i.e., truly human patterns of mourning, marrying and fighting, of being a prince, a father, a son and so on. However, men are by no means conceived as being mere standardized units mechanically carrying out prescribed routines in the service of some cosmic or social law. Nor are they self-sufficient, individual souls who happen to consent to a social contract. Men become truly human as their raw impulse is shaped by *li*. And *li* is the fulfillment of human impulse, the civilized expression of it —not a formalistic dehumanization. *Li* is the specifi-

cally humanizing form of the dynamic relation of man-to-man.

The novel and creative insight of Confucius was to see this aspect of human existence, its form as learned tradition and convention, in terms of a particular revelatory image: *li*, i.e., "holy rite," "sacred ceremony," in the usual meaning of the term prior to Confucius.

In well-learned ceremony, each person does what he is supposed to do according to a pattern. My gestures are coordinated harmoniously with yours—though neither of us has to force, push, demand, compel or otherwise "make" this happen. Our gestures are in turn smoothly followed by those of the other participants, all effortlessly. If all are "self-disciplined, ever turning to *li*," then all that is needed—quite literally—is an initial ritual gesture in the proper ceremonial context; from there onward everything "happens." What action did Shun (the Sage-ruler) take? "He merely placed himself gravely and reverently with his face due south; that was all." (15:4) Let us consider in at least a little detail the distinctive features of action emphasized by this revelatory image of Holy Rite.

It is important that we do not think of this effortlessness as "mechanical" or "automatic." If it is so, then, as Confucius repeatedly indicates, the ceremony is dead, sterile, empty: there is no *spirit* in it. The truly ceremonial "takes place"; there is a kind of spontaneity. It happens "of itself." There is life in it because the individuals involved do it with seriousness and sincerity. For ceremony to be authentic one must "participate in the sacrifice"; otherwise it is as if one "did not sacrifice at all." (3:12) To put it another way, there are two contrasting kinds of failure in carrying out *li*: the ceremony may be awkwardly performed for lack of learning and skill; or the ceremony may have a surface slickness but yet be dull, mechanical for lack of serious purpose and commitment. Beautiful and effective ceremony requires the personal "presence" to be fused with learned ceremonial skill. This ideal fusion is true *li* as sacred rite.

Confucius characteristically and sharply contrasts the ruler who uses *li* with the ruler who seeks to attain his ends by means of commands, threats, regulations, punishments and force. (2:3) The force of coercion is manifest and tangible, whereas the vast (and sacred) forces at work in *li* are invisible and intangible. *Li* works through spontaneous coordination rooted in reverent dignity. The perfection in Holy Rite is esthetic as well as spiritual.

Having considered holy ceremony in itself, we are now prepared to turn to more everyday aspects of life. This is in effect what Confucius invites us to do; it is the foundation for his perspective on man.

I see you on the street; I smile, walk toward you, put out my hand to shake yours. And behold—without any command, stratagem, force, special tricks or tools, without any effort on my part to make you do so, you spontaneously turn toward me, return my smile, raise your hand toward mine. We shake hands—not by my pulling your hand up and down on your pulling mine but by spontaneous and perfect cooperative action. Normally we do not notice the subtlety and amazing complexity of this coordinated "ritual" act. This subtlety and complexity become very evident, however, if one has had to learn the ceremony only from a book of instructions, or if one is a foreigner from a nonhandshaking culture.

Nor normally do we notice that the "ritual" has "life" in it, that we are "present" to each other, at least to some minimal extent. As Confucius said, there are always the general and fundamental requirements of reciprocal good faith and respect. This mutual respect is not the same as a conscious feeling of mutual respect; when I am *aware* of a respect for you, I am much more likely to be piously fatuous or perhaps self-consciously embarrassed; and no doubt our little "ceremony" will reveal this in certain awkwardnesses. (I put out my hand too soon and am left with it hanging in midair.) No, the authenticity of the mutual respect does not require that I consciously feel respect or focus my attention on my respect for you; it is fully expressed in the correct "live" and spontaneous performance of the *act*. Just as an aerial acrobat must, at least for the purpose at hand, possess (but not think about his) complete trust in his partner if the trick is to come off, so we who shake hands, though the stakes are less, must have (but not think about) respect and trust. Otherwise we find ourselves fumbling awkwardly or performing in a lifeless fashion, which easily conveys its meaninglessness to the other.

Clearly it is not necessary that our reciprocal respect and good faith go very far in order for us to accomplish a reasonably successful handshake and greeting. Yet even here, the sensitive person can often plumb the depths of another's attitude from a handshake. This depth of human relationship expressible in a "ceremonial" gesture is in good part possible because of the remarkable specificity of the ceremony. For example, if I am your former teacher, you will spontaneously be rather obvious in walking toward me rather than waiting for me to walk toward you. You will allow a certain subtle reserve in your handshake, even though it will be warm. You will not slap me on the back, though conceivably I might grasp you by the shoulder with my free hand. There are indescribably many subtleties in the distinctions, nuances and minute but meaningful variations in gesture. If we do try to describe these subtle variations and their rules, we immediately sound like Book 10 of the *Ana-*

lects, whose ceremonial recipes initially seem to the modern American reader to be the quintessence of quaint and extreme traditionalism. It is in just such ways that social activity is coordinated in civilized society, without effort or planning, but simply by spontaneously initiating the appropriate ritual gesture in an appropriate setting. This power of *li*, Confucius says, depends upon prior learning. It is not inborn.

The effortless power of *li* can also be used to accomplish physical ends, though we usually do not think of it this way. Let us suppose I wish to bring a book from my office to my classroom. If I have no magic powers, I must literally take steps—walk to my office, push the door open, lift the book with my own muscles, physically carry it back. But there is also magic—the proper ritual expression of my wish which will accomplish my wish with no such effort on my part. I turn politely, i.e., ceremonially, to one of my students in class and merely express in an appropriate and polite (ritual) formula my wish that he bring me the book. This proper ceremonial expression of my wish is all; I do not need to force him, threaten him, trick him. I do not need to do anything more myself. In almost no time the book is in my hands, as I wished! This is a uniquely human way of getting things done.

The examples of handshaking and of making a request are humble; the moral is profound. These complex but familiar gestures are characteristic of human relationships at their most human: we are least like anything else in the world when we do not treat each other as physical objects, as animals or even as subhuman creatures to be driven, threatened, forced, maneuvered. Looking at these "ceremonies" through the image of *li*, we realize that explicitly sacred rite can be seen as an emphatic, intensified and sharply elaborated extension of everyday *civilized* intercourse. . . .

In general, what Confucius brings out in connection with the workings of ceremony is not only its distinctively human character, its linguistic and magical character, but also its moral and religious character. Here, finally, we must recall and place at the focus of our analysis the fact that for Confucius it is the imagery of Holy Ceremony that unifies and infuses all these dimensions of human existence. Perhaps a modern Westerner would be tempted to speak of the "intelligent practice of learned conventions and language." This has a fashionably value-free, "scientific" ring. Indeed the contemporary analytical philosophers tend to speak this way and to be suitably common-sensical and restrained in their style. But this quite fails to accomplish what Confucius's central image did.

The image of Holy Rite as a metaphor of human existence brings foremost to our attention the dimension of the holy in man's existence. There are several dimensions of Holy Rite which culminate in its holiness. Rite brings out forcefully not only the harmony and beauty of social forms, the inherent and ultimate dignity of human intercourse; it brings out also the moral perfection implicit in achieving one's ends by dealing with others as beings of equal dignity, as free coparticipants in *li*. Furthermore, to act by ceremony is to be completely open to the other; for ceremony is public, shared, transparent; to act otherwise is to be secret, obscure and devious, or merely tyrannically coercive. It is in this beautiful and dignified, shared and open participation with others who are ultimately like oneself (12:2) that man realizes himself. Thus perfect community of men—the Confucian analogue to Christian brotherhood—becomes an inextricable part, the chief aspect, of Divine worship—again an analogy with the central Law taught by Jesus.

Confucius wanted to teach us, as a corollary, that sacred ceremony in its narrower, root meaning is not a totally mysterious appeasement of spirits external to human and earthly life. Spirit is no longer an external being influenced by the ceremony; it is that that is expressed and comes most alive *in* the ceremony. Instead of being diversion of attention from the human realm to another transcendent realm, the overtly holy ceremony is to be seen as the central symbol, both expressive of and participating in the holy as a dimension of all truly human existence. Explicitly Holy Rite is thus a luminous point of concentration in the greater and ideally all-inclusive ceremonial harmony of the perfectly humane civilization of the *Tao*, or ideal Way. Human life in its entirety finally appears as one vast, spontaneous and holy Rite: the community of man. This, for Confucius, was indeed an "ultimate concern"; it was, he said, again and again, the only thing that mattered, more than the individual's life itself. (3:17; 4:5, 6, 8)

6.9 CONFUCIAN WOMEN

We included as one of our sources (Reading 6.3.2) Pan Chao's *Lessons for Women*, which, even though written by a renowned female Confucian scholar, presented lessons reflecting a deeply entrenched patriarchal value system. The New Confucians, as we noted earlier, recognize the need to reform Confucianism with respect to the views of women. There is a long history and well-established Confucian literature stemming from Pan Chao that addresses the problems and needs of women. The instructional literature is an important source for contemporary historians interested in gender issues and religion.

In our final selection, Theresa Kelleher, a professor of religion and Asian studies at Manhattanville College, shares some of her research into traditional Chinese instructional literature for women. She shows how the position of women in traditional Confucian thought was reinforced by relating that position to the supposed cosmic order. Confucianism is not alone among religions in seeking sanctions for the *way things are* by showing that they are the *way things are supposed to be.*

THERESA KELLEHER

Confucianism

READING QUESTIONS

1. What three aspects of the cosmic order especially impressed Confucians, and what "lessons" for conducting one's life did these aspects of the cosmic order teach?
2. According to classical Confucianism, what were the implications of the cosmic order and its lessons for the life of women?
3. In what ways did Confucianism during the Han dynasty attempt to bring women "into the mainstream of the tradition"?
4. What sorts of stories about "good" girls and boys in contrast to "bad" girls and boys were you taught by your religious tradition (if you have one) or by your society? How do they compare to some of the stories told in the Confucian tradition?
5. What is the "new element" with respect to both women and men that Neo-Confucianism introduces?
6. Do you agree with Kelleher that there is a "positive legacy" for women in the Confucian tradition? Why or why not?
7. If you read the selection on ritual by Fingarette (Reading 6.8), compare his approach to Confucianism with Kelleher's approach. Fingarette is a philosopher, and Kelleher is a historian interested in feminist issues and theories. Focus specifically on how their approaches differ.

This chapter will examine the position of women in Confucianism, focusing primarily on the classical period and to a lesser extent on its later phase, Neo-Confucianism. As I shall show, women played a central role in Confucianism by virtue of their place in both the cosmic order and in the family. Nevertheless, since Confucianism was a patriarchal religious tradition, its estimation of women's nature was by and large a low one. Richard Guisso has summed up the negative attitudes toward women which appear in the canonical texts of early Confucianism, the Five Classics, as follows: "The female was inferior by nature, she was dark as the moon and changeable as water, jealous, narrow-minded, and insinuating. She was indiscreet, unintelligent, and dominated by emotion. Her beauty was a snare for the unwary male, the ruination of states."

I have chosen not to dwell so much on these negative attitudes as on the actual religious path set forth for women in the tradition. I will give particular attention to the types of attitudes and behavior considered desirable for a good Confucian woman and the models put forth for women to emulate. To do so, I will draw on various instructions for women found in the classical ritual texts and in pieces written by women for women, as well as biographies of exemplary women.

There are, of course, limitations in the use of these sources. They were all in support of the dominant male teachers and were addressed to an elite group in society. Social historians have pointed out the cruel use to which some of these teachings were put at different periods of Chinese history to make the lot of women difficult. Although there were surely discrepancies between the ideals articulated in the texts and the realities of women's lives in Chinese history, we have evidence that many women did take these teachings seriously, fervently believed in them, and were even willing to die to honor them. For this reason, though other readings of the texts are possible (and even necessary) to fully understand the position of women in Confucianism, I will keep to a fairly straightforward description of the texts and their teachings, supplying occasional critical commentary.

Since the basic religious orientation of Confucianism may not be well understood by many and since such an understanding is necessary if one is to appreciate the part women played in the tradition, I will begin with a brief overview of basic Confucian teachings. I will do so in terms of the cosmic order of Heaven and earth, the human order, which parallels the cosmic order with its roots in the family and its fullest expression in the state, and lastly, the proper response of humans to these two orders.

The cosmic order in its fullest sense is seen as comprised of the triad of Heaven, earth, and the human. Humans are intimately linked to Heaven and earth, but not in the same way as they are related to the divine in the West. The call of the human community is not to worship Heaven and earth, but to learn from them, imitate their behavior, and thus form a human order modeled upon the cosmic order. Three aspects of the cosmic order especially impressed the Confucians as lessons worth learning in the human order.

First, Heaven and earth were seen as fundamentally life-giving; they continually bring new life into being, nurture and sustain it, and bring it to its completion. The fundamental optimism of Confucianism that life is good—indeed, that life is the most precious gift of all—comes from this sense of the universe as being fundamentally oriented toward the production and promotion of life.

The second aspect of the cosmic order valued by the Confucians was that everything in life is relational. Nothing comes into being in isolation, and nothing survives in isolation. Both the creative and the nurturing process depend on the coming together of two different elements in a relationship. Now the relationship between Heaven and earth is the most primal and most creative one in the universe. But these bodies do not function as equals; rather, they observe a hierarchy, with Heaven as the superior, creative element, positioned high above, and earth as the inferior, receptive element, positioned down below. What mattered was the overall effectiveness of the relationship rather than which was superior or inferior.

The third aspect of the cosmic order which impressed the Confucians was the orderly fashion in which it worked, with harmony rather than conflict prevailing among its parts. Each part seemed patterned to work for the good of the whole and yet at the same time to realize its own nature. It appeared to the Confucians that the parts observed a type of deference, or "polite form," with each other. For example, the sun dominates the day but yields its place to the moon at night with an absence of strife. Each of the four seasons gets its turn to dominate part of the year, but then gives way, or defers, to the season that follows.

In sum, the cosmic order was seen as life-giving, relational, and harmonious in the interaction of its parts. All these concepts formed the cornerstone of the Confucian ordering of human society.

The capacity of humans to be life-giving, for human life to be passed down from generation to generation in an unbroken chain, was an awesome thing for Confucians. The most direct and profound experience of this for any human was the gift of life at birth from one's parents. Birth brought one into this continuum of life, which was much larger than any one individual life. One felt oneself caught up in a flow of life which connected one to countless generations before and many more to come. A worshipful attitude was thus directed toward the progenitors of life: in the most concrete sense, one's own parents, but also their parents and their parents' parents. This reverence and gratitude for life formed the basis of ancestor worship.

The family, as the nexus of this life-giving activity and the custodian of the chain of life, thus came to be enshrined as a sacred community and was reverenced in a way that few religious traditions of the world have reverenced it. All other social groupings, including the state, had their basis in the family, and indeed, were often seen in terms of the family metaphor. Since Confucianism had no priesthood or special houses of worship, the roles of husband and wife took on a sacerdotal character. Marriage was a vocation to which all were called. Just as one received life at birth, one was to pass on that life to the next generation. Not to do so was a serious offense. As the philosopher Mencius said, "There are three things which are unfilial, and to have no posterity is the greatest of them" (Mencius 4A:26). As we shall see, this sense of the primacy of marriage and the sacredness of the family had an immense impact on the lives of women in Confucianism.

The second lesson that Confucians learned from the cosmic order was the relational aspect of things. All humans exist in relationships; there are no solitary individuals. These relationships are not just any relationships, but five very specific ones, known as the "Five Cardinal Relationships." The family generates three of them, and society generates the other two. Man and woman come together as husband and wife. They produce children, thus establishing the parent-child relationship as well as the older-younger sibling relationship. These bonds form the basis of the political relationship of ruler and subject and the social one of friend and friend.

For the Confucians, these relationships were not just biological or social; more importantly, they were moral. Since humans are not like plants and animals, they need more than food and shelter to sustain themselves—they need the empathetic response and support of other humans. Confucians had a profound awareness of the capacity of humans to nurture (be life-giving) or tear down (be life-destroying) in their interactions with others. Confucius thus made as the focus of his teachings in the Analects the virtue of *jen*, variously translated as "benevolence," "humaneness," "humanity," "love," or even just "virtue." The Chinese character for jen is composed of two elements: a human being on the left and the word for "two" on the right. The implication is that humans are structured to be in relationship, that our fundamental being is wrapped up in the existence of others. We

are called upon to be as responsible and as empathetic as possible, both for the sake of the other and for our own good. One of the descriptions of jen given by Confucius explains it thus:

> Now the man of perfect virtue, wishing to be established himself, seeks also to establish others; wishing to be enlarged himself, he seeks also to enlarge others. To be able to judge of others by what is nigh in ourselves: this may be called the art of virtue. (Analects 6:28)

Thus the Confucians were puzzled and disturbed when Buddhism made its way to China with its monastic system, which called for males to leave home and lead a celibate existence away from any family or social context.

The actual practice of jen in the Five Cardinal Relationships varied because of the hierarchical nature of these relationships. The same sense of hierarchy that exists in the cosmic order was seen as existing in the human order. Except for the friend-friend relation, all the others were conceived of as hierarchical in nature, with one party in the superior position and the other in the inferior position. This hierarchy was seen as necessary if the relationships were to work. Those who occupied the superior positions were parents, rulers, husbands, and older siblings; those in the inferior positions were children, subjects, wives, and younger siblings. Children were exhorted to be filial to their parents, subjects loyal to their rulers, wives submissive to their husbands, and younger siblings respectful to their older siblings. While most moral teachings in Confucianism were directed to those in the inferior positions, persons in the superior positions were obliged to use their superior status for the well-being of the other.

The third aspect of the cosmic order which impressed Confucians was the order and harmony which prevailed among the various elements, the correct positioning of each part in relation to the whole. Desirous of establishing the same order and harmony in the human community, from the family up to the state, Confucians attempted to choreograph the gestures, speech, and behavior of human beings with ritual. Here ritual included not just the more overtly religious ceremonials associated with coming-of-age ceremonies, weddings, funerals, and ancestral sacrifices (the four major rituals in Confucianism), but also what Westerners would put in the category of comportment and good manners. The classical ritual texts (notably, the Book of Rites, the Book of Etiquette and Ceremonial, the Rites of Chou) are filled with directives on the correct and proper behavior for every conceivable human interaction. The range extends from details for children to follow in serving their parents on a day-to-day basis in the household to the correct protocol for officials at court. While Confucius was all too aware of the dangers of formalism to which such a heavy emphasis on ritual could lead, nevertheless, he feared leaving the carrying out of virtue to chance. How as a child to be filial? Did he have to figure that duty out anew each day? Though one's understanding of filial piety should deepen over one's lifetime, one must begin with patterns to follow, both to ensure the smooth running of the household and also to initiate a person into a sense of what filial piety consists. Similar directions could be applied to the other relationships, including that of husband and wife.

From this brief presentation of the basic teachings of Confucianism, we see that the cosmic order is the primary source of divine revelation and the model for the human order, that the family is perceived as the nexus of the sacred community, and that all humans, both male and female, operate in a highly contextual, hierarchical, and choreographed setting. Relationships and the behavior considered appropriate to them are spelled out in quite specific terms. The religious pursuit for a Confucian is not to leave the world, but to realize the fullness of his or her humanity by a total immersion in human life, beginning with the family and extending outward to society through public service. By so doing, one achieves a mystic identification with the cosmic order, and one is "able to assist in the transforming and nourishing powers of Heaven and earth" (Doctrine of the Mean, ch. 22).

This, then, is the context in terms of which I will base my discussion of the role of women in Confucianism. I will show how that role was said to mirror the cosmic order, how women were identified in terms of their roles in the network of human relationships rather than as individuals, and how their behavior was informed by the elaborate ritual code.

In the cosmic order of things, the feminine as yin constitutes one of the two primary modes of being. This feminine force is identified with the earth, with all things lowly and inferior. It is characterized as yielding, receptive, and devoted, and it furthers itself through its sense of perseverence (Book of Changes, *k'un* hexagram). Though inferior to the masculine yang principle, the yin principle is nevertheless crucial and indispensable to the proper workings of the universe. From this cosmic pattern it was deduced that the position of women in the human order should be lowly and inferior like the earth, and that the proper behavior for a woman was to be yielding and weak, passive and still like the earth. It was left for men to be active and strong, to be initiators like Heaven. Though men were considered superior, they could not do without women as their complementary opposites.

In the human order, women were seen only in the context of the family, while men were seen in the wider social-political order. And within the family, a woman was subject to the "three obediences": as a daughter she was subject to her father; as a wife, to her husband; and when older, to her son. If the Confucian calling for men was "the way of the sages" (*sheng-tao*), for women it was "the wifely way" (*fu-tao*). The Chinese word for "wife" shows a woman with a broom, signifying the domestic sphere as her proper place. Marriage was indeed the focal point of a woman's life, and she was identified in terms of her role as wife, along with her two related roles as daughter-in-law and mother. In theory, females as step-daughters did not have much status within their natal families because, destined as they were to join the ranks of another family at marriage, they would never be official members of their natural families (no tablet would ever stand for them on the family's ancestral altar).

All childhood education for females was solely to prepare them for their future roles as wives and mothers. In contrast to boys, who went out of the house at age 10 for their education in history and the classics, girls remained at home, sequestered in the female quarters and under the guidance of a governess. They learned good manners and domestic skills like sewing and weaving.

> A girl at the age of ten ceased to go out [from the women's apartments]. Her governess taught her [the arts of] pleasing speech and manners, to be docile and obedient, to handle the hemper fibres, to learn [all] woman's work, how to furnish garments, to watch the sacrifices, to supply the liquors and sauces, to fill the various stands and dishes with pickles and brine, and to assist in setting forth the appurtenances for the ceremonies. (Book of Rites, ch. 12)

At age 15, according to this chronology, a girl would receive the hair pin in a coming-of-age ceremony. At 20 she was to marry. Three months before her marriage, a young woman was to be instructed in the four aspects of womanly character: virtue, speech, comportment, and work.

Both for the woman and the families, marriage and the wedding ceremony were extremely important events. As mentioned earlier, marriage marked the formation of a new link in the family chain of life, the sacred passing on of one generation to the next. The emphasis was on this sense of linkage or continuity rather than on any sense that marriage was the start of something new; that is why the Book of Rites says that no one congratulates anyone at the time of marriage. In addition, the Book of Rites comments on marriage as follows:

The ceremony of marriage was intended to be a bond of love between two [families of different] surnames, with a view, in its retrospective character, to secure the services in the ancestral temple, and in its prospective character, to secure the continuance of the family line. Therefore, the superior men (the ancient rulers), set a great value upon it. (Book of Rites, ch. 44)

Because the event had repercussions not just in the existing human order but also in the cosmic order and with the ancestors, the ceremony had to be done with careful attention to detail so that it would have its proper effect. Below are several of the most important details.

When the groom is about to set forth to fetch his bride, he receives the following command from his father: "Go meet your helpmeet, and so enable me to fulfill my duties in the ancestral temple. Be diligent in taking the lead as husband, but with respectful consideration, for she is the successor of your mother. Thus will the duties of the women in our family show no signs of decay" (I-li, or Book of Etiquette and Ceremonial, 4B). The groom then sets forth to the home of his bride. It is important that he take the initiative in this matter to remind all the parties that as husband, he is to be the active agent like Heaven, while the wife is to be the passive agent like earth.

> Faithfulness is requisite in all service of others, and faithfulness is specially the virtue of a wife. Once mated with her husband, all her life she will not change her feeling of duty to him, and hence, when the husband dies, she will not marry again. (Book of Rites, ch. 11)

A good deal of the reason for this was that a woman's bond in marriage was not just with her husband, but also with his family. Thus, even with his death, she had duties to his living relations and his ancestors. Though women were encouraged not to remarry, the social sanctions against those who did, in classical and medieval Chinese history, were not nearly as heavy as they were to become in later Chinese history under the influence of Neo-Confucianism.

Such was the wifely way as outlined in the ritual texts of classical Confucianism. During the Han dynasty (206 B.C.E.–220 C.E.) when Confucianism was first made a state orthodoxy, there was a more conscious attempt to bring women into the mainstream of the tradition and to give them more specialized instructional writings and biographies of women to emulate. Specifically, we have in the Han dynasty two pieces, Instructions for Women

(Nü-chieh) by Pan Chao, and Biographies of Exemplary Women (Lieh-nü chuan) by Liu Hsiang. . . .

As Pan Chao's Instructions became the prototype of later instructional texts for women, so did the Biographies of Exemplary Women kept by the scholar-official Liu Hsiang (77–6 B.C.E.) with respect to collections of female biographies. This collection, which drew upon a variety of sources from the legendary past to his own day, presents biographies of over a hundred women, grouped according to seven types. The first six types are of good, moral women (exemplary mothers, worthy and astute women, benevolent and wise women, women of propriety, women of sexual integrity, and intellectual women), and the seventh group is of bad, wicked women.

This text is fairly remarkable. Even though it groups women into types, and even though most of the women are celebrated for some contribution they make to men, still, it is no mean thing that such a large number of lively women who show themselves skillful in the arts of moral persuasion, have a keen moral sense, and are ready to act on their beliefs are honored in the sociopolitical realm.

To appreciate the distinctiveness of this text, I wish to provide the reader with a sampling of the biographies, beginning with two of the model mothers from the first chapter. These two models give us a sense of how Confucians regarded the duties of a mother. The first is T'ai-jen, the mother of one of the classical sage-kings, who was honored for her ability in "prenatal instruction." Believing that the moral character of the child was formed during pregnancy, an expectant mother was urged to pay special attention to her attitudes and behavior during that period.

> A woman with child did not lie on her side as she slept; neither would she sit sidewise nor stand on one foot. . . . She did not let her eyes gaze on lewd sights nor let her ears listen to depraved sounds. At night she ordered the blind musicians to chant poetry. (Lieh-nü chuan 1:4a)

Because T'ai-jen excelled in doing these things, her son "King Wen grew up and became an illustrious sage."

The next model mother is the most celebrated mother in Chinese history, the widowed mother of the great philosopher Mencius. Aware of the influence the environment had on the moral formation of children, she moved their residence three times before coming on one suitable for her son's upbringing. In their first two places of residence, one near a graveyard and one near a market place, Mencius had spent his time playing undertaker and businessman, two professions a good Confucian mother would hardly want for her son. Finally, she moved near a school, where Mencius engaged in play more along the Confucian lines of teacher and ritualist.

Several other incidents are given to show her vigilance in the care of her son, but the one which most endears her to women is one which takes place after Mencius was married. One day he entered his wife's room and found her not fully dressed as propriety would dictate, and he left immediately in disgust. Aware that in his stubbornness he would never return to her on his own, the wife appealed to Mencius's mother. Mencius's mother, with her down-to-earth, balanced moral sense, took her son aside and pointed out to him that while his wife might have transgressed the dictates of propriety, so had he by not giving her fair warning that he was approaching. "Mencius apologized and kept his wife. The superior person commented that Mencius's mother understood propriety and excelled in the way of the mother-in-law" (1:11a).

Elsewhere, in chapters 2, 3, and 6, we are presented with women, mostly wives, who excel in dispensing valuable moral advice to men, often in attempts to reform their conduct in the domestic or political sphere. These women are skillful in the art of persuasion, show that they are fully conversants with Confucian moral teachings, and even display a type of savvy in terms of the hard political realities of their day (which, for most of these biographies, is the chaotic and violent Warring States period, roughly 500–220 B.C.E.). Among these women, we find wives of rulers who criticize their husbands for failing in their role as father to the people, or for being inept in selecting good, capable advisors, or for shortsightedness in planning military campaigns. A daughter proves herself more astute about marriage politics than her father.

Many of these women are astute enough to realize that they must be indirect in their approach if their advice is to be taken seriously by the men in their lives. One wife, disturbed that her husband finds her so attractive that he neglects his duties at court to be with her, tried to reform him by making a public display of her guilt. In the palace tribunal, she tears off her hair ornaments and earrings, and has her governess deliver a statement of her guilt to her husband. "The stupidity and licentious heart of your wife have manifested themselves. It has come to such a pass that she causes the King to fail in propriety and to come late to court, so that it is seen that the King enjoys the beauty of women and has forgotten virtue" (2:1a). In so taking responsibility on herself, she awakens the king to his own responsibility in the matter. He refuses to accept her accusation and immediately reforms his ways, thereby becoming a more effective ruler.

In contrast to those wives who excel at advising and reforming their husbands, chapters 4 and 5 are filled with women dealing with their own sense of personal honor. These chapters have a great dramatic sense, with women often taking their own lives to protect their honor. While both chapter headings have a word meaning "chastity" (*chen* in chapter 4 and *chieh* in chapter 5), the interpretation of "chastity" has a broader sense than the narrow one of sexual continence, embracing a more general sense of integrity or honor.

Some of these women illustrate a strict adherence to proper ritual behavior as in the case of the widow who, when her room catches fire one night, will not leave the room because, according to ritual procedures, a woman does not go out at night unless accompanied by a matron and governess. Declaring herself willing to risk death rather than go against right principle, she perishes in the fire. She is praised as one who has perfectly realized the "wifely way" (4:1b–2a) Another example is that of the wife of the Duke of Ch'u. While he is away from home, a terrible flood threatens his home so he sends a messenger with others to relocate his wife. But because the messenger has forgotten the proper credentials, the wife refuses to go with him. She does so even though she is aware that her refusal almost certainly means death by drowning. She does indeed die in the flood, but is celebrated by her husband and others for preserving her chastity (4:6a–b).

Other biographies deal more explicitly with the matter of faithfulness to husbands, dead or alive. There is the woman of Wei who learns only when she has reached the gates of the town that her prospective husband has just died. Though she is advised to return home to her parents, she asserts her prerogative as his wife to enter his household, carry out the mourning rites for him, and to remain on as a member of the household. Her dead husband's younger brother proposes marriage to her, but she staunchly refuses, even when her own brothers pressure her to do so. "My heart is not a stone, it cannot be rolled. My heart is not a mat, it cannot be folded away" (4:2a–b).

There is also the case of the wife who refuses to obey her mother's order to return home when she learns that her husband has contracted leprosy. "If my husband is unfortunate, then his misfortune is mine. Why should I leave him? The way of the bride is that after one marriage cup of wine with the groom, she does not change in a lifetime. If unfortunately she meets with one having an incurable disease, she does not change her resolve" (4:2b–3a).

The suicides and killings continue in chapter 5, but here women are caught in divided loyalties to the various men in their lives. In one example, a wife's brother comes and murders her husband, takes over his kingdom, and then tries to take his sister back to his own kingdom. For her, the dilemma is that if she ignores what happened to her husband and excuses her brother, she will be going against righteousness; and yet, if on account of the loss of her husband she became angry with her brother, she will go against sibling love. What should she do so that she can be true to both men? With tears to Heaven, the woman goes out and kills herself (5:5b–6a). A second example is that of the "chaste woman of the capital." Her husband's enemy sees a way of getting revenge by exploiting the virtuous nature of the wife. He captures her father and threatens to kill him if she doesn't help him get to her husband. Her dilemma is that if she doesn't obey her father, she will be unfilial and he will be killed; if she obeys him, she will be unrighteous and her husband will be killed. Either way she will lose. She pretends to cooperate, advising the enemy where her husband will be sleeping on a certain night. She has her husband sleep elsewhere that night and arranges that it is she who is murdered, not her husband. Thus able to be faithful to both men, the woman earns the reputation of being humane and filial (5:11a–b).

From this sample of biographies from the first six chapters of this text, we have seen a variety of strong, moral women. In the domestic scene, they have shown themselves to be wise and able teachers of their sons and husbands; in the political sphere, they have proven themselves to be skillful and astute advisers. Often they have appeared more faithful in carrying out their Confucian duty than have the men, some even going so far as to give their lives on behalf of some Confucian principle. These are women with moral consciences who have the courage of their convictions. Thus does Liu Hsiang honor women as custodians of family and state morality.

But if he gives most of his attention to exemplary women (trying to exercise the power of positive thinking?), he does not completely leave out evil, selfish, wicked women. The last chapter of the text is given over to examples of "dangerous" women, women whose beauty distracts from their official duties and occasions the downfall of kingdoms. Among the example given are the concubines of the bad last rules of the Hsia and Shang dynasties (second millenium B.C.E.), Mo-hsi, the concubine of King Chieh, and Tan-chi, the concubine of King Chou. Not only do these two women ensnare the men in a life of sensual pleasure, but they also encourage sadistic treatment of servants and ministers. When the minister Pi-kan remonstrates with King Chou about his orgies, Tan-chi goads King Chou to have Pi-kan cut

open to see if it is true that a sage has seven orifices (7:1a–2a). . . .

These women in the last chapter are the antithesis of the others, caring nothing for the betterment of the men in their lives, wrapped up instead in their own insatiable desires for sensual pleasure. They threaten the moral fabric of society, and rather than being the custodians of family and state morality, are its destroyers.

The texts that this paper has discussed so far can all be seen as attempts to bring women into the mainstream of male-dominated Confucianism. Though the modern reader might well have doubts as to whether they truly gave women much dignity in their own rights, still, when compared with the later position of women in Neo-Confucianism, they reflect a broad and generous approach to women. We turn now to take a brief look at women and Neo-Confucianism.

With the fall of the Han dynasty in 220 C.E., Confucianism was eclipsed by Buddhism and Taoism in the area of religion. It was not to play a significant role in that area until its reemergence in the form of Neo-Confucianism in the Sung dynasty (960–1279 C.E.). When it did reemerge in this form, a great shift had occurred which was to have a profound effect on the lives of women.

The early Neo-Confucians zealously worked to revitalize Confucianism to reclaim the territory it had earlier lost to the Buddhists. Their challenge was to reestablish the family and the state as the locus of religious duty. They attacked the Buddhists for selfishly trying to escape from the world rather than direct their energies to building up the human order. Nevertheless, they were quite impressed with the depths of Buddhist spirituality. How could they blend the best of the two? The Neo-Confucianism that resulted was a more overtly religious tradition than earlier Confucianism and was concerned more with metaphysical matters, human interiority, and religious practices such as meditation. There was a new sense of the profound depths of the human self, but with it a great awareness of the dangers and obstructions which hinder the full development of the self. They saw these dangers in terms of human desires and passions. As a result, in Neo-Confucianism there is a greater preoccupation with self-discipline and with controlling one's desires.

This great wariness about human desires and passions was directed to the area of human relationships, the cornerstone of Confucian religiosity. Ch'eng I (1033–1107), one of the leading Sung Neo-Confucians, reflects this wariness in the following statement which appears in the most famous anthology of Neo-Confucian writings, Reflections on Things at Hand (Chin-ssu lu):

In family relationships, parents and children usually overcome correct principles with affection and supplant righteousness with kindness. Only strong and resolute people can avoid sacrificing correct principles for the sake of personal affection. (Chin-ssu lu 6:1b)

Here we see a new element. In classical Confucianism, one fulfilled oneself by immersing oneself in the network of human relationships. Now there is more ambivalence about these relationships, a sense that they may be a source of obstruction rather than a contribution to one's pursuit of sagehood.

Women could not but be influenced by this change, especially because one of the most intimate ties of a Confucian male was with his wife. Women came to be seen as activators of desires both sensual and affective. There was a felt need to ensure that they controlled their desires and not upset men's progress toward sagehood. Thus the moral code for women, while in many ways a continuation of the earlier, classical one, focused to an almost obsessive degree on chastity. And within this, the chastity of widows was singled out for special emphasis.

To be sure, chastity had been an important virtue for women in the classical period, as we have seen in the Biographies of Exemplary Women, and widows were exhorted to remain faithful to their husbands by not remarrying. But nothing in the classical period can match the degree of preoccupation with chastity that Neo-Confucianism exhibited. The most chilling statement in this regard was made by Ch'eng I concerning the remarriage of widows. He is asked whether a widow can remarry in the extenuating circumstance that she is poor, all alone, and about to starve to death. Ch'eng I responds: "This theory has come about only because people of later generations are afraid of starving to death. But to starve to death is a very small matter. To lose one's integrity, however, is a very serious matter" (Chin-ssu lu 6:3a).

The models of women presented in an influential primer for young men, the Elementary Learning (Hsiao-hsüeh), compiled by the most famous Sung dynasty Neo-Confucian Chu Hsi (1130–1200), staunchly promote this moral code. In one case, we have a woman who progressively mutilates her body with each new exertion of pressure by her parents to remarry. First she cuts off her hair, then her ears, and finally her nose, all the while defiantly asserting her determination to remain faithful to her dead husband. Another example is of two unmarried sisters who are abducted by bandits. They both resist rape, the first by hurling herself off a high cliff and the second by dashing herself on the rocks (there is plenty of blood and gore in these tales) (Hsiao-

hsüeh 6:11a–12a). Since the bond of marriage is not just with the husband but with his parents as well, we are also presented with model widows who further prove their faithfulness by giving unstinting care to their mother-in-laws, even in the worst of conditions. One woman's husband dies in war while she is still young, leaving her childless. Rather than succumb to her parent's pressure to remarry, she cares for her mother-in-law even though it entails a life of poverty for her. What little she has at the time of her mother-in-law's death she sells to give the mother-in-law a proper funeral (6:10a–b). Another woman is praised for trying to ward off ten strong bandits when they attack her mother-in-law. She is able to succeed in saving the mother even though she herself is almost beaten to death (6:11b–12a).

What is noticeably absent among these models are mature, astute women of the kind who dispense good advice, who are skillful in the arts of persuasion, and who involve themselves in the political realm. There are no wise, discerning mothers. There are only nun-like martyrs in their young adulthood. This more dramatic and ascetical tone, I must add, also pervades the models set up for men to emulate. . . .

The legacy of Confucianism in the modern period is a complicated one. By the late nineteenth and early twentieth century, China was in a state of decline, overwhelmed by problems of poverty, overpopulation, corruption, and loss of morale in the government, and imperialism by Western powers. Radicals and reformers turned on Confucianism as one of the prime sources of their problems. Since the position of women was also seen as at an all-time low, as evidenced in the widespread practices of footbinding, female infanticide, and the buying and selling of women, women also turned against the tradition. Probably no other socioreligious tradition has been attacked in such a large-scale, systematic way. Mao Tse-tung was astute enough to see the potential in women as a revolutionary group and achieved much of his success from the support of women. The People's Republic of China has made sweeping reforms to improve the status of women in society, and has included large numbers of them in the work force and in political office. However, as several recent books have shown, much remains to be done to give women full equality. The recent one-child policy has brought to the surface the traditional bias in favor of male heirs.

But the larger question for us is the future of Confucianism. Does it indeed have a future? Can it exist in a scientific and technological world that does not reflect its cosmic orientation? Can it exist apart from the traditional Chinese political and family system? Despite all the repudiation of Confucianism in modern China, do many of its teachings persist, albeit in Communist form?

If there is no future for Confucianism, then there is no use asking what future role women might play in it. Indeed, there are few Chinese women today who want to identify themselves with Confucianism, linked as it is with the oppression of women. But will there come a time when the atmosphere is not so highly charged and when Chinese women will want to evaluate the positive legacy of their tradition as well? From the outsider's point of view, there is such a positive legacy. Though Confucianism contributed to the victimization of women, it also gave them a sense of self-discipline, esteem for education, and respect for public service that has enabled them to enter into today's political and social realm in the number and with the effectiveness that they have.

The Confucian tradition, with its appreciation for the gift of life, with its profound humanistic spirit, its sense of religious practice as building the human community, and its sense of the relational quality of things, has much to contribute to our global religious heritage. The challenge of giving women a more equitable place within that tradition remains. It seems obvious that unless that challenge is met, the appeal of many aspects of Confucianism will be greatly diminished.

PRONUNCIATION GUIDE

There are two methods in wide use today for romanticizing (translating into a Latin-based alphabetical system) Chinese words. One is called Wade-Giles and the other pinyin. I have used Wade-Giles spelling even though it is older than pinyin and is slowly being replaced by pinyin because most of my sources use it. Thus it minimizes confusion. However, Wade-Giles does require a pronunciation guide because some of the sounds indicated by the letters do not, to an English speaker, correspond to the sound in Chinese.

a as in father
e as in end
i as in the initial e in eve
o as in go
u as in rude
ü as in menu
ai as in ice
ao as in out
ou as in obey
ch pronunced as j
k pronunced as g
p pronunced as b
t pronounced as d
ts or tz pronounced as tz or dz
hs pronounced like sh
j pronounced like r
ch', k', p', ts', tz' pronounced as in English

KEY TERMS AND CONCEPTS

Analects (*Lun-yü*) The name for a collection of Confucius's sayings and one of the **Four Books.**

ch'eng The virtue of sincerity, or truthfulness.

ch'i A primary energy or force that may be thought of as both material and spiritual in Western terms.

chiao Usually translated as "teaching" or sometimes as "religion."

chih The Confucian virtue of understanding.

chung The Confucian virtue of loyalty.

chün-tzu A "noble person." Sometimes translated as "honorable person," "superior person," or "gentleman."

Five Agents (Five Elements) The elemental forces of the universe: water, earth, metal, fire, and wood.

Five Classics The classical literature derived from a time preceding Confucius consisting of the *Book of Changes, Book of History, Book of Poetry* or *Odes, Classic Rites* (includes *Ceremonials, Book of Rites,* and *Institutes of Chou*), and the *Spring-Autumn Annals.*

Four Books A widely influential collection of Confucian writings: *The Great Learning, Doctrine of the Mean, Analects,* and *Mencius.*

hun The upper soul or heavenly soul expressed in intelligence and as a vital force in the power to breathe, in contrast to *p'o.*

jen A primary Confucian concept that can be translated as humanity, human-heartedness, love, benevolence, altruism, and, in general, virtue. It is the general virtue out of which various moral virtues come.

kuei See *kuei-shen.*

kuei-shen Literally means ghosts and deities but is used in a variety of ways to indicate spiritual beings in general. In ancient times, *shen* usually referred to heavenly beings and *kuei* to spirits of deceased humans. In popular religion, *kuei* means something like demons and *shen* refers to good deities. In Confucianism, *kuei* often refers to positive spiritual forces and *shen* to negative ones. Some hold that at death the *hun* becomes *kuei* and the *p'o* becomes *shen.*

li Can be used to mean principle of conduct, rule of conduct, rules of propriety, good manners, civility, ceremonies, rituals, and rites. Philosophically, when it is used in contrast to *ch'i,* it means principle, reason, law, order, or pattern.

p'o The lower or earthly soul expressed in bodily movements. See *hun* and *kuei-shen.*

shen See *kuei-shen.*

shu The virtue of reciprocity.

T'ai-chi Often translated as the Great Ultimate.

tao Literally means the path along which one walks. As an abstract concept, it came to designate the right way. It can be used to refer to the right moral path or the right way to live as well as the way of nature or of heaven.

Ti Can mean emperor and often translated as Lord.

yang Can refer to the sun or the sunny side of a slope. As an abstract principle, it came to designate anything positive, active, strong, male, and creative. It is the complement of *yin.*

yin Can refer to the moon or the shady side of a slope. As an abstract principle, it came to designate anything negative, passive, weak, female, and receptive. It is the complement of *yang.*

SUGGESTIONS FOR FURTHER READING

Berthrong, John H. *Transformations of the Confucian Way.* Boulder, Colo.: Westview Press, 1998. A study of the historical development of Confucian thought.

Chang, Wing-tsit. "Confucian Thought." In *The Encyclopedia of Religion,* edited by Mircea Eliade, vol. 4, pp. 15–24. New York: Macmillan, 1987. An insightful treatment of the classical period.

Hall, David L., and Roger T. Ames. *Thinking Through Confucius.* Albany: State University of New York Press, 1987. A critical interpretation of the conceptual structure behind Confucius's thinking.

Taylor, Rodney Leon. *The Religious Dimensions of Confucianism.* Albany: State University of New York Press, 1990. Taylor focuses on the religious aspects of the Confucian tradition.

Thompson, Laurence G. *Chinese Religion: An Introduction.* 3rd ed. Belmont, Calif.: Wadsworth, 1996. A good introduction to Chinese religion in general with informative chapters on Confucianism or what Thompson calls the literati tradition.

Tu, Wei-ming. *Humanity and Self-Cultivation: Essays in Confucian Thought.* Berkeley, Calif.: Asian Humanities Press, 1978. Collected essays on various aspects of Confucianism as it relates to the process of fulfilling the human potential for humaneness.

RESEARCH PROJECTS

1. Select any one of the authors of the source material included in this chapter and do further research on his or her life, times, influence, and views. Write a report summarizing what you have found out. For example, you may wish to read Nancy Lee Swann's *Pan Chao: Foremost Woman Scholar of China* (New York: Russell & Russell, 1968), which provides information on Pan Chao's ancestry, life, and writings, then write your report on this interesting and influential Confucian woman.

2. Imagine growing up in a Confucian family and town. Write an account of what you think your life would be like.

3. View the video *A Confucian Life in America: Tu Wei-ming* available from Films for the Humanities and Sciences, 1994 (Princeton, N.J.) and write a report on what you learn.

Taoist Ways of Being Religious

INTRODUCTION

In the center of a home in Taiwan there is a room with an altar. On that altar are statues of ancient-looking men with long robes and beards. Into the room come two men. One listens as the other tells him about an illness that medicines have not been able to cure. After the illness has been described, and some questions asked and answered, one of the men, called a master, dips a brush in red ink and quickly draws a sign on a little piece of yellow paper. This sign is called a *fu* and is a talismanic symbol for a particular energy drawn from the body of the master. The paper is burned and the ashes dissolved in water, which is drunk by the sick man. Both men are confident that health will return because the *fu* is a specially selected energy distilled from the vital energy of the master and given to the sick man in order to restore his health. There is no charge for this service, even though the master has given from his own life force in order to restore the life force of another.

This description is based on a common ritual described in Kristofer Schipper's *The Taoist Body*. Curing rituals are the stock and trade of many religious practitioners the world over. Some might classify this particular one as a folk religious curing-ritual, others as part of Chinese popular religion. However, the master is a Taoist priest and Schipper refers to it as a Taoist ritual.

What exactly is Taoism? Some claim it is a sophisticated philosophy, and others that it is a degenerate form of a sophisticated philosophy. Some claim it is a form of popular or folk religion, and others that it is a political movement developed and supported by the imperial court for its own purposes. While some say it is primarily a misguided medical and alchemical attempt to attain health, longevity, and even immortality, others argue it is a messianic movement offering salvation for the masses. Some think it is an

unsystematic mass of beliefs, rituals, and other practices that has grown up more or less by chance, changing radically from century to century. The *Harper-Collins Dictionary of Religion* defines Taoism as "a traditional component of Chinese culture embracing a broad array of moral, social, philosophical, and religious values and activities," which is broad enough to include just about everything mentioned above.

It used to be common among scholars to distinguish between philosophical Taoism and religious Taoism, but the most recent scholarship recognizes that the difference between the two is not as clear as once thought. In the past ten years, the scholarship on Taoism by Western scholars has increased dramatically, and it is changing our understanding and appreciation of a unified tradition of thought, experience, and practice that has creatively reinvented itself to meet the demands of changing times and places.

7.1 AN OVERVIEW

In 142 a man named Chang Tao-ling claimed that a deity he called the Highest Venerable Lord appeared to him. This deity, Tao-ling maintained, was a manifestation of the Tao, or Way of Reality, about whom the ancient sage Lao Tzu wrote. In fact, Lao Tzu himself was an incarnation of the Tao. Tao-ling went on to establish one of the first organized Taoist schools or sects called Orthodox Unity, or **Celestial Masters.** It still exists today.

The Highest Venerable Lord may have appeared "out of the blue" to Chang Tao-ling, but that does not mean that there were no precursors to organized Taoism. The ancient philosophers Lao Tzu and Chuang Tzu, whose major works date from the fourth and third centuries B.C.E., laid the foundations on which Tao-ling described the world as created and sustained by the Tao, which literally means way, road, or path.

In the Former Han dynasty (206–8 B.C.E.), wandering healers and ascetics called *fang-shih* became famous for their abilities in a variety of arts including astrology, dream interpretation, acupuncture, pharmacology, dietetics, exorcisms, and the like. They sought longevity of the body and open channels to the world of gods and spirits. They too left an indelible mark on Taoism.

Then, around the beginning of the common era, a number of messianic movements emerged promising that the increasingly political and economic stresses of the time would soon end in a utopian Great Peace. Thousands of people took to the dusty roads of China, visionaries received numerous revelations, sacred talismans for protection and good luck were circulated, and rebellions against the prevailing authorities erupted. The insurrection of the Yellow Turbans, or Tao of Great Peace, in 184 is probably the most famous rebellion. It was cruelly smashed, as were many others. The Celestial Masters was one of these messianic movements, although less politically inclined than some of them. It somehow managed to survive as the others died.

Laurence G. Thompson, Professor Emeritus, University of Southern California, presents an overview of religious Taoism in the following selection. He quotes liberally from the sources thereby giving us a rich taste of the many fascinating Taoist ways of being religious.

LAURENCE G. THOMPSON

The Taoist Tradition

READING QUESTIONS

1. As you read, make a list of all the words and ideas you do not understand or are uncertain about. Discuss them with a classmate, look them up in a dictionary, or bring them up in class for discussion and clarification.

2. According to Thompson, what is the goal of Taoism?
3. What is *wai-tan*, and how does it differ from *nei-tan?*
4. According to Thompson, why are the alchemical practices of Taoism more than protoscience?
5. What is the theory behind "Taoist yoga"?
6. What are the two main functions of the Taoist professional or clergy?
7. What is the difference between *fa-shih* and *tao-shih?*
8. Describe both the esoteric and exoteric meaning of *chiao.*

It is essential to understand that Taoism is not the same as "popular religion." The pervasive influence of various Taoistic principles in the popular culture should not obscure the special features that set Taoism apart as an organized, specialized religion. Such special features include a nearly two thousand-year-old tradition of ordained priesthood; the accumulation of an enormous "Bible" of esoteric texts comprehensible only to those with special competence; a grand liturgical tradition based on the ritual texts; a well-defined eremitic tradition; and many distinctive techniques conducive to the ultimate goal of transformation to transcendent immortality. We shall attempt, in what follows, to delineate the features of Taoism as a Way to ultimate transformation and then to depict the nature of its interactions with religious life in the communities.

The premise of religious Taoism is that life is good and to be enjoyed. The individual self is not set apart from the rest of nature but is, like all things, a product of *yin* and *yang* as the creative processes of *tao*. Neither the ego nor the rest of the phenomenal world is illusory —both are completely real. *The religious quest is for liberation of the spiritual element of the ego from physical limitations, so that it may enjoy immortality or at least longevity.* In other words, the goal is the triumph of the *yang* over *yin*. When one has attained this liberation, this triumph, one may choose either to remain in the physical body to enjoy mundane pleasures or to wander freely in the realm of space, to visit or dwell in one of the fabled abodes of the immortals.

It may seem difficult to reconcile this religious Taoism with the whole purport of the classic Taoist texts *The Old Master (Lao Tzû)*, i.e., the *Scripture of the Tao and Its Individuating Power (Tao Tê Ching)*, and *Master Chuang (Chuang Tzû)*. And yet, although the authors of these profoundly philosophical works would certainly have been bemused by many of the theories and practices of the religion that later claimed them as founders, it is, in fact, easy to find in their writings numerous passages that lend themselves to mystical and even esoteric interpretations. A literal, as opposed to a symbolic or poetic, reading could find both the goal of immortality and some techniques for attaining it in such passages as the following:

One who does not lose his [proper] place endures for long; One who [apparently] dies but does not perish is long-lived. (*The Old Master* 33)

. . .

I have heard that one who is good at taking care of his life will not encounter wild bulls or tigers when traveling by land, and will not [be wounded] by weapons when in the army. [In his case] wild bulls will find no place in which to thrust their horns, tigers no place in which to put their claws, and weapons no place in which to insert their points. And why? Because in him there is no place (literally, no ground) of death. (*The Old Master* 50)

. . .

Attain utmost emptiness and preserve earnest stillness. (*The Old Master* 16)

. . .

Block the road, shut your gate, subdue your ardor, do away with your inner divisions, dim your light, and become one with the dusty world. (*The Old Master* 56)

. . .

[Controlled] exhaling and inhaling; disgorging old [breath] and taking in new; bearlike lurchings and birdlike stretchings are performed solely for the sake of longevity. These are what specialists in guiding [the vital breath] and men who nourish the form [in hope of attaining] the longevity of Ancestor P'êng like to do. (*Master Chuang*, scroll 15, "The Will Constrained"; *Chuang Tzû, K'ô Yi*)

. . .

Master Lieh traveled by charioteering on the wind with light and wonderful skill. (*Master Chuang*, scroll 1, "Taking It Easy"; *Chuang Tzû, Hsiao Yao Yu*)

. . .

In the mountains of Miao-ku-shê (supposedly in the Northern Sea—i.e., an island of the immortal transcendents) there live spiritlike men with flesh and skin like ice and snow, gentle and weak as unmarried maidens. They do not eat the five grains but inhale the wind and drink the dew. They ride on the breaths of the clouds and chariot on flying dragons, traveling beyond the Four Seas. (*Master Chuang*, scroll 1)

. . .

My Master, Master Lieh, asked the Guardian of the Pass, saying, The Perfect Man (i.e., the Taoist adept) walks under water without hindrance, treads on fire without being burned, and moves about on the heights without fear. May I ask how he has attained to this? The Guardian of the Pass replied, It is by the safeguarding of his pure vital breath. (*Master Chuang*, scroll 19, "The Fulfillment of Life"; *Chuang Tzû, Ta Shêng*)

. . .

The True Man (another term for the Taoist adept) breathes from his heels, while the masses of men breathe from their throats. (*Master Chuang*, scroll 6, "The Great Master"; *Chuang Tzû, Ta Tsung Shih*)

. . .

When he succeeded in transcending his own being, apprehension [of the true condition of things] dawned on him, and when that apprehension had dawned, he was able to perceive the One. When he succeeded in perceiving the One he was able [to understand] the nonexistence of "past" and "present." Understanding the nonexistence of past and present he was able to enter into the awareness of no death or birth. (*Master Chuang*, scroll 6)

The historical relationship between this sort of thinking as found in the first Taoist philosophers and the formulation of specific techniques for achieving the goals at which it hinted is obscure. The goal itself must, of course, be as old as humankind, but the kinds of practices characteristic of the religious Taoist system in China were perhaps developed no earlier than three to four centuries B.C.E. These practices have been divided into two inclusive categories: The first was called "outer elixir" (**wai-tan**); this involved the concoction of a drug of immortality. The second was called "inner elixir" (**nei-tan**), which was the refining by various means of the spiritual essence within the body in order to liberate this spiritual essence from its physical shackles.

WAI-TAN

The search for the elixir of immortality, closely related to, or identical with, "the philosopher's stone," apparently began in China and eventually spread to the West. The alchemical elixir, when ingested, would prolong life indefinitely; the alchemical philosopher's stone would be able to transmute base metals into gold. Gold was the common denominator. In the case of the elixir, the symbolism of gold was that of indestructible, incorruptible life. The hope of making cheaper ingredients into the most valuable needs no symbolism.

The earliest literary reference to the elixir is found in the first great history of China, written by Ssû-ma Ch'ien in the mid-second century B.C.E.:

At this time [133 B.C.] Li Shao-jün was also received in audience by Emperor [Wu], because, by worshipping the Stove and by a method of [not eating] grain [products], he said he knew how to avoid old age. . . .

[Li] Shao-jün spoke to the Emperor, saying You should worship the Stove and then you can make [spiritual] beings present themselves; when [spiritual] beings have presented themselves, cinnabar powder can be metamorphosed into gold . . . ; when this gold has been made, it can be used for vessels for drinking and eating, and will increase the length of your life; when the length of your life has been increased, the immortals of Peng-lai in the midst of the ocean can thereupon be given audience; when they have been given audience, by [making the sacrifices] *fêng* and *shan* you will never die. The Yellow Lord did this. Your subject has traveled on the ocean and had an audience with Master An-chi. Master An-chi fed your servant jujubes as large as melons. Master An-chi is an immortal who is in conununication with those on [the isle of] Peng-lai. When it suits him, he appears to people, and when it does not suit him, he remains hidden. . . .

Whereupon the Son of Heaven [Emperor Wu], for the first time worshipped the Stove in person, sent gentlemen [possessors] of recipes . . . out into the ocean to seek for Master An-chi and similar [beings from the isle of] Peng-lai, and paid attention to metamorphosing powdered cinnabar and potions of various drugs into gold.

The activities of the alchemists were of direct concern to the State, which was anxious to prevent counterfeiting of gold money. For this reason such activities were proscribed on penalty of public execution. The alchemists, therefore, to avoid prosecution and to protect an esoteric lore, kept their operations secretive, relaying their formulas orally or writing them down in a language so occult and obscure that none but initiates could find them intelligible. One rare text, dating from the mid-second century C.E., contains the following explanation of the elixir theory:

Tan-sha (Red Sand, cinnabar, mercury sulfide) is of wood and will combine with gold (metal). Gold (metal) and water live together; wood and fire keep one another company. [In the beginning] these four were in a confused state. They came to be classified as Tigers and Dragons. The numbers for the Dragons, which are *yang* (positive, male), are odd, and those for the Tigers, which are *yin* (negative, female), are even.

The blue liver is the father and the white lungs are the mother. The red heart is the daughter, the yellow spleen is the grandfather, and the black kidneys are the son. The son is the beginning of the *wu-hsing* (the Five Elements). The *three* things are of the same family and they all are of the ordinal numbers *Wu* and *Chi*.

Another passage from the same work pictures the alchemist at work, his ingredients in the cauldron, and explains the efficacy of the elixir:

Circumference three-five, diameter one tenth of an inch, mouth four-eight, two inches, length one and two-tenths feet, and thickness equal throughout. With its belly properly set, it is to be warmed up gradually. *Yin* (negativeness) is above and *yang* (positiveness) runs below. The ends are strongly heated and the middle mildly warmed. Start with seventy, and with thirty, and two hundred and sixty. There should be thorough mixing.

The *yin* . . . fire is white and produces the *huang-ya* (Yellow Sprout) from the lead. Two-seven gathers to bring forth the man. When the brain [head] is properly tended for the required length of time, one will certainly attain the miracle. The offspring, living securely in the center, plies back and forth without coming out of doors. By degrees he grows up and is endowed with a pure nature. He goes back to the one to return to his origin. . . .

Respectful care should be accorded, as by a subject to his ruler. To keep up the work for a year is indeed a strenuous task. There should be strict protection, so as not to get lost. The Way is long and obscurely mystical, at the end of which the *Ch'ien* (positiveness, male) and the *K'un* (negativeness, female) come together. The taking of so small a quantity of it as would cover the edge of a knife or spatula will be enough to confer tranquility on the *hun-p'o* (man's animal spirit), give him immortality, and enable him to live in the village of the immortals.

. . . Careful reflection is in order, but no discussion with others should take place. The secret should be carefully guarded and no writing should be done for its conveyance. . . .

When the aspirant is accomplished, he will ride on the white crane and the scaled dragon to pay respects to the Immortal Ruler in the Supreme Void. There he will be given the decorated diploma which entitles him to the name of a *Chên-jen* (True Man).

Had alchemy been no more than a technique for producing the elixir, it could be considered as simply protoscience and not as religion; but, in fact, the adepts of this technique were never simply experimenters with material substances. The major treatise of the alchemical school, written by one Kô Hung (253–333?) under the pen name Pao P'u Tzû, or The Master Who Holds in His Arms the Uncarved Block, contains many specifications such as the following:

> The rules of immortality demand an earnest desire for quietness, loneliness, nonactivity and forgetfulness of one's own body.
>
> The rules of immortality require that one extend his love to the creeping worm and do no harm to beings with the life-fluid. . . .
>
> The rules of immortality require that one entirely abstain from flesh, give up cereals and purify one's interior.
>
> The rules of immortality demand universal love for the whole world, that one regard one's neighbor as one's own self.

As in all religions, there is a moral imperative in this search for immortality through alchemy:

> He who aspires after immortality should, above all, regard as his main duties: loyalty, filial piety, friendship, obedience, goodness, fidelity (all good "Confucian" virtues). If one does not lead a virtuous life but exercises himself only in magical tricks, he can by no means attain long life. If one does evil, should this be of a grave nature, the god of the fate would take off one chi (300 days, according to translator's note), and for a small sin he would take off a suan (three days) of one's life. . . .
>
> If the number of good actions is not yet completed, he will have no profit from them, although he takes the elixir of immortality.

The life to be led by the aspirant is described by the same authority:

> This Way is of utmost importance. You must teach it only to those who are wise and virtuous. . . . Whoever receives this instruction, must as a pledge throw a golden effigy of a man and of a fish into a river which flows eastwards. He must smear on his mouth the blood of a victim to pledge allegiance to the cause. . . . One must compound the cinnabar in a famous mountain, uninhabited by human beings, in the company of not more than three persons. First, one must fast for a hundred days, washing and bathing in water mixed with five odoriferous substances and thus effect absolute purity. Avoid strictly proximity to filthy things and observe isolation from the vulgar crowd. Furthermore,

disbelievers of the Way should not be given any information, for these would slander and spoil the elixir, and thus the Medicine will fail.

NEI-TAN

The quest for the elixir continued on for centuries, becoming increasingly conceived more in spiritual than in physical terms. This development is summed up by Waley, who calls *nei-tan* "esoteric alchemy":

> *Exoteric alchemy* [i.e., *wai-tan*] . . . uses as its ingredients the tangible substances mercury, lead, cinnabar and so on . . . [whereas] *esoteric alchemy* . . . uses only the "souls" of these substances. . . . Presently a fresh step is made. These transcendental metals are identified with various parts of the human body, and alchemy comes to mean in China . . . a system of mental and physical re-education. This process is complete in the *Treatise on the Dragon and Tiger* (lead and mercury) of Su Tung-p'o, written c. 1100: "The dragon is mercury. He is the semen and the blood. He issues from the kidneys and is stored in the liver. His sign is the trigram *k'an*. The tiger is lead. He is breath and bodily strength. He issues from the mind and the lungs bear him. His sign is the trigram *li*. When the mind is moved, then the breath and strength act with it. When the kidneys are flushed then semen and blood flow with them."
>
> In the thirteenth century alchemy (if it may still so be called) no less than Confucianism is permeated by the teachings of the Buddhist Meditation Sect [i.e., Ch'an]. The chief exponent of the Buddhicized Taoism is Ko Ch'ang-kêng, also known as Po Yü-chuan. In his treatise . . . he describes three methods of esoteric alchemy: (1) the body supplies the element lead; the heart, the element mercury. Concentration supplies the necessary liquid; the sparks of intelligence, the necessary fire. "By this means a gestation usually demanding ten months may be brought to ripeness in the twinkling of an eye." . . . (2) The second method is: The breath supplies the element lead, the soul [*shên*] supplies the element mercury. The cyclic sign [*wu*] "horse" supplies fire; the cyclic sign [*tzu*] "rat" supplies water. (3) The semen supplies the element lead. The blood supplies mercury; the kidneys supply water; the mind supplies fire.
>
> "To the above it may be objected," continues Ko Ch'ang-kêng, "that this is practically the same

as the method of the Zen Buddhist. To this I reply that under Heaven there are no two Ways, and that the Wise are ever of the same heart."

Although *wai-tan*, an alchemy of substances, thus becomes more and more a technique for cultivating the "inner chemistry" of the body, it must not be assumed that this latter was historically an outgrowth of the former. On the contrary, . . . inner cultivation was already a feature of ancient Taoist philosophy. From these hints, the later adepts of religious Taoism developed a variety of yoga, based on a theory that may be called "spiritual physiology." This in turn formed the foundation for the protoscience of traditional Chinese medicine. The objective of Taoist yoga was, as we have said, liberation of the *yang* soul (that is, the *shên*) from the hindrances of the *yin*, or gross physical body, and thus it was, in fact, a development of the ancient concepts. That is, it had always been presumed that such a liberation was accomplished by death, but the religious Taoists believed it could be accomplished in this very life.

In the spiritual physiology of religious Taoism, the life-force was identified with such obviously vital components as breath, blood, and semen. To preserve life these components must be conserved, and the obstructions to their continuing nourishment of the *shên* must be reduced and finally eliminated. The peculiarity about the religious Taoist notion of breath was that it was not merely inhalation and exhalation of an exterior substance but that it was a progressive "using up" of the allotment of life-spirit with which one was born. Taoist yoga therefore endeavored to conserve the breath. In the same way exhaustion of the semen was equivalent to exhaustion of the life-spirit; therefore, adepts used a technique to retain it instead of ejaculating it during the sexual act. Not only did this prevent exhaustion of the life-spirit, but the method of retention was positively beneficial as well. It was believed that pressure on the urethra at the moment of ejaculation forced the semen back up through the spinal passage to the brain, where it nourished the **Field of Cinnabar** supposed to be located there. Through this circulation of the semen (as of the breath) throughout the various passages and organs predicated by Taoist physiological and anatomical theory, the practitioner was continually rejuvenated.

The same purpose lay behind the various gymnastic routines of Taoist devotees, some of which have been widely adopted in East Asia. The so-called Chinese boxing (*t'ai-chi ch'üan*), a slow-motion ballet performed by countless men and women every morning in China, is like the setting-up exercises used in the West. Its rationale, however, is that just described. Such Taoist gymnastics, when combined with the injunctions of the Old Master to be nonassertive, "weak, like water," and so forth, further led to techniques of bodily combat that have recently become popular among some Westerners, particularly that called the "yielding way" (*rou-tao* in Chinese, or *jūdō* in Japanese).

The Taoist adept attempted to reduce his intake of food as far as possible, because the consumption of food merely contributed to maintenance of the physical body and produced excreta that clogged the various interior passages, which were to be kept open wide for circulation of the life-forces. Even cereals were to be avoided because the body was inhabited by maleficent spirits (*kuei*), who were nourished by cereals.

The notion of the body being inhabited by both beneficent and malevolent spirits was further extended to the conception of the body as a microcosm corresponding to the macrocosm of the universe. Such an imaginative conception might have had its origin, at least in part, in certain passages of *Master Chuang*, where the relativity of things is most powerfully delineated:

> There is nothing in the world larger than the tip of an autumn down; but Mt T'ai is small. There is no life so long as that which is cut off in youth. Ancestor P'êng (the Chinese Methuselah) may be considered to have died prematurely. Heaven-and-Earth were created together with me. The myriad things-and-beings and I are one. (*Master Chuang*, scroll 2, "An Essay on the Relativity of Things"; *Chuang Tzû, Ch'i Wu Lun*)

However, the same sort of thinking was stimulated by the paradoxes beloved of the philosophers of the sophist type who flourished in the fourth and third centuries B.C.E. And even in the more socially oriented thought of Master Mêng, one finds this curious passage: "The ten thousand things (i.e., all things) are complete within us."

At the highest level, among Taoists of superior intellectual and spiritual attainments, the religious quest led not only to the goal of immortality but to a mystical absorption in *tao* itself. Although the meditational techniques of Taoism were strongly influenced by Buddhism in later times, ultimately resulting in the Buddho-Taoist techniques of Ch'an, it seems certain that some form of meditation was already practiced in China long before the arrival of the Indian religion. What is hinted at in *The Old Master* seems to become explicit in *Master Chuang*:

> [Yen] Hui said, May I venture to ask about "fasting the mind"? Chung-ni (i.e., Master K'ung) replied, Concentrate the will. Do not listen with the ears but listen with the mind. Do not listen with the mind but listen with the vital breath. Hearing stops at the ears, the mind stops at tallying [with a stimulus],

but the vital breath is empty and awaits something. It is just the *Tao* that gathers in this emptiness, and this emptiness is the "fasting of the mind." (*Master Chuang*, scroll 4, "Society and the Times"; *Chuang Tzû, Rên Chien Shih*)

. . .

Sloughing off limbs and trunk, driving out intellectual apprehension, abandoning form and rejecting knowledge, identifying with the Great Pervader: this is what is meant by sitting in forgetfulness. (*Master Chuang*, scroll 6)

. . .

Light is produced in the empty room and felicity stops and abides there. If for a time it does not, this is called galloping about while sitting. When the eyes and ears are directed inward and the "knowledge" of the mind is cast out, the very spirits will come to lodge. (*Master Chuang*, scroll 4)

INSTITUTIONALIZATION OF TAOISM

The quest for transcending the limitations of the flesh that has been described thus far was based on esoteric interpretations of certain ancient texts and carried on by means of various techniques that Western scholars have called alchemy. These interpretations and practices constituted the essence of Taoism as a religious Way and required no professional ordination. Indeed, lay devotees of the arts of longevity or immortality must always have been far more numerous than the professional religious. By itself this sort of effort—corresponding in general intent to the search in the West for the "philosopher's stone" or the "fountain of youth"—would not have produced an institutionalized religion. That Taoism did become institutionalized may be ascribed to two major historical developments. On the one hand, the solitary retreats of recluses evolved into whole communities of aspirants living under the guidance of renowned masters, and as one result of this situation, the teachings of the latter were written down to become gospel texts of a Taoist Canon. On the other hand, a new type of religious specialist emerged in the "theocratic" regimes that arose during the time of troubles of the Later Han dynasty, in the second century of the common era.

By far the most important of these regimes for the history of Taoism was that established in the far western province of Ssuch'uan by one Chang Ling or Chang Tao-ling. It is Chang Tao-ling who must be identified, if any one figure can be, as the founder of Taoist religion in the institutionalized form. He stands conveniently for this purpose at the borders of history and legend, and in

the latter area he has been deified as one of popular Taoism's most puissant spiritual powers. Historically, it seems that he did gain political control over a considerable territory, which he administered through a bureaucracy whose officials were more religious than secular in authority. These officials, although deriving organizationally from the practices of the Han imperium, are said to have acted most importantly in the capacity of parish priests. They, like Chang Tao-ling, were evangelists of a new religion of faith healing and ritual adapted to the needs of the masses. Apparently this addition to the age-old popular religion was eagerly embraced by the multitudes, perhaps because it was the first time that their rulers had concerned themselves with the common people. Now, the services of common mediums, shaman-exorcists, and sorcerers were in a sense brought under the aegis of respectable, literate priest-officials, who could bring an unprecedented spiritual power to bear in popular religion. It was this literacy, or mastery of texts, that distinguished the Taoists (we shall use this term hereafter to designate the professional religious and not "believers" in general) from lower-level religious practitioners. At the same time, it was the involvement of the Taoists in the communities that made their services an integral part of the popular religion.

The original chief of these community priests, Chang Tao-ling, assumed a title that was to endure as the most prestigious both within and outside the Taoist institution: **T'ien Shih.** This title, obviously derived by analogy with the imperial title of T'ien Tzû (Son of Heaven), meant the Master Designated by the [Three] Heavens. It remained the hereditary property of the Chang lineage, was given official recognition by many imperial regimes throughout history, especially since the Sung dynasty, and is still acknowledged to have unique authority.

The great majority of Taoists remain in society to act as ritualists for the communities in which they live. They are identified as receiving a number of different ritual traditions, but that purporting to trace back to Chang Tao-ling, called the T'ien-Shih Chêng-yi Tao, or Way of the Orthodox One of the Master Designated by the Heavens, holds pride of place. Most important, it has been the T'ien Shih who has been the recognized source of orthodox ordination, which he would confer on aspirants in accordance with their mastery of specific texts from the whole range of sectarian traditions. On the other hand, Taoists who chose to leave the world and live secluded in monasteries in order to pursue the alchemical techniques that would gain them personal immortality might be said more closely to resemble Buddhist monks. The major tradition of this style of Taoist career was the Ch'üan-chên Chiao, or Sect of Total Perfection.

THE TAOIST AS EXORCIST
AND RITUALIST

The two main functions of the Taoist are exorcism and protection of the well-being and security of the mortal world against the attacks of *kuei*, and performance of rituals on behalf of clients and community. Although both of these functions are also carried on by lower-level religious specialists, the Taoist is recognized to have more effective power under his control for exorcism and protection, and only he knows the complicated rubrics of the major liturgies. He is, to put it in brief, a better-educated specialist than those others, especially by virtue of his book learning. This was, of course, an outstanding qualification in those days when the mere ability to read and write made a person exceptional and constituted the very basis for qualifying one to enter elite status in the society. It should be stressed that the profession of Taoist is very much more demanding in its preparation than those of medium, shaman, or the like. While these latter may have literally no preparatory training but simply be "possessed" by their familiar deity—or even substitute only a convincing assertion of their occult powers for such possession—the Taoist has to undergo a long period of textual studies, supplemented by the oral instructions of his mentor. The latter is customarily his own father as, in common with most professions involving specialized technical knowledge in traditional China, the professional secrets were kept within the family. Following this long apprenticeship, the aspirant would seek service under an eminent master, in order to become his successor. His ordination was an impressive ceremony, preceded by many days of isolation and fasting and publicly performed during a sacrificial "mass" called *chiao*, which lasted a minimum of three days.

. . . The basis for the Taoist's control over *kuei* and *shên* was a form of "name magic," an interesting survival, in a sophisticated religion, of a very ancient, even primitive, notion. He could summon and dismiss the deities of **macrocosm** (the universe) and **microcosm** (his own body) by virtue of his knowledge of their names, true descriptions, and functions. He further controlled them by means of cabalistic writing, the talismans or charms called *fu*. These *fu* were, in effect, orders or commands issued by the Taoist by virtue of his authority in the spiritual realm, and thereby they kept away *kuei* and invoked the beneficence of *shên*. . . .

It should be noted that there is generally understood to be a distinction between those Taoists (commonly called "Red-heads" in Taiwan) who are found practicing exorcism and other popular rites in the busy temples on an everyday basis and the supposedly higher-class Taoists (called "Black-heads" in Taiwan) who alone are competent to perform the extended liturgies of the *chiao*. The former will wear a red scarf tied about the head (or waist) and carry a buffalo horn, which they blow in loud blasts, while the latter are seen attired in their formal sacerdotal vestments complete with black "mandarin cap" with gold-colored knob. The essential distinction between the two types is that the former (called *fa-shih*, or occult specialists), knowing only the more rudimentary texts, are ordained in low rank and cannot perform the greater liturgies, while the latter have mastered the texts qualifying them to perform those greatly more complex and religiously profound rituals. However, the superior ranked *tao-shih* (Taoist masters) are, of course, able to carry out the popular rites that are the specialty of their inferiors and often do not disdain to do so in consideration of the pecuniary rewards.

The greater rituals whose liturgies are set forth in the advanced texts are known as *chiao* and **chai**. There apparently was not much difference between these two forms historically. A contemporary Chinese scholar, Liu Chih-wan, has suggested the following distinction: "Taking the broadest view, the difference in the results sought by the two [forms of ritual] is simply that their emphases are not the same: The *chai* places its emphasis upon the prayers of the individual for blessings and the salvation of the dead; whereas the emphasis of the *chiao* is upon the prayers of the public (i.e., the community) for averting calamities and ensuring tranquillity. [Thus] each has its special emphasis." According to the American authority Michael Saso, himself an ordained *tao-shih*, although the two sets of rituals are both performed during the several-day festivals in the communities in Taiwan, the *chiao* has as its purpose "to win blessing from heaven and union with the transcendent Tao," whereas the *chai* is intended "to free the souls from hell." A special feature of the latter is that it concludes with a great feast for the souls of those in purgatory, called by the Buddhist term *p'u-tu*.

The *chiao* has both esoteric and exoteric levels of meaning. For the Taoist himself, it is a procedure whereby he personally attains mystical union with Tao, or in other words, a form of *nei-tan*. To the public it is an impressive ceremonial and magical performance whereby the supreme powers of the universe are called down into the temple for a State visit and petitioned to give their spiritual support to the community. At the same time, while these highly formalized, canonically prescribed events are being enacted within a temple—which, incidentally, is only for this occasion made off-limits to the public—the people are themselves participating in the rituals according to traditional lay roles, and the joint efforts of priests and people comprise a total community "happening," a great festival both sacred and profane.

In Taiwan today such *chiao* are the most exciting and colorful affairs carried on in the communities. Like medieval European fairs, they combine the religious, the aesthetic, and the purely sensual, and they last for at least three days and nights. Large structures called *t'an,* or altars, are erected in vacant lots or fields, dedicated to major deities, and at night brightly illuminated. They are facades or skeletons of bamboo covered with cloth and paper, colorfully decorated with all sorts of ingenuous folk art. Every so often the Taoist retinue emerges from the temple to perform some public section of the liturgies, much to the enjoyment of the people. Huge crowds arrive, many from distant places, to share in the excitement. Everywhere the local people have set out their household offerings on tables at the roadside, of which pride of place goes to monstrous pigs that have been fattened for just this occasion and that are spread-eagled in hairless nudity on special stands. There are noisy theatricals, fortune-telling booths, hawkers of every kind, and carnival amusements. Day and night this animated scene astonishes by its vitality and the prodigality with which these people of so little material substance spend for their festival. The persistent theme of the festival as a whole is the dominance of the dead. Not only are canonical texts of merit and repentance for salvation of souls constantly being read by the Taoists during the entire *chiao,* but all of that mountain of food and drink set out by the households of the entire community is for the souls of the dead. The ancestors are of course expected to enjoy this feast, but there are many souls who must be appeased for fear of their vengeance—the spirits of those who have been deprived of their due sacrifices and the spirits of those who must suffer punishment in purgatory. Dominating the scene before the temple stands the figure of Ta Shih, the metamorphosed Kuan Shih Yin as King of these Ghosts, charged with keeping them in order when they flock to the feast prepared for them by the community. To that feast they have been invited by signal lamps and pennants hung on tall posts and by paper boats sent burning out on the waters. Not until these dangerous spirits have been respectfully banqueted on the essences of the sacrifices can the community feel secure and the hoped-for benefits of the *chiao* be assured.

We may seem here to have left the topic of the religious vocation and to have returned to religion in the community. But it will be seen that it is in fact the roles of exorcist and ritualist for the community that have constituted the profession, the raison d'etre, of the Taoist and ensured the continuing vitality of his public vocation through the centuries.

SOURCES

The source material for Taoism is massive. The official collection or canon of Taoist literature (*Tao-tsang*), published in 1445, is composed of 1,120 volumes and 1,476 titles. It is divided into three primary parts called the "Three Caverns" in which one will find moral codes, revelations from gods and goddesses, textual commentaries, ritual instructions, alchemical recipes, meditation instruction, philosophical musing, and much more.

Over the years there have been many supplements to the *Tao-tsang* and there is much literature pertaining to Taoism that is not part of the canon. The material I have selected is organized historically and covers a variety of themes. It includes both influential and representative material touching on some of the main themes of Taoism such as the Tao, discipline, meditation, physical practices, rituals, longevity, and immortality.

The promise of Taoism is freedom and immortality. The serious Taoist seeks to be free from conventional modes of thought and ways of living, hoping one day to live among the glorious immortals. The path to freedom and immortality is long and complex. Along the way the serious adept must discipline both body and mind, transforming not only her or his life in this world, but also securing a place in the world to come.

7.2 THE EARLY FOUNDATIONS

Although, as we noted earlier, the revelation on which the Taoist movement called Celestial Masters is based did not take place until 142, that revelation is intimately tied to earlier ideas. Among them are ideas attributed to two brilliant sages, Lao Tzu and Chuang Tzu. We must start with this foundation because its authority has been vital to Taoism for more than 2,000 years.

Even before Chang Tao-ling had his vision of Lao Tzu in 142, people had been inspired by the writings of Lao Tzu and Chuang Tzu. We have records of vivid visionary journeys inspired by the imagery of these two great sages. One, called "Far-Off Journey," relates a trip into a soundless, invisible Great Beginning.

7.2.1 The Way and Its Power

Imagine that you are instructed to describe the source of all things. You might begin by thinking about the things you know about like rocks, trees, cats, books, chairs, people, and the like. Could any one of these things be the source of all things? It seems unlikely because all of these things are limited by time, space, and matter. Is the source of all things limited too? If it is, how could it be the source of everything? Perhaps it is best to say that the source of all things is unlimited. Does that mean it is spaceless, timeless, and immaterial? If it is, how can we describe it except by saying what it is not?

Lao Tzu, the legendary author of the **Tao Te Ching,** faced this problem of describing the source of all. He gave it a name—the Tao, or Way—and he talked about its power (Te), but in the final analysis he knew that it is really the Nameless.

According to Taoist tradition, Lao Tzu, was an older contemporary of Confucius living in sixth century B.C.E. China. Supposedly he worked as an archivist for most of his life, and, when he became disturbed by the degeneration of his society, he decided to leave China by the "Western Gate." Before the gatekeeper would let him pass, the gatekeeper persuaded him to write down his wisdom concerning the Tao and its power. Later generations reported numerous sightings of the departed Lao Tzu, and soon a wealth of legends began to circulate about him, including one in which he instructed Confucius in the proper understanding of the Tao. After Lao Tzu purportedly went through the Western Gate, he traveled to India and there became known as the Buddha. Eventually he became an immortal deity, or, rather, he returned to his original state since it was rumored that he was really a deity incarnate all the while people had thought him mortal. However, he still appears in visions to people at crucial times to instruct them in the Way.

The Taoist tradition claims that the *Tao Te Ching* is the oldest text in the Taoist canon, dating from around 250 B.C.E. It is sometimes called the *Lao-tzu,* after its alleged author, and is popularly known as "The Five Thousand Character Classic" because it contains around five thousand characters. It is the foundational text of Taoism.

The *Tao Te Ching* has been translated numerous times and interpreted in a variety of ways. The text as we have it now is divided into two parts. The first deals with the Tao (Way) and the second with its Te (power or virtue). The selections that follow focus on the notion of the Tao, since this "nameless name" has played such a central role in Taoism.

LAO TZU

Tao Te Ching

READING QUESTIONS

1. Why is the Tao that can be told not the eternal Tao?
2. What does it mean to manage affairs without action?
3. What kinds of metaphors are used to characterize Tao?
4. If we model our life after Tao, what sort of life would it be?
5. What is the order of production of the ten thousand things?

1

The Tao that can be told of is not the eternal Tao;
The name that can be named is not the eternal name.
The Nameless is the origin of Heaven and Earth;
The Named is the mother of all things.

Therefore let there always be non-being, so we may
  see their subtlety,
And let there always be being, so we may see their
  outcome.
The two are the same,
But after they are produced, they have different names.
They both may be called deep and profound.
Deeper and more profound,
The door of all subtleties!

From Chan, Wing-tsit, *A Source Book of Chinese Philosophy.* Copyright © 1963 by Princeton University Press; renewed 1991. Reprinted by permission of Princeton University Press. Footnotes and commentary omitted.

2

When the people of the world all know beauty as
 beauty,
There arises the recognition of ugliness.
When they all know the good as good,
There arises the recognition of evil.
Therefore:
 Being and non-being produce each other;
 Difficult and easy complete each other;
 Long and short contrast each other;
 High and low distinguish each other;
 Sound and voice harmonize each other;
 Front and behind accompany each other.
 Therefore the sage manages affairs without action
 And spreads doctrines without words.
 All things arise, and he does not turn away from
  them.
 He produces them but does not take possession of
  them.
 He acts but does not rely on his own ability.
 He accomplishes his task but does not claim credit
  for it.
 It is precisely because he does not claim credit that
  his accomplishment remains with him. . . .

4

Tao is empty (like a bowl).
 It may be used but its capacity is never exhausted.
 It is bottomless, perhaps the ancestor of all things.
 It blunts its sharpness,
 It unties its tangles.
 It softens its light.
 It becomes one with the dusty world.
 Deep and still, it appears to exist forever.
 I do not know whose son it is.
 It seems to have existed before the Lord. . . .

6

The spirit of the valley never dies.
 It is called the subtle and profound female.
The gate of the subtle and profound female
 Is the root of Heaven and Earth.
It is continuous, and seems to be always existing.
Use it and you will never wear it out. . . .

8

The best (man) is like water.
 Water is good; it benefits all things and does not
  compete with them.
It dwells in (lowly) places that all disdain.
This is why it is so near to Tao.

(The best man) in his dwelling loves the earth.
In his heart, he loves what is profound.
In his associations, he loves humanity.
In his words, he loves faithfulness.
In government, he loves order.
In handling affairs, he loves competence.
In his activities, he loves timeliness.
It is because he does not compete that he is without
 reproach. . . .

11

Thirty spokes are united around the hub to make a
 wheel,
 But it is on its non-being that the utility of the
  carriage depends.
Clay is molded to form a utensil,
 But it is on its non-being that the utility of the
  utensil depends.
Doors and windows are cut out to make a room,
 But it is on its non-being that the utility of the room
  depends.
Therefore turn being into advantage, and turn non-
 being into utility. . . .

14

We look at it and do not see it;
 Its name is The Invisible.
We listen to it and do not hear it;
 Its name is The Inaudible.
We touch it and do not find it;
 Its name is The Subtle (formless).

These three cannot be further inquired into,
And hence merge into one.
Going up high, it is not bright, and coming down low,
 it is not dark.
Infinite and boundless, it cannot be given any name;
It reverts to nothingness.

This is called shape without shape,
Form without objects.
It is The Vague and Elusive.
Meet it and you will not see its head.
Follow it and you will not see its back.
Hold on to the Tao of old in order to master the
   things of the present.
From this one may know the primeval beginning
   (of the universe).
This is called the bond of Tao. . . .

16

Attain complete vacuity.
Maintain steadfast quietude.

All things come into being,
And I see thereby their return.
All things flourish,
But each one returns to its root.
This return to its root means tranquillity.
It is called returning to its destiny.
To return to destiny is called the eternal (Tao).
To know the eternal is called enlightenment.
Not to know the eternal is to act blindly to result in
   disaster.
He who knows the eternal is all-embracing.
Being all-embracing, he is impartial.
Being impartial, he is kingly (universal).
Being kingly, he is one with Nature.
Being one with Nature, he is in accord with Tao.
Being in accord with Tao, he is everlasting
And is free from danger throughout his lifetime. . . .

22

To yield is to be preserved whole.
To be bent is to become straight.
To be empty is to be full.
To be worn out is to be renewed.
To have little is to possess.
To have plenty is to be perplexed.
Therefore the sage embraces the One
And becomes the model of the world.
He does not show himself; therefore he is luminous.
He does not justify himself; therefore he becomes
   prominent.

He does not boast of himself; therefore he is given
   credit.
He does not brag; therefore he can endure for long.

It is precisely because he does not compete that the
   world cannot compete with him.
Is the ancient saying, "To yield is to be preserved
   whole," empty words?
Truly he will be preserved and (prominence and credit)
   will come to him. . . .

25

There was something undifferentiated and yet
   complete,
Which existed before heaven and earth.
Soundless and formless, it depends on nothing and
   does not change.
It operates everywhere and is free from danger.
It may be considered the mother of the universe.
I do not know its name; I call it Tao.
If forced to give it a name, I shall call it Great.
Now being great means functioning everywhere.
Functioning everywhere means far-reaching.
Being far-reaching means returning to the original
   point.

Therefore Tao is great.
Heaven is great.
Earth is great.
And the king is also great.
There are four great things in the universe, and the
   king is one of them.
Man models himself after Earth.
Earth models itself after Heaven.
Heaven models itself after Tao.
And Tao models itself after Nature. . . .

34

The Great Tao flows everywhere.
It may go left or right.
All things depend on it for life, and it does not turn
   away from them.
It accomplishes its task, but does not claim credit for it.
It clothes and feeds all things but does not claim to be
   master over them.
Always without desires, it may be called The Small.

All things come to it and it does not master them; it
  may be called The Great.
Therefore (the sage) never strives himself for the great,
  and thereby the great is achieved. . . .

37

Tao invariably takes no action, and yet there is nothing
  left undone.
If kings and barons can keep it, all things will transform
  spontaneously.
If, after transformation, they should desire to be active,
I would restrain them with simplicity, which has no
  name.
Simplicity, which has no name, is free of desires.
Being free of desires, it is tranquil.
And the world will be at peace of its own accord. . . .

42

Tao produced the One.
The One produced the two.
The two produced the three.
And the three produced the ten thousand things.
The ten thousand things carry the yin and embrace
  the yang, and through the blending of the material
  force they achieve harmony. . . .

7.2.2 Mystical Tales

After the *Tao Te Ching*, the *Chuang Tzu* is the second
most important foundational text of Taoism. It is attributed to the philosopher **Chuang Tzu** after whom
it is named. It is unlikely that Chuang Tzu, who lived
in the fourth century B.C.E., is responsible for all of
the thirty-three chapters in the book, but most scholars agree that the so-called "inner chapters" (chapters 1–7) may well be from his mouth, if not his brush.

The *Chuang Tzu* is a remarkable book. It is full
of funny stories, brilliant philosophical asides, wry
observations, illustrative anecdotes, tips on living,
contradictory riddles, and questions upon questions
upon questions. It is skeptical and mystical, brilliant
and dark, stable and fluid, ancient and postmodern. It
is constantly undermining itself while undermining

its undermining. It is very much like the Tao itself.
Then again, it is not.

As you might imagine, the interpretations of the
Chuang Tzu vary greatly. Some read the text as deeply
mystical, teaching us to see the unity of all opposites.
Others read the text as deeply skeptical, teaching
us to doubt all conceptions of truth and reality. Still
others think the *Chuang Tzu* teaches a radical value
relativism that undermines all philosophical and religious claims to reveal absolute values. Burton Watson, whose translation I use, says in his introduction
that the *Chuang Tzu* seeks to point the way to freedom from the baggage of conventional values. As you
read, apply these various interpretations and see if
they make sense of the text.

CHUANG TZU

Chuang Tzu

READING QUESTION

1. Write a brief commentary on these passages from
   chapter 2, stating what you think they mean.

Now I am going to make a statement here. I don't know
whether it fits into the category of other people's statements or not. But whether it fits into their category or
whether it doesn't, it obviously fits into some category.
So in that respect it is no different from their statements.
However, let me try making my statement.

There is a beginning. There is a not yet beginning to
be a beginning. There is a not yet beginning to be a not
yet beginning to be a beginning. There is being. There
is nonbeing. There is a not yet beginning to be non-
being. There is a not yet beginning to be a not yet beginning to be nonbeing. Suddenly there is being and
nonbeing. But between this being and nonbeing, I don't
really know which is being and which is nonbeing. Now
I have just said something. But I don't know whether

Republished with permission of Columbia University Press,
562 W. 113th St., New York, NY 10025. *Chuang Tzu: Basic
Writings*, translated by Burton Watson, 1964/1996. Reproduced by permission of the publisher via Copyright Clearance
Center, Inc. Pp. 38–45. Footnotes edited.

what I have said has really said something or whether it hasn't said something.

There is nothing in the world bigger than the tip of an autumn hair, and Mount T'ai is little. No one has lived longer than a dead child, and P'eng-tsu died young.[1] Heaven and earth were born at the same time I was, and the ten thousand things are one with me.

We have already become one, so how can I say anything? But I have just *said* that we are one, so how can I not be saying something? The one and what I said about it make two, and two and the original one make three. If we go on this way, then even the cleverest mathematician can't tell where we'll end, much less an ordinary man. If by moving from nonbeing to being we get to three, how far will we get if we move from being to being? Better not to move, but to let things be!

The Way has never known boundaries; speech has no constancy. But because of [the recognition of a] "this," there came to be boundaries. Let me tell you what the boundaries are. There is left, there is right, there are theories, there are debates, there are divisions, there are discriminations, there are emulations, and there are contentions. These are called the Eight Virtues. As to what is beyond the Six Realms,[2] the sage admits it exists but does not theorize. As to what is within the Six Realms, he theorizes but does not debate. In the case of the *Spring and Autumn*, the record of the former kings of past ages, the sage debates but does not discriminate. So [I say,] those who divide fail to divide; those who discriminate fail to discriminate. What does this mean, you ask? The sage embraces things. Ordinary men discriminate among them and parade their discriminations before others. So I say, those who discriminate fail to see.

The Great Way is not named; Great Discriminations are not spoken; Great Benevolence is not benevolent; Great Modesty is not humble; Great Daring does not attack. If the Way is made clear, it is not the Way. If discriminations are put into words, they do not suffice. If benevolence has a constant object, it cannot be universal. If modesty is fastidious, it cannot be trusted. If daring attacks, it cannot be complete. These five are all round, but they tend toward the square.[3]

Therefore understanding that rests in what it does not understand is the finest. Who can understand discriminations that are not spoken, the Way that is not a

way? If he can understand this, he may be called the Reservoir of Heaven. Pour into it and it is never full, dip from it and it never runs dry, and yet it does not know where the supply comes from. This is called the Shaded Light.

So it is that long ago Yao said to Shun, "I want to attack the rulers of Tsung, K'uai, and Hsü-ao. Even as I sit on my throne, this thought nags at me. Why is this?"

Shun replied, "These three rulers are only little dwellers in the weeds and brush. Why this nagging desire? Long ago, ten suns came out all at once and the ten thousand things were all lighted up. And how much greater is virtue than these suns!"

Nieh Ch'üeh asked Wang Ni, "Do you know what all things agree in calling right?"

"How would I know that?" said Wang Ni.

"Do you know that you don't know it?"

"How would I know that?"

"Then do things know nothing?"

"How would I know that? However, suppose I try saying something. What way do I have of knowing that if I say I know something I don't really not know it? Or what way do I have of knowing that if I say I don't know something I don't really in fact know it? Now let me ask *you* some questions. If a man sleeps in a damp place, his back aches and he ends up half paralyzed, but is this true of a loach? If he lives in a tree, he is terrified and shakes with fright, but is this true of a monkey? Of these three creatures, then, which one knows the proper place to live? Men eat the flesh of grass-fed and grain-fed animals, deer eat grass, centipedes find snakes tasty, and hawks and falcons relish mice. Of these four, which knows how food ought to taste? Monkeys pair with monkeys, deer go out with deer, and fish play around with fish. Men claim that Mao-ch'iang and Lady Li were beautiful, but if fish saw them they would dive to the bottom of the stream, if birds saw them they would fly away, and if deer saw them they would break into a run. Of these four, which knows how to fix the standard of beauty for the world? The way I see it, the rules of benevolence and righteousness and the paths of right and wrong are all hopelessly snarled and jumbled. How could I know anything about such discriminations?"

Nieh Ch'üeh said, "If you don't know what is profitable or harmful, then does the Perfect Man likewise know nothing of such things?"

Wang Ni replied, "The Perfect Man is godlike. Though the great swamps blaze, they cannot burn him; though the great rivers freeze, they cannot chill him; though swift lightning splits the hills and howling gales shake the sea, they cannot frighten him. A man like this rides the clouds and mist, straddles the sun and moon, and wanders beyond the four seas. Even life and death

---

[1] The strands of animal fur were believed to grow particularly fine in autumn: hence "the tip of an autumn hair" is a cliché for something extremely tiny. P'eng-tsu [is] the Chinese Methuselah. . . .

[2] Heaven, earth, and the four directions, i.e., the universe.

[3] All are originally perfect, but may become "squared," i.e., impaired, by the misuses mentioned.

have no effect on him, much less the rules of profit and loss!"

Chü Ch'üeh-tzu said to Chang Wu-tzu, "I have heard Confucius say that the sage does not work at anything, does not pursue profit, does not dodge harm, does not enjoy being sought after, does not follow the Way, says nothing yet says something, says something yet says nothing, and wanders beyond the dust and grime. Confucius himself regarded these as wild and flippant words, though I believe they describe the working of the mysterious Way. What do you think of them?"

Chang Wu-tzu said, "Even the Yellow Emperor would be confused if he heard such words, so how could you expect Confucius to understand them? What's more, you're too hasty in your own appraisal. You see an egg and demand a crowing cock, see a crossbow pellet and demand a roast dove. I'm going to try speaking some reckless words and I want you to listen to them recklessly. How will that be? The sage leans on the sun and moon, tucks the universe under his arm, merges himself with things, leaves the confusion and muddle as it is, and looks on slaves as exalted. Ordinary men strain and struggle; the sage is stupid and blockish. He takes part in ten thousand ages and achieves simplicity in oneness. For him, all the ten thousand things are what they are, and thus they enfold each other.

"How do I know that loving life is not a delusion? How do I know that in hating death I am not like a man who, having left home in his youth, has forgotten the way back?

"Lady Li was the daughter of the border guard of Ai.[4] When she was first taken captive and brought to the state of Chin, she wept until her tears drenched the collar of her robe. But later, when she went to live in the palace of the ruler, shared his couch with him, and ate the delicious meats of his table, she wondered why she had ever wept. How do I know that the dead do not wonder why they ever longed for life?

"He who dreams of drinking wine may weep when morning comes; he who dreams of weeping may in the morning go off to hunt. While he is dreaming he does not know it is a dream, and in his dream he may even try to interpret a dream. Only after he wakes does he know it was a dream. And someday there will be a great awakening when we know that this is all a great dream. Yet the stupid believe they are awake, busily and brightly assuming they understand things, calling this man ruler, that one herdsman—how dense! Confucius and you are

both dreaming! And when I say you are dreaming, I am dreaming, too. Words like these will be labeled the Supreme Swindle. Yet, after ten thousand generations, a great sage may appear who will know their meaning, and it will still be as though he appeared with astonishing speed.

"Suppose you and I have had an argument. If you have beaten me instead of my beating you, then are you necessarily right and am I necessarily wrong? If I have beaten you instead of your beating me, then am I necessarily right and are you necessarily wrong? Is one of us right and the other wrong? Are both of us right or are both of us wrong? If you and I don't know the answer, then other people are bound to be even more in the dark. Whom shall we get to decide what is right? Shall we get someone who agrees with you to decide? But if he already agrees with you, how can he decide fairly? Shall we get someone who agrees with me? But if he already agrees with me, how can he decide? Shall we get someone who disagrees with both of us? But if he already disagrees with both of us, how can he decide? Shall we get someone who agrees with both of us? But if he already agrees with both of us, how can he decide? Obviously, then, neither you nor I nor anyone else can know the answer. Shall we wait for still another person?

"But waiting for one shifting voice [to pass judgment on] another is the same as waiting for none of them. Harmonize them all with the Heavenly Equality, leave them to their endless changes, and so live out your years. What do I mean by harmonizing them with the Heavenly Equality? Right is not right; so is not so. If right were really right, it would differ so clearly from not right that there would be no need for argument. If so were really so, it would differ so clearly from not so that there would be no need for argument. Forget the years; forget distinctions. Leap into the boundless and make it your home!"

Penumbra said to Shadow, "A little while ago you were walking and now you're standing still; a little while ago you were sitting and now you're standing up. Why this lack of independent action?"

Shadow said, "Do I have to wait for something before I can be like this? Does what I wait for also have to wait for something before it can be like this? Am I waiting for the scales of a snake or the wings of a cicada? How do I know why it is so? How do I know why it isn't so?"

Once Chuang Chou dreamt he was a butterfly, a butterfly flitting and fluttering around, happy with himself and doing as he pleased. He didn't know he was Chuang Chou. Suddenly he woke up and there he was, solid and unmistakable Chuang Chou. But he didn't know if he was Chuang Chou who had dreamt he was a butterfly,

---

[4] She was taken captive by Duke Hsien of Chin in 671 B.C., and later became his consort.

or a butterfly dreaming he was Chuang Chou. Between Chuang Chou and a butterfly there must be *some* distinction! This is called the Transformation of Things.

7.2.3 Ecstatic Travel

Taoists practice three different kinds of meditation: concentrative meditation, insight meditation, and **ecstatic journeys.** The first type is called "guarding the One" and involves learning how to fix one's mind on a single point. It is similar to Hindu and Buddhist *samadhi* practices. The second type, which appears to be borrowed from Buddhism, involves developing insight into the "true nature of things" by learning how to observe or witness self and others from the viewpoint of Taoism. Ecstatic travel involves spiritual journeys into the otherworld. The adept has an "out of body experience" in which he or she travels to the heavens and moves among the gods.

Ecstatic spirit travel probably derives from ancient shamanistic practices. Shamans developed various techniques for traveling to spirit worlds in order to find answers to various questions or bring back power for healing. Later, these journeys were linked with the physical journeys taken by emperors through their realm. Such journeys established the power and control of the emperors by making their presence known in the far reaches of their kingdoms.

A classical account of ecstatic travel ("Far-Off Journey") is found in a collection of ritual songs titled *Songs of the Chu* (also called *Songs of the South*), which date from the third century B.C.E. and later. They were compiled by a poet from South China named Ch'ü Yüan. A story recounts how Ch'ü Yüan drowned himself in despair over the corruptness of the world, having been unfairly slandered and banished from court. His death is associated with the Dragon Boat festival held in midsummer. During the festival, boat races reenact fishermen's attempts to save Ch'ü Yüan.

We do not know the author of "Far-Off Journey," but he or she draws on the imagery found in both the *Tao Te Ching* and the *Chuang Tzu*. One important concept found in all three writings is **wu-wei,** or nonaction (sometimes translated as "actionless action"). The Tao acts without acting, which means acting freely and without force. It is to allow or permit natural action to occur rather than to control and shape a situation by force. Both rulers and the ruled should model their own action after the Tao.

The journey you are about to undertake leads you not only to the realm of nonaction but also beyond. It not only takes you to the realm of the gods but transcends that realm as well. You come in contact with accomplished adepts and learn how to command the deities. Racing across the cosmos, traveling in all directions, surveying many marvels, you finally enter the silence of the Great Beginning.

Far-Off Journey

READING QUESTIONS

1. Outline the structure of this poem. How does it start? How does it end? What happens in the middle?
2. What part of the poem do you find most gripping? Why?
3. How might experiences of ecstatic travel and their accounts function in religion?

Wrought with afflictions of the wonts of this age
I long to rise softly and journey afar,
But my meager powers are of trifling avail.
On what might I ride to soar upwards?
Confronting sunken depravity, a morass of corruption,
Alone and depressed, in whom might I confide?
Through the night I am wakeful and sleepless,
And my soul is restive until dawn;
I ponder the unfathomable reaches of heaven and earth,
Mourn the endless travails of human existence,
Lament those people already departed, whom I had
   never met,
And those yet to come, whom I would never know.
Pacing about, my thoughts adrift,
Nervously anxious and oddly pensive,
My thoughts run wild and unsettled,
And my heart is sadly despondent.
My spirit flashes forth and does not return,
And my physical frame withers and is left behind.
Reflecting inwardly I remain steadfast,
Searching for the source of the true vital force.
In silent vacuity and tranquillity I find quiet joy;

From *Chinese Religion: An Anthology of Sources*, edited by Deborah Sommer (New York: Oxford University Press, 1995), pp. 91–94. Copyright © 1995 Oxford University Press. Reprinted by permission.

With still nonaction I accomplish things naturally. . . .
I am in awe of the regularity of heaven's seasons,
Of that shining ethereal brightness, in its westward
   journey;
But a light frost is settling, sinking downward,
And I worry lest my fragrant flowers fall early.
Would that I could drift and roam,
Forever passing the years with no particular design.
But with whom might I enjoy my few remaining
   fragrances?
At dawn, I unloose my feelings into the prevailing
   winds. . . .
I dine on the six vital forces and drink mists and vapors,
Rinse my mouth with the principal yang forces and
   imbibe the morning haze.
I safeguard the halcyon clarity of the spiritual and
   numinous,
And refined vital forces enter and coarser dregs are
   expelled.
Flowing with the gentle breezes, I roam about with
   them;
Arriving at the Southern Aerie, I stop at once,
And seeing Master Wang, I stay the night.
I ask him how the one vital force can be harmonized
   with virtue,
And he says, "The way can be received, but it cannot
   be transmitted to others.
It is so small that it has no inner space, so large that it
   has no outer limits.
When the soul is without artifice, one can deal with
   things naturally;
When the unitary vital force permeates the spirit,
   sustain it throughout the night.
Abide in vacuity prior to nonaction,
And everything will come to completion.
This is the gate of virtue."
I hear this and treasure it; I continue on,
Quickly preparing to set out.
I soon see the Feathered People of the Cinnabar Hills
And linger in that ancient deathless land.
I wash my hair in Boiling Valley,
And at night dry my bodily self at Nine Yang Forces;
I inhale the subtle secretions of the Flying Springs,
And embrace the shining emblems of the jade regalia.
The jade's colors radiate, casting a luster on my face;
My subtle essences, purified, start to strengthen;
My material self melts and dissolves, frothing away,
And my spirit floats about, loose and free.
I admire the warm, radiant virtues of the southern land,
And the winter blossoming of the beautiful cassia tree.
There desolate mountains are uninhabited by beasts,
And silent wildernesses harbor no human beings.

Bearing my corporeal soul, I ascend the mists of dawn,
And spread upon a floating cloud, I journey upward.
I order the porter of the gates of heaven to open his
   doors,
Swing back the gates, and keep a lookout for me.
I summon Feng Lung and place him in my vanguard
And ask him where Great Subtlety lies.
Collecting my redoubled yang forces, I enter the
   palace of the Lord;
I visit Temporal Origins and purview the City of
   Clarity.
Setting out at dawn, I stop at the Court of Grand
   Ceremony,
And by evening draw nigh to the Gate of Subtlety.
Marshalling a company of ten thousand chariots,
Rolling forward en masse at an even gallop,
I drive eight dragons, beautiful and sleek,
In a chariot strung with waving serpentine cloud banners
And mounted with bold rainbows of multicolored
   streamers,
Their five colors arrayed in dazzling brightness.
My inside steeds arch proudly, lowering and tossing;
The outside team writhes spiritedly, prancing.
Charging off, we ride tightly bunched and then fan out
   in a fray,
And the colorful stampede takes off.
Taking up the reins and unleashing the whip,
I set off to see Kou Mang.
Passing Grand Luminosity, I wheel to the right,
Sending Fei Lien ahead to clear the way.
As the light brightens just before sunrise,
I traverse the diameter of heaven and earth;
The Earl of the Wind courses ahead as my vanguard,
Sweeping away the dusts and ushering in clear coolness;
Soaring phoenixes bear my banners aloft,
And I encounter Ju Shou at the Western August
   Heavens.
Grasping a broom-star as my standard
And wielding aloft the Dipper's handle as my ensign,
In a glittering coruscation wending high and low,
I roam onward, scattering the flowing waves of mist.
Daylight clouds into darkness
As I summon Hsüan Wu to race in my retinue,
Charge Wen Ch'ang to direct the maneuvers at the
   rear guard,
And appoint a host of spirits to flank me on both sides.
The road spans far into the distance,
And I check the pace as I veer sharply upward.
At my right the Master of Rains serves as my scout,
And on the left, the Duke of Thunder is my escort.
Wanting to traverse the entire world, I forget to return
   home;

My thoughts are carefree and unconstrained,
And inwardly I rejoice and am at peace with myself,
Delighting in my own contentment.
But pacing the azure clouds, drifting and roaming,
I suddenly catch a glimpse of my old homeland;
My charioteers and grooms long for it, and my own
  heart grows sad.
Even the outside horses, turning back to look, do not
  go on.
Thinking of my old home, I envision it in my thoughts,
Drawing a deep breath as I hide my tears.
With a troubled countenance, I still advance upward,
Restraining my will and regaining composure.
Aiming for the Flaming Spirit, I gallop straight for it,
Heading toward the Southern Mountains.
I survey the barren reaches beyond space,
The floating mirages that drift of their own accord,
But Chu Jung warns me to turn back.
So I remount, bidding the simurgh to invite Fu Fei;
Strumming "In Many Ponds" and playing "Uplifting
  the Clouds,"
Two maidens present the Nine Shao Songs.
I bid the spirits of the Hsiang River to play the drum
  and zither,
And order the God of the Sea to dance with P'ing-i.
Lines of black dragons and sea-serpents weave in
  and out,
Their bodies wriggling and swaying in serpentines.
Lady Rainbow brightens ever more beautifully
As the simurgh soars and flies above
And the music rises in limitless crescendos.
I roam again, sporting to and fro,
Rolling onward at an even pace, galloping excitedly.
Striding ahead to the boundary limits at the Gate of
  Coldness;
Rushing forth swiftly with the wind at Clear Springs,
I follow Chuan Hsü over tiers of ice.
Crossing the land of Hsüan Ming, I diverge from
  my path;
Mounting the latitudes, I turn to look back,
Summoning Ch'ien Lei to manifest himself
To go before me and level the road.
I have traversed the Four Vastnesses,
Made a circuit of the Six Deserts,
Ascended to the lightning's cracks,
And descended into the Great Ravine.
Peaks rise high below, but there is no earth;
Empty vastness soars above, but there is no heaven.
Glancing this way and that, I see nothing;
Listening anxiously, I hear nothing.
Going beyond nonaction, I attain clarity,
And dwell in the Great Beginning.

7.3 TAOISM EXPANDS

As we have seen, Chang Tao-ling's revelation in 142 was the beginning of the Celestial Masters school of Taoism. In 364 a medium named Yang Hsi began to receive revelations from the Heaven of Highest Clarity, and, with those revelations, the second major Taoist school began. It was called, appropriately enough, the Highest Clarity (*Shang Ch'ing*) school. **Highest Clarity** practice aimed at transferring humans into the realms of the immortals by the use of visualizations, ecstatic journeys, and even by the ingestion of highly poisonous alchemical elixirs.

A few decades after Yang Hsi's revelations, yet another Taoist school formed around the revelations of Ge Chao-fu. Known as the Numinous Treasure (*Ling-bao*) school, it integrated Highest Clarity scriptures with some Buddhist ideas. Its practice was much simpler than that of Highest Clarity, requiring the recitation of its scriptures and participation in its rites, rather than arduous meditation exercises and alchemical elixirs, in order for humans to be perfected.

With the *Ling-bao* movement, Taoism emerged for the first time as an organized religion of *all* China. Copying from popular Buddhist movements, its leaders built monasteries, compiled scriptures, created representations of Taoist gods, and established order among its membership during the fifth and sixth centuries.

7.3.1 Commenting on the Tao

Commentaries are acts of interpretation and are vital for keeping a religion that is based on scriptures alive. As times change, the foundational scriptures must be reinterpreted to fit the changed circumstances. In a very real sense, commentaries constitute acts of rewriting scriptures because, wittingly or unwittingly, commentators rewrite the meaning of a text to reflect their own concerns.

The Celestial Masters remained an isolated and localized community for many years after Chang Tao-ling's encounter with a returned Lao Tzu. Eventually they were forced, by political and military circumstances, to spread out into a larger geographic area. As the community broke up and spread, it carried its ideas and practices with it, and soon new converts were entering the ranks. These new members needed to know about the values, beliefs, and practices of their newfound faith, and so instruction manuals were required.

The next selection (*Hsiang-erh*) is the earliest known Taoist commentary on the foundational scripture (*Tao Te Ching*) of the Celestial Masters school. It is less a commentary than a treatise in its own right that uses the *Tao Te Ching* as a point of departure in order to instruct new converts. Some attribute the authorship to either Chang Tao-ling or his grandson Chang Lu. The manuscript dates to the late fifth or early sixth century, but we do know versions were in existence prior to 255.

The graphs *hsiang* and *erh* can mean "thinking of or contemplating you" and may refer to the adepts' need to contemplate the celestial deities or may reassure the adepts that the celestial deities are thinking of them. Perhaps both.

Before you read the selection, here is a note about the translation. You will encounter the word *pneuma*, which the translator has used to translate the Chinese word *ch'i*. *Pneuma* means breath or spirit in Greek, and *ch'i* can mean a variety of things in Chinese, including material energy, spiritual energy, or the vital force or power that gives life. *Ch'i* appears in all things, but one of its most immediate manifestations in animals is the breath. Hence, learning how to control the breath meant learning how to control *ch'i*, and learning how to control *ch'i* meant, for the Taoists, the possibility of creating a longer and healthier life.

One further note. The translator has used pinyin spelling. Thus, Tao is spelled Dao.

CELESTIAL MASTER

Hsiang-erh Commentary

READING QUESTIONS

1. The commentary is on various lines of the *Tao Te Ching*. Compare the comments to the lines in two or three instances and describe how the author has gone beyond the surface meaning of the line. For example, the author comments on the line "Then all is regulated" by interpreting it as a political comment equivalent to "the kingdom will be regulated."

From *Early Daoist Scripture*, by Stephen R. Bokenkamp (Berkeley: University of California Press, 1997), pp. 78–83. © 1997 by The Regents of the University of California. Reprinted by permission of the publisher. Footnotes edited.

2. What purpose do you think the author had in mind when writing this commentary?

Not seeing that which is desirable will make your heart unruffled.

. . . Not desiring to see something is like not seeing it at all. Do not allow your heart to be moved. If it is moved, restrain it. [If you do so,] though the Dao departs, it will return again. But if you follow the wild promptings of your heart, the Dao will leave for good.

The Sage regulates through emptying his heart and filling his belly,

The heart is a regulator. It may hold fortune or misfortune, good or evil. The belly is a sack for the Dao; its pneumas constantly wish to fill it. When the heart produces ill-omened and evil conduct, the Dao departs, leaving the sack empty. Once it is empty, deviance enters, killing the person. If one drives off the misfortune and evil in the heart, the Dao will return to it and the belly will be filled.

through weakening his will and strengthening his bones.

The will follows the heart in possessing both good and evil. The bones follow the belly in accommodating pneuma. When a strong will produces evil, the pneumas depart and the bones are desiccated. If one weakens the evil will, the pneumas return and marrow fills the bones.

He constantly causes the people to be without knowledge, without desire;

When the Dao is cut off and does not circulate, deviant writings flourish and bribery arises. Then the people contend in their avarice and in their desire to study these writings. Consequently, their bodies are placed into grave danger. Such things should be prohibited. The people should not know of deviant writings; nor should they covet precious goods. Once this is accomplished, the kingdom will be easy to rule. The transformative influence of those above over those below will be like a wind through the slender grasses. If you wish this, the essential thing is that you should know to keep faith with the Dao.

and causes the knowledgeable not to dare inaction.

If his highness tirelessly keeps faith with the Dao, the knowledgeable, even though their hearts have been perverted, will still outwardly mark right and wrong. Seeing his highness acting reverently, they will dare not act otherwise.

Then all is regulated.

In this manner, the kingdom will be regulated.

Employ the Dao as it rushes in. Further, do not allow it to overflow.

The Dao values the centrally harmonious. You should practice it in inner harmony. Your will should not flood over, for this is a transgression of the precepts of the Dao.

Be deep, resembling the primogenitor of the myriad things.

This refers to the Dao. When one practices the Dao and does not transgress the precepts, one is deep like the Dao.

Blunt its sharp edges; release its vexations.

The "sharp edge" refers to the heart as it is plotting evil. "Vexations" means anger. Both of these are things in which the Dao takes no delight. When your heart wishes to do evil, blunt and divert it; when anger is about to emerge, forgive and release it. Do not allow your five viscera to harbor anger and vexation. Strictly control yourself by means of the precepts of the Dao; urge yourself on with the [hope of] long life. By these means you will reach the desired state. The stirring of vexations is like the rapid vibrations of lute strings; this is why it leads to excess. You should strive to be slow to anger, for death and injury result from these violent urges. If the five viscera are injured by anger, the Dao is not able to govern. This is why the Dao has issued such heavy injunctions against anger and why the Dao teaches about it so diligently.

The five viscera are injured when the five pneumas [which fill them]—those of metal, wood, water, fire, and earth—are rendered inharmonious. When these are harmonious, they give birth to one another; when they clash, they attack one another. When you give vent to anger or follow your emotions, one of these pneumas will always issue forth. It issues from one of the viscera and then attacks the others. The victorious pneuma will then form an illness and kill you. If you are strong in yang, a declining pneuma will emerge to attack an ascendant pneuma and there will be no injury from the anger. Even so, in this way you are only a hair's breadth from death. If you are weak, an ascendant pneuma will emerge to attack a declining pneuma and disaster will result.

Harmonize your radiances; unify your dust.

When one's emotions are unmoved and one's joy and anger do not issue forth, the five viscera harmonize and are mutually productive. This is to be of one radiance and of one dust with the Dao.

Be deep and still and so perpetually present.

One who is still in this fashion endures perpetually without perishing.

Do you not yet know whose child I am? My image preceded the Thearchs.

"I" refers to the Dao, as does the phrase "preceded the Thearchs." The ten thousand things all alike originated in it, the nameless. It is not yet known which children from which families will be able to practice this Dao. Those who are able to practice it will pattern themselves on the Dao and will be as if they existed before the Thearchs.[1]

Heaven and earth are inhumane; they treat the myriad things as straw dogs.

Heaven and earth are patterned on the Dao. They are humane to all those who are good, inhumane to all those who do evil. Thus, when they destroy the myriad things, it is the evil whom they hate and whom they view as if they were grass or domestic dogs.

The Sage is inhumane; he treats the common people as if they were straw dogs.

The Sage models himself on heaven and earth. He is humane to good people, inhumane toward evil people. When kingly governance turns to destruction and evil, [the Sage] also views the king as a straw dog. Thus people should accumulate meritorious actions so that their essences and [internal] spirits communicate with heaven. In this way, when there are those who wish to attack and injure them, heaven will come to their aid. The common run of people are all straw dogs; their essences and spirits are unable to communicate with heaven. The reason for this is that, as robbers and thieves with evil intentions dare not be seen by government officials, their essences and spirits are not in touch with heaven, so that when they meet with dire extremities, heaven is unaware of it.

The Yellow Thearch was a humane sage and knew the inclinations of later generations, so he plaited straw to make a dog and hung it above the gate, desiring

---

[1] The "Thearchs" (*Di*) were, as early as the Shang period, regarded as the ascended ancestors of the king. From 221 B.C.E. on, living emperors adopted the title. In Daoism, *Di* are the god-kings of the heavens. In this text, the Yellow Thearch occupies a special place. . . . Although these lines are commonly taken to refer to the Dao, our commentator in effect reads them in two ways simultaneously; once as a description of the Dao, and the second time as a description of those who are able to successfully emulate the Dao. This is a reading strategy used throughout the commentary.

thereby to indicate that within these gates in later generations, all would be straw dogs. But people did not understand what the Yellow Thearch meant to imply. They merely copied this practice without reforming their evil hearts.[2] This is certainly a great evil.

The space between heaven and earth, is it not like a bellows?

The pneumas of the Dao reside in this space—clear, subtle, and invisible. All blood-bearing beings receive them in reverence. Only the ignorant do not believe this. As a result the space is here compared to a bellows. When the smelter works the bellows, air moves through the tube—that is, the hollow bamboo pipe—with a sound. [Although there is something there,] it cannot be seen. This is why it is here taken as a metaphor, meant to explain the matter for the ignorant.

Void, it cannot be exhausted. The more movement there is, the more it emits.

The clear pneumas are invisible, as if they were void. Yet their breathing never is exhausted. The more they move, the more it is that emerges.

Those with great learning are again and again depleted; best maintain the middle.

Those possessing great knowledge are superficial and ornate. They do not know how to hold to the Dao or to perfect the body. Once they live out their span of years, they will invariably be "depleted" [i.e., die]. "Again and again" means [that this has happened] more than once. It is better to study life, to maintain the centrally harmonious Dao.

Desiring that one's spirits do not die—this is called the mysterious feminine.

Gu [valley] means desire. Essence congeals to form [internal] spirits. If you desire to keep these spirits from perishing, you should congeal your essences and maintain them. The "feminine" is earth. The inborn nature of its body is stable. Women are patterned on it; therefore [their sexual organs] do not become rigid. If a man wishes to congeal his essence he should mentally pattern himself on earth and be like a woman. He should not work to give himself priority.

The gate of the mysterious feminine is the root of heaven and earth—

The "feminine" refers to the earth. Women are patterned after it. The vagina is the "gate," the comptroller of life and death. It is the very crux [of existence] and thus is called "the root." The penis is also called "the root." . . .

___

7.3.2 Immortality, Alchemy, and Merit

Taoist claims about people who could live ten thousand years and secret elixirs of immortality were bound to raise a few eyebrows. Both Buddhists and Confucianists scoffed at what they saw as superstition and the sad neglect of morality. The teachings of Taoism were, they believed, inferior not only to their own teachings but to the teachings of many other philosophical and religious schools as well.

Ko Hung (253–333?) took up these skeptical challenges in his *Pao-p'u Tzu (The Philosopher Who Embraces Simplicity)*. He offers a defense of the possibility of immortality, a justification of both external and internal alchemy, a detailed essay on the importance of morality, and comments on the relation of Taoism to other schools. His work paved the way for further elaboration of the Taoist religion and reinforced the notion that philosophy and religion are not as far apart as some might suppose.

KO HUNG

The Philosopher Who Embraces Simplicity

READING QUESTIONS

1. How does Pao-p'u Tzu answer the question about the possibility of immortality?
2. What do you think is the main point of the essay on alchemy?

___

[2] According to standard commentaries, "straw dogs" were dogs made of plaited grass used in a scapegoat ritual. . . . The commentary, in tracing this popular practice back to a misunderstood warning from the Yellow Thearch, indicates at the same time that all who continue this practice are marking themselves as "disciples of the straw dog" and outside of the Dao.

Republished with permission of Columbia University Press, 562 W. 113th St., New York, NY 10025. *Sources of the Chinese Tradition*, compiled by Wm. Theodore De Bary, Wing-tsit Chan, and Burton Watson. Volume 1, 1960. Reproduced by permission of the publisher via Copyright Clearance Center, Inc. Pp. 258–265. Footnotes omitted.

3. How would you characterize Ko Hung's views on morality and merit?
4. How does Pao-p'u Tzu answer the question about the relationship of Taoism and Confucianism?

THE BELIEF IN IMMORTALS

Someone asked: Is it really possible that spiritual beings and immortals (*hsien*) do not die?

Pao-p'u Tzu said: Even if we had the greatest power of vision, we could not see all the things that have corporeal form. Even if we were endowed with the sharpest sense of hearing, we could not hear all the sounds there are. Even if we had the feet of Ta-chang and Hsu-hai [expert runners], what we had already trod upon would not be so much as what we have not. And even if we had the knowledge of [the sages] Yü, I, and Ch'i-hsieh, what we know would not be so much as what we do not know. The myriad things flourish. What is there that could not exist? Why not the immortals, whose accounts fill the historical records? Why should there not be a way to immortality?

Thereupon the questioner laughed heartily and said: Whatever has a beginning necessarily has an end, and whatever lives must eventually die. . . . I have only heard that some plants dry up and wither before frost, fade in color during the summer, bud but do not flower, or wither and are stripped of leaves before bearing fruit. But I have never heard of anyone who enjoys a life span of ten thousand years and an everlasting existence without end. Therefore people of antiquity did not aspire to be immortals in their pursuit of knowledge, and did not talk of strange things in their conversation. They cast aside perverse doctrines and adhered to what is natural. They set aside the tortoise and the crane [symbols of immortality] as creatures of a different species, and looked upon life and death as morning and evening. . . .

Pao-p'u Tzu answered: . . . Life and death, beginning and end, are indeed the great laws of the universe. Yet the similarities and differences of things are not uniform. Some are this way and some are that. Tens of thousands of varieties are in constant change and transformation, strange and without any definite pattern. Whether things are this way or that, and whether they are regular or irregular in their essential and subsidiary aspects, cannot be reduced to uniformity. There are many who say that whatever has a beginning must have an end. But it is not in accord with the principle [of existence] to muddle things together and try to make them all the same. People say that things are bound to grow in the summer, and yet the shepherd's-purse and the water chestnut wilt. People say that plants are bound to wither in the winter, and yet the bamboo and the cypress flourish. People say whatever has a beginning will have an end, and yet Heaven and earth are unending. People say whatever is born will die, and yet the tortoise and the crane live forever. When the yang is at its height, it should be hot, and yet the summer is not without cool days. When the yin reaches its limit, it should be cold, and yet even a severe winter is not without brief warm periods. . . .

Among creatures none surpasses man in intelligence. As creatures of such superior nature, men should be equal and uniform. And yet they differ in being virtuous or stupid, in being perverse or upright, in being fair or ugly, tall or short, pure or impure, chaste or lewd, patient or impatient, slow or quick. What they pursue or avoid in their interests and what their eyes and ears desire are as different as Heaven and earth, and as incompatible as ice and coals. Why should you only wonder at the fact that immortals are different and do not die like ordinary people? . . . But people with superficial knowledge are bound by what is ordinary and adhere to what is common. They all say that immortals are not seen in the world, and therefore they say forthwith that there cannot be immortals. [2:1a–4a]

Among men some are wise and some are stupid, but they all know that in their bodies they have a heavenly component (*hun*) and an earthly component (*p'o*) of the soul. If these are partly gone, man becomes sick. If they are completely gone, man dies. If they are partially separated from the body, the occult expert has means to retain and restrict them. If they are entirely separated, there are principles in the established rites to recall them. These components of the soul as entities are extremely close to us. And yet although we are born with them and live with them throughout life, we never see or hear them. Should one say that they do not exist simply because we have not seen or heard them? [2:12a]

[From *Pao-p'u Tzu*, 2:1a–4a; 12a]

ALCHEMY

The immortals nourish their bodies with drugs and prolong their lives with the application of occult science, so that internal illness shall not arise and external ailment shall not enter. Although they enjoy everlasting existence and do not die, their old bodies do not change. If one knows the way to immortality, it is not to be considered so difficult. [2:3b–4a]

Among the creatures of nature, man is the most intelligent. Therefore those who understand [creation] slightly can employ the myriad things, and those who get to its depth can enjoy [what is called in the *Lao Tzu*] "long life and everlasting existence" [ch. 59]. As we know that the best medicine can prolong life, let us take it to obtain immortality, and as we know that the tortoise and the crane have longevity, let us imitate their activities to increase our span of life. . . . Those who have obtained Tao are able to lift themselves into the clouds and the heavens above and to dive and swim in the rivers and seas below. [3:1a, 5a]

Pao-p'u Tzu said: I have investigated and read books on the nourishment of human nature and collected formulas for everlasting existence. Those I have perused number thousands of volumes. They all consider reconverted cinnabar [after it has been turned into mercury] and gold fluid to be the most important. Thus these two things represent the acme of the way to immortality. . . . The transformations of the two substances are the more wonderful the more they are heated. Yellow gold does not disintegrate even after having been smelted a hundred times in fire, and does not rot even if buried in the ground until the end of the world. If these two medicines are eaten, they will strengthen our bodies and therefore enable us not to grow old nor to die. This is of course seeking assistance from external substances to strengthen ourselves. It is like feeding fat to the lamp so it will not die out. If we smear copperas on our feet, they will not deteriorate even if they remain in water. This is to borrow the strength of the copper to protect our flesh. Gold fluid and reconverted cinnabar, however, upon entering our body, permeate our whole system of blood and energy and are not like copperas which helps only on the outside. [4:1a–3a]

It is hoped that those who nourish life will learn extensively and comprehend the essential, gather whatever there is to see and choose the best. It is not sufficient to depend on cultivating only one thing. It is also dangerous for people who love life to rely on their own specialty. Those who know the techniques of the *Classic of the Mysterious Lady* and the *Classic of the Plain Lady* [books on sexual regimen no longer extant] will say that only the "art of the chamber" will lead to salvation. Those who understand the method of breathing exercises will say that only the permeation of the vital power can prolong life. Those who know the method of stretching and bending will say that only physical exercise can prevent old age. And those who know the formulas of herbs will say that only medicine will make life unending. They fail in their pursuit of Tao because they are so onesided. People of superficial knowledge think they have enough when they happen to know of only one way and do not realize that the true seeker will search unceasingly even after he has acquired some good formulas. [6:4a]

[From *Pao-p'u Tzu*, 2:3b–4a; 3:1a, 5a; 4:1a–3a; 6:4a]

THE MERIT SYSTEM

Furthermore, as Heaven and earth are the greatest of things, it is natural, from the point of view of universal principles, that they have spiritual power. Having spiritual power it is proper that they reward good and punish evil. Nevertheless their expanse is great and their net is wide-meshed. There is not necessarily an immediate response [result] as soon as this net is set in operation. As we glance over the Taoist books of discipline, however, all are unanimous in saying that those who seek immortality must set their minds to the accumulation of merits and the accomplishment of good work. Their hearts must be kind to all things. They must treat others as they treat themselves, and extend their humaneness (*jen*) even to insects. They must rejoice in the fortune of men and pity their suffering, relieve the destitute and save the poor. Their hands must never injure life, and their mouths must never encourage evil. They must consider the success and failure of others as their own. They must not regard themselves highly, nor praise themselves. They must not envy those superior to them, nor flatter dangerous and evil-minded people. In this way they may become virtuous and blessed by Heaven; they may be successful in whatever they do, and may hope to become immortal.

If, on the other hand, they hate good and love evil; if their words do not agree with their thoughts; if they say one thing in people's presence and the opposite behind their backs; if they twist the truth; if they are cruel to subordinates or deceive their superiors; if they betray their task and are ungrateful for kindness received; if they manipulate the law and accept bribes; if they tolerate injustice but suppress justice; if they destroy the public good for their selfish ends; if they punish the innocent, wreck people's homes, pocket their treasures, injure their bodies, or seize their positions; if they overthrow virtuous rulers or massacre those who have surrendered to them; if they slander saints and sages or hurt Taoist priests; if they shoot birds in flight or kill the unborn in womb or egg; if in spring or summer hunts they burn the forests or drive out the game; if they curse spiritual beings; if they teach others to do evil or conceal their good deeds or endanger others for their own security; if they claim the work of others as their own; if they spoil people's happy affairs or take away what others love; if they cause division in people's families or disgrace others in order to win; if they overcharge or underpay; if they set fire or inundate; if they injure people with trickery or coerce the weak; if they repay good with evil; if they take things by force or accumulate wealth through robbery and plunder; if they are unfair or unjust, licentious, indulgent, or perverted; if they oppress orphans or mistreat widows; if they squander inheritance and accept charity; if they cheat or deceive; if they love to gossip about people's private affairs or criticize them for their defects; if they drag Heaven and earth into their affairs and rail at people in order to seek vindication; if they fail to repay debts or play fair in the exchange of goods; if they seek to gratify their desires without end; if they hate and resist the faithful and sincere; if they disobey orders from above or do not respect their teachers; if they ridicule others for doing good; if they destroy people's crops or harm their tools so as to nullify their utility, and do not feed people with clean food; if they cheat in weights or measures; if they mix spurious articles with genuine; if they take dishonorable advantage; if they tempt others to steal; if they meddle in the affairs of others or go beyond their position in life; if they leap over wells or hearths [which provide water and fire for food]; if they sing in the last day of the month [when the end should be sent off with sorrow] or cry in the first day of the month [when the beginning should be welcomed with joy]; if they commit any of these evil deeds; it is a sin.

The Arbiter of Human Destiny will reduce their terms of life by units of three days or three hundred days in proportion to the gravity of the evil. When all days are deducted they will die. Those who have the intention to do evil but have not carried it out will have three-day units taken just as if they had acted with injury to others. If they die before all their evil deeds are punished, their posterity will suffer for them. [6:5b–7a]

Someone asked: Is it true that he who cultivates the way [to become an immortal] should first accomplish good deeds?

Pao-p'u Tzu answered: Yes, it is true. The middle section of the *Yu-ch'ien ching* says: "The most important thing is to accomplish good works. The next is the removal of faults. For him who cultivates the way, the highest accomplishment of good work is to save people from danger so they may escape from calamity, and to preserve people from sickness so that they may not die unjustly. Those who aspire to be immortals should regard loyalty, filial piety, harmony, obedience, love, and good faith as their essential principles of conduct. If they do not cultivate moral conduct but merely devote themselves to occult science, they will never attain everlasting life. If they do evil, the Arbiter of Human Destiny will take off units of three hundred days from their allotted life if the evil is great, or units of three days if the evil is small. Since [the punishment] depends on the degree of evil, the reduction in the span of life is in some cases great and in others small. When a man is endowed with life and given a life span, he has his own definite number of days. If his number is large, the units of three hundred days and of three days are not easily exhausted and therefore he dies later. On the other hand, if one's allotted number is small and offences are many, then the units are soon exhausted and he dies early."

The book also says: "Those who aspire to be terrestrial immortals should accomplish three hundred good deeds and those who aspire to be celestial immortals should accomplish 1,200. If the 1,199th good deed is followed by an evil one, they will lose all their accumulation and have to start all over. It does not matter whether the good deeds are great or the evil deed is small. Even if they do no evil but talk about their good deeds and demand reward for their charities, they will nullify the goodness of these deeds although the other good deeds are not affected." The book further says: "If good deeds are not sufficiently accumulated, taking the elixir of immortality will be of no help." [3:7b–8a, 10a–b]

[From *Pao-p'u Tzu*, 3:7b–10b; 6:5b–7a]

TAOISM IN RELATION TO OTHER SCHOOLS

Someone said: If it were certain that one could become an immortal, the sages would have trained themselves to be such. But neither Duke Chou nor Confucius did so. It is clear that there is no such possibility.

Pao-p'u Tzu answered: A sage need not be an immortal and an immortal need not be a sage. The sage receives a mandate [from Heaven], not to attend to the way of everlasting life, but to remove tyrants and eliminate robbers, to turn danger into security and violence into peace, to institute ceremonies and create musical systems, to propagate laws and give education, to correct improper manners and reform degenerate customs, to assist rulers who are in danger of downfall and to support those states that are about to collapse. . . . What the ordinary people call sages are all sages who regulate the world but not sages who attain Tao. The Yellow Emperor and Lao Tzu were sages who attained Tao, while

Duke Chou and Confucius were sages who regulated the world. [12:1a–b]

Someone asked: Which is first and which is last, Confucianism or Taoism?

Pao-p'u Tzu answered: Taoism is the essence of Confucianism and Confucianism is an appendage to Taoism. First of all, there was the "teaching of the yin-yang school which had many taboos that made people constrained and afraid." "The Confucianists had extensive learning but little that was essential; they worked hard but achieved little." "Mo-ism emphasized thrift but was difficult to follow," and could not be practiced exclusively. "The Legalists were severe and showed little kindness"; they destroyed humanity and righteousness. "The teachings of the Taoist school alone enable men's spirits to be concentrated and united and their action to be in harmony with the formless. . . . Taoism embraces the good points of both Confucianism and Mo-ism and combines the essentials the Legalists and Logicians. It changes with the times and responds to transformations of things. . . . Its precepts are simple and easy to understand; its works are few but its achievements many." It is devoted to the simplicity that preserves the Great Heritage and adheres to the true and correct source. [10:1a–b]

[From *Pao-p'u Tzu*, 10:1a–b; 12:1a–b]

7.3.3 Immortal Ladies

Fully accomplished Taoist adepts become immortal. When their allotted time on earth is over or when a summons suddenly arrives from the celestial court, the **immortals** ascend from this world to become heavenly hosts and serve in the celestial administration of the universe.

However, as long as these immortals are here and must live among ordinary mortals, they exhibit some very unusual characteristics. They have powers far above the ordinary. They are, in short, supermen and superwomen.

Biographies of these immortals became popular literature among the Chinese and the stories circulated far and wide, much like the stories of saints in the Middle Ages and superheroes in our own time. The story that follows is from an early collection called *Biographies of Spirit Immortals*. Originally compiled in the fourth century, it was lost and reassembled in the sixth century. One of the more interesting and entertaining stories is about "The Lady of Great Mystery." Although women were second-class citizens in

ancient China, within Taoism they could attain ranks of great importance, as we shall soon see.

The Lady of Great Mystery

READING QUESTION

1. What religious purpose do you think stories like this served, and what might be their social functions?

The Lady of Great Mystery had the family name Zhuan and was personally called He. When she was a little girl she lost first her father and after a little while also her mother.

Understanding that living beings often did not fulfill their destined lifespans, she felt sympathy and sadness. She used to say: "Once people have lost their existence in this world, they cannot recover it. Whatever has died cannot come back to life. Life is so limited! It is over so fast! Without cultivating the Tao, how can one extend one's life?"

She duly left to find enlightened teachers, wishing to purify her mind and pursue the Tao. She obtained the arts of the Jade Master and practiced them diligently for several years.

As a result she was able to enter the water and not get wet. Even in the severest cold of winter she would walk over frozen rivers wearing only a single garment. All the time her expression would not change, and her body would remain comfortably warm for a succession of days.

The Lady of Great Mystery could also move government offices, temples, cities, and lodges. They would appear in other places quite without moving from their original location. Whatever she pointed at would vanish into thin air. Doors, windows, boxes, or caskets that were securely locked needed only a short flexing of her finger to break wide open. Mountains would tumble, trees would fall at the pointing of her hand. Another short gesture would resurrect them to their former state.

One day she went into the mountains with her disciples. At sunset she took a staff and struck a stone. The stone at once opened wide, leading into a grotto-world

---

fully equipped with beds and benches, screens and curtains. It also had a kitchen and larder, full with wine and food. All was just like it would be in the world of everyday life.

The Lady of Great Mystery could travel ten thousand miles, yet at the same time continue to stay nearby. She could transform small things to be suddenly big, and big things to be small. She could spit fire so big it would rise up wildly into heaven, and yet in one breath she could extinguish it again.

She was also able to sit in the middle of a blazing fire, while her clothes would never be even touched by the flames. She could change her appearance at will: one moment she was an old man, the next a small child. She could also conjure up a cart and horse to ride back and forth in if she did not want to walk.

The Lady of Great Mystery perfectly mastered all thirty-six arts of the immortals. She could resurrect the dead and bring them back to life. She saved innumerable people, but nobody knew what she used for her dresses or her food, nor did anybody ever learn her arts from her. Her complexion was always that of a young girl; her hair stayed always black as a raven. Later she ascended into heaven in broad daylight. She was never seen again. (7.27a)

7.4 TAOISM FLOURISHES

Imperial favor reached its height during the T'ang dynasty (618–907) and Taoism flourished. The founder of the dynasty was named Li, the supposed surname of Lao Tzu, and so he was honored as a descendant of the immortal and divine Lao Tzu himself. He called himself the Most High Emperor of Mystic Origin and ranked himself above Confucius and Buddha. Princes, dukes, and other nobles were required to study the *Tao Te Ching*, and Taoist temples were built throughout the empire. In 742 Lao Tzu's illustrious followers were canonized as saints and immortals, and this included Chuang Tzu (who, one imagines, would have found all of this quite amusing).

7.4.1 The Path

In the mid T'ang dynasty, Ssu-ma Cheng Chen, a famous patriarch of the Highest Clarity school, published an essay recommending the practices outlined by someone called the Master of Heavenly Seclusion. Although we do not know (and neither did Ssu-ma Cheng Chen) who this person is, his or her essay is the first well-organized and clear summary of the

Taoist path. It has remained both popular and influential ever since and its guidelines are followed by practitioners today.

The Master of Heavenly Seclusion

READING QUESTIONS

1. What is spirit immortality?
2. What is the path of simplicity?
3. What do fasting and abstention mean?
4. What is meant by seclusion?
5. How is "sitting in oblivion" related to visualization and imagination?
6. Why do you think Taoists believe that the goal of spirit liberation can be attained by these practices?

1. SPIRIT IMMORTALITY

All people from birth are endowed with the energy of emptiness. Originally their essence and enlightenment are of penetrating awareness, learning has no obstructions, and the "spirit" is pure. Settle this spirit within and let it shine without! You will naturally become different from ordinary people. You will be a spirit immortal! Yet even as a spirit immortal, you are still human.

To accomplish spirit immortality you must cultivate the energy of emptiness. Never let the common world defile it. Find spirit immortality in spontaneously following your nature. Never let false views obstruct your path.

Joy, anger, sadness, happiness, love, hate, and desires are the seven perversions of the emotions. Wind, damp, cold, heat, hunger, satiation, labor, and idleness are the eight perversions of energy. Rid yourself of them! Establish immortality!

2. SIMPLICITY

The *Book of Changes* says: "The way of heaven and earth is simple." What does this mean?

The Master of Heavenly Seclusion says: "Heaven and earth are above my head and beneath my feet. When I

From Livia Kohn, "The Teaching of T'ien-yin-tzu," *Journal of Chinese Religions* (1987) 15:1–28. Reprinted by permission.

open my eyes I can see them. I can speak of them without complex devices. Thus I say: Consummate simplicity is the virtue of immortality."

What path should be used to seek this? He says: "Without seeking you cannot know; without a path you cannot attain the goal. All students of spirit immortality must first realize simplicity. Teachings that are marvelous, artful, and attractive only lead people astray. They do not lead to the root. They could never be my teaching."

3. GRADUAL PROGRESS TOWARD THE GATE OF THE TAO

In the *Book of Changes*, there is the hexagram called "Progressive Advance." Lao Tzu speaks of the "Marvelous Gate." Human beings should cultivate inner perfection and realize their original natures. They should not expect sudden enlightenment. Rather, they progress gradually and practice the techniques in peace. The following five are the progressive gateways to the Tao.

The first is fasting and abstention.
The second is seclusion.
The third is visualization and imagination.
The fourth is sitting in oblivion.
The fifth is spirit liberation.

What does fasting and abstention mean? It means cleansing the body and emptying the mind.
What does seclusion mean? It means withdrawing deep into the meditation chamber.
What does visualization and imagination mean? It means taming the mind and recovering original nature.
What does sitting in oblivion mean? It means letting go of the personal body and completely forgetting oneself.
What does spirit liberation mean? It means spirit pervasion of all existence.

Practice according to these five and perfect step one, then only proceed to step two. Perfect step two, then gradually move on to step three. Perfect step three, then approach step four. Perfect step four, then finally pass on to step five. Thus you attain spirit immortality!

4. FASTING AND ABSTENTION

Fasting and abstention not only mean to live on vegetables and mushrooms. Cleansing the body is not just bathing to remove the dirt. Rather, the method is to regulate the food so that it is perfectly balanced, to massage the body so that it glows in health.

All people are endowed with the energy of the five agents. They live on things that consist of the five agents. From the time they enter the womb people breathe in and out; blood and essence circulate in their bodies. How could one stop eating and yet attain long life?

Ordinary people do not realize that to abstain from food and nourish on pure energy are only temporary measures of the Taoists. These things do not mean that we completely abstain from all grain. We speak of fasting and abstention from food, yes. But we refer to the purification of nourishment and the moderation of intake. If one is hungry one eats—but never to satiation. Thus we establish a balanced diet.

Don't eat anything not well cooked! Don't eat strongly flavored dishes! Don't eat anything rotten or conserved! These are our basic abstentions. Massage your skin with your hands so that it becomes moist and hot! This drives out the cold energy and makes the body radiate with a glow.

Refrain from long sitting, long standing, long exhaustive labor! All these are basic abstentions. They serve to balance and regulate the body. If the body is strong, energy is whole. Thus, fasting and abstention are the first gateway to the Tao.

5. SECLUSION

What is meant by seclusion? It has nothing to do with living in ornate halls, in cavernous buildings, on double matting and thick carpeting. It means sitting with one's face to the south, sleeping with one's head to the east, complying in everything with the harmonious rhythm of yin and yang.

Light and darkness should be in balance. The room should not be too high. If it is too high, yang is predominant and there will be too much light. The room should not be too low. If it is too low, yin is predominant and there will be too much darkness. The reason for this precaution is that, when there is too much light, the material souls will be harmed. When there is too much darkness, the spirit souls will suffer. People's three spirit souls are yang, their seven material souls are yin. Harm them with light and darkness, and they will get sick.

When things are arranged in the proper balanced way, we have a chamber of seclusion. Still, don't forget how various the energies of heaven and earth can be. There may be, for example, a violent yang that attacks the flesh. Or there may be a lascivious yin that overpowers the body. Be wary and guard against these!

During the progressive advance of cultivation and nourishment there is no proper seclusion unless these instructions are carried out. Thus the Master of Heavenly Seclusion says:

"The room I live in has windows on all four sides. When wind arises I close them; as soon as the wind has died down I open them again. In front of my meditation seat a curtain is suspended; behind it a screen has been placed. When it is too light I draw the curtain to adjust the brightness inside. When it gets too dark I roll the curtain up again to let light in from outside.

"On the inside I calm my mind, on the outside I calm my eyes. Mind and eyes must be both completely at peace. If either light or darkness prevails, there are too many thoughts, too many desires. How could I ever calm myself inside and out?" Thus, in studying the Tao, seclusion marks the second step.

6. Visualization and Imagination

Visualization is to produce a vision of one's spirit. Imagination means to create an image of one's body. How to do this? Close your eyes and you can see your own eyes. Collect the mind and you can realize your own mind. Mind and eyes should never be separate from the body; they must not harm the spirit: this is what visualization and imagination are for.

Ordinary people, to the end of their days, direct their eyes only toward others. Thus their minds wander outside. When the mind is concerned only with outer affairs, it also causes the eyes to continue looking at things outside. Brightly sparkling, their light floats around and never reflects back on themselves. How can people not become sick from this and end up dying prematurely?

Therefore, "return to the root means tranquility, and tranquility means to recover life." To recover life and perfect one's inner nature is called "the gate of all subtleties." Thus, with the step of visualization and imagination the task of learning the Tao is half completed.

7. Sitting in Oblivion

Sitting in oblivion is the perfection of visualization and imagination. It is also the utter oblivion of visualization and imagination.

To put the Tao into action but not oneself act—isn't that the meaning of sitting? To see something and not act on it—isn't that the meaning of oblivion?

Why do we speak of not acting? Because the mind remains free from agitation. Why do we speak of not seeing? Because the body is completely obliterated.

Someone asks: "If the mind is unmoving, does it have the Tao then?" The Master of Heavenly Seclusion remains silent and does not answer.

Another asks: "If the body is obliterated, does it have the Tao then?" The Master of Heavenly Seclusion closes his eyes and does not look.

Then someone awakens to the Tao and, in withdrawing, says: "The Tao is really in me. What person is this 'me'? What person actually is this Master of Heavenly Seclusion?"

Thus, self and other are both forgotten. Nothing is left to shine forth.

8. Spirit Liberation

Step one, fasting and abstention, is called liberation through faith. Without faith, the mind cannot be liberated.

Step two, seclusion, is called liberation through tranquility. Without tranquility, the mind cannot be liberated.

Step three, visualization and imagination, is called liberation through insight. Without insight, the mind cannot be liberated.

Step four, sitting in oblivion, is called liberation through absorption. Without absorption, the mind cannot be liberated.

When the four gates of faith, tranquility, insight, and absorption have been pervaded by the spirit, then we speak of spirit liberation. By "spirit" we mean that which arrives without moving and is swift without hurrying. It pervades the rhythm of yin and yang and is as old as heaven and earth.

When the three forces, heaven, earth, and humanity, are combined, changes occur. When the myriad beings are equalized, then the Tao and the Virtue are active. When the one original nature of all is realized, there is pure suchness. Enter into suchness and return to non-action.

The Master of Heavenly Seclusion says: "I am born with the changes; I will die with the changes. In accordance with the myriad beings I move; going along with the myriad beings I rest. Pervasion comes from the one original nature; perfection comes from the one original nature. Through spirit I am liberated from all: life and death, movement and rest, pervasion and perfection."

Among human beings the liberated are spirit immortals: in heaven they are heavenly immortals; on earth they are earth immortals; in water they are water immortals. Only when they pervade all are they spirit immortals.

The path to spirit immortality consists of these five progressive gateways. They all lead to one goal only.

7.4.2 Gods and Goddesses

The gods and goddesses of Taoism are personifications of *yin* and *yang* energy. Although there are many deities of different ranks, two deities—the Lord King of the East and the Queen Mother of the West—embody the *yang* and *yin* forces all the deities represent.

The **Queen Mother,** in different forms, was known as a powerful deity from very ancient times, but she was not paired with her male counterpart (Lord King) until the Han dynasty (206 B.C.E.–220 C.E.). The following biography of the Queen Mother comes from the late T'ang dynasty. It is found in the *Records of the Assembled Immortals of the Heavenly Walled City,* written by Tu Kuangtin (850–933), an important Taoist liturgist and chronicler of the late T'ang.

As you read this selection, you may get visions of the imperial palaces of ancient China. This is not surprising because ideas of Heaven are modeled after human society. So, if you want to imagine heaven, what better place to look than the imperial palaces.

TU KUANGTIN

The Queen Mother of the West

READING QUESTIONS

1. Why do you think many religions, including Taoism, describe their heavens in such luxurious terms?
2. What is the Queen Mother's life like?
3. What message is contained in the story about the help the Queen Mother gives to the Yellow Emperor?

From Suzanne Cahill, "Practice Makes Perfect: Paths to Transcendence for Women in Medieval China," *Taoist Resources* (1990) 2.2:23–42. Reprinted by permission.

The goddess Mother of Metal is the Ninefold Numinous and Greatly Wondrous Mother of Metal of Tortoise Mountain. Sometimes she is also called the Greatly Numinous and Ninefold Radiant Mother of Metal of Tortoise Terrace. Another common name of hers is Queen Mother of the West. She is, in fact, the incarnate wondrousness of the innermost power of the west, the ultimate venerable of all-pervading yin-energy.

In old times, the energy of the Tao congealed in quietude and deepened into an organized structure. Resting in non-action, it desired to unfold and guide the mysterious accomplishments of creation, to bring forth and raise the myriad beings.

First it took the perfected true energy of the innermost power of the east and transformed it into the Lord of Wood. The Lord of Wood was born on the shore of the Bluegreen Sea, in the void of fresh-green spiritual power. Born from the energy of highest yang harmony, he rules in the east. Because of this, he is also called the Lord King of the East.

Then the Tao took the perfected wondrous energy of the innermost power of the west and transformed it into the Mother of Metal. The Mother of Metal was born on the shore of Yonder River on the Divine Continent. Jue is her surname, and Kou the clan to which she belongs. As soon as she was born, she soared up in flight. Born from the energy of highest yin spiritual power, she rules in the west. Because of this she is also called the Queen Mother of the West.

In the beginning, she derived her substance from great nonbeing. She floated along in spirit and was mysteriously hidden in the midst of the west's confused chaos of primordial energy. Then she divided the pure essential energy of the great Tao, to connect it back together again and form herself a body.

She and the Lord King of Wood and the East rule the two primal energies [yin and yang], nourish and raise heaven and earth, mold and develop the myriad beings.

The Queen Mother embodies the deepest foundation of the weak and yielding; she represents the origin of the ultimate yin. Therefore she rules over the direction of the west. She mothers and nourishes all kinds of beings, whether in heaven above or on the earth below, whether in any of the three worlds or in any of the ten directions. Especially all women who ascend to immortality and attain the Tao are her dependents.

The palaces and towers she resides in are located on Pestle Mountain in the Tortoise Mountain Range, in the splendid parks of Mount Kunlun with its hanging gardens and lofty atmosphere. Here there is a golden city a thousand levels high, with twelve-storied jade buildings and towers of jasper essence. There are halls of radiant lucid jade, nine-storied mysterious terraces, and purple kingfisher cinnabar chambers.

On the left, the palace compound is surrounded by the Fairy Pond; on the right, it is ringed by the Kingfisher River. Beneath the mountain, the weakwater stream rushes along in nine layers, its waves and swells a hundred thousand feet high. Without a whirlwind carriage on feathered wheels, no one can ever reach here.

The jade towers rise up all the way into the heavens; the luscious terraces reach into the empyrean. The buildings' eaves are of green gems; the chambers inside of vermilion-purple stone. Joined gems make colorful curtains, while a steady bright moon irradiates them on all four sides.

The Queen Mother wears a flowered *sheng* headdress and has marvelous ornaments suspended from her belt. Her attendants on the left are immortal maidens; her attendants on the right are feathered lads. Gem-studded canopies glimmer with their mutual reflections; feathered banners shade the courtyard.

Beneath the balustrades and staircases of the palaces, the grounds are planted with white bracelet trees and a cinnabar diamond forest. There are a myriad stalks of emptiness-pure greenery, a thousand stems of turquoise-jade trees. Even when there is no wind, the divine reeds spontaneously harmonize sounds, clinking like jade belt-pendants. They naturally produce the spheric timbres of the eight harmonies.

The Divine Continent where the Queen Mother was born is southeast of Mount Kunlun. Thus the *Erya Dictionary* claims: "The land of the Queen Mother of the West is directly beneath the sun. This place and the subsolar land are the same." It also says: "The Queen Mother has disheveled hair and wears a *sheng* headdress. She has tiger's teeth and is good at whistling." Now, this describes really the Queen Mother's envoy, the white tiger spirit of the direction of metal. Such are not in fact the Queen Mother's true looks!

To ensure her power, the Heavenly King of Primordial Beginning bestowed upon her the primordial lineage record of the myriad heavens and the Tortoise Mountain registers of ninefold radiance. He empowered her to control and summon the myriad spirit forces of the universe, to assemble and gather the perfected and the sages of the world, to oversee all covenants and examine the people's quality of faith.

Moreover, she presides over all formal observances in the various heavens as well as at all audiences and banquets held by the celestial worthies and supreme sages. In addition, it is her duty to supervise the correcting and editing of the sacred scriptures in heaven, to reflect due divine light on the proceedings. Her responsibility covers all the treasured scriptures of Highest Clarity, the jade writs of the Three Caverns, as well as the sacred texts that are bestowed at ordination.

Formerly the Yellow Emperor punished the Wormy Rebel when he rose and usurped power. Before he was subdued, the Wormy Rebel brought forth many magical transformations. He raised the wind, summoned the rain, puffed forth smoke, and spat mist, so that the generals and soldiers of the Yellow Emperor's army were greatly confused. Thereupon the emperor returned home and rested in a valley of Mount Tai. Bewildered, he lay down in deep distress.

Seeing his plight, the Queen Mother sent out an envoy wearing a dark fox cloak to give him a talisman. It said:

Great Unity just ahead!
Heavenly Unity just behind!
Obtain it and excel!
Attack and overcome!

The talisman was three inches wide and one foot long. It shone like jade with a greenish lustre. Cinnabar drops like blood formed a glistening pattern on it. The Yellow Emperor hung it at his waist.

When he had done this, the Queen Mother commanded a woman with a human head and the body of a bird to go to him. She introduced herself as the Mysterious Lady of the Nine Heavens and gave the emperor the plan of cosmic yin and yang. This included information also on the five basic human intentions and the three palaces within. In addition, she bestowed upon him various arts: how to calculate the times of attack and withdrawal with the help of Great Unity and how to control all space and time through pacing the Northern Dipper in the sky. Beyond that, she taught him the way to use a number of talismans of concealment, the five divine talismans of the Numinous Treasure, and the divine writ ensuring the five kinds of victory.

Thus equipped, the Yellow Emperor easily subdued the Wormy Rebel in Middleland. He then destroyed the descendents of the Divine Farmer and executed the Fiery Emperor's great-grandson at Blockspring. Thereafter all under heaven was greatly at peace.

The Yellow Emperor then built his capital at Dripping Deer in the Upper Valley. After he had thus been settled peacefully for a number of years, he received another envoy from the Queen Mother. This time the white tiger spirit came to him. Riding a white tiger, he descended to the emperor's courtyard. He bestowed upon him the cosmic maps of the unified empire.

Toward the end of his years, the Queen Mother moreover gave him the perfect true Tao of purity, tranquility, and non-action. Its instructions were:

Do not stop drinking and gobbling up food—and
your body will never be light.

Do not stop fretting and worrying—and your spirit
  will never be pure.
Do not stop craving for sounds and sights—and
  your heart will never be calm.
No calm in your heart—and your spirit will never be
  numinous.
No numen in your spirit—and the Tao cannot work
  its wonders.
Success is not in homage to the stars or worship of
  the Dipper.
That rather makes you suffer and exhausts your body.
Success is in deepening the spirit powers of your
  heart.
There is no effort needed—the Tao of immortality
  is there!
Now you can live long!

7.4.3 Ascension

Before you can join the Heavenly Immortals, you
must ascend. Stories of ascensions abound in Taoism and fascinated many because of their miraculous
qualities and for their confirmation of Taoist teachings and techniques. One finds eyewitness accounts
of sudden and unexpected ascensions, and stories of
Taoist masters publicly announcing and planning
their ascension with great drama.

The story that follows (recorded by Tu Kuangtin
in his *Records of the Assembled Immortals of the Heavenly
Walled City*), about the ascension of a Taoist priestess,
is particularly dramatic. Unlike other ascension accounts that indicate the physical body is left behind,
the "Flower Maiden" takes her corpse with her, astonishing all who watch.

TU KUANGTIN

The Flower Maiden

READING QUESTIONS

1. What impresses you most about this story?
2. Many different religions have ascension stories.
   What role do you think such stories play?

From Suzanne Cahill, "Practice Makes Perfect: Paths to Transcendence for Women in Medieval China," *Taoist Resources*
(1990) 2.2:23–42. Reprinted by permission.

In the ninth year of Kaiyuan [721], Huang Lingwei,
known as the Flower Maiden, wished to ascend through
transformation. So she said to her disciples: "My journey to immortality is coming close. I cannot stay here
much longer. After my body has been transformed, do
not nail my coffin shut, but just cover it with crimson
netted gauze."

The next day she came to an end without even being
sick. Her flesh and muscles were fragrant and clear; her
body and energy were still warm and genial. A strange
fragrance filled the courtyard and halls.

Her disciples followed her orders and did not nail the
coffin shut. Instead, they simply covered it with crimson
netted gauze.

Suddenly they all heard a massive clap of thunder.
When they looked at the coffin, there was a hole about
as big as a hen's egg in the gauze, and in the coffin itself
only her shroud and some slips of wood were left. In the
ceiling of the room, there was a hole big enough for a
person to pass through.

They duly presented an offering of a gourd at the
place of her ascension. After several days it sprouted
creepers and grew two fruits that looked like peaches.

Each time the anniversary of her death came around,
wind and clouds swelled up and suddenly entered the
room.

7.5 TAOISM ABIDES

After the heyday of the T'ang dynasty, the fortunes
of Chinese religions and culture faced troubled times
due to a rebellion in 755. By 960 the Song dynasty
reestablished political stability and, realizing the need
for a strong social order, the rulers of the Song emphasized "harmonizing the three teachings."

Many new sects of Taoism sprung up, especially in
South China. Among them was the Complete Perfection or **Perfect Truth** (*Ch'üan-chen*) monastic school,
which emphasized the practice of inner alchemy and
the integration of the three teachings. It obtained a
position of great influence, especially under the Mongol rulers. It still exists today along with the Celestial
Masters as one of the two surviving forms of organized Taoism.

While the fortunes of Taoism have waxed and
waned over the centuries and reached their lowest
point after the establishment of the People's Republic in this century, Taoism has not, contrary to many
predictions, died. In fact, it is making a comeback

as many of its ancient practices have become popular once more as both medical and spiritual techniques.

In a recent visit to the White Cloud Temple in Beijing, home of the Chinese Daoist Association and chief temple of the Perfect Truth sect, I observed many young monks attending the various shrines. There was a steady stream of laypeople offering incense and praying. The temple gift shop sold religious items such as tapes of chanting, statues of goddesses and gods, incense holders, books, good-luck charms, meditation beads, and even a Christian crucifix to hang around your neck.

7.5.1 Floating with the Tao

Ponder the statement "The bird is controlled by the air." Close your eyes and imagine a bird carried aloft by the wind, soaring on the currents. Does it look like fun? Do you feel the freedom? Without flying, the bird flies. Can we live like that?

Wang Ch'ung-yang (1112–1170), founder of Perfect Truth Taoism, thinks we can. Wang studied both Confucianism and Buddhism before becoming a Taoist adept. He recommends to his monastic followers that they read Taoist literature as well as Buddhist and Confucian texts. The influence of all of these viewpoints can be seen in the "Fifteen Teachings," which follows. In it, Wang teaches others how to float like the bird held aloft by the wind.

WANG CH'UNG-YANG

Fifteen Teachings

READING QUESTIONS

1. What are the differences between the two kinds of wandering?
2. What are the ecological implications of Wang's advice about residences and coverings?
3. How does Wang blend the ideas of Taoism, Confucianism, and Buddhism?
4. Do you think this would be a good way to live? Why or why not?

ON THE CLOISTERED LIFE

All those who choose to leave their families and homes should join a Taoist monastery, for it is a place where the body may find rest. Where the body rests, the mind also will gradually find peace; the spirit and the vital energy will be harmonized, and entry into the Way (*Tao*) will be attained.

In all action there should be no overexertion, for when there is overexertion, the vital energy is damaged. On the other hand, when there is total inaction, the blood and vital energy become sluggish. Thus a mean should be sought between activity and passivity, for only in this way can one cherish what is permanent and be at ease with one's lot. This is the way to the correct cloistered life.

ON CLOUD-LIKE WANDERING

There are two kinds of wandering. One involves observing the wonders of mountains and waters; lingering over the colors of flowers and trees; admiring the splendor of cities and the architecture of temples; or simply enjoying a visit with relatives and friends. However, in this type of wandering the mind is constantly possessed by things, so this is merely an empty, outward wandering. In fact, one can travel the world over and see the myriad sights, walk millions of miles and exhaust one's body, only in the end to confuse one's mind and weaken one's vital energy without having gained a thing.

In contrast, the other type of wandering, cloud-like wandering, is like a pilgrimage into one's own nature and destiny in search of their darkest, innermost mysteries. To do this one may have to climb fearsome mountain heights to seek instruction from some knowledgeable teacher or cross tumultuous rivers to inquire tirelessly after the Way. Yet if one can find that solitary word which can trigger enlightenment, one will have awakened in oneself perfect illumination; then the great matters of life and death will become magnificent, and one will become a master of the Perfect Truth. This is true cloud-like wandering. . . .

ON RESIDENCE AND COVERING

Sleeping in the open air would violate the sun and the moon, therefore some simple thatched covering is necessary. However, it is not the habit of the superior man to live in great halls and lavish palaces, because to cut down the trees that would be necessary for the building of such grand residences would be like cutting the arteries of the earth or cutting the veins of a man. Such deeds would only add to one's superficial external merits while actually damaging one's inner credits. It would be like drawing a picture of a cake to ward off hunger or piling up snow for a meal—much ado and nothing gained. Thus the Perfect Truth Taoist will daily seek out the palace hall within his own body and avoid the mundane mind which seeks to build lavish external residences. The man of wisdom will scrutinize and comprehend this principle.

ON COMPANIONSHIP

A Taoist should find true friends who can help each other in times of illness and take care of each other's burials at death. However he must observe the character of a person before making friends with him. Do not commit oneself to friendship and then investigate the person's character. Love makes the heart cling to things and should therefore be avoided. On the other hand, if there is no love, human feelings will be strained. To love and yet not to become attached to love—this is the middle path one should follow.

There are three dimensions of compatibility and three of incompatibility. The three dimensions of compatibility are an understanding mind, the possession of wisdom, and an intensity of aspiration. Inability to understand the external world, lack of wisdom accompanied by foolish acts, and lack of high aspiration accompanied by a quarrelsome nature are the three dimensions of incompatibility. The principle of establishing oneself lies in the grand monastic community. The choice of a companion should be motivated by an appreciation of the loftiness of a person's mind and not by mere feelings or external appearance.

ON SITTING IN MEDITATION

Sitting in meditation which consists only of the act of closing the eyes and seating oneself in an upright position is only a pretense. The true way of sitting in meditation is to have the mind as immovable as Mount T'ai all the hours of the day, whether walking, resting, sitting, or reclining. The four doors of the eyes, ears, mouth, and nose should be so pacified that no external sight can be let in to intrude upon the inner self. If ever an impure or wandering thought arises, it will no longer be true quiet sitting. For the person who is an accomplished meditator, even though his body may still reside within this dusty world, his name will already be registered in the ranks of the immortals or free spirits (hsien) and there will be no need for him to travel to far-off places to seek them out; within his body the nature of the sage and the virtuous man will already be present. Through years of practice, a person by his own efforts can liberate his spirit from the shell of his body and send it soaring to the heights. A single session of meditation, when completed, will allow a person to rove through all the corners of the universe.

ON PACIFICATION OF THE MIND

There are two minds. One is quiet and unmoving, dark and silent, not reflecting on any of the myriad things. It is deep and subtle, makes no distinction between inner and outer, and contains not a single wandering thought. The other mind is that mind which, because it is in contact with external forms, will be dragged into all kinds of thoughts, pushed into seeking out beginnings and ends—a totally restless and confused mind. This confused mind must be eliminated. If one allows it to rule, then the Way and its power will be damaged, and one's Nature and Destiny will come to harm. Hearing, seeing, and conscious thoughts should be eliminated from all activities, from walking, resting, sitting, or reclining.

ON NURTURING ONE'S NATURE

The art of cultivating one's Nature is like that of playing on the strings of a musical instrument: too great a force can break the string, while too weak a pull will not produce any sound; one must find the perfect mean to produce the perfect note. The art of nurturing one's Nature is also like forging a sword: too much steel will make the sword too brittle while too much tin will make it too malleable. In training one's Nature, this principle must be recognized. When it is properly implemented, one can master one's Nature at will.

ON ALIGNING THE FIVE PRIMAL ENERGIES

The Five Primal Energies are found in the Middle Hall. The Three Primal Energies are located at the top of the head. If the two are harmonized, then, beginning with the Green Dragon and the White Tiger [the supreme Yin-Yang pair], the ten thousand gods in the body will be arranged in perfect harmony. When this is accomplished, then the energy in the hundred veins will flow smoothly. Cinnabar [symbol for Nature] and mercury [symbol for Destiny] will coalesce into a unity. The body of the adept may still be within the realm of men, but the spirit is already roving in the universe.

ON THE UNION OF NATURE AND DESTINY

Nature is spirit. Destiny is material energy. When Nature is supported by Destiny it is like a bird buoyed up and carried along by the wind—flying freely with little effort. Whatever one wills to be, one can be. This is the meaning in the line from the *Classic of the Shadowy Talismans:* "The bird is controlled by the air." The Perfect Truth Taoist must treasure this line and not reveal its message casually to the uninitiated. The gods themselves will chide the person who disobeys this instruction. The search for the hidden meaning of Nature and mind is the basic motif of the art of self-cultivation. This must be remembered at all times.

ON THE PATH OF THE SAGE

In order to enter the path of the sage, one must accumulate patiently, over the course of many years, merit-actions and true practices. Men of high understanding, men of virtue, and men who have attained insight may all become sages. In attaining sagehood, the body of the person may still be in one room, but his nature will already be encompassing the world. The various sages in the various Heavens will protect him, and the free spirits and immortals in the highest realm of the Non-Ultimate will be around him. His name will be registered in the Hall of the Immortals, and he will be ranked among the free spirits. Although his bodily form is in the world of dust, his mind will have transcended all corporal things.

ON TRANSCENDING THE THREE REALMS

The Three Realms refer to the realms of desire, form, and formlessness. The mind that has freed itself from all impure or random thoughts will have transcended the first realm of desire. The mind that is no longer tied to the perception of objects in the object-realm will have transcended the realm of form. The mind that no longer

is fixed upon emptiness will further transcend the realm of formlessness. The spirit of the man who transcends all three of these realms will be in the realm of the immortals. His Nature will abide forever in the realm of Jade-like Purity.

ON CULTIVATING THE BODY OF THE LAW

The Body of the Law is formless form. It is neither empty nor full. It has neither front nor back and is neither high nor low, long nor short. When it is functioning, there is nothing it does not penetrate. When it is withdrawn into itself, it is obscure and leaves no trace; it must be cultivated in order to attain the true Way. If the cultivation is great, the merit will be great; if the cultivation is small, the merit will be small. One should not wish to return to it, nor should one be attached to this world of things. One must allow Nature to follow its own course.

ON LEAVING THE MUNDANE WORLD

Leaving the mundane world is not leaving the body; it is leaving behind the mundane mind. Consider the analogy of the lotus; although rooted in the mud, it blossoms pure and white into the clear air. The man who attains the Way, although corporally abiding in the world, may flourish through his mind in the realm of sages. Those people who presently seek after non-death or escape from the world do not know this true principle and commit the greatest folly.

The words of these fifteen precepts are for our disciples of aspiration. Examine them carefully!

7.5.2 The Great Tao Has No Form

The societies in which we live all have a certain amount of hierarchical structure to them. Some are more egalitarian than others, but all have some sort of structure, formal and informal, from the lowest to the highest levels. Chinese society, for a good portion of its history, exhibits a well-defined hierarchical structure stretching from the poor peasant to the emperor.

When Taoists speak of transcendence, they usually imagine moving up in a way analogous to someone bettering their lot in the social order. The pious

Taoist, however, is bettering his or her lot for all eternity, and the goal is to obtain earthly, then heavenly immortality. However, even in Heaven there is a hierarchy, and there the heavenly immortal Taoist has to repeat the earthly process by diligent work. Is there an end to advancement? Is there a place where the quest for transcendence stops? Is there something so transcendent that one cannot imagine going beyond it? Does one attain it by effort or by effortless action (*wu-wei*)? Perhaps the best way to get "ahead" is to be content with where one is.

The following text is a Taoist liturgical text that has been memorized and chanted in Taoist monasteries since the Song dynasty (960–1260). It is particularly popular in the Perfect Truth monastic school, and, because it extols the virtues of purity and tranquility, is titled *Scripture of Purity and Tranquility*. This text teaches the monks or nuns who chant it what sort of life they should live while in this world by making an analogy to the ultimate transcendent, the Great Tao.

Scripture of Purity and Tranquility (Ching-ching Ching)

READING QUESTIONS

1. What are the exhortations and warnings found in this liturgy?
2. Can you find Buddhist ideas in this text? What are they?
3. This liturgy reveals a quest for transcendence. How would you characterize that transcendence?

The Great Tao has no form;
It brings forth and raises heaven and earth.
The Great Tao has no feelings;
It regulates the course of the sun and the moon.

The Great Tao has no name;
It raises and nourishes the myriad beings.

I do not know its name—
So I call it Tao.

The Tao can be pure or turbid, moving or tranquil.
Heaven is pure, earth is turbid;
Heaven is moving, earth is tranquil.
The male is moving, the female is tranquil.

Descending from the origin,
Flowing toward the end,
The myriad beings are being born.

Purity—the source of turbidity,
Movement—the root of tranquility.

Always be pure and tranquil;
Heaven and earth
Return to the primordial.

The human spirit is fond of purity,
But the mind disturbs it.
The human mind is fond of tranquility,
But desires meddle with it.

Get rid of desires for good,
And the mind will be calm.
Cleanse your mind,
And the spirit will be pure.

Naturally the six desires won't arise,
The three poisons are destroyed.
Whoever cannot do this
Has not yet cleansed his mind,
His desires are not yet driven out.

Those who have abandoned their desires:
Observe your mind by introspection—
And see there is no mind.

Then observe the body,
Look at yourself from without—
And see there is no body.

Then observe others by glancing out afar—
And see there are no beings.

Once you have realized these three,
You observe emptiness!

Use emptiness to observe emptiness,
And see there is no emptiness.
When even emptiness is no more,
There is no more nonbeing either.

Without even the existence of nonbeing
There is only serenity,
Profound and everlasting.

When serenity dissolves in nothingness—
How could there be desires?

When no desires arise
You have found true tranquility.

In true tranquility, go along with beings;
In true permanence, realize inner nature.
Forever going along, forever tranquil—
This is permanent purity, lasting tranquility.

In purity and tranquility,
Gradually enter the true Tao.
When the true Tao is entered,
It is realized.

Though we speak of "realized,"
Actually there is nothing to attain.
Rather, we speak of realization
When someone begins to transform the myriad beings.

Only who has properly understood this
Is worthy to transmit the sages' Tao.

The highest gentleman does not fight;
The lesser gentleman loves to fight.
Highest Virtue is free from Virtue;
Lesser Virtue clings to Virtue.

All clinging and attachments
Have nothing to do with the Tao or the Virtue.

People fail to realize the Tao
Because they have deviant minds.
Deviance in the mind
Means the spirit is alarmed.

Spirit alarmed,
There is clinging to things.
Clinging to things,
There is searching and coveting.

Searching and coveting,
There are passions and afflictions.
Passions, afflictions, deviance, and imaginings
Trouble and pester body and mind.

Then one falls into turbidity and shame,
Ups and downs, life and death.
Forever immersed in the sea of misery,
One is in eternity lost to the true Tao.

The Tao of true permanence
Will naturally come to those who understand.
Those who understand the realization of the Tao
Will rest forever in the pure and tranquil.

7.5.3 Taoist Breathing Techniques

As the twenty-first century opens, Taoist practices
remain important as both spiritual and medical techniques. Many exercises aimed at developing and fo-

cusing the body's vital energy (*ch'i*) abound. One of
the most popular is called **Ch'i-kung**. Mental control,
relaxed postures, and, above all, regulated breathing
are paramount features of *Ch'i-kung*. Practitioners
believe that by focusing the *ch'i* on weakened or ill
parts of the body, health can be restored.

Ch'i-kung's popularity stems, in part, from the
experience and writings of Jiang Weiqiao, known as
Master Yinshi. He was a sickly child whose health
worsened as he grew older. After reading an ancient
text on inner alchemy, he decided to practice the exercises, adapting them to his own situation. His health
improved, and he stopped the practices. His health
got worse again and, at age twenty-two, he caught tu-
berculosis, a disease that had already killed his brother.
He started his exercises again in earnest and was cured.

Master Yinshi first published his guide to these
exercises in 1914 under the title *Quiet Sitting with
Master Yinshi*. It has been made a part of the supple-
ment to the Taoist canon and provides a particularly
clear account of those parts of the exercises involving
breathing. The techniques he describes have been
modified and applied in a wide variety of settings
to help people deal with everything from stopping
smoking to battling cancer.

JIANG WEIQIAO

*Quiet Sitting
with Master Yinshi*

READING QUESTIONS

1. Create your own set of reading questions for this
   selection and answer them.
2. Why do you think these breathing exercises might
   be beneficial?

Breathing is one of the most essential necessities of
human life, even more so than food and drink. Ordinary
people are quite familiar with the idea that food and

Reprinted by permission of the State University of New York
Press, from *The Taoist Experience: An Anthology* by Livia Kohn
(Ed.), pp. 136–141. © 1993 State University of New York.
Notes omitted. All rights reserved.

drink are important to maintain life, that they will starve if left without it for a while. But they hardly ever turn around to think about the importance of breathing and that air is even more essential to life than anything else.

This has to do with the fact that in order to obtain food and drink people have to go to work and earn money, so they come to value these things as important commodities. Breathing, on the other hand, is done by taking in the air of the atmosphere of which there is no limit and which cannot be exhausted. There is no need to labor and pay for the air we breathe; thus people tend to overlook the importance of this function.

Yet if you stop eating and drinking, you may still survive for a couple of days, even as long as a whole week. However, if you stop up your nostrils and mouth you will be dead within minutes. This fact alone shows that breathing is far more important than food.

In discussing methods of breathing, two main types can be distinguished: natural breathing and regulated breathing.

NATURAL BREATHING

One exhalation and one inhalation are called one breath. The respiratory organs in the body are the nose on the outside and the lungs on the inside. The two wings of the lungs are positioned within the upper torso so that through the motion of the respiration the entire area expands and contracts. Such is the law of nature. However, in ordinary people, the respiration never expands or contracts the lungs to their full capacity. They only use the upper section of the lungs while their lower section hardly ever is employed at all. Because of this they cannot gain the full advantage of deep breathing, their blood and body fluids are not refreshed, and the various diseases gain easy entry. Any of this has as yet nothing to do with natural breathing.

Natural breathing is also called abdominal breathing. Every single inhalation, every single exhalation must always go deep down into the stomach area. During inhalation, when the air enters the lungs, they are filled to capacity and as a result their lower section expands. This in turn presses against the diaphragm and pushes it downward. Therefore, during inhalation, the chest area is completely relaxed while the stomach area is curved toward the outside.

Again, during exhalation the stomach area contracts, the diaphragm is pushed upward against the lungs and thereby causes the old and turbid breath to be expelled from their depth. Once it is all dispersed outside, no used air remains within. Therefore in this kind of breath-

ing, although it makes use mostly of the lungs, it is the area of the stomach and the diaphragm which expands and contracts. This is the great method of breathing naturally by which the blood and the body fluids are kept fresh and active.

Not only during and prior to meditation should this method be employed, but always: whether walking, staying, sitting, or lying down, one can breathe deeply and naturally in any given circumstance.

Breathing Instructions

1. Contract the lower abdomen when breathing out. Thereby the diaphragm is pushed upward, the chest area is tensed, and all used breath, even from the lower part of the lungs, is expelled entirely.

2. Breathe in fresh air through the nostrils. Let it fill the lungs to capacity so that the diaphragm is pushed down and the stomach area expands.

3. Gradually lengthen and deepen your inhalations and exhalations. The stomach will get stronger and more stable. Some people say that one should hold the breath for a short moment at the end of an inhalation. This is called stopping respiration. According to my own experience, this is not good for beginners.

4. As you go along, let the respiration gradually grow subtler and finer until the entering and leaving of the breath is very soft. With prolonged practice you will cease to be consciously aware of the respiration and feel as if you weren't breathing at all.

5. Once the state of non-respiration is reached, you can truly be without inhalations and exhalations. Even though you have special organs for breathing, you won't feel any longer that you are using them. At the same time the breath will by and by come to enter and leave through all the body. This is the perfection of harmonious breathing. However, as a beginner you should never try to attain this intentionally. Always obey nature and go along with what you can do.

REGULATED BREATHING

Regulated breathing is also known as "reversed breathing." It resembles natural breathing in that it is very deep and soft and should always reach as far as the stomach area. On the other hand, it reverses the movements of the stomach. The upward and downward movement of the diaphragm is accordingly different from its activity during natural breathing. It is called "reversed" precisely because it reverses the pattern proper to natural breathing.

Practical Instructions

1. Exhale slow and far, let the stomach area expand freely, and make sure that the stomach is strong and full.

2. Let the lower abdomen be full of breath, the chest area slack, and the diaphragm completely relaxed.

3. Inhale slowly and deeply into the diaphragm. Let the fresh air fill the lungs so that they expand naturally. At the same time contract the abdomen.

4. As the lungs are filled with breath they will press down, while the stomach, contracted, will push up. The diaphragm is therefore pressed in from above and below; its movement is thereby getting subtler and subtler.

5. When the chest area is fully expanded, the stomach region may be contracted, yet it should not be entirely empty. Independent of whether you inhale or exhale, the center of gravity must always be solidly established beneath the navel. Thus the stomach area remains strong and full.

6. All respiration should be subtle and quiet. Especially during the practice of quiet sitting it should be so fine that you don't hear the sound of your own breathing. In the old days some people claimed that inhalations should be slightly longer than exhalations. Nowadays some say that exhalations should be slightly longer than inhalations. As far as I can tell, it is best to keep their length equal.

To summarize: Independent of whether you practice natural breathing or regulated breathing, the aim is always to activate the diaphragm. In the case of regulated breathing, the diaphragm is worked by means of human power. It reverses natural breathing and thus causes the diaphragm to stretch even farther, to move even more smoothly. For this reason I never enter my meditation practice without first practicing regulated breathing for a little while.

This is also the reason why I have recommended its use in my book. Since its publication many students have begun the practice. Some found the prescribed breathing exercises useful, others didn't. For this reason, always remain aware that even though regulated breathing is controlled by the human mind, it cannot be learned by human means alone. It is not a mere distortion of natural breathing, but its development, and should be learned in accordance with nature.

BREATHING EXERCISES

Both natural and regulated breathing have the following eight instructions in common:

1. Sit cross-legged and erect; take the same posture as in quiet sitting.

2. First breathe short breaths, then gradually lengthen them.

3. All breaths should be slow and subtle, quiet and long. Gradually they enter deeper into the abdomen.

4. Always inhale through the nose. Do not inhale through the mouth. The nose is the specific organ of respiration. There are tiny hairs on the inside of the nostrils which are easily blocked and obstructed. The mouth, on the other hand, is not made primarily for respiration, and if you use it for breathing it will usurp the proper function of the nose. This in turn will lead to the gradual obstruction of the nose. More than that, by breathing through the mouth any number of bacteria and dirt particles will enter the body, and diseases are easily conceived. Therefore always keep the mouth closed, not only during breathing and meditation practice.

5. Once your breathing gets purer and warmer with prolonged practice, lengthen the individual breaths. The limit of lengthening is reached when it takes you a whole minute to breathe in and out one single breath. However, never forget that this cannot be forced.

6. The practice of slow and subtle breathing can be continued any time, any place.

7. During quiet sitting there should be no thoughts and no worries. If you have to pay constant attention to your respiration, the mind cannot be truly calm. Therefore it is best to practice breathing before and after every sitting.

8. Before and after quiet sitting, practice respiration. Pick a place that has good fresh air. Take about five to ten minutes for the exercise.

BREATHING AND THE LOWERING OF THE PIT OF THE STOMACH

In my discussion of posture above [in a separate section], I already spoke about the reason why the pit of the stomach should be lowered. Nevertheless, since this lowering is also of central importance in breathing, I come back to it now. Generally, if the pit of the stomach is not lowered, the respiration cannot be harmonized. Then the effectiveness of quiet sitting will not come to bear.

Repeating thus what I said before, students should pay attention to the following points:

1. During the breathing exercise, beginners should be aware of the pit of the stomach being firm and solid. It thus interferes with the breath, which cannot be harmonized properly. This is because the diaphragm is not yet able to move up and down freely. A beginner should overcome this difficulty with determination and not falter before it.

2. Should you become aware that your breathing is obstructed in this way, never try to force it open. Rather, let it take its natural course by gently focusing your attention on the lower abdomen.

3. Relax your chest so that the blood circulation does not press upon the heart. The pit of the stomach will then be lowered naturally.

4. Practice this over a long period. Gradually the chest and the diaphragm will feel open and relaxed. The breathing will be calm and subtle, deep and continuous. Every inhalation and exhalation will reach all the way to the center of gravity below the navel. This, then, is proof that the pit of the stomach has been effectively lowered.

CONTEMPORARY SCHOLARSHIP

Contemporary scholarship on Taoism is growing by leaps and bounds. More texts are being translated, more detailed histories compiled, more careful philological studies undertaken than ever before. The Western bias favoring the more philosophical aspects of Taoism is slowly giving way to a closer examination of Taoist liturgical traditions. Along with this explosion of knowledge about Taoism, an increased interest in Chinese popular religion has developed.

Increased interest in gender studies along with the new scholarship on Taoism naturally leads to exploring the topic of women and Taoism. In the *Tao Te Ching*, the Tao is often described in feminine imagery and symbolism, and, as we have seen, there have been impressive female Taoist masters. We shall look at one example of scholarship on Taoism and women.

One continuing problem in the study of Chinese religions involves determining the precise relationship between Taoism and Chinese popular religion. Laurence Thompson (Reading 7.1) says they are not to be confused. However, Kristofer Schipper, who is both an ordained Taoist priest and a scholar of Taoism, writes, "Taoism . . . can be seen as the most elevated expression of Chinese popular religion" (*The Taoist Body*, p. 2). The second selection that follows, while not directly treating the problem of how Taoism relates to popular religion, does give us an overview of key elements in Chinese popular religion. As you read it, look for connections with Taoism.

7.6 WOMEN AND TAOISM

Chinese literature tells many tales of women who have learned the secrets of the Tao. The Tao itself is called "Mother," and female divinities generously populate Taoist literature. Powerful dragon goddesses save the world, and Hsi Wang Mu, the Queen Mother of the West, rules over the Taoist immortals. Clearly there is much in the Taoist tradition to interest scholars who are particularly concerned with issues of gender.

Barbara E. Reed, who is a professor of religion at St. Olaf College and author of the next selection, is just such a scholar. She did graduate work at the University of Iowa and at the National Taiwan Normal University. She is particularly interested in symbolism, especially as it relates to women, found in the Chinese Taoist and Buddhist traditions.

BARBARA E. REED

Women in Taoism

READING QUESTIONS

1. What are the views of women found in Taoist philosophical literature?
2. How does the way we think of the relationships between *yin* and *yang* relate to the relationships between men and women?

Reprinted by permission of the State University of New York Press, from *Women in World Religions* by Arvind Sharma (Ed.). © 1987 State University of New York. Barbara E. Reed, "Taoism," pp. 161–166, 172–180. Notes omitted. All rights reserved.

3. How can sexuality be used for religious ends?
4. What role do female deities play in Taoism?
5. Why do you think that there seems to be a more positive view of women in Taoism than in Confucianism?

The Valley Spirit never dies.
It is named the Mysterious Female.
And the Doorway of the Mysterious Female
Is the base from which Heaven and Earth sprang.
It is there within us all the while;
Draw upon it as you will, it never runs dry.

(Tao te ching VI)

Any religious or philosophical tradition that symbolizes cosmic and personal creativity as the "Mysterious Female" has great potential for attracting women's participation. Taoism not only uses female images for creative powers, but also advocates the harmony and equality of all opposites, including male and female. Women's historical fate in Taoism is especially interesting because it developed within the extremely patriarchal culture of Confucian China.

Taoism is the native religious tradition of China. It has shaped Chinese culture along with the native philosophical tradition of Confucianism and the imported Buddhist religion. According to tradition, Taoism was founded by the legendary Lao tzu in the sixth century B.C.E. But its roots are traceable to ancient shamanistic practices, deities, and myths which were incorporated into a rich tradition of philosophy, ritual, and magic. The Taoist tradition has several interacting strands: the mystical and philosophical texts, such as the Tao te ching (compiled ca. third century B.C.E.) and the Chuang tzu (fourth century B.C.E.), the Taoist religious sects dating from the second century C.E., and various techniques of exorcising malevolent spirits and attaining immortality.

WOMEN IN TAOIST PHILOSOPHICAL LITERATURE

The two great classics of Taoist philosophy, the Tao te ching and Chuang tzu, extol the way of nature as the path to happiness. The mysterious way of nature is called Tao. One can know Tao by yielding to and following nature. One should act spontaneously, naturally, without purpose. These two Taoist texts describe similar paths to simplicity and happiness, but they address themselves to different audiences and use radically different styles.

The Tao te ching uses feminine imagery and traditional views of female roles to counter destructive male behavior. Chuang tzu illustrates the Tao by describing anecdotes in the lives of individuals who manifest the Tao.

The Tao te ching is a short, cryptic text addressed to the ruler. One who has the responsibility of rule could, it suggests, create a simple and happy society by allowing the Tao to govern. The mysterious Tao can transform all things spontaneously if the ruler does not intervene with obstructive behavior. The Sage Ruler says: "So long as I love quietude, the people will of themselves go straight. So long as I act only by inactivity the people will of themselves become prosperous" (Tao te ching LVII). To communicate the Tao, the path of quietude and inactivity, the Tao te ching relies heavily on female imagery. Ultimately, the Tao is ineffable: "The Way that can be told of is not an Unvarying Way." But the Tao manifests itself in creativity and in spontaneous, nonaggressive human behavior. The Tao te ching symbolizes this behavior in concrete images from nature: water, the uncarved block, the child, the female, the mother, the valley, the dark, the bellows, the door, the empty vessel, the mare, and the hen. Most of these symbols are explicitly female, and all of them point to the potentiality associated with female reproduction or the unqualified nature of motherly love. Ellen Chen has shown that in many ways the Tao represents the Great Mother, the creative power of the female.

Creation in the Tao te ching is the production of all things from the womb of the Mother. The Tao is named the "Mother," the "dark," and the "mysterious." She is the "doorway" through which things enter the visible world. All things were created by her and continue to rely on her for their sustenance. The creativity of the Tao depends on the womb of creation, on its emptiness, its potentiality. The Tao is nonbeing in the Taoist understanding of nonbeing as the potential for new being —not in the usual Western sense of the negation of being. The Tao as empty has unlimited potentiality.

The Way is like an empty vessel
That yet may be drawn from
Without ever needing to be filled.
It is bottomless; the very progenitor of all things in the world.

(Tao te ching IV)

Tao as nonbeing is the beginning of all things and should also be that to which all things return. Unless one realizes that nonbeing is the sacred quality of female creative power, the return to the darkness of nonbeing appears to be a morbid search for annihilation. The return to original nonbeing is truly the return to authentic existence. Perhaps the goal of returning to the Tao is rooted in an earlier worship of the mother goddess. Because the cycle of return is grounded in the creative power of the Tao, it has none of the terror or meaninglessness associated with Hindu conceptions of life in continuing cycles. As [Mircea] Eliade has suggested, the terror of cyclical views of time occurs only when the sacred nature of the cosmos has been forgotten. The Tao te ching does not envision a primordial beginning with specific gods and goddesses. The creative powers of the beginning are instead symbolized by the abstract Mother, the Tao. She provides the comfort and meaning for the return to the beginning.

Nonbeing and being are both described with female imagery. Tao as the nameless (nonbeing) is beyond categories, but in attempting to describe it the text uses images of the dark and mysterious female. Tao as the named (being) is the source of all things. In Ellen Chen's view, the creativity of the nameless Tao as Mother is based on her emptiness, and the creativity of the named Tao (being) is based on its potentiality. The Mother is nonbeing, and her child of unlimited potential is being.

The spirit and creativity of the Mother is also found within all her creatures.

> The Valley Spirit never dies.
> It is named the Mysterious Female.
> And the Doorway of the Mysterious Female
> Is the base from which Heaven and Earth sprang.
> It is there within us all the while;
> Draw upon it as you will, it never runs dry.
>
> (Tao te ching VI)

The Taoist follows the Tao by acting as a child and clinging to the Mother's breast. The way to act in the world is to follow the role traditionally assigned to women in society—to be weak, flexible, and lowly. Creative power comes from these positions, not from positions of strength, hardness, or superiority. "He who knows the male, yet cleaves to what is female/Becomes like a ravine, receiving all things under heaven." The lowly position is identified with women but is advocated for all—particularly for the ruler, to whom the entire text is addressed. If the ruler acts passively, all things spontaneously follow the creative principle within them.

The Tao te ching takes a negative view toward the achievements of traditionally male-dominant Chinese civilization—its books, laws, and travel. And it views the traditional love of the mother as the model for the relationship of the Tao to all creation. The Tao, like the love of a mother, makes no distinctions; it embraces both the "good" and the "bad." One who follows Tao also refrains from judgments and accepts all things that come

from the mother. Traditional sex roles and biological differences are recognized but denied determinative status. All people (male or female) should take the role of the infant clinging to the Mother or of the female animal beneath the male in order to live in harmony in the world and to return to the Tao.

The Tao te ching uses both female biological characteristics and traditional socially defined characteristics to symbolize the Taoist path. The biological imagery of the womb and breast dominates images of the Tao; the social role of passivity dominates the images of the person who follows the Tao.

Chuang tzu does not use female imagery to communicate the Tao. Whereas the Tao te ching uses universal female images abstracted from nature to counter the normal way of perceiving and acting, Chuang tzu teaches in concrete anecdotes. The text illustrates Tao by describing people who have lived in harmony with it. Although women are mentioned, most of the characters are men. But all those who follow Tao act in the yielding and spontaneous way suggested by the Tao te ching. Chuang tzu expands the meaning of returning to the Tao by expressing a joyful acceptance of the mysterious transformation called "death." One should yield to all things brought about by the Tao, even death.

There are two items in Chuang tzu that are particularly interesting for this investigation of women in Taoism. First, Chuang tzu mentions a myth of a utopian matrilinear society in which people "knew their mothers, but not their fathers." Second, Chuang tzu sees no sex restrictions for the immortal beings who are an important part of later popular legends and religious Taoism. Hsi Wang Mu, the Queen Mother of the West, appears as one who found Tao and became immortal. And there is also an old woman with the complexion of a child who knew Tao and tried to teach it to a sage.

The Tao te ching and Chuang tzu both reject the aggressive, highly structured societies of their times in favor of lives of simplicity close to nature. With no value placed on social hierarchy, there is no place for the denigration of women. In fact, in the Tao te ching women serve as models.

YIN AND YANG

The complementary principles of yin and yang are important in most of Chinese thought and religion. They are not unique to Taoism, but in Taoism they are fundamental. Yin is the dark side, the cold, the damp, the female. Yang is the sunny side, the hot, the dry, the male.

In Taoist thinking, yin and yang are the complementary principles of the cosmos. The ideal is balance, not the victory of one over the other. In the Tao te ching the balance is grounded in the yin, which has the lower position. In Chuang tzu the alternation of the two, such as life and death, is accepted as the transformation of the Tao. Neither is superior—the yin state of death is as acceptable as the yang state of life. One cannot exist without the other; they are both part of the wondrous Tao.

The yin-yang duality of balance is strikingly different from Western conceptions of conflict dualism. In Western dualism, the victory of good over evil is based on a conflict that separates everything and everyone into two opposing sides that cannot exist in peace. Violence, whether physical or mental, may be necessary for the victory of one side over the other. There is no room for compromise with the other side—"You are either for us or against us," as the saying goes. This conflict dualism gives great hope to those on the side of "good" because there is the assurance that good is stronger than evil. Good, usually represented as God, will win in the end. The closer the end, the more hope for the forces of good.

Taoist harmony is a radically different goal than the victory of good over evil. It is based on a complementary dualism rather than a conflict dualism. There are two sides, but they depend on each other for their existence. The goal is the balancing of the two sides, the mutual interaction of the two forces. This complementary dualism has been the core of much east Asian religion and philosophy. It is the yin-yang model that originated in ancient China. One attains harmony in society and nature through the balancing of the positive forces of yang and the negative forces of yin. The cooperative actions of male and female, summer and winter, the sun and rain are examples of this complementary dualism, in which neither side is better than nor independent of the other. Yin and yang are viewed as female and male principles or forces, but women and men contain both principles and need the harmony of the two for physical and mental health.

The idea of the balance and relativity of yin and yang is difficult to maintain. In later Confucian thought and in some religious Taoism, yang is evaluated as the superior. In the Taoist quest for immortality, the relativity of individual life and death is superseded by the development of techniques for holding off death by the accumulation of yang. Breathing exercises, special diets, laboratory alchemy, and sexual practices were all developed in the context of yin-yang theory to prolong life and to attain individual immortality.

Even though the desire for the yang principle of life dominates, however, the importance of the yin principle never dies. Taoist techniques for attaining immortality are based on the cooperation of yin and yang and maternal creativity. The union of yin and yang in sexual intercourse is one technique to produce an immortal body and serves as the paradigm for others. In laboratory alchemy, the crucible functions as the womb, the elements of cinnabar and lead as female and male sexual fluids, and the alchemic firing process as the sexual technique. The equal importance of yin and yang is central to most Taoist paths to immortality. Both yin and yang could be absorbed through the skin to further the Taoist's progress toward immortality. The Classic of the Five Sacred Talismans (Ling-pao wu fu ching) of the third or fourth century suggests that the adept "breathe" in yang from the light of the sun and yin from the light of the moon at midnight. . . .

VIEWS OF THE BODY

Religions often associate women more closely than men with the physical body. Whenever body is contrasted with spirit, this association means lower status for women. Fear and guilt about the body is then transferred to the female sex. Taoism does not have a body-spirit dualism. The complementary duality of yin and yang is within nature. The physical world is highly valued, and the physical human body in its most purified form is the Taoist's goal.

The natural universe is the transformation of yin and yang. It is the body of the Tao. The individual human body is a microcosm of the universe, and it undergoes the same transformations, is controlled by the same forces, and is of highest value. The goal of immortality in religious Taoism is not the immortality of a disembodied spirit; it is the prolongation of life in a purified physical body. Just as gold is the incorruptible and highest form of metal, the bodies of the highest Celestial Immortals are of the purest, most incorruptible substance.

The division of male and female in the body of the universe is most clearly the division of Heaven and Earth. Heaven and Earth are the father and mother of the macrocosm and are equally important. In the earliest Taoist scripture, the T'ai-p'ing ching, the Master says, "Father and mother are equally human beings, and Heaven and Earth are both 'celestial.'" The respect for Mother Earth is as important as that for Heaven, which traditionally had been associated with moral law and natural order. In this scripture, followers are prohibited from digging wells because it would be equivalent to wounding one's own mother. People must be content with the natural springs which serve as the nipples of Mother Earth. This Taoist vision of the world is clearly wholistic. Each being is part of the larger body of the universe, and to harm any part of the universe is to harm oneself, one's siblings, or one's own parents.

Taoism views even women's bodies and sexuality positively. Women's menstrual blood is powerful, not impure as in many religions. Menstrual blood is the essence (*ching*) of the woman, which she can use to increase her life span if she can nurture it; semen serves the same function for men. The bodily fluids of men and women are equally valuable as the sources of natural life and immortal life. Both menstrual blood and semen provide the raw material for creating an embryo for an immortal body. Human sexuality is valued as the obvious means of creation and is given religious and philosophical meaning. Sexual intercourse is the primary form of the interaction of yin and yang and thus represents the mysterious Tao.

The female body as symbol for creativity in the Tao te ching is not lost in the religious movement of Taoism. The Tao as the dark womb of creation is often given more mythological form. In a fifth century Taoist text (San-t'ien nei-chieh ching), creation proceeds from non-being, which produces the Three Breaths, which in turn produce the Jade Mother of Divine Mystery. The Jade Mother then gives birth to the legendary Lao tzu, who creates the world. In this type of myth, the creativity of the Tao manifests itself as a specific woman—the mother of Lao tzu. Early birth legends of Lao tzu do not mention a father but only his mother, from whom he took the surname Li. Elsewhere Lao tzu himself is Mother Li and gives birth to himself.

If the female body represents the creative power of the Tao, then it could be the model for all Taoists. In some instances, men apparently tried to imitate the physical characteristics of women. This imitation goes beyond the use of women's traditionally passive social role as a model. The Hsiang-erh commentary on the Tao te ching says that men should cultivate a female character, and modern lore tells of Taoist practices leading to the atrophy of male genitals or to old Taoist men urinating in a female position. In Chuang tzu, when the Taoist character Lieh tzu reaches the highest level of understanding he takes the place of his wife in the kitchen, but even more extreme is the case in the *Lü-chu chih* in which the man Lü T'ung-pin actually claims he is pregnant. Pregnancy is a basic Taoist model for attaining immortality. A Taoist, male or female, creates and nurtures an immortal embryo within the corruptible physical body. According to this model, males must become females, at least metaphorically, to achieve their goal of deathlessness.

Sometimes sexual transformation did go the other way in Taoism. A text from about the eighteenth century proposes Hsi Wang Mu's ethical and physiological path to immortality specifically to women Taoists, but the end of the path is the rejuvenated form of a young boy rather than a young girl.

FEMALE ADEPTS

Women such as Hsi Wang Mu attained the secret of Tao and thus immortality in legendary times. Chinese literature is full of women who have learned the secrets of Tao in historical times, either accidentally or through the study of alchemy or meditation. One source for these stories is Pao p'u-tzu, written by Ko Hung in the fourth century. He was a scholar who defended the claims of esoteric Taoism, especially the belief that normal human beings can attain the status of Immortals through Taoist arts. He argues that just because some people have not seen Immortals is no proof that they do not exist; they do exist, because people have reported their existence. Some of the stories he offers as proof describe female adepts who have learned the secrets of immortality.

Ko Hung reports a second-hand story of a 4-year-old girl who learned the secret of prolonging life. Her father, Chan Kuang-ting, had to flee from disaster, but his young daughter was unable to make the difficult trip. He abandoned her in a tomb with a few months' supply of food and drink and then fled. After three years the father returned and went to the tomb to collect his daughter's bones for burial. At the tomb he found his daughter alive and well. She explained that at first she was hungry but that then she imitated a large tortoise in the corner of the tomb that stretched its neck and swallowed its own breath. This story is used to prove that tortoises, known for their longevity in China, possess specific techniques leading to long life. It also demonstrates that gender is not relevant to the ability to master the Taoist arts leading to extreme longevity.

Another story tells of an amazing 200-year-old woman captured by hunters during the Han dynasty (202 B.C.E.–220 C.E.). She was naked and covered with thick black hair. When questioned, she told her unusual story.

> I was originally a Ch'in concubine. Learning that with the arrival of bandits from the East the King of Ch'in would surrender and the palace would be burned, I became frightened and ran away to the mountains where I famished for lack of food. I was on the point of dying when an old man taught me how to eat the leaves and fruits of pines. At first it

was bitter and unpleasant, but I gradually grew used to it until it produced lack of hunger and thirst. In the winter I suffered no cold, and in the summer I felt no heat.

Unfortunately this woman, who proved to be nearing immortality, was taken back to the court and fed a normal diet, whereupon she lost her hair and died. Ko Hung tells us that if left alone she would have become an Immortal.

The last story of a woman using Taoist arts in Pao p'u-tzu is that of a girl from a family who possessed the esoteric knowledge of Taoist alchemy. A Han courtier, Ch'eng Wei, married her but failed to convince her to give him the secrets. She believed her own efforts in the laboratory were successful because she was fated to master the Tao, but she did not believe that he was so fated. He harassed her to give him the secrets until she went crazy, fled, and later died.

A tale from the I-yüan gives further evidence of female adepts. The tale tells of a shrine to a certain Lady Mei-ku in the third century B.C.E. Mei-ku was an accomplished Taoist master who could walk on water. She once broke the law of the Tao, and her husband killed her in rage and threw her body in a lake. A shaman placed her corpse in a lakeside shrine, and thereafter she would appear twice a month standing on the water. Fishing and hunting were then prohibited in this area because the shaman said that Lady Mei-ku hated to see animals suffer and die as she had.

These four stories have one thing in common: all the women have experienced crises within a family relationship. The crisis that motivates or ends the practice of Taoist arts is caused by a male member of her family—father, husband, or patron/lover. These stories linking the practice of Taoist arts with family crises and the need for survival are similar to the stories of modern shamanesses who seek communication with the spirits only after family crises and financial necessity.

Not all women experienced crises in their search for the secrets of the Tao. The Taoist canon contains several texts that describe meditation techniques for any woman to follow. Women are important in these meditation texts as both practitioners and as representations of visualized deities.

The meditation techniques of religious Taoism demonstrate that the spiritual powers are not identified with one sex. The spirits that rule the internal world of the body and the external world of the universe are both male and female. Neither immortality nor spiritual powers are gender specific. The female spirits include various jade maidens, fairies, goddesses, and powerful spirit-generals who aid women and men in their meditation. These female spiritual beings are as diverse as the male spirits. Many are beautiful and even erotic maidens. Some are terrifying and ugly female spirits. An example of the diversity is found in Michael Saso's description of a ritual to counter black magic used by a contemporary Taoist priest. Of the six spirit-generals called on to fight the battle against evil, two are women. General Hsiao-lieh is a beautiful woman: "She is eight feet tall, and her face is white and clear complexioned, with pretty features and delicate eyes." General Kang-Hsien is hideous: "She is ten feet tall, with the face of an ugly woman, yellow hair, and large protruding white teeth." However, although differing in beauty, both women are courageous and strong. Here beauty is not associated with weakness.

Some meditation texts have separate spirits for women and men. The goals and techniques of the meditation are the same; only the register of spirits to be visualized differs. In the T'ai-p'ing ching women and men may both meditate on the Primordial one, or women may visualize the internal spirits that control the body as female and the men may visualize them as male. Another example of separate but equal participation in meditation requires marriage for the highest level of participation. When first initiated into the sect, young children receive a register of 1 or more spirit generals for meditation. At the second childhood initiation, they receive a register of 10 generals. At adolescence, sex distinctions begin, and women receive a register of 75 Superior Powers while the men receive 75 Superior Immortals. The highest station is not for the individual but for the married couple whose combined register amounts to 150 spirit generals. This practice follows the model of the complementarity of male and female, yang and yin, in which both are equal and necessary.

Sexual techniques were also used to prolong life and sometimes even to form an incorruptible embryo for a new existence. The state of Taoist texts and current research make it difficult to fully understand women's participation in the sexual techniques or their understanding of them. Much literature focuses on male techniques of preventing ejaculation and using the yang semen and the yin essence absorbed from the female during intercourse. All people have an essence within them, and when it is exhausted, they die. The essence for the man is his semen; the essence for the woman is her menstrual blood. Sexual intercourse is important for the nourishing of the essence, but only if it is done right. The Immortal P'eng-tsu recommends to men that they choose young women who do not know the techniques themselves because women who know the technique will seek to prolong their own lives and not give up their essence. The physical techniques for women are not as clear as the suggested male techniques for preventing ejaculation. But women were obviously using these techniques for their own benefit, as they used other Taoist meditative disciplines. Lest these Taoists seem to be involved in continual sexual orgies, we must add that the texts contain many restrictions limiting when these practices could be performed. The restricted days, based on regular monthly and yearly prohibitions, number over two hundred a year. In addition, there are restrictions based on weather and personal circumstances that reduce the possible days to only a few per year.

Taoist women found communal living most conducive to following these methods leading to immortality. Life in convents appealed even to high-ranking women during the T'ang dynasty (618–907 c.e.). Daughters of T'ang emperors T'ai Tsung and Jui Tsung chose to become Taoist priestesses. A new convent was built for Jui Tsung's daughters, who took the Taoist titles "Jade Realized Princess" and "Golden Transcendent Princess." Many T'ang Taoist priestesses were known for their beauty and dressed in the same rich costumes worn by the immortal goddesses whom they sought to imitate. T'ang poetry depicts them in their crowns and splendid cloaks as they seek their true love—immortality:

> To go off in search of transcendence—
> Halcyon filigrees and golden comb are discarded:
> She enters among the steep tors;
> Fog rolls up—as her yellow net-gauze cloak;
> Clouds sculptured—as her white jade crown.

Sexual intercourse was one form of inner alchemy practiced in Taoist convents that created, not surprisingly, suspicion and hostility in outsiders. This form was later superceded by an inner alchemy for combining the yin and yang within a woman's own body without intercourse. A text written around 1798 by Liu I-ming explains that a woman's menstrual blood alone was enough to create an immortal body. By this time, Confucian and Buddhist influences had permeated Taoist communal life. A list of rules for Taoist nuns from the late eighteenth century requires them to abstain from wine and meat, remain celibate, and preserve their hymens if possible.

Even with the increased restrictions, some Chinese continued to see Taoist nuns as models of transcendence. Liu T'ieh-yün (1857–1909) in the last chapters of his novel *The Travels of Lao Ts'an* (translated as "A nun of Taishan" by Lin Yutang, 1950), depicted a young Taoist nun as the embodiment of the freedom, self-determination, and compassion that he sought in a new China.

FEMALE DEITIES

Taoist texts, Chinese mythology, and popular literature are filled with female divinities. Most have been related to Taoism at either the popular level or in the rituals. Ancient China was filled with powerful dragon women, river goddesses, and rain goddesses who lived on the cloudy peaks of mountains. Edward Schafer has shown how the state cult of medieval China turned these goddesses into abstract and asexual deities and how T'ang prose and poetry depicted them as man-destroying evil creatures often disguised as beautiful women.

One example of a transformed creature is Nü-kua, a dragon goddess who, according to ancient Chinese mythology, created humanity and repaired the world. Huainan-tzu, the eclectic Taoist work of the second century b.c.e, contains the legend of her saving the world.

> In very ancient times, the four pillars [at the compass points] were broken down, the nine provinces [of the habitable world] were split apart, Heaven did not wholly cover [Earth] and Earth did not completely support [Heaven]. Fires flamed without being extinguished, waters inundated without being stopped, fierce beasts ate people, and birds of prey seized the old and weak in their claws. Thereupon Nü-kua fused together stones of the five colors with which she patched together azure Heaven. She cut off the feet of a turtle with which she set up the four pillars. She slaughtered the Black Dragon in order to save the province of Chi [the present Hopei and Shansi provinces in North China]. She collected the ashes of reeds with which to check the wild waters.

Nü-kua not only saved the world; in another myth, she also created humanity out of yellow mud. The fate of this powerful and benevolent dragon was unkind. She was preserved primarily as one of the three emperors of the golden age—covered with robes and deprived of her serpentine and female characteristics.

Some early goddesses survived better. Hsi Wang Mu (Queen Mother of the West) was first mentioned in Chuang tzu, and a full mythology and cult devoted to her developed by about 100 c.e. Chinese artists depicted her with a royal headdress and seated on a half-dragon and half-tiger creature. As symbols of yin and yang, the tiger and dragon represent the cosmic transformations over which Hsi Wang Mu reigns. Chinese worshippers believed her to be the source of immortality: she could provide the desired potion to eliminate death. Her gift of immortality was first mentioned in the third century b.c.e. text Mu t'ien tzu chuan, which describes the meeting between the divine Queen of the West and the earthly King Mu of Chou. King Mu offered precious gifts, and she responded with the promise of immortality and marriage. Hsi Wang Mu's meetings with King Mu are part of a larger cycle of Chinese myths of seasonal meetings between rulers and goddesses or between stellar gods and goddesses. These myths also reflect the ancient Chinese fertility rites, during which young men and women celebrated the beginning of the new season with poetry contests and sexual intercourse. The seasonal interaction of yin and yang brings both agricultural and human fertility.

The attraction and mythology of Hsi Wang Mu continued, and she became the Fairy Queen of all the Taoist Immortals. A biography of her from the fourth or fifth century describes her life and paradise in detail. Her paradise in the K'un-lun mountains is filled with magical beauty: jade towers, silk tents, charming music, and the youthful men and women who serve as attendants for the benevolent Queen. Hsi Wang Mu was also known for her concern for women's problems: she was invoked in Taoist rituals to dispel the White Tiger deity who causes miscarriages in women. Hsi Wang Mu's cult did not survive, but she continues to exist in Chinese literature and art as the Queen of all Immortals who cultivates the peaches of immortality. She is one of the characters in the popular novel *Journey to the West.*

Nature goddesses have also survived—the Mother of Lightning, the Old Woman Who Sweeps Heaven Clear, the Woman in the Moon, and the Mother of the Pole Star. Stellar deities are central to Taoist rituals, and the Mother of the Pole Star, Toumu, is one of the most important. As patroness of the contemporary Taoist Master Chuang, she appears on his altar as an eight-armed, four-headed goddess—a deity of awesome power.

Chinese domestic rituals often involve goddesses, usually paired with a male god to reflect yin-yang duality. The kitchen god and his wife keep records of the deeds of the household to ensure that justice is done—his wife is responsible for the records of the women of the family. Another couple, the Lord and Lady of the Bed, are worshiped for fertility and marital happiness. A solitary goddess, the goddess of the latrine, is sometimes worshiped by girls seeking a good husband. Although Taoism has encouraged such domestic rituals, there is nothing in them unique to Taoism.

Two goddesses enshrined in Taoist temples continue to be important in providing protection for the individual. The Empress of Heaven (T'ien-hou) protects sailors, aided by a deity who can see for one thousand *li* (Chinese mile) and one who can hear for one thousand li. Her cult has been popular since the eleventh century.

The Sacred Mother (Sheng-mu) or Lady Mother (Nainai niang-niang) protects women and children and is assisted by the popular goddess who brings children to women who worship her. These two Taoist goddesses avert disaster and send children just like the Buddhist *bodhisattva* Kuan-yin, who is given female form in China. . . .

7.7 RELIGION ON THE GROUND

A woman lights three sticks of incense and intones a prayer while clasping her hands above her head. She closes her eyes, joins her fingers, with the exception of the thumbs, at the fingertips, and enters a trance. Two women, who are sisters, wait expectantly. They have asked this woman, who is a medium, to contact their dead mother about some family problems, in particular, why a third sister, who lives elsewhere, has not answered their letters. The medium announces that their mother is occupied elsewhere but that their grandfather wishes to speak with them. Next, the medium recounts a brief history of the family in order to ensure the right spirit has been contacted, and the seance proceeds once all present are assured it is the correct spirit.

This brief description of a seance that occurred in Hong Kong in the 1940s is described by V. R. Burkhardt in *Chinese Creeds and Customs.* There is nothing remarkable about it, and seances like this occur every day throughout the world in many different religious settings. In this case, the religious setting is Chinese, but should this event be characterized as Buddhist, Confucian, or Taoist? Many Western scholars would argue that it is not a part of any organized religious tradition but is a part of Chinese popular religion.

As we noted earlier, some scholars draw a sharp distinction between Chinese Taoism and Chinese popular religion, but other scholars view them as closely related. Whatever their exact relationship may be, there undoubtedly has been mutual influence. The actual religious practices of most of the Chinese people are a blending of Confucian, Buddhist, Taoist, and popular practices.

We have learned something about Buddhism, Confucianism, and Taoism in China. However, we have not focused directly on popular religion. This final essay, by Daniel L. Overmyer, provides a brief description of popular religion.

DANIEL L. OVERMYER

Popular Religion

READING QUESTIONS

1. Where are the activities associated with Chinese popular religion carried out?
2. Who are the gods of popular religion, and what do they symbolize?
3. Who are the demons, and what function do they perform?
4. What is sectarian popular religion like?
5. What role does the Great Mother goddess play in sectarian popular religion?

Nevertheless, even if some intellectuals did not place much emphasis on religion, various kinds of rituals and beliefs continued to be important for the vast majority of the population. As far back as the records go, we read of a variety of religious activities practiced by all except a few of the more strict scholars, priests, monks, including ancestor worship, sacrifices to spirits of sacred objects and places, belief in ghosts and demons, **exorcism,** divination, and the use of spirit-mediums. By the eleventh century (Song period) these practices had been blended together with Buddhist ideas of karma and rebirth and Daoist teachings about many levels of gods to form the popular religious system common from then on. Chinese popular religion is carried out in the midst of ordinary social life, in family, village, and city neighborhoods. It has no full-time specialists but is led by people who have other jobs, such as a farmer who may serve on a temple managerial committee, or a mechanic who works as a spirit-medium at night. There are popular religious temples where the gods are believed to live, but they usually have no resident clergy, just a caretaker or two. They are run and paid for by local people, who hire Daoist priests or Buddhist monks to perform special rituals. Worship in these temples is by individuals or families in the area who bring food offerings and incense to pray for blessings whenever they feel the need, though most come on the first or fifteenth of the

lunar month or on festival days. In such temples there are no congregations or group worship, and usually no reciting of scriptures. In any event, most popular rituals are done at home before the family altar or at the shrine of the locality god who is responsible just for one field or neighborhood.

The gods of popular religion are almost all the spirits of former human beings who have been deified, unlike the star gods of Daoism or the natural powers worshiped in the state religion. Since these gods were once human, they understand the needs of their worshipers, and furthermore they need their offerings and recognition if they are to keep their position as gods. Under Daoist influence popular gods were organized into a system like offices in a bureaucracy, each responsible for a specific function, such as healing smallpox, bringing children, or protecting fishermen. This system is ruled by the **Jade Emperor** in heaven, parallel to the emperor on earth. The Jade Emperor appoints the spirits of virtuous people to divine offices, which they hold temporarily until they are promoted for doing well or demoted for not being effective. In fact, if people feel their prayers are not being answered, they can abandon a god, or even a temple, and look for aid somewhere else. The offices remain much the same, but gods to fill them appear and disappear.

These gods are symbols of order, and many of them are believed to be equipped with weapons and celestial troops, as are some Daoist deities as well. Such force is necessary because beneath the gods is a vast array of demons, hostile influences that bring disease, suffering, and death—in a word, disorder. Ultimately the gods are more powerful, but these demons are violent and unruly and can be subdued only through repeated commands and dramatic rituals of exorcism. Most demons, or *gui*, are the spirits of the restless dead who died unjustly or whose bodies are not properly cared for; they cause disruption in order to draw attention to their problems. Other demons represent natural forces that can be dangerous, such as mountains and wild animals. Since these harmful spirits are believed to cause most illnesses, fires, and destructive weather, much effort is devoted to keeping them under control. A common method for driving them away is for a spirit-medium or Daoist priest to write out a charm in the name of a powerful god, a charm that is really a command such as might be issued by an emperor. Such a charm says something like, "I, the Jade Emperor, hereby order the evil and crooked forces causing this illness to leave immediately. This order has the power to smash and drive away all demons." The priest reads the charm aloud, then burns it so that its message is communicated to the sky through the smoke. There is a dramatic split in popular religion between the forces of good and evil. Most people in China had to struggle just to survive every day, so they easily felt threatened and did all they could to fight back, from working hard in their fields and protesting against unfair landlords to hiring a spirit-medium to heal a daughter's fever. This spirit of struggle has a lot to do with the success of Chinese people today.

There is another kind of Chinese popular religion, organized as sects or denominations similar to Protestant Christian groups in North America and Europe that are led and supported by ordinary people. These sects, still active in Taiwan, have their own books of scripture, which they chant or sing from in group worship. People join these associations as individuals looking for their own religious satisfaction, whereas in general popular religion there are no members, just families who worship in a village temple because they happen to live there. The sects go back in Chinese history to groups like the Yellow Turbans at the end of the Han dynasty, but they took their present shape in the thirteenth century under Buddhist influence. Some evangelistic monks started organizing groups of followers outside the monasteries, teaching them Buddhist beliefs in simple form, mostly about Amitabha's paradise. These groups grew so rapidly that more conservative monks became jealous and reported them to the government, which outlawed them because it was uneasy about any organized associations among the people. Once the sects were declared illegal, it was difficult for orthodox monks to work with them, so they were left on their own, They picked up a lot of ideas from Daoism and popular religion and tried to protect themselves by forming communes to raise their own food. When they were attacked by police or troops, some of them resisted with weapons, and even raided towns themselves; the government considered them just bandits or rebels. Perhaps because of this pressure, some sects started emphasizing Maitreya, the future Buddha, whom they said was coming soon to bring in a new world where they would be safe and happy. In the fourteenth century a few sects rebelled against the Mongols in the name of Maitreya, which confirmed their bad reputation with the government.

However, for the most part, the sects were peaceful and provided a way for some people to be more religious if they wanted to be and go directly to paradise at death, without going through purgatory first. By the sixteenth century the beliefs of most of these groups were centered on a great mother goddess who created the world and humankind and loves everybody as her own children. Unfortunately her children have forgotten the Mother, their real parent, and where they came from, and so they lead sinful lives and get into trouble because of sex,

drinking, dishonesty, and stealing. Sectarian scriptures were regarded as having been revealed by the Mother or her messengers to remind people of who they are, how they should live, and how they can be saved. Those who believe the message should join the sect and share the good news with others. These scriptures were passed on from one sect leader to the next and used as the basis of preaching, ritual, and discussion. Sect members were supposed to be more pious and good than their neighbors; their perception of themselves was very different from that of the government.

KEY TERMS AND CONCEPTS

Note: See the Key Terms and Concepts and the Pronunciation Guide at the end of chapter 6 for more information on Chinese words and meanings.

Celestial Masters A Taoist school still in existence whose leaders trace their lineage to Chang Taoling, who first claimed **Lao Tzu** appeared to him in 142.

chai Rituals and prayers offered for individuals and intended to secure good fortune and other blessings.

chiao A major Taoist ritual in which the priest renews a community's beneficial relationship or covenant with the Three Pure Ones who are supreme Taoist deities and a source of blessings.

Ch'i-kung Breathing techniques designed to promote a healthy and peaceful life.

Chuang Tzu The name of an early Chinese philosopher and the title of a book attributed to him.

ecstatic journey An elaborate visualization practice involving out-of-body experiences and marvelous travels. It probably relates to ancient shamanistic practices.

exorcism The ritual expulsion of evil spirits or demons from a person or place.

fa-shih Taoist specialists in the occult or hidden sciences who cannot perform the greater liturgies such as the *chiao*.

Field of Cinnabar The head, chest, and abdomen are important power areas in inner alchemy and associated with the cinnabar (mercuric sulfide) of outer alchemy.

fu Written talismans or charms used in Taoist rituals.

Highest Clarity One of the more important Taoist sects (*Shang Ch'ing*) that no longer exists, but whose writings and practices are still part of the Taoist canon.

immortals Humans who have become deified. They may live on earth and/or in the celestial realms. Some function as patrons of various professions and crafts.

Jade Emperor The ruler of the gods and supreme deity of popular Chinese religion.

Lao Tzu Legendary Chinese philosopher who supposedly authored the *Tao Te Ching*, a basic text in Taoism.

macrocosm The universe viewed as a whole. In other words, the cosmic large scale structure or order.

microcosm Some part of the universe thought to mirror in structure the whole of the universe. For example, some think that human beings or society reflect the cosmic structure.

nei-tan The practice of inner or spiritual alchemy whose purpose is to transform a mortal into an immortal.

Perfect Truth A monastic school of Taoism dating from the thirteenth century and still in existence.

p'u-tu A Buddhist term used by Taoists to refer to the great feast for the dead offered at the close of a *chai* ritual.

Queen Mother of the West The designation for an important Taoist goddess.

t'ai-chi ch'üan A Chinese form of exercise consisting of slow-motion ballet movements and coordinated breathing. Sometimes called "Chinese boxing."

Tao Te Ching (*The Way and Its Power*) One of the classics of Taoism. Authorship is unknown, but it is attributed to **Lao Tzu**. Sometimes titled *Lao Tzu*.

T'ien Shih Means "Master Designated by the Heavens" and is usually shortened to Heavenly or Celestial Masters. It is a title that Chang Tao-ling, founder of the Celestial Masters school, assumed and has been passed on to his successors.

wai-tan Outer alchemical practices.

wu-wei Literally means "no action" and is used by Taoists to describe how the Tao "acts" and how the ideal human should learn to act. Primarily refers to acting without force or artificial constraint.

SUGGESTIONS FOR FURTHER READING

Baldrian, Farzeen. "Taoism." In *The Encyclopedia of Religion*, edited by Mircea Eliade, vol. 14, pp. 288–306. New York: Macmillan, 1987. Articles include an overview of major ideas and the history of Taoist development and literature.

Ching, Julia. *Chinese Religions*. Maryknoll, N.Y.: Orbis Books, 1993. Chapters 5 and 6 provide a good overview of Taoism.

Cleary, Thomas, ed. *Immortal Sisters: Secrets of Taoist Women*. Boston: Shambhala, 1989. Translations of texts by and about Taoist women.

Kohn, Livia. *Early Chinese Mysticism: Philosophy and Soteriology in the Taoist Tradition*. Princeton, N.J.: Princeton University Press, 1992. A good but advanced study of Taoist mysticism and theories of salvation (soteriology) by a leading scholar.

Robinet, Isabelle. *Taoism: Growth of a Religion*. Translated by Phyllis Brooks. Stanford, Calif.: Stanford University Press, 1997. Although advanced this is one of the best studies available on the history of Taoism. Robinet has been called one of the foremost contemorary scholars of Taoism.

Saso, Michael R. *Blue Dragon, White Tiger: Taoist Rites of Passage*. Washington, D.C.: Taoist Center, 1990. A study of Taoist ceremonies by a scholar and a Taoist.

Schipper, Kristofer. *The Taoist Body*. Translated by Karen C. Duval. Berkeley: University of California Press, 1993. First published in French in 1982, this important study combines the insights of a scholar with the views of an ordained Taoist priest.

RESEARCH PROJECTS

1. Do a comparative study of Taoist and Christian mysticism.
2. Do a Web search for information about Taoism, and write a report describing and evaluating some of the resources you find.
3. View the video *The Dragon Boat Festival*, which is about the life and death of Ch'ü Yüan, who is credited with the *Songs of Chu* (*Songs of the South*). Write a report on what you learn. (The video is available from the University of Washington Press, P.O. Box 50096, Seattle, WA, 98145.)

Appendix

Religion on the Web

The resources on the World Wide Web are both fleeting and untrustworthy. The addresses I have annotated below will aid the student who wishes to explore religion in cyberspace. However, some will have changed or no longer exist by the time this book reaches publication. Those seeking more information should consult Patrick Durusau's *High Places in Cyberspace: A Guide to Biblical and Religious Studies, Classics, and Archaeological Resources on the Internet*, 2nd ed. (Atlanta, Ga.: Scholars Press, 1998) for information on searching the internet, browsers, creating Web resources, E-mail discussion lists, and URLs. See **http://schemesh.scholar.emory.edu/scripts/high places.html** for updates.

GENERAL RESOURCES

http://religion.rutgers.edu/vir
"Virtual Religion Index: Links for Research on Religion" is a tool providing hyperlinks to homepages, major subsites, documents, and directories in religion. It is a good starting point for resources relating to the academic study of religion available on the Web.

http://www.freenet.edmonton.ab.ca/~cstier/religion/toc.htm
"A Guide to the Best Religious Studies Resources on the Internet" provides links to resources that the creators regard as the most useful sources for undergraduates seeking more information on the major religions of the world including Buddhism, Christianity, Hinduism, Islam, Judaism, Confucianism, Taoism, and others.

http://www.wlu.ca/~wwwrandc/internet_links.html
"Religious Studies Internet Links" is a well-organized listing that provides not only directories for the major religions but also course syllabi, multimedia resources, departments, societies, and current religious news.

http://scholar.cc.emory.edu/
"TELA" (Scholars Press) is the official Web site for the Scholars Press and sponsoring societies such as the American Academy of Religion, the Society of Biblical Literature, the American Philological Association, the American Schools of Oriental Research, and the American Society of Papyrologists. This is an important and essential site for students of religion.

http://www.academicinfo.net/religindex.html
"Religion: A Directory of Internet Resources for the Study of Religion" provides a good list with hundreds of links to directories, historical studies, bibliographies, sacred texts, and other documents on religions. It is particularly useful for interdisciplinary topics such as "Women and Religion" or "Art and Religion."

http://www.arda.tm
"American Religion Data Archive" lists dozen of influential studies on American religion and allows you to view, print, or download important data files. This project is supported by the Lilly Endowment.

http://www.human.toyogakuen-u.ac.jp/~acmuller/
This site, maintained by Charles Muller of Toyo Gakuen University, provides a listing of many of the most important resources for Buddhism, Confucianism, and Taoism.

BUDDHISM

http://ciolek.com/WWWVC-Buddhism.html
This is an outstanding database with electronic texts,

information, and links on nearly every aspect of Buddhism.

http://www.human.toyogakuen-u.ac.jp/~acmuller/ebti.htm

This site allows access to the Electronic Buddhist Text Initiative (EBTI), a collection of major Buddhist online text projects organized by Lewis Lancaster of the University of California at Berkeley.

http://kaladarshan.arts.ohio-state.edu

"John C. and Susan L. Huntington Archive of Buddhist and Related Art" is an image-intensive site containing almost 300,000 original color slides and black-and-white photographs of Asian art and architecture drawn from the Huntington Archive.

CHRISTIANITY

http://www.iclnet.org/pub/resources/christian-history.html

"Early Christian Texts" is an excellent site for the study of Christianity in its early and medieval periods. It provides full-text versions of creeds and the writings of early theologians.

http://goon.stg.brown.edu/bible_browser/pbeasy.shtml

This search tool allows users to locate words or phrases in any of eight versions of the Bible.

http://www.hti.umich.edu/relig/mormon.html

This is a searchable electronic version of the Book of Mormon that allows users to browse specific sections.

http://www.vpm.com/thawes

"Theology on the Web" is a useful collection of links relating to Christianity.

CONFUCIANISM AND TAOISM

http://www-personal.monash.edu.au/~sab/index.html

"Chinese Philosophy Page" seeks to provide all the information available on the internet about Chinese philosophy and related subjects.

http://www.clas.ufl.edu/users/gthursby/taosim

"Taoism WWW Virtual Library" may well be the most comprehensive source of information on Taoism on the Web.

HINDUISM

http://www.hindunet.org

A general directory with links to information on many facets of Hinduism including art, temples, and organizations.

http://rbhatnagar.csm.uc.edu:8080/scriptures.html

"The Hindu Electronic Scriptures Reference Center" provides the full texts in English translation of several Hindu scriptures including the *Ramayana* and *Mahabharata*. The Hindu Students Council, an international, nonprofit religious organization, produces part of this site (called the Hindu Universe).

ISLAM

http://goon.stg.brown.edu/quran_browser

"Qur'an Browser" is a searchable database of the Qur'an with a choice of translations.

http://www.princeton.edu/~humcomp/alkhaz.html

"Al-Khazina: The Treasury" is an educational Web site with links to information on the Qur'an, *Hadith*, and *Hajj* databases, along with historical charts, maps, and photographs.

http://wings.buffalo.edu/student-life/sa/muslim/isl/texts.html

A number of different links to the hypertext version of the Qur'an along with sound files of the recitations of the Qur'an.

JUDAISM

http://www.shamash.org/trb/judaism.html

The most complete directory of links to Jewish resources, both academic and general, on the Web.

http://world.std.com/~alevin/jewishfeminist.html
For those with a specific interest in Jewish feminism, this site provides a wealth of resources and information.

NATIVE AMERICAN

http://www.academicinfo.net/nativeam.html#religions
This connection through the directory of the study of religions will link you to a variety of useful sources on Native American religions.